Physics for JavaScript Games, Animation, and Simulations

With HTML5 Canvas

Dev Ramtal

Adrian Dobre

Apress·

Physics for JavaScript Games, Animation, and Simulations: with HTML5 Canvas

ISBN-13 (pbk): 978-1-4302-6337-1

ISBN-13 (electronic): 978-1-4302-6338-8

President and Publisher: Paul Manning
Lead Editor: Ben Renow-Clarke
Technical Reviewer: Brian Danchilla
Developmental Editor: Anne Marie Walker
Editorial Board: Steve Anglin, Mark Beckner, Ewan Buckingham, Gary Cornell, Louise Corrigan, Jim DeWolf, Jonathan Gennick, Jonathan Hassell, Robert Hutchinson, Michelle Lowman, James Markham, Matthew Moodie, Jeff Olson, Jeffrey Pepper, Douglas Pundick, Ben Renow-Clarke, Dominic Shakeshaft, Gwenan Spearing, Matt Wade, Steve Weiss
Coordinating Editor: Christine Ricketts
Copy Editor: James Compton
Compositor: SPi Global
Indexer: SPi Global
Artist: SPi Global
Cover Designer: Anna Ishchenko

Distributed to the book trade worldwide by Springer Science+Business Media New York, 233 Spring Street, 6th Floor, New York, NY 10013. Phone 1-800-SPRINGER, fax (201) 348-4505, e-mail orders-ny@springer-sbm.com, or visit www.springeronline.com. Apress Media, LLC is a California LLC and the sole member (owner) is Springer Science + Business Media Finance Inc (SSBM Finance Inc). SSBM Finance Inc is a Delaware corporation.

For information on translations, please e-mail rights@apress.com, or visit www.apress.com.

Apress and friends of ED books may be purchased in bulk for academic, corporate, or promotional use. eBook versions and licenses are also available for most titles. For more information, reference our Special Bulk Sales–eBook Licensing web page at www.apress.com/bulk-sales.

Any source code or other supplementary material referenced by the author in this text is available to readers at www.apress.com. For detailed information about how to locate your book's source code, go to www.apress.com/source-code/.

To the memory of my father

— DR

To my beloved family

— AD

Contents at a Glance

Contents

About the Authors

Dev Ramtal has been coding physics for over two decades. Alongside his academic research background in mathematical and computational physics, he has a long history of web development experience since building his first website back in 1997. Dev has a PhD in Physics from the University of London and lives in the UK with his family.

Adrian Dobre has more than 18 years of experimental and computational modeling experience in fluid dynamics. Adrian holds a PhD in Engineering Science from the University of Western Ontario, Canada. He currently lives in Bucharest, Romania, with his family.

About the Technical Reviewer

Brian Danchilla is a web developer and consultant (www.briandanchilla.com/hire) providing custom solutions, troubleshooting, and training. He is a strong analytical thinker and holds a double degree in mathematics and computer science.

In a field where continuous learning is a requirement, Brian has authored *Beginning WebGL for HTML5* (Apress, 2012), coauthored *Pro PHP Programming* (Apress, 2011), and been a technical reviewer for a handful of other titles.

When not programming, Brian likes to play guitar, jog, and travel. He resides in Saskatoon, Canada, with his wife Tressa and their dog Meisha.

Acknowledgments

We are extremely grateful to all the individuals who have helped turn this book from an idea into physical reality. An enormous amount of work goes into producing a book, of which writing it is only one part. We were fortunate to have the support of such a fantastic team at Apress—we won't mention any names for fear of missing anyone.

We would also like to thank our respective families for their patience and encouragement during the writing of this book.

Introduction

We hope you will enjoy reading—and using—this book as much as we enjoyed writing it. Creating physics-based simulations is a lot of fun—there is great satisfaction in writing a few lines of code and then seeing them bring inanimate objects to life, behaving as they do in the real world! This is a striking demonstration that the natural world is governed by simple laws, and that we have at least an approximate grasp of those laws. The ability to replicate the real world in a computer program gives us great power as programmers. The aim of this book is to provide you with tools that will make you feel that awesome sense of power. Whether you want to build convincing animations, games that behave realistically, or accurate simulators, you will find herein plenty of tools, examples, and ideas that should be of help.

This book is based closely on our earlier book, *Physics for Flash Games, Animation, and Simulations* (Apress, 2011). Although the physics content has not changed, the numerous examples in the book have been rewritten from scratch in JavaScript for rendering in an HTML5 canvas. The last two chapters also include some WebGL examples, with the help of the three.js JavaScript library. All the examples are designed for use in a web browser. Although we don't give any examples of mobile apps, the examples given can be easily adapted for mobile devices.

While the popularity of JavaScript is on the rise, there is currently a lack of resources for creating physics-based animation using JavaScript. The excellent book by Billy Lamberta and Keith Peters, *Foundation HTML5 Animation with JavaScript* (Apress, 2011), contains good coverage of physics-related topics and provides a great introduction to the subject. It seemed to us that there was also a need for a book that explored physics further and in greater depth, and that catered to more demanding applications such as accurate simulators or more complex game programming. After all, there are several "game physics" books written for other programming languages, such as C++ and Java, so why not JavaScript? This book is meant to fill that gap.

We should make it clear at the outset that this is primarily a book about applying physics to your coding projects; hence we tend to focus less on producing attractive visual effects and more on modeling real physics. Some of the animations in the book may not be very pretty or smooth from a visual perspective, but they do contain a lot of physics you can apply! By the same token, there is little emphasis on writing elegant code—rather we prefer to keep the coding simple and clean, so that the physics content may not be obscured by over-clever programming. The approach we adopt attempts to make serious physics accessible. But although we don't shy away from going into technical information, with all of the accompanying math, we hope to have done so in a way that is simple and straightforward.

Inevitably, because of space and time restrictions, there are topics that we were not able to include or that we didn't explore in detail. Nevertheless, the book covers an awful lot of ground, taking you from coding a simple bouncing ball animation in a few lines of code in the first chapter to a highly accurate simulation of the solar system in the final chapter. We hope you enjoy the journey in between!

What this book will (and won't) teach you

Physics for JavaScript Games, Animation, and Simulations teaches you how to incorporate physics into your programming. It does not teach you how to program. It does not teach you JavaScript. We assume that you have at least some programming experience, preferably with JavaScript (or a similar programming language). And although this book teaches you how to implement physics into your games (as well as other projects), it is not about game programming per se.

We do not assume any previous knowledge of physics, and we assume only basic school-level math knowledge. One chapter is dedicated to explaining some of the more difficult math concepts and tools that you are likely to need in the book. All the physics concepts and knowledge you will need are explained in a self-contained way. Numerous applications are given throughout the book with full source code to illustrate the application of the principles learned.

Overview of this book

This book is divided into four parts:

Part I: "The Basics" (Chapters 1–4) introduces the necessary background in basic math and physics concepts upon which the rest of the book builds. For completeness, it also covers selected topics in JavaScript that are most pertinent to physics programming.

Part II: "Particles, Forces, and Motion" (Chapters 5–10) begins by formulating the laws of physics that govern the motion of particles under any type of force (Chapter 5). The next five chapters then apply those laws to make objects move under the action of a variety of forces including gravity, friction, drag, buoyancy, wind, springs, central forces, and many more. The main focus in this section is on simulating the motion of individual particles and other simple objects.

In Part III: "Multi-Particle and Extended Systems" (Chapters 11–13), we show you how to model more complicated systems, including multiple interacting particles and extended objects. In these systems the constituent particles and objects may not simply co-exist but also interact with one another, mutually influencing their motion. These interactions include collisions, short-range forces, and long-range forces. This part includes a discussion of particle systems, rigid bodies, and deformable bodies.

Part IV: "Building More Complex Simulations" (Chapters 14–16) is devoted to building more complex simulations, where accuracy and/or realism is especially important, not just visual effects. This part includes a discussion of integration schemes and other numerical and technical issues such as scale modeling and 3D. Part IV ends with a chapter that includes some example simulation projects, which the reader is encouraged to build upon.

Source code and examples

All the code for this book can be downloaded from the book's page on the Apress website: www.apress.com. An up-to-date version of the code will also be maintained on github.com.

We encourage you to modify and build upon the example codes given. We also invite you to share your codes, and have set up the following page on our website where you can find and contribute more code and examples: www.physicscodes.com/jsbook.

The Basics

CHAPTER 1

∎∎∎

Introduction to Physics Programming

You've picked up this book because you are interested in implementing physics in your programming projects. But why would you want to do that? What can it do for you? And how difficult will it be? This chapter will provide answers to these questions.

Topics covered in this chapter include the following:

- **Why model real physics?** This section will explain some of the reasons why you might want to add physics to your projects.

- **What is physics?** Here we lift the veil of mystery and explain in simple terms what physics is. We also tell you, in a nutshell, what you'll need to know before you can write code involving physics.

- **Programming physics.** Thankfully, programming physics is not as difficult as you might imagine, once you understand some basic principles. This section explains what you'll need to do.

- **A simple example.** As a concrete example, we'll code up a simple animation involving physics, using a minimum of code.

Why model real physics?

There are a number of reasons why you might be interested in modeling physics using JavaScript. Here are some of the most common:

- To create realistic animation effects

- To create realistic games

- To build simulations and models

- To generate art from code

Let us look at each in turn.

Creating realistic animation effects

Thanks to the HTML5 canvas element, it is now possible to create animations without the need for plug-ins such as Flash. With a little JavaScript and some familiarity with physics, it is also possible to make animations that look and behave like the real thing. For example, suppose you are animating a scene in which someone kicks a ball and it bounces off the ground. You could try to create an animation that mimics the ball's behavior, but however hard you might try, it would probably look less than realistic. With just a little bit of coding and some knowledge of elementary physics, you could produce a far more realistic animation. And if, like the authors, you are programmers rather than designers, you might even find it easier! We'll show you just how easy it can be in the example at the end of this chapter.

Creating realistic games

Web-based games are extremely popular. As the capabilities of modern web browsers continue to improve, better and more powerful games can be built. Hardware acceleration and 3D support are just two of the emerging developments that have the potential to improve the online gaming user experience dramatically. But apart from performance and appearance, it is equally important for games to feel and look realistic. If a player throws a ball, it should fall according to the law of gravity; if a player fires a torpedo underwater, it should move differently from a ball falling in air. In other words, your game needs to incorporate real physics.

How do you build physics awareness into your games? This book will show you how.

Building simulations and models

A *computer simulation* or *computer model* is a program that attempts to imitate certain key aspects of a physical system. Simulations vary in completeness or accuracy, depending on purpose and resources. Let's take a flight simulator program as an example. We would expect a flight simulator designed for training pilots to be much more comprehensive and accurate than one designed for a game. Simulations are extremely common in e-learning, training, and scientific research. In the final chapter of this book, you'll build simulations—namely a submarine, a basic flight simulator, and a model of the solar system. In fact, many of the coded examples throughout the book are simulations, even if generally simpler.

Generating art from code

Generative art has gained popularity in recent years. A lot of fun can be had with some basic physics—for example, elaborate visual effects and motions can be produced using particles (small graphic objects that you can create and animate with code) and different kinds of forces. These effects can include realistic-looking animation such as smoke and fire, as well as more abstract examples of generative art that can be created using a mixture of algorithms, randomness, and user interaction. Adding some physics in the mix can result in enhanced realism and/or richer effects.

We will explore the world of generative art and provide additional tools and algorithms that can be used to create original and interesting effects such as particle trajectories in complex force fields.

What is physics?

Physics is the most fundamental of the sciences. In a broad sense, physics is the study of the natural laws that govern how things behave. More specifically, it concerns itself with space, time, and matter (defined as any "stuff" that exists in space and time). One aspect of physics is to formulate general laws that govern the behavior of matter, its interactions, and its motion in space and time. Another aspect is to use these laws to predict the way specific things move and interact—for example, the prediction of eclipses from the laws of gravity or how airplanes are able to fly from the laws of aerodynamics.

Physics is a vast subject, and in a book of this nature we cannot do more than scratch the surface. Fortunately, most of the physics that you will probably need to know falls within a branch known as *mechanics*, which is one of the easiest to understand. Mechanics governs the way in which objects move and how that motion is influenced by effects in the environment. Because most games and animations include motion, mechanics is clearly of relevance in developing algorithms for making objects behave realistically in code.

Everything behaves according to the laws of physics

Without getting too philosophical, it is fair to say that the laws of physics are truly universal, as far as physicists have been able to observe. What this means is that everything *must* behave according to physics. This is different from say, the laws of biology, which pertain only to living things. A stone thrown in the air, a planet orbiting the Sun, the workings of the human body, and the operation and motion of a man-made machine must all obey the laws of physics. Moreover, many seemingly diverse phenomena are governed by the same subset of laws. In other words, a single law or group of laws can explain many types of observed facts or patterns of behavior in the physical world. For example, a falling stone and a planet orbiting the Sun both obey the laws of gravity. Another example is that all electrical, magnetic, and radiation phenomena (such as light and radio waves) are governed by the laws of electromagnetism.

The laws can be written as math equations

The great thing is that the laws of physics can be written as mathematical equations. Okay, that may not sound too great if you don't like math! But the point here is that for a law to be useful, it has to be made precise. And math equations are as precise as anything can be. There is no possible ambiguity in how to apply a law that is expressed mathematically, in contrast with the laws that are fought over in courtrooms! Second, this means that centuries of developments in mathematics prove to be applicable to physics, making it possible to solve many physics problems. Third, and what is of most relevance for us: math equations are readily convertible into code.

Predicting motion

Let's get more specific. As a JavaScript programmer, you are mostly interested in how things move. Much of physics deals with how things move under the action of different types of influences. These "influences" can be from other things and from the environment. Examples include gravity, friction, and air resistance. In physics we have a special name for these influences: they are called *forces*. The really good news is that the forces have precise mathematical forms. Although the motion of objects is usually complicated, the underlying mathematical laws that describe the forces are usually quite simple.

The general relationship between force and motion can be written symbolically as follows:

motion = function{**forces**}

Here the use of the word *function* is not intended to represent an actual code function. Rather, it is meant to emphasize two things. First, it signifies a cause-and-effect relationship. Forces cause objects to move in different ways. Second, it also points to an algorithmic relationship between forces and motion in code, in that the motion of an object can be seen as the output of a function with forces as input. In practical terms, it means this: specify the forces acting on an object and put them in a mathematical equation, and then you can calculate the motion of the object.

■ **Note** Motion is effect. Force is cause. The motion of an object is the result of the forces acting on it. The mathematical relationship between force and motion is known as the "Law of Motion."

To be able to put the principle stated in this note to use, you need to know the following:

- **Definitions.** The precise definitions of *motion* and *force*.

- **The law of motion.** In other words, the precise mathematical form of the function that relates a force to the motion it produces.

- **Force laws.** In other words, how to calculate the forces. There are equations that tell you how to calculate each type of force.

So there are two kinds of laws you need to know about: laws of motion and force laws. You will also need to know the proper concepts (known as *physical quantities*) to describe and analyze motion and forces and the relationship between them. Finally, you will need to know the mathematics for manipulating and combining these quantities. We'll cover the relevant math in Chapter 3, the basic physics concepts in Chapter 4, the laws of motion in Chapter 5, and the force laws for various types of forces in Chapters 6–10.

Programming physics

So, how do you code physics? Do you program the motion, or the forces, or both? And what does it involve?

Once you know some basic physics (and some relevant math), coding it is not much different or more difficult than what you are used to as a programmer, provided you do it in the right way. Let's take some time to explain what this "right way" is by describing what is involved in simulating real physics and how it is done through steps involving math equations, algorithms, and code.

The difference between animation and simulation

Some wise guy once said "A picture is worth a thousand words" or something like that. One could extend this by saying "A movie is worth a thousand pictures." A movie (or *animation*) adds so much more to our perception than a static image because it includes the element of change in time, an extra dimension. But there is a sense in which an animation is still static rather than dynamic. No matter how many times you play it, the animation has the same beginning and the same end. Everything happens in exactly the same way. While we might see a progression in capturing the real world from written words to visual images to animated movies, there is still something missing: the power to interact with the medium and to influence the outcome in a way that duplicates the behavior of things in real life. This next step is what we call *simulation*. As we use the word in this book, simulation entails realism and also interactivity. When you simulate something, you don't just depict how it behaves under one set of conditions; you allow for many, even infinitely many, conditions. Building interactive simulations including physics makes things behave as they do in the real world: interacting with the environment and with the user to produce diverse and complex outcomes.

There is more. If you really pay attention to accuracy, you can even build a simulation that is so realistic it can be used as a virtual lab. You'll be able to experiment with it to learn how things actually work out there in the real world, on your computer! In fact, you will build such simulations in this book.

The laws of physics are simple equations

We have already said that the laws of physics are mathematical equations. The good news is that most of the laws (and hence the equations) you'll come across are actually quite simple. The apparently bad news is that these laws can produce very complex motions. In fact, that is probably a good thing, too; otherwise the universe would have been a rather boring place.

For example, the laws that govern gravity can be written down as just two simple-looking equations (they are given in Chapter 6). But they are responsible for the motion of the Moon around the Earth, the motion of planets around the Sun, and the motion of stars in a galaxy. The net effect of all these motions, plus the gravitational interactions between different celestial bodies, is to create very complicated motions that arise from just two equations.

Equations can be readily coded up!

We are now in a position to answer the first two questions asked at the beginning of this section. The laws of motion and forces are simple; the actual motions they produce are complex. If you know the laws, you can calculate the motions under different conditions. Hence, it makes much more sense to code the laws and forces, rather than the motions that result from them.

Animation attempts to reproduce the motion of an object directly. Simulation programs the laws of motion and then *derives* the motion of the object. It is much easier to code up the cause of motion than its effect. Moreover, an animation generally depicts a single scenario. But a simulation can potentially handle an infinite number of different scenarios.

■ **Note**   Simple laws of motion and simple force laws can give rise to complex motions. It is therefore generally easier to code the laws rather than the motions. Hence, paradoxically, simulation can be easier than animation.

Simulation is like playing God. You re-create a virtual world, not by blindly duplicating all the behavior you see, but by reproducing the laws that govern the way things behave and then letting it all happen.

The four steps for programming physics

To answer the third question we asked at the beginning of this section, the process of programming physics can be broken down into four steps, as shown schematically in Figure 1-1.

Figure 1-1. Steps in programming physics

The first step is to identify the physics principles that apply to the situation you are modeling. This can be tricky if you have no physics background. This book will help you: it is not just a how-to book but is also intended to teach you some physics. The second step is to recall, research, or derive the relevant equations. Obviously, this step involves some math. Don't worry; we'll give you all the help you need! The third step is to develop *algorithms* to solve the equations. Sometimes the equations can be solved *analytically* (we'll explain what that means in later chapters), in which case the algorithms are pretty straightforward. More often, one needs to employ *numerical methods*, which can be simple or less so, depending on the problem and on the desired level of accuracy. Although the first two steps may seem obvious, the third step is often overlooked. Indeed, many developers may even be unaware of its existence or necessity. Again, we'll spend some time on this aspect, especially in Part IV of the book. The fourth and last step is to write the code in your favorite programming language. You are already good at this, aren't you?

A simple physics simulation example

To see how the process depicted in Figure 1-1 works in practice, we will now look at a simple example. We'll set ourselves the task of simulating the motion of a ball thrown to the ground, using just a few lines of code.

To start with, let's picture the scenario that we are trying to model, the way it behaves in reality. Suppose you throw a volleyball in the air. How does it move? You've probably noticed that such a ball does not move in a straight line, but traces out a curved path. Moreover, the ball appears to move slowly at the top of the curve and quickly at the bottom, near the ground. When it hits the ground it usually bounces, but always reaches a lesser height than that from which it fell. Before we try to reproduce this motion, let us look more closely at the physics causing it.

The physics of a bouncing ball

As you already know by now, forces are what cause things to move. So the first clue to understanding why the volleyball moves the way it does is to find out what forces are acting on it. As you'll learn later, there are generally many forces acting together on objects in everyday situations. But in this case there is one force that is much more important than any other. It's the force of gravity that the Earth exerts on the ball.

So let us assume that gravity is the only force acting on the ball once it has been thrown in the air. Thankfully, gravity acts in a straightforward way. Close to the Earth's surface, as in the present example, it is a constant force that points vertically downward. Its effect is therefore to pull objects downward, making them *accelerate* as they do so. Accelerate? Yes, that means it increases the speed of the object. As we'll discuss in much greater detail in later chapters, gravity increases the vertical speed of an object by a constant amount in each second. But because gravity acts downward, it does not affect the horizontal speed of an object.

Every time the ball hits the ground, the latter exerts a *contact force* on it (a contact force is a force that two solid objects exert on each other when in direct contact). This force acts upward for a very brief time. Unlike gravity, it is not easy to model this contact force directly. Therefore, we'll simplify things and model its effect instead. Its effect is to reverse the motion of the ball from downward to upward while reducing the speed of the ball.

Coding up a bouncing ball in 2D

To simplify the scenario and the resulting code, we'll pretend we're living in a 2D world. An object in 2D can move along two independent directions: horizontal and vertical. We'll denote the position of the ball at any given time by two numbers, x and y, where x refers to the horizontal position, and y refers to the vertical position. We'll denote the speed at which the ball is moving along these two directions as vx and vy.

According to what we said, each time the clock ticks, gravity will cause vy to increase by a constant amount, but vx will remain the same.

Because vx and vy are speeds, they tell us how much the object moves each time the clock ticks. In other words, at each tick of the clock, x increases by an amount vx, and y increases by an amount vy.

This implements the effect of gravity. To implement the effect of the ground, what we have to do is reverse the sign of vy and reduce its magnitude each time the ball hits the ground. And, believe it or not, that's pretty much it.

Some code at last!

The JavaScript code for the example depicted in Figure 1-2 is included in the `bouncing-ball.js` file, which may be downloaded together with all other source code in the book at `apress.com`.

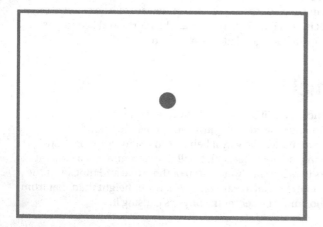

Figure 1-2. *The bouncing ball created by this example*

Here is the code that does it all:

```javascript
var canvas = document.getElementById('canvas');
var context = canvas.getContext('2d');
var radius = 20;
var color = "#0000ff";
var g = 0.1; // acceleration due to gravity
var x = 50;  // initial horizontal position
var y = 50;  // initial vertical position
var vx = 2;  // initial horizontal speed
var vy = 0;  // initial vertical speed

window.onload = init;

function init() {
    setInterval(onEachStep, 1000/60); // 60 fps
};
function onEachStep() {
    vy += g; // gravity increases the vertical speed
    x += vx; // horizontal speed increases horizontal position
    y += vy; // vertical speed increases vertical position
    if (y > canvas.height - radius){ // if ball hits the ground
        y = canvas.height - radius; // reposition it at the ground
        vy *= -0.8; // then reverse and reduce its vertical speed
    }
    if (x > canvas.width + radius){ // if ball goes beyond canvas
        x = -radius; // wrap it around
    }
    drawBall(); // draw the ball
};
function drawBall() {
    with (context){
        clearRect(0, 0, canvas.width, canvas.height);
        fillStyle = color;
        beginPath();
        arc(x, y, radius, 0, 2*Math.PI, true);
        closePath();
        fill();
    };
};
```

We'll explain fully in the next chapter all the elements of the JavaScript code as well as the HTML5 markup in which it is embedded. The important lines that contain the physics are those with the comments next to them. The variable g is the acceleration due to gravity. Here we've set a value that will give an animation that looks visually correct. The next lines set the initial horizontal and vertical position and speeds of the ball. All the physics action is taking place in the aptly named function onEachTimestep(), which is executed at the frame rate set for the movie. Here we increase vy but not vx because gravity only acts vertically. Then we update the ball's position by increasing x and y by amounts vx and vy, respectively. The subsequent pieces of code take care of the bouncing, and recycle the ball if it leaves the canvas. The ball is erased and redrawn at each time step by the function drawBall(), the innards of which will become clear in the next chapter, together with the rest of the code.

Run the code and see the result. It looks pretty realistic, doesn't it? How does the ball know how to behave with so few instructions? This is like magic. We challenge you to create the same effect without physics!

Is it really that easy? Wait! We've barely scratched the surface of what's possible. There are plenty of ways to improve the simulation to make it even more realistic, but they require more physics and more coding. For example, you could add friction so that the ball's horizontal speed reduces as it moves along the ground. Suppose you are building a game that includes balls moving around. You might want the ball to feel the effect of air resistance and to be blown by wind in addition to moving under the effect of gravity. You might want it to behave properly if thrown into water, sinking and then rising, and oscillating on the water surface before coming to rest and floating. There might be lots of balls colliding. Or you might want to create an accurate simulation that school students can use to learn about gravity. In that case, you would need to pay careful attention to implement proper boundary effects as well as accurate and stable time-stepping algorithms. By the time you finish the book, you will be able to do all these and more. And you'll know what you are doing. We promise.

Summary

Physics encapsulates the laws of nature in mathematical form. These laws are simple and can be readily coded. Hence, it is generally easy to create effects that look realistic.

Programming physics involves four steps: identifying what physics principles you need, writing down the relevant equations, devising a numerical algorithm for solving the equations, and writing the code. So it involves knowledge and skills in four different areas: physics, math, numerical methods, and programming. This book gives you help in the first three areas; you are assumed to have some proficiency in the fourth: general programming in JavaScript.

Having said this, the next chapter will provide a rapid overview of selected topics in JavaScript and HTML5, emphasizing aspects that are especially relevant for physics programming.

CHAPTER 2

■ ■ ■

JavaScript and HTML5 Canvas Basics

This chapter gives a brief review of the elements of JavaScript and HTML5 that we will make the most use of in the rest of this book. It is not meant to be a comprehensive tutorial on JavaScript; instead, it is a summary of what you need to know to understand the code examples in the book. The other aim of this chapter is to cover relevant aspects of the HTML5 canvas element and JavaScript that will set the context for applying physics.

This chapter was written with the assumption that the reader has at least a basic knowledge of HTML and JavaScript. If you are an experienced JavaScript programmer, you can safely skip most of this chapter, perhaps skimming over some of the material at the end on the canvas element and animating with code. On the other hand, if you haven't done any programming with JavaScript before, we suggest you pick up one of the books mentioned in the summary at the end. If you have programmed in another language, you will benefit from going through the chapter in some detail. While the overview on its own won't make you a proficient JavaScript programmer, it should enable you to use and build upon the code examples in the book without much difficulty.

Topics covered in this chapter include the following:

- **HTML5 and canvas:** HTML5 is the latest standard of HTML, and brings exciting new features to the web browser. The most important addition for our purpose is the canvas element, which enables rendering of graphics and animation without the need for external plug-ins.

- **JavaScript objects:** Objects are the basic building blocks of JavaScript. "Things" in the real world can be represented as objects in JavaScript. Objects have properties. They can also do things by means of methods.

- **JavaScript language basics:** For completeness, the basic constructs of JavaScript and their syntax are reviewed, such as variables, data types, arrays, operators, functions, math, logic, and loops.

- **Events and user interaction:** We briefly review some basic concepts and syntax, giving examples of how to make things happen in response to changes in the program or user interaction.

- **The canvas coordinate system:** This is the equivalent of space in the canvas world. Objects can be positioned on a canvas element using its 2D rendering context. We review the differences between the canvas coordinate system and the usual Cartesian coordinate system in math.

- **The canvas drawing API:** The ability to draw things using only code is a powerful tool, especially when combined with math and physics. Some of the most common methods of the canvas-drawing application programming interface (API), which will be used throughout the book, are briefly reviewed here.

- **Producing animation using code:** We review different methods for producing animation using code, and explain the main method we'll use for physics-based animation in the rest of the book.

HTML5, the canvas element, and JavaScript

HTML5 is the latest incarnation of the HTML standard, and it brings lots of new capabilities to the web browser. We will only present the bare minimum of what you, as a prospective physics programmer using JavaScript, need to know to exploit the most important feature for animation purposes—the canvas element.

A minimal HTML5 document

For the purpose of this book, you need to know surprisingly little of HTML5. Here is an example of a minimal HTML5 document. Assuming you are familiar with basic HTML markup, much of it should make sense. Note the very simple form of the doctype declaration compared to that of earlier HTML versions.

```
<!doctype html>
<html>
  <head>
    <meta charset="utf-8">
    <title>A minimal HTML5 document</title>
  </head>
  <body>
    <h1>Hello HTML5!</h1>
  </body>
</html>
```

The HTML5 documents that we will use in this book won't be much more complicated than this! Essentially, we'll add a few more tags for including a canvas element, CSS styling, and JavaScript code.

The canvas element

One of the most exciting additions to the HTML5 specification is the canvas element, which enables rendering graphics, and hence animation, in the web browser without the need for external plug-ins such as the Flash Player. To add a canvas element to an HTML5 document couldn't be simpler. Just include the following line in the body part of the document:

```
<canvas id="canvas" width="700" height="500"></canvas>
```

This produces a canvas instance of the specified dimensions that can be accessed in the Document Object Model (DOM) via its specified ID.

You can style the canvas in the same way as any regular HTML element. In the example canvas-example.html (source files can be downloaded from the http://apress.com web site), we have linked a CSS file named style.css by inserting the following line in the head section:

```
<link rel="stylesheet" href="style.css">
```

If you look in the file style.css, you'll find that we have chosen different background colors for the body section and the canvas element, so that we can better see the latter against the background of the former.

There's nothing stopping you from adding more than one canvas element to a single HTML5 document. You could even overlap or overlay different canvas instances. This technique can prove very useful for certain purposes, for example to render a fast-moving animation against a fixed background. The file canvas-overlap.html shows a simple example of this, with the file style1.css specifying the required CSS positioning code for the two canvas instances (see Figure 2-1 in the next section).

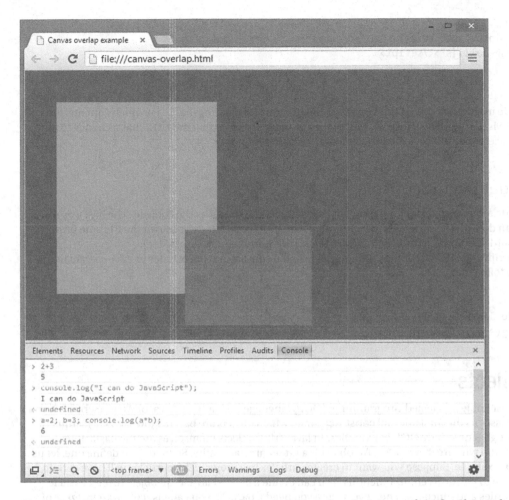

Figure 2-1. *Top: Two overlapping canvas elements. Bottom: JavaScript console in the Chrome browser*

Adding JavaScript

You can add JavaScript to an HTML5 document in two ways: by embedding the code within a `<script></script>` tag within the HTML file itself, or by linking to an external file that contains the JavaScript code. We'll adopt the latter practice in this book. Let's take another look at the bouncing ball example from the last chapter. Here is the HTML file for that example in its entirety (`bouncing-ball.html`):

```
<!doctype html>
<html>
<head>
<meta charset="utf-8">
<title>Bouncing ball</title>
<link rel="stylesheet" href="style.css">
</head>
```

```
<body>
<canvas id="canvas" width="700" height="500"></canvas>
<script src= "bouncing-ball.js"></script>
</body>
</html>
```

Note the line of code in the body part of the script that links to the file bouncing-ball.js, which contains the JavaScript code. This line is placed right before the end of the closing body tag so that the DOM has a chance to fully load before the script is executed. You have already seen that script in Chapter 1.

The JavaScript debugging console

Modern browsers provide a very useful tool for debugging JavaScript code, known as the console. The best way to learn about what you can do with the console is to experiment with it. To launch the console in the Chrome browser, use the following keyboard shortcut: Control-Shift-J (Win/Linux) or Command-Option-J (Mac).

You can type JavaScript code directly at the command line in the console and press Enter to have it evaluated (see Figure 2-1). Try the following:

```
2 + 3
console.log("I can do JavaScript");
a=2; b=3; console.log(a*b);
```

JavaScript objects

If you've programmed in an object-oriented programming (OOP) language such as C++, Java, or ActionScript 3.0, you have been exposed to classes as the fundamental constructs upon which objects are based. However, JavaScript is a classless language, although it does have OOP capabilities. In JavaScript, objects themselves are the basic units.

So what are objects, and why are they useful? An object is a rather abstract entity. So before we define one, let us explain it by means of an example. Suppose you want to create particles in a project. The particles will have certain properties and will be able to perform certain functions. You can define a general JavaScript *object* (called Particle, say) that has these properties and functions. Then every time you need a particle, you can just create an *instance* of the Particle object. The following sections describe how to do these things.

Objects and properties

We can generalize from the example just given to define an *object* in JavaScript as a collection of *properties*. A property may in turn be defined as an association between a name and a value. The scope of what constitutes the value of a property is rather generous; it can also include functions—see the next section. This makes objects quite versatile.

In addition to existing JavaScript objects, you can create custom objects with custom properties at will. Examples of predefined objects include String, Array, Date and the Math object (which we'll discuss later in this chapter). To create a new object, you can use two alternative forms of syntax, either

```
obj = new Object();
```

Or

```
obj = {};
```

Either of these creates an *instance* of Object. The resulting object obj has no properties. To ascribe properties and corresponding values to it, as well as to access those properties subsequently, we use the dot notation:

```
obj.name = "First object";
obj.length = 20;
console.log(obj.name,obj.length);
```

An alternative syntax is bracket notation:

```
obj["name"] = "First object";
obj["length"] = 20;
```

Functions and methods

We have seen how to assign properties to objects, but how can we make an object do something? That's where functions come in. A function is a block of code that is executed when the function's name is called. The general syntax for a function definition is the following:

```
function functionName(){
    code block
}
```

Optionally, functions can carry any number of *arguments* or *parameters*:

```
function functionName(arg1, arg2){
    code block
}
```

And they can return a value by using a *return* statement, for example:

```
function multiply(x,y){
    return x*y;
}
```

In this example, multiply(2,3) would return the value of 6.

Going back to objects, we define a *method* as a property of an object that is a function. Hence, methods allow objects to do stuff. A method is defined in the same way as a function, but additionally needs to be assigned as a property of an object. This can be done in a number of ways. One syntax is this:

```
objectName.methodName = functionName;
```

For example, to assign the multiply() function as a property of the obj object, we can type

```
obj.multiply = multiply;
```

The function multiply is now a method of obj (we could have used a different method name), and obj.multiply(2,3) would then return 6. We'll come across other ways to assign methods to objects in the next section when we look at constructors.

Prototypes, constructors, and inheritance

An important concept in OOP is that of *inheritance*, which allows you to build a new object from an existing object. The new object then inherits the properties and methods of the old object. In class-based languages, inheritance applies to classes—this is known as classical inheritance. In JavaScript, objects inherit directly from other objects—this is achieved by means of an internal object known as a *prototype*. Hence, inheritance in JavaScript is prototype-based.

The prototype is actually a property of any function. A function is also an object and hence has properties. Properties ascribed to a function's prototype are automatically inherited by new objects constructed from the function object. A function object that is intended to be used for constructing new objects is therefore called a *constructor*. There is nothing special about a constructor function—any function can be used as a constructor. But there is a widespread convention to denote constructors by function names starting with a capital letter.

Here is an example that shows the syntax in action:

```
function Particle(pname){
    this.name = pname;
    this.move = function(){
        console.log(this.name + " is moving");
    };
}
```

This code creates a constructor `Particle` with a property name and a method `move()`. The keyword `this` ensures that these properties are accessible outside the constructor. Any instance of the `Particle` object can then be created by the `new` keyword, and it automatically inherits these properties, as shown in this example:

```
particle1 = new Particle("electron");
particle1.name; // returns "electron"
particle1.move(); // returns "electron is moving"
```

To add new properties to the parent object so that they are inherited by all instances of the object, you need to assign those properties to the parent object's prototype. For example, to add a new property `mass` and a new method `stop()` to the `Particle` object, we can type:

```
Particle.prototype.mass = 1;
Particle.prototype.stop = function(){console.log("I have stopped");};
```

These are then available to all instances of `Particle`, even those instantiated previously, for example:

```
particle1.mass; // returns 1
```

Note that the value of `particle1.mass` can thereafter be changed independently of the default value inherited from `Particle.prototype.mass`, for example:

```
particle1.mass = 2;       // returns 2
Particle.prototype.mass; // returns 1;
```

Other properties can be added to the instance and do not, of course, propagate to the parent object or to other instances. For example, this line:

```
particle1.spin = 0;
```

adds a new property called `spin` to `particle1` and gives it the value of 0. Other instances of `Particle` will not have that property by default.

Static properties and methods

In the example from the preceding section, suppose we assign a new property directly to Particle (and not its prototype), for example:

```
Particle.lifetime = 100;
```

This statement creates a *static* property of Particle that is accessible without the need to instantiate the object. On the other hand, instances of Particle do not inherit the static property.

Naturally, static methods can also be defined. For example, suppose you have the following static method in an object called Physics:

```
function calcGravity(mass,g) {
    return(mass*g);
}
Physics.calcGravity = calcGravity;
```

The function Physics.calcGravity(4, 9.8) would then give you the gravity force on a 4kg object on planet Earth.

The Math object is an example of a built-in JavaScript object that has static properties and methods, such as Math.PI and Math.sin().

Example: a Ball object

As an example of the principles discussed in the last few sections, the file ball.js contains code that creates a Ball object:

```
function Ball (radius, color) {
    this.radius = radius;
    this.color  = color;
    this.x      = 0;
    this.y      = 0;
    this.vx     = 0;
    this.vy     = 0;
}
Ball.prototype.draw = function (context) {
    context.fillStyle = this.color;
    context.beginPath();
    context.arc(this.x, this.y, this.radius, 0, 2*Math.PI, true);
    context.closePath();
    context.fill();
};
```

Note that the Ball object has been given six properties and one method. The drawing code has been placed in the Ball.draw() method, and takes one compulsory argument, the canvas context on which the ball is to be drawn.

The file ball-object.js provides a simple example of the creation of a ball instance from the Ball object:

```
var canvas = document.getElementById('canvas');
var context = canvas.getContext('2d');
var ball = new Ball(50,'#0000ff');
```

17

```
ball.x = 100;
ball.y = 100;
ball.draw(context);
```

We'll make use of this `Ball` object extensively throughout the book, making various modifications to it along the way. As an example, the file `bouncing-ball-object.js` is a modification of the bouncing ball simulation of Chapter 1 to make use of the `Ball` object—take a look!

JavaScript frameworks, libraries, and APIs

If you've had any contact with JavaScript you are probably aware of the existence of numerous libraries and frameworks, such as jQuery and MooTools. These offer the advantage of providing a set of core functionality for commonly needed tasks. However, each has its own learning curve; hence, we will not generally make use of existing libraries or frameworks in this book (the notable exception is when we explore 3D in Chapter 15). Rather, as we proceed through the various chapters, we will create a small library of math- and physics-related objects from scratch.

Likewise, numerous JavaScript APIs exist that bring extended functionality to the web browser. Of particular note is the WebGL API, which uses the HTML5 canvas element to provide 3D graphics capabilities. WebGL is based on OpenGL ES 2.0, and includes shader code that is executed on a computer's GPU (Graphics Processing Unit). WebGL coding is outside of the scope of this book. However, in Chapter 15 we'll make use of a JavaScript library that will greatly simplify the task of creating 3D animations in conjunction with WebGL.

JavaScript language basics

In this section, we review essential code elements in the JavaScript language. Special emphasis is placed on their relevance to math and physics.

Variables

A variable is a container that holds some data. Here data might mean different things, including numbers and text. A variable is defined, or *declared*, using the `var` keyword:

```
var x;
```

Subsequently, x may be *assigned* some value. For example:

```
x = 2;
```

This assignment can be done together with the following variable declaration or anywhere else in the code:

```
var x = 2;
```

One can also perform arithmetic on x; for example, the following code multiplies x by a number, adds the result to another variable y, and assigns the result to a third variable z:

```
z = 2*x + y;
```

This resembles algebra, with some notable differences. The first difference is purely a matter of syntax: We use the operator * to multiply 2 and x. More about operators soon.

The second difference is more subtle and relates to the meaning of an assignment. Although the preceding code may look superficially like an algebraic equation, it is important to note that an assignment is not an equation. The difference can be highlighted by considering an assignment like this one:

```
x = x + 1;
```

If this were an algebraic equation, it would imply that 0 = 1, an impossibility! Here, what it means is that we increase the value of x (whatever it is) by 1.

Variables in JavaScript can have values other than numeric values. The type of value that a variable can hold is called its *data type*.

Data types

Variables in JavaScript have dynamic data types. This means that they can hold different data types at different times. Data types in JavaScript can be divided into two categories: *primitive* and *nonprimitive*. The primitive data types are Number, String, Boolean, Undefined, and Null (the latter two are sometimes referred to as special data types); nonprimitive data types include Object, Array, and Function (which are all types of objects). Table 2-1 lists all these data types. The data type of a variable can be determined by the typeof operator.

Table 2-1. *Data Types in JavaScript*

Data Type	Description
Number	64-bit double-precision floating-point number
String	A sequence of 16-bit characters
Boolean	Has two possible values: true and false, or 1 and 0
Undefined	Returned for a nonexistent object property or a variable without a value
Null	Has only one value: null
Object	Holds a collection of properties and methods
Array	An object consisting of a list of data of any type
Function	A callable object that executes a block of code

Numbers

Unlike in many other programming languages, there is only one numeric data type in JavaScript: Number. There is no distinction between integers and floating-point numbers, for instance.

The Number type is a double-precision 64-bit floating-point number according to the IEEE 754 specification. It is able to store both positive and negative real numbers (not only whole numbers, but those with fractional parts, too). The maximum value that Number can store is 1.8×10^{308}. Given that the number of atoms in the visible universe is estimated to be "only" 10^{80}, this should be enough even for the biggest scientific calculations! It also allows for numbers as small as 5×10^{-324}.

The Number data type also includes the following special values: NaN (not a number), Infinity, and –Infinity. NaN signifies that a numeric value has not been assigned. You'd get NaN as a result of a mathematical operation that produces nonreal or undefined results (for example, by taking the square root of –1 or dividing 0 by 0). Infinity is the result of dividing a nonzero number by 0. You will get positive or negative infinity depending on the sign of the number you are dividing by zero.

19

Strings

A String is a group of characters. For example, the following

```
var str = "Hello there!";
console.log(str);
```

would give this output: "Hello there!"

Note that the value of a String must be enclosed within quotes (single or double). Double quotes can be contained in strings enclosed by single quotes and vice-versa.

Booleans

A Boolean can have only one of two values: true or false. For example:

```
var bln = false;
```

Note that the value true or false is not enclosed within quotes; it is not a string. Particular care must be taken, because JavaScript variables are of dynamic type. Hence, if bln is later assigned the following value:

```
bln = "true";
```

it will become a string variable because of the quotes!

Undefined and Null

The Undefined data type has a single value: undefined. A nonexistent property, or a variable that has been declared but not assigned a value, assumes a value of undefined. A function without a return statement returns undefined. The unsupplied argument of a function also assumes an undefined value.

The Null data type also has a single value: null. A crucial difference between null and undefined is that null is assigned to a variable intentionally, for example

```
var noVal = null;
```

Using the typeof operator on a variable with a null value reveals an Object type rather than an Undefined type or a Null type.

Objects, Functions, and Arrays

We have already come across objects and functions earlier in this chapter. Just like functions, arrays are particular types of objects. An array is an object that holds a collection of items. Suppose you have to keep track of a number of particles in your animation. You could do that by naming them individually as particle1, particle2, particle3, and so on. That might work fine if you have a few particles, but what if you have 100 or 10,000? That's where an array comes in handy. You can just define an array called particles, for example, and put all the particles in there.

A simple way to create an array is by specifying the array elements as a comma-separated list enclosed by square brackets:

```
var arr = new Array();
arr = [2, 4, 6];
arr[1]; // gives 4
```

As the preceding code snippet shows, the resulting array elements are then accessed by arr[*n*], where *n* is an unsigned integer called the *array index*. Note that the array index starts from 0, so that the first array element is arr[0]. Array elements can also be assigned values individually, for example to create a fourth array element and assign it a value of 8:

```
arr[3] = 8;
```

There are several other ways of creating arrays. There are also many rules for the manipulation of arrays and array elements. We'll come across examples of those soon.

You can also create multidimensional arrays, by creating arrays whose elements are also arrays. The following example creates a two-dimensional array from two one-dimensional arrays:

```
var xArr = new Array();
var yArr = new Array();
xArr     = [1,2];
yArr     = [3,4];
var zArr = new Array(xArr,yArr);
zArr[0][1]; // gives 2
zArr[1][0]; // gives 3
```

Note that we've created the third array in a different way, by passing the array elements directly as arguments in Array().

It is possible to add different types of data into the same array. That's because arrays in JavaScript are not typed, unlike in some other languages like C++ and Java.

Operators

You can perform basic arithmetic with numbers with the usual operators (+, -, * and /, respectively) for adding, subtracting, multiplying, and dividing numbers.

There are also a number of other, less obvious operators. The modulo operator % gives the remainder when a number is divided by another. The increment operator (++) increases the value of a number by 1, and the decrement operator (--) reduces the value of a number by 1.

```
var x = 5;
var y = 3;
x%y; // gives 2
var z;
z = x++; // assigns the value of x to z, then increments x
console.log(z); // gives 5
z = ++x // increments the value of x, then assigns it to z
console.log(z); //gives 7
```

Operators can also be combined with assignment. For example:

```
var a = 1;
a = a + 1;
console.log(a); // gives 2
a += 1;         // shortened form of a = a + 1
console.log(a); // gives 3
```

```
a = 4*a;
console.log(a); // gives 12
a *= 4;          // shortened form of a = a*4
console.log(a); // gives 48
```

Math

Besides the basic operators described in the last section, the `Math` object contains many more mathematical functions.

Table 2-2 gives some common examples of `Math` functions and what they do. In the next chapter you will encounter many more `Math` methods, such as trigonometric, exponential, and logarithmic functions.

Table 2-2. *Math Methods*

Method	What it returns
`Math.abs(a)`	absolute value of a
`Math.pow(a,b)`	a to the power of b
`Math.sqrt(a)`	square root of a
`Math.ceil(a)`	smallest integer that is larger than a
`Math.floor(a)`	largest integer that is smaller than a
`Math.round(a)`	nearest integer to a
`Math.max(a,b,c,...)`	largest of a, b, c, ...
`Math.min(a,b,c,...)`	smallest of a, b, c, ...
`Math.random()`	a pseudo-random number n, where $0 <= n < 1$

The last method, `Math.random()`, is an interesting one. It generates a random number between 0 and 1, including 0 but excluding 1. Strictly speaking, the number is pseudorandom because generating it follows an algorithm. But it is good enough for most purposes you're likely to use it for.

Here is an example of how to use the `Math.random()` method. In `bouncing-ball-random.js`, we have made a simple modification so that each time the animation runs, the ball has a different initial velocity. We do this by initializing the horizontal and vertical speeds as follows:

```
vx = Math.random()*5;
vy = (Math.random()-0.5)*4;
```

The first line sets the initial horizontal speed to be between 0 and 5. The second line sets the vertical speed between –2 and 2. What does a *negative vertical speed* mean? It means a speed in the direction opposite to the direction of increasing *y*. Because in the canvas coordinate system *y* increases as we go down (as we'll see later in this chapter), negative vertical speed means that the object moves upward. So each time you reload the page, you'll see the ball initially move up or down with a different horizontal and vertical speed.

Logic

In any programming language, logic is an essential part of coding. Logic enables code to take different actions based on the outcome of some expression.

The simplest way to implement logic in JavaScript is through a basic if *statement*, which has the following structure:

```
if (logical expression){
    do this code
}
```

An if statement basically checks if a logical expression is true. For example, in the bouncing-ball.js code, there is the following logic:

```
if (y > canvas.height - radius){
    y = canvas.height - radius;
    vy *= -0.8;
}
```

This tests whether the ball's vertical position is below the floor level and, if so, repositions the ball exactly at the floor level and then multiplies its vertical speed by –0.8. In this example, the logical expression to be tested is y > canvas.height – radius, and > is a *logical operator* that means "greater than."

Other commonly used logical operators include < (less than), == (equal to), <= (less than or equal to), >= (greater than or equal to), and != (not equal to). There is also a strict equality operator ===, which differs from the equality operator == in that it takes the data type into account when comparing two variables.

Care must be taken not to confuse the equality operator == with the assignment operator =. This is a common source of mistakes and consequent debugging frustration!

There are also && (and) and || (or) operators, which enable you to combine conditions:

```
if (a < 10 || b < 20){
    c = a+b;
}
```

There are more elaborate forms of the if statement. The if else statement is of this form:

```
if (logical expression){
    do this if expression is true
} else {
    do this if expression is false
}
```

You can also use an if else if ... else statement to check for different possibilities:

```
if (a == 0){
    do this if a is zero
} else if (a < 0 ) {
    do this if a is negative
} else if (a > 0) {
    do this if a is positive
} else {
    do this if a is NaN
}
```

Other logical constructs include the *switch* and the *ternary conditional operator*, but we won't be using them in this book.

Try this exercise: modify the `bouncing-ball-random.js` code to recycle the ball so that when it disappears at the right boundary, it starts again at the initial location but with a new random velocity. The answer is in `bouncing-ball-recycled.js`.

Loops

Just like logic, looping is an essential ingredient of programming. One of the things that make computers useful is their capability to repeat operations over and over again, much more quickly than humans, and without ever getting bored. They do it by *looping*.

In JavaScript there are several kinds of loops. We'll review just a couple of those here.

The for *loop* is the one that we'll make most use of. Here is an example of a for loop, used for summing the first 100 positive integers:

```
var sum = 0;
for (var i = 1; i <= 100; i++) {
    sum += i;
}
console.log(sum);
```

The first line initializes the value of the variable sum to 0. The next line sets up the loop—the variable i is a counter, set to start at 1 (you could start it from 0 or any other integer), up to and including 100, and told to increment by 1 (i++) on each step. So the loop executes 100 times, each time adding the current value of i to sum.

Looping over elements of an array is an especially useful technique. Suppose you want to animate five bouncing balls rather than one. To see how you'd do it, take a look at the code in `bouncing-balls.js`, which builds upon the code in `bouncing-ball-object.js`.

The main idea is to modify the init() function so that we create a bunch of balls, give each one a position and velocity, and put them into an array named balls using the push() method:

```
function init() {
    balls = new Array();
    for (var i=0; i<numBalls; i++){
        var ball = new Ball(radius,color);
        ball.x = 50;
        ball.y = 75;
        ball.vx = Math.random()*5;
        ball.vy = (Math.random()-0.5)*4;
        ball.draw(context);
        balls.push(ball);
    }
    setInterval(onEachStep, 1000/60); // 60 fps
};
```

Naturally, the event handler (see the section "Event listeners and handlers" later in this chapter) is also modified to loop over all the balls:

```javascript
function onEachStep() {
    context.clearRect(0, 0, canvas.width, canvas.height);
    for (var i=0; i<numBalls; i++){
        var ball = balls[i];
        ball.vy += g;
        ball.x += ball.vx;
        ball.y += ball.vy;
        if (ball.y > canvas.height - radius){
            ball.y = canvas.height - radius;
            ball.vy *= -0.8;
        }
        if (ball.x > canvas.width + radius){
            ball.x = -radius;
        }
        ball.draw(context);
    }
};
```

Don't worry that the balls just pass through each other when they meet. That's because your code doesn't know about collision detection yet! We'll fix that in a later chapter.

Note that in order to use a for loop, you need to know exactly how many times you want to loop. If you don't, or if you have array keys which are discontinuous, then there are other options, such as for ... in, for each ... in, and while loops. We won't describe the first two as we don't make use of them in this book.

In a while loop, you tell the loop to execute as long as some condition is true, no matter how many times through the loop are needed. The basic structure of a while loop is as follows:

```javascript
while (some condition) {
    do something
}
```

For example, suppose you want to know the minimum number of consecutive integers you must sum, starting from 1, to obtain at least 1000. Here is a while loop to do this:

```javascript
var sum = 0;
var i = 1;
while (sum < 1000) {
    sum += i;
    i++;
}
console.log(i-1);
```

You can also use a while loop in the same way as a for loop, to perform an operation a fixed number of times, for example, to sum the first 100 positive integers:

```javascript
var sum = 0;
var i = 1;
while (i <= 100) {
    sum += i;
    i++;
}
console.log(sum);
```

Be careful with while loops— if the condition is always true, you'll end up with an infinite loop, and the code will never stop executing!

A variation is a do ... while loop, in which the condition is checked after the loop instead of before. This ensures that the code within the loop executes at least once:

```
do {
    do something
} while (some condition);
```

Events and user interaction

An *event* allows a given course of action to be replaced by a different course of action. User interaction, for example via the keyboard or mouse, generates special event types. Events and user interaction contribute in a major way to making interactive media as interesting as they are. JavaScript can be used to react to HTML DOM events.

Event listeners and handlers

There are two aspects to event management: tracking events and responding to them. *Event listeners* "listen" to events, and *event handlers* take the appropriate action. The listeners are HTML DOM elements. The syntax for setting up a particular DOM element as a listener for a particular event is as follows:

```
someElement.addEventListener(event_type, handler [, useCapture]);
```

The different types of events that can be specified as event_type will be discussed in the next section. Here handler is simply a function that is called whenever an event of type event_type happens. The third argument, useCapture, is usually optional; however, in some older browser implementations it is not. Hence, we will always specify it as false in this book. The value of useCapture determines how events bubble up the DOM tree, and it need not concern us here.

You can also remove an event listener in exactly the same way, replacing addEventListener by removeEventListener:

```
someElement.removeEventListener(event_type, handler [, useCapture]);
```

User interaction: keyboard, mouse, and touch events

The events that we're generally interested in are keyboard, mouse, and touch events. These types of events are great because they allow the user to interact with an animation or simulation. We don't have space for reviewing all the different types of events, and will merely provide some examples to explain the usage. The reader is referred to the books mentioned at the end of this chapter for more detailed information. As a simple example, suppose we want to pause the bouncing ball animation when the user clicks and holds down the mouse, and resume it when the mouse is released. This can be achieved easily using the 'mousedown' and 'mouseup' events. Just modify the init() method as follows:

```
function init() {
    canvas.addEventListener('mousedown',stopAnim,false);
    canvas.addEventListener('mouseup',startAnim,false);
    startAnim();
};
```

and include these event handlers:

```
function startAnim() {
    interval = setInterval(onEachStep, 1000/60); // 60 fps
}
```

```
function stopAnim() {
    clearInterval(interval);
}
```

The code is in bouncing-ball-pause.js.

Drag and drop

Often one wants to drag and move an object in an interactive animation. A simple trick to do that is to force the position of the object to match that of the mouse cursor when the mouse is pressed on the object and moved around. To illustrate the method, we will modify the bouncing-ball-object.js code, so that now you can click the ball, move it anywhere on the stage, and then release it again.

To do this, make the following changes. First, add the following code block to the init() function:

```
canvas.addEventListener('mousedown', function () {
    canvas.addEventListener('mousemove',onDrag,false);
    canvas.addEventListener('mouseup',onDrop,false);
}, false);
```

This sets up a 'mousedown' event listener, which in turn sets up 'mousemove' and 'mouseup' listeners. Then add the following event handlers:

```
function onDrag(evt){
    isDragging = true;
    ball.x = evt.clientX;
    ball.y - evt.clientY;
}
function onDrop(){
    isDragging = false;
    canvas.removeEventListener('mousemove',onDrag,false);
    canvas.removeEventListener('mouseup',onDrop,false);
}
```

The clientX and clientY properties provide a simple way to track the mouse location. The isDragging Boolean variable must be declared and set to false at the beginning of the code:

```
var isDragging = false;
```

As its name indicates, isDragging tells us if the object is being dragged. This is needed to stop the physics part of the code from executing while dragging is taking place. Hence, we wrap the physics code in the following if block in function onEachStep:

```
if (isDragging==false){
    execute physics code
}
```

You will also need to set the initial values of vx and vy to zero, the initial value of ball.y to canvas.height - radius (so that it is initially stationary on the ground), and ball.x to any suitable value so that it is visible on the stage. The modified code is in bouncing-ball-drag-drop.js. Try it out. You will notice a couple of oddities—first, the ball moves to the mouse position even if you click outside the ball; second, the ball's center jumps to the mouse location. You will be able to fix these issues when you learn how to work out the distance between two points in the next chapter.

The canvas coordinate system

In the real world things exist in space. In the HTML5 world the equivalent is that objects exist on the canvas element. To know how to position objects on canvas, it is necessary to understand the canvas coordinate system.

The canvas coordinate system is somewhat different from the usual Cartesian system of coordinates in math. In normal coordinate geometry, the x-coordinate runs from left to right, and the y-coordinate runs from bottom to top (see Figure 2-2b). In canvas, however, the y-coordinate runs in the opposite way, from top to bottom (see Figure 2-2a). The origin is in the top-left corner of the visible stage.

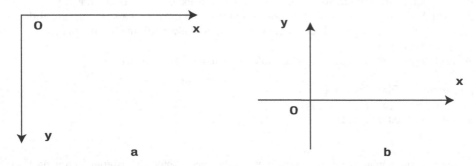

Figure 2-2. *2D coordinate systems compared: (a) in canvas and (b) math*

The usual Cartesian system is called a *right-handed coordinate system* because if you hold your right hand with your fingers partly closed and your thumb pointing out of the paper, your fingers will point from the positive x-axis to the positive y-axis. By implication, the coordinate system in canvas is a *left-handed coordinate system.*

Another oddity in the canvas coordinate system is that angles are measured in a clockwise sense from the direction of the positive x-axis (see Figure 2-3a). The usual convention in math is that angles are measured counterclockwise from the positive x-axis (see Figure 2-3b).

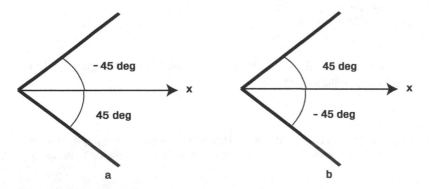

Figure 2-3. *Angles as measured in (a) canvas and (b) math coordinate systems*

The canvas drawing API

The canvas drawing *application programming interface (API)* allows you to draw things such as shapes and fills using JavaScript. The canvas drawing API provides a rich set of functionality through a relatively small number of methods. We will only go through a few for illustrative purposes here.

The canvas context

The object that allows access to the canvas drawing API is the *canvas rendering context.* The API is nothing but a collection of properties and methods of that object. The first two lines of code in bouncing-ball.js in Chapter 1 show how to access the canvas context:

```
var canvas = document.getElementById('canvas');
var context = canvas.getContext('2d');
```

The string '2d' in the canvas element's getContext method is self-explanatory: the HTML5 standard specifies a 2D drawing API, which is supported by all modern browsers.

The canvas context has a number of properties and methods—rather than list all of them, we'll pick just a few to illustrate how we can accomplish certain common drawing tasks.

Drawing lines and curves

The following are a few essential properties and methods of the canvas context for drawing basic shapes using lines and curves:

- The strokeStyle property specifies the line color in CSS-style format. The default value is '#000000' (black).

- The lineWidth property specifies the line thickness in pixels. The default value is 1.

- The beginPath() method resets the current path. A path is a collection of subpaths. Each subpath is a set of points connected by straight or curved lines.

- The closePath() method closes the current subpath and starts a new one from the end of the closed subpath.

- The moveTo(x, y) method moves the cursor to the specified location (x, y) without drawing anything, that is, it creates a new subpath from the specified point.

- The lineTo(x, y) method draws a straight line from the current location to the new location (x, y) specified in its argument, that is, it adds a new point to a subpath and connects that point to the previous point in the subpath with a straight line.

- The arc(x, y, radius, startAngle, endAngle, anticlockwise) method adds an arc to the path with center (x, y), and of the specified radius. The starting and ending angles are in radians (see chapter 3). The anticlockwise parameter is a boolean: if true, the arc is drawn in a counterclockwise direction; if false, it is drawn in a clockwise direction.

- The rect(x, y, w, h) method creates a new closed rectangular subpath with the upper-left corner at (x, y) and width w and height h.

- The stroke() method renders the current subpath using the current stroke styles.

- The strokeRect(x, y, w, h) method combines the last two methods to render an outline of the specified rectangle.

As a simple example, to draw a blue 2-pixel straight line from the point (50, 100) to (250, 400), you would do something like this:

```
context.strokeStyle = '#0000ff';
context.lineWidth = 2;
context.beginPath() ;
```

```
context.moveTo(50, 100);
context.lineTo(250, 400);
context.stroke();
```

Note that if the `stroke()` method is not invoked, then nothing will be rendered, and the path will be invisible! As an exercise, try drawing a grid using these methods. See the code in `drawing-api-grid.js`.

Creating fills and gradients

Producing fills is a straightforward process with the aid of the following commands:

- The `fillStyle` property gets or sets the style for filling shapes. It can be a color or a gradient.

- The `fill()` method fills subpaths using the current fill style.

- The `fillRect(x, y, w, h)` method creates a filled rectangle with the upper-left corner at `(x, y)` and width `w` and height `h`, using the current fill style.

The following code snippet produces a green rectangle with a blue border:

```
context.strokeStyle = '#0000ff';
context.lineWidth = 2;
context.beginPath() ;
context.moveTo(50, 50);
context.lineTo(150, 50);
context.lineTo(150, 200);
context.lineTo(50, 200);
context.lineTo(50, 50);
context.stroke();
context.fillStyle = '#00ff00';
context.fill();
```

And this single additional line of code will produce a green rectangle without a border:

```
context.fillRect(250,50,150,100);
```

You can use the following additional methods for creating gradients:

- The `createLinearGradient(x0, y0, x1, y1)` method creates a linear gradient object, where `(x0, y0)` is the start point and `(x1, y1)` is the end point of the gradient.

- The `createRadialGradient(x0, y0, r0, x1, y1, r1)` method creates a radial gradient object, where `(x0, y0)` and `r0` are the center and radius of the starting circle, and `(x1, y1)` and `r1` are the center and radius of the ending circle of the gradient.

- The `Gradient.addColorStop(offset, color)` method adds the specified color and offset position in a canvas gradient object. The offset is a decimal number between 0 and 1, where 0 and 1 represent the start and end points in a gradient.

The following example creates a ball with a radial gradient, against a background "sky" represented using a linear gradient (see Figure 2-4).

Figure 2-4. *A linear gradient and a radial gradient produced using the canvas drawing API*

```
gradient = context.createLinearGradient(0,0,0,500);
gradient.addColorStop(0,'ffffff');
gradient.addColorStop(1,'0000ff');
context.fillStyle = gradient;
context.fillRect(0,0,700,500);

gradient1 = context.createRadialGradient(350,250,5,350,250,50);
gradient1.addColorStop(0,'ffffff');
gradient1.addColorStop(1,'ff0000');
context.fillStyle = gradient1;
context.arc(350,250,50,0,2*Math.PI,true);
context.fill();
```

Animating using the canvas context

So far we have been drawing static shapes—but how do we animate objects on the canvas? The approach is very basic—simply erase everything and redraw over and over again! This can be accomplished using the `clearRect()` method: The `clearRect(x, y, w, h)` method clears the pixels on a canvas context within a rectangle with the upper-left corner at (x, y) and width w and height h.

The following line of code clears the entire content of the canvas element:

```
context.clearRect(0,0,canvas.width,canvas.height);
```

Repeated application of `clearRect()` before each time step then creates an empty canvas context to draw on. The next section describes how to do the time-stepping.

Producing animation using code

Producing animation using code is one of the main themes of this book. In addition, since our focus is to produce physics-based animation, we need a method to measure the advancement of time. We need a clock. We have already introduced the `setInterval()` function, which to some extent accomplishes this task. So let's begin by looking at this and related functions.

Using JavaScript timers

The "old" classic way of animating in JavaScript involves the use of a timer function, There are a couple of those: setTimeout() and setInterval(). The latter is what we have been using in the examples so far.

- The setTimeout(func,timeDelay) function will execute the specified function func() once after a delay of timeDelay (in milliseconds).

- The setInterval(func,timeDelay) function will execute the specified function func() repeatedly after successive delays of timeDelay (in milliseconds).

- The corresponding functions clearTimeout(timerId) and clearInterval(timerId) clear the setTimeout() and setInterval() timers respectively, where timerId is a variable to which they are assigned.

The generic syntax for the use of these functions is demonstrated here:

```
intervalID = setInterval(func,timeDelay);
function timeDelay(){
     some code
}
clearInterval(intervalId);
```

We have already encountered the use of setInterval() in various versions of the bouncing ball simulation. A stripped-down example of the use of setInterval for animation is given in the file timer-example.js.

We can specify the time delay in the setInterval() function as 1000/fps, where fps is the *frame rate* of the animation, that is, the number of updates or frames per second.

How is the frame rate related to the perceived speed of an animation? To answer this question, we'll need to do some simple math. Suppose that we want to move an object at a constant velocity of 100 pixels per second, and suppose that the frame rate of the animation is 50 fps. Let's increment the object's horizontal position by vx per frame as in the bouncing ball example:

```
function onEachStep(){
     ball.x += vx;
}
```

In other words, vx is the horizontal velocity in units of pixels per frame. What value must we give vx? Well, the velocity in units of pixels per second is 100, and there are 50 frames per second. So the value of vx is 100/50 or 2. In general, we have the following relationship:

(Velocity in pixels per second) = (Velocity in pixels per frame) × (Frame rate in fps)

Okay, so if we set vx = 2, we should see the ball moving at 100 pixels per second. The speed in pixels per second is what we actually perceive on the screen. However, there is no guarantee that the frame rate at which the movie runs will be exactly the frame rate that is set. Suppose that your machine is slow or there are other things running on it, so that the actual frame rate is closer to 30 fps. This gives an actual velocity of only 60 pixels per second. Your object appears to be moving slower. Hence, setting the frame rate in a setInterval() function does not guarantee the speed of an animation. We will look at how to resolve this problem shortly. But first we'll introduce another, more recent, method of animation using JavaScript—the requestAnimationFrame() method.

Using requestAnimationFrame()

In recent years, a new API has emerged among web browsers, allowing developers to create HTML5 animations that benefit from browser-based optimizations, allowing significant performance gains over the old setInterval() and setTimeout() methods.

The function `requestAnimationFrame(someFunction)` calls the function `someFunction()` before redrawing the browser screen. Some browser implementations also include a second parameter to specify the HTML5 element to which the redrawing applies, for example `requestAnimationFrame(someFunction, canvas)`.

To create an animation loop using `requestAnimationFrame()`, you just include it within the function that it calls! For example:

```
function animFrame(){
    requestAnimationFrame(animFrame,canvas);
    onEachStep();
}
```

The `onEachStep()` function is the one that contains the animation code. As an example, the `timer-example.js` code has been modified to use `requestAnimationFrame()`, and the resulting code is given in `frame-example.js`. This is an important example, since we will use the basic code setup within it as the basis for most of the animations in the rest of the book. We therefore reproduce the code in its entirety here for quick reference:

```
var canvas = document.getElementById('canvas');
var context = canvas.getContext('2d');
var ball;

window.onload = init;

function init() {
    ball = new Ball(20,"#0000ff");
    ball.x = 50; ball.y = 250;
    ball.vx = 2;
    ball.draw(context);
    animFrame();
};
function animFrame(){
    requestAnimationFrame(animFrame,canvas);
    onEachStep();
};
function onEachStep() {
    ball.x += ball.vx;
    context.clearRect(0, 0, canvas.width, canvas.height);
    ball.draw(context);
};
```

Despite the superior performance of the `requestAnimationFrame()` function compared to `setInterval()` and `setTimeout()`, it suffers from the limitation that there is no built-in way to control the frame rate. A simple trick to constrain the frame rate is to nest the `requestAnimationFrame()` function within a `setTimeout()` function. In the previous example, we can modify the `animFrame()` function to the following:

```
function animFrame(){
    setTimeout(function() {
        requestAnimationFrame(animFrame,canvas);
        onEachStep();
    }, 1000/60);
}
```

This of course does not guarantee that the frame rate will be exactly 60 fps. One of the main problems is that the time interval between timer events actually includes the time it takes to execute all the code within the event handler on top of the specified delay. If there is a lot of code in your event handler, it might mean your timer ticking rate is substantially slower than you specified.

Using getTime() to compute elapsed time

Bad timekeeping can really mess up your physics. For really accurate timekeeping, what we need is a way to measure actual elapsed time. Fortunately, there is a simple way to do this: using the getTime() function. And the method can be used with either setInterval() or requestAnimationFrame().

The getTime() function is a method of the built-in JavaScript Date object, and it returns an integer equal to the number of milliseconds that have elapsed since midnight on 1 January 1970. So if you call Date.getTime() twice, in different parts of the code, and work out the difference in the returned value, that would give you the time that has elapsed between those two calls.

How does that help us with animation? The point is that we can calculate the actual time that has elapsed since an object's position was last updated. Then we can use that time to calculate the amount by which to move it.

To see this in action, getTime-example.js modifies the frame-example.js code to animate the motion of a ball moving at constant horizontal velocity vx. Here is the modified event handler:

```
function onEachStep() {
    var t1 = new Date().getTime(); // current time in milliseconds
    dt = 0.001*(t1-t0); // time elapsed in seconds since last call
    t0 = t1; // reset t0
    ball.x += ball.vx * dt;
    context.clearRect(0, 0, canvas.width, canvas.height);
    ball.draw(context);
};
```

We added three lines here. The first line gets the current time in milliseconds by invoking Date().getTime(). The second line works out the time elapsed dt (this notation will become clear in the next chapter) since the last time the call to onEachStep() was made. Here t0 is a variable initialized to new Date().getTime() before the start of the animation. The next line resets t0 so that it can be used for the next call.

You'll see also that we modified the code that updates the ball's position. We're now adding an amount vx*dt to the ball's current position instead of vx, as before. What's going on here? Well, this is the whole point of calculating the elapsed time dt. You see, previously we were interpreting the velocity vx as pixels moved per frame (if using requestAnimationFrame) or per tick (if using setInterval). In doing so, we were assuming that the frames or ticks were of fixed duration, and that duration was just what we specified in the frame rate or timer delay parameter. As long as those assumptions work, we can use frames or timer ticks as a good proxy for time, and thinking of velocity in terms of pixels per frame or timer tick is a good idea. But what we're saying is this: let's get back to thinking about velocity in the correct way, as pixels moved per second. Therefore, in dt seconds, the distance moved is vx*dt, so that the new position is this:

```
ball.x += vx*dt;
```

The advantage of going back to the real meaning of velocity is that the motion is always computed correctly, independently of the frame rate or timer tick rate. This technique will come in handy when we start looking at more complex physics. But even with this simple example, you can see how the animation reflects real physics by varying the value of ball.vx, and seeing how the ball moves exactly at the specified velocity in pixels per second.

Here is the code for getTime-example.as in its entirety:

```
var canvas = document.getElementById('canvas');
var context = canvas.getContext('2d');
var ball;
var t;

window.onload = init;

function init() {
    ball = new Ball(20,"#0000ff");
    ball.x = 50; ball.y = 250;
    ball.vx = 200;
    ball.draw(context);
    t = new Date().getTime(); // initialize value of t
    animFrame();
};
function animFrame(){
    requestAnimationFrame(animFrame,canvas);
    onEachStep();
};
function onEachStep() {
    var dt = (new Date().getTime() - t)/1000; // time elapsed in seconds since last call
    t = new Date().getTime(); // reset t
    ball.x += ball.vx * dt;
    context.clearRect(0, 0, canvas.width, canvas.height);
    ball.draw(context);
};
```

Precalculating motion

As you'll now be aware, the methods for animating objects with code we're using work by calculating updates to the object's position "on the fly." It might also be possible to precalculate the motion of an object and animate it afterward. This can be done by using a for or while loop to represent time-stepping, calculating the particles position at each step and saving the position coordinates in an array.

Why would you want to do that? It can be useful, for example, if calculations take too long to perform and cannot fit within a reasonable frame rate.

The downside of this method is that it doesn't work with interactivity. Because user interaction is usually an important aspect of physics-based applications, we won't generally use this approach.

Summary

Wow! This chapter has been a whirlwind tour through vast stretches of JavaScript and the HTML5 canvas. Hopefully, you've now gained an appreciation of how they can be useful for physics-based animation.

If you've struggled with any of the material in this chapter, we highly recommend that you brush up on your knowledge of JavaScript and HTML5. Here are a couple of books that we particularly recommend for beginners:

- *Foundation HTML5 Canvas: For Games and Entertainment,* by Rob Hawkes (Apress, ISBN: 978-1430232919).

- *Foundation HTML5 Animation with JavaScript,* by Billy Lamberta and Keith Peters (Apress, ISBN: 978-1430236658).

CHAPTER 3

∎ ∎ ∎

Some Math Background

Programming even the simplest physics inevitably involves some math. Therefore, we assume that readers of this book are comfortable with math notation and have at least some math knowledge. This knowledge need not be very sophisticated; familiarity with basic algebra and simple algebraic manipulations of equations and formulas is the most important requirement and will be assumed without review. In addition, some appreciation of coordinate geometry and the basics of trigonometry and vectors would provide a good foundation. In case you need it, this chapter provides a review or refresher of these topics. Prior knowledge of calculus is a bonus, but is not essential; similarly for numerical methods. We provide an overview of the basic concepts involved in these topics at a level sufficient to apply them in physics programming.

Topics covered in this chapter include the following:

- **Coordinates and simple graphs:** Math functions and their graphs crop up constantly in physics applications. We review some common math functions and plot their graphs using a custom JavaScript graph-plotting object. We also show how to make an object move along any curve described by a mathematical equation.

- **Basic trigonometry:** Trigonometry crops up a lot in graphics and animation in general, and is pretty much an indispensable tool in physics-based animation. In this section, we'll review some trigonometry essentials that will be used in later chapters. We'll also get to play with trig functions such as sin and cos to produce some cool animation effects.

- **Vectors and vector algebra:** Vectors are useful because physics equations can be expressed, manipulated, and coded up more simply using them. After a review of vector concepts, we'll construct a JavaScript Vector2D object that will be used throughout the rest of the book.

- **Simple calculus ideas:** Calculus deals with things that change continuously, including motion. It is, therefore, a natural tool to apply to physics. Calculus is usually considered part of advanced math. So we'll give only an overview of the basic concepts here to show how they can be implemented in physics equations and in code.

Although this chapter consists of review material, much of it covers application of the math in JavaScript and physics. Therefore, even if you have a solid math background, we recommend that you at least skim through this chapter to see how we apply the math.

In our attempt to illustrate the application of otherwise abstract math concepts to physics, we have picked some examples of physics concepts that will be explained more fully in later chapters. So don't worry if you don't immediately get everything that we'll cover here; you can always come back to this chapter as needed.

Coordinates and simple graphs

Coordinate geometry provides a way to visualize relationships expressed as mathematical functions or equations. This section will review some things you'd have covered in your school math classes, but mixed with a lot of JavaScript code to emphasize the application of those math concepts.

To get started, let's remember how to plot functions on graphs. Say you want to plot the graph of the function $y = x^2$. The first thing you must do is to decide what range of values you want to plot. Suppose you want x to range from –4 to 4. Then what you might have done at school is tabulate the values of x and the corresponding values of y that you get by using $y = x^2$. Then you might have plotted each (x, y) pair of values as a dot on graph paper and then joined the dots to make a smooth curve. Don't worry; we won't ask you to do this here. Instead of reaching for graph paper, let's do it with JavaScript!

Building a plotter: the Graph object

The Graph object is a custom object we created that does just what its name suggests: draw graphs. You're welcome to have a look at the code, but what it does is quite simple: it has methods that draw a set of axes and major and minor grid lines using the drawing API. It also has a method to plot data. The Graph object takes nine arguments in its constructor:

```
Graph(context,xmin, xmax, ymin, ymax, x0, y0, xwidth, ywidth)
```

The first argument is simply the canvas context on which any instance of the Graph object is to be drawn. The next four arguments (xmin, xmax, ymin, ymax) denote the minimum and maximum desired values of x and y. The next two parameters (x0, y0) denote the coordinates of the origin in the canvas coordinate system, in pixels. The final two parameters specify the width and height of the graph object in pixels.

The function drawgrid() takes four numeric arguments, which specify the major and minor divisions:

```
drawgrid(xmajor, xminor, ymajor, yminor)
```

It draws corresponding grid lines and labels the values at the relevant major grid locations.

The function drawaxes() takes two optional arguments that specify the text labels on the axes as strings. It draws the axes and labels them, the default labels being "x" and "y".

```
drawaxes(xlabel, ylabel)
```

An example will make the usage clear. Suppose we want to plot the function $y = x^2$ over the range of values specified for x from –4 to 4. Then the corresponding range of values of y would be from 0 to 16. This tells us that the graph should accommodate positive and negative values for x, but only needs to have positive values for y. If the available area is 550 by 400 pixels, a good position to place the origin would be at (275, 380). Let's choose the width and height of the graph to be 450 and 350 so that it fills most of the available space. We will set the range in x and y (xmin, xmax, ymin, and ymax) to be (–4, 4, 0, 20). Sensible choices for (xmajor, xminor, ymajor, and yminor) are (1, 0.2, 5, and 1):

```
var graph = new Graph(context, -4, 4, 0, 20, 275, 380, 450, 350);
graph.drawgrid(1, 0.2, 5, 1);
graph.drawaxes('x','y');
```

You can find the code in graph-example.js, from this book's download page on http://apress.com. Go on, try it yourself and change the parameters to see the effect. It's not really hard, and you'll soon get the hang of it.

Plotting functions using the Graph object

What we've done so far is to make the equivalent of a piece of graph paper, with labeled axes on it. To plot a graph, we use the Graph object's plot() method. This method plots pairs of values of x and y and optionally joins them with a line of specified color:

```
public function plot(x, y, color, dots, line)
```

The values of x and y are to be specified as separate arrays in the first two arguments. The third, optional, parameter color is a string that denotes the color of the plot. Its default value is "#0000ff", representing blue. The last two parameters, dots and line, are optional Boolean parameters. If dots is true (the default), a small circle (radius 1 pixel) is drawn at each point with the specified color. If line is true (the default), the points are joined by a line of the same color. If you look at the code, you'll see that the dot is drawn using the arc() method, and the line is drawn using the lineTo() method.

Let's now plot the graph of $y = x^2$:

```
var xvals = new Array(-4,-3,-2,-1,0,1,2,3,4);
var yvals = new Array(16,9,4,1,0,1,4,9,16);
graph.plot(xvals, yvals);
```

There's our graph, but it looks a bit odd and is not a smooth curve at all. The problem is that we don't have enough points. The lineTo() method joins the points using a straight line, and if the distance between adjacent points is large, the plot does not look good.

We can do better than that by computing the array elements from within the code. Let's do this:

```
var xA = new Array();
var yA = new Array();
for (var i=0; i<=100; i++){
    xA[i] = (i-50)*0.08;
    yA[i] = xA[i]*xA[i];
}
graph.plot(xA, yA, "0xff0000", false, true);
```

We've now used 101 x-y pairs of values instead of just 9. Note that we have subtracted the index i by 50 and multiplied the result by 0.08 to give the same range in x as in the previous array xvals(that is, from –4 to 4). The result is shown in Figure 3-1. As you can see, the plot gives a smooth curve. This particular curve has a shape called a *parabola*. In the next few sections, we'll use the Graph class to produce plots for different types of math functions.

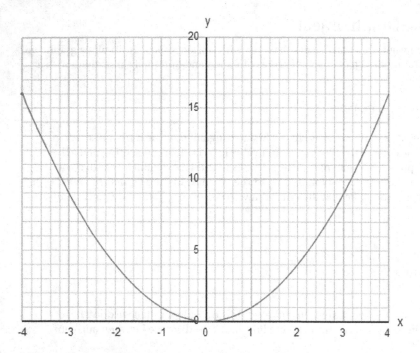

Figure 3-1. *Plotting the function y = x² using the Graph object*

Drawing straight lines

We'll start with linear functions, such as $y = 2x + 1$. Type the following code or copy it from graph-functions.js:

```
var canvas = document.getElementById('canvas');
var context = canvas.getContext('2d');

var graph = new Graph(context,-4,4,-10,10,275,210,450,350);
graph.drawgrid(1,0.2,5,1);
graph.drawaxes('x','y');
var xA = new Array();
var yA = new Array();
for (var i=0; i<=100; i++){
    xA[i] = (i-50)*0.08;
    yA[i] = f(xA[i]);
}
graph.plot(xA,yA,'#ff0000',false,true);

function f(x){
    var y;
    y = 2*x + 1;
    return y;
}
```

Note that we've moved the math function to a JavaScript function called f() to make things slightly easier to see and modify.

The graph is a straight line. If you wish, play around with different linear equations of the form $y = ax + b$, for different values of a and b. You'll see that they are always straight lines.

Where does the line meet the y-axis? You'll find that it is always at $y = b$. That's because on the y-axis, $x = 0$. Putting $x = 0$ in the equation gives $y = b$. The value b is called the *intercept* on the y-axis. What is the significance of a? You'll find out later in this chapter, in the section on calculus.

Drawing polynomial curves

You've already seen that the equation $y = x^2$ gives a parabolic curve. Experiment with `graph-functions.js` by plotting different quadratic functions of the form $y = ax^2 + bx + c$, for different values of a, b and c, for example:

```
y = x*x - 2*x - 3;
```

You may need to change the range of the graph. You'll find that they are all parabolic. If the value of a is positive, you will always get a bowl-shaped curve; if a is negative, the curve will be hill-shaped.

Linear and quadratic functions are special cases of polynomial functions. In general, a polynomial function is created by adding terms with different powers of x. The highest power of x is called the *degree* of the polynomial. So a quadratic is a degree 2 polynomial. Higher polynomials have more twists and turns; for example, this polynomial will give you the plot shown in Figure 3-2:

```
y = -0.5*Math.pow(x,5) + 3*Math.pow(x,3) + x*x - 2*x - 3;
```

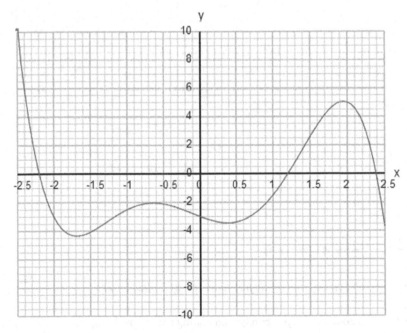

Figure 3-2. *A polynomial curve* $y = -0.5\,x^5 + 3x^3 + x^2 - 2x - 3$

Things that grow and decay: exponential and log functions

There are many more exotic types of functions that display interesting behavior. One interesting example is the exponential function, which crops up all over physics. It is defined mathematically by

$$y = e^x$$

You might be wondering what e stands for. It's a special number approximately equal to 2.71828. In this respect, e is a math constant like π, which cannot be written down in exact decimal form, but is approximately equal to 3.14159. Constants such as π and e appear all over physics.

The exponential function is also sometimes written as $\exp(x)$. JavaScript has a built in `Math.exp()` function. It also has a `Math.E` static constant with the value of 2.718281828459045.

Let's plot `Math.exp(x)` then!

As you can see from Figure 3-3, the graph of $\exp(x)$ goes to zero as x becomes more negative and increases more rapidly as x becomes more positive. You've heard of the term *exponential growth*. This is it. If you now plot $\exp(-x)$, you'll see the reverse: as x increases from negative to positive values, $\exp(-x)$ decays rapidly to zero. This is *exponential decay*. Note that when x is 0, both $\exp(x)$ and $\exp(-x)$ are exactly equal to 1. That's because any number to the power of zero is equal to 1.

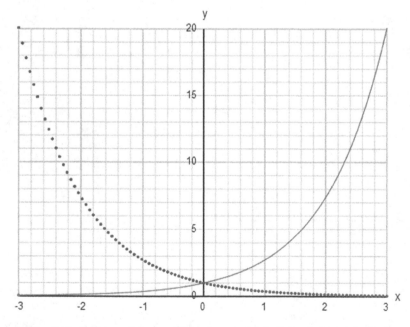

Figure 3-3. *Exponential growth function exp(x) (solid curve) and decay function exp(-x) (dotted curve)*

Nothing stops us from combining functions, of course, and you can get interesting shapes by doing that. For example, try plotting the exponential of $-x^2$:

$$y = \exp\left(-x^2\right)$$

This gives a bell-shaped curve (technically it's called a *Gaussian curve*), as shown in Figure 3-4. It has a maximum in the middle and falls rapidly toward zero on either side. In Figure 3-4, the curve appears to fall to zero because of the limited resolution of the plotted graph. In reality, it never gets to exactly zero because exp($-x^2$) becomes vanishingly small for large positive and negative values of x, but never becomes exactly zero.

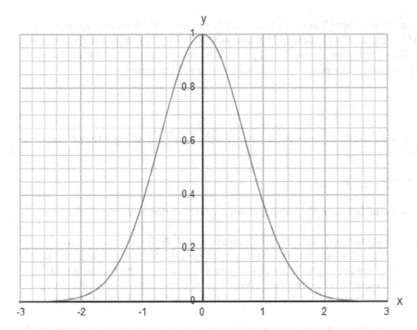

Figure 3-4. *The bell-shaped (Gaussian) function exp($-x^2$)*

Making an object move along a curve

Let's have some fun and make a ball move along a curve. To do this, we have restructured graph-functions.js and added three new functions to the new code move-curve.js:

```
function placeBall(){
    ball = new Ball(6,"#0000ff");
    ball.x = xA[0]/xscal+ xorig;
    ball.y = -yA[0]/yscal + yorig;
    ball.draw(context);
}

function setupTimer(){
    idInterval = setInterval(moveBall, 1000/60);
}

function moveBall(){
    ball.x = xA[n]/xscal + xorig;
    ball.y = -yA[n]/yscal + yorig;
    context.clearRect(0, 0, canvas.width, canvas.height);
    ball.draw(context);
```

```
        n++;
        if (n==xA.length){
            clearInterval(idInterval);
        }
}
```

The function `placeBall()` is called after `plotGraph()` in `init()` and simply places a `Ball` instance at the beginning of the curve. Then `setupTimer()` is called after `placeBall()`, and exactly as its name suggests, it sets up a timer, using the `setInterval()` function. The event handler `moveBall()` runs at every `setInterval()` call and moves the ball along the curve, clearing the `setInterval()` instance when it reaches the end of the curve.

Fun with hills

You can make an object move along the curve of any function you like; for example $y = x^2$. But let's go crazy and try something more fun, such as this degree 6 polynomial:

```
y = 0.2*(x+3.6)*(x+2.5)*(x+1)*(x-0.5)*(x-2)*(x-3.5);
```

You can see that this is a degree 6 polynomial because if you expand out the factors, the term with the highest power of x will be $0.2\,x^6$.

Run the code with this function to see the animation. Does that give you any ideas? Perhaps you could use a curve to represent a hilly landscape and build a game where you try to push a ball over the hills. The only problem is that the curve shoots off to very large values at the ends. This is inevitable with polynomials. The reason is that for large positive or negative values of x, the highest term (in this case, $0.2\,x^6$) will always dominate over the rest. So, in this example, we'll get very large values because of the effect of the $0.2\,x^6$ term. In the math jargon, the curve "blows up" in those limits.

Let's remedy this by multiplying the whole thing by a bell function of the type $\exp(-x^2)$, which, as you know, tends to zero at the ends:

```
y = (x+3.6)*(x+2.5)*(x+1)*(x-0.5)*(x-2)*(x-3.5)*Math.exp(-x*x/4);
```

Figure 3-5 shows what we get. Cool. The bell function flattens the curve at the ends, solving our problem. Note that we've divided the x^2 within the `exp()` by 4. This is to broaden the bell shape; otherwise, it would kill off the polynomial too quickly, leaving fewer hills. Remove the 4 or replace it with 2 to see what we mean. Try also changing the 4 to 5 or 6 to see the opposite effect.

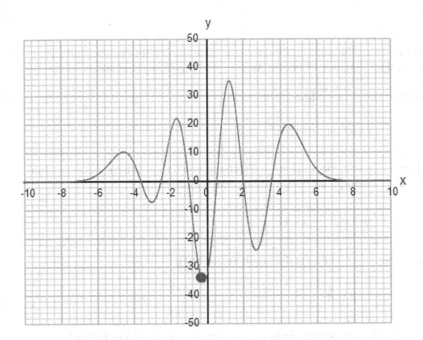

Figure 3-5. *Animating a ball on a curve created by multiplying a polynomial and a Gaussian*

Here is another way you can modify the curve: multiply it by another factor of *x* (and an appropriate number to keep it within the range being displayed):

```
y = 0.5*x*(x+3.6)*(x+2.5)*(x+1)*(x-0.5)*(x-2)*(x-3.5) *Math.exp(-x*x/4);
```

This modifies the curve in a different way. Because *x* is small near the origin and large away from it, by multiplying the function by *x*, we tend to reduce the hills closer to the origin and increase the relative height of the hills farther away. You might notice another change: the value of *y* for large negative *x* is now negative, and the landscape starts with a valley instead of a hill because by introducing that extra factor of *x*, the dominant term in that function is now $0.5\,x^7$. Compare that with the previous $0.2\,x^6$. When the power of the dominant term is odd, it will be negative for negative values of *x*. But when the power is even, it will be positive even if *x* is negative. Check this out by multiplying by another factor of *x* to get this:

```
y = 0.1*x*x*(x+3.6)*(x+2.5)*(x+1)*(x-0.5)*(x-2)*(x-3.5) *Math.exp(-x*x/4);
```

If you multiply the function by a negative number, you'll reverse the whole curve.

There is clearly enormous flexibility in what you can do with functions to create different types of shapes. Hopefully, you might find some use for them! Perhaps build that game that shoots balls over hills. Or maybe get rid of the graph and curve to produce some cool math-based animations without giving away how you've done it.

Beyond its use for plotting known functions, the Graph object will come in handy as a useful diagnostic tool to help you visualize what your code is actually calculating, more intuitively and in much greater detail than the humble console.log() function can do. It can help you to understand the logic or physics in your code, and to identify any potential problems. Think of it as a dashboard or instrument panel like the ones in a car or plane, and soon you'll be using it more than you think!

The trouble with circles

Let's now try to move an object around a circle using the same method we've used in the previous two sections. That should be simple enough, right? First, we need the equation of a circle. You can find this in any elementary geometry textbook.

The equation of a circle of radius r and with origin at (a, b) is given by this:

$$(x-a)^2 + (y-b)^2 = r^2$$

If you try to follow exactly the same procedure as in the previous two sections, you'll want to have y as a function of x. Recalling your algebra, you should be able to manipulate the preceding equation to get this:

$$y = b + \sqrt{r^2 - (x-a)^2}$$

To keep the task simple, choose $a = b = 0$, and $r = 1$ (center at the origin, radius of 1):

$$y = \sqrt{(1-x^2)}$$

Now let's plot the graph. You'll want to use the same scaling on both axes so that your circle does not look distorted. If you do just that and run the code, you'll get something that looks partially correct, but with a couple of strange problems. The first is that you only end up with a semicircle, not the whole circle. The second problem is that the ball takes a little while to appear, and then it disappears at the end. Figure 3-6 shows the resulting plot.

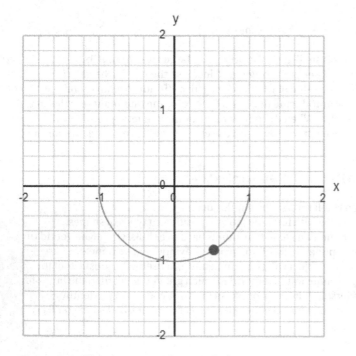

Figure 3-6. *First attempt to plot a circle*

Let's deal with the latter problem first. This strange ball behavior arises because we've gone outside the range for which the equation makes sense. If you look at the preceding equation, you'll see that if the magnitude of x is larger than 1, we have the square root of a negative number, which does not give you a real number. So the ball has nowhere to go when that happens!

In contrast to the functions you saw previously, a circle is confined to a limited region of the plane. In math jargon, the function is not defined outside of that range. Let's fix the code by calculating the value of the function only for values of x in the range $-1 <= x <= 1$. This is easily done in the loop that calculates the values of the function. Take a look at move-circle.js. This is the modified code that ensures that x is restricted to the correct range:

```
for (var i=0; i<=1000; i++){
    xA[i] = (i-500)*0.002;
    yA[i] = f(xA[i]);
}
```

The first problem is trickier. The creation of only a semicircle arises because when we take the square root to get the previous equation, we should have included the negative as well:

$$y = \pm\sqrt{\left(1 - x^2\right)}$$

The trouble is that you can't have a function returning two different values at the same time. There is another problem, this time to do with the animation. You might have noticed that the ball appears to move quickly along some parts of the circle and slowly elsewhere. This isn't usually what we want to see. It arises because we have been incrementing x in equal amounts. But where the curve is "steep," the same increment in x leads to a larger increment in y compared with where the curve is more "level."

Usually we'd want to make an object move in a circle at a uniform rate. Is there a way to know how the position of the ball depends on time and the rate of rotation? There is. It's time to learn about parametric equations.

Using parametric equations

The basic problem we had in the last section was that we know y as a function of x, but do not know how either x or y depends on time. What we are after is a pair of equations of this form, where $f(t)$ and $g(t)$ are functions of time:

$$x = f(t)$$

$$y = g(t)$$

They are called *parametric equations* because x and y are expressed in terms of another parameter t, which in this instance represents time. From these parametric equations, it should be possible to recover the equation connecting x and y. But the reverse is not necessarily true. Parametric equations are not unique; there might be different pairs of parametric equations that work.

We'll give you an answer here. Although it won't make full sense until you've done some trigonometry and we've covered the concept of angular velocity (in the next section), here it is (where r is the radius of the circle and ω is the so-called angular velocity, which is basically a rate of rotation around the circle):

$$x = r\sin\left(\omega t\right)$$

$$y = r\cos\left(\omega t\right)$$

Note that we are using concepts here that will be fully explained only later in this chapter. Therefore, although the concepts might not be completely clear now, they should become so soon enough.

Let's choose $r = 1$ and $w = 1$, and modify the code to compute x and y accordingly (see move-circle-parametric.js):

```
for (var i=0; i<=1000; i++){
    var t = 0.01*i;
    xA[i] = Math.sin(t);
    yA[i] = Math.cos(t);
}
```

This does the job perfectly (see Figure 3-7). The multiplicative factor that computes time t from the counter i is chosen to produce at least one complete revolution. Of course, you don't have to do it this way. You can get rid of the arrays and the loop altogether and just compute x and y on the fly. But it's good to know that there *is* another way to animate an object with code apart from computing its position on the fly. This method can prove useful, for example, if the computations are too time-consuming; they could then be done and the positions stored in an array (as done previously) during an "initialization" period, to be animated subsequently in the usual way.

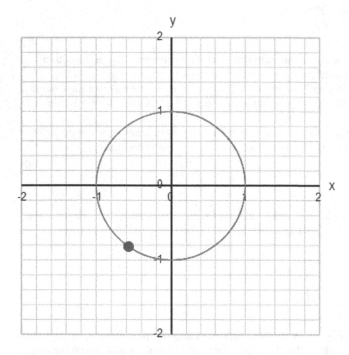

Figure 3-7. *Moving an object around a circle using parametric equations*

Finding the distance between two points

A common problem is to find the distance between two objects given their locations, which is needed in collision detection, for example. Some physical laws also involve the distance between two objects. For example, Newton's law of gravitation (covered in Chapter 6) involves the square of the distance between two objects.

Fortunately, there is a simple formula, based upon the Pythagorean Theorem, which allows us to calculate the distance between two points. The Pythagorean Theorem is actually a theorem about the lengths of the sides of triangles. Specifically, it applies to a special type of triangle known as a *right triangle,* or *right-angled triangle,* which has one angle that is 90 degrees. The longest side of the triangle, called the *hypotenuse,* is always opposite the 90-degree angle (see Figure 3-8).

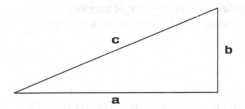

Figure 3-8. *A right triangle*

The Pythagorean Theorem states that if we take each of the other sides, square their lengths, and add the result, we would get the square of the length of the longest side. Stated as a formula, it is the following, where c is the length of the hypotenuse, and a and b are the lengths of the other two sides:

$$a^2 + b^2 = c^2$$

Figure 3-9 shows how we use this formula to calculate the distance between two points: by drawing a right triangle. If the coordinates of the two points are $(x1, y1)$ and $(x2, y2)$, the length of the two shorter sides are $(x2 - x1)$ and $(y2 - y1)$, respectively.

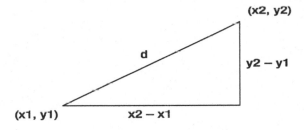

Figure 3-9. *Using the Pythagorean Theorem to calculate the distance between two points*

Therefore, the length of the hypotenuse, which is actually the distance d between the two points, is given by this:

$$d^2 = (x2 - x1)^2 + (y2 - y1)^2$$

The distance d is then obtained by taking the square root of the previous expression. That's it. What's more, this formula can be readily generalized to 3D to give the following:

$$d^2 = (x2 - x1)^2 + (y2 - y1)^2 + (z2 - z1)^2$$

Note that it does not matter if we take $(x1 - x2)^2$ instead of $(x2 - x1)^2$, and similarly for the other terms, because the square of a negative number is the same as that of the corresponding positive number.

Basic trigonometry

Trigonometry is a branch of math that technically deals with the properties of triangles and the relationships between the lengths of their sides and their angles. Put this way, trigonometry may not sound very special, but it is, in fact, an indispensable part of your toolset as an animation or game programmer. For example, we used trigonometric functions previously in the parametric equations that produced uniform motion around a circle.

You probably remember the basics from your school days, such as the theorem that the sum of interior angles in a triangle is 180 degrees. But perhaps you may not remember what a sine function is. This section will review the essentials of the subject.

Degrees and radians

Everyone knows that there are 360 degrees in a complete revolution. Far fewer people know that 360 degrees equal 2π radians (or maybe have never even heard of a radian). So let's start by explaining what a radian is.

The short explanation is this: a *radian* is a unit of angular measure (just like a degree is). Here's how the two measures are related:

2π radians is equal to 360 degrees

so π radians is equal to 180 degrees

so 1 radian is equal to $180/\pi$ degrees, which is approximately 57.3 degrees

Now you might not feel very comfortable with the idea of a radian at all. Why do we need such a weird unit for angle? Don't we all know and love the degree? Well, the point is that the degree is just as arbitrary—why are there 360 degrees in a circle? Why not 100?

In fact, the radian is in many ways a more "natural" unit of angle. This follows from its definition: the angle subtended at the center of a circle by an arc that is equal in length to its radius. See Figure 3-10.

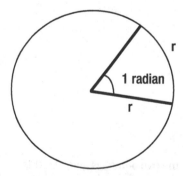

Figure 3-10. *A radian is the angle subtended at the center of a circle by an arc of length equal to the circle's radius*

You will frequently need to convert between degrees and radians. So, here is the conversion formula:

(angle in degrees) = (angle in radians) × 180 / π

(angle in radians) = (angle in degrees) × π / 180

The sine function

The trigonometric functions are defined in terms of the sides of a right triangle. Referring to Figure 3-11, you know that the hypotenuse (hyp) is the longest side of the triangle and is opposite the right angle. Pick one of the other angles, say x. Then, in relation to angle x, the far side that does not touch x is called the opposite (opp). The near side that does touch x is called the adjacent (adj). Note that opposite and adjacent are in relation to your chosen angle (x in this case). In relation to the other angle, the roles of opposite and adjacent are reversed. On the other hand, the hypotenuse is always the longest side.

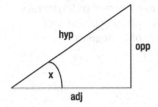

Figure 3-11. *Definition of hypotenuse, adjacent, and opposite sides of a right triangle*

The sine function is defined simply as the ratio of the length of the opposite side to that of the hypotenuse:

$$\sin(x) = \frac{\text{opp}}{\text{hyp}}$$

Now you could draw lots of right triangles for different angles x, measure opp and hyp, calculate their ratio, and tabulate and plot $\sin(x)$ to see what it is like. But surely you'll prefer to dig out that `Graph` object and plot `Math.sin()`. This is what we've done in `trig-functions.js`.

Figure 3-12 shows what we get. We've plotted between –720 degrees (–4π radians) and 720 degrees (4π radians) to show the periodic nature of the function. The period (the interval over which it repeats) is 360 degrees, or 2π radians. The curve is like a smooth wave.

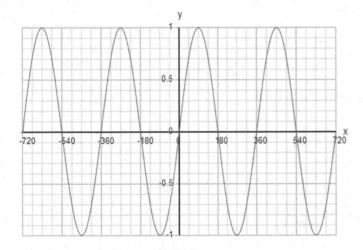

Figure 3-12. *The graph of a sine function*

Note that $\sin(x)$ is always between –1 and 1. It can never be larger than 1 in magnitude, because opp can never be larger than hyp. We say that the peak *amplitude* of a sine wave is 1. The value of $\sin(x)$ is zero at 0 degrees and every 180 degrees thereafter and before.

51

The cosine function

Similar to sine, the cosine function is defined as the ratio of the length of the adjacent side to that of the hypotenuse:

$$\cos(x) = \frac{\text{adj}}{\text{hyp}}$$

The graph shown in Figure 3-13 is similar to that of sin (x), except that cos (x) appears to be shifted by 90 degrees with respect to sin (x). In fact, it turns out that cos $(x - \pi/2) = \sin(x)$. Go ahead and prove it by plotting this function. This shows that cos and sin differ only by a constant shift. We say they have a *phase difference* of 90 degrees.

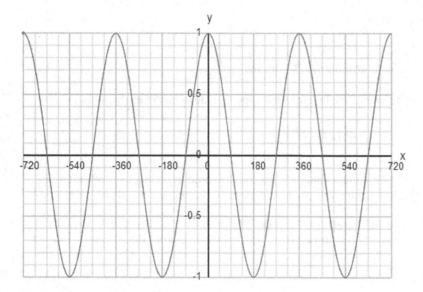

Figure 3-13. *The graph of a cosine function*

The tangent function

A third common trig function is the tangent function, defined as follows:

$$\tan(x) = \frac{\text{opp}}{\text{adj}}$$

This definition is equivalent to this:

$$\tan(x) = \frac{\sin(x)}{\cos(x)}$$

If you plot the graph of tan x, it might look a bit weird at first sight (see Figure 3-14). Ignore the vertical lines at 90 degrees, and so on. They shouldn't really be there. The graph is still periodic, but it consists of disjointed branches every 180 degrees. Also, tan (x) can take any value, not just a value between –1 and 1. What happens at 90 degrees is that tan (x) becomes infinite. Going back to the definition of tan (x), this is because for 90 degrees, adj is zero, so we end up dividing by zero.

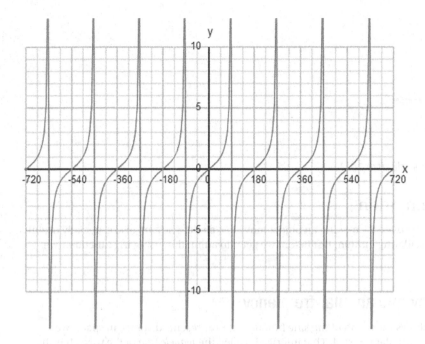

Figure 3-14. *The graph of a tangent function*

You probably won't use tan nearly as much as sin and cos. But you will definitely use its inverse, which we'll introduce next.

The inverse trig functions

It is frequently necessary to find an angle given the value of the sin, cos, or tan of that angle. In math, this is done using the inverse of the trig functions, called arcsin, arccos, and arctan, respectively.

In JavaScript, these functions, which are called Math.asin(), Math.acos(), and Math.atan(), take a number as argument. Obviously, the number must be between -1 and 1 for Math.asin() and Math.acos(), but can be any value for Math.atan().

Note that the inverse trig functions return an angle in radians, so you have to convert to degrees if that's what you need.

There is another inverse tan function in JavaScript: Math.atan2(). What is the difference, and why do we need two of them?

Math.atan() takes a single argument, which is the ratio opp/adj for the angle you are computing. Math.atan2() takes two arguments, which are the actual values of opp and adj, if you happen to know them. So, why is Math.atan2() needed—can't you just do Math.atan(opp/adj)?

To answer this question, do the following:

```
console.log(Math.atan(1)*180/Math.PI);
console.log (Math.atan2(2,2)*180/Math.PI);
console.log (Math.atan2(-2,-2)*180/Math.PI);
```

All three lines of code have an opp/adj ratio of 1, but you'll find that the first two will return 45 degrees, while the third will return -135 degrees. What's going on is that the third option specifies that the angle points upward and to the left, and because angles are measured in a clockwise direction from the positive *x*-axis in the canvas coordinate system, the angle is actually -135 degrees (see Figure 3-15). Now, you'd have no way of telling this to the Math.atan() function, because it takes only one argument: 1, the same as for 45 degrees.

Figure 3-15. *Understanding the result of* `Math.atan2(-2,-2)`

Using trig functions for animation

You've already seen how sin and cos can be used for making an object move in a circle. They are also especially useful for producing any kind of repeating or oscillating motion. But before we get into animation using trig functions, we need to introduce some new concepts.

Wavelength, period, frequency and angular frequency

Take a look again at Figure 3-12, which shows the graph of the sine function. If *x* represents distance in space, we have a sine wave in space that repeats at a regular interval. That interval is called the *wavelength* of the wave. It is the distance between adjacent similar points, for example, the distance between successive crests.

If we instead plot the sine function against time, the repeating interval is a time scale called the *period* of the wave. For example, if this were a ball that's moving up and down, the period (denoted by the symbol *T*) would be the time it takes to return to its initial position. Let's call this a *cycle*.

Now, suppose that a cycle takes 0.5 seconds, which we can state as *T* = 0.5 seconds. How many cycles does the ball complete in 1 second? Well, obviously 2. That's how many half-seconds there are in a second. This is called the *frequency* of the motion (denoted by the symbol *f*).

It is not difficult to see that, in general, the frequency is given by the reciprocal of the period:

$$f = \frac{1}{T}$$

Now, it turns out that you can always think of the up-and-down motion of the ball as the projection of the position of another imaginary ball that is moving at a constant rate in a circle (see Figure 3-16). One cycle in an oscillation (wave-like motion) then corresponds to a complete revolution around the circle. Thinking in terms of the angle moved by the circling ball, that's 2π radians. Because the ball moves *f* cycles per second, and each cycle is 2π radians, this means that the ball goes through 2π*f* radians per second. This is called the *angular frequency* or *angular velocity* of the motion (usually denoted by the Greek letter ω, omega). It tells you the angle, in radians, through which the circling ball moves in each second.

$$\omega = 2\pi f = \frac{2\pi}{T}$$

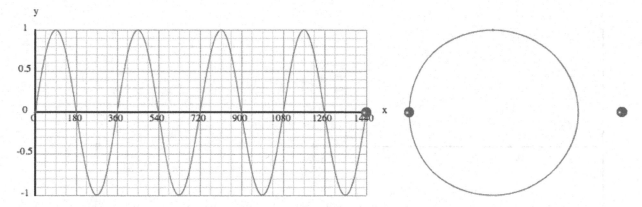

Figure 3-16. *Relationship between oscillation, circular motion, and a sine wave*

Finally, because ω is the angle through which the imaginary ball moves per second, in *t* seconds the ball will have moved through ω *t* radians. So, if it starts out at an angle of 0 radians, at *t* seconds its projected displacement is equal to sin (ω *t*):

$$y = \sin(\omega t)$$

If we know the angular frequency of the oscillation, we can calculate the position of the ball at any time if its initial position is known. Of course, if we know the period or frequency instead, we can work out the angular frequency from the preceding formula.

Let's look at some examples. For these examples, we're using `trig-animations.js`, which is a modification of `move-curve.js`. We will now show, side by side, a 2D animation as well as its 1D version, in which you just move an object along one direction.

Oscillations

Basic oscillations (wave motion in 2D) are pretty straightforward to achieve with just a sine or cosine function. Such an oscillation is called a *simple harmonic motion (SHM)*. The oscillation consists of a wave with a single frequency. Try it out with `trig-animations.js`:

```
function f(x){
    var y;
    y = Math.sin(x*Math.PI/180);
    return y;
}
```

You can produce waves of different frequencies by multiplying the argument by different factors.

Damped oscillations

Oscillations with a sine wave go on forever. If you want to make them die out with time, you can just multiply the sine by an exponential with a negative coefficient:

```
y = Math.sin(x*Math.PI/180)*Math.exp(-0.002*x);
```

You can experiment by changing the coefficient 0.002 to a smaller or larger number. Figure 3-17 shows a typical pattern you might see.

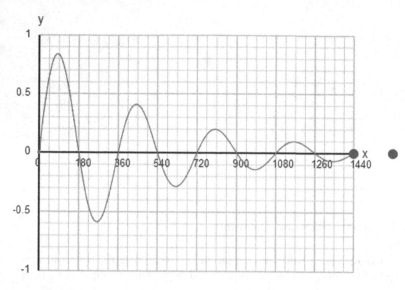

Figure 3-17. *Damped oscillations using sin(x) and exp(-x)*

Combining sine waves

You can produce all kinds of exotic effects by combining sine and cosine waves. Here's an example of a combination:

```
y = Math.sin(x*Math.PI/180) + Math.sin(1.5*x*Math.PI/180);
```

Or try two sine waves with nearly the same angular frequency:

```
y = 0.5*Math.sin(3*x*Math.PI/180) + 0.5*Math.sin(3.5*x*Math.PI/180);
```

This gives you a "beats" motion; a rapid oscillation upon which is superimposed a slower oscillation (see Figure 3-18).

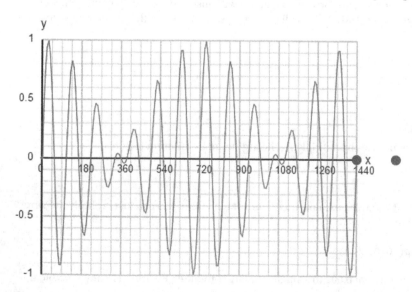

Figure 3-18. *Pattern produced by superimposing two sine waves of nearly equal frequency*

It is possible to produce all sorts of repeating patterns using a combination of sine waves. There is a mathematical technique called *Fourier analysis* that allows you to work out what combination of sine waves you need to produce a particular pattern. The resulting sum of sine waves is called a *Fourier series*.

For example, you can produce something that looks like a square wave (a *step function* wave) by adding sine waves in the following way:

```
y = Math.sin(x*Math.PI/180) + Math.sin(3*x*Math.PI/180)/3 + Math.sin(5*x*Math.PI/180)/5;
```

The more waves you add, the closer the result will be to a square wave. For example, add the next term in the series (Math.sin(7*x*Math.PI/180)/7) to see what you get.

We wrote a little function, fourierSum(N,x), that computes the Fourier sum to N terms for the square wave.

```
function f(x){
    var y;
    y = fourierSum(10,x);
    return y;
}
function fourierSum(N,x){
    var fs=0;
    for (var nn=1; nn<=N; nn=nn+2){          fs += Math.sin(nn*x*Math.PI/180)/nn;
    }
    return fs;
}
```

Figure 3-19 shows what you get with *N* = 10. With a value of *N* = 1000, the curve is an almost perfect square wave.

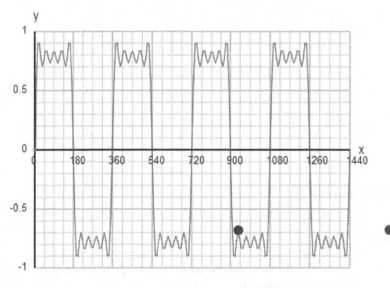

Figure 3-19. *Fourier series pattern for a square wave with N = 10*

Vectors and basic vector algebra

Vectors are useful math constructs that simplify how we need to deal with many physical quantities like velocity and force, which will be discussed in detail in the next chapter. *Vector algebra* consists of rules for manipulating and combining vectors. You've already met vectors informally, when you dealt with velocity components. Let's now introduce vectors more formally.

What are vectors?

Vectors can be most intuitively illustrated using the example of displacements. The concept of displacement will be covered in detail in Chapter 4, but essentially it refers to movement for a given distance and in a given direction. Here is an example.

Suppose that Bug, the ladybug, is crawling on a piece of graph paper. Bug starts at the origin and crawls for a distance of 10 units; then he stops. Bug then resumes crawling for a further distance of 10 units before stopping again. How far is Bug from the origin? One might be tempted to say 20 units. But what if Bug crawled upward the first time and to the right the second time? (See Figure 3-20). Clearly 20 units is the wrong answer. By using the Pythagorean Theorem, the answer is actually $\sqrt{(10^2 + 10^2)}$, or roughly 14.1 units.

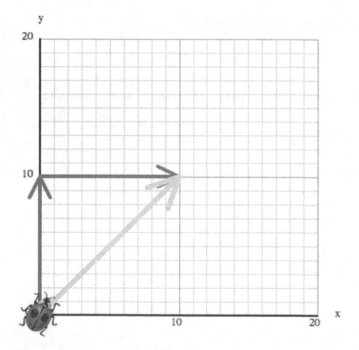

Figure 3-20. *The direction of displacement matters!*

You can't simply add the two distances, because you also need to take into account the direction in which Bug moves. To analyze displacements, you need a magnitude and a direction.

In math we abstract this idea into the concept of a *vector*, which is a quantity that has a magnitude and a direction.

Displacements are not the only vectors. Many of the basic concepts of motion, such as velocity, acceleration, and force, are vectors (they will be discussed in the next chapter). This section outlines the algebra of vectors as abstract mathematical objects, regardless of whether they are displacements, velocities, or forces. With a little grasp of vector algebra, you can simplify calculations by reducing the number of equations that you have to deal with. This saves time, reduces the likelihood of errors, and simplifies life.

Vectors vs. scalars

Vectors are often contrasted with *scalars*, which are quantities that have a magnitude only. Distance or length is a scalar—you need only one number to specify it. But displacement is a vector because you need to specify the direction of the displacement. Pictorially, vectors are often represented as directed straight lines—a line with an arrow on it.

Note that a vector is characterized uniquely by its magnitude and direction. That means that two vectors with the same magnitude and direction are considered to be equal, irrespective of where they are in space (see Figure 3-21a). In other words, the location of a vector does not matter. There's one exception to this rule, however: the *position vector*. The position vector of an object is the vector that joins a fixed origin to that object, so it's a displacement vector in relation to a fixed origin (see Figure 3-21b).

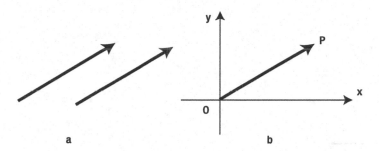

Figure 3-21. *(a) Parallel vectors of equal length are equal; (b) Position vectors relate to the origin*

Adding and subtracting vectors

In the Bug example, what is the sum of the two displacements? The natural answer is that it is the resultant displacement as given by the vector that points from the initial to the final position (refer to Figure 3-20). What if Bug now moves a distance of 5 units downward? You might say that the resultant displacement is the vector that points from the beginning (the origin, in this case) to the destination. This is the so-called head-to-tail rule:

> To add two or more vectors, join them so that they are "head-to-tail," moving them around if necessary (as long as their direction does not change, that is they remain parallel to their original direction). The sum or resultant vector is then the vector that joins the starting point to the ending point.

To subtract a vector from another vector, we just add the negative of that vector. The negative of a vector is one with the same magnitude but pointing in the opposite direction.

Subtracting a vector from itself (or the sum of a vector and its negative) gives you the *zero vector*—a vector of zero length and arbitrary direction.

Let's look at an example. Suppose that after Bug has moved 10 units upward, he decides to move 10 units at an angle of 45 degrees instead (see Figure 3-22). What is the resultant displacement? Now that is trickier: you can't directly apply the Pythagorean Theorem because you don't have a right triangle any more. You could use some more complicated trigonometry, or draw the vectors accurately and take a ruler and measure the resultant distance and angle.

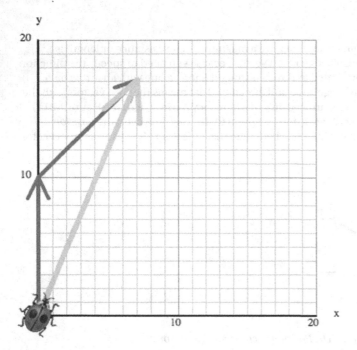

Figure 3-22. *Addition of vectors*

In practice, that's not how you'll be doing it, though. Adding and subtracting vectors is much easier using vector components. So let's take a look at vector components now.

Resolving vectors: vector components

As mentioned before, a vector has a magnitude and a direction. What this means in 2D is that you need two numbers to specify a vector. Take a look at Figure 3-23. The two numbers are the length r of the vector and the angle θ that it makes with the positive x-axis. But we can also specify the two numbers as the extent of the vector in the x- and y- direction, denoted by x and y respectively. These are called the *vector components*.

Figure 3-23. *Vector components*

The relation between (r, θ) and (x, y) can be obtained with the simple trigonometry discussed in the previous section. Looking at Figure 3-23 again, we know this:

$$\cos(\theta) = x/r$$
$$\sin(\theta) = y/r$$

This gives the following:

$$x = r\cos(\theta)$$
$$y = r\sin(\theta)$$

Working out the vector components in this way from the magnitude and angle of a vector is known as "resolving the vector" along the x- and y-axes. Actually, you can resolve a vector along any two mutually perpendicular directions. But most of the time, we'll be doing that along the x- and y-axes.

There are many different notations for vectors, and it's easy to get bogged down with notation. But in JavaScript you just have to remember that a vector has components. So any notation that helps you remember that is just as good as any other. We'll use the following notation for compactness, denoting vectors using bold letters and denoting their components by enclosing them using square brackets:

$$\mathbf{v} = [a, b]$$

In 3D, you need not two, but three, components to specify a vector, so we write this:

$$\mathbf{v} = [a, b, c]$$

Position vectors

The position vector of an object is a vector pointing from the origin to that object. Hence, we can write the position vector in terms of the coordinates of the object. In 2D:

$$\mathbf{r} = [x, y]$$

In 3D:

$$\mathbf{r} = [x, y, z]$$

Adding vectors using components

Here's how you add two vectors using components:

$$[a, b] + [c, d] = [a + c, b + d]$$

Pretty simple, isn't it? Why this is so should be clear from Figure 3-24. You separately add the horizontal components and the vertical components of the two vectors you're adding. This gives you the components of the resultant vector.

Figure 3-24. *Adding vectors using components*

As an example, applying this to the Bug displacement problem shown in Figure 3-22 gives the following displacement, which you can easily verify on the graph:

$$[0,10]+[7,7]=[7,17]$$

Feel free to practice doing vector additions with pen and paper; after going through a few, the process should become obvious and help you build your intuition about vectors and vectors components.

Similarly, vector subtraction using components is simply this:

$$[a,b]-[c,d]=[a-c,b-d]$$

Multiplying a vector by a number

Multiplying a vector by a number just multiplies each of its components by that number:

$$4[a,b,c]=[4a,4b,4c]$$

In particular, if we multiply a vector by –1, we get this, which gives the negative of that vector:

$$-[a,b,c]=[-a,-b,-c]$$

Dividing a vector by a number N is just the same as multiplying the vector by the reciprocal $1/N$ of that number.

Vector magnitude

The *magnitude* (length) of a vector is given by applying the Pythagorean Theorem to its components:

In 2D, the magnitude of $[x, y]$ is $\sqrt{x^2 + y^2}$; or in JavaScript code: `Math.sqrt(x*x+y*y)`.

In 3D, the magnitude of $[x, y, z]$ is $\sqrt{x^2 + y^2 + z^2}$; or in JavaScript code: `Math.sqrt(x*x+y*y+z*z)`.

Note that if we divide a vector by its magnitude, we get a vector of length one unit in the same direction as the original vector. This is called a *unit vector*.

Vector angle

Calculating the angle of a vector from its components is no more difficult than calculating its magnitude. In JavaScript, this can be done most easily using the `Math.atan2()` function.

The angle of a vector $[x, y]$ is given by `Math.atan2(y, x)`. Beware—you need to specify the arguments as y first and then x.

Multiplying vectors: Scalar or dot product

Is it possible to multiply two vectors? The answer is yes. Mathematicians have defined a "multiplication" operation called *scalar product*, in which two vectors produce a scalar. Recall that a scalar only has a magnitude and no direction; in other words, it is basically just a number. The rule is that you multiply the corresponding components of each vector and add the results:

$$[x1, y1] \bullet [x2, y2] = x1 \cdot x2 + y1 \cdot y2$$

The scalar product is denoted by a dot, so it is also called the *dot product*.

Expressed in terms of vector magnitudes and direction, the dot product is given by the following, where θ is the angle between the two vectors, and $r1$ and $r2$ are their lengths:

$$[x1, y1] \bullet [x2, y2] = r1 \cdot r2 \cdot \cos(\theta)$$

The geometrical interpretation of the scalar product is that it's the product of the length of one vector with the projected length of the other (see Figure 3-25).

Figure 3-25. *The scalar product between two vectors*

This is useful when you need to find the angle between two vectors, which you can obtain by equating the right sides of the previous two equations and solving for θ. In JavaScript, you just do this:

```
angle = Math.acos((x1*x2+y1*y2)/(r1*r2))
```

Note that if the angle between two vectors is zero (they are parallel), $\cos(\theta) = 1$, and the dot product is just the product of their magnitudes.

If the two vectors are perpendicular, then $\cos(\theta) = \cos(\pi/2) = 0$, and so the dot product is zero. This is a good test to check if two vectors are perpendicular or not. All these formulas and facts carry over to 3D, with the dot product given by the following:

$$[x1, y1, z1] \bullet [x2, y2, z2] = x1 \cdot x2 + y1 \cdot y2 + z1 \cdot z2$$

Scalar products crop up in several places in physics. We'll come across an example in the next chapter, with the concept of *work*, which is defined as the dot product of force and displacement. So, although the dot product may appear somewhat abstract and mysterious as a math construct, it will hopefully make more intuitive sense when you come across it again in an applied context in Chapter 4.

Multiplying vectors: Vector or cross product

In 3D, there is another type of product, known as the *vector product* because it gives a vector instead of a scalar. The rule is quite a bit trickier.

If you have two vectors $\mathbf{a} = [x1, y1, z1]$ and $\mathbf{b} = [x2, y2, z2]$, and their vector product is given by a vector $\mathbf{c} = \mathbf{a} \times \mathbf{b} = [x, y, z]$, the components of $\mathbf{c}$ are given by the following:

$$x = y1 \cdot z2 - z1 \cdot y2$$
$$y = z1 \cdot x2 - x1 \cdot z2$$
$$z = x1 \cdot y2 - y1 \cdot x2$$

Now this is not exactly intuitive, is it? There sure is some logic to it, as with everything in math. But trying to explain it would be too much of a diversion. So let's just accept the formula.

The vector product is also called the *cross product* because of the "cross" notation used to denote it. The vector product of two vectors $\mathbf{a}$ and $\mathbf{b}$ gives a third vector that is perpendicular to both $\mathbf{a}$ and $\mathbf{b}$.

In terms of vector magnitudes and directions, the cross product is given by this:

$$\mathbf{a} \times \mathbf{b} = a\,b\sin(\theta)\,\mathbf{n}$$

where a and b are the magnitudes of $\mathbf{a}$ and $\mathbf{b}$ respectively, θ is the smaller angle between $\mathbf{a}$ and $\mathbf{b}$, and $\mathbf{n}$ is the unit vector perpendicular to $\mathbf{a}$ and $\mathbf{b}$ and oriented according to the right-hand rule (see Figure 3-26): hold your right hand with the forefinger pointing along the first vector $\mathbf{a}$, and your middle finger pointing in the direction of $\mathbf{b}$. Then $\mathbf{n}$ will point in the direction of the thumb, held perpendicular to $\mathbf{a}$ and $\mathbf{b}$.

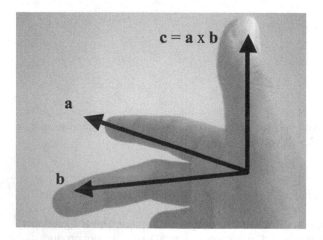

Figure 3-26. *The right-hand rule for the vector product*

Note that the cross product is zero when θ = 0 (because sin (0) = 0). Hence, the cross product of two parallel vectors gives the zero vector.

Like the scalar product, vector products appear in several places in physics; for example in rotational motion.

Building a Vector object with vector algebra

We built a lightweight Vector2D object endowed with all the relevant vector algebra in 2D. Here is the code (see vector2D.js). The method names have been chosen to make intuitive sense.

```
function Vector2D(x,y) {
    this.x = x;
    this.y = y;
}

// PUBLIC METHODS
Vector2D.prototype = {
    lengthSquared: function(){
        return this.x*this.x + this.y*this.y;
    },
    length: function(){
        return Math.sqrt(this.lengthSquared());
    },
    clone: function() {
        return new Vector2D(this.x,this.y);
    },
    negate: function() {
        this.x = - this.x;
        this.y = - this.y;
    },
    normalize: function() {
        var length = this.length();
        if (length > 0) {
            this.x /= length;
            this.y /= length;
        }
        return this.length();
    },
    add: function(vec) {
        return new Vector2D(this.x + vec.x,this.y + vec.y);
    },
    incrementBy: function(vec) {
        this.x += vec.x;
        this.y += vec.y;
    },
    subtract: function(vec) {
        return new Vector2D(this.x - vec.x,this.y - vec.y);
    },
    decrementBy: function(vec) {
        this.x -= vec.x;
        this.y -= vec.y;
    },
```

```
        scaleBy: function(k) {
            this.x *= k;
            this.y *= k;
        },
        dotProduct:     function(vec) {
            return this.x*vec.x + this.y*vec.y;
        }
};

// STATIC METHODS
Vector2D.distance = function(vec1,vec2){
    return (vec1.subtract(vec2)).length();
}
Vector2D.angleBetween = function(vec1,vec2){
    return Math.acos(vec1.dotProduct(vec2)/(vec1.length()*vec2.length()));
}
```

The file `vector-examples.js` contains some examples of the usage of the `Vector2D` object. You will soon see plenty of examples of its use throughout the book.

Simple calculus ideas

As stated at the beginning of this chapter, we do not assume that all readers will have a background in calculus. If you do, that is certainly handy; but we still recommend that you skim through this section, especially the code examples and the section on discrete calculus, to see how we apply calculus in code. If calculus is completely new to you, this section is designed as a gentle overview of some of the basic concepts. So although you won't be able to "do" calculus just by reading this section, you will hopefully gain enough understanding to appreciate the meaning of physics formulas that involve calculus. Additionally, you will be introduced to discrete calculus and the subject of numerical methods, which will provide a foundation for approaching more complex physics simulations.

So what is calculus? In one sentence, it's a mathematical formalism for dealing with quantities that change continuously with respect to other quantities. Because physics deals with laws that relate some quantities to other quantities, calculus is clearly relevant.

Calculus consists of two parts. Differential calculus (or *differentiation*) deals with the rate of change of quantities. Integral calculus (or *integration*) deals with continuous sums. The two are related by the fundamental theorem of calculus, which states that integration is the reverse of differentiation.

That all sounds very mysterious if you've never come across calculus before, so let's start from something you know to give you a gentle introduction to the subject. By the end of this chapter, these statements will make much more sense to you.

Slope of a line: gradient

The idea of rate of change is an important concept in physics. If you think of it, we are trying to formulate laws that tell us how, for example, the motion of a planet changes with time; how the force on the planet changes with its position, and so on. The key words here are "changes with." The laws of physics, it turns out, contain the rate of change of different physical quantities such as position, velocity, and so on.

Informally, "rate of change" tells us how quickly something is changing. Usually we mean how fast it's changing in time, but we could also be interested in how "fast" something changes with respect to some other quantity, not just time. For example, as a planet moves in its orbit, how quickly does the force of gravity change with its position?

So, in math terms, let's consider the rate of change of a quantity y with respect to another quantity x (where x could be time t or some other quantity). To do this, we'll use graphs to help us visualize relationships more easily.

Let's start with two quantities that have a simple, linear, relationship with each other; that is, they are related by

$$y = ax + b$$

As you saw in the coordinate geometry section, this implies that the graph of y against x is a straight line. The constant b is the y-intercept; the point at which the line intersects the y-axis. We'll now show that the constant a gives a measure of the rate of change of y with x.

Look at Figure 3-27. Of the two lines, in which one is y changing faster with x?

Figure 3-27. *The gradient (slope) of a line*

Clearly it's A, because it is "steeper," so the same increase in x leads to a larger increase in y. The steepness of the slope of the line therefore gives a measure of the rate of change of y relative to x. We can make this idea precise by defining the rate of change as follows:

Rate of change = (change in y) / (change in x)

It is customary to use the symbol Δ to denote "change in," so we can write this:

$$\text{Rate of change} = \frac{\Delta y}{\Delta x}$$

Let's give the rate of change a shorter name; let's call it *gradient*. Here's the idea: take any two points on the line with coordinates $(x1, y1)$ and $(x2, y2)$, calculate the difference in y and the difference in x and divide the former by the latter:

$$\text{Gradient} = \frac{y2 - y1}{x2 - x1}$$

With a straight line, you'll find that no matter which pair of points you take, you'll always get the same gradient. Moreover, that gradient is equal to a, the number that multiplies x in the equation $y = ax + b$.

This makes sense because a straight line has a constant slope, so it should not matter where you measure it. This is a very good start. We've got a formula for calculating the gradient or rate of change. The only problem is that it is restricted to quantities that are linearly related to each other. So how do we generalize this result to more general relationships (for example, when y is a nonlinear function of x?)

Rates of change: derivatives

You already know that the graph of a nonlinear function is a curve instead of a straight line. Intuitively, a curve's slope is not constant—it changes along the curve. Therefore, whatever the rate of change or gradient of a nonlinear function might be, it is not constant but depends on x. In other words, it is also a function of x.

Our objective now is to find this *gradient function*. In a math course, you'd do some algebra and come up with a formula for the gradient function. For example, you can start with the function $y = x^2$ and show that its gradient function is $2x$. But because you're not in a math course, let's do that with code instead. But first, we need to define what we mean by the gradient of a curve.

Because the gradient of a curve changes along the curve, let's focus on a fixed point P on the curve (Figure 3-28).

Figure 3-28. *The gradient of a curve*

Then let's pick any other point Q near point P. If we draw a line segment joining P and Q, the slope of that line approximates the slope of the curve. If we imagine that Q approaches P, we can expect the gradient of the line segment PQ to be closer and closer to the gradient of the curve at P.

What we are doing, in effect, is using the formula for the gradient of a line we had before and reducing the intervals Δx and Δy:

$$\text{Gradient} = \frac{\Delta y}{\Delta x} = \frac{y2 - y1}{x2 - x1}$$

We can then repeat this process at different locations for the point P along the curve to find the gradient function. Let's do this now in `gradient-function.js`:

```
var canvas = document.getElementById('canvas');
var context = canvas.getContext('2d');

var numPoints=1001;
var numGrad=50;
var xRange=6;
var xStep;

var graph = new Graph(context,-4,4,-10,10,275,210,450,350);
graph.drawgrid(1,0.2,2,0.5);
graph.drawaxes('x','y');
var xA = new Array();
var yA = new Array();
// calculate function
xStep = xRange/(numPoints-1);
for (var i=0; i<numPoints; i++){
    xA[i] = (i-numPoints/2)*xStep;
    yA[i] = f(xA[i]);
}
graph.plot(xA,yA,'#ff0000',false,true); // plot function
```

```
// calculate gradient function using forward method
var xAr = new Array();
var gradA = new Array();
for (var j=0; j<numPoints-numGrad; j++){
    xAr[j] = xA[j];
    gradA[j] = grad(xA[j],xA[j+numGrad]);
}
graph.plot(xAr,gradA,'#0000ff',false,true); // plot gradient function

function f(x){
    var y;
    y = x*x;
    return y;
}

function grad(x1,x2){
    return (f(x1)-f(x2))/(x1-x2);
}
```

The relevant lines are the ones that compute the gradient function, and the function grad(). This function simply computes the gradient $(y2 - y1) / (x2 - x1)$ given $x1$ and $x2$ as input. The line that decides which points to use is the following:

```
gradA[j] = grad(xA[j],xA[j+numGrad]);
```

Here numGrad is the number of grid points that Q is away from the point P (the point at which we are evaluating the gradient). Obviously, the smaller the value of numGrad, the more accurate the calculated gradient will be.

We have used a total of 1,000 grid points in an x-interval of 6 (from -3 to 3). That gives us a step size of 0.006 units per grid point. Let's use numGrad=1 to start with. This is the smallest possible value. Running the code plots the gradient function alongside the original function $y = x^2$. The graph of the gradient function is a straight line passing through the origin. When $x = 1$, $y = 2$, when $x = 2$, $y = 4$, and so on. You can probably guess that the equation of the line is $y = 2x$. Now any calculus textbook will tell you that the gradient function of $y = x^2$ is $y = 2x$. So this is good. You've successfully calculated your first gradient function!

Now change the value of numGrad to 50. You'll see that the computed gradient function line shifts a bit; it's no longer $y = 2x$. Not too good. Try reducing numGrad. You'll find that a value of up to about 10 gives you something that looks very close to $y = 2x$. That's a step size of $10 \times 0.006 = 0.06$. Anything much larger than this and you'll start losing accuracy.

Let's finish off this section by introducing some more terminology and notation. The gradient function is also called the *derived function* or *derivative* with respect to x. We'll use these terms interchangeably. The process of calculating the derivative is called *differentiation*.

We showed that the ratio $\Delta y/\Delta x$ gives the gradient of a curve at a point provided that Δx and Δy are small. In formal calculus, we say that $\Delta y/\Delta x$ tends to the gradient function as Δx and Δy go to zero.

To express the fact that the gradient function is really a limiting value of $\Delta y/\Delta x$, we write it like this:

$$\frac{dy}{dx}$$

This is the standard notation for the derivative of function y with respect to x. Another notation is y' ("y prime"); or if we write $y = f(x)$, the derivative can also be denoted by f' ("f prime").

There is nothing stopping you from calculating the derivative of a derivative. This is called the second derivative, and is written as follows:

$$\frac{d^2y}{dx^2}$$

In fact, as you'll find out in the next chapter, velocity is the derivative of position (with respect to time), and acceleration is the derivative of velocity. So acceleration is the second derivative of position with respect to time. In the notation, $v = dx/dt$, $a = dv/dt$, so $a = d^2x/dt^2$.

We calculated the derivative of a scalar function, but you can also differentiate vectors. You just find the derivative of each vector component separately.

For example, $vx = dx/dt$, $vy = dy/dt$, and $vz = dz/dt$ are the three velocity components. We can write this more compactly in vector form as follows, where $\boldsymbol{v} = [vx, vy, vz]$ and $\boldsymbol{r} = [x, y, z]$:

$$\mathbf{v} = \frac{d\mathbf{r}}{dt}$$

Discrete calculus: difference equations

What we did while calculating the gradient function in the preceding code is an example of discrete calculus: calculating the derivative using *numerical methods*. A numerical method is basically an algorithm for performing a mathematical calculation in an approximate way using code. This is needed if we don't have an exact formula for the quantity we are calculating.

In the preceding example, we had $y = x^2$ and needed to calculate y' using the discrete form of the derivative:

$$y' = \frac{dy}{dx} \approx \frac{\Delta y}{\Delta x}$$

To do this, we used a *difference equation* of the following form:

$$y'(n) = \frac{y(n+1) - y(n)}{x(n+1) - x(n)}$$

This is called a *forward difference scheme* because we are calculating the derivative at step n by using values of the function at the next step $n+1$.

There are many other difference schemes. Let's try a central difference scheme:

$$y'(n) = \frac{y(n+1) - y(n-1)}{x(n+1) - x(n-1)}$$

It's called a central difference scheme because we're picking a point on either side of the point P at which we're evaluating the gradient. Here is the code that does this:

```
// calculate gradient function using centered method
var xArc = new Array();
var gradAc = new Array();
for (var k=numGrad; k<numPoints-numGrad; k++){
    xArc[k-numGrad] = xA[k];
    gradAc[k-numGrad] = grad(xA[k-numGrad],xA[k+numGrad]);
}
```

If you run this code, you'll see that it gives you the same answer as the previous scheme for numGrad = 1 (recall that numGrad is the number of grid points between P and Q, and that the smaller it is, the more accurate the computed gradient will be). But if you now try larger values of numGrad, you'll find that it's still pretty accurate for a value as large as 250, which amounts to a grid size of 1.5. Compare that with the maximum step size of 0.06 for the forward difference scheme—it's 25 times larger!

This shows that the central difference scheme is much more accurate than a forward scheme. Figure 3-29 shows the derivatives calculated by the two methods for numGrad = 50. Note that we are plotting two different kinds of things on this graph: the original function y and its gradient function dy/dx. Hence, the labeling on the y-axis. The line that passes exactly through the origin is the gradient function obtained by using the central difference scheme. With your knowledge of coordinate geometry, you should be able to deduce that it's a plot of the function $2x$. In other words, $dy/dx = 2x$. Anyone who's done any calculus will instantly recognize $2x$ as the gradient function of $y = x^2$, our original function—so the central difference scheme is doing very well. The other line, which is computed using the forward difference scheme, has a bit of an offset, though, which means it will have an error associated with it. This is called a *numerical integration error*. Of course, there is an error associated with all numerical schemes. But in this case, the error due to the central difference scheme is so small that it is not visible on the plot. We'll go into much more detail on numerical accuracy in Chapter 14.

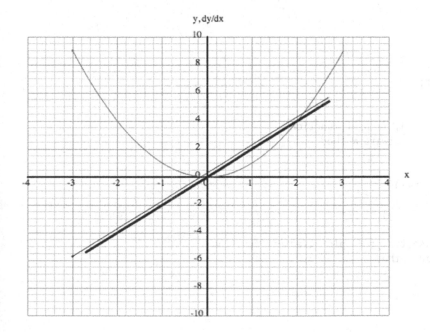

Figure 3-29. *Derivatives computed by the forward (thin line) and central (thick line) difference schemes*

Doing sums: integrals

Now we ask this question: Is it possible to do the reverse? Suppose we know the derivative of a function; can we find the function? The answer is yes. This is called *integration*. Again, usually in math you'll do that using analytical methods. But here we'll integrate numerically by using code.

As an example of numerical integration, let's reverse the preceding forward difference scheme to find $y(n+1)$, which gives this:

$$y(n+1) = y(n) + y'(n) \cdot \left[x(n+1) - x(n) \right]$$

Now y' is given, so we can calculate $y(n+1)$ from the previous $y(n)$. So you can see that this will be an iterative process in which we increment the value of y. It's a sum, and that's what integration is. The result of integration is called the *integral*, just as the result of differentiation is called the *derivative*.

Let's apply this to the derivative $y' = 2x$. We should be able to recover the function $y = x^2$. Here's the code that does this:

```
var canvas = document.getElementById('canvas');
var context = canvas.getContext('2d');

numPoints=1001;
var numGrad=1;
var xRange=6;
var xStep;

var graph = new Graph(context,-4,4,-10,10,275,210,450,350);
graph.drawgrid(1,0.2,2,0.5);
graph.drawaxes('x','y');
var xA = new Array();
var yA = new Array();
// calculate function
xStep = xRange/(numPoints-1);
for (var i=0; i<numPoints; i++){
    xA[i] = (i-numPoints/2)*xStep;
    yA[i] = f(xA[i]);
}
graph.plot(xA,yA,'#ff0000',false,true); // plot function
// calculate gradient function using forward method
var xAr = new Array();
var gradA = new Array();
for (var j=0; j<numPoints-numGrad; j++){
    xAr[j] = xA[j];
    gradA[j] = grad(xA[j],xA[j+numGrad]);
}
graph.plot(xAr,gradA,'#0000ff',false,true); // plot gradient function
// calculate integral using forward method
var xAi = new Array();
var integA = new Array();
xAi[0] = -3;
integA[0] = 9;
```

```
for (var k=1; k<numPoints; k++){
    xAi[k] = xA[k];
    integA[k] = integA[k-1] + f(xA[k-1])*(xA[k]-xA[k-1]);
}
graph.plot(xAi,integA,'#00ff00',false,true); // plot integral

function f(x){
    var y;
    y = 2*x;
    return y;
}
function grad(x1,x2){
    return (f(x1)-f(x2))/(x1-x2);
}
function integ(x1,x2){
    return (f(x1)-f(x2))/(x1-x2);
}
```

The full source code is in integration.js. One thing you'll notice is that you have to specify the starting point. This is clear from the preceding equation; because $y(n+1)$ depends on $y(n)$, you need to know the value of $y(0)$ (and $x(0)$) to begin with. This is called an *initial condition*. You always have to specify an initial condition when you are integrating. In the code we did that by specifying that $x(0) = -3$ and $y(0) = 9$. Try another initial condition and see what you get; for example, $x(0) = -3$, $y(0) = 0$.

This example might appear artificial, but in fact it describes an actual physical example: throwing a ball vertically upward. The function $f(x)$ denotes the vertical velocity, and its integral is the vertical displacement. In fact, the derivative $f'(x)$ is the acceleration. If you compute it (as we've done in the code), you'll find that it's a constant—a straight line with the same value of y for all x, as the acceleration due to gravity is constant. And in case you haven't guessed what x stands for in this example, it represents time. The initial condition $x(0) = -3$, $y(0) = 9$ represents the initial position of the ball. Now it's clear why you need an initial condition in the first place and why different initial conditions give different curves. Of course, with x representing time, you'd probably start with $x(0) = 0$. If you feel so inclined, go ahead and animate a ball using the integrated values of y to show that it really produces a ball thrown upward. One thing you'd need to do is to scale y so that it extends over enough pixels on the canvas element.

You could start with the constant acceleration $f'(x)$ and integrate it to get the velocity and then integrate the velocity to get the displacement. In fact, this is what we did, in a simplified way, in the first example of the book: bouncing-ball.js back in Chapter 1.

The forward scheme that we used in both examples (integration.js and bouncing-ball.js) is the simplest integration scheme possible. In Chapter 14, we'll go into considerable detail on numerical integration and different integration schemes.

Summary

Wow! Well done for surviving this chapter. You now have a remarkable set of tools at your disposal. Hopefully, you can begin to see the potential for applying these ideas and methods. No doubt you have many ideas of your own.

In case you've had difficulty with some of the material in this chapter, don't worry. Things will become much clearer when you see the concepts applied in practice in later chapters. You might want to come back to this chapter again to refresh your memory and reinforce your understanding.

You're now ready for physics. So take a well-deserved break and, when you feel ready, let's move on to the next chapter.

CHAPTER 4

■■■

Basic Physics Concepts

The previous two chapters covered a great deal of background material about JavaScript coding and math tools. This chapter will provide a gentle overview of basic physics to establish the final set of key concepts you'll need to get started with physics-based programming. Along the way, we will illustrate some of these concepts using JavaScript examples and will build useful physics objects that will be used throughout the book.

Topics covered in this chapter include the following:

- **General physics concepts and notation:** Physics deals with measurable quantities. This brief section reviews some basic facts about the nature of physical quantities and their units, and explains the use of scientific notation for expressing the values of physical quantities.

- **Things—particles and other objects in physics:** Things in physics are modeled using idealized concepts such as *particles*. We build a JavaScript `Particle` object that implements appropriate particle properties and methods, and extend it to create a visible `Ball` object.

- **Describing motion—kinematics:** This section explains the concepts and methods needed to describe and analyze motion. It contains some essential definitions and formulas that any prospective physics programmer must know.

- **Predicting motion—forces and dynamics:** To predict motion, you need to understand what causes it: force. Dynamics is the study of force and motion. By specifying the forces acting on an object, you can compute its motion.

- **Energy concepts:** Energy is a powerful concept in physics and enables us to solve some otherwise tricky problems in a simple way.

General physics concepts and notation

This short section reviews some general concepts and establishes some essential terminology and notation that apply across all of physics.

Physical quantities and units

In physics, when you talk about length or mass or energy, you want to be as precise as possible. Ideally, you want to be able to measure or calculate the things that you talk about. For example, the size of an object is not just a quality; it's a quantity. Physical quantities are measurable properties. They can be given a numerical value, or magnitude.

There is something else that a physical quantity must have: a unit. For example, we don't just say that the length of a particular table is 2; we say (in most of the world) it is 2 *meters*. Meter (m) is the unit. Why do we need a unit? A unit does two things. First, it tells us what kind of thing we are talking about. Meter tells us we are dealing with a length, not a temperature or something else. Second, the unit establishes a reference against which we are comparing the magnitude of the quantity. When we say that a table's length is 2 m, what we are really saying is that the length is twice as long as that of a reference that we call the meter. All measurements are only meaningful against some reference that we compare with.

As you might imagine, there are different choices of units. For example, to measure lengths or distances, you can use meters or feet. The usual unit of length in scientific literature is the meter (m) and its subdivisions and multiples, such as centimeter (cm) and kilometer (km). The key thing is to use consistent units, not mix different types of units. Otherwise, we can use any system of units that is appropriate. For example, in computer graphics and animation work, we usually measure distances in pixels.

In the previous chapter, you came across scalars and vectors. Just to recap briefly, a *vector* is a mathematical object that has a magnitude and a direction, whereas a *scalar* is one that only has a magnitude. Physical quantities can be scalar quantities or vector quantities. An example of a vector quantity, referred to in the preceding chapter, is displacement. You'll come across more examples later in this chapter.

Scientific notation

You frequently encounter very large as well as very small numbers in physics. For example, the speed of light is approximately 300 000 000 m/s. Instead of writing all these zeros, we usually write this as 3×10^8 m/s. The 10^8 ("ten to the power of 8") is 1 followed by 8 zeros, which equates to 100 million. This is known as *scientific notation*. The idea is to write large or small numbers in this form, where A is greater or equal to 1 but less than 10, and B is a positive or negative integer:

$$A \times 10^B$$

As shown in the example, if B is positive, 10^B is 1 followed by B zeros. What if B is a negative integer? In that case, we place the 1 in the Bth position after the decimal place, with zeros before it: for instance, 10^{-4} is the same as 0.0001.

As an example, the mass of an electron (the tiny particle that circles the center of atoms) is approximately 9.1×10^{-31} kg.

In JavaScript, you write this as 9.1e-31 and the velocity of light as 3e8. The "*e*" here must not be confused with the number *e* introduced in the previous chapter, which is Math.E in JavaScript. Here, *e* is used to denote the power of 10 by which we multiply the number preceding it.

Things: particles and other objects in physics

To describe and model the real world, physics has to have some representation of physical things. The theories of physics are conceptual and mathematical models of reality. They consist of concepts that are idealizations from the things that exist in real life. One such idealization is the concept of a particle. Although we'll focus exclusively on particles in this section, to put them in context, here is a list of the variety of "things" you'll come across in this book:

- **Particles:** Starting from this section, much of this book will deal with *particles*. We say more about particles shortly, but in a nutshell they can be thought of as indivisible units that exist at discrete points in space. Therefore, they are distinguished from more complex objects that can be extended or can consist of multiple parts. Particles move in a simple way: they can basically just change their position. This is also known as *translation*.

- **Rigid bodies:** A *rigid body* is an extended object whose size and shape cannot be changed easily, such as a table or car. Rigid bodies can move by translation like particles, but in addition they can undergo rotation. Rigid body motion will be covered in Chapter 13.

- **Deformable bodies:** Like rigid bodies, *deformable bodies* can translate and rotate, but in addition their shape and/or size can also change. Examples include a rubber ball, a rag doll, or a piece of cloth. An approach to model deformable bodies will be discussed in Chapter 13.

- **Fluids:** *Fluids* differ from the objects described previously in that they have no well-defined size or shape, but have the ability to flow from one part of space to another. Because any part of a fluid can move, it is much more difficult to simulate fluid motion accurately. But sometimes it is possible to "cheat" by modeling fluids using particles. This is the approach we take in Chapter 12 to create some interesting fluid visual effects.

- **Fields:** Fields are more abstract entities. In a broad sense, a *field* is some physical quantity that exists continuously over space. For example, we will explore the concept of a *force field* in Chapter 10.

What is a particle?

Because we are going to do lots of things with particles, let's discuss them a bit more. What are particles? Probably the first things that might come to mind are tiny entities such as electrons. In physics these are called fundamental or elementary particles. That's not necessarily what we are talking about here.

The sense in which we are going to use the word *particle* is as a mathematical idealization for any physical object whose inner structure or composition is not important for whatever problem we are considering. This might include atoms, or billiard balls, or even stars in a galaxy! In that sense, a particle is basically just a set of properties that characterize the object as an individual thing.

Particle properties

Let's be more precise about what we mean by the last statement in the preceding section. What properties are we talking about? A particle has the following properties:

- **Position:** A particle has to be somewhere! That means it must have coordinates x and y (and z in 3D).

- **Velocity:** Particles move, so they have a velocity. We define velocity formally in the next section; for now just note that it is a vector with components, just like position.

- **Mass:** As a physical thing, a particle must also have mass.

- **Charge:** Some elementary particles, such as electrons, also have a property called an *electric charge*, which makes them experience an interesting type of force known as the electromagnetic force. Because we'll play with that force in this book, we want to give our particles a charge property, too.

- **Others (spin, lifetime, and so on):** There are other properties we could include, taking inspiration from elementary particles in physics. But for now, we'll stick with the properties listed here.

This background gives us enough ingredients to start building some JavaScript objects to represent particles and their behaviors, although some of the particle properties and motion concepts introduced as we do so will be covered in greater depth only as we progress through the chapter.

To start with, we will create a `Particle` object that implements the particle properties just described. We will then create a `Ball` object that extends `Particle`, drawing graphics so that `Ball` instances can be seen, while behaving as particles. Finally, we will show how to make particles move.

Building a Particle object

We need to create object properties based on the physical properties such as mass, charge, position, and velocity described in the preceding section. We should be able to read as well as modify these properties. Table 4-1 shows the properties we want to create.

Table 4-1. *Properties of the Particle object*

Property	Type	Possible Values and Meaning
mass	Number	Any positive value (default 1)
charge	Number	Any value: positive, negative or zero (default)
x	Number	Any value; *x*-component of position
y	Number	Any value; *y*-component of position
vx	Number	Any value (default 0); *x*-component of velocity
vy	Number	Any value (default 0); *y*-component of velocity
pos2D	Vector2D	Any Vector2D value; 2D position vector
velo2D	Vector2D	Any Vector2D value; 2D velocity vector

The choice of some of these properties and their possible values requires some explanation. It is clear that mass cannot be negative or zero because every particle has mass. As you will see in Chapter 10, charge can be positive, negative, or zero. A particle with a charge of zero would behave as if it had no charge at all.

Having extolled the virtues of vectors in the previous chapter, we'd be hypocrites not to use them. Therefore, we create position and velocity vectors pos2D and velo2D as Vector2D objects from their respective components.

The implementation of these properties proceeds as follows. To begin with, we define the Particle mass, charge, x, y, vx and vy properties in its constructor:

```
function Particle(mass,charge){
    if(typeof(mass)==='undefined') mass = 1;
    if(typeof(charge)==='undefined') charge = 0;
    this.mass = mass;
    this.charge = charge;
    this.x = 0;
    this.y = 0;
    this.vx = 0;
    this.vy = 0;
}
```

We want to be able to set the mass and charge of our particles when we create them, so it makes sense to use a constructor and feed those as parameters in the constructor. Note that the values of mass and charge of a Particle instance default to 1 and 0 respectively, while the position and velocity components are all initially assigned the value of 0.

The pos2D and velo2D properties are added to the Particle prototype via getters and setters:

```
Particle.prototype = {
    get pos2D (){
        return new Vector2D(this.x,this.y);
    },
    set pos2D (pos){
        this.x = pos.x;
        this.y = pos.y;
    },
    get velo2D (){
        return new Vector2D(this.vx,this.vy);
    },
```

```
    set velo2D (velo){
        this.vx = velo.x;
        this.vy = velo.y;
    }
};
```

(Note that you may get an error with the use of these getters/setters if you use Internet Explorer, particularly IE8 or earlier.) Through these accessors, you can get or set the pos2D property of a Particle instance called particle simply by typing **particle.pos2D**, and similarly for the velo2D property. Naturally, you can read or assign the position coordinates of a Particle instance either using the pos2D vector of its components x and y, and similarly for velo2D. That's all there is to the Particle object.

The file particle-example.js contains examples of the usage of the Particle object. You'll need to launch the JavaScript console to see output from the code.

To simplify code for updating a particle's pos2D or velo2D value, we added a couple of methods, multiply(k) and addScaled(vec, k), to the Vector2D object (where vec is a Vector2D and k is a Number). The vec1.multiply(k) method multiplies vector vec1 by the scalar k, and vec1.addScaled(vec, k) adds k times vec to vec1.

For example, to update the position of a Particle instance called particle, write this:

```
particle.pos2D = particle.pos2D.add(particle.velo2D.multiply(dt));
```

Or do this, which involves a single method call addScaled() rather than the two method calls multiply() and add():

```
particle.pos2D = particle.pos2D.addScaled(particle.velo2D, dt);
```

These are equivalent to the component form:

```
particle.x += particle.vx * dt;
particle.y += particle.vy * dt;
```

Extending the Particle object

What we've done in the preceding section is great stuff, but you haven't seen any particles yet. That's because our particles are currently invisible. The Particle object has deliberately been kept to a minimum level of complexity. It's time now to extend it and include something that we can see. To do this, we'll reinvent the Ball object by making some modifications to the old version that we used in previous chapters.

The Ball object

Instead of starting with the existing Ball object from previous chapters, it is easier to start with the Particle object and add some extra properties and methods to turn it into something visible. First we add a radius and a color property similar to the Ball object in Chapter 3. Then we introduce an additional property gradient, a Boolean, which specifies whether the Ball object is to be drawn with a gradient or not. Finally, we add the draw() method to Ball's prototype, augmented to include options to draw the ball with or without a gradient. The full code for the Ball object then looks like this:

```
function Ball(radius,color,mass,charge,gradient){
    if(typeof(radius)==='undefined') radius = 20;
    if(typeof(color)==='undefined') color = '#0000ff';
    if(typeof(mass)==='undefined') mass = 1;
```

```
        if(typeof(charge)==='undefined') charge = 0;
        if(typeof(gradient)==='undefined') gradient = false;
        this.radius = radius;
        this.color = color;
        this.mass = mass;
        this.charge = charge;
        this.gradient = gradient;
        this.x = 0;
        this.y = 0;
        this.vx = 0;
        this.vy = 0;
}

Ball.prototype = {
    get pos2D (){
        return new Vector2D(this.x,this.y);
    },
    set pos2D (pos){
        this.x = pos.x;
        this.y = pos.y;
    },
    get velo2D (){
        return new Vector2D(this.vx,this.vy);
    },
    set velo2D (velo){
        this.vx = velo.x;
        this.vy = velo.y;
    },
    draw: function (context) {
        if (this.gradient){
            grad = context.createRadialGradient(this.x,this.y,0,this.x,this.y,this.radius);
            grad.addColorStop(0,'#ffffff');
            grad.addColorStop(1,this.color);
            context.fillStyle = grad;
        }else{
            context.fillStyle = this.color;
        }
        context.beginPath();
        context.arc(this.x, this.y, this.radius, 0, 2*Math.PI, true);
        context.closePath();
        context.fill();
    }
};
```

As you can see, the constructor takes five optional arguments: radius, color, mass, charge, and gradient, with default values of 20, '#0000ff', 1, 0, and false, respectively. The Boolean gradient option determines whether the ball is drawn with a gradient fill or a simple fill. The actual drawing takes place in the draw() method, as before.

Here we have created the Ball object from scratch by simply copying the properties and methods of Particle. A smarter method is to emulate classical inheritance using the Object.create() method to create the Ball object with the Particle prototype:

```
Ball.prototype = Object.create(Particle.prototype);
Ball.prototype.constructor = Ball;
```

The Ball object can then be augmented with the additional draw() method thus:

```
Ball.prototype.draw = function (context) {
    // code as before
}
```

We demonstrate this method of creating the Ball object in the file ball2.js. To use it, simply include the ball2.js file instead of ball.js in the relevant HTML file. Remember to also include the particle.js file. Whether you use ball.js or ball2.js in future examples is purely a matter of personal preference and will not affect the results in any way.

Using the Ball object

Using the Ball object is quite straightforward. This code snippet creates a ball object, initializes its position, and draws it:

```
var ball = new Ball(20,'#ff0000',1,0,true);
ball.pos2D = new Vector2D(150,50);
ball.draw(context);
```

This piece of code produces a bunch of balls of random size and location, and puts them in an array so that they can be referenced in later code (see Figure 4-1):

```
var balls = new Array();
var numBalls = 10;
for (var i=1; i<=numBalls; i++){
    var ball;
    var radius = (Math.random()+0.5)*20;
    var color = '#0000ff';
    ball = new Ball(radius,color,1,0,true);
    ball.pos2D = new Vector2D(Math.random()*canvas.width,Math.random()*canvas.height);
    ball.draw(context);
    balls.push(ball);
}
```

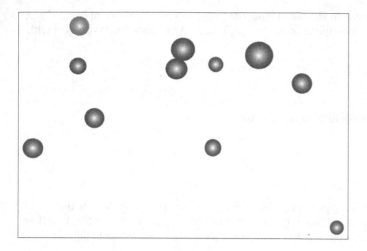

Figure 4-1. *A random bunch of Ball objects*

The code for these examples is in `ball-test.js`. To run this code, the `ball-test.html` file makes use of the `ball.js` file, whereas `ball-particle-inheritance-test.html` uses `ball2.js` (see the previous section).

Moving particles

The `Ball` instances depicted in Figure 4-1 look cool, but they're just sitting there and not doing much. We need to get them moving. To make `Particle` (and `Ball`) instances move is not difficult in principle: we just need to set up an animation loop and update the particle's position and redraw it every timestep. To do this, we will use an animation loop based on the `requestAnimationFrame()` method, together with the `Date.getTime()` method to compute time intervals accurately. We suggest that you take a look at the last example in Chapter 2, `getTime-example.js`, to refresh your memory about the basic logic and code structure. The example code in `ball-move.js` builds upon the code in `getTime-example.js` (Chapter 2) and is shown here in its entirety:

```
var canvas = document.getElementById('canvas');
var context = canvas.getContext('2d');

var ball;
var t;
var t0;
var dt;
var animId;
var animTime = 5; // duration of animation

window.onload = init;

function init() {
    ball = new Ball(20,'#ff0000',1,0,true);
    ball.pos2D = new Vector2D(150,50);
    ball.velo2D=new Vector2D(30,20);
```

```
        ball.draw(context);
        t0 = new Date().getTime();
        t = 0;
        animFrame();
};

function animFrame(){
        animId = requestAnimationFrame(animFrame,canvas);
        onTimer();
}
function onTimer(){
        var t1 = new Date().getTime();
        dt = 0.001*(t1-t0);
        t0 = t1;
        t += dt;
        if (t < animTime){
                move();
        }else{
                stop();
        }
}
function move(){
        ball.pos2D = ball.pos2D.addScaled(ball.velo2D,dt);
        context.clearRect(0, 0, canvas.width, canvas.height);
        ball.draw(context);
}
function stop(){
        cancelAnimationFrame(animId);
}
```

Much of the code deals with setting up the time-keeping, as described in Chapter 2, and should therefore be familiar. The init() function creates a Ball instance, initializes its position and velocity, and draws it on the canvas. It then initializes the time variables and calls the animFrame() function, which sets up the animation loop. The onTimer() function, which fires at every timestep, computes the time interval elapsed (in seconds) since the first call, dt, and then updates the time duration from the beginning of the simulation, t (in seconds). The latter is computed by summing all the elapsed time intervals dt up to the current one. The onTimer() function also contains an if loop that then calls the move() function if the total elapsed time of the simulation is less than a specified duration animTime, and calls a stop() function otherwise, which terminates the animation loop. The move() function updates the ball's position vector based on its velocity vector, erases everything on the canvas, and redraws the ball object. Open the file ball-move.html in a web browser and you will see a ball moving at a constant velocity across the canvas.

The basic setup for the time-keeping in this code will be used over and over again in future examples. The next example, balls-move.js, extends the code to make several balls move at the same time. The only substantial changes take place in the init() and move() methods:

```
function init() {
        balls = new Array();
        for (var i=0; i<numBalls; i++){
                var radius = (Math.random()+0.5)*20;
                var ball = new Ball(radius,'#0000ff',1,0,true);
```

```
            ball.pos2D = new Vector2D(canvas.width/2,canvas.height/2);
            ball.velo2D = new Vector2D((Math.random()-0.5)*20,(Math.random()-0.5)*20);
            ball.draw(context);
            balls.push(ball);
        }
        t0 = new Date().getTime();
        t = 0;
        animFrame();
};
```

In init(), a number of balls are now created and their position and velocity are initialized. They are then placed into an array named balls, as in the example in the previous section. This time, the array is actually used in the move() function:

```
function move(){
        context.clearRect(0, 0, canvas.width, canvas.height);
        for (var i=0; i<numBalls; i++){
            var ball = balls[i];
            ball.pos2D = ball.pos2D.addScaled(ball.velo2D,dt);
            ball.draw(context);
        }
}
```

As you can see, we loop over all the elements of balls to update the position of each ball and redraw it on the canvas element. Run the code by opening the file balls-move.html in a browser and you'll see balls of different sizes moving out from the same initial location.

In all these examples, the balls move at a constant velocity. The really interesting situation is when the velocity changes with time; we'll do that soon in this chapter. But first we need to introduce some motion concepts.

Describing motion: kinematics

In this section, we will start to describe motion more formally using precise concepts, equations, and graphs. The description of motion is called *kinematics*. In kinematics, we are not concerned with what causes motion, but only with how to describe it. The next section, "Predicting motion: forces and dynamics," will look at the cause of motion: force.

Concepts: displacement, velocity, speed, acceleration

Up to now, we've talked about things like velocity and acceleration rather loosely. It's time now to say precisely what we mean by these quantities.

Here are the main concepts that require definition in kinematics:

- Displacement

- Velocity (and the associated concept of speed)

- Acceleration

These physical quantities rest upon more fundamental concepts—position, distance, and time—that are taken as self-evident and do not require definition. For vector quantities, there is a fourth basic concept: angle, which defines a direction in space.

Displacement

Displacement is a vector quantity associated with the motion of an object. To be more precise, it's the vector connecting the initial position with the final position of the object. Remember the example of Bug from Chapter 3? Bug moves a distance of 10 units along the *y*-axis from the origin—that's a displacement. From there, it then undergoes another displacement of 10 units to the right (in the positive *x* direction).

In this example, the net or resultant displacement of Bug is then $\sqrt{(200)}$, or approximately 14.1 units at an angle of 45 degrees. But the net distance it moves is, of course, 20 units. This example illustrates the difference between displacement and distance. In general, an object might move along any complicated trajectory: the distance moved would then be the length along the trajectory, whereas the displacement would always be the vector joining the initial position to the final position of the object (see Figure 4-2).

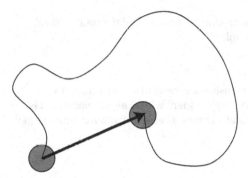

Figure 4-2. *Displacement vector (arrow) contrasted with distance along trajectory*

Displacement is usually denoted by the symbol **s** or **x**, and its magnitude as *s* or *x*. The usual unit of displacement (and distance) is the meter and its multiples (for example, km) and fractions (cm, mm, and so on). On canvas, where you've got a stage on a computer screen rather than real space, you'll think of distance and displacement in terms of pixels, which we'll often abbreviate as px.

Velocity

Velocity is defined as the rate of change of displacement with time. It tells you how quickly something is moving, but also in what direction it is moving. Hence, velocity is a vector quantity.

The usual symbol for velocity is **u** or **v**; for its magnitude, *u* or *v*.

Remember what rate of change means in calculus? It's the gradient function, or derivative. Therefore, velocity is the derivative of displacement with time. In calculus notation we write this as

$$\mathbf{v} = \frac{d\mathbf{s}}{dt}$$

Again, this derivative is the limit of the ratio $\Delta\mathbf{s}/\Delta t$ as the time interval Δt (and therefore also the displacement change $\Delta\mathbf{s}$) becomes small. So, for finite intervals, we can write

$$\mathbf{v} = \frac{\Delta\mathbf{s}}{\Delta t}$$

This gives us the average velocity over the time interval Δt, whereas $\mathbf{v} = d\mathbf{s}/dt$ gives us the instantaneous velocity at a given time. In the special case where velocity is constant, the average velocity is equal to the instantaneous velocity at any time.

As mentioned before, the usual unit for velocity in physics is meters per second (m/s), although km/hr and miles/hr are commonly used in everyday life. In a canvas context, the measure of time is still the second, but the measure of distance is the pixel. So, you'll usually think of velocity in terms of pixels per second (px/s).

In computer code, we are always dealing with discrete intervals, so we are really dealing with average velocities. But if we use a small enough time interval, the average is close to the instantaneous value. One can rearrange the preceding equation to give $\Delta\mathbf{s}$ in terms of $\mathbf{v}$ and Δt:

$$\Delta\mathbf{s} = \mathbf{v}\,\Delta t$$

This equation tells us that the displacement increment is given as the product of velocity and the time interval. This is exactly what we do in the move() method in the ball-move.js example:

```
ball.pos2D = ball.pos2D.addScaled(ball.velo2D,dt);
```

You might also recognize this as being equivalent to integrating in time using the forward scheme (refer to Chapter 3). That makes perfect sense—because velocity is the derivative of displacement with time, displacement is the integral of velocity with time. We'll use this integration scheme, specifically known as an *Euler scheme*, until we get to Part IV of the book.

Speed

Speed is the scalar version of velocity; it has no direction. *Speed* is defined as the rate of change of distance with time, or, in other words, as distance moved per unit of time. The unit of speed is the same as that of velocity.

The average speed of an object is the total distance travelled divided by the total time taken:

$$\text{average speed} = \frac{\text{total distance travelled}}{\text{total time taken}}$$

In this book, most of the time we'll be dealing with velocity and velocity components rather than speed.

Acceleration

Acceleration is defined as the rate of change of velocity with time. It tells you how fast an object's velocity is changing. If you're driving a car at a constant velocity of 20 m/s (approximately 45 miles/hr) in a straight line, you're not accelerating—the acceleration is zero. But if you apply the accelerator and increase the car's speed from 20 m/s to 30 m/s in 10 seconds, the average acceleration is $(30 - 20)/10$ m/s per second, or 1 m/s^2. This means that the velocity increases by 1 m/s in each second. Acceleration can also be negative; in that case, the velocity magnitude decreases.

The calculus definition of acceleration is

$$\mathbf{a} = \frac{d\mathbf{v}}{dt}$$

and the discrete version is

$$\mathbf{a} = \frac{\Delta\mathbf{v}}{\Delta t}$$

These equations are similar to those for velocity, with displacement replaced by velocity. Like the corresponding equations for velocity, $\mathbf{a} = \Delta\mathbf{v}/\Delta t$ gives us the average acceleration over the time interval Δt, whereas $\mathbf{a} = d\mathbf{v}/dt$ gives us the instantaneous acceleration at a given time.

■ **Note** In the special case where acceleration is constant, the average acceleration is equal to the instantaneous acceleration. We'll illustrate this fact in the next section.

Reversing the previous equation gives this:

$$\Delta\mathbf{v} = \mathbf{a}\,\Delta t$$

Interpreted as a discrete equation, this gives us an integration scheme for updating velocity given the acceleration. This is how you would code it in JavaScript using Vector2D:

```
particle.velo2D = particle.velo2D.add(acc.multiply(dt));
```

or

```
particle.velo2D = particle.velo2D.addScaled(acc, dt);
```

Here acc is a variable representing acceleration. It is a Vector2D object. Suppose we use a fixed value:

```
var acc:Vector2D = new Vector2D(0,10);
```

This will make our particles accelerate downward at a rate of 10 px/s^2, simulating the effect of gravity.

Because acceleration is the rate of change of velocity, it is nonzero if the direction of motion changes, even if the speed is constant. A common example is that of an object moving at constant speed in a circle. Because the object's direction of motion changes, its velocity changes. Therefore, its acceleration is not zero. We'll look at this situation in detail in Chapter 9.

Combining vector quantities

Because displacement, velocity, and acceleration are vector quantities, it goes without saying that they must be combined (added or subtracted) using vector methods. You saw an example of how this is done in the previous chapter, so we won't repeat it here.

Why would you want to combine these quantities? You'll frequently want to add displacements and velocities to calculate their total (also known as their *resultant*). Again, you saw an example of resultant displacement in Chapter 3. An example of a situation in which you would want to add velocities is that of a boat on a flowing river. The resultant velocity of the boat is then given by the vector sum of its velocity in the water with the velocity of the water current (see Figure 4-3).

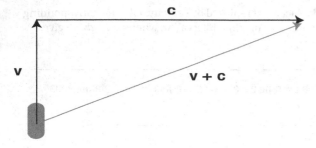

Figure 4-3. *Resultant velocity*

You'll need to use vector subtraction when calculating relative velocities. Suppose you have spaceship A chasing another spaceship B, moving at different velocities **a** and **b** in space (see Figure 4-4). What is the velocity of B relative to A? That's the velocity of B from the point of view of A. In other words, it's the velocity of B in a frame of reference in which A is not moving (we say it's *at rest*). A little quiet thinking should convince you that it's given by the velocity of B minus that of A, in a vector sense: **b** - **a**. Figure 4-4 shows you what **b** - **a** means geometrically: it's the same as **b** + (-**a**), and because (-**a**) points opposite to **a** with the same magnitude, we end up with **b** - **a** pointing in the direction shown. This is the velocity of B as seen by A from its point of view.

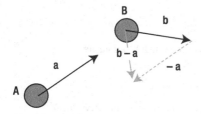

Figure 4-4. *Relative velocity*

Describing motion using graphs

The motion of an object can be represented graphically in different ways. For a particle moving in two dimensions, you can plot its *y*-coordinate against its *x*-coordinate at different times. The resulting graph would, of course, just give you the trajectory of the particle.

You can also plot the components of displacement, velocity, or acceleration against time. These graphs can tell us useful information about how the particle moves.

You will soon see examples in which we make use of the Graph object that we introduced in the previous chapter to create such plots.

Equations of motion for uniform acceleration

For the special case of motion under constant acceleration (also known as *uniform motion*), it is possible, starting only from the definitions of velocity and acceleration, to arrive at a very useful set of equations. These equations of motion can be used to analyze problems in which the acceleration is constant, including the motion of bodies falling under gravity and the motion of projectiles.

We could just state the equations of motion and ask you to accept them. But you might understand them better if you see where they come from. And it's not really difficult; you just need to do a tiny amount of algebra. The starting point is the definition of average acceleration:

$$\mathbf{a}_{av} = \frac{\Delta \mathbf{v}}{\Delta t}$$

If the acceleration is constant, $\mathbf{a}_{av}$ is also equal to the instantaneous acceleration $\mathbf{a}$ at any time t.

Let's now establish our initial conditions by saying that at time $t = 0$ (initially), $\mathbf{s} = 0$ (zero initial displacement), and $\mathbf{v} = \mathbf{u}$ (the initial velocity is denoted by $\mathbf{u}$).

Therefore at time t, we have $\Delta \mathbf{v} = \mathbf{v} - \mathbf{u}$, and $\Delta t = t - 0 = t$, so that

$$\mathbf{a} = \frac{(\mathbf{v} - \mathbf{u})}{t}$$

It is now easy to change the subject of this formula to get this:

$$\mathbf{v} = \mathbf{u} + \mathbf{a} t$$

This formula gives us the velocity $\mathbf{v}$ at any time t, given the initial velocity $\mathbf{u}$ and the (constant) acceleration $\mathbf{a}$.

It would be nice to have a similar equation for displacement too. Can it be done? Yes, you just need to apply the same trick, this time starting from the definition of average velocity:

$$\mathbf{v}_{av} = \frac{\Delta \mathbf{s}}{\Delta t}$$

Now we have $\Delta \mathbf{s} = \mathbf{s} - 0 = \mathbf{s}$, and $\Delta t = t - 0 = t$, which gives

$$\mathbf{v}_{av} = \frac{\mathbf{s}}{t}$$

Because the velocity increases linearly, the average velocity $\mathbf{v}_{av}$ is just $\frac{1}{2}$ $(\mathbf{u} + \mathbf{v})$, the average of the initial and final velocities. Substituting into the preceding equation gives this:

$$\mathbf{s} = \frac{1}{2}(\mathbf{u} + \mathbf{v})t$$

Now you can use the formula already derived ($\mathbf{v} = \mathbf{u} + \mathbf{a} t$) to substitute for $\mathbf{v}$. Do this and simplify, and you should get this:

$$\mathbf{s} = \mathbf{u} t + \frac{1}{2}\mathbf{a} t^2$$

Now sit down and admire this remarkable result of your hard work. What you have here is a formula that tells you the displacement **s** of a particle at any time *t*, in terms of the initial velocity **u** of the particle and the (constant) acceleration **a**.

This will equal the position vector of the particle at time *t* if it starts out at the origin at time *t* = 0. In general, if the particle starts out at location **pos0** = (*x*0, *y*0, *z*0) at time *t* = 0, its position vector **pos** = (*x*, *y*, *z*) at time *t* will be given by the following, in pseudocode:

```
pos = u * t  + 0.5 * a * t * t + pos0
```

This gives you the position of the particle as an exact analytical equation. There is no need to use numerical integration in this case.

You can code up this solution directly in vector form (as we do), or split it into components if you prefer. In pseudocode, you get this in 3D (in 2D just ignore the *z* component):

```
x = ux * t + 0.5 * ax * t * t + x0
y = uy * t + 0.5 * ay * t * t + y0
z = uz * t + 0.5 * az * t * t + z0
```

Before we leave this section, you should know that there is a third formula that sometimes proves useful. The two formulas derived previously ($\mathbf{v} = \mathbf{u} + \mathbf{a}\,t$, and $\mathbf{s} = \mathbf{u}\,t + \frac{1}{2}\,\mathbf{a}\,t^2$) give you the velocity **v** and the displacement **s**, each as a function of time t. If you eliminate the time *t* between these two equations, you can get an equation for *v* and *s* in terms of each other:

$$v^2 = u^2 + 2\,\mathbf{a} \bullet \mathbf{s}$$

Note that this one is a scalar equation, not a vector equation.

■ **Caution**   As mentioned earlier, the equations of motion derived in this section are valid only for constant acceleration. If the acceleration changes with time, they will give the wrong answer.

Example: Applying the equations to projectile motion

It's time for an example. Let's apply the preceding equations to model the motion of a projectile such as a cannonball. To do this, we'll neglect all other forces except gravity. In that case, the force on the projectile at any time during its flight is constant. This will give it a constant acceleration (you'll understand fully why in the next chapter).

We do not model the explosive force that shoots the cannonball in the first place. That force is very brief, and its effect is to impart an initial velocity **u** to the cannonball.

In this special case, the equations for the position of the projectile in component form reduce to this, in pseudocode:

```
x = ux * t + x0
y = uy * t + 0.5 * g * t * t + y0
z = uz * t  + z0
```

Because the acceleration due to gravity points vertically downward, its *x* and *z* components *ax* and *az* are zero, and *ay* = *g*. If you use vectors, you simply need to specify the acceleration vector as (0, *g*, 0) in 3D and (0, *g*) in 2D in the equation **pos** = **u** * *t* + 0.5 * **a** * *t* * *t* + **pos0**.

Let's use these formulas to code a simple projectile simulation. The code is in `projectile-test.js` and is reproduced here:

```javascript
var canvas = document.getElementById('canvas');
var context = canvas.getContext('2d');

var ball1;
var ball2;
var t;
var t0;
var dt;
var animId;
var pos0 = new Vector2D(100,350);
var velo0 = new Vector2D(20,-80);
var acc = new Vector2D(0,10); // acceleration due to gravity
var animTime = 16;

window.onload = init;

function init() {
    ball1 = new Ball(15,'#000000',1,0,true);
    ball1.pos2D = pos0;
    ball1.velo2D = velo0;
    ball2 = new Ball(15,'#aaaaaa',1,0,true);
    ball2.pos2D = pos0;
    ball2.velo2D = velo0;
    ball1.draw(context);
    ball2.draw(context);
    t0 = new Date().getTime();
    t = 0;
    animFrame();
};

function animFrame(){
    animId = requestAnimationFrame(animFrame,canvas);
    onTimer();
}
function onTimer(){
    var t1 = new Date().getTime();
    dt = 0.001*(t1-t0);
    t0 = t1;
    if (dt>0.2) {dt=0;}; // fix for bug if user switches tabs
    t += dt;
    if (t < animTime){
        move();
    }
}
function move(){
    // numerical solution - Euler scheme
    ball1.pos2D = ball1.pos2D.addScaled(ball1.velo2D,dt);
    ball1.velo2D = ball1.velo2D.addScaled(acc,dt);
```

```
        // analytical solution
        ball2.pos2D = pos0.addScaled(velo0,t).addScaled(acc,0.5*t*t);
        ball2.velo2D = velo0.addScaled(acc,t);
        // display
        context.clearRect(0, 0, canvas.width, canvas.height);
        ball1.draw(context);
        ball2.draw(context);
}
```

In the init() function, the code creates two balls (one gray and one black), which are initially positioned at the same location (100, 350), have the same initial velocity (20, –80), and are subjected to the same downward acceleration (0, 10) to simulate gravity. In the move() function, the positions and velocity of these two balls are updated differently. For the first ball, we implement the Euler integration scheme (as discussed in the section on velocity) for updating the velocity by adding the acceleration times the current time interval dt. Similarly for the position of the ball. For the second ball, we assign a new current position based on the exact analytical formula **pos** = **u** * t + 0.5 * **a** * t * t + **pos0**. No numerical approximation is then involved.

Before you run the code, note the following additional line of code in onTimer():

```
if (dt>0.2) {dt=0;};
```

This is a fix for a bug that arises if the user switches browser tabs and then returns. When this happens, requestAnimationFrame() ceases to be active until the user returns to the current tab, so that the animation "freezes" on the current frame. However, when the user returns the elapsed time dt is still computed as the difference between the last call to getTime() and the current time, resulting in an artificially large value of dt in that frame. The code in the move() function then updates the particle's position using the same velocity over the large time interval dt. This would have been fine if the velocity *were* constant, as in the ball-move.js example we saw earlier in this chapter. But in general, as in the present example, the velocity would in reality be changing due to acceleration. The artificially large value of dt would then result in unphysical deviations or "jumps" in the position of the particle from where it should be. The previous line of code fixes this problem simply by setting the value of dt to 0 if its value happens to be larger than a threshold value of 0.2 seconds. The value of 0.2 is essentially arbitrary, and you can use any value you like as long as it is much larger than the typical value of dt when the animation is running normally (here that would be of order 20 milliseconds, which is ten times less than 0.2 seconds) and much smaller than the time it takes to switch to a new tab and back.

If you run the code, you'll see both balls start off together and move in a parabolic path as projectiles are supposed to do. As the simulation progresses, you'll see them begin to separate slightly, as pictured in Figure 4-5, because of numerical errors due to the Euler scheme.

Figure 4-5. Simulating the motion of a projectile with both numerical and analytical solutions

The gray ball is exactly where it should be because it follows the exact analytical solution of the equation of motion. Now you probably won't normally care about the difference. But if you're building an accurate simulation of projectiles or a game of billiards, you would. The difference in position shown in Figure 4-5 is after only 16 seconds of run time. If you were to run this for a few minutes and include bouncing or collisions with other particles, your particle would soon be in places it shouldn't be.

So, what can be done about this if your simulation or game requires high accuracy? If your simulation is simple enough for an analytical solution to exist (as in the present example), using that solution would solve the problem. However, in the vast majority of scenarios, analytical solutions do not exist. In those cases, you need to use a more accurate integration scheme than the Euler scheme.

Chapter 14, in Part IV of the book, covers some more accurate integration schemes. But before we get there, we will use the Euler scheme in most of the examples because Euler is the simplest and quickest scheme, and our main aim in much of the book prior to Part IV is to demonstrate physics effects without necessarily worrying too much about absolute accuracy. As we go along, we will point out examples in which the lack of accuracy may be especially important, although we will defer any solutions to Chapter 14.

The choice of integration scheme is not the only consideration if you are worried about numerical accuracy. Errors can also arise due to the algorithms for dealing with sudden changes such as bouncing and collisions. We'll discuss these other sources of error and how they can be dealt with later in the book.

More motion-related concepts: inertia, mass, and momentum

So far, we've been limited to a few motion concepts, and the progress we can make just with those is rather restricted. The greatest power comes with the notion of forces and how they affect motion. We'll introduce that approach in a conceptual way in the next section and then develop it fully in the next chapter.

Before we do so, we need to introduce two new concepts that act as a connection between motion and the forces that produce them: *mass* and *momentum*.

Let's start with mass. In physics, mass has a very specific meaning: it is a measure of inertia. *Inertia* (literally "laziness") is resistance to motion. The more massive an object is, the more it resists motion—it is more difficult to push a car than a bike. So we say that the mass of a car is larger than that of a bike. The usual unit of mass in physics is the kilogram (kg). The usual symbol for mass is m.

In physics, the mass of an object is not the same as its weight. Weight is actually a force, the force of gravity that the Earth exerts on it. Mass is a scalar; weight is a vector. We'll come back to this in the next section.

The momentum of an object, denoted usually by the symbol $\mathbf{p}$, with magnitude p, is defined as the product of its mass and its velocity. It is a vector quantity.

$$\mathbf{p} = m\,\mathbf{v}$$

Because it is equal to a scalar (mass) times velocity, it has the same direction as that of the velocity vector.

Informally, momentum is a measure of the "quantity of motion" that a body possesses—for the same velocity, a car has "more motion" than a bike because it is more difficult to stop the car. Momentum is important for two reasons: it is intimately connected with force, and there is a law known as the *law of conservation of momentum* that's very useful for solving problems such as collisions between particles. We'll take a close look at momentum and its conservation in the next chapter.

Predicting motion: forces and dynamics

In the preceding section, we could "solve" the projectile problem by obtaining a formula for the position of the projectile as a function of time. That was possible because we knew the acceleration—it was constant and was equal to g, the acceleration due to gravity.

The problem of predicting the motion of an object basically boils down to calculating the acceleration at each time $\mathbf{a}(t)$, whether by some analytical formula or by some numerical procedure. Once we know $\mathbf{a}$, we know how to do the rest—we can integrate numerically (using the Euler or some other scheme) or use an analytical solution if one exists.

In the case of gravity near the Earth's surface, you now know that $a = g$, so that's nice and simple. But how can we calculate the acceleration of an object in general? Before we can give the answer, we need to talk a bit more about forces.

The cause of motion: forces

A *force* is an abstract concept in physics that denotes "something" that makes things move. To be more precise, if a bit mysterious, forces change the way things move. The meaning of this statement will be made clear in just a moment.

Intuitively, you can think of a force as some kind of push or pull. Gravity is a force; it pulls you toward the Earth. Friction is another type of force; it pushes against a moving object.

Forces can be measured and calculated. The unit of force is the newton, denoted by the symbol N.

Forces are useful because knowing the forces acting on a body allows prediction of its motion. How this is done will be explained next.

The relationship between force, mass, and acceleration

Let's go back to the question we asked at the beginning of this section. How can we work out the acceleration of an object? The answer turns out to be surprisingly simple:

$$\mathbf{F} = m\,\mathbf{a}$$

$\mathbf{F}$ is the total force acting on an object, m is its mass, and $\mathbf{a}$ is the acceleration produced by the force. That's it. This is a remarkable formula, probably the most important in this book. It's remarkable because it connects motion (more precisely, acceleration) with its cause (force) in probably the simplest way you can imagine.

The equation $\mathbf{F} = m\mathbf{a}$ is a special case of Newton's second law of motion. It's the most common form of this law. In the next chapter, we'll look at the general form of the law.

You can rewrite the formula as follows, which you can use to calculate the acceleration $\mathbf{a}$ given the mass m of an object and the force $\mathbf{F}$ acting on it:

$$\mathbf{a} = \frac{\mathbf{F}}{m}$$

As we discussed in Chapter 1, the motion of an object is a function of the forces acting on the object:

$$\mathbf{motion} = \text{function}\{\mathbf{forces}\}$$

Well, $\mathbf{a} = \mathbf{F}/m$ is exactly what that means. That's our function. Forces cause acceleration; they cause the velocity of an object to change. And that's how we calculate that change in motion.

This formula is consistent with our conceptual idea of force and mass as respectively causing and resisting motion. For a given force, the acceleration produced is less for a larger mass because we'll be dividing the force by a larger number.

The next question is this: how do we know the force $\mathbf{F}$? Well, in fact, there are many different types of forces. Luckily, there are formulas for each type of force. The formulas come from physics theories or experiments. For us, it does not matter where they come from, of course. The point is that we can calculate all the forces acting on an object at any time and then add them all up to give the total or resultant force $\mathbf{F}$. We then divide this total force $\mathbf{F}$ by the mass m of the object; that gives us the acceleration $\mathbf{a}$ of the object. Problem solved.

Types of forces

In Part II of the book, we'll be looking at different types of forces in a lot of detail. Here are some quick examples.

Gravity is perhaps the most obvious example of a force. The force of gravity acting on an object is also known as its weight. The Earth (or any other planet or star) exerts a gravitational force on any object near it that is in proportion to the mass of that object. So the weight of an object of mass m is given by

$$\text{Weight} = m\,\mathbf{g}$$

where $\mathbf{g}$ is a vector that points vertically downwards with constant magnitude g.

Using $\mathbf{a} = \mathbf{F}/m$, this gives $\mathbf{a} = m\mathbf{g}/m = \mathbf{g}$. In other words, the weight of an object (the force of gravity on it) produces an acceleration of $\mathbf{g}$ if it's the only force acting on the object. This shows that $\mathbf{g}$ is actually an acceleration, known as the *acceleration due to gravity*. Near the Earth's surface, it has a magnitude of approximately 9.81 m/s². Note that the mass m of the object "drops out"—all objects fall with the same acceleration regardless of their mass or size (as long as other forces such as air resistance are negligible compared with gravity).

Another common type of force is a *contact force*, which is the force that an object experiences when it comes into direct physical contact with another object. This occurs, for example, when you push something, when two objects collide, or when two things are pressed together by another force (for example, a book pressing against a table because of its weight). If you are reading a physical copy of this book, lay it on the table. The reason it does not fall through the table is that the latter is exerting an upward contact force that balances the force of gravity on the book.

Another type of contact force is friction, which acts when two objects that are in contact move relative to each other. If you push the book along the table, friction is the force that resists the motion of the book. We'll look at contact forces in Chapter 7.

There are also several examples of forces caused by fluids, such as pressure, drag (a type of frictional force), and upthrust. We'll look at these forces in detail in Chapter 7.

Then there are electric and magnetic forces, which can also act together as an electromagnetic force. These forces are exerted and experienced by particles and objects that possess a physical property called *electric charge*. In fact, apart from gravity, all the everyday forces such as contact forces, fluid forces, and so on originate from the electromagnetic forces that atoms and molecules exert on each other. We'll look at these forces in Chapter 10 and see how they can be used to produce interesting effects.

Combining forces: force diagrams and resultant force

In the equation $\mathbf{F} = m\mathbf{a}$, $\mathbf{F}$ is the total or resultant force. Because force is a vector quantity, the resultant force due to two or more forces must be obtained by vector addition, as described in Chapter 3.

A vector diagram that shows the forces acting on a body is called a *force diagram*. Force diagrams can be useful tools because they help us to work out the resultant force. The point is that it does not matter if the forces acting on a body are of different types. You can add gravity to friction and drag, for example, as long as you do so using vector addition.

As vectors, forces can be "resolved" or "decomposed" into perpendicular components, as explained in Chapter 3. Sometimes it might prove helpful to analyze a problem by resolving forces into their components and combining all the horizontal and vertical components separately.

Figure 4-6 shows an example of a force diagram. It shows the forces acting on an object sliding down an inclined plane. There are three forces acting on this object: its weight $m\mathbf{g}$, which acts downward; a frictional force $\mathbf{f}$ exerted by the surface, which acts opposite to the direction of its motion; and a contact force $\mathbf{R}$, which the surface exerts upon it, acting perpendicular to the surface. Note that you don't care about the force that the object exerts on the surface. If you are modeling the motion of an object, you care only about the forces acting on it, not the forces exerted by it.

Figure 4-6. *Force diagram for a body sliding down an inclined plane*

If you were to simulate the motion of an object such as the one shown in Figure 4-6 (perhaps a car going downhill), how would you do it? As always, with a bit of common-sense logic, some physics formulas, and some code. We won't go into detail about the physics and coding (we'll save that for Chapter 7, when we look at friction and contact forces in detail), but here is the common-sense part. From experience, you know that the object will slide along the surface while always maintaining contact. So it makes sense to resolve the forces along the plane. Well, **f** is already along the plane; **R** is perpendicular to it and so has no component along it; the component of gravity force (weight) is *mg* sin 30° down the incline. Hence, the magnitude of the resultant force down the incline is given by

$$F = m\,g\,\sin(30°) - f$$

Of course, you'll need to know how to calculate the frictional force **f**. We'll tell you that in Chapter 7. Once you know **f**, you can calculate the acceleration **a** = **F**/*m*, as you must surely know by now.

Forces in equilibrium

Sometimes, with two or more forces acting on an object, it so happens that the vector sum (resultant) of the forces is zero. In that case the forces are said to be in *equilibrium*. In terms of the motion of the body, it's as if no forces were acting on it.

Let's go back once more to the equation **a** = **F**/*m*. The equation implies that if the resultant force **F** = 0, then **a** = 0. Therefore, if there is no resultant force acting on a body, the body does not accelerate. In other words, *its velocity does not change, whatever it is*. This means two things. First, if the object is not moving (if it's at rest), it will remain at rest. But also, if the object was already moving at some velocity, it will maintain that velocity and neither accelerate nor decelerate (which is really a negative acceleration). The latter conclusion might come as a surprise to you; we'll pick up on it again when we discuss Newton's laws of motion in the next chapter.

Figure 4-7 shows two examples of an object in equilibrium while under the action of more than one force. In the first example, a book rests motionless on a level table, so it must experience at least two forces that add up to zero. You know that one of them must be the force of gravity, which acts downward. There is another force, a contact force **R** that the table exerts on the book that acts upward, opposing the force of gravity exactly.

Figure 4-7. *Examples of forces in equilibrium*

The second, slightly more complicated example again shows an object at rest. But this time there are three forces acting on it. The object is suspended by means of two strings. So there is a tension force in each string as well as the force of gravity acting on the object. If you add up the three forces, their vector sum must be zero. And if you resolve each force into horizontal and vertical components and then add all the horizontal components together and all the vertical components together, both will add up to zero.

The example in Figure 4-8 shows the force diagram for a plane flying at constant velocity. From the previous discussion, we again deduce that the resultant force on it *must* be zero, no matter how many forces there are or how complicated they are. In fact there are four main forces acting on the plane: a forward thrust, an opposing drag, a downward weight, and an upward lift. *Lift* balances the weight of the plane, and *thrust* balances the drag force on the plane. It may sound a bit counterintuitive that the thrust and drag are equal. In fact, thrust must exceed drag only when the plane is accelerating, for example during take-off and ascent. But once the plane has reached a uniform velocity, thrust is needed only to overcome drag.

Figure 4-8. *Forces on a plane moving at constant velocity are also in equilibrium*

Example: Object falling under gravity and drag

All this discussion of forces might appear somewhat abstract, and you are probably eager to see how it's all applied in practice. Although we'll have plenty of examples in Part II, let's look at a simple example now to whet your appetite. Don't worry if you don't understand everything immediately: it will all make complete sense after you've seen a few more examples in Part II.

In this example, a ball is dropped in a fluid such as air and, as it falls, it experiences a downward force of gravity W and an upward drag force D (see Figure 4-9). Gravity is, of course, constant and given by this:

$$W = m\,g$$

Figure 4-9. *A ball falling in air, experiencing forces of gravity W and drag D*

We'll have more to say about the drag force in Chapter 7; for now we just borrow the following formula:

$$D = -k\,v$$

In other words, the drag force is proportional to the velocity of the ball through the fluid (the minus sign indicates that the drag force is opposite in direction to the velocity, and k is a constant of proportionality). Using these two formulas, we can make the following deductions. Initially, the ball is at rest, so the drag force on it is zero. As the ball falls, it accelerates under gravity, so its velocity increases, and so does the drag force *D*. Eventually (if the ball falls long enough without hitting the ground), the drag force will become equal to the force of gravity, so the two will balance. At that point, we'll have equilibrium, so the acceleration will be zero, as discussed in the previous section. The ball will then continue falling at a constant velocity, known as *terminal velocity*. This is what we expect to happen according to physics theory, but can we reproduce it in a simulation?

To demonstrate that we indeed can simulate the ball's motion under the action of these forces, we will animate its fall while simultaneously plotting its velocity and acceleration as time progresses. Take a look at the code in the file forces-example.js and the markup in the file forces-example.html, in which it is embedded.

First you'll notice that we have two canvas instances in the HTML file, with IDs of canvas and canvas_bg. The canvas instance is placed exactly on top of canvas_bg and made transparent (see the style file style1.css to find out how this is done). The idea is that we will place a static Graph instance on canvas_bg, and animate the ball on canvas. Note also that we have to include the graph.js file in addition to vector2D.js and ball.js in the HTML file.

The code in forces-example.js builds upon previous examples but also adds some important new elements. The init() function looks like this:

```
function init() {
    ball = new Ball(15,'#000000',1,0,true);
    ball.pos2D = new Vector2D(75,20);
    ball.velo2D=new Vector2D(0,0);
    ball.draw(context);
    setupGraphs();
    t0 = new Date().getTime();
    t = 0;
    animFrame();
};
```

This is very familiar: what's new here is the addition of the setupGraphs() method, which sets up a couple of Graph instances on canvas_bg on which to plot the velocity and acceleration of the ball as it falls:

```
function setupGraphs(){
    //graph = new Graph(context,xmin,xmax,ymin,ymax,xorig,yorig,xwidth,ywidth);
    graphAcc = new Graph(context_bg,0,30,0,10,150,250,600,200);
    graphAcc.drawgrid(5,1,5,1);
    graphAcc.drawaxes('time (s)','acceleration (px/s/s)');
    graphVelo = new Graph(context_bg,0,30,0,25,150,550,600,200);
    graphVelo.drawgrid(5,1,5,1);
    graphVelo.drawaxes('time (s)','velocity (px/s)');
}
```

The animFrame() function called in init(), which sets up the animation, is essentially the same as in the previous projectile example, but the time-stepping move() method now looks different:

```
function move(){
    moveObject();
    calcForce();
    updateAccel();
    updateVelo();
    plotGraphs();
}
```

For pedagogical reasons mainly, we've split the code into separate functions whose tasks should be evident from their names. First, the moveObject() method updates the ball's position and redraws it, and it looks like this:

```
function moveObject(){
    ball.pos2D = ball.pos2D.addScaled(ball.velo2D,dt);
    context.clearRect(0, 0, canvas.width, canvas.height);
    ball.draw(context);
}
```

This does nothing new that we haven't seen before. The significant additions are the three methods calcForce(), updateAccel(), and updateVelo(), which look like this:

```
function calcForce(){
    force = new Vector2D(0,ball.mass*g-k*ball.vy);
}
function updateAccel(){
    acc = force.multiply(1/ball.mass);
}
function updateVelo(){
    ball.velo2D = ball.velo2D.addScaled(acc,dt);
}
```

As you can see, these functions respectively compute the resultant downward force using $F = mg - kv$, the acceleration using $a = F/m$, and the new velocity using $\Delta v = a \, \Delta t$. So we subject the ball instance to the two forces of gravity and drag, calculate their resultant force, and then calculate the acceleration and velocity. The position is updated at the next timestep in the moveObject() method.

The final method, plotGraphs(), plots the vertical components of acceleration and velocity on the respective Graph instances on canvas_bg:

```
function plotGraphs(){
    graphAcc.plot([t], [acc.y], '#ff0000', false, true);
    graphVelo.plot([t], [ball.vy], '#ff0000', false, true);
}
```

Run the code, and you will see something like Figure 4-10. As the ball falls, it initially accelerates at the value of $g = 10$ (as set in the code) and its velocity starts to increase sharply. But then the drag force starts increasing; this reduces the resultant downward force and therefore the downward acceleration, causing the velocity to increase less rapidly. About 10 seconds into the simulation, the acceleration has fallen to zero because the drag force has now grown enough to exactly balance the downward force of gravity. From then onward, the ball's velocity is constant at the value of 20 px/s. This is all just as described previously, so the simulation really works! In fact, the value of the terminal velocity is exactly as predicted by physics theory.

Figure 4-10. *Simulating a ball falling under gravity and drag*

To see this, we reason that when terminal velocity is reached:

$$\text{drag} = \text{gravity},$$

and so

$$k\,v = m\,g$$

This gives $v = mg/k$. In our simulation, $m = 1$, $g = 10$ and $k = 0.5$. This gives $v = 20$ px/s, exactly as computed by the simulation. Not bad at all for a first example on forces, don't you agree?

Energy concepts

We've talked a lot about forces, but there is another physics concept that is perhaps equally important: *energy*. From our point of view, the important thing is that energy concepts sometimes provide an alternative way to solve problems that can prove tricky or even impossible to solve using the approach of forces. Just as you saw with momentum, this is because there is a powerful law of conservation of energy (which we'll talk about shortly). In fact, conservation of energy and momentum can be applied together to solve problems involving collisions, as we shall see in Chapter 5 and, in more detail, in Chapter 11.

Unlike momentum, energy is a bit trickier to define. Before we can do so, we need to introduce a closely related concept—that of *work*.

The notion of work in physics

We've often said that force causes motion, but we've also seen that a force can exist in equilibrium with other forces, so that motion cannot occur. To distinguish the motion-producing effect of a force from that of merely balancing another force, we introduce the concept of work.

In physics, we say that *work* is done by a force when it produces motion in the direction along which it acts. The amount of work done W is then defined as the product of the force magnitude F and the displacement s in the direction of the force:

$$W = F s$$

That may sound a bit abstract, so let's look at an example. Let's say a stone is dropped from a certain height h above the ground (see Figure 4-11).

Figure 4-11. *An object dropped from rest at a height h above the ground*

Then the weight of the stone (the force of gravity on it) does work by displacing it downward. According to the preceding definition, the amount of work done in falling a distance h to the ground is therefore given by the following formula, because here $F = mg$ and $s = h$:

$$W = F s = m g h$$

Because work is the product of a force and a distance (and recalling that the unit of force is the newton, N), its unit is Nm (newton times meter). This unit also has a special name, the joule (J). So, J = Nm. Work is a scalar quantity.

What if the displacement is not in the same direction as the force? For example, what if the stone is thrown at an angle rather than dropped vertically downward? Then the work done is given as the product of the force and the projection of the displacement in its direction (see Figure 4-12).

Figure 4-12. *Work done is the scalar product of force and displacement*

You might recognize this as the dot product between **F** and **s**, where θ is the angle between the force **F** and the displacement **s**:

$$W = \mathbf{F} \bullet \mathbf{s} = F\, s \cos(\theta)$$

Hence, if the angle θ is zero, then W = F s (because cos (0) = 1). But if θ is 90 degrees, then cos θ = 0, so W = 0. In other words, the work done by a force is zero if the displacement is perpendicular to the force.

■ **Note**   The resultant acceleration must always be in the direction of the resultant force. However, the resultant motion (displacement) may or may not be in the direction of the resultant force.

The capacity to do work: energy

Now that we know what work is, the definition of energy is simple: Energy is the capacity to do work. Take the example of the stone dropped from a height: because it can do work by falling it must possess energy just by being above the ground. This energy is called *potential energy* (usually abbreviated as PE, with symbol E_p). Similarly, a moving object can do work by colliding with another object, exerting a contact force during the collision and causing it to move under the action of this force. Hence, moving bodies also have energy, known as *kinetic energy* (usually abbreviated as KE, with symbol E_k).

In fact, *work causes a transfer or conversion of energy*. For example, applying a force to make an object move imparts kinetic energy to it. This causes a decrease in energy for the agent applying the force. This is expressed generally in the *work-energy theorem*:

Energy transferred = work done

In symbols:

$$\Delta E = \Delta W$$

Because we are equating energy and work, it follows that energy has the same unit as work: the joule (J). Like work, energy is a scalar quantity.

Energy transfer, conversion, and conservation

Just as there are many types of forces, there are also many types of energy. Examples include light energy, thermal energy, nuclear energy, and so on. But usually we will be concerned with only two forms of energy: kinetic and potential energy. At a fundamental microscopic level, all forms of energy are manifestations of these two basic forms.

Energy can be transferred from one body to another. Energy can also be converted from one form to another. Whether energy is transferred or converted, total energy is always conserved.

An example of *energy transfer* is the collision of two particles, where one of the particles loses KE and the other gains KE. An *elastic* collision is defined as one in which the total *kinetic* energy is conserved (KE is not converted into other forms of energy as a result of the collision); otherwise, the collision is *inelastic*. Therefore, if the collision is elastic, the amount of KE gained by one is exactly equal to that lost by the other.

As an example of *energy conversion*, a body released from a certain height loses potential energy but gains kinetic energy as it accelerates downward—its PE is converted to KE. If the body falls only under the action of the gravitational force, the gain in KE is exactly equal to the loss in PE; the total energy, kinetic plus potential, remains constant. If there are other forces, such as friction (due to air resistance), a small amount of energy is converted to thermal energy in the body and the surrounding air by doing work against friction. The total energy in all forms still remains the same. This is known as the *principle of conservation of energy*.

This principle is so important, let's state it once more, in a more general way:

> **Principle of Conservation of Energy:** Energy can be converted from one form to another or transferred from one body to another during interactions, but the total energy of a closed system is constant.

"Closed system" means a system that has no interaction outside of itself. Within the system, the interactions and exchanges can be as many or as complicated as can occur and the principle will still hold. For example, if you have hundreds of particles colliding with each other in a closed system, the principle will hold. If you have zillions of molecules interacting in an isolated gas, the principle still holds.

Potential and kinetic energy

Because potential energy and kinetic energy are so important, let's see how we can calculate them. Let's start with potential energy. When we discussed the concept of work, recall that the work done by an object falling from a height h above ground was shown to be equal to mgh. Now, because work done is equal to energy transferred, the object must have possessed that amount of energy before it fell. Because it was dropped from rest at height h, its velocity was initially zero and so it had no kinetic energy to start with. Hence, its energy was all potential energy to start with. We therefore conclude that an object of mass m at a height h above the ground has an amount of potential energy given by

$$E_p = m\,g\,h$$

This is our formula for potential energy.

Let's now work out a formula for kinetic energy. Consider the same example of the falling stone. Neglecting energy lost by friction, the kinetic energy of the stone just before it hits the ground must equal the potential energy it had initially (because it does not have any PE at the ground, so it must all have been converted to KE). So the final KE is also equal numerically to mgh. Here h is the distance that the stone has fallen. Because KE is energy possessed due to motion, we really want a formula for KE as a function of the velocity the stone has, not the displacement it has undergone. Remember the formula connecting velocity and displacement? Using $v^2 = u^2 + 2\,\mathbf{a}\cdot\mathbf{s}$, and noting that $u = 0$, $a = g$, and $s = h$, we get $v^2 = 2gh$.

Using this, all we need to do now is replace gh by $\frac{1}{2}v^2$ and we end up with this:

$$E_k = \frac{1}{2}m\,v^2$$

This is the formula for the kinetic energy of a body of mass m moving at a velocity v.

Power

The final concept we'll introduce is that of *power*. In talking about energy, we seem to have given up the concept of time. We've talked about work being done and energy being exchanged or transferred, but without reference to how fast it happens. Power introduces time in the energy approach.

Power is defined as the rate of doing work. In calculus notation, the power P is therefore given by the following:

$$P = \frac{dW}{dt}$$

Or, in discrete form:

$$P = \frac{\Delta W}{\Delta t}$$

In words, P is defined as work done divided by time taken. From this definition, the unit of power is therefore J/s. This unit has a special name. It's called the watt (W). Another commonly used unit is the horsepower (HP). Power is a scalar quantity, just like energy.

We can reverse the last formula to obtain the work done in a time interval Δt when power P is deployed:

$$\Delta W = P\Delta t$$

Power is a very useful concept for analyzing the operation of machines, such as vehicles. Suppose that a machine is doing work by exerting a force F and moving its point of application at a velocity v in the direction of F. Then, the work done is $\Delta W = F\Delta s$. (Note: this is just the formula $W = Fs$ written for small changes ΔW and Δs.)

From the definition of power as the rate of doing work, the power output of the machine is therefore this:

$$P = \frac{\Delta W}{\Delta t} = \frac{F\Delta s}{\Delta t}$$

And because $\Delta s/\Delta t = v$, we end up with this formula:

$$P = F v$$

So the power deployed by the machine is equal to the product of the force F it applies and the velocity v it produces.

You usually need to apply power concepts if you are simulating machines engineered by humans, such as cars and boats.

Example: A rudimentary "car" simulation

We conclude this chapter by showing you a simple example of how to apply power and energy concepts to simulate motion, without the explicit use of forces. In this example, you will apply power to a Ball object (the car) to accelerate it against frictional and other power losses, in the same manner as you press the gas pedal of your car to keep it moving.

The code for this example is in the file energy-example.js and is shown here in full:

```
var canvas = document.getElementById('canvas');
var context = canvas.getContext('2d');
var canvas_bg = document.getElementById('canvas_bg');
var context_bg = canvas_bg.getContext('2d');

var car;
var t;
var t0;
var dt;
var animId;
var graph;
var force;
var acc;
var g = 10;
var k = 0.5;
var animTime = 60; // duration of animation

var powerLossFactor=0.1;
var powerApplied=50;
var ke;
var vmag;
var mass;
var applyThrust=false;

window.onload = init;

function init() {
    car = new Ball(15,'#000000',1,0,true);
    car.pos2D = new Vector2D(50,50);
    car.velo2D=new Vector2D(20,0);
    car.draw(context);

    mass = car.mass;
    vmag = car.velo2D.length();
    ke = 0.5*mass*vmag*vmag;
    window.addEventListener('keydown',startThrust,false);
    window.addEventListener('keyup',stopThrust,false);
    setupGraphs();

    t0 = new Date().getTime();
    t = 0;
    animFrame();
};

function setupGraphs(){
    //graph = new Graph(context,xmin,xmax,ymin,ymax,xorig,yorig,xwidth,ywidth);
    graph= new Graph(context_bg,0,60,0,50,100,550,600,400);
    graph.drawgrid(5,1,5,1);
    graph.drawaxes('time (s)','velocity (px/s)');
}
```

```
function startThrust(evt){
    if (evt.keyCode==38){
        applyThrust = true;
    }
}
function stopThrust(){
    applyThrust = false;
}

function animFrame(){
    animId = requestAnimationFrame(animFrame,canvas);
    onTimer();
}
function onTimer(){
    var t1 = new Date().getTime();
    dt = 0.001*(t1-t0);
    t0 = t1;
    if (dt>0.2) {dt=0;}; // fix for bug if user switches tabs
    t += dt;
    //console.log(dt,t,t0,animTime);
    if (t < animTime){
        move();
    }else{
        stop();
    }
}
function move(){
    moveObject();
    applyPower();
    updateVelo();
    plotGraphs();
}

function moveObject(){
    car.pos2D = car.pos2D.addScaled(car.velo2D,dt);
    context.clearRect(0, 0, canvas.width, canvas.height);
    car.draw(context);
}
function applyPower(){
    if (applyThrust){
        ke += powerApplied*dt;
    }
    ke -= powerLossFactor*vmag*vmag*dt;
}
function updateVelo(){
    vmag = Math.sqrt(2*ke/mass);
    car.vx = vmag;
}
```

```
function plotGraphs(){
    graph.plot([t], [car.vx], '#ff0000', false, true);
}
function stop(){
    cancelAnimationFrame(animId);
}
```

Most of the code should be familiar from previous examples. The `init()` method includes extra code that sets up keydown and keyup event listeners. The corresponding event handlers set the value of a Boolean variable applyThrust to true if the up-arrow key is pressed and to false otherwise.

Some convenience variables are used in the code: mass (the mass of the particle), vmag (its velocity magnitude), ke (its kinetic energy), powerApplied (the applied power), and powerLossFactor (a coefficient we use to calculate the power loss due to friction and other factors). The values of vmag and ke are initialized in `init()`. We have given the ball an initial velocity of 20 px/s in the x-direction. The mass of the ball is 1 unit.

The most important, and novel, parts of the code are the two methods applyPower() and updateVelo(), which are called at every timestep within the move() method.

In applyPower(), we are updating the kinetic energy of the ball. The applyThrust Boolean variable tells us if the up-arrow key is pressed; if so, the KE is updated by multiplying the power by the time interval dt. What we are doing here is applying this formula:

$$\Delta E_k = P\Delta t$$

You might not immediately recognize this formula, but it is obtained by equating the work done $\Delta W = P\Delta t$ with the kinetic energy gained according to the work-energy theorem, as discussed earlier. Conceptually, what is happening is that the applied power is doing mechanical work on the ball, which results in an increase in its kinetic energy.

In applyPower(), you will notice that we also *reduce* the kinetic energy of the ball by an amount equal to powerLossFactor*vmag*vmag*dt. This is equivalent to applying a power loss given by the following, where k is a constant corresponding to powerLossFactor:

$$P = -k\,v^2$$

This formula comes from applying the formula $P = F\,v$ we saw in the last section and modeling the total of all resistive forces (such as friction and drag) by $F = -k\,v$, as a force proportional to the velocity of the ball (see Chapter 7). This is a crude approximation, but it will do for the purpose of our simple example.

The updateVelo() method first computes the velocity magnitude from the updated kinetic energy by this formula, which is obtained by reversing the formula for kinetic energy $E_k = \dfrac{1}{2}\,m\,v^2$:

$$v = \sqrt{2E_k/\mathrm{m}}$$

It then updates the ball's velocity accordingly.

There is also code for setting up a Graph instance and plotting a graph of the horizontal velocity component of the ball as the simulation progresses. These pieces of code are straightforward, so we will not go into them here.

If you run the code, you will find that the ball starts moving, but its velocity is gradually reduced, owing to the effect of the power loss. If you then press and hold down the up-arrow key, the applied power will cause an increase in the ball's KE, making it accelerate. If the power is applied continuously, eventually the velocity will tend to a constant value, but if the up-arrow key is released, the velocity will reduce again, as shown in Figure 4-13. This behavior mirrors the operation of a car accelerator in a simple way.

Figure 4-13. *A rudimentary car simulation*

Summary

That was another long overview chapter, and you've now learned an awful lot of physics concepts. This chapter completes Part I of the book. The next chapter will bring together what you've learned so far to lay out the principles of how to simulate a wide range of forces and motions.

Get ready for the real action!

PART II

Particles, Forces, and Motion

CHAPTER 5

■■■

The Laws Governing Motion

Chapter 4 provided some of the general conceptual background for describing and analyzing motion. That background included a discussion of motion-related concepts such as velocity, acceleration, and force. In this chapter, we'll use those concepts to formulate the physics laws that will allow you to calculate the motion of particles under any type of force. The next five chapters will then apply the laws to a number of different forces. We'll illustrate the application of the principles with brief examples, with the aim of building on them in the next few chapters.

We have deliberately kept this chapter brief and focused on the fundamental laws and principles that you will need to apply to the examples in this part of the book and beyond. You can come back to this chapter as needed to refresh your understanding of the underlying physics principles, as you work your way through their applications in the rest of the book.

Topics covered in this chapter include the following:

- **Newton's laws of motion:** Newton's three laws provide the link between force and motion. These laws allow us to predict the motion of objects under the action of known forces.

- **Applying Newton's laws:** We show you how to implement Newton's laws of motion numerically in code and illustrate their use with a couple of examples.

- **Newton's second law as a differential equation:** In physics textbooks, Newton's second law is sometimes expressed as a differential equation and solved analytically using calculus. We briefly discuss the connection between that formulation and our numerical method, and illustrate it with an example.

- **The principle of conservation of energy:** We apply the principle of conservation of energy to motion by considering the potential and kinetic energy of moving particles.

- **The principle of conservation of momentum:** We take a look at conservation of momentum and its application to a simple example involving collisions.

- **Laws governing rotational motion:** We'll note briefly that the preceding laws can be extended to objects undergoing rotational motion. We do not discuss rotation here, but will do so in later chapters.

Newton's laws of motion

Newton's three laws of motion, formulated in his classic book *Principia Mathematica* in 1687, provide the link between force and motion. You might recall that we said in the previous chapter that the formula $\mathbf{F} = m\mathbf{a}$ provides that link. This formula is actually the second of Newton's three laws of motion. In fact, it is a special form of that law. In this chapter, we'll go a bit deeper, looking at the general form of Newton's second law as well as the two other laws.

Newton's first law of motion (N1)

The first law of motion tells you what happens if there is no force acting on an object (see Figure 5-1). Think of an object that is at rest and not moving. If you don't apply any force to it (in other words, if you leave it alone), what do you think will happen? That's right—nothing. Things don't suddenly start moving on their own. This is basically what the first law says. Common sense? But wait, there is more. Suppose the object is already moving and there is no force on it. What would happen to it? Everyday experience might tempt you into thinking that the object would slow down and finally stop. So you might be surprised to hear that the first law says that the object would carry on moving at its initial velocity as long as there is no force on it!

Figure 5-1. *Schematic illustration of Newton's first law of motion*

This proposition seems to run somewhat counter to our everyday experience. For example, a ball rolling on the ground always comes to rest. In fact, it does so because friction with the ground is causing it to slow down. In the absence of friction, the ball would carry on indefinitely. This can be demonstrated by minimizing friction with the underlying surface—for example, by using marbles on a perfectly smooth horizontal surface. The marbles then move in a straight line for long distances without significant decrease in their velocity.

Another way of putting this is that you don't need a force for an object to *continue* moving at constant velocity. You only need a force to make it *change* its velocity—for example, by starting to move, or speeding up or slowing down. In other words, you only need a force to make an object accelerate (or decelerate).

Armed with this insight, we can formulate Newton's first law of motion succinctly in the following form, which covers both the cases of an object at rest and of one moving at constant velocity:

N1: If the resultant force acting on an object is zero, its acceleration is zero. $\mathbf{F} = \mathbf{0}$ implies $\mathbf{a} = \mathbf{0}$.

This law is so important that we'll say it in yet another way: If no resultant force acts on an object, its velocity must be constant (including zero). Conversely, if an object has a constant velocity (which may be zero), you know for certain that the resultant force on it must be zero.

Finally, note that we said that the *resultant force* is zero. We're not saying that no forces are acting on the object. As you saw in Chapter 4, two or more forces acting on the same object can be in equilibrium so that their resultant is zero. In such a case, the first law will still hold. It does not distinguish between no resultant force and no force at all.

To put these concepts into context, the moveObject() method in the last two examples in Chapter 4 implements the first law; it takes a particle and moves it at its velocity forever. It knows nothing about forces.

Newton's second law of motion (N2)

Newton's second law of motion builds upon the first law (see Figure 5-2). The first law tells you what happens when no resultant force acts on an object. The second law tells you what happens when a resultant force does act on an object. It tells you that the object's motion changes. But that's not all. It tells you exactly by what amount it changes—it gives you an exact formula connecting the force applied and the change in motion produced.

Figure 5-2. *Schematic illustration of Newton's second law of motion*

Recall from the last chapter that momentum (with the symbol $\mathbf{p}$ and defined as $\mathbf{p} = m\mathbf{v}$) represents the "quantity of motion" that an object possesses. Newton's second law connects the force applied to the change in momentum it produces. We won't go into how Newton arrived at that formula, but here it is:

N2: If a resultant force F acts on an object, its momentum changes so that the rate of change of momentum is equal to the force applied: $\mathbf{F} = d\mathbf{p}/dt$.

This is the general form of Newton's second law, and it may appear somewhat unintuitive, at least until you get used to it! In Calculus-speak, this tells us that the applied force is equal to the time derivative of momentum. Essentially, the time derivative of momentum tells us how fast the momentum is changing on an instantaneous basis. This means that the force being applied at any given time is equal to the change in momentum per unit time.

We have seen similar formulas before. For example, $\mathbf{v} = d\mathbf{s}/dt$ and $\mathbf{a} = d\mathbf{v}/dt$. Newton's second law is exactly of the same form: $\mathbf{F} = d\mathbf{p}/dt$. Note that the preceding equations for velocity and acceleration are actually *definitions*, whereas $\mathbf{F} = d\mathbf{p}/dt$ is a *law* that tells us how things behave in the real world.

In this general form, the second law might seem quite different from the first law. In the first law, we were talking about acceleration, and now we are talking about rate of momentum change. There is actually a link between the two when we apply the second law to objects whose mass doesn't change, such as particles.

To see the link, recall again that momentum is defined by $\mathbf{p} = m\mathbf{v}$. For a particle, the mass m is constant. In that case, the rules of calculus tell us that $d\mathbf{p}/dt = m\,d\mathbf{v}/dt$. If you're into calculus, what we've done here is to calculate the (time) derivative of $\mathbf{p}$, which must be equal to the derivative of $m\mathbf{v}$ (because these two things are equal: $\mathbf{p} = m\mathbf{v}$). But m is constant, so the derivative of $m\mathbf{v}$ is equal to m times the derivative of $\mathbf{v}$. You probably recall that $d\mathbf{v}/dt = \mathbf{a}$ (the definition of acceleration). Therefore, we conclude that for a particle, $d\mathbf{p}/dt = m\mathbf{a}$. Because Newton assures us that $\mathbf{F} = d\mathbf{p}/dt$, we've recovered our old friend $\mathbf{F} = m\mathbf{a}$. So here is the special form of Newton's second law of motion:

N2 (special): If a resultant force $\mathbf{F}$ acts on an object of constant mass m, it produces an acceleration a given by the formula $\mathbf{F} = m\mathbf{a}$.

If you now compare this form of the second law with the statement of the first law given in the last section, you'll see that N1 is really just a special case of N2. Starting with $\mathbf{F} = m\mathbf{a}$ and putting $\mathbf{F} = 0$ gives $m\mathbf{a} = 0$, and hence $\mathbf{a} = 0$. In other words, $\mathbf{F} = 0$ gives $\mathbf{a} = 0$, which is exactly what the first law says. So the first law is "contained" within the second law. Good; that's one fewer law to worry about!

You'll use Newton's second law in the form of $\mathbf{F} = m\mathbf{a}$ most of the time. But bear in mind that it's not the most general form of the law—it applies only if the mass m does not change. There is a third form of the law that applies when instead of an object of fixed mass m, you have a stream of substance moving at a certain velocity. For example, the exhaust gases from a rocket are pushed out at a constant velocity $\mathbf{v}$ relative to the rocket. Because $\mathbf{v}$ is now constant, calculus rules tell us that $d\mathbf{p}/dt = \mathbf{v}\,dm/dt$. Therefore, the force on the gases is given by $\mathbf{F} = \mathbf{v}\,dm/dt$, where dm/dt is the rate of change of mass (the mass of gas released per second). We'll use this form of Newton's second law to model a rocket in Chapter 6:

N2 (alternate): The force $\mathbf{F}$ needed to move any substance at a rate of dm/dt at constant velocity $\mathbf{v}$ is given by $\mathbf{F} = \mathbf{v}\,dm/dt$.

Despite its simplicity, Newton's second law is arguably the most important law in Newtonian mechanics. It's almost magical how it connects forces and motion. But it is also utterly useless unless we know how to work out the forces acting on an object. We need *force laws*. We'll look at some examples of force laws shortly. But before we do that, you want to know about Newton's third law, don't you?

Newton's third law of motion (N3)

In the preceding chapter, we said that force is the cause of changes in motion. As you have just seen, Newton's second law makes that statement much more precise, giving us a formula for calculating the change in motion arising from a given force. But so far, we haven't said much about where forces come from. Many forces arise because of the presence of other objects. Newton's first and second laws tell us how an object's motion responds to an applied force. Newton's third law tells us how two objects interact by exerting forces on each other. Here it goes:

> **N3:** If a body A exerts a force **F** on another body B, body B must in turn exert an equal and opposite force –**F** on body A.

What this means is that forces between objects always exist as an *action-reaction pair*. Both forces exist *simultaneously*; there is no delay between them. And even if their magnitudes and directions change with time, they remain equal and opposite at all times.

Newton's third law of motion is frequently misunderstood and misquoted. One of the common mistakes is to think that action and reaction forces "balance" each other. In fact, in an action-reaction pair, the forces act on *different* objects. Therefore, it is wrong to think that they "balance" or "cancel" each other. In other words, they are not in equilibrium. Each force acts on a different object and affects its motion individually. Subtleties like these make Newton's third law somewhat difficult to understand deeply at an abstract level. But it helps a lot to see how the law is applied in analyzing specific problems. For example, Newton's third law is applied to analyze the interaction between two particles in the section "The principle of momentum conservation" that follows. You will also see it applied in the analysis of different examples throughout the book.

Here are some examples of action-reaction pairs of forces:

- Two colliding bodies exert equal and opposite forces on each other, even if they have different masses, as depicted in Figure 5-3.

Figure 5-3. *Schematic illustration of Newton's third law of motion*

- The Earth is exerting a force of gravity on you equal to your weight. This implies that you are also exerting an equal and opposite force of gravity on the Earth!

- In a rocket, the engine exerts a downward force on the exhaust gases, which in turn exerts an equal and opposite force on the rocket, propelling it forward.

Applying Newton's laws

Practically the whole of the rest of this book is about applying Newton's laws of motion. Here, we'll just establish the method, create some force functions, and illustrate their application with some simple examples.

General method for applying F = ma

To analyze a problem for applying **F** = m**a**, use the following procedure:

1. Draw a diagram representing the interacting objects in the problem.

2. Choose the object whose motion is to be calculated and indicate using arrows all the forces acting *on* it due to other objects. Ignore the forces exerted *by* the object on other objects. This gives you a force diagram, as described in Chapter 4.

3. Calculate the resultant force **F** on the object (using vector addition, as described in Chapter 3) and apply the second law **F** = m**a** to calculate the acceleration **a**.

In principle, that's all there is to it. You have to do steps 1 and 2 using pen and paper. Let's use JavaScript to help us do step 3.

Coding up motion under any force

What we need in order to achieve step 3 in the previous section is a general piece of code that allows you to calculate the forces on a particle, find their resultant, and hence compute their acceleration. You can then use the acceleration to update the velocity and position of the particle. Recall the sense in which we are using the term "particle," as discussed in Chapter 4: any object whose inner structure is irrelevant from the point of view of the simulation. So, for our purposes, a particle could be a ball as well as a planet.

The general code structure for doing this will look very similar to the move() method in the example forces-example.js in the preceding chapter:

```
function move(){
    moveObject();
    calcForce();
    updateAccel();
    updateVelo();
}
```

As discussed, the moveObject() method simply moves the particle according to its existing velocity:

```
function moveObject(){
    particle.pos2D = particle.pos2D.addScaled(particle.velo2D,dt);
    context.clearRect(0, 0, canvas.width, canvas.height);
    particle.draw(context);
}
```

The rest of the code computes the force, works out the acceleration, and updates the velocity, ready to be used in the moveObject() method on the next timestep. The job of calcForce() is to calculate the resultant force on the particle. We'll look at that last. The updateAccel() method updates the acceleration once we know the force. How do we do that? Of course, using $\mathbf{F} = m\mathbf{a}$ to give $\mathbf{a} = \mathbf{F}/m$. So, with acc and force defined as Vector2D objects, updateAccel() is just a one-liner:

```
function updateAccel(){
    acc = force.multiply(1/particle.mass);
}
```

Recalling from Chapter 4 that $\Delta\mathbf{v} = \mathbf{a}\Delta t$, the updateVelo() method is just as simple:

```
function updateVelo(){
    particle.velo2D = particle.velo2D.addScaled(acc,dt);
}
```

Finally, the calcForce() method should calculate each force acting on the particle and then add them up to give their resultant, the force variable. The code that goes into calcForce() will depend on the problem and the forces involved. In the forces-example.js code in Chapter 4, calcForce() looked like this:

```
function calcForce(){
    force = new Vector2D(0,particle.mass*g-k*ball.vy);
}
```

In that simple example we just specified the force directly. But as our examples get more complicated, it will be useful to bunch together the different kinds of force laws we'll come across into static methods in a single object that we'll call Forces. To invoke the action of a particular force we can then do something like this:

```
function calcForce(){
    force = Forces.zeroForce();
}
```

All this method currently does is to set the force to zero. It does this using the Forces.zeroForce() method, which produces a Vector2D object with zero components. Of course, we haven't said much about the Forces object yet, so let's do that now.

The Forces object

Exactly what goes into calcForce()depends on the problem at hand, but it always involves specifying the forces on the particle and then adding them up. So, let's build a new object to help us with these tasks.

The object we'll build will basically just contain static methods for different types of forces. So we'll name the object Forces, appropriately enough:

```
function Forces(){
}
```

In general, the force on a particle could depend on the particle properties (size, position, velocity, mass, charge), as well as on properties of the environment it is in, or on properties of other objects. These properties will need to be specified as arguments in the relevant methods.

Let's look at some examples. First, let's create a zero force. This is a force with a magnitude of zero, and therefore with components equal to zero.

Here is the static method that will make one:

```
Forces.zeroForce = function() {
    return (new Vector2D(0,0));
}
```

Next, let's create a gravity force method:

```
Forces.constantGravity = function(m,g){
    return new Vector2D(0,m*g);
}
```

The force of gravity on an object of mass m is given by mg and points downward. Hence, we give the values of m and g as arguments and are given back a vector with the vertical (y) component being mg and the horizontal (x) component being zero. You'll note that we've named the function constantGravity instead of simply gravity. This is because we are reserving the name *gravity* for the more general form of the force of gravity, which you'll learn about in Chapter 6. The form of gravity given by mg is near-Earth gravity, as experienced by objects near the surface of the Earth. You'll learn more about this in the next chapter.

As another example, let's look at *drag*, which is the resistive force experienced by an object moving in a fluid such as air or water. We'll take a much deeper look at drag in Chapter 7, but for now let's just say that at low speeds the drag force is given by $-k\mathbf{v}$. That's a constant k times the velocity $\mathbf{v}$ of an object. The minus sign signifies that the drag force is in the opposite direction to the velocity. Let us create a function for this type of drag force, which we call linearDrag.

Here is the static method `linearDrag`:

```
Forces.linearDrag = function(k,vel){
    var force;
    var velMag = vel.length();
    if (velMag > 0) {
        force = vel.multiply(-k);
    }else {
        force = new Vector2D(0,0);
    }
    return force;
}
```

As you can see, the `linearDrag` function takes two arguments: the drag constant k (a Number) and the velocity `vel` (a Vector2D) of the object.

Next, we create a static method `add()` for adding any number of forces:

```
Forces.add = function(arr){
    var forceSum = new Vector2D(0,0);
    for (var i=0; i<arr.length; i++){
        var force = arr[i];
        forceSum.incrementBy(force);
    }
    return forceSum;
}
```

The `add()` method takes as argument an array of forces arr. It loops through the array, adding the forces in turn and returning the final vector sum. This is all we need for now. In the next few chapters, we'll be adding many more force functions as static methods of the `Forces` object. To use the `Forces` object, don't forget to add the file `forces.js` (available along with all the source code at `http://apress.com`) in your HTML file.

A simple example: projectile with drag

To demonstrate how to use the Forces class, let's look at a simple example that brings together what we've been discussing in the previous two sections. Suppose we want a particle to move under gravity while experiencing the drag force (such as an object thrown or falling through a fluid such as air or water). The file `forces-test.js` shows how to do that:

```
var canvas = document.getElementById('canvas');
var context = canvas.getContext('2d');

var ball;
var t;
var t0;
var dt;
var animId;
var force;
var acc;
var g = 10;
var k = 0.1;
var animTime = 10; // duration of animation
```

```
window.onload = init;

function init() {
     ball = new Ball(15,'#0000ff',1,0,true);
     ball.pos2D = new Vector2D(50,400);
     ball.velo2D = new Vector2D(60,-60);
     ball.draw(context);
     t0 = new Date().getTime();
     t = 0;
     animFrame();
};
function animFrame(){
     animId = requestAnimationFrame(animFrame,canvas);
     onTimer();
}
function onTimer(){
     var t1 = new Date().getTime();
     dt = 0.001*(t1-t0);
     t0 = t1;
     if (dt>0.2) {dt=0;};
     t += dt;
     if (t < animTime){
          move();
     }else{
          stop();
     }
}
function move(){
     moveObject();
     calcForce();
     updateAccel();
     updateVelo();
}
function stop(){
     cancelAnimationFrame(animId);
}
function moveObject(){
     ball.pos2D = ball.pos2D.addScaled(ball.velo2D,dt);
     context.clearRect(0, 0, canvas.width, canvas.height);
     ball.draw(context);
}
function calcForce(){
     var gravity = Forces.constantGravity(ball.mass,g);
     var drag = Forces.linearDrag(k,ball.velo2D);
     force = Forces.add([gravity, drag]);
}
function updateAccel(){
     acc = force.multiply(1/ball.mass);
}
function updateVelo(){
     ball.velo2D = ball.velo2D.addScaled(acc,dt);
}
```

The new physics here takes place in the calcForce() method, where we include the forces of gravity and linear drag by making use of the relevant static methods of the Forces class. So we've invoked Forces.constantGravity(), using $g = 10$ and the particle mass. We've also invoked Forces.linearDrag() using $k = 0.1$. Then we added the two forces by passing them as an array argument to the Forces.add() method and assigned the result to the force variable.

Run the code and you will see a ball being thrown upward; it is then pulled down by gravity and slowed down by drag.

To appreciate the effect that the additional drag force has on the ball's motion, replace the last two lines in calcForce() with the following line:

```
force = gravity;
```

This makes the ball move under gravity only. If you now run the code, you will see the ball following a parabolic trajectory, as in the projectile simulation in Chapter 4.

On the other hand, if you keep the drag force and increase the drag coefficient k to 0.5, the drag force will have a more extreme effect, quickly killing the horizontal motion of the ball and making it fall almost vertically thereafter—similar to what a balloon might do if you hit it upward.

This simple example demonstrates how easy it is to make use of the Forces object to build simulations, and how you can get different effects by changing the forces and their parameters in the calcForce() method.

Just to give you an idea of how flexible and powerful this approach is, let's look at a somewhat more complicated example.

A more complicated example: floating ball

The example we are going to look at involves throwing a ball about in air or water and making it behave as it would do in real life. This example uses more physics than we've covered, so we won't go into the details of the physics or coding involved, leaving a more complete discussion for Chapter 7. At this stage, we just want to whet your appetite by showing you what can be done with a fairly small amount of straightforward coding using the approach outlined in this section.

The source code for this example is in the file floating-ball.js. Before we look at this, a quick word on the HTML setup to give the desired visual environment as shown in Figure 5-4. As you can see from this screenshot, we have a rectangular area that represents water, and a ball which appears to be partially immersed in it. To achieve this visual effect, the water is drawn on a transparent canvas instance canvas_fg which is in the foreground, with the animation taking place on a different canvas instance named canvas. Take a look at the files floating-ball.html and style2.css to see how this is achieved.

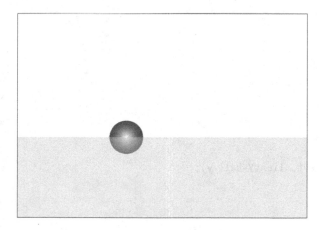

Figure 5-4. *The floating ball simulation*

Here is the full code of floating-ball.js:

```javascript
var canvas = document.getElementById('canvas');
var context = canvas.getContext('2d');
var canvas_fg = document.getElementById('canvas_fg');
var context_fg = canvas_fg.getContext('2d');

var ball;var t0;
var dt;
var animId;
var force;
var acc;
var g = 50;
var k = 0.01;
var rho = 1.5;
var V = 1;
var yLevel = 300;
var vfac = -0.8;

window.onload = init;

function init() {
    // create a ball
    ball = new Ball(40,'#0000ff',1,0,true);
    ball.pos2D = new Vector2D(50,50);
    ball.velo2D = new Vector2D(40,-20);
    //ball.velo2D = new Vector2D(20,-60);
    ball.draw(context);
    // create water
    context_fg.fillStyle = "rgba(0,255,255,0.5)";
    context_fg.fillRect(0,yLevel,canvas.width,canvas.height);
    // set up event listeners
    addEventListener('mousedown',onDown,false);
    addEventListener('mouseup',onUp,false);
    // initialize time and animate
    initAnim();
};

function onDown(evt) {
    ball.velo2D = new Vector2D(0,0);
    ball.pos2D = new Vector2D(evt.clientX,evt.clientY);
    moveObject();
    stop();
}

function onUp(evt) {
    ball.velo2D = new Vector2D(evt.clientX-ball.x,evt.clientY-ball.y);
    initAnim();
}
```

```
function initAnim(){
    t0 = new Date().getTime();
    animFrame();
}
function animFrame(){
    animId = requestAnimationFrame(animFrame,canvas);
    onTimer();
}
function onTimer(){
    var t1 = new Date().getTime();
    dt = 0.001*(t1-t0);
    t0 = t1;
    if (dt>0.2) {dt=0;};
    move();
}
function move(){
    moveObject();
    calcForce();
    updateAccel();
    updateVelo();
}
function stop(){
    cancelAnimationFrame(animId);
}

function moveObject(){
    ball.pos2D = ball.pos2D.addScaled(ball.velo2D,dt);
    context.clearRect(0, 0, canvas.width, canvas.height);
    ball.draw(context);
}
function calcForce(){
    //force = new Vector2D(0,ball.mass*g-k*ball.vy);
    var gravity = Forces.constantGravity(ball.mass,g);
    var rball = ball.radius;
    var xball = ball.x;
    var yball = ball.y;
    var dr = (yball-yLevel)/rball;
    var ratio; // volume fraction of object that is submerged
    if (dr <= -1){ // object completely out of water
        ratio = 0;
    }else if (dr < 1){ // object partially in water
        //ratio = 0.5 + 0.5*dr; // for cuboid
        ratio = 0.5 + 0.25*dr*(3-dr*dr); // for sphere
    }else{ // object completely in water
        ratio = 1;
    }
    var upthrust = new Vector2D(0,-rho*V*ratio*g);
    var drag = ball.velo2D.multiply(-ratio*k*ball.velo2D.length());
    force = Forces.add([gravity, upthrust, drag]);
    //force = Forces.add([gravity, upthrust]);
```

```
    if (xball < rball){
        ball.xpos = rball;
        ball.vx *= vfac;
    }
    if (xball > canvas.width - rball){
        ball.xpos = canvas.width - rball;
        ball.vx *= vfac;
    }
}
function updateAccel(){
    acc = force.multiply(1/ball.mass);
}
function updateVelo(){
    ball.velo2D = ball.velo2D.addScaled(acc,dt);
}
```

Without going into the details, you can see that we have a more complicated calcForce() method that includes three forces: gravity, upthrust, and drag. There is also some logic in calcForce() that tells the code how to work out the forces on the ball depending on where it is. Additionally, there is some logic to tell the code what to do at the boundaries. Finally, there are a number of parameters to do with the different forces. On the whole, though, this is certainly not an overly complex piece of code, and it should be possible for you to get the gist of what it's doing.

The onDown() and onUp() methods allow the user to interact with the simulation by clicking the mouse. If you click anywhere on the canvas, the ball will immediately move there. If you hold down the mouse button, drag the cursor, and then release the mouse, the ball is imparted a velocity numerically equal to the distance between the ball and the point at which the mouse is released.

Run the simulation and play around to see how much it behaves like the real thing, all accomplished with a relatively small amount of code. It's fun!

Newton's second law as a differential equation

This section is especially meant for readers who want to understand the connection between what we are doing here and what you would typically find in physics textbooks or on physics web sites or Wikipedia. It provides a more in-depth understanding of the material but is not strictly required in the rest of the book. You can safely skip it if you wish.

If you are a serious physics programmer, it's likely that you'll find yourself digging into physics textbooks or online sources at some point or other, perhaps in search of some formula or to look for solutions to specific problems. Now, if you are looking for the solution of any problem involving Newton's second law, chances are that you will come across differential equations, and pages of math to solve them analytically. How does all that math relate to our approach of solving Newton's law numerically as discussed in the preceding section? In the next two subsections we explain the connection conceptually, and then illustrate it using a concrete example.

Taking a deeper look at F = ma

A differential equation contains derivatives of quantities. Solving differential equations is in general more complicated than solving ordinary algebraic equations because it involves integration (refer to Chapter 3).

Newton's second law, in the form $\mathbf{F} = m\mathbf{a}$, might appear superficially like a simple algebraic equation.

However, it is useful to remember that acceleration is actually the derivative of velocity, $\mathbf{a} = d\mathbf{v}/dt$, so that we can also write Newton's second law as

$$m\frac{d\mathbf{v}}{dt} = \mathbf{F}$$

This is a so-called first-order differential equation with respect to velocity because it involves the first derivative of velocity. Recalling that $\mathbf{v} = d\mathbf{s}/dt$, we can then write the previous equation as

$$m\frac{d^2\mathbf{s}}{dt^2} = \mathbf{F}$$

This is now a second-order differential equation with respect to displacement, because it involves the second derivative of displacement (refer to Chapter 3).

In general, the force $\mathbf{F}$ can be a function of position and velocity. You will see an example of such a force function shortly.

You will sometimes see Newton's second law expressed in these forms if you look in physics textbooks. In principle, the preceding differential equations can be solved by integrating analytically or numerically to yield the displacement $\mathbf{s}$ and velocity $\mathbf{v}$ as a function of time. Most physics textbooks focus on analytical solutions. But an analytical solution is possible only in special cases and it requires application of calculus integration techniques. On the other hand, it is always possible to solve the differential equation numerically. In fact, this is what we are doing in the examples we have looked at. Specifically, we are integrating the first form of the differential equation in the updateVelo() method and then integrating the velocity to give the displacement in the moveObject() method.

The next example will illustrate a case in which we can solve Newton's second law both analytically and numerically. We'll use this example to show you what a typical analytical solution of this differential equation might look like. We'll also compare the exact analytical solution with the numerically integrated solution to see how good the latter is.

Example: Falling under gravity and drag revisited

This example builds upon the one described in the previous chapter, in which we simulated the fall of a ball under the combined forces of gravity and drag, and showed that it attained terminal velocity as predicted by simple physics theory. Here we'll update the example to compare the detailed analytical solution with the simulation.

The differential equation in this case is as follows (note that this is a 1D case; hence there is no need to use vector notation):

$$m\frac{d^2s}{dt^2} = mg - kv$$

Or in first-order form in terms of velocity:

$$m\frac{dv}{dt} = mg - kv$$

The analytical solution of this equation is given in many physics textbooks (for those interested, a derivation can be downloaded as supplementary material from www.physicscodes.com). For an object dropped from rest, it is this:

$$v = \frac{mg}{k}\left[1 - \exp(-k\,t/m)\right]$$

When the time t is large, the exponential term tends to zero (recall the review of the exponential function in Chapter 3). Therefore, according to this equation, v tends to a limiting value of mg/k, which is of course the terminal velocity. So the solution agrees with what we found in Chapter 4. In addition, it now tells us the velocity at any time t, not just the terminal velocity.

This solution can in turn be integrated to give the displacement s at any time t. The result is this:

$$s = \frac{mg}{k}\left[t + \frac{m}{k}\exp(-k\,t/m) - \frac{m}{k}\right]$$

These analytical solutions for the displacement *s* and velocity *v* may now be compared with the simulated results. In `forces-example2.js`, we updated `forces-example.js` from Chapter 4 to make this comparison. We have also used the `Forces` methods in `calcForce()`; otherwise, the physics is identical to that in `forces-example.js` because the same forces (gravity and drag) are involved.

The relevant code is the function `plotGraphs()`, which plots graphs to compare the analytical and numerical values of *s* and *v*:

```
function plotGraphs(){
    graphDisp.plot([t], [ball.y-y0], '#ff0000');
    graphDisp.plot([t], [m*g/k*(t+m/k*Math.exp(-k/m*t)-m/k)], '#0000ff');
    graphVelo.plot([t], [ball.vy], '#ff0000');
    graphVelo.plot([t], [m*g/k*(1-Math.exp(-k/m*t))], '#0000ff');
}
```

In this code we are plotting the vertical displacement of the ball, which is `ball.y` minus its initial value y0, as well as its value as given by the analytical solution on the `Graph` instance `graphDisp`. Similarly, `graphVelo` displays the vertical velocity as computed by the code and the analytical solution. The simulation is shown in Figure 5-5. The agreement between the two is so good that the respective curves lie on top of each other in both graphs. So we're happy that in this case the simple Euler integration scheme implemented in the code is actually doing a pretty decent job.

Figure 5-5. *Comparing numerical and analytical solutions for a ball falling under gravity and drag*

The principle of energy conservation

We introduced energy and its conservation in the previous chapter. The key point to reiterate here is that we can apply the principle of conservation of energy to work out how things move and how they interact with other things.

It's also important to remember that the principle can apply to the conversion of energy between different forms, as well as to the transfer of energy between different objects. Here is a statement of the principle once more, in a slightly different form:

> **Principle of Energy Conservation:** In any conversion of energy between different forms, or in transfer of energy between different objects, the total amounts of energy before and after the conversion or transfer are always equal.

A particularly useful form of the principle is when the energy conversion or transfer involves only potential and kinetic energy. We refer to PE and KE collectively as *mechanical energy*.

Conservation of mechanical energy

Although the principle of conservation of energy in its general form is powerful and is always true, it may be difficult to apply in practice because it is not always easy to calculate all the energy forms involved in an interaction. For example, think of the energy transformations involved when a ball is dropped, falls through air, and bounces off a surface. The ball initially has PE and, as it falls through air, the PE is gradually converted into KE as it accelerates because of gravity. A small amount of energy is also converted into heat due to friction (drag) through the air. When it hits the surface, a large amount of energy may be transferred to the surface. Some more of the energy is usually converted into heat on impact, and some may be converted into sound as well. Now, we'll steer clear of trying to calculate things like heat and sound energy because that can get pretty complicated. But sometimes, if they can be assumed to be small, we only need to deal with PE and KE. In that case, we say that mechanical energy is conserved.

Conservation of mechanical energy is a particularly useful principle because it involves the energy forms associated with motion (KE) and position (PE). We'll look at two examples of its application in this chapter. One is the elastic collision of two particles, when the total kinetic energy of the particles is conserved. We'll look at this in the later section "The principle of momentum conservation." The other example is the motion of a projectile (ignoring drag due to air resistance). Let's look at this example now.

Example: Energy changes in a projectile

To simplify the example, let's assume the projectile is launched vertically upward from ground level with some initial velocity u. Then we have a 1D problem with constant acceleration under gravity, and we can use the 1D version of the analytical equations of motion introduced in Chapter 4:

$$v = u + a t$$

$$s = u t + \frac{1}{2} a t^2$$

Here $s = h$, the height of the projectile above ground, and $a = -g$, where g is the acceleration due to gravity. So we can write this:

$$v = u - g t$$

$$h = u t - \frac{1}{2} g t^2$$

It is now straightforward to calculate the PE and KE of the projectile at any time by using the following:

$$E_p = m\,g\,h$$

$$E_k = \frac{1}{2}m\,v^2$$

Here is code that computes and plots the PE, KE, and their sum for 10 seconds, using values of $m = 1$, $g = 10$ px/s^2, and $u = 50$ px/s. The source code is in projectile-energy.js.

```
var canvas = document.getElementById('canvas');
var context = canvas.getContext('2d');
var canvas_bg = document.getElementById('canvas_bg');
var context_bg = canvas_bg.getContext('2d');

var ball;

var animId;
var graph;
var m = 1;  // particle mass
var g = 10; // gravity
var u = 50; // initial velocity
var groundLevel = 350;
var n = 0;
var tA = new Array();
var hA = new Array();
var peA = new Array();
var keA = new Array();
var teA = new Array();

window.onload = init;

function init() {
    ball = new Ball(10,'#000000',m,0,true);
    ball.pos2D = new Vector2D(550,groundLevel);
    ball.draw(context);
    setupGraph();
    setupArrays();
    animFrame();
};
function setupGraph(){
    //graph = new Graph(context,xmin,xmax,ymin,ymax,xorig,yorig,xwidth,ywidth);
    graph = new Graph(context_bg,0,10,0,1500,50,350,450,300);
    graph.drawgrid(1,0.5,500,100);
    graph.drawaxes('t','p.e., k.e., total');
}

function setupArrays(){
    var t;
    var v;
```

```
        for (var i=0; i<=100; i++){
            tA[i] = i*0.1;
            t = tA[i];
            v = u - g*t;
            hA[i] = u*t - 0.5*g*t*t;
            peA[i] = m*g*hA[i];
            keA[i] = 0.5*m*v*v;
            teA[i] = peA[i] + keA[i];
        }
    }

function animFrame(){
    setTimeout(function() {
        animId = requestAnimationFrame(animFrame,canvas);
        animate();
    }, 1000/10);
}
function animate(){
    moveObject();
    plotGraphs();
    n++;
    if (n==hA.length){
        stop();
    }
}

function moveObject(){
    ball.y - groundLevel-hA[n];
    context.clearRect(0, 0, canvas.width, canvas.height);
    ball.draw(context);
}

function plotGraphs(){
    graph.plot([tA[n]], [peA[n]], '#ff0000', true, false);
    graph.plot([tA[n]], [keA[n]], '#0000ff', true, false);
    graph.plot([tA[n]], [teA[n]], '#000000', true, false);
}

function stop(){
    cancelAnimationFrame(animId);
}
```

The code should be easy to understand. Note that we have limited the frame rate to 10 fps by nesting the call to requestAnimationFrame() and animate() within a setTimeout() function. This slows the animation enough to enable the ball's motion to be visually matched to the corresponding location on the plots. In Figure 5-6, we show the three plots as a function of time. The series of dots that curves upward is the PE, the series that curves downward is the KE, and the one that is horizontal (constant) is the total energy (the sum of PE and KE). From these plots, we learn that, when the projectile is initially launched at the ground, it has zero PE and maximum KE Then, for the first 5 seconds as it rises, its PE increases at the expense of its KE. At exactly 5 seconds, its KE is zero, signifying that it is momentarily at rest. This happens when it reaches its highest point. It then starts falling down again. As it does so, its PE starts falling again, and its KE increases as it speeds up toward the ground. Throughout its motion, the sum of the PE and KE is constant, as indicated by the horizontal series of dots. This demonstrates the conservation of energy.

Note that the sum of PE and KE is only constant because we've omitted drag effects. If you include drag, then you'll find that the sum of PE and KE decreases slightly with time. If you're extra keen, you can show this by adding a drag term and integrating the equations of motion numerically to give v and h as a function of time.

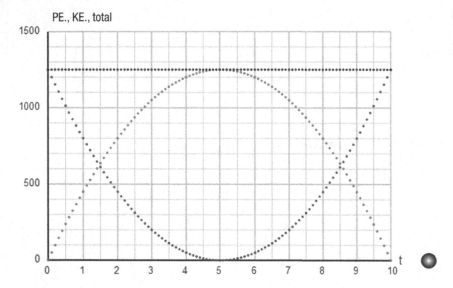

Figure 5-6. *Energy graphs for a projectile—downward curve: KE; upward curve: PE; constant line: total*

The principle of momentum conservation

As mentioned in the preceding chapter, there is a conservation principle for momentum just like the one for energy. Let's state the principle first and then explain it:

> **Principle of Momentum Conservation:** For any system of interacting particles, the total momentum of all the particles remains constant, as long as no external forces act on the system.

"Interacting particles" means that the particles influence each other by exerting forces on each other. The forces can be of any type; for example, gravitational forces between stars in a galaxy. The principle is true regardless of the nature of the forces between the particles. Once you define your system, the particles in that system may be mutually subjected to any number of internal forces between themselves—the total momentum of that system will be conserved as long as there are no forces from external agents.

Conservation of momentum is closely connected with Newton's laws of motion. In fact, under certain conditions, it may be derived from Newton's laws. Let's see how.

The starting point is Newton's second law $\mathbf{F} = d\mathbf{p}/dt$, which we can write in the discrete form $\mathbf{F} = \Delta\mathbf{p}/\Delta t$. Multiplying both sides by Δt gives this:

$$\mathbf{F}\,\Delta t = \Delta\mathbf{p}$$

This is, of course, just Newton's second law written in a slightly different form, for a small but finite time interval Δt. What it tells us is that if a force $\mathbf{F}$ acts on a particle for a small duration Δt, multiplying $\mathbf{F}$ by Δt gives you the change in momentum $\Delta\mathbf{p}$ of the particle. We call the quantity $\mathbf{F}\Delta t$ the *impulse* due to the force. The preceding relationship is called the *impulse-momentum theorem*.

Next, imagine two particles interacting (exerting forces on each other; for example by colliding), as depicted in Figure 5-7. From Newton's third law of motion, they exert equal and opposite forces simultaneously on each other. If they exert forces **F** and –**F** on each other for a time interval of Δt, they experience impulses of –**F** Δt and **F** Δt, respectively. From the impulse-momentum theorem, this implies that they exchange momentum, gaining –Δ**p** and Δ**p**, respectively. The total momentum of both particles is still the same, however, because one gains exactly the negative amount that the other gains; in other words, the momentum lost by one particle is gained by the other. This argument extends to any number of interacting particles, so we have the principle of conservation of momentum.

$-\mathbf{F}\,\Delta t = -\Delta\mathbf{p}$ ⟵ ⬤⬤ ⟶ $\mathbf{F}\,\Delta t = \Delta\mathbf{p}$

Figure 5-7. *Two interacting particles exchanging momentum*

Examples of momentum conservation include the following:

- An apple falling to Earth acquires downward momentum at each instant. Considering the apple-Earth system, the Earth itself must "fall" toward the apple to compensate. But because the mass of the Earth is so large, its velocity toward the apple is tiny.

- The exhaust gases from a rocket and the rocket itself get equal momentum changes in opposite directions.

- In an explosion, the total momentum of all the fragments must equal the momentum of the whole object before the explosion. If the object was initially at rest, the total momentum (as a vector sum of the momenta of all the fragments) after the explosion is still zero.

To give you a feel for how you'll be applying this principle in practice, here is a numerical example. Suppose you fire a bullet of mass 40 g from a rifle of mass 1.6 kg, and the exit velocity of the bullet is 80 m/s. What is the recoil velocity of the rifle?

Let's denote the mass and velocity of the bullet by m and v, respectively. And we'll denote the mass and velocity of the rifle by M and V, respectively. Initially, both are at rest so that the total momentum is zero.

The principle of conservation of momentum therefore implies that the final momentum should be zero, too:

$$M\,V + m\,v = 0$$

This equation can be easily rearranged to give this:

$$V = -\frac{m\,v}{M}$$

Substituting the values of m, v and M give the following:

$$V = -0.04 \times 80\,/\,1.6\ \text{m/s} = -2\ \text{m/s}$$

Therefore, the recoil velocity of the rifle is –2 m/s. The minus sign means that it is in the opposite direction to the velocity of the bullet.

Example: 1D elastic collision between two particles

Conservation of momentum is especially useful in handling collisions between particles. A *collision* is a special type of interaction in which particles exert large forces on each other for a very brief duration.

The entirety of Chapter 11 is dedicated to collisions. Here we'll look briefly at the simplest case of elastic collisions between two particles in 1D. *Elastic* in this context means that kinetic energy is conserved. In other words, no energy is converted to other forms (such as heat) during the collision. Momentum is, of course, always conserved.

Let's say the masses of the particles are $m1$ and $m2$, their initial velocities before collision are $u1$ and $u2$, and their final velocities after collision are $v1$ and $v2$ (see Figure 5-8). Applying conservation of momentum then tells us that

$$m1\cdot v1 + m2\cdot v2 = m1\cdot u1 + m2\cdot u2$$

Applying conservation of kinetic energy gives this:

$$\frac{1}{2}m1\cdot v1^2 + \frac{1}{2}m2\cdot v2^2 = \frac{1}{2}m1\cdot u1^2 + \frac{1}{2}m2\cdot u2^2$$

Remember that the formula for kinetic energy is $1/2\ m\ v^2$.

Before collision: m1, u1   m2, u2

After collision: m1, v1   m2, v2

Figure 5-8. *Change in particle velocities caused by a collision*

What we have here are two equations containing two unknown quantities: the final velocities $v1$ and $v2$ of the two colliding particles. Everything else is known. These equations can be solved to give a general formula for $v1$ and $v2$ in terms of the known quantities $m1$, $m2$, $u1$, and $u2$. But we'll save that for Chapter 11.

For now, let's discuss the case where $m1 = m2$; that is, the two particles have the same mass. In that case, one can show that $v1 = u2$ and $v2 = u1$; in other words, the final velocity of particle 1 is equal to the initial velocity of particle 2, and vice versa. Particles of the same mass that collide elastically simply swap their velocities!

We'll now build an example that implements this special case. The code is in `collisions-test.js`. Since it is a bit different from the other examples you've encountered so far, we reproduce the full code here before discussing it:

```
var canvas = document.getElementById('canvas');
var context = canvas.getContext('2d');
var t0;
var dt;
var animId;
var radius = 15; // ball radius
var balls = new Array();

window.onload = init;

function init() {
    makeBalls();
    t0 = new Date().getTime();
    animFrame();
};

function makeBalls(){
    setupBall('#0000ff',new Vector2D(50,200),new Vector2D(30,0));
    setupBall('#ff0000',new Vector2D(500,200),new Vector2D(-20,0));
    setupBall('#00ff00',new Vector2D(300,200),new Vector2D(10,0));
}
```

```
function setupBall(color,pos,velo){
    var ball = new Ball(radius,color,1,0,true);
    ball.pos2D = pos;
    ball.velo2D = velo;
    ball.draw(context);
    balls.push(ball);
}

function animFrame(){
    animId = requestAnimationFrame(animFrame,canvas);
    onTimer();
}
function onTimer(){
    var t1 = new Date().getTime();
    dt = 0.001*(t1-t0);
    t0 = t1;
    if (dt>0.2) {dt=0;};      checkCollision();
    move();
}
function move(){
    context.clearRect(0, 0, canvas.width, canvas.height);
    for (var i=0; i<balls.length; i++){
        var ball = balls[i];
        ball.pos2D = ball.pos2D.addScaled(ball.velo2D,dt);
        ball.draw(context);
    }
}
function checkCollision(){
    for (var i=0; i<balls.length; i++){
        var ball1 = balls[i];
        for (var j=i+1; j<balls.length; j++){
            var ball2 = balls[j];
            if (Vector2D.distance(ball1.pos2D,ball2.pos2D)<=ball1.radius+ball2.radius){
                var vtemp = ball1.velo2D;
                ball1.velo2D = ball2.velo2D;
                ball2.velo2D = vtemp;
            }
        }
    }
}
```

Here we are creating and initializing three balls in the function makeBalls(), using a special function setupBalls() to minimize code repetition. To make things a bit more interesting, we create three balls aligned horizontally and give them different horizontal velocities. The animation loop code looks nothing out of the ordinary, but the onTimer() method that fires every timestep now contains an additional function checkCollision() in addition to the move() method.

In checkCollision(), we test for collisions between pairs of particles in the array. To do this, we use the Vector2D.distance(vec1,vec2) static method, which computes the distance between two points with position vectors vec1 and vec2. The logic of the collision detection algorithm is simple: if the distance between the centers of the two particles is less than or equal to the sum of their radii, it means they've collided. We then swap the velocities of the two particles.

As an aside, the `Vector2D.distance()` method computes the distance between two points by an appeal to the Pythagorean Theorem (see Chapter 3), as the following listing of relevant `Vector2D` methods shows:

```
Vector2D.prototype = {
    lengthSquared: function(){
        return this.x*this.x + this.y*this.y;
    },
    length: function(){
        return Math.sqrt(this.lengthSquared());
    },
}
Vector2D.distance =  function(vec1,vec2){
    return (vec1.subtract(vec2)).length();
}
```

If you run the code, you'll see that, initially, all three balls get closer together. They then suffer three successive collisions that swap the velocities of each colliding pair. In the end, they all move away from each other.

Laws governing rotational motion

In this chapter, we have focused on translational motion, in which the object being considered changes its position. But what if an object rotates about a center or (if it's an extended object) revolves on itself about some axis?

It turns out that analogous principles for rotational kinematics, dynamics, and conservation principles exist. For example, the analog of Newton's laws of motion can be written down for rotational motion. Analogous to momentum, there is a quantity called *angular momentum* and it is also conserved.

We'll look at rotational mechanics in Chapters 9 and 13.

Summary

This chapter laid the foundation for simulating the motion of particles under any type of force. The laws of motion and conservation principles discussed here can be applied in many different scenarios. In the remaining chapters in Part II, we'll apply those laws to simulate the motion of objects under the action of a wide variety of force laws.

CHAPTER 6

■ ■ ■

Gravity, Orbits, and Rockets

Starting in this chapter, you'll explore many different forces and the types of motion they produce. Here we focus exclusively on the force of gravity. You'll learn how gravity makes things move both on Earth and in space. And before you know it, you'll be able to code up orbits and rockets!

Topics covered in this chapter include the following:

- **Gravity:** Gravity, or gravitation, is the force that the Earth exerts on all objects near it. But there is a lot more to gravity than we've discussed so far.

- **Orbits:** An example of the effect of gravity is to keep planets in their orbits around the Sun. Learn how to easily build simple orbit simulations.

- **Local gravity:** How gravity behaves at the local scale, near the surface of the Earth.

- **Rockets:** Build a simple rocket, launch it, and make it orbit a planet.

Gravity

As inhabitants of a planet, we are aware of *gravity* perhaps more than any other force. Gravity, also known as *gravitation*, will play a part in most of the simulations you'll build in this book. In fact, you've already come across several examples. However, in all the cases you've met so far, we've dealt with gravity as it exists near the surface of the Earth—as a constant force. It's now time to take a deeper look at gravity.

Gravity, weight, and mass

Let's first recap briefly what you have already learned about gravity in the previous chapters. If an object has mass m, then Earth exerts a force on it that points vertically downward. The magnitude of this force of gravity is equal to mg, where g is a constant equal to approximately 9.81 m/s² near the Earth's surface. This force is also called the weight of the object.

The constant g is equal to the acceleration that any object would experience if it were to move under the sole effect of gravity. We can see this by using Newton's second law, $F = ma$. If the resultant force F is just the force of gravity, then $F = mg$. Hence, we have this:

$$m\,a = m\,g$$

And dividing both sides by m gives us this:

$$a = g$$

This result tells us that all objects moving under the action of gravity as the only force experience the same acceleration regardless of their mass, or indeed, of any other properties. So, assuming all other forces can be neglected, if you drop a hammer and a house from the same height, both would accelerate at the same rate and therefore fall at the same time!

Of course, if you drop a feather, it will take much longer to fall. That's because there is an upward drag force due to air that opposes its fall. There is also a drag force in the cases of a stone or a house, but in those cases that force is negligibly small compared with their weight, and so has a negligible impact on their motion. If you were to drop a feather and a hammer on the Moon, where there is no air and therefore no drag, they would both fall at the same time. In fact, the astronaut David Scott did exactly that during the Apollo 15 mission. You can even see a video of this feat on NASA's web site or on YouTube (search for "hammer and feather").

Newton's universal law of gravitation

The Earth is not the only object that exerts a force of gravity. Newton taught us that any object exerts a gravitational pull on any other object. So not only does the Earth exert a gravitational force on us, but each of us also exerts a gravitational force on the Earth, and indeed on each other, too!

Newton gave an exact formula for calculating the gravitational force between any two objects, which is the force law for gravity:

$$F = G \frac{m_1 m_2}{r^2}$$

In this formula, m_1 and m_2 are the masses of the objects involved, and r is the distance between their centers. The symbol G is a universal constant with the value of approximately 6.67×10^{-11} Nm^2/kg^2. It is called the *gravitational constant*. By *universal*, we mean that it has the same value irrespective of the properties of the interacting objects. Newton postulated that the same formula, with the same value of G, holds for any two objects—from tiny particles to planets and stars. Hence, we call it *Newton's universal law of gravitation*.

Let's try to understand what this formula is telling us. First of all, the gravitational force F is proportional to the masses m_1 and m_2 of the two objects. Therefore, the larger those masses are, the larger the force will be. Second, the force is inversely proportional to the square of their distance apart; that means we are dividing by r^2. Therefore, the greater the distance between the two objects, the smaller the force will be (because we'll be dividing a number by the square of a very large number). Third, because we are multiplying by a small number G (6.67×10^{-11} is equal to 0.0000000000667), the force will be tiny except when very large masses are involved. So, gravity is a very weak force, except when at least one of the objects has a very large mass.

To give you an idea of what we mean, let's calculate the gravitational force between two persons (whom we'll call Joe1 and Joe2) of mass 80 kg each standing a distance of 1 m apart, and compare it with the gravitational force that the Earth exerts on each of them.

Using the previous formula, the force between Joe1 and Joe2 is given by $F = 6.67 \times 10^{-11} \times 80 \times 80 / 1^2$ N $= 4.3 \times 10^{-7}$ N (approximately). That's 0.43 millionth of a newton.

The force that the Earth exerts on each is, of course, equal to their weight: $mg = 80 \times 9.81$ N $= 785$ N (approximately). You can also work it out using the previous formula and the mass (5.97×10^{24} kg) and radius (6.37×10^6 m) of the Earth as F $= 6.67 \times 10^{-11} \times 5.97 \times 10^{24} \times 80 / (6.37 \times 10^6)^2$ N $= 785$ N. That's nearly 2 billion times larger!

We haven't said anything about the direction of the force yet. Newton said that the force always acts along the line that joins the centers of the two objects (see Figure 6-1).

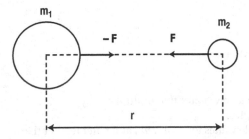

Figure 6-1. *Newton's law of universal gravitation*

Also note that the forces on Joe1 and Joe2 form an action-reaction pair. So Joe1 exerts a force of 4.3×10^{-7} N on Joe2, and vice versa, with the two forces being equal and opposite—and similarly for the force between each of the two Joes and the Earth.

Creating the gravity function

We'll now create a static method of the Forces object that will implement gravity in the form of Newton's law of gravitation. The method will take as input the variables that go into the force law for gravity, namely G, m_1, m_2, and r. It must return a vector force. Therefore, we need a vector form for Newton's law of gravitation that implements the fact that the force points along the line joining the two objects. Let's just give the formula and explain it afterward:

$$\mathbf{F} = -G\frac{m_1 m_2}{r^3}\mathbf{r}$$

Comparing that with the previous formula for the force law for gravity, what we've done is write the force as a vector; then we multiplied the force magnitude by $-\mathbf{r}/r$. Recall from Chapter 3 that $\mathbf{r}/r$ is a unit vector in the direction of $\mathbf{r}$, where $\mathbf{r}$ here is the position vector of one of the objects relative to the location of the other object.

As shown in Figure 6-2, $\mathbf{r}$ is the difference in the position vectors of the two objects, and r is its magnitude, which is simply the distance between the two objects. Recall that there are two forces, not one: the force on object 1 due to object 2, and vice versa. These two forces have the same magnitude but the opposite direction. We always define $\mathbf{r}$ to be the position vector of the object on which the force is acting, relative to the object that is exerting the force. We need the minus sign because that force is directed in the opposite direction to $\mathbf{r}$.

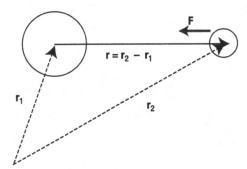

Figure 6-2. *Vector form of Newton's law of universal gravitation*

Here is the static method to implement the gravity force:

```
Forces.gravity = function(G,m1,m2,r){
    return r.multiply(-G*m1*m2/(r.lengthSquared()*r.length()));
}
```

We just use the `multiply()` method of the `Vector2D` object to return a new vector that multiplies **r** by $(-G\, m_1 m_2/r^3)$. Let's now use this `gravity()` method in the next few examples.

Before we can apply the `gravity` function, we have to choose suitable values for G, m_1, m_2, and r. Remember that we are modeling motion on a computer screen. Therefore we have to scale physical values appropriately so that we get the right amount of motion on the screen in a sensible time. For example, if we were simulating the motion of the Earth around the Sun, we wouldn't want to use the real values of all the variables, such as the mass of the Sun, and so on. Doing that would mean we'd have to wait for a year to see the Earth go once around the Sun!

In Part IV, we'll show you how to create a scaled computer model properly. For now, we'll simplify the approach and make some suitable choices just to make the motion look roughly right on the screen. To do this, we'll choose our own units for all the variables of the model.

Let's start with the distance r. That's an easy one—the natural unit to use here is pixels. This leaves us with mass and G. We can give G any value we like, so let's choose $G = 1$. Having made these two choices, we now need to choose suitable values for the masses so that the right amount of motion is produced to be noticeable on the screen. Let's look at an example: orbits!

Orbits

With our gravity function, it's very easy to create a realistic-looking orbital simulation. Figure 6-3 shows a screenshot of what we'll create: a planet orbiting a sun, against a background of fixed stars. For simplicity, we assume that the sun remains fixed. In reality, as we saw previously, both the sun and the planet will experience a gravitational force of the same magnitude but in opposite directions (with the force on each one pointing toward the other). So both the planet and the sun will move. But if the mass of the sun is much larger than that of the planet, the motion of the sun will be so small it will hardly be perceivable, anyway. That's because $F = ma$ again, so that the acceleration $a = F/m$. Thus, if the mass m is very large, the acceleration a will be very small. So to save coding and CPU time, we can neglect the motion of the sun altogether.

Figure 6-3. *A planet orbiting a stationary sun*

The orbits code

The code to achieve a basic orbit simulation is simpler than you think. The file `orbits.js` contains the code, shown here in its entirety:

```javascript
var canvas = document.getElementById('canvas');
var context = canvas.getContext('2d');
var canvas_bg = document.getElementById('canvas_bg');
var context_bg = canvas_bg.getContext('2d');

var planet;
var sun;
var m = 1; // planet's mass
var M = 1000000; // sun's mass
var G = 1;
var t0,dt;

window.onload = init;

function init() {
    // create 100 stars randomly positioned
    for (var i=0; i<100; i++){
        var star = new Ball(Math.random()*2,'#ffff00');
        star.pos2D= new Vector2D(Math.random()*canvas_bg.width,Math.random()*canvas_bg.height);
        star.draw(context_bg);
    }
    // create a stationary sun
    sun = new Ball(70,'#ff9900',M,0,true);
    sun.pos2D = new Vector2D(275,200);
    sun.draw(context_bg);
    // create a moving planet
    planet = new Ball(10,'#0000ff',m,0,true);
    planet.pos2D = new Vector2D(200,50);
    planet.velo2D = new Vector2D(70,-40);
    planet.draw(context);
    // make the planet orbit the sun
    t0 = new Date().getTime();
    animFrame();
};

function animFrame(){
    animId = requestAnimationFrame(animFrame,canvas);
    onTimer();
}
function onTimer(){
    var t1 = new Date().getTime();
    dt = 0.001*(t1-t0);
    t0 = t1;
    if (dt>0.1) {dt=0;};
    move();
}
```

```
function move(){
    moveObject(planet);
    calcForce();
    updateAccel();
    updateVelo(planet);
}

function moveObject(obj){
    obj.pos2D = obj.pos2D.addScaled(obj.velo2D,dt);
    context.clearRect(0, 0, canvas.width, canvas.height);
    obj.draw(context);
}
function calcForce(){
    force = Forces.gravity(G,M,m,planet.pos2D.subtract(sun.pos2D));
}
function updateAccel(){
    acc = force.multiply(1/m);
}
function updateVelo(obj){
    obj.velo2D = obj.velo2D.addScaled(acc,dt);
}
```

The code is very straightforward. First, we create a group of 100 stars as Ball instances and place them randomly on the stage. This is, of course, purely for aesthetic reasons. If you don't like stars, go ahead and get rid of them. Next we create a sun as another Ball instance, setting its radius to 70 pixels and its mass to 1,000,000. We position the sun at (275, 200). By default, the velocity of the sun is zero. Then we create a planet as a Ball instance, set its radius to 10, and set its mass to 1. The initial position and velocity of the planet are then set.

The animation loop is similar to previous examples; the only difference is that we've chosen to pass the planet as a parameter in moveObject() and updateVelo(), just for some variety. Remember that updateAccel() implements Newton's second law, $\mathbf{F} = m\mathbf{a}$, to make a particle move under forces specified in the calcForce() method. In the calcForce() function we specify the gravity force exerted by the sun on the planet as the only force. In the Forces. gravity() method, we pass the values of G (set to 1), the masses of the two objects, and the position vector of the planet relative to that of the sun: planet.pos2D.subtract(sun.pos2D).

Go ahead and run the code—it really works!

Observe that the planet tries to move away at its initial velocity, but is pulled back by the sun's gravity. You might wonder why the planet does not fall into the sun. Well, in fact it is "falling" toward the sun all the time but, because of its initial position and velocity, it "misses" the sun every time. Notice also that the planet travels faster when it's near the sun. This happens because the force of gravity is larger and therefore its acceleration is larger closer to the sun.

This code produces a realistic orbit simulation because it has basically all the physics governing orbital motion under gravity. And the physics really boils down to just four equations:

$$\mathbf{F} = -G\frac{M\,m}{r^3}\,\mathbf{r}$$

$$\mathbf{F} = m\,\mathbf{a}$$

$$\mathbf{a} = \frac{d\mathbf{v}}{dt}$$

$$\mathbf{v} = \frac{d\mathbf{s}}{dt}$$

In these equations, m is the mass of the planet, and M is the mass of the sun. The first two equations are laws, and the last two are just definitions. To recap, this is what our code is doing at each timestep: From the first law, you compute the gravitational force. You then use the second law to compute the acceleration. Knowing the acceleration, you integrate the third equation to compute the velocity. Finally, knowing the velocity, you integrate the fourth equation to give the displacement. This tells you where you must move your particle at each timestep.

Try changing the parameters in the code to see their effect. For example, you can change the masses of the planet and the sun, or the initial position and velocity of the planet. We've chosen the mass of the sun to be 1,000,000 times that of the planet. This is a realistic ratio; for example, the mass of the Sun is 330,000 times that of the Earth and 6,100,000 times that of Mercury.

Change the mass of the sun to 2,000,000. The planet is pulled closer to the sun because the force of gravity is proportional to the mass of the sun. Doubling the sun's mass doubles the force of gravity and therefore the acceleration toward the sun. Conversely, if you decrease the mass of the sun to 900,000, you'll see that the sun's pull on the planet is weaker, so that the planet wanders farther away.

Now change the mass of the planet instead. Make it 0.001 and then 1000. You'll see that the mass of the planet has no effect on its motion. What's going on is that you are increasing the force on the planet by increasing its mass, but then you must divide the larger force by its larger mass. Take a look at the first two equations above. In the first one, you multiply by the mass of the planet to calculate the gravitational force. In the second one, you then need to divide that force by the same mass to calculate the acceleration. The net result is that the acceleration is independent of the mass of the planet. This is just as it should be. It's the astronomical equivalent of the hammer-and-feather experiment we mentioned at the beginning of this chapter.

Does this mean that the motion is unchanged even if the planet's mass is comparable to that of the sun? No, not really. Remember the approximation we made at the beginning? We assumed that the mass of the sun was much larger than that of the planet, so that we could neglect the sun's motion under the gravitational force exerted on it by the planet. If the planet's mass is a sizeable fraction of the sun's mass, we'll need to model the motion of the sun too, even if we are just interested in the planet's motion! That's because as the sun moves around, its distance from the planet will change, which will modify the force on the planet. What we've done so far is to model *one-body motion*. To deal with this problem, we'll need to model *two-body motion*. It's not really that much more difficult, and we'll do that later. We'll even look at the motion of a large number of particles under mutual gravitational forces in a later chapter.

Next, experiment with different initial velocities for the planet. For example, changing the velocity vector to (70, –40) gives a more circular orbit, similar to the Earth's orbit. A velocity of (85, –40) gives a highly elongated orbit like that of a comet. Later in the book we'll show you how to work out the exact velocity you need to produce a circular orbit.

If the velocity of the planet is small, it will get sucked into the sun. For example, change the velocity to (0,0). The planet accelerates toward the sun's center, as it should do, but then something weird happens when it actually gets there. For example, it might bounce back or fly off at high speed. This is an unphysical behavior, and it happens because we have not accounted for the finite size of the objects in the code. Because Newton's law of gravitation is proportional to $1/r^2$, the force becomes larger as the distance r becomes smaller. For example, when r is 10 pixels, $1/r^2$ has the value of 0.01; when r is 1, $1/r^2$ is 1; and when r is 0.1, $1/r^2$ is 100. So when r approaches zero (when the centers of the two particles nearly coincide), the gravitational force becomes indefinitely large. At the same time, the vector $\mathbf{r}$, which is the position vector pointing from the sun to the planet, becomes so small that numerical errors make its direction unpredictable. Therefore, the planet suffers a large acceleration in some apparently random direction at the center of the sun.

This is a general problem that you'll encounter with a force law like Newton's law of gravitation. The way you deal with it depends on precisely what you want to model. If something is falling into the sun, chances are you'd want to make it disappear when it does so—that's simple enough to code up, and you don't need any special physics. If something is colliding with a solid planet like the Earth, it will burn up in the Earth's atmosphere, create a crater, or smash up the Earth, depending on its size. Any of this would be rather tricky to model in a precise way, although you could conceivably create some movie-style special effects! If something is falling into one of the gas giants like Jupiter or Saturn, you might want to model how gravity varies *inside* the planet. We'll see an example of how you might be able to do that later in this chapter.

Escape velocity

It turns out that if the velocity magnitude of a planet is less than a certain critical value, it will always be "caught" by the gravitational attraction of the sun, either orbiting or ending up in a collision with the sun. The critical value above which a planet would escape the sun's gravity is called the *escape velocity*. The formula for the escape velocity is given by the following, where M is the mass of the sun and r is the distance from its center:

$$v = \sqrt{\frac{2GM}{r}}$$

So the escape velocity is a function of distance from the center of the attracting body.

Note that whatever we said about a planet orbiting the sun applies more generally to any object orbiting another object under the force of gravity—for example, a satellite (natural or artificial) orbiting a planet. Hence, using the preceding formula, the escape velocity of any object at the Earth's surface is given by the following, where M_e and r_e are the mass and radius of the Earth, respectively:

$$v = \sqrt{\frac{2GM_e}{r_e}}$$

Putting in the values for G, M_e, and r_e into the above formula gives $v = 11.2$ km/s. This is the escape velocity at the Earth's surface: if you could throw a projectile with a velocity at least equal to this velocity, it would escape the Earth's gravity. For comparison, the escape velocity from the surface of the Sun is 618 km/s. By contrast, the escape velocity from the surface of Eros (a near-Earth asteroid with dimensions of approximately 34 km × 11 km × 11 km) is a mere 10 m/s. You could drive off the asteroid in a car!

Going back to the Orbits simulation, $G = 1$, the mass of the sun is 1,000,000, and the planet is initially at a distance of $\sqrt{(75^2 + 150^2)} = 167.7$ pixels from the sun. So the escape velocity at the initial location of the planet is $\sqrt{(2 \times 1 \times 1000000 / 167.7)} = 109.2$ pixels per second. You can check this with the simulation. First, change the initial velocity of the planet to (80, 0), so that its magnitude is 80. The planet will orbit the sun. Now increase the initial velocity magnitude to 100 by changing the velocity to (100, 0). The planet will move farther from the Sun but will still orbit it. Even if you change the velocity to (105, 0) and wait long enough (about five minutes or so), the planet will disappear from the edge of the canvas, but will eventually come back to complete an orbit. But if you increase the velocity magnitude beyond 109.2, it will never come back. We don't advise you to wait!

Two-body motion

So far, we've made a single object move under the gravitational attraction of another object. But we know that gravitational forces come as an action-reaction pair, so the other object must also experience an equal and opposite force. The result is that the other object will also move. It is fairly straightforward to modify the orbits.js code to implement this. The resulting code is in the file two-masses.js:

```
var canvas = document.getElementById('canvas');
var context = canvas.getContext('2d');
var canvas_bg = document.getElementById('canvas_bg');
var context_bg = canvas_bg.getContext('2d');
```

```
var ball1;
var ball2;
var r1 = 10;
var r2 = 40;
var m1 = 1;
var m2 = 60;
var G = 100000;
var t0, dt;

window.onload = init;

function init() {
    var ball1Init = new Ball(r1,'#9999ff',m1,0,true);
    ball1Init.pos2D = new Vector2D(150,200);
    ball1Init.draw(context_bg);

    var ball2Init = new Ball(r2,'#ff9999',m2,0,true);
    ball2Init.pos2D = new Vector2D(350,200);
    ball2Init.draw(context_bg);

    ball1 = new Ball(r1,'#0000ff',m1,0,true);
    ball1.pos2D = ball1Init.pos2D;
    ball1.velo2D = new Vector2D(0,150);
    ball1.draw(context);

    ball2 = new Ball(r2,'#ff0000',m2,0,true);
    ball2.pos2D = ball2Init.pos2D;
    ball2.velo2D = new Vector2D(0,0);
    ball2.draw(context);

    t0 = new Date().getTime();
    animFrame();
};

function animFrame(){
    animId = requestAnimationFrame(animFrame,canvas);
    onTimer();
}
function onTimer(){
    var t1 = new Date().getTime();
    dt = 0.001*(t1-t0);
    t0 = t1;
    if (dt>0.1) {dt=0;};
    move();
}
function move(){
    context.clearRect(0, 0, canvas.width, canvas.height);
    moveObject(ball1);
    moveObject(ball2);
    calcForce(ball1,ball2); // calc force on ball1 due to ball2
    update(ball1);
```

```
        calcForce(ball2,ball1); // calc force on ball2 due to ball1
        update(ball2);
}

function update(obj){
        updateAccel(obj.mass);
        updateVelo(obj);
}

function moveObject(obj){
        obj.pos2D = obj.pos2D.addScaled(obj.velo2D,dt);
        obj.draw(context);
}
function calcForce(obj1,obj2){
        force = Forces.gravity(G,obj1.mass,obj2.mass,obj1.pos2D.subtract(obj2.pos2D));
}
function updateAccel(m){
        acc = force.multiply(1/m);
}
function updateVelo(obj){
        obj.velo2D = obj.velo2D.addScaled(acc,dt);
}
```

What we've done here is basically simple. We create a couple of Ball instances, ball1 and ball2, and then make each ball move under the gravity exerted by the other. From the values specified previously, ball2 has a radius 4 times larger than ball1 and a mass 60 times larger. Also, ball1 has an initial velocity of (0, 150), whereas ball2 is initially stationary. We also create two more Ball instances, ball1Init and ball2Init, to indicate the initial positions of their respective counterparts in a lighter color.

Comparing two-masses.js with orbits.js, you'll see that we have restructured some of the animation loop and physics code. To begin with, the calcForce() method now takes two arguments: the first argument is the ball that experiences the force; the second argument is the ball that exerts the force. The updateAccel() method now also takes an argument, the mass of the object whose acceleration is being calculated. For convenience we've also introduced a new function update(), which groups together calls to updateAccel() and updateVelo(). The move() method makes successive calls to moveObject(), calcForce() and update() for each ball. Note carefully the order in which these function calls are made—the order is important! We leave it as an exercise for you to figure out why and to experiment with what happens if you change the order of the function calls.

The other thing we've done here is to change the value of G to 100,000. You can give G any value you want if you compensate by using appropriate values for the masses to create the desired effect.

If you run the code, you'll see that ball1 orbits ball2, while the latter appears to wobble. This makes sense. Both ball1 and ball2 experience the same force at any given time, but because ball2 is 60 times larger than ball1, its acceleration is 60 times less (applying $a = F/m$). Therefore, ball2 moves much less than ball1, as the screenshot in Figure 6-4 suggests. Note that the two balls experience a net slow drift vertically downward. This is due to conservation of momentum (see Chapter 5): the total initial momentum is nonzero (ball1 is initially moving vertically downward while ball2 is initially at rest), so this vertically downward momentum must be conserved at all times, even as ball2 moves. You can easily eliminate this drift by imparting to ball2 an initial velocity such that the total initial momentum of the system is zero, that is, $m1 \times u1 + m2 \times u2 = 0$. Hence, the initial vertical velocity of ball2 is $u2 = -m1 \times u1/m2 = -1 \times 150/60 = -2.5$ px/s. Implement this by adding the following line of code after ball2 is created:

```
ball2.velo2D = new Vector2D(0,-2.5);
```

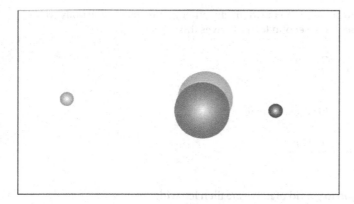

Figure 6-4. *Two-body motion (lighter images show initial positions of respective balls)*

If you now rerun the code, you will find that the residual drift has disappeared, and that ball2 experiences only a slight wobble as a result of the gravitational force exerted by ball1.

Now make the mass and size of ball2 the same as those of ball1 by modifying the appropriate line so that it reads thus:

```
ball2 = new Ball(r1,'#ff0000',m1,0,true);
```

Then change the initial velocities of the two balls by making the following changes to the code:

```
ball1.velo2D = new Vector2D(0,10);
ball2.velo2D = new Vector2D(0,-10);
```

If you now run the code, you'll find that the two balls orbit each other in a strange sort of dance, alternately coming together and then moving farther away. What is happening is that they are orbiting a common center, known as their *center of mass*. In fact, this was also happening when the balls had different masses; but the center of mass then was within the large ball, so that it appeared to wobble.

Local gravity

We are most familiar with gravity close up. How does local, near-Earth gravity relate to what you've learned so far? In this section, we establish the connection between Newton's universal law of gravitation and the formula $F = mg$ that we previously used for gravity. This will lead us to clarify the significance of the acceleration due to gravity g. We'll then discuss how g varies with distance from the center of the Earth, and how it differs on other celestial bodies.

The force of gravity near the Earth's surface

Time to come back to Earth! At the beginning of this chapter (as well as in previous chapters), we said that the force of gravity near the Earth on an object of mass m is given by $F = mg$, with g being approximately 9.81 m/s². Then, for most of this chapter so far, we've been using Newton's law of universal gravitation, which says that the gravitational force is given by $F = Gm_1m_2/r^2$. How do we reconcile those two different formulas?

The answer is that they are both correct. If M is the mass of the Earth (or any other planet or celestial body we're considering), and m is the mass of an object on or near it, the second formula gives this:

$$F = \frac{G M m}{r^2}$$

This has to give the same force as $F = mg$. Therefore, this must be true:

$$m g = \frac{G M m}{r^2}$$

Now we can divide both sides of this equation by m to get rid of it. We are then left with this:

$$g = \frac{G M}{r^2}$$

This formula shows that g is related to the mass M of the Earth and the distance r from its center. It tells us that g is actually a "nickname" for GM/r^2.

If an object is sitting on the Earth's surface, its distance from the Earth's center is equal to the radius of the Earth. The mass of the Earth is 5.974×10^{24} kg and its radius is 6.375×10^6 m.

Therefore, using the last formula, the value of g at the Earth's surface is given by this, which is the exact value that was quoted before:

$g = 6.67 \times 10^{-11} \times 5.974 \times 10^{24} / (6.374 \times 10^6)^2 = 9.81$ m/s^2

Therefore, $F = mg$ is consistent with Newton's law of universal gravitation.

Because it is always pointing toward the Earth's center, gravity acts vertically downward wherever we are on or near the Earth's surface (see Figure 6-5).

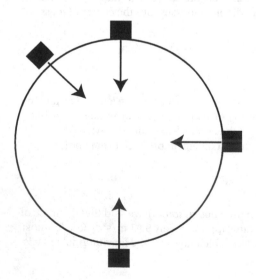

Figure 6-5. *Near-Earth gravity*

Variation of gravity with height

The formula $g = GM/r^2$ tells us that we can use $F = mg$ to calculate the force of gravity at any distance from the Earth, provided that we account for the variation of g with distance from the center of the Earth.

If an object is at a height h above the surface of the Earth, its distance from the Earth's center is given by the following, where R is the radius of the Earth:

$$r = R + h$$

Therefore, the value of g at a height h above the Earth's surface is given by this:

$$g = \frac{G M}{(R+h)^2}$$

Because the value of g at the Earth's surface is 9.81 m/s², a little bit of algebra gives the two equivalent formulas:

$$g = 9.81 \frac{R^2}{(R+h)^2}$$

$$g = 9.81 \frac{R^2}{r^2}$$

Using this formula, you can show that the value of g at the height of the International Space Station, which is 350 km above the Earth's surface, is about 8.8 m/s². The value of g at the distance of the Moon (384,000 km away) is approximately 0.0026 m/s². Remember that g gives you the acceleration of an object under gravity, and this acceleration is independent of the mass of the object. So, if the Moon were replaced with a football, it would experience the same acceleration.

You might be curious to know how g varies *within* the Earth. A simple model shows that g decreases approximately linearly from the surface of the Earth down to zero at the Earth's center. The formula is as follows, where R is the radius of the Earth:

$$g = 9.81 \frac{r}{R}, \quad \text{for } r < R$$

Figure 6-6 shows the variation of g with normalized distance r/R from the Earth's center. As you can see, g increases linearly from the center of the Earth up to its surface (where $r/R = 1$ and $g = 9.81$). It then decreases rapidly with the inverse square of distance from the Earth's center.

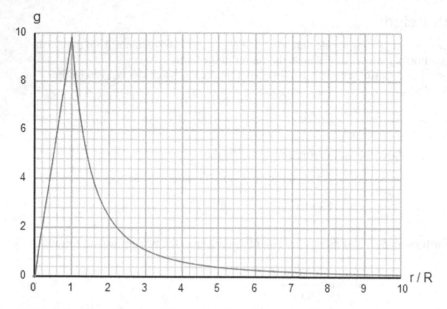

Figure 6-6. *Variation of g with distance from the center of the Earth*

Gravity on other celestial bodies

The formula $g = GM/r^2$ allows you to calculate the value of g on other celestial bodies such as planets and stars, if you know their mass and radius.

Table 6-1 shows the approximate value of g on the surface of a few celestial bodies. These values show that the Sun's gravity is about 28 times that of Earth, while the Moon's is about one-sixth that of Earth. The value of g on the surface of Jupiter, the largest planet in the solar system, is about 2.5 times that of Earth. Ceres and Eros are asteroids, and their gravity is extremely weak: Earth's gravity is about 36 times that of Ceres and more than 1660 times that of Eros.

Table 6-1. *Gravity on Selected Celestial Bodies*

Celestial Body	Value of g in m/s²
Earth	9.81
Sun	274
Moon	1.6
Jupiter	25
Ceres	0.27
Eros	0.0059

Rockets

Rockets are used for a variety of purposes, including launching spacecraft and missiles or as fireworks. In all rocket types, the rocket is propelled by exhaust formed from burning propellants within the rocket. In what follows, we give a very simplified account of the physics involved in rocket motion and show you how to put together a simple rocket simulation that can be incorporated in your games.

It *is* rocket science!

Without going into engineering details on the operation of various types of rocket engines, let's just say that hot gases at high pressure are produced and pushed through a nozzle at high velocity. By Newton's third law, the exhaust gases push back upon the rocket, propelling it forward. The forward force generated is called the *thrust*.

Apart from the thrust, there may be other forces on the rocket, depending on where it is and how it's moving. Gravity is one of them. If the rocket is traveling through the Earth's atmosphere, it will also experience a retarding drag force as well as a lift force (see the next chapter). We'll neglect the effects of drag and lift here.

On Earth, there will also be effects due to the variation of pressure with altitude, which will affect the thrust, drag, and lift. We'll neglect those effects, too.

As the rocket rises, the strength of the gravity that it experiences decreases in the manner described earlier in this chapter. We will account for this effect.

Rockets generally carry a substantial proportion of their mass as fuel. Therefore, the mass of a rocket will vary substantially as the fuel gets used up. This decrease in mass will affect the acceleration of the rocket and must therefore be included in the modeling.

Modeling the thrust of a rocket

To model the thrust on a rocket, we make use of the alternate form of Newton's second law given in Chapter 5.

Remember that the force needed to move a substance at the rate of dm/dt at a velocity $\mathbf{v}$ is given by the formula $\mathbf{F} = \mathbf{v}\,dm/dt$. The exhaust gases from a rocket exit at an *effective exhaust velocity* $\mathbf{v}_e$ and at a mass rate dm/dt that can be controlled. Therefore, the force on the gases is given by this:

$$\mathbf{F} = \mathbf{v}_e \frac{dm}{dt}$$

Using Newton's third law, the thrust on the rocket is therefore given by this:

$$\mathbf{F} = -\mathbf{v}_e \frac{dm}{dt}$$

The minus sign in the preceding vector equation means that the thrust generated is in the opposite direction to the exhaust velocity.

There may also be side thrusters on a rocket to provide a sideways thrust as needed. These work on the same principle as the main engine.

Building a rocket simulation

Okay, let's build a rocket simulation! But before you jump up and down in glee, please note that we'll just focus on the physics here; we leave it as an exercise for you to come up with the nice graphics and special effects.

Once again we'll start with the `orbits.js` file, make some modifications, and save the new file as `rocket-test.js`. Here's what it should look like:

```
var canvas = document.getElementById('canvas');
var context = canvas.getContext('2d');
var canvas_bg = document.getElementById('canvas_bg');
var context_bg = canvas_bg.getContext('2d');
```

```javascript
var rocket;
var massPlanet;
var centerPlanet;
var radiusPlanetSquared;
var G = 0.1;
var dmdt = 0.5;
var dmdtSide= 0.1;
var fuelMass = 3.5;
var fuelSideMass = 3.5;
var fuelUsed = 0;
var fuelSideUsed = 0;
var ve = new Vector2D(0,200);
var veSide = new Vector2D(-100,0);
var applySideThrust = false;
var showExhaust = true;
var orientation = 1;
var animId;
var t0, dt;

window.onload = init;

function init() {
    // create 100 stars randomly positioned
    for (var i=0; i<100; i++){
        var star = new Ball(1,'#ffff00');
        star.pos2D= new Vector2D(Math.random()*canvas_bg.width,Math.random()*canvas_bg.height);
        star.draw(context_bg);
    }
    // create a stationary planet planet
    planet = new Ball(100,'#0033ff',1000000);
    planet.pos2D = new Vector2D(400,400);
    planet.draw(context_bg);
    massPlanet = planet.mass;
    centerPlanet = planet.pos2D;
    radiusPlanetSquared = planet.radius*planet.radius;
    // create a rocket
    rocket = new Rocket(12,12,'#cccccc',10);
    rocket.pos2D = new Vector2D(400,300);
    rocket.draw(context,showExhaust);
    // set up event listeners
    window.addEventListener('keydown',startSideThrust,false);
    window.addEventListener('keyup',stopSideThrust,false);
    // launch the rocket
    t0 = new Date().getTime();
    animFrame();
};

function animFrame(){
    animId = requestAnimationFrame(animFrame,canvas);
    onTimer();
}
```

```
function onTimer(){
    var t1 = new Date().getTime();
    dt = 0.001*(t1-t0);
    t0 = t1;
    if (dt>0.1) {dt=0;};
    move();
}
function move(){
    moveObject();
    calcForce();
    updateAccel();
    updateVelo();
    updateMass();
    monitor();
}

function moveObject(){
    rocket.pos2D = rocket.pos2D.addScaled(rocket.velo2D,dt);
    context.clearRect(0, 0, canvas.width, canvas.height);
    rocket.draw(context,showExhaust);
}
function calcForce(){
    var gravity = Forces.gravity(G,massPlanet,rocket.mass,rocket.pos2D.subtract(centerPlanet));
    var thrust = new Vector2D(0,0);
    var thrustSide = new Vector2D(0,0);
    if (fuelUsed < fuelMass){
        thrust = ve.multiply(-dmdt);
    }
    if (fuelSideUsed < fuelSideMass && applySideThrust){
        thrustSide = veSide.multiply(-dmdtSide*orientation);
    }
    force = Forces.add([gravity, thrust, thrustSide]);
}
function updateAccel(){
    acc = force.multiply(1/rocket.mass);
}
function updateVelo(){
    rocket.velo2D = rocket.velo2D.addScaled(acc,dt);
}
function updateMass(){
    if (fuelUsed < fuelMass){
        fuelUsed += dmdt*dt;
        rocket.mass += -dmdt*dt;
    }
    if (fuelSideUsed < fuelSideMass && applySideThrust){
        fuelSideUsed += dmdtSide*dt;
        rocket.mass += -dmdtSide*dt;
    }
}
```

```
function monitor(){
    if (showExhaust && fuelUsed >= fuelMass){
        showExhaust = false;
    }
    if (rocket.pos2D.subtract(centerPlanet).lengthSquared() < radiusPlanetSquared){
        stop();
    }
}
function startSideThrust(evt){
    if (evt.keyCode==39){ // right arrow
        applySideThrust = true;
        orientation = 1;
    }
    if (evt.keyCode==37){ // left arrow
        applySideThrust = true;
        orientation = -1;
    }
}
function stopSideThrust(evt){
    applySideThrust = false;
}
function stop(){
    cancelAnimationFrame(animId);
}
```

The initial setup in init() is pretty similar to that in orbits.js, except that we now have a stationary planet in place of the sun and a rocket in place of the planet. Note that the rocket is an instance of the Rocket object, which we will look at a little later. We have introduced a couple of event listeners in init(). These listen for keydown and keyup events respectively. The corresponding event handlers startSideThrust() and stopSideThrust() set the value of a Boolean parameter applySideThrust. Whenever the right or left arrow key is pressed and held down, the applySideThrust Boolean variable is set to true; applySideThrust reverts to false when the keys are released. This variable will control the thrust applied by the side thrusters. The variable orientation is given an integer value of +1 or –1 to distinguish between right and left key presses. This variable determines the direction of the applied thrust.

In calcForce(), we specify the forces on the rocket and add them up as usual. The first force is the force of gravity that the planet exerts on it. Then there is the main thrust and side thrust. The main thrust is applied as long as there is fuel; the amount of fuel is set in the variable fuelMass. The side thrust is applied if there is fuel and if applySideThrust is true. In either case, the thrust is calculated using the formula $\mathbf{F} = -\mathbf{v}_e \, dm/dt$. The amount of fuel, exhaust velocity, and mass rate are set independently for the main thrusters and the side thrusters. (In reality, the exhaust velocity and mass rates can be varied to control the thrust, but for simplicity we've taken them to be fixed here.)

There are a couple of new function calls in the move() method. First, it calls a new method updateMass(). It needs to do this because the mass of the rocket is changing. The code in updateMass() checks whether there is any fuel left in the main and side thrusters; if so, it increments the mass of fuel used and decrements the mass of the rocket by the same amount. For the side thrusters, it also checks whether applySideThrust is true.

The second new function called in move() is monitor(). This method does two checks. First, it checks whether all the fuel in the main tank has been used up and, if so, it sets the value of the showExhaust Boolean variable to false, so that the exhaust will no longer be displayed at the next drawing update. The drawing of the rocket, with or without the exhaust, is done by the function call rocket.draw(context,showExhaust) in moveObject().

The second thing monitor() does is check whether the rocket collides with the planet; if so, it simply invokes the stop() method, which stops the timestepping, freezing all motion.

If you run the simulation, you'll see that the rocket is launched automatically. It moves very slowly at first; then both its velocity and its acceleration increase until its fuel is used up. It then slows down under the gravitational pull of the planet. If you don't do anything, it will fall back to the planet. If you press the right or left arrow keys, a side thrust will be applied to the right or left, respectively. If you apply too much or too little side thrust, the rocket will either escape the planet's gravity or be pulled back into a collision course with the planet. See if you can make the rocket orbit the planet (Figure 6-7)! This involves applying the right amount of side thrust at the right time.

Figure 6-7. *A rocket orbiting a planet!*

The Rocket object

Finally, let's take a quick look at the Rocket object that creates a visible rocket. Embarrassingly, our "rocket" is simply a triangle, with another (transparent) triangle attached at the end to represent gases from the exhaust. But please go ahead and create a better-looking version if you feel the urge to exercise your artistic skills at this point.

Here is the full source code in rocket.js:

```
function Rocket(width,height,color,mass){
    if(typeof(width)==='undefined') width = 20;
    if(typeof(height)==='undefined') height = 40;
    if(typeof(color)==='undefined') color = '#0000ff';
    if(typeof(mass)==='undefined') mass = 1;
    this.width = width;
    this.height = height;
    this.color = color;
    this.mass = mass;
    this.x = 0;
    this.y = 0;
    this.vx = 0;
    this.vy = 0;
}
Rocket.prototype = {
    get pos2D (){
        return new Vector2D(this.x,this.y);
    },
```

```
    set pos2D (pos){
        this.x = pos.x;
        this.y = pos.y;
    },
    get velo2D (){
        return new Vector2D(this.vx,this.vy);
    },
    set velo2D (velo){
        this.vx = velo.x;
        this.vy = velo.y;
    },
    draw: function (context,firing) {  // firing is a Boolean
        if (firing){
            var exhaust=new
            Triangle(this.x,this.y+0.5*this.height,this.width,this.height,'#ffff00',0.8);
            exhaust.draw(context);
        }
        var capsule = new Triangle(this.x,this.y,this.width,this.height,this.color);
        capsule.draw(context);
    }
};
```

Rocket draws a rocket using parameter values for width, height and color, supplied as arguments in the constructor. The code looks very similar to that for the Ball object, but with a different draw() method, which takes two parameters: context and firing. The Boolean parameter firing determines whether the 'exhaust' is drawn or not. Both the rocket body and the exhaust are drawn as triangles using a convenient Triangle object, which you can find in our growing objects library. Feel free to take a look at the code in triangle.js.

It's easy to see how this simple simulation can be developed into an interesting game. Besides improved graphics and special effects, you could add extra features and controls for greater realism. With this in mind, we need to point out that there are several limitations in the way we implemented some of the operational features of the rocket. For a simple online game, these limitations probably won't be a big deal, but they might well matter if you are trying to build a realistic simulator. In any case, it's worth knowing about them.

We've already mentioned that we have fixed the thrust of the rocket in this demonstration, although in reality it can be controlled by varying the speed of exhaust and the mass rate of the ejected gases. More importantly, the directions of the main and side thrusts have been implemented in a way that is, strictly speaking, incorrect. The main thrust of a rocket acts along its axis no matter what the angle of the rocket is, and its side thrust will be at some specified angle relative to the rocket's angle. What we did in this simplified simulation is to fix the main and side thrust to act in the vertical (y) and horizontal (x) directions, regardless of the inclination of the rocket. We also neglected the effects of air pressure, drag, and lift when the rocket is moving in an atmosphere.

Another obvious simplification we made is to put the whole rocket into orbit. In reality, space-borne rockets include one or more disposable tanks that are dropped when their fuel is used up. We leave this as an exercise for you. The Rocket class could be enhanced functionally, too. For example, it might make sense to include the amount of fuel, fuel used, exhaust velocity, and mass rate as properties of Rocket instead of hard-coding them into rocket-test.js.

Finally, the examples we coded in this chapter are realistic in that they contain the correct physics equations, but the values chosen for the various parameters are not necessarily to scale. For example, in the orbits simulation, the sizes of the planet and the sun are grossly exaggerated in comparison with their distances. This was necessary in order to see both the objects and their motion on a computer screen. Scaling issues are discussed in detail in Part IV of the book.

Summary

This chapter showed you the richness and variety that the gravitational force can exhibit, and the different types of motion it can produce. In a fairly short chapter, you've been able to code up orbits, two objects moving in interesting ways under their mutual gravity, and a rocket simulation from launch to orbit.

It's amazing how much fun can be had with a just a few physics formulas and a little bit of code. You now have a taste of what can be done, even with a single force such as gravity. We'll play more with gravity in later chapters. Meanwhile, we'll introduce a lot of other forces in the next chapter.

CHAPTER 7

■ ■ ■

Contact and Fluid Forces

In the previous chapter, we looked in some detail at gravity, which is a force that acts at a distance. Except for gravity, however, most of the forces that we encounter in our daily lives arise from direct contact with other objects, either solids or fluids. Because on this planet we are usually in contact with a solid floor and are surrounded by fluid, either air or water, it is surely a good thing to know what forces they exert on things. This chapter will look at these forces.

Topics covered in this chapter include the following:

- **Contact forces:** Contact forces are forces that two solid objects exert on each other when in direct contact. Examples include normal forces, friction, and tension.

- **Pressure:** Fluids exert pressure. Any object in the fluid experiences a force due to this fluid pressure.

- **Upthrust or buoyancy:** Upthrust, also known as buoyancy, is the resultant pressure force experienced by a body that is partially or fully immersed in a fluid.

- **Drag:** An object moving through a fluid experiences a retarding force that tends to oppose its motion. This is the drag force.

- **Lift:** An object moving through a fluid may experience another force perpendicular to the direction of motion, known as the lift force. The lift force is what makes airplanes fly.

- **Wind:** Although wind is not itself a force, it does exert a force on any object over which it blows. Wind also produces turbulence, which can cause an object to move erratically.

As this list indicates, these varieties of forces include interactions between solid objects as well as interactions between a solid object and a fluid, in both cases as a result of direct physical contact. But technically, the term *contact force* is reserved for a force that exists between two solid objects. Only the first section will deal with contact forces in this technical sense. Most of the chapter will then focus on forces exerted by fluids on solid objects. That's partly because the latter are more complex, but they also manifest in a richer variety, with interesting features and effects. In looking at fluid forces, we'll restrict our attention to forces that solid objects experience in a fluid. We do not consider the forces acting on the fluid and the effect these forces have on the fluid itself. Fluid motion is a more complicated problem and is not treated in this book.

Here are just some of the simulations you'll be able to create after reading this chapter: motion with friction, floating objects, bubbles, balloons, parachutes, lift forces, wind, and turbulence effects. You will also know most of the physics you need to build a submarine simulation (see Chapter 16).

Contact forces

Simply stated, a contact force is a force experienced by a solid object from contact with another solid object. Pushing and pulling involve contact forces. So does running, or simply standing. Collisions involve large contact forces that operate for a very small duration.

Normal contact forces

When two solid objects are brought into contact, each of them exerts a normal force on the other that prevents them from merging together. The magnitude of the normal force depends on the force with which the two objects are pushed together.

■ **Note** Before we do anything else, we must explain that the word normal here is meant in the mathematical sense of the word, which is perpendicular rather than the opposite of abnormal.

An example of a normal contact force is the reaction that the floor exerts on you. In fact, that force is why we are aware of our weight. Without the normal reaction from the floor (and therefore without the normal force), we would fall through the floor.

Now, whenever we introduce a new force in this book, we'll give you a way to calculate it. That's how you can simulate it. If you cannot calculate a force, there is no point in talking about it!

How do you calculate the normal force? It depends on the situation. Unlike gravity, it has no universal formula that will tell you what the normal force is. Usually, you can deduce it from the other forces acting on the object.

Here is an example. Consider a book resting on a flat horizontal table (see Figure 7-1). There are two main forces acting on the book: the force of gravity $W = mg$ exerted by the Earth and acting vertically downward, and the normal contact force N exerted by the table on the book acting vertically upward (the normal contact force is usually denoted by N or R). Because the book does not move, the resultant force on it must be zero (Newton's first law of motion). Therefore, we can deduce that the normal force N in this case is equal in magnitude to the weight W of the book.

Figure 7-1. *The normal contact force acting on a book resting on a table*

The normal force will change if, for example, the table is tilted. You'll see in the first example in this chapter ("Sliding down a slope") how to calculate the normal force in such a case.

Tension and compression

Tension in strings is another contact force. If you tie an object with a piece of string and then suspend the object by holding the other end of the string (see Figure 7-2), the string exerts a pull on the object that prevents it from falling down. The string can only do this if it is taut. By Newton's third law of motion, the object exerts an equal and opposite force on the string. The force on the string is called tension. Informally, we also refer to the force that the string exerts on the object as tension. The effect of tension on the string itself is to stretch it slightly. If the object stops moving, then the tension must be equal to the weight of the object. If the object is very heavy, the tension may stretch the string to breaking point.

Figure 7-2. *Tension in a string*

Springs also experience tension. Springs are designed so that large extensions are produced for relatively small tensions. Because a spring will tend to regain its normal length when stretched, it will pull back on the object that is stretching it. The opposite of tension is compression. Springs can also be compressed; they then exert a push on the object compressing them.

Springs are both great fun and extremely useful for producing a variety of effects. In fact, the next chapter is devoted exclusively to springs and spring-like motion.

Friction

Frictional forces are forces that resist the relative movement of two bodies that are in contact or the movement of a body through a fluid. For example, if you push a book along a table, it will slow down and come to a stop. That's because of the frictional force that the table surface exerts on it. The friction between two solid objects is also called *dry friction*. Fluids such as air or water also exert a frictional force, known as *viscous fluid drag*.

We'll discuss fluid drag later in this chapter. In this section, we'll look at dry friction between two solid objects and how we can model it.

As discussed, friction is a force that resists the relative motion of two objects in contact with each other. This implies that the frictional force on an object will act in a direction opposite to its motion. But an object does not necessarily have to move in order to experience friction. If an object is experiencing a force that *tends* to move it against another object, it can also experience friction, even if it does not actually move. In fact, it is friction that stops it from moving. So there are actually two types of friction: friction experienced by a stationary object, and friction experienced by a moving object. We call them *static* and *kinetic* friction, respectively.

Modeling static and kinetic friction

We model both types of friction using the concept of a *coefficient of friction*. Let's start with *kinetic friction* because it is a bit simpler.

Common experience tells us that there will be more friction if we press two surfaces together while trying to slide one over the other. That's because the two objects "stick together" more if pressed together. It's also clear that the amount of friction will depend upon the material making up the object. Rubber, for example, would give more friction than glass. It should therefore come as no surprise to learn that the magnitude of the frictional force F is given by the following, where N is the normal force between the two objects and C_k is a number that depends on the two surfaces, known as the coefficient of kinetic friction:

$$F = C_k N$$

By Newton's third law, a force of the same magnitude acts on both objects; for each object, the force acts in a direction to oppose its motion relative to the other object. Kinetic friction is also sometimes referred to as *dynamic* or *sliding* friction.

Static friction is a bit different. Whereas the kinetic frictional force has just one value for a given pair of surfaces and normal contact force, the static frictional force can take on any value up to a maximum value. The maximum value is given by the following:

$$F_{max} = C_s\, N$$

This is similar in form to the formula for kinetic friction, but with a different coefficient, known as the *coefficient of static friction*. Its value is usually larger than the corresponding value of C_k for the same two surfaces. Hence, the maximum static frictional force is larger than the kinetic frictional force.

To understand static versus kinetic friction, consider the following thought experiment. Suppose you are pushing an object in contact with a surface. If the force you apply has a magnitude less than F_{max} as given by the preceding formula, the frictional force will be equal to the applied force, so that the resultant force is zero and the object does not move. If you now push harder so that the applied force is greater than the value of F_{max}, the frictional force will be equal to F_{max} (because it cannot exceed that maximum value). Therefore, the frictional force cannot completely balance the applied force, and the object will begin to accelerate under the resultant force. As soon as it starts moving, the frictional force will reduce to a value equal to the magnitude of the kinetic friction. Hence, the resultant force will suddenly increase, and the object will accelerate faster. If you've ever tried to move a piece of heavy furniture, you will readily appreciate this fact: it is easier to push once it's already moving. That's because kinetic friction is less than the maximum value of static friction.

Coefficients of friction

Some examples of coefficients of friction are given in Table 7-1. The key point is that the values are generally less than 1. It is very rare for the coefficient of friction to be larger than 1, because that would imply a frictional force larger than the normal contact force holding the two objects together.

Table 7-1. *Static and Kinetic Coefficients of Friction*

Materials	C_s	C_k
Wood on wood	0.25–0.5	0.2
Steel on steel	0.74	0.57
Rubber on concrete	1.0	0.8
Glass on glass	0.94	0.4
Ice on ice	0.1	0.03

Note that although the values are representative of the materials cited, actual coefficients of friction may vary because of the nature of the surface of actual objects. For game programming purposes, this does not present a big problem.

It is impossible to give a comprehensive list of friction coefficients; but if what you need is not listed here it should be easy to find it online.

Example: Sliding down a slope

Time for an example! You can now apply what you learned about normal contact forces and friction to simulate an object sliding down an inclined plane. First, let's apply the physics concepts to this particular example.

The physics

The force diagram for this simulation is shown in Figure 7-3. As indicated on the diagram, there are three forces acting on the object: gravity $m\mathbf{g}$, normal contact force $\mathbf{N}$, and friction $\mathbf{f}$. Because the object moves in a straight line along the surface, the resultant force acts along the surface. There is no resultant force perpendicular to the surface.

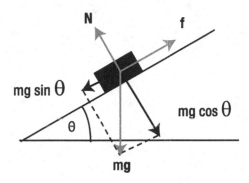

Figure 7-3. *Force diagram for an object sliding down an inclined plane*

Therefore, resolving the forces along the surface gives the magnitude of the resultant force F as follows, where θ is the angle of the inclined plane:

$$F = mg\sin(\theta) - f$$

Resolving forces perpendicular to the surface must give a zero resultant, so that the normal contact force N is balanced by the component of gravity perpendicular to the surface. Note that friction f acts along the surface, so its component perpendicular to the surface is zero. Hence,

$$N = mg\cos(\theta)$$

The magnitude of the frictional force f is given by the following when the object is moving:

$$f = C_k\, N$$

If it is not moving, the resultant force F along the surface must be zero, so f has to balance the component of gravity along the surface. From the preceding equation, setting $F = 0$ gives this:

$$f = mg\sin(\theta)$$

It will be true up to a maximum value of the following:

$$f = C_s\, N$$

If the value of the gravity component ($mg\sin(\theta)$) exceeds this critical value ($C_s N$), f will have the latter value, at least momentarily. As soon as the object starts moving, f will have the value $C_k N$.

Now that you know the physics and have the relevant formulas, you can start coding. This will be a two-step process, pretty similar to what you did in the previous chapter. First, you'll create the visual setup; then you'll write the code that drives the simulation.

Creating the visual setup

The code is in a file called sliding.js. After declaring and initializing the canvas, context and other variables, we handle the visual setup in the init() function:

```
var canvas = document.getElementById('canvas');
var context = canvas.getContext('2d');
var canvas_bg = document.getElementById('canvas_bg');
var context_bg = canvas_bg.getContext('2d');

var ball;
var m = 1;           // mass of ball
var g = 10;          // acceleration due to gravity
var ck = 0.2;        // coeff of kinetic friction
var cs = 0.25;       // coeff of static friction
var vtol = 0.000001 // tolerance
// coordinates of end-points of inclined plane
var xtop = 50; var ytop = 150;
var xbot = 450; var ybot = 250;
var angle = Math.atan2(ybot-ytop,xbot-xtop); // angle of inclined plane
var t0,dt;

window.onload = init;

function init() {
    // create a ball
    ball = new Ball(20,'#0000ff',m,0,true);
    ball.pos2D = new Vector2D(50,130);
    ball.velo2D = new Vector2D(0,0);
    ball.draw(context);
    // create an inclined plane
    context_bg.strokeStyle = '#333333';
    context_bg.beginPath();
    context_bg.moveTo(xtop,ytop);
    context_bg.lineTo(xbot,ybot);
    context_bg.closePath();
    context_bg.stroke();
    // make the ball move
    t0 = new Date().getTime();
    animFrame();
};
```

In init() we create a ball and a line (the latter on a different canvas element, the background), and place the ball on the line. The angle of the line is calculated using the end points and the Math.atan2() function and stored in the angle variable. If you are unsure about what is happening here, take a look at the subsection "The inverse trig functions" in Chapter 3 again. Finally, we make the ball move down the inclined line by invoking the animFrame() function.

Coding the animation

The animFrame() function does its usual job of setting up the animation loop, and the relevant code is very much like the examples in the previous chapter, but just to remind you we reproduce the code here:

```
function animFrame(){
    animId = requestAnimationFrame(animFrame,canvas);
    onTimer();
}
function onTimer(){
    var t1 = new Date().getTime();
    dt = 0.001*(t1-t0);
    t0 = t1;
    if (dt>0.2) {dt=0;};
    move();
}
function move(){
    moveObject(ball);
    calcForce();
    updateAccel();
    updateVelo(ball);
}
function moveObject(obj){
    obj.pos2D = obj.pos2D.addScaled(obj.velo2D,dt);
    context.clearRect(0, 0, canvas.width, canvas.height);
    obj.draw(context);
}
function updateAccel(){
    acc = force.multiply(1/m);
}
function updateVelo(obj){
    obj.velo2D = obj.velo2D.addScaled(acc,dt);
}
```

This is almost the entire animation code, and you can see that nothing has changed so far. The only change is in the calcForce() function, which contains the new physics:

```
function calcForce(){
    var gravity = Forces.constantGravity(m,g);
    var normal = Vector2D.vector2D(m*g*Math.cos(angle),0.5*Math.PI-angle,false);
    var coeff;
    if (ball.velo2D.length() < vtol){  // static friction
        coeff = Math.min(cs*normal.length(),m*g*Math.sin(angle));
    }else{  // kinetic friction
        coeff = ck*normal.length();
    }
    var friction = normal.perp(coeff);
    force = Forces.add([gravity, normal, friction]);
}
```

The calcForce() method calculates the three relevant forces gravity, normal, and friction at each timestep and then adds them up to get the resultant force by using the Forces.add() method. The calculation of the normal and friction forces requires explanation. For the normal force, we are using a new method of Vector2D called vector2D(), which is defined as follows:

```
Vector2D.vector2D = function(mag,angle,clockwise){
    if (typeof(clockwise)==='undefined') clockwise = true;
    var vec = new Vector2D(0,0);
    vec.x = mag*Math.cos(angle);
    vec.y = mag*Math.sin(angle);
    if (!clockwise){
        vec.y *= -1;
    }
    return vec;
}
```

This method takes two required Number arguments, mag and angle (in radians), and an optional Boolean argument clockwise, and returns a Vector2D object which is a 2D vector with the specified magnitude and angle. It does this by converting from the (magnitude, angle) representation to the component representation of a vector (refer to the section "Resolving vectors," in Chapter 3). The clockwise parameter tells vector2D() whether the angle is taken in a clockwise direction (the default) or in a counterclockwise direction.

Using the previous formulas and Figure 7-3, we know that the magnitude of the normal force is equal to $mg \cos(\theta)$, and its angle is equal to $\pi/2 - \theta$ (that's 90° – θ, in radians) taken in an anticlockwise sense. Therefore, the normal force is given by this:

```
var normal = Vector2D.vector2D(m*g*Math.cos(angle),0.5*Math.PI-angle,false);
```

The friction force is perpendicular to the normal force and has a magnitude of coeff*N, where coeff is the coefficient of friction and N is the magnitude of the normal force. It is therefore given by the following, where perp() is another new method we created in the Vector2D class (which we shall describe shortly) and coeff is equal to $C_k N$ when the object starts moving; and is equal to $mg \sin(\theta)$, up to a maximum of $C_s N$, when the object is not moving:

```
var friction = normal.perp(coeff);
```

This is implemented in the following way:

```
if (ball.velo2D.length() < vtol){  // static friction
    coeff = Math.min(cs*normal.length(),m*g*Math.sin(angle));
}else{  // kinetic friction
    coeff = ck*normal.length();
}
```

Note that we make use of the Math.min() function to implement the fact that for static friction, coeff is equal to either $mg \sin(\theta)$, or $C_s N$, whichever is smaller.

The perp() method of Vector2D is defined like this:

```
Function perp(u,anticlockwise){
    if (typeof(anticlockwise)==='undefined') anticlockwise = true;
    var length = this.length();
    var vec = new Vector2D(this.y, -this.x);
```

```
    if (length > 0) {
        if (anticlockwise){ // anticlockwise with respect to canvas coordinate system
            vec.scaleBy(u/length);
        }else{
            vec.scaleBy(-u/length);
        }
    }else{
        vec = new Vector2D(0,0);
    }
    return vec;
}
```

This definition implies that if vec is a Vector2D object, and k is a number, vec.perp(k) returns a Vector2D object that is perpendicular to vec and of length k, with a counterclockwise orientation to vec (in the canvas coordinate system). Referring to Figure 7-4, which shows a screenshot of the setup, normal.perp(coeff) therefore gives a vector of magnitude coeff directed up the slope, just as the frictional force should be.

Figure 7-4. An object sliding down a slope

When checking to see if the object is not moving, we don't actually check that its velocity is zero but that it's smaller than some small value vtol (set at 0.000001 in the code). The value of g is set at 10 and, assuming both the sliding object and the surface are made of wood, we choose ck = 0.2 and cs = 0.25.

If you run the code with the given choice of values for the parameters, you'll see that nothing happens. The object just stays there. How can this be? To understand this, take another look at Figure 7-3. It is clear that the object can slide only if the component of gravity along the slope exceeds the maximum static friction. In other words, it will slide if the following condition is true:

$$mg \sin(\theta) > C_s N$$

Because $N = mg \cos(\theta)$, this is equivalent to the following:

$$mg \sin(\theta) > C_s mg \cos(\theta)$$

Dividing both sides of this inequality by $mg \cos(\theta)$ gives this:

$$\tan(\theta) > C_s$$

So the object will slide only if the tangent of the slope angle is greater than the coefficient of static friction. Now you can calculate $\tan(\theta)$ from the values of xtop, ytop, xbot, and ybot as follows:

$$\tan(\theta) = \frac{ybot - ytop}{xbot - xtop} = \frac{250 - 150}{450 - 50} = 0.25$$

This is exactly equal to the value of C_s specified in the code. Therefore, gravity is not sufficient to overcome the force of friction, and the object does not slide. If you increase the angle of the slope slightly, the object will slide. For example, if you change the value of ybot to 260, this will give tan $(\theta) = 110/400 = 0.275$, which is larger than the value of C_s. Give it a go!

In this example, the object slides along a surface without rolling. Rolling involves rotational motion of a rigid body (it will be discussed in Chapter 13).

Pressure

The rest of this chapter will deal with forces that originate from pressure, more specifically fluid pressure. Technically, pressure is associated with solids as well as liquids and gases. But the concept is especially useful in relation to fluids, so it tends to be associated more with liquids and gases.

The meaning of pressure

So what is *pressure*? It is the normal (perpendicular) force per unit area exerted on the surface of an object. The origin of that perpendicular force can be different in different cases. Pressure due to solids and liquids is usually due to the force of gravity. Pressure in gases is due to collisions by gas molecules.

The key question is this: how can we calculate pressure and thus the forces on an object in a fluid? Once we can do that, we can try to simulate the motion of an object in a fluid.

Based on this definition of pressure, if a force F acts normally to a surface with area A, the average pressure P on the surface is given by the following:

$$P = \frac{F}{A}$$

Because pressure is force divided by area, its unit is N/m². This unit has a special name: the pascal, or Pa.

What if F acts at an angle to the normal? Then you need to resolve F to find the component along the normal, and that normal component is what you use in the preceding formula. This gives us a method for calculating the pressure if we know the force, and vice versa.

Pressure is not restricted to fluids (although fluid pressure will be our main concern in this chapter), and it is actually easier to introduce the method of calculating pressure using a simple illustrative example of a solid object.

Suppose that a cuboid (box) of length l, width w, height h, and mass m sits on a table (see Figure 7-5). What is the pressure it exerts on the table?

Figure 7-5. *A box sitting on a table*

The force it exerts on the table is equal to its weight, and that force is perpendicular to the table surface, so we have $F = mg$. The area $A = lw$. Hence, the pressure P is given by this:

$$P = \frac{mg}{A} = \frac{mg}{lw}$$

Density

We can make some more progress by introducing the concept of density.

Density is defined as mass per unit volume. Density gives you a way of comparing the relative "heaviness" of different substances—you can take the same volume of each substance and compare how much each weighs.

We use the Greek symbol ρ (rho) for density. So, based on the definition, we can write:

$$\rho = \frac{m}{V}$$

Because density is a mass divided by a volume, its unit is kg/m³. Because things expand when heated, especially liquids and gases, the density of a fluid varies with temperature (and also with pressure). At 20°C and standard atmospheric pressure, the density of water is approximately 1000 kg/m³, and that of air is approximately 1.2 kg/m³. That means a box measuring 1m × 1m × 1m (of volume 1 m³) would hold 1000 kg (1 ton) of water and 1.2 kg of air.

Manipulating the above formula gives this:

$$m = \rho V$$

It also gives this:

$$V = \frac{m}{\rho}$$

We'll use these formulas frequently in the rest of this chapter.

Just like pressure, the concept of density applies to solids as well as liquids. Going back to the preceding illustrative example of the cuboid, we can replace the mass m in the formula for pressure by using $m = \rho V = \rho lwh$ because the volume of the cuboid is $V = lwh$:

$$P = \frac{mg}{lw} = \frac{\rho lwhg}{lw} = \rho gh$$

This is a very useful formula. It gives the pressure exerted by a regular object (in this case, a cuboid) on a surface in terms of three known quantities: the density of the object, the acceleration due to gravity, and the height of the object. Note that we could have used another shape other than a box, as long as it had a regular cross-section A. The area A would cancel out in the same way, leaving the same formula: $P = \rho gh$.

In the next section, we'll find that this formula is actually even more general, and also applies to the pressure exerted by fluids, provided that we reinterpret h.

Variation of pressure with depth in a fluid

Instead of a solid, now consider a column of liquid of the same shape as the solid in the last section.

Exactly the same math applies, and we again end up with the following, where P is the pressure underneath the column of fluid, ρ is the density of the fluid, and h is the height of the fluid column:

$$P = \rho g h$$

Now mentally transport yourself to the ocean.

At a depth h beneath the sea surface, there is a column of water of height h above. Hence, the pressure at depth h below the surface is given by the same formula:

$$P = \rho g h$$

Note that this is the pressure due to the water only. There is also an additional pressure due to the air above the water surface. This is atmospheric pressure, which we can denote by A. Then the total pressure at a depth h in the ocean is $A + \rho gh$, assuming the density of water is constant with depth. This formula shows that pressure in a fluid increases with depth, which makes perfect sense because there is more fluid above that is "weighing down."

The same is true in the atmosphere, too. The air pressure we feel at the surface of the Earth is due to the column of air above our heads. Standard atmospheric pressure is approximately 100 kPa, or 100,000 Pa. This is sometimes simply called 1 atmosphere (atm).

Because the density of water is 1000 kg/m³, and g is approximately 10 m/s², using the formula $P = \rho gh$ tells us that 10 m of water will exert approximately the same pressure as 1 atm. So, at an ocean depth of 10 m, the pressure will be 2 atm, including the pressure of the air above.

Static and dynamic pressure

So far, when we've talked about pressure in a fluid, we've been referring to *static pressure*. The formula $P = \rho gh$ applies to static pressure. Static pressure is defined at any point in a flow, and it is isotropic; that is, it has the same value in any direction. It exists even in static fluids (fluids that are at rest).

In a moving fluid, there is another kind of pressure, known as *dynamic pressure*. Dynamic pressure is due to the flow of fluid. For example, the flow of water from a tap gives rise to dynamic pressure. When the water hits the sink, it exerts a force on the sink. Similarly, the wind exerts a force due to the dynamic pressure associated with it. The formula for the dynamic pressure at any point in a fluid is the following, where v is the velocity of the fluid at that point:

$$P = \frac{1}{2} \rho v^2$$

The same is true for an object moving with velocity v in a fluid; it's the relative velocity between the object and the fluid that matters.

The total pressure in a moving fluid is the sum of the static and the dynamic pressure.

Upthrust (buoyancy)

After this background on pressure and density, we are now ready to introduce the forces due to fluids. So let's start with upthrust, also known as buoyancy.

Here is a simple experiment for you to do in the bath. Try pushing a hollow ball under water. What do you feel? You should feel a force trying to push the ball back upward. This is the upthrust force. Now let go of the ball. What happens? It pops back up and oscillates at the water surface before settling down. You will create such an effect soon.

Upthrust is also responsible for making us feel lighter in the swimming pool or bath. It acts upward, opposing the force of gravity.

What causes upthrust? The physical origin of upthrust is the difference in pressure that exists at different heights in a fluid. To see what we mean, take a look at Figure 7-6a, which shows an object partially immersed in a fluid such as water. The pressure on the top face of the object is equal to atmospheric pressure A and pushes the object downward, while the pressure on the bottom surface is equal to $A + \rho gh$, where ρ is the density of the fluid and h is the depth to which the object is submerged. This pressure acts upward, so that there is a net upward pressure equal to ρgh. Hence, because force = pressure × surface area, there is a resultant upward force U due to this pressure difference given by the following (where S is the area of the top and bottom faces of the object—assumed to be equal here for simplicity):

$$U = \rho \, g \, h \, S$$

This is the upthrust or buoyancy force.

Note that because pressure is isotropic, it also acts on the sides of the object. But the pressures on opposite sides are equal and opposite at each height, so their effects are cancelled. Similar conclusions hold if the object is completely immersed in a fluid (see Figure 7-6b), including objects in air. That's basically because pressure increases with depth in a fluid, so the pressure at the base of a submerged object will always be greater than that at its top. So there will be a net upward pressure on the object due to the fluid.

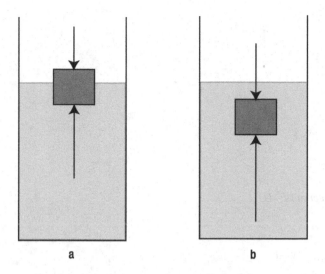

Figure 7-6. *An object immersed in a fluid experiences upthrust due to a pressure difference*

Archimedes' Principle

Let's revisit the last formula we derived in the preceding section. The magnitude of the upthrust U was found to be given by $U = \rho ghS$. Now h is the height of the submerged portion of the object and S is its cross-sectional area (which we assume to be constant for simplicity). Hence, hS is equal to the volume V of the submerged portion of the object. So we can write this:

$$U = \rho\, g\, h\, S = \rho\, g\, V$$

But then $\rho V = m$, the mass of the *fluid* whose place has been taken by the submerged portion of the object, so we can now write this:

$$U = m_{\text{fluid}}\, g$$

This is just the weight of the displaced fluid. Hence, we have derived Archimedes' principle:

> **Archimedes' principle:** The upthrust on an object immersed in a fluid is equal to the weight of fluid it displaces.

Archimedes was an ancient Greek scientist, mathematician, and all-round genius. According to legend, upon discovering this principle, he jumped out of his bath shouting "Eureka!", which means "Found it!"

Apparent weight

Upthrust leads to the phenomenon of *apparent weight*. Figure 7-7 illustrates the concept. Any object that is partially or completely immersed in a fluid will experience an upward upthrust force U that opposes the downward force of gravity W on it.

Figure 7-7. *Upthrust reduces the apparent weight of an object to W – U*

Hence, the apparent weight of the object is given by

$$W_{apparent} = W - U$$

The phenomenon of apparent weight is responsible for why we feel lighter in the bath or a swimming pool. Exploiting the apparent weight effect, astronauts train while submerged in a giant water tank to simulate reduced or zero gravity.

Submerged objects

Objects that are completely immersed (submerged) in a fluid obviously displace their own volume of fluid.

The apparent weight of a completely immersed object can therefore be written as follows because both the object and the displaced fluid have the same volume V:

$$W_{apparent} = W - U = m_{object}\, g - m_{fluid}\, g = \rho_{object}\, V\, g - \rho_{fluid}\, V\, g$$

It can therefore be written in the following form:

$$W_{apparent} = \left(\rho_{object} - \rho_{fluid}\right) V\, g$$

This is a very useful formula that gives the resultant downward force, or apparent weight, of an object submerged in a fluid in terms of their densities and the volume of the submerged object.

From this formula, we can deduce:

- If the density of the object is greater than that of the fluid, the apparent weight will be positive (i.e. downward) but less than the real weight. You can experience this lower apparent weight in the bath or a swimming pool.

- If the density of the object is *much* greater than that of the fluid, the apparent weight is nearly equal to the real weight because the upthrust is negligible compared to the weight of the object. For example, the upthrust on a stone in air can usually be neglected.

- If the density of the object is exactly equal to that of the fluid, the apparent weight will be zero, and so the object will float in the fluid.

- If the density of the object is less than that of the fluid, the apparent weight is negative (it acts upward) and so the object will rise. For example, air bubbles in water have a very large upthrust compared with their weight because the density of air is much lower than that of water, and so they rise quickly.

Floating objects

A special form of Archimedes' principle applies for floating bodies. This is the so-called law of flotation.

Law of flotation: A floating object displaces its own weight of fluid.

Here's the logic. A floating body has no *net* force acting on it; otherwise, it would either rise or sink. Because the only two forces acting on it are its weight and upthrust, they must balance. Hence, the upthrust on a floating body must equal the weight of the body. By Archimedes' principle, this implies that the weight of fluid displaced is equal to the weight of the body. So the apparent weight of a floating object is zero—it "feels weightless."

As discussed previously, this is also the situation when a body is submerged in a fluid with a density equal to the body's own density. In fact, an object that is floating on the surface of a liquid, such as a ship on water, has an "effective density" that is the same as that of the water, even though it may be made of metal with a higher density than that of water. That's because the part of the ship below the water surface also includes air enclosed within the ship's interior, which lowers its average density.

Example: Balloon

We've had quite a bit of theory, so let's look at an example. This example (shown in Figure 7-8) simulates a simple hot-air balloon. Hot-air balloons work, well, by heating air. The heated air has a density less than that of the ambient air, so it rises. By controlling the temperature of the air in the balloon, you can control its density and therefore the upthrust on it.

Figure 7-8. *Simulating a hot-air balloon*

The code for this simulation is found in balloon.js. The init() function creates the visual background shown in Figure 7-8 and creates a balloon as a Ball object, initially at rest on the ground. It also sets up keydown and keyup event listeners, with the corresponding keydown event listener responding to UP and DOWN arrow presses by respectively increasing or decreasing the balloon's density rhoP from its initial value of 1.1. The air density rho is kept constant at 1.2. You can take a look at the code for more details.

You could probably write the animation code without too much help by now. The only substantial change here is the calcForce() method, which specifies two forces (gravity and upthrust) and then adds them up:

```
function calcForce(){
    var gravity = Forces.constantGravity(m,g);
    var V = m/rhoP; // volume of air displaced
    var upthrust = Forces.upthrust(rho,V,g);
    force = Forces.add([gravity, upthrust]);
}
```

The `upthrust` is calculated using the newly created `Forces.upthrust()` static function, which basically uses the formula $U = \rho g V$, where ρ (variable `rho`) in the code is the density of the fluid and V (variable `V` in the code) is the volume of air displaced. This is the volume of the balloon because it is completely immersed in air. So `V` is calculated using the mass of the balloon and its effective density `rhoP`, using the formula volume = mass/density. The effective density `rhoP` is the density of the whole balloon, including any load it carries (not just the density of the air in it).

The critical parameter in the simulation is the ratio of the balloon density to ambient air density `rhoP/rho`. If the effective balloon density `rhoP` is smaller than the air density `rho` (that ratio is smaller than 1), the balloon will rise. If `rhoP` is larger than `rho`, it will sink.

To make the simulation more interactive, we've also included a call in `move()` to the function `changeBalloonDensity()` that lets you increase and decrease the density `rhoP` of the balloon by pressing the up and down arrow keys, respectively. The code outputs the value of the ratio (`rhoP/rho`) to the console whenever `rhoP` is changed. See if you can make the balloon rise and then remain stationary at some height.

There is something missing in this simulation. The balloon rises too fast; it basically accelerates under the effect of the excess upthrust force, so its upward velocity keeps on rising. In reality, it will be slowed down by drag. So let's take a look at how we can include drag effects.

Drag

Trying to model drag can prove somewhat confusing for someone who is not familiar with fluid dynamics. One reason is that there is not just one, but several types of drag. Depending on the object and flow you are simulating, you might need to consider different types of drag.

Another source of difficulty is that a lot of what we know about drag is based on empirical work. The laws of drag were discovered by doing lots of experiments, and not as part of a beautiful universal theory like gravity.

The bottom line is that you will bump into formulas that were developed from experimental results that you just have to accept without argument.

For most of what we'll do in this book, we'll use one of two drag laws: one that holds for low velocities (or so-called *laminar flow*) and another (more common) one that holds for higher velocities (or so-called *turbulent flow*).

Drag law for low velocities

For an object moving through a fluid at very low velocities, the flow around the object is *laminar*, or streamlined. This generates relatively low drag. The drag force then obeys Stokes' law, which says that the drag force is proportional to the velocity of the object. For a spherical object, the Stokes' drag formula is the following, where r is the radius of the sphere and the Greek letter η denotes a property of the fluid known as *viscosity* (more precisely, *dynamic viscosity*):

$$\mathbf{F} = -6\,\pi\,\eta\,r\,\mathbf{v}$$

Note that dynamic viscosity is also denoted by the Greek letter μ. The viscosity of a fluid is a measure of the resistance it offers to objects moving through it. Intuitively, it represents the "thickness" of the fluid. So the viscosity of water is higher than that of air, and the viscosity of oil is higher than that of water. Therefore, an object moving at the same velocity through water experiences a greater drag force than through air. The formula also tells us that a larger object experiences more drag because the parameter r is greater for a larger object.

To use this formula in an accurate simulation, you need to know the viscosity of the fluid in which your object is moving. Like density, viscosity depends on temperature. At 20°C, the dynamic viscosity of water is 1.0×10^{-3} kg/(ms), and that of air is 1.8×10^{-5} kg/(ms)—about 1/55 as much.

In coding this drag force, we will lump together all the factors, multiplying the velocity into a single factor denoted by k, so that the linear drag law becomes the following, where $k = 6\pi\eta r$ for a sphere:

$$\mathbf{F} = -k\,\mathbf{v}$$

Writing the linear drag law in this form is in fact more general because it then also applies to other, nonspherical objects, for which k is not given by this formula. By choosing suitable values for k, we can model the linear drag force on objects of any shape.

This is basically the form of drag that we coded into the Forces.linearDrag() function back in Chapter 5:

```
Forces.linearDrag = function(k,vel){
    var force;
    var velMag = vel.length();
    if (velMag > 0) {
        force = vel.multiply(-k);
    }else {
        force = new Vector2D(0,0);
    }
    return force;
}
```

Drag law for high velocities

Stokes' drag law holds only for low velocities. At higher velocities, the flow around the immersed object becomes *turbulent*, generating eddies that disturb the flow and make it chaotic. The drag force law is then different from that of laminar flow and is proportional to the square of the velocity of the object. The drag formula is given by the following, where ρ is the density of the fluid, A is the frontal area of the object (the area on which the fluid impacts as the object moves through it), and C_d is a parameter called the *drag coefficient*, which depends on characteristics of the object such as its shape, surface properties, and characteristics of the flow:

$$\mathbf{F} = -\frac{1}{2}\rho A C_d \, v \, \mathbf{v}$$

Note that the formula involves the product of the velocity $\mathbf{v}$ with its magnitude v. This gives a vector of magnitude v^2 in the direction of $\mathbf{v}$. Hence, the drag force law is quadratic in the velocity, with a magnitude given by this:

$$F = \frac{1}{2}\rho A C_d \, v^2$$

In this form, it is clear that quadratic drag depends on dynamic pressure $P = 1/2 \, \rho v^2$, and indeed we can write this:

$$F = P A C_d$$

As mentioned previously, the drag coefficient C_d can depend on a large number of factors. Its value is found by experiment for particular objects and setups. For example, the drag coefficient of a sphere can range from 0.07 to 0.5. Similarly, you can find the drag coefficients for a large number of object shapes (both in 2D and in 3D) in physics or engineering textbooks or websites.

As for the laminar drag formula, we'll simplify the previous formula by defining a drag constant k for high velocities as the following:

$$k = \frac{1}{2}\rho A C_d$$

So the drag law for high velocities can be written in this form:

$$\mathbf{F} = -k \, v \, \mathbf{v}$$

We now define a second drag force function called Forces.drag(), which looks as follows:

```
Forces.drag = function(k,vel) {
    var force;
    var velMag = vel.length();
    if (velMag > 0) {
        force = vel.multiply(-k*velMag);
    }
    else {
        force = new Vector2D(0,0);
    }
    return force;
}
```

Which drag law should I use?

We have described two drag laws, linear and quadratic, saying the former applies at low velocities and the latter at high velocities. But so far we've been rather vague about what "low" and "high" mean. What is the "critical velocity" that distinguishes between low and high?

To answer this question, we introduce the concept of the *Reynolds number* of a flow. In simple terms, the Reynolds number tells us whether a flow is laminar or turbulent. Therefore it tells us, among other things, whether a linear or a quadratic drag law applies. The Reynolds number, denoted by the symbol Re, is defined by the following equation, where u is a characteristic velocity associated with the flow, d is a characteristic length scale, and the Greek symbol ν (nu) is the so-called *kinematic viscosity* of the fluid:

$$\mathrm{Re} = \frac{u\,d}{\nu}$$

The kinematic viscosity is defined as the ratio of the dynamic viscosity and the density of the fluid:

$$\nu = \frac{\mu}{\rho}$$

Using the values of dynamic viscosity and density given before, we can deduce that at 20°C the kinematic viscosity of water is 1.0×10^{-6} m²/s and that of air is 1.5×10^{-5} m²/s.

The choice of what velocity u and what length scale d to use to calculate the Reynolds number depends on the problem. For an object such as a sphere moving in a fluid, u is just the velocity of the object and d is a linear dimension (the diameter for a sphere).

Now it is found experimentally that laminar flow dominates, and therefore Stokes' law for linear drag holds when the Reynolds number is much less than 1. Using the formula for the Reynolds number and setting Re = 1, this implies that the critical velocity that determines which drag law applies is given by

$$u_c \approx \frac{\nu}{d}$$

If the velocity of the object is much less than this critical value v_c, the drag law is linear; if it is much larger than v_c, the drag law is quadratic. If the velocity is intermediate between those two limits, a combination of both laws can be used.

As an example, the diameter of a soccer ball is 22 cm, or 0.22 m. Using the values of the kinematic viscosity of water and air given previously, we deduce that the critical velocity for such a ball is 0.0045 mm/s in water and 0.068 mm/s in air (yes, those are in millimeters per second). These are tiny velocities, so for all practical purposes you can assume that a ball this size moving in water or air will always obey a quadratic drag law. This also applies to most everyday objects moving at normal velocities in air or water.

On the other hand, a ball bearing of diameter 1 mm falling in glycerin (which has a kinematic viscosity of 1.2×10^{-3} m^2/s at 20°C) has a critical velocity of 1.2 m/s. That's a much greater critical velocity. The maximum velocity that the ball bearing reaches (its terminal velocity) is much less than this. Therefore, the linear drag law applies in this case.

Adding drag to the balloon simulation

As shown in the previous section, the drag law that is appropriate for most everyday objects moving in air or water is the quadratic drag law, as coded in the Forces.drag() function. It is a very simple matter to add drag to the last example of the balloon simulation. We simply update calcForce() as follows:

```
function calcForce(){
    var gravity = Forces.constantGravity(m,g);
    var V = m/rhoP; // volume of air displaced
    var upthrust = Forces.upthrust(rho,V,g);
    var drag = Forces.drag(k,balloon.velo2D);
    force = Forces.add([gravity, upthrust, drag]);
}
```

The new variable k is the drag constant. In the sample code provided, we give it the value of 0.01. If you run the simulation with these modifications, you'll see that the balloon no longer rises at an accelerating rate. The addition of the drag force slows down its ascent, and the effect is more realistic.

Example: Floating ball

Let's now go back to the floating ball simulation we introduced in Chapter 5 to illustrate the effect of drag, together with upthrust and gravity. The code simulates the motion of a ball that is thrown, dropped, or released in water.

The code is in the file floating-ball.js. The visual and interactive aspects of the code were discussed in Chapter 5. Here we'll focus on the physics, which is essentially contained in the calcForce() method:

```
function calcForce(){
    var rball = ball.radius;
    var xball = ball.x;
    var yball = ball.y;
    var dr = (yball-yLevel)/rball;
    var ratio;                               // volume fraction of object that is submerged
    if (dr <= -1){                           // object completely out of water
        ratio = 0;
    }else if (dr < 1){                       // object partially in water
        //ratio = 0.5 + 0.5*dr;              // for cuboid
        ratio = 0.5 + 0.25*dr*(3-dr*dr);     // for sphere
    }else{                                   // object completely in water
        ratio = 1;
    }
    var gravity = Forces.constantGravity(ball.mass,g);
    var upthrust = new Vector2D(0,-rho*V*ratio*g);
    var drag = ball.velo2D.multiply(-ratio*k*ball.velo2D.length());
    force = Forces.add([gravity, upthrust, drag]);
```

```
    // bouncing off walls
    if (xball < rball){
        ball.xpos = rball;
        ball.vx *= vfac;
    }
    if (xball > canvas.width - rball){
        ball.xpos = canvas.width - rball;
        ball.vx *= vfac;
    }
}
```

The section of code consisting of the two if blocks at the end of calcForce() handles bouncing of the ball off the walls. The four lines of the code before that should be evident: we are calculating the three forces (gravity, upthrust, and drag) that act on the ball and then adding them up to obtain the resultant force. The new piece of physics here is the inclusion of a factor called ratio, which is the fraction by volume of the ball that is submerged in the water. This is used to compute the upthrust in the water (according to Archimedes' principle), and the drag in the water (assuming that this is also proportional to the volume fraction that is submerged—it is actually a fairly crude approximation, but will help keep the algorithm much simpler). For simplicity, we neglect the upthrust and drag forces that the ball might experience in air. It is not difficult to see how they could be included too, if needed. All this should be easy to follow; the subtlety is in the code that calculates ratio.

To calculate ratio, you need to do some geometrical thinking. Take a look at Figure 7-9, which represents a cuboid and a sphere partially immersed in water. In our animation, assuming that coordinates of the corresponding objects are at the center of the objects, we need a formula that gives ratio in terms of the position of the objects and the position of the water level.

Figure 7-9. *Objects partially immersed in water*

To do this, it turns out to be convenient to first define a parameter dr that tells you how much the center of the object is above or below the water level, as a fraction of the radius of the ball (or half-height of the cuboid). So dr is defined as the following, where r is the half-height of the object (and is equal to the radius for the ball):

$$dr = \frac{\text{position of object - water level}}{\text{half-height of object}} = \frac{d}{r}$$

A little bit of thinking should convince you that dr = -1 means that the object (whether ball or cuboid) is just completely out of the water, and that dr = 1 means that it is just completely submerged in the water. Therefore, if dr <= -1, ratio is zero, and if dr >= 1, ratio is 1. The trickier part is when the object is partially submerged. In the case of a cuboid, simple geometry tells us that (yes, you can work it out yourself):

$$\text{ratio} = 0.5 + 0.5\,dr$$

In the case of a sphere, it's a bit more complicated to work out (you need to do a bit of calculus), but here is the formula:

$$\text{ratio} = 0.5 + 0.25\,dr\,(3 - dr^2)$$

That's all we need.

In the code, the volume V of the ball is set to 1, and its mass is also 1. Therefore, its density (equal to mass/volume) is 1. The density of the water is set to 1.5. Therefore, because the density of the ball is less than that of the water, it will float.

In floating-ball.js, the initial position and velocity of the ball are given as follows:

```
ball.pos2D = new Vector2D(50,50);
ball.velo2D = new Vector2D(40,-20);
```

This puts the ball initially above the water and imparts a velocity with an upward component and a component to the right. If you run the code, you'll see that the ball then follows a curved (parabolic) path in the air until it hits the water. It then slows down suddenly because of the drag and upthrust in the water, sinking a bit and then rising again to the surface and oscillating on the water surface until it stops. A screenshot of the simulation is shown in Figure 7-10.

Figure 7-10. *A floating ball*

The simulation is so realistic that you can experiment with it to learn about the physics involved! Click anywhere above the water to move the ball there. Then release it above the water. It will fall into the water, decelerate, rise, and again oscillate on the water surface a few times before stopping. The higher you drop it, the further it will sink. Now click underwater and release it. It will rise to the surface and again oscillate a few times before stopping.

You can also play around by changing the initial conditions or the values of the parameters. For example, change the mass of the ball to 2 or the volume to 0.5, so that the density is 2. The ball will then sink instead of floating because its density is greater than the density of the water, which is 1.5.

Want to try something different? What would happen if the ball were very light? Try it. Reduce the density to 0.5 by increasing the volume to 2. What happens when you release the ball under water? It shoots out into the air, before falling back into the water. If you've ever tried doing this with a real ball, you'll know that it's a real effect. Our simulation is so realistic it can be used to perform "virtual experiments". And we haven't even paid any attention to numerical accuracy (which we'll look at in Part IV of the book).

This example is particularly instructive in that it shows how a simulation that includes the relevant physics can behave pretty much like the real thing would do in real life. The simulation knows how to deal with any change in initial conditions or parameters, without the need for you to tell it anything more! This is the power of real physics simulation. It gives you a lot for your money, perhaps more than you'd expect—and it's much easier than faking it!

Terminal velocity

As you discovered in the preceding examples, the presence of the drag force means that the velocity of a rising or falling object cannot increase indefinitely. To understand why, consider the case of an object released from a height (far from the ground) and falling under gravity. This example was discussed in Chapter 4 and elaborated upon in Chapter 5, but it is worth a recap here to gain a deeper understanding, now that you know more about the drag force. In particular, the previous discussions were in terms of the linear drag formula; it is useful to know how the results generalize to quadratic drag, and also when upthrust is taken into account.

In Figure 7-11, there is a downward gravity force $W = mg$ acting on the object, and an upward drag force D. The drag force has a magnitude given by kv at very low velocities but more usually by kv^2. Now initially the velocity of the object is zero, so that the drag force is zero. As it accelerates under gravity, its velocity increases and therefore the drag force increases, too. This reduces the resultant downward force to $W - D$ and therefore reduces the acceleration. Because the force of gravity is constant, as the velocity increases, there will be a point at which the drag force will be equal to gravity; in other words, the resultant force $W - D$ will be zero, so the acceleration of the object will be zero. In other words, it will eventually move at a constant velocity: the terminal velocity.

Figure 7-11. *Force balance giving rise to terminal velocity*

As shown in Chapter 4, it is easy to work out the magnitude of the terminal velocity. It is the value of v at which $W - D = 0$. Because $W = mg$, if we use $D = kv$, we get this:

$$m g = k v$$

So that

$$v = \frac{m g}{k}$$

This is the terminal velocity for laminar flow. It holds for an object moving in a fluid with high viscosity (such as oil). If we use the drag law for higher velocities, $D = kv^2$, we instead get

$$m g = k v^2$$

It then implies that

$$v = \sqrt{\frac{m\,g}{k}}$$

We can also generalize these formulas to include upthrust (see Figure 7-12) by replacing the weight $W = mg$ by the absolute value of the apparent weight $W_{apparent} = (\rho_{object} - \rho_{fluid})\,V\,g$.

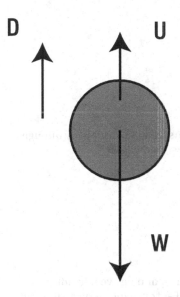

Figure 7-12. *Force balance with upthrust*

If you are doing a simulation in which the object attains terminal velocity very quickly, you may get away with just giving the object a constant velocity equal to the terminal velocity by making use of the preceding formulas. This will preserve the physical realism of the simulation (if the initial acceleration is not important) while cutting down the computing time significantly. For example, bubbles rising in water attain terminal velocity very rapidly and can be simulated in this way if there are no other forces apart from gravity, upthrust, and drag.

As discussed in Chapter 5, the motion of an object under gravity, upthrust, and drag can be solved analytically using calculus to give not only the terminal velocity but also the velocity at any time. For example, for an object dropped from rest in a fluid, the analytical solution assuming linear drag and neglecting upthrust is given by

$$v = \frac{mg}{k}\left[1 - \exp(-k\,t/m)\right]$$

This gives the velocity of the object at time t after being dropped. The solutions with quadratic drag and including upthrust look a bit more complicated, and you can find them in physics textbooks.

Example: Parachute

Parachutes work by exploiting the fact that the drag force is proportional to the area of an object. Going back to the formula for quadratic drag $\mathbf{F} = -kv\mathbf{v}$, with the drag constant k given by $k = 1/2\,\rho A C_d$, we can see that the larger the area of an object, the greater the drag force will be. Opening a parachute suddenly increases the surface area exposed to the air, thereby increasing the value of k. This greatly increases the drag force and therefore slows down a parachutist.

Our present example is an educational exercise to illustrate this principle. Take a look at the init() function in parachute.js:

```
function init() {
    ball = new Ball(20,'#0000ff',m);
    ball.pos2D = new Vector2D(650,50);
    ball.velo2D=new Vector2D(0,0);
    ball.draw(context);
    setupGraph();
    window.addEventListener('mousedown',openParachute,false);
    t0 = new Date().getTime();
    t = 0;
    animFrame();
};
```

This simply creates a Ball instance (to represent a skydiver!) and then animates its fall in the usual way through animFrame() and related motion code. The calcForce() method adds gravity, upthrust, and drag:

```
function calcForce(){
    var gravity = Forces.constantGravity(m,g);
    var drag = Forces.drag(k,ball.velo2D);
    var upthrust = Forces.upthrust(rho,V,g);
    force = Forces.add([gravity, upthrust, drag]);
}
```

In addition, an event listener is set up in init() for a mousedown event. In the corresponding event handler openParachute(), the radius of the parachute is increased by a factor equal to linearFactor (which is given the value of 3 in the code), and the value of the drag constant k is increased by a factor equal to the square of linearFactor (by 9). The event listener is then removed.

```
function openParachute(evt){
    k *= linearFactor*linearFactor;
    ball.radius *= linearFactor;
    window.removeEventListener('mousedown',openParachute,false);
}
```

This means that the parachute is made three times bigger (by radius) and the drag constant is made nine times greater the first time the user clicks the mouse. Finally, a Graph object is set up in setupGraph(), which is called in the init() function, and used to plot the vy component of the parachute's velocity at each time by calling the plotGraph() method within the move() method.

If you now run the code (without opening the parachute) you'll find that the parachute accelerates quickly at first, then more slowly until it reaches a constant velocity (terminal velocity) about 10 seconds into the fall. The value of the terminal velocity is approximately 30 pixels per second. If you then click to "open the parachute," it will become bigger and immediately slow down, reaching a new lower terminal velocity of approximately 10 pixels per second in a few seconds. The terminal velocity is the same whenever you open the parachute: it's independent of time, only depending on the mass m of the parachute, the acceleration due to gravity g, and the drag constant k through the formula $v = \sqrt{(mg / k)}$. Figure 7-13 shows a typical shape of the velocity-time graph.

Figure 7-13. *Velocity-time graph for a parachute*

Lift

You saw that the drag force depends upon the dynamic pressure. There is another force that also depends on the dynamic pressure: it's called lift. More precisely, it is the difference in dynamic pressure on opposite sides of an object that is responsible for these forces. Whereas the drag force on an object acts opposite to the velocity of the object, the lift force acts perpendicular to the velocity (see Figure 7-14). Now, because there is always a difference in the dynamic pressure between the front and back of a moving object, there is always a drag force on a moving object. However, if an object is perfectly symmetrical along an axis in the direction of motion, the flow (and therefore the dynamic pressure) on either side of the object will be exactly the same. In that case, there is no lift force. But any asymmetry in the flow—for example, caused by an asymmetrical wing shape (for aircraft) or angle of attack, will give rise to a lift force perpendicular to the direction of motion.

Figure 7-14. *Drag and lift force on an object moving in a fluid*

The lift force is what enables airplanes to fly. In that case, the direction of motion is usually horizontal, so the lift force acts vertically upward and balances the weight of the plane. But lift does not always have to act vertically upward. Depending on the direction of motion, it can act in any direction.

Lift is sometimes confused with upthrust. In fact, upthrust is sometimes mistakenly referred to as lift. Like upthrust, lift arises because of a difference in pressure. Upthrust is caused by the difference in static pressure between the top and bottom of an object that is due to the weight of the displaced fluid (buoyancy); but lift is caused by the difference in dynamic pressure between opposite sides of an object that lie along the direction of its motion. This causes a difference in the static pressure between the opposite sides mentioned earlier. Thus, whereas upthrust is always upward (as its name suggests), that is not necessarily so for lift. More crucially, the physics laws and therefore the formulas that govern these two forces are completely different. Consider this: lift is the force that makes an airplane fly; upthrust is the force that makes a balloon float; the mechanisms are different in the two cases.

Lift coefficients

The lift force is modeled in terms of a lift coefficient, in exactly the same way as quadratic drag. Hence the magnitude of the lift force can be written as follows, where C_L is the *lift coefficient* and A is the area of the object along the direction of motion (rather than perpendicular to it as for drag):

$$F = \frac{1}{2} \rho\, A\, C_L\, v^2$$

Like the drag coefficient C_d, the lift coefficient C_L depends on a variety of factors. For aircraft, the important variables are wing shape and angle of attack.

As we did for the drag force, we can define a lift constant $k = 1/2\, \rho A C_L$, which then enables us to write the magnitude of the lift force as $F = kv^2$.

The direction of the lift force is perpendicular to the direction of the velocity. Taking this into account, we can define a Forces.lift() function as follows:

```
Forces.lift = function(k,vel) {
    var force;
    var velMag = vel.length();
    if (velMag > 0) {
        force = vel.perp(k*velMag);
    }
    else {
        force = new Vector2D(0,0);
    }
    return force;
}
```

Example: An airplane

Let's now demonstrate how the lift force can make an airplane fly. The file airplane.js contains the code for a basic flight demonstration. We'll just reproduce the key parts of the code here. First, take a look at the variable declarations/initializations and the init() function:

```
var plane;
var m = 1;
var g = 10;
var kDrag = 0.01;
var kLift = 0.5;
var magThrust = 5;
var groundLevel = 550;
var t0,dt;

window.onload = init;

function init() {
    makeBackground();
    makePlane();
    t0 = new Date().getTime();
    animFrame();
};
```

The variable names should be self-explanatory. The makeBackground() and makePlane() methods produce the visual setup you can see in Figure 7-16. In makePlane(), a plane is created as an instance of the Plane object and placed on the "runway" with an initial velocity of zero. You are welcome to take a look at the plane.js file to see what the code for the Plane object looks like (or even improve on it, if you feel so inclined!). But the visual details are not important for our present purpose. What really matters is how to make the plane fly. This is initiated, as ever, by the animFrame() and related methods. The only new code here is in calcForce().

As depicted in Figure 7-15, there are four main forces on an airplane in flight: gravity (W), thrust (T), drag (D), and lift (L). When the airplane is on the ground, there is also the normal contact force due to the ground. Hence, the calcForce() method computes these forces and adds them up:

```
function calcForce(){
    var gravity = Forces.constantGravity(m,g);
    var velX = new Vector2D(plane.vx,0);
    var drag = Forces.drag(kDrag,velX);
    var lift = Forces.lift(kLift,velX);
    var thrust = new Vector2D(magThrust,0);
    var normal;
    if (plane.y >= groundLevel-plane.height){
        normal = gravity.multiply(-1);
    }else{
        normal = new Vector2D(0,0);
    }
    force = Forces.add([gravity, drag, lift, thrust, normal]);
}
```

Figure 7-15. The four forces on a airplane in flight

Gravity is straightforward as usual. The drag and lift forces are computed in a simplified way, by considering only the horizontal component of the airplane's velocity. Also, the airplane is assumed to be horizontal at all times, with an angle of attack that is zero. The thrust is modeled as a constant force. Finally, the normal force is set to be equal and opposite to gravity when the plane is on the ground, and zero otherwise.

When you run the simulation, you'll see that the plane takes off only when it has attained a high enough velocity to create sufficient lift to overcome its weight (see Figure 7-16). If you reduce the magnitude of the thrust magThrust to 3 or 4, the plane moves along the runway, but it never takes off. Under the horizontal thrust and drag forces, it attains a maximum horizontal velocity (similar to terminal velocity) that is insufficient to generate enough lift to overcome its weight.

Figure 7-16. *Plane flying thanks to the lift force*

To reiterate, we've made a lot of simplifications in this example. We'll build a much more complete and realistic flight simulator in the final chapter, in which we'll also look at the drag, lift, and thrust forces on an airplane in more detail.

Wind and turbulence

Wind is not itself a force, but it can generate forces. Wind is the movement of air, and it has an associated velocity at each point in space and time. It can be quite complicated, but fairly realistic effects can be achieved even with simple models of the wind. A constant wind blowing over a stationary object can be viewed in a similar way to an object moving through air, with the direction reversed. It generates drag and lift forces in a similar way.

Force due to the wind

As you saw at the beginning of the chapter, moving fluids have an associated dynamic pressure. Wind is nothing but moving air. When wind blows on an object or surface, it therefore exerts a force due to the dynamic pressure.

How do we calculate this force? According to what we said, only the relative velocity matters. So, the force exerted by the wind is just the drag force in reverse, where **w** is the wind velocity:

$$F = \frac{1}{2} \rho A C_d \, w \, \mathbf{w}$$

Hence, we can use the drag force function to model wind, using the wind velocity and a negative drag constant k.

Wind and drag

An object moving in air will, of course, still experience drag, even in the presence of wind. Therefore, the net force due to the motion of the object and that of the air (wind) will be the drag force taking as reference the relative velocity between the object and the air. Therefore, the combined force due to wind and drag is given by the following, where $|\mathbf{w} - \mathbf{v}|$ denotes the magnitude of the vector $(\mathbf{w} - \mathbf{v})$:

$$F = \frac{1}{2} \rho A C_d |\mathbf{w} - \mathbf{v}| (\mathbf{w} - \mathbf{v})$$

Note that |**w** - **v**| is *not* usually equal to the difference $(w - v)$ in the magnitudes of **w** and **v**.

We can use the drag force function to compute the combined effect of wind and drag by using the relative velocity between an object and the air.

Steady and turbulent flow

We now know how to calculate the force on an object in the presence of wind given the wind velocity. But how do we model the wind velocity **w** itself?

The answer is that it depends on the situation we are modeling. The behavior of the wind is rather complicated because it varies both in space and in time. Wind depends on complex atmospheric conditions as well as obstacles such as buildings and trees. However, for most purposes, you'd probably want to keep things as simple as you can get away with. So we'll discuss only some simple ways of modeling the wind velocity.

The simplest model of the wind is to assume that the velocity **w** is constant both in space and time. This corresponds to what is called a uniform and steady flow. A slightly more complicated model is to assume a steady flow (still constant in time) that is constant horizontally but varies with height. This model would account for the fact that the wind speed is lower near the ground and becomes higher farther up.

In the real world, the wind is usually not steady but consists of gusts that blow apparently randomly. The gusts produce what is called turbulent flow, which can make things move in complex ways.

Example: Air bubbles in a steady wind

In this example, we'll model a steady and uniform wind blowing some bubbles in air. The file bubbles-wind.js contains the code. Since it is a little different than in previous examples (because it involves multiple particles), we reproduce the code in full here:

```
var canvas = document.getElementById('canvas');
var context = canvas.getContext('2d');

var bubbles; var t0;
var dt;
var force;
var acc;
var numBubbles = 10;
var g = 10;
var rho = 1;
var rhoP = 0.99;
var kfac = 0.01;
var windvel = new Vector2D(40,0);

window.onload = init;

function init() {
    bubbles = new Array();
    var color = 'rgba(0,200,255,0.5)';
    for (var i=0; i<numBubbles; i++){
        var radius = Math.random()*20+5;
        var V = 4*Math.PI*Math.pow(radius,3)/3;
        var mass = rho*V;
        var bubble = new Ball(radius,color,mass,0,true);
```

```
                bubble.pos2D = new Vector2D(Math.random()*canvas.width,Math.random()*canvas.height);
                bubble.velo2D = new Vector2D((Math.random()-0.5)*20,0);
                bubble.draw(context);
                bubbles.push(bubble);
        }
        to = new Date().getTime();
        animFrame();
};

function animFrame(){
        requestAnimationFrame(animFrame,canvas);
        onTimer();
}
function onTimer(){
        var t1 = new Date().getTime();
        dt = 0.001*(t1-to);
        to = t1;
        if (dt>0.2) {dt=0;};
        move();
}
function move(){
        context.clearRect(0, 0, canvas.width, canvas.height);
        for (var i=0; i<numBubbles; i++){
                var bubble = bubbles[i];
                moveObject(bubble);
                calcForce(bubble);
                updateAccel(bubble.mass);
                updateVelo(bubble);
        }
}
function moveObject(obj){
        obj.pos2D = obj.pos2D.addScaled(obj.velo2D,dt);
        obj.draw(context);
}
function updateAccel(mass){
        acc = force.multiply(1/mass);
}
function updateVelo(obj){
        obj.velo2D = obj.velo2D.addScaled(acc,dt);
}
function calcForce(particle){
        var V = particle.mass/rhoP;
        var k = Math.PI*particle.radius*particle.radius*kfac;
        var gravity = Forces.constantGravity(particle.mass,g);
        var upthrust = Forces.upthrust(rho,V,g);
        var relwind = windvel.subtract(particle.velo2D);
        var wind = Forces.drag(-k,relwind);
        force = Forces.add([gravity, upthrust, wind]);
}
```

In init() we're creating a lot of bubbles as Ball objects and giving each a random radius. (If you have a slow computer, you may want to reduce the number of bubbles!) Their volume and mass are then calculated using the formula for the volume of a sphere and the density of the bubbles, which is specified as 0.99. The bubbles are given a random position and a small random horizontal velocity. Then they are collected into an array, which is then used in the move() method to apply the methods moveObject(), calcForce(), updateAccel() and updateVelo() to each bubble in turn.

In the calcForce() method, three forces are calculated and added: gravity, upthrust, and the wind (drag) force. The upthrust is calculated using the volume of each bubble, worked out using the formula volume = mass/density. To compute the force due to wind, the relative velocity relwind is computed by subtracting the bubble's current velocity from the velocity of the wind windvel, which is given as a constant horizontal vector. The wind/drag force is then calculated by using Forces.drag() with a negative drag coefficient -k and the relative velocity as arguments. Note that k includes a factor equal to the bubble's projected area, taking into account that the drag force is proportional to the area of an object.

If you run the simulation, you'll see that the bubbles drift in the direction of the wind while rising slowly, as you'd expect (see Figure 7-17). Play with the wind velocity and other parameters to see how the motion is modified.

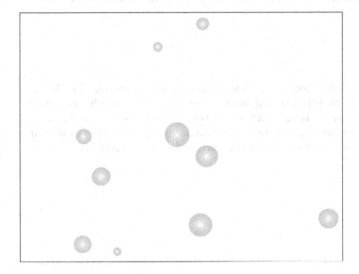

Figure 7-17. *Bubbles in a steady wind*

Modeling turbulence

Turbulence is a complex phenomenon. In fact, it is so complex that you need huge supercomputers with hundreds of processors to compute turbulent flows accurately even for simple configurations. On the other hand, there are numerous approaches for modeling turbulence in an approximate way. One simple approach is to use random numbers.

You can produce effects that look like turbulence by superimposing random noise on an otherwise steady wind field. This exploits the statistical properties of turbulence, which can usually be represented by decomposing the wind velocity at any time in the following way, where $\mathbf{w}_{steady}$ is a steady part and $\mathbf{w}_{fluctuating}$ is a time-varying part that captures the turbulent fluctuations:

$$\mathbf{w} = \mathbf{w}_{steady} + \mathbf{w}_{fluctuating}$$

The steady part $\mathbf{w}_{steady}$ is just a constant vector, as we modeled in the previous bubbles simulation. We can model $\mathbf{w}_{fluctuating}$ by a vector whose components are random numbers that are updated at each timestep. To do this in the bubbles simulation, just add the following line of code in calcForce() before the line that computes relwind:

```
windvel = new Vector2D(20 + (Math.random()-0.5)*1000,(Math.random()-0.5)*1000);
```

We did this and saved the new file as bubbles-turbulence.js. We also added some code to indicate the variation of the wind vector **w** in a function showArrow() called from move(). The code produces a line in the middle of the stage directed along the instantaneous wind direction and with length proportional to the magnitude of the wind velocity.

The preceding line of code specifies the wind velocity **w** as the sum of a steady wind vector (20, 0) that blows to the right at 20 pixels per second, and a random wind vector (Math.random()-0.5)*1000,(Math.random()-0.5)*1000) with x and y components that range from –500 to 500 pixels per second. The wind velocity is the same at all locations on the stage.

Experiment by changing these values to whatever you like. The magnitude of the steady wind (here set by the value of 20) gives the bubbles a steady drift. The magnitude of the fluctuations (here set by the factor of 1000), controls the gustiness of the wind and makes the bubbles fluctuate. You can produce a fairly convincing turbulence effect in this way.

Summary

This chapter introduced a number of forces that act on solid objects in contact with other solid objects or with fluids. If you are simulating nearly anything on Earth, chances are you'll need to model these forces. What you learned in this chapter has given you a solid foundation upon which you can build to create more complex effects and simulations. In the final chapter, you will have the opportunity to develop more complete simulations using the physics explained here. Meanwhile, in the next chapter, you will be introduced to a new type of force that produces oscillatory (spring-like) motion.

CHAPTER 8

Restoring Forces: Springs and Oscillations

Springs are among the most useful tools you'll come across, especially for creating interesting physics effects. A great many systems can be modeled using springs and spring-like motion. Therefore, learning the basics of spring motion is time well spent. But beware: springs are strangely addictive!

Topics covered in this chapter include the following:

- **Free oscillations:** An object will oscillate under the action of a spring force, also known as a *restoring force.*

- **Damped oscillations:** Damping dissipates the energy of oscillations so that they die out with time.

- **Forced oscillations:** Oscillations can be driven by external forces that sustain them against damping forces.

- **Coupled oscillators:** Interesting effects can be produced by using multiple springs and objects coupled together.

Springs and oscillations: Basic concepts

We introduced oscillations back in Chapter 3, while discussing sinusoidal waves and their combinations (refer to the section "Using trig functions for animation"). An *oscillation* is a repeating motion around some central position. Simple examples of oscillating systems include a pendulum and a swing.

Oscillations abound in natural systems, too: trees oscillate under a blowing wind, and floating objects oscillate on the water surface because of passing waves. Man-made mechanisms that include springs involve oscillations. Hence, there is an intuitive association between oscillations and springs; in fact, we will use the terms *oscillations* and *spring-like motion* interchangeably. This association is more than verbal: oscillating systems can usually be modeled using virtual "springs."

Spring-like motion

You've already met spring-like motion in this book, probably without realizing it. The floating ball simulation in the preceding chapter provided an example in which the ball oscillated on the water surface in a spring-like fashion. Many other things undergo spring-like motion: the suspension mechanism of a car; and the swaying of a tree, its branches, and their leaves in the wind. Other things, although they don't necessarily appear to be spring-like, can nevertheless be modeled using springs: deformable bodies such as ropes, clothes, and hair. Surely then, there must be common characteristics that these systems exhibit that make them amenable to modeling using springs. So, what are the general characteristics of oscillating systems?

Restoring force, damping, and forcing

An oscillating system will usually involve the following ingredients:

- An *equilibrium position* in which an object would remain if it were not moving.

- A *restoring force* that pulls the object back toward the equilibrium position if it is displaced.

- A *damping force* that reduces the oscillations with time.

- A *driving force* that displaces the object from its equilibrium position.

Of those, the first two are essential to generate oscillations, whereas the last two may or may not be present, depending on the system. Although more complex systems may not appear to show these characteristics, they can be composed of (or be modeled by) component parts that do—for example, a rope can be represented as a chain of springs.

In understanding the roles of the restoring force, damping, and forcing, a relevant concept is that of *amplitude*. The amplitude of an oscillation is the maximum displacement from the equilibrium position. If you pull a swing away from its equilibrium position and then let go, the initial displacement will be the amplitude of the oscillation.

The restoring force changes the displacement with time, but it does not change the amplitude (maximum displacement). The amplitude depends on the amount of energy in the system. A damping force takes away energy from the system and therefore reduces the amplitude with time. This is what would happen if, after initially displacing it, you left the swing to oscillate on its own. A driving force puts energy into the system and therefore tends to increase the amplitude of the oscillations. With both damping and forcing being present, it is possible for the energy put into the system to compensate exactly for the energy lost by damping. In that case, the amplitude remains constant with time, as if only a restoring force were present. In the swing example, this is achieved by pushing the swing periodically with the right amount of force.

Hooke's law

In most oscillating systems, the force law that governs the restoring force is known as Hooke's law (because a gentleman named Robert Hooke discovered it at some point in history).

Hooke's law is quite simple. We'll explain it for springs first because that's the original form of the law. Take a look at Figure 8-1, which shows a spring of natural length l, fixed at one end, that is then stretched by an amount x, so that its length becomes $l + x$.

Figure 8-1. *A stretched spring experiences a restoring force proportional to the extension x*

Hooke's law says that the spring will be pulled back by a force of magnitude F given by this equation:

$$F = -k\,x$$

In other words, the restoring force is proportional to the extension x. The constant of proportionality k is known as the *spring constant*, and it is a measure of the stiffness of the spring. The greater the value of k is, the greater the force will be for a given extension, so that the spring will be pulled back more strongly when stretched.

The minus sign indicates that the force is in the opposite direction to the extension. So if the spring is compressed instead, the force will push back to increase its length.

The vector form of the equation is this, where now **r** is interpreted as the displacement vector of the free endpoint of the spring:

$$\mathbf{F} = -k\,\mathbf{r}$$

For most of what we'll do in this chapter (and probably for what you'll want to do, too), we won't care much about the actual spring. What we'll be more interested in is the motion of a particle attached to the end of a spring. How would such an object move? As every kid knows, it will oscillate about the equilibrium position.

In fact, we could get rid of the spring altogether and just consider the effect of the restoring force on the particle. This is what we'll do in many examples. In such a case, the displacement vector **r** in Hooke's law is interpreted as the displacement from the equilibrium position about which the particle is oscillating, as shown in Figure 8-2.

Figure 8-2. *A particle oscillating about an equilibrium position*

A word of warning before we end this section: it should not be assumed that all oscillations obey Hooke's law; many don't. However, a great many types of moving systems follow Hooke's law, at least approximately. So we'll stick with Hooke's law in this chapter.

Free oscillations

Let's start by modeling *free oscillations*. What that means is that the system oscillates purely under the action of the restoring force, without any other force. Of course, for an object to oscillate, something (an applied force) must have moved it away from its equilibrium position in the first place. But what we are interested in here is what happens after that initial forcing is removed and the oscillating system is left to itself.

The spring force function

To begin with, we need to create a new force function in the Forces object for the restoring force. Let's call it spring(). It is a very simple function:

```
Forces.spring = function(k,r){
    return r.multiply(-k);
}
```

The function spring() takes two arguments, which are the spring constant k and the displacement vector r (this is just the vector **r** in the previous formulas). It returns the restoring force $\mathbf{F} = -k\,\mathbf{r}$.

Let's now use that function to create a basic oscillator.

Creating a basic oscillator

You know what's coming next, don't you? Here is some code extracted from the file basic-oscillator.js that creates the object that we want to oscillate as a Ball object called ball (we're omitting the standard lines on the canvas and context variables). We don't actually create a spring (in the visual sense) but instead another Ball object that we call attractor, whose position will be the equilibrium position. Both have an initial velocity of zero and are placed some distance apart by giving them different position vectors pos2D:

```
var ball;
var displ;
var center = new Vector2D(0.5*canvas.width,0.5*canvas.height);
var m = 1;
var kSpring = 1;
var t0, dt;
var acc, force;
var animId;

window.onload = init;

function init() {
    // create a ball
    ball = new Ball(15,'#0000cc',m,0,true);
    ball.pos2D = new Vector2D(100,50);
    ball.draw(context);
    // create an attractor
    var attractor = new Ball(2,'#000000');
    attractor.pos2D = center;
    attractor.draw(context_bg);
    // make the ball move
    t0 = new Date().getTime();
    animFrame();
}
```

The animation code is pretty standard; the only novelty is in the calcForce() method:

```
function calcForce(){
    displ = ball.pos2D.subtract(center);
    force = Forces.spring(kSpring,displ);
}
```

This code is very simple: it first calculates the displacement vector displ of the object relative to the attractor and then uses it to calculate the spring force that the attractor exerts on the object. The parameter kSpring is the spring constant k.

Run the code and you'll see the ball oscillate about the attractor, as expected. Now change the spring constant value from 1 to 10. This gives you a stiff spring. If you run the code again, you'll see the ball oscillate faster. If you want it to oscillate at a different amplitude, just change the initial position in basic-oscillations.js.

Next change the value of k back to 1, then change the initial velocity of the ball to (200,0):

```
ball.velo2D = new Vector2D(200,0);
```

When you run the code, you should now see the ball "orbit" the attractor in some sort of oval trajectory. It's a bit like what you saw with gravity in Chapter 6. Both gravity and the spring force are attractive forces that always act toward a point. But gravity *decreases* with distance, whereas the spring force *increases* with distance. That's because gravity is proportional to $1/r^2$, whereas the spring force is proportional to r, where r is the distance from the center of attraction.

Simple harmonic motion

The type of oscillatory motion you've just seen is technically called *simple harmonic motion* (SHM). An object undergoes SHM if the only force acting on it is the spring force, as was the case in the previous example.

Because the only force in SHM is the restoring force $\mathbf{F} = -k\mathbf{r}$, and Newton's second law says that $\mathbf{F} = m\mathbf{a}$, these two equations together tell us that for SHM the following is true:

$$m\,\mathbf{a} = -k\,\mathbf{r}$$

Dividing both sides of this equation by m gives this:

$$\mathbf{a} = -\frac{k}{m}\mathbf{r}$$

Here m is the mass of the oscillating particle, and k is the spring constant, so the ratio k/m is a constant. This equation therefore tells us that the acceleration of the oscillating particle is proportional to its displacement vector from the center. The constant of proportionality is negative, meaning that the acceleration is always opposite to the displacement vector (it always points toward the center because the displacement vector always points away from the center by definition). See Figure 8-3.

Figure 8-3. *The acceleration in SHM always points toward the center, opposite to displacement*

Remember back in Chapter 3 where we talked about derivatives and said that acceleration is the second derivative of displacement? This means the following is true:

$$\mathbf{a} = \frac{d^2\mathbf{r}}{dt^2}$$

Therefore we can write the SHM equation $\mathbf{a} = -(k/m)\mathbf{r}$ in the equivalent form:

$$\frac{d^2\mathbf{r}}{dt^2} = -\frac{k}{m}\mathbf{r}$$

Stating it this way makes it clear that the equation that governs SHM is a second-order differential equation, as described in Chapter 5. What the animation code in basic-oscillator.js has been doing is to solve this second-order differential equation numerically using the Euler scheme (again as described in Chapter 5).

In fact the preceding differential equation can also be solved analytically to give a formula for the displacement as a function of time. This is an exercise in college-level calculus, and here is the solution, where $\mathbf{A}$ and $\mathbf{B}$ are constant vectors that depend on the initial conditions, and ω is the angular velocity of the oscillation (see Chapter 3):

$$\mathbf{r} = \mathbf{A}\cos(\omega t) + \mathbf{B}\sin(\omega t)$$

Hence, SHM consists of the sum of a sine and a cosine function. This is not surprising because SHM is basically an oscillatory motion and, as you know from Chapter 3, sin and cos are oscillatory functions. The value of ω sets the frequency and therefore the period of oscillation, whereas the values of $\mathbf{A}$ and $\mathbf{B}$ set the amplitude of the oscillations (the maximum displacement of the object from its equilibrium position).

Anyone with a little knowledge of calculus can immediately write down the velocity vector $\mathbf{v}$ by differentiating the preceding expression for $\mathbf{r}$ because $\mathbf{v} = d\mathbf{r}/dt$. The result is this:

$$\mathbf{v} = -\omega\mathbf{A}\sin(\omega t) + \omega\mathbf{B}\cos(\omega t)$$

What are the values of $\mathbf{A}$, $\mathbf{B}$, and ω? $\mathbf{A}$ and $\mathbf{B}$ are set by the initial conditions that you specify for the displacement and velocity of the object at the start (the values of $\mathbf{r}$ and $\mathbf{v}$ at time $t = 0$). Let's call the initial displacement vector $\mathbf{r}_0$ and the initial velocity vector $\mathbf{v}_0$. If we now put $t = 0$ into the preceding equations for $\mathbf{r}$ and $\mathbf{v}$ because $\cos(0) = 1$ and $\sin(0) = 0$, we get this:

$$\mathbf{r}_0 = \mathbf{A}$$

We also get the following:

$$\mathbf{v}_0 = \omega\mathbf{B}$$

This tells us right away that $\mathbf{A} = \mathbf{r}_0$ and $\mathbf{B} = \mathbf{v}_0/\omega$.

If you were to solve that differential equation, you would also find that the angular velocity ω is actually given by this formula:

$$\omega = \sqrt{\frac{k}{m}}$$

This is called the *natural frequency* of the system. If the oscillating system is given an initial perturbation (to move the object away from its equilibrium position), but is thereafter left on its own, it will oscillate at that frequency and only at that frequency in the absence of other influences such as damping.

Now, if you remember (again from Chapter 3) that $\omega = 2\pi f$ and $f = 1/T$, where f is the frequency (the number of oscillations per second) and T is the period of oscillation (the time to complete one oscillation), you can use the preceding formula to obtain both the frequency and period of the oscillation in terms of the parameters k and m:

$$f = \frac{1}{2\pi}\sqrt{\frac{k}{m}}$$

$$T = 2\pi\sqrt{\frac{m}{k}}$$

These formulas tell you that if you increase the spring stiffness k, the frequency of the oscillations will increase and its period will decrease (it will oscillate faster). If you increase the mass of the oscillating particle instead, the reverse will happen, and it will oscillate more slowly. Go ahead and try it!

These are the only two parameters that affect the frequency and period; the initial position and velocity of the object do not. You might think that if the object is initially farther away from the center it will take longer to complete one oscillation. But not with SHM. What happens is that if the object is farther away, it experiences a greater acceleration at the start so that on average it acquires a greater velocity, which compensates for the longer distance it has to travel to complete one oscillation. Skeptical? Try it by timing the oscillations with a stopwatch or outputting the time.

In fact, we can do better than that. Let's plot a graph.

Oscillations and numerical accuracy

To plot a graph, we modify `basic-oscillations.js` by changing the initial position of the oscillating object as follows:

```
object.pos2D = new Vector2D(100,50);
```

We also alter the position of the attractor:

```
var center = new Vector2D(0.5*canvas.width,50);
```

After adding some extra bits of code to plot a graph showing the displacement of the object against time, and to run the simulation for a fixed duration (20 s), we then save the file as `free-oscillations.js`.

Here is the code that sets up and plots the graph:

```
function setupGraph(){
    //graph= new Graph(context,xmin,xmax,ymin,ymax,xorig,yorig,xwidth,ywidth);
    graph = new Graph(context_bg,0,20,-250,250,50,300,600,300);
    graph.drawgrid(5,1,50,50);
    graph.drawaxes('t (s)','displacement (px)');
}
function plotGraph(){
    graph.plot([t], [displ.x], '#ff0000', false, true);
    graph.plot([t], [displ.y], '#0000ff', false, true);
}
```

The `plotGraph()` method, which is called at each timestep, invokes the `plot()` method of Graph to plot the x and y coordinates of the displacement of the ball relative to the attractor.

If you now run the code, you'll see something like Figure 8-4. Sure enough, the horizontal displacement (x) of the object with time is a sinusoidal wave, as we said in the previous section. The vertical displacement is always zero because of the initial condition we chose. But it's easy to change it by giving the object an initial vertical component of velocity or a different initial vertical position. Then the y displacement would also vary sinusoidally. You can also change the values of k, m, and the initial position of the object to verify the statements we made at the end of the previous section about how the frequency and period of oscillations vary (or not) with these parameters.

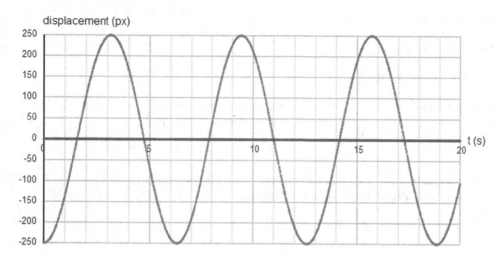

Figure 8-4. *Plotting the displacement of an oscillating object as a function of time*

Let's now see how accurate our simulation is by comparing the trajectory of the oscillating object with what the analytical solution given in the previous section predicts.

To do this, we first modify free-oscillations.js to free-oscillations2.js by changing the initial velocity of the oscillating object as follows:

```
object.velo2D=new Vector2D(0,50);
```

Then we add code that calculates the values of **A**, **B**, and ω (defined as variables A, B and omega in the code) using the previously given equations $\omega = \sqrt{(k/m)}$, $\mathbf{A} = \mathbf{r}_0$, and $\mathbf{B} = \mathbf{v}_0/\omega$. This is done in the init() method, which therefore contains these additional lines:

```
omega = Math.sqrt(kSpring/m);
A = ball.pos2D.subtract(center);
B = ball.velo2D.multiply(1/omega);
```

We then modify the code to create two Graph objects graphX and graphY (set up in a suitably modified setupGraph() method), on which we plot the *x* and *y* displacements, respectively, in plotGraph(). In the plotGraph() method, we then insert the following additional lines to plot the *x* and *y* components of the analytical solution $\mathbf{r} = \mathbf{A} \cos(\omega t) + \mathbf{B} \sin(\omega t)$:

```
var r = A.multiply(Math.cos(omega*t)).add(B.multiply(Math.sin(omega*t)));
graphX.plot([t], [r.x], '#00ff00', false, true);
graphY.plot([t], [r.y], '#ff00ff', false, true);
```

If you now run the code, you'll see the object orbiting the attractor in an elongated orbit, and you'll see a pair of graphs for each of the horizontal and vertical displacements of the object. In each pair of graphs, one corresponds to the analytical solution computed by the specified formulas, whereas the other corresponds to the numerical solution as computed by the simulation. You can see that they are quite close to each other, practically overlapping (see Figure 8-5). Euler integration is not doing such a bad job in this case.

Figure 8-5. *Comparing the numerical and analytical solutions for the oscillator*

However, if you now change the value of kSpring to 20, for example, so that the "spring" is stiffer and the object moves faster, you'll see that the difference between the two is more significant, signaling that Euler is losing accuracy. If you try a value for kSpring greater than about 100, then you may find that Euler gives you complete rubbish, and the object ends up in the wrong place at the wrong time. So here you begin to see that you can get the wrong physics if you are not careful with your integrator, especially in the case of springs. You'll see how to overcome this problem in Chapter 14. Meanwhile, for the rest of this chapter we'll avoid very high values of the spring constant.

Damped oscillations

In the previous examples, the oscillations just go on forever. In practice, this rarely happens. Oscillating systems are usually *damped*. That means the oscillations are reduced and die out in time as energy is removed from the system. This is similar to the drag force, which dissipates the kinetic energy of a moving object and makes it slow down. To implement damping in our springs, we need a damping force.

Damping force

The *damping force* is usually modeled as being proportional to the velocity of the moving object. This means that, at any instant in time, it is given by the following equation, where c is a constant known as the damping coefficient, and the minus sign indicates that the force is in the opposite direction to the velocity:

$$\mathbf{F} = -c\,\mathbf{v}$$

Notice that this is exactly the same form as the force law for linear drag. We could, therefore, use the linearDrag() function to implement damping in spring motion. However, although drag is certainly a form of damping, it is not physically the only form of damping, although the two terms are sometimes used interchangeably. Drag is the resistive force exerted by a fluid on a moving object immersed in it. Spring damping, on the other hand can be caused by external factors such as fluid drag or external friction, or to internal factors such as internal friction, which arise from the molecular material properties of springs. In fact, you could have both internal damping due to spring resistance and drag due to fluid resistance side by side (with different coefficients, of course). For example, a mass suspended on a spring and oscillating in a fluid such as air or water experiences both internal friction and fluid drag. For these reasons, we prefer to create a separate function for damping. The form of this function is identical to that for linearDrag(), as shown in this listing:

```
Forces.damping = function(c,vel){
    var force;
    var velMag = vel.length();
    if (velMag>0) {
        force = vel.multiply(-c);
    }
    else {
        force = new Vector2D(0,0);
    }
    return force;
}
```

The effect of damping on oscillations

We'll now modify free-oscillations.js to handle damping in addition to the spring force. The new file is called damped-oscillations.js, and basically introduces a new force: damping. So one difference from free-oscillator.js is that it declares a damping coefficient cDamping and assigns it a value:

```
var cDamping = 0.5;
```

The other difference is that it includes a damping force in calcForce() and adds it to the spring force to work out the resultant force:

```
function calcForce(){
    displ = ball.pos2D.subtract(center);
    var restoring = Forces.spring(kSpring,displ);
    var damping = Forces.damping(cDamping,ball.velo2D);
    force = Forces.add([restoring, damping]);
}
```

That's it. If you run the code with kSpring = 10 and cDamping = 0.5, you'll see something like what's shown in Figure 8-6. The oscillations die out in time, and the object eventually settles at the equilibrium position, as you'd expect.

Figure 8-6. *Damped oscillations*

At this point, you should play with the damping constant cDamping to see what you get. Choose a lower value, and you'll see the oscillations persist longer, whereas a higher value will kill them off sooner. You might think that the greater the value of *c*, the quicker the object will stop. In fact, there is a critical value of *c* for which the oscillations die in the minimum time. At this value, there are no oscillations at all. The object simply moves smoothly to the equilibrium position without oscillating beyond it. This is called *critical damping*, and an example is shown in Figure 8-7. For kSpring = 10 in our simulation, the critical value of cDamping is about 5.5, and the object reaches its equilibrium position in about 1.5 seconds. If you increase cDamping beyond this critical value, for example to 10 or 20, you'll see that the object actually takes longer to reach its equilibrium location. This is because the increased damping slows it down so much that, although it does not go beyond the equilibrium position, it takes longer to get there. Critical damping is a very useful phenomenon that's applied in things like damping mechanisms in doors.

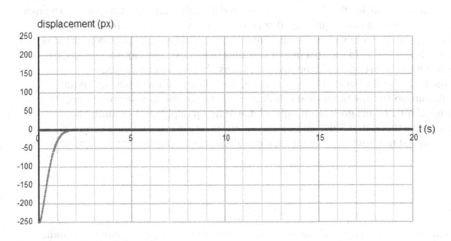

Figure 8-7. *Critical damping*

Analytical solutions for oscillations with damping

This brief section is for enthusiasts. You may safely skip it if complicated formulas are not your thing. The point of this section is to show you how the analytical solution quoted previously for free oscillations changes in the presence of damping, and how well our simulation does at reproducing it. Thus, it is more educational than practical.

Newton's second law for oscillations under a spring force $\mathbf{F} = -k\mathbf{r}$, together with a damping force $\mathbf{F} = -c\mathbf{v}$ is the following:

$$m\,\mathbf{a} = -k\,\mathbf{r} - c\,\mathbf{v}$$

This can be written in terms of derivatives as (after dividing both sides by m):

$$\frac{d^2\mathbf{r}}{dt^2} = -\frac{k}{m}\mathbf{r} - \frac{c}{m}\frac{d\mathbf{r}}{dt}$$

The analytical solution of this differential equation is given by the following:

$$\mathbf{r} = \left[\mathbf{A}\cos(\omega_d t) + \mathbf{B}\sin(\omega_d t) \right] \exp(-\gamma\,\omega_0\,t)$$

where the constants γ, ω_0, ω_d, $\mathbf{A}$ and $\mathbf{B}$ are given by the following:

$$\gamma = \frac{c}{2\sqrt{m\,k}}$$

$$\omega_0 = \sqrt{\frac{k}{m}}$$

$$\omega_d = \omega_0 \sqrt{1 - \gamma^2}$$

$$\mathbf{A} = \mathbf{r}_0$$

$$\mathbf{B} = \frac{(\mathbf{v}_0 + \gamma\,\omega_0\,\mathbf{r}_0)}{\omega_d}$$

Comparing this with the previous solution without damping, you'll notice that there is an additional exponential factor in the expression for $\mathbf{r}$, which is responsible for the decay in the sinusoidal oscillations (see Chapter 3). The new parameter γ is due to the damping. In the absence of damping, $c = 0$ and so $\gamma = 0$; the solution then reduces to that without damping. Note also that the angular frequency of the oscillations is now ω_d (because it appears in the sine and cosine), which is less than the natural frequency ω_0 in the absence of damping (which was previously denoted by ω).

We coded up these equations in a modified version of free-oscillations.js that we call damped-oscillations2.js. Take a look at the code if you wish. If you run the code, you'll find that there is again some discrepancy between this analytical solution and the numerical solution computed by the simulation. In fact, sometimes you might find that the oscillating object goes seemingly wild, ending up in places it shouldn't be. The important take-away message from all this is that Euler integration simply does not cut it when it comes to simulations like this, except for the simplest motions. In Chapter 14, we shall discuss alternative integration schemes that overcome this problem.

Forced oscillations

In the presence of damping, the oscillations of a system will die out in time. Therefore, a force is needed to sustain oscillations or to initiate them in the first place. That's called a driving force, or forcing.

Driving forces

Driving forces can be of any form, so let's denote them simply by $\mathbf{f}(t)$. This simply means that the force is a function of time without specifying the form of the force law at all.

For example, we could have a periodic force of the form $\mathbf{f} = \mathbf{A}\cos(\omega t) + \mathbf{B}\sin(\omega t)$, where $\mathbf{A}$ and $\mathbf{B}$ are constant vectors that give the amplitude (maximum magnitude) and direction of the force, and ω is the angular frequency of the forcing. This could, for example, represent an oscillator interacting with and driving another, such as a periodic wind blowing over a suspension bridge and causing it to vibrate.

Let's start with an example.

Example: A periodic driving force

We'll start by modifying damped-oscillations2.js. We do not want to plot the analytical solutions here, so we get rid of the relevant lines in plotGraph(), but we'll keep the three lines that compute gamma, omega0, and omegad in the init() method. These are the variables corresponding to the constants γ, ω_0, and ω_d. After deleting any unnecessary variable declarations, we rename the file as forced-oscillations.js.

Remember that omega0 (ω_0) is the natural angular frequency of the undamped system, and omegad (ω_d) is the angular frequency with damping. Let's begin by adding the following lines to calcForce():

```
var forcing = new Vector2D(200*Math.cos(2*omegad*t)+200*Math.sin(2*omegad*t),0);
force = Forces.add([restoring, damping, forcing]);
```

This adds a driving force of the form $\mathbf{f} = \mathbf{A}\cos(\omega t) + \mathbf{B}\sin(\omega t)$, with $\mathbf{A}$ and $\mathbf{B}$ both of magnitude 200 and in the x direction (we need fairly large values to see a noticeable difference of the forcing on the oscillations), and $\omega = 2\,\omega_d$. So we are forcing the system with a driving force that varies sinusoidally with time at an angular frequency that is twice the frequency of the damped system.

Run the code, and you'll see that the oscillations start to die out as they did before without the forcing. Then, after a while, the object starts to oscillate at around twice the frequency it did before, but with a much smaller amplitude. This carries on indefinitely. So, the effect of the sinusoidal driving force is to eventually make the system oscillate at the driving frequency (albeit at reduced amplitude), rather than the frequency that the system would prefer to oscillate at on its own. You can try this with different forcing frequencies. For example, if you use $\omega_d/2$, half the damped system's frequency, the oscillations will eventually have a frequency of half the initial, unforced frequency. The conclusion is that if you force a system to oscillate at a frequency other than its natural frequency, it will still oscillate but at a reduced amplitude.

Now make the forcing frequency exactly equal to ω_d by modifying the forcing vector to this:

```
var forcing = new Vector2D(200*Math.cos(omegad*t)+200*Math.sin(omegad*t),0);
```

When you run the code, you'll now see that the oscillations quickly settle into equilibrium at the original frequency ω_d and maintain a large, constant amplitude without decaying. The system is now "happy" because it is forced at exactly the frequency it likes to oscillate. Hence, it settles down quickly and oscillates with a large amplitude. So, although damping reduces the energy of the system, forcing puts energy back into the system and sustains the oscillations.

When the forcing frequency is equal to the natural frequency of the oscillating system, we have what is called *resonance*. It happens in lots of situations, from pushing a child's swing to the tuning of radio circuits. Resonance can have bad effects, too, such as unwanted vibrations in bridges due to periodic wind gusts. In fact, resonance due to wind gusts was infamously responsible for the collapse of the Tacoma Narrows Bridge in Washington in 1940.

Example: A random driving force

Next, let's try a random forcing. This is as easy as replacing one line of code. Let's try this first:

```
var forcing = new Vector2D(1000*Math.random(),0);
```

This applies a random force of up to 1,000 units in the positive *x* direction (to the right). If this were the only force, it would send the object flying off to the right, never to be seen again. But the presence of the restoring force (as its name suggests) pulls the object back toward the attractor. In fact, because the restoring force is proportional to the displacement from the attractor, the farther away the object moves, the stronger it gets pulled back. This creates an interesting effect that you'll surely want to experiment with. Because we made the force act only to the right, the object will spend most of its time on the right side of the attractor, although it occasionally gets pulled slightly to the left.

To make the oscillations more symmetrical around the attractor, simply change that line of code to this:

```
var forcing = new Vector2D(1000*(Math.random()-0.5),0);
```

This produces a random force with an *x* component between –500 and +500, where the minus sign means that the force is directed to the left instead of to the right. Run the code, and you'll get a nonperiodic oscillator (the object oscillates without regularity).

Finally, let's make the object oscillate under a random force in 2D by modifying the same line of code to the following:

```
var forcing = new Vector2D(1000*(Math.random()-0.5),1000*(Math.random()-0.5));
```

If you run the code, you'll see that the system quickly goes into a state where the oscillations in the *x* and *y* directions are of comparable magnitude, with the object hovering around the attractor (see Figure 8-8). The object is kicked in different directions at every timestep, but it is also pulled back toward the attractor. It's not allowed to get away, no matter how large the forcing is, because the farther it goes the more strongly it gets pulled back. That's an interesting effect. It's some kind of crazy random orbiting motion. Or maybe even like a bee buzzing around a flower. Play with that one for sure!

Figure 8-8. *Oscillator with random forcing*

Gravity as a driving force: bungee jumping

Let's now move on to something a little different: bungee jumping! Someone jumps off a bridge or similar structure tied to an elastic cord whose other end is tied to a fixed support on the structure. The elastic cord has a natural unstretched length, say cordLength. So if the distance of the jumper from the fixed support is less than cordLength, gravity and drag are the only forces on the jumper. But once that distance exceeds cordLength, the elastic (spring) force will come into effect, and pull the jumper back.

So here gravity is acting as the driving force, so that $f(t) = mg$, where m is the mass of the jumper. It's a constant forcing, unlike the types of forcing discussed before. The main damping mechanism is provided by drag through the air, so it can be implemented using the Forces.drag() method. Finally, the spring force is applied only if the jumper's distance from the fixed support exceeds the natural unstretched length of the cord, cordLength. This distance may be less than cordLength initially (before the jumper jumps off some supporting structure), but also whenever the jumper bounces back high enough.

Because this example is a little different from the last few, we'll list the full source code and then go through the main points. The file is called simply bungee.js:

```
var canvas = document.getElementById('canvas');
var context = canvas.getContext('2d');

var jumper;
var fixedPoint;
var displ = new Vector2D(0,0);
var center = new Vector2D(0.5*canvas.width,50);
var mass = 90;
var g = 20;
var kDamping = 0.02;
var kSpring = 25;
var cordLength = 100;
var t0, dt;
var acc, force;
var animId;

window.onload = init;

function init() {
    // create a bungee jumper
    jumper = new StickMan();
    jumper.mass = mass;
    jumper.pos2D = center;
    jumper.draw(context);
    // create a fixedPoint
    fixedPoint = new Ball(2,'#000000');
    fixedPoint.pos2D = center;
    fixedPoint.draw(context);
    // make the ball move
    t0 = new Date().getTime();
    animFrame();
};
```

```
function animFrame(){
    animId = requestAnimationFrame(animFrame,canvas);
    onTimer();
}
function onTimer(){
    var t1 = new Date().getTime();
    dt = 0.001*(t1-t0);
    t0 = t1;
    if (dt>0.2) {dt=0;};
    move();
}
function move(){
    context.clearRect(0, 0, canvas.width, canvas.height);
    drawSpring(jumper);
    moveObject(jumper);
    calcForce(jumper);
    updateAccel();
    updateVelo(jumper);
}
function drawSpring(obj){
    fixedPoint.draw(context);
    context.save();
    if (displ.length() > cordLength){
        context.lineStyle = '#999999';
        context.lineWidth = 2;
    }else{
        context.lineStyle = '#cccccc';
        context.lineWidth = 1;
    }
    context.moveTo(center.x,center.y);
    context.lineTo(obj.x,obj.y);
    context.stroke();
    context.restore();
}
function moveObject(obj){
    obj.pos2D = obj.pos2D.addScaled(obj.velo2D,dt);
    obj.draw(context);
}
function calcForce(obj){
    displ = obj.pos2D.subtract(center);
    var gravity = Forces.constantGravity(mass,g);
    var damping = Forces.drag(kDamping,obj.velo2D);
    var extension = displ.subtract(displ.unit().multiply(cordLength));
    var restoring;
    if (displ.length() > cordLength) {
        restoring = Forces.spring(kSpring,extension);
    }else{
        restoring = new Vector2D(0,0);
    }
    force = Forces.add([gravity, damping, restoring]);
}
```

```
function updateAccel(){
    acc = force.multiply(1/mass);
}
function updateVelo(obj){
    obj.velo2D = obj.velo2D.addScaled(acc,dt);
}
```

Notice that we are creating two objects here: a fixed point and a jumper. The jumper is an instance of StickMan, a poor man's version of a man, which you are welcome to improve upon by editing the file stickman.js.

First, note the large value we used for the spring constant kSpring (25). That's because we've specified the mass of the jumper as 90 in bungee.js, instead of 1 as in all the previous simulations. This mirrors the fact that, if you want to make a big guy oscillate at the end of an elastic cord, the cord had better be pretty stiff!

Looking next at the calcForce() method, we see that we are including gravity, damping, and restoring forces, as discussed previously. The first two are implemented in a straightforward way as usual. There are two differences in how we calculate the restoring force compared with earlier examples. First, the displacement vector that must be used to calculate the restoring force is now the displacement vector of the end point of the elastic cord (the extension), as explained at the beginning of this chapter, not the displacement of the object from the fixed support. Therefore, we first calculate that extension as a vector in the following line:

```
var extension = displ.subtract(displ.unit().multiply(cordLength));
```

Note the cunning use of the unit() method, newly added to the Vector2D object, where vec.unit() returns a vector of unit length in the direction of vector vec.

We then supply extension as the second argument in Forces.spring().

The second difference is that the restoring force is nonzero only if the object is farther from the support than the length of the cord. That's the same as saying that displ.length() > cordLength. This explains the code within the if block:

```
if (displ.length() > cordLength) {
    restoring = Forces.spring(kSpring,extension);
}else{
    restoring = new Vector2D(0,0);
}
```

The other new feature is that we've included a drawSpring() method, called within the move() method, that draws a line to represent the elastic cord at each timestep. The line is drawn thinner and fainter when the cord is unstretched. As usual, run the code and feel free to play with the parameters. The initial position of the object is the same as that of the fixed support. This makes the object oscillate in a vertical straight line (it makes the oscillations 1D). To make it 2D, simply change the initial x-coordinate of the object in bungee.js; for example:

```
object.pos2D = new Vector2D(300,50);
```

A screenshot of the demo is shown in Figure 8-9.

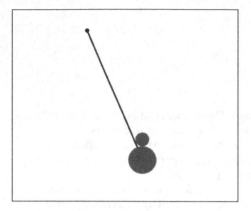

Figure 8-9. *A bungee jump simulation*

Example: Driving force by user interaction

User interaction can also be viewed as some kind of forcing. In the following example, we will build a simulation in which the user can click and drag the object and release it in any location. This will disturb the system, setting it to oscillate.

It is fairly straightforward to modify the bungee simulation to do what we want here. We'll call the new file `dragging-oscillations.js`. Among other modifications, we change the mass of the object to 1 and add code to enable dragging. Take a look at the file if you want to see how this is done—the details are not particularly interesting for our present purposes. The main point here is that the code changes enable you, the user, to exert a driving force whenever you feel like by dragging and releasing the object. Hence, the forcing is not specified by a mathematical function but is a product of random human interaction.

The essential physics does not change, however, as reflected in the `calcForce()` method:

```
function calcForce(obj){
    displ = obj.pos2D.subtract(center);
    var gravity = Forces.constantGravity(mass,g);
    var damping = Forces.drag(kDamping,obj.velo2D);
    var extension = displ.subtract(displ.unit().multiply(springLength));
    var restoring = Forces.spring(kSpring,extension);
    force = Forces.add([gravity, damping, restoring]);
}
```

In `calcForce()`, we include gravity as before, while damping is included using the `Forces.damping()` function. We then calculate the extension of the spring and feed it into the restoring force as before. However, because this is a spring that can also be compressed and is not an elastic cord, we apply the restoring force even if the extension is negative, so we have deleted the `if` statement we had in the previous bungee example.

Run the code and you'll see the object fall down under gravity and be pulled back again by the spring, oscillating with reducing amplitude due to the damping. If you drag the object and release it, it oscillates again thanks to the forcing.

Coupled oscillators: Multiple springs and objects

In all the examples so far, we've considered only a single object and spring system. Effects get even more interesting when you couple more than one object and spring system together. In fact, you can create extended systems based on objects with masses connected by springs. In the next subsection, you'll see an example of what can be done. Then we'll look at more complicated examples in Chapter 13 when we model deformable bodies.

Example: A chain of objects connected by springs

What you'll create is shown in Figure 8-10: a number of balls connected by springs, with the first ball connected to a support. The support will then be moved around, causing the chain of suspended balls to move around, too.

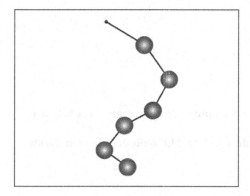

Figure 8-10. *A chain of objects held together by springs*

The forces that will be modeled include gravity, damping, and restoring force. The springs will have a natural length, as in the last couple of examples. Each ball will therefore experience gravity, damping, a restoring force due to a spring above, and another restoring force due to a spring below (except for the last ball). The springs themselves will be assumed to be massless.

The code is in a file called `coupled-oscillations.js`. We first list the variable declarations and `init()` function:

```
var canvas = document.getElementById('canvas');
var context = canvas.getContext('2d');

var balls;
var support;
var center = new Vector2D(0.5*canvas.width,50);
var g = 20;
var kDamping = 0.5;
var kSpring = 10;
var springLength = 50;
var numBalls = 6;
var t0, t, dt;
var acc, force;
var animId;

window.onload = init;
```

```
function init() {
    // create a support
    support = new Ball(2,'#000000');
    support.pos2D = center;
    support.draw(context);
    // create a bunch of balls
    balls = new Array();
    for (var i=0; i<numBalls; i++){
        var ball = new Ball(15,'#0000ff',1,0,true);
        ball.pos2D = new Vector2D(0.5*canvas.width,100+60*i);
        ball.pos2D = new Vector2D(0.5*canvas.width+60*i,100+60*i);
        ball.draw(context);
        balls.push(ball);
    }
    // make the balls move
    t0 = new Date().getTime();
    t = 0;
    animFrame();
}
```

As in the previous two examples, we first create a Ball object to act as a support. Then we create a whole bunch of Ball objects and put them in an array called balls.

We've made a few structural changes to the animation part of the code, which we also reproduce here in full for ease of reference:

```
function animFrame(){
    animId = requestAnimationFrame(animFrame,canvas);
    onTimer();
}
function onTimer(){
    var t1 = new Date().getTime();
    dt = 0.001*(t1-t0);
    t0 = t1;
    if (dt>0.2) {dt=0;};
    t += dt;
    move();
}
function move(){
    context.clearRect(0, 0, canvas.width, canvas.height);
    drawSpring();
    for (var i=0; i<numBalls; i++){
        var ball = balls[i];
        moveObject(ball);
        calcForce(ball,i);
        updateAccel(ball.mass);
        updateVelo(ball);
    }
}
function drawSpring(){
    support.draw(context);
    context.save();
    context.lineStyle = '#999999';
```

```
        context.lineWidth = 2;
        context.moveTo(center.x,center.y);
        for (var i=0; i<numBalls; i++){
            var X = balls[i].x;
            var Y = balls[i].y;
            context.lineTo(X,Y);
        }
        context.stroke();
        context.restore();
}
function moveObject(obj){
        obj.pos2D = obj.pos2D.addScaled(obj.velo2D,dt);
        obj.draw(context);
}
function calcForce(obj,num){
        var centerPrev;
        var centerNext;
        if (num > 0){
            centerPrev = balls[num-1].pos2D;
        }else{
            centerPrev = center;
        }
        if (num < balls.length-1){
            centerNext = balls[num+1].pos2D;
        }else{
            centerNext = obj.pos2D;
        }
        var gravity = Forces.constantGravity(obj.mass,g);
        var damping = Forces.damping(kDamping,obj.velo2D);
        var displPrev = obj.pos2D.subtract(centerPrev);
        var displNext = obj.pos2D.subtract(centerNext);
        var extensionPrev = displPrev.subtract(displPrev.unit().multiply(springLength));
        var extensionNext = displNext.subtract(displNext.unit().multiply(springLength));
        var restoringPrev = Forces.spring(kSpring,extensionPrev);
        var restoringNext = Forces.spring(kSpring,extensionNext);
        force = Forces.add([gravity, damping, restoringPrev, restoringNext]);
}
function updateAccel(mass){
        acc = force.multiply(1/mass);
}
function updateVelo(obj){
        obj.velo2D = obj.velo2D.addScaled(acc,dt);
}
```

Note the changes in the move() method, which loops over the elements of the balls array to apply the moveObject(), calcForce(), updateAccel() and updateVelo() methods to each ball in turn. We have modified the method calcForce() by including another argument, which is a Number. In move(), when we call calcForce(), we then include an additional parameter i, which is the index number of the relevant particle in the array. Why do we need to do this? For each ball, we need to calculate the spring force exerted by the springs connected to it from the previous and the next balls. Therefore, it would be handy if we knew exactly which ball we're dealing with, and therefore which balls are before and after it. That's what the extra parameter achieves.

In calcForce(), we take into account the fact that each object experiences a restoring force due to its nearest neighbors, by first defining variables centerPrev and centerNext. We give these the positions of the balls just before and just after the current ball, by using the array index num that is passed as a parameter in calcForce(). For the first ball, centerPrev is given the position of the fixed support; for the last ball, centerNext is given the position of the current ball. We then use the values of centerPrev and centerNext to calculate the displacement vectors of the ball from the previous and the next balls in the usual way. Then the spring extension from the natural length of the spring springLength is worked out for each spring as in the last two examples. Finally, the spring force due to each spring is calculated using Forces.spring() and added to the gravity and damping forces.

The drawSpring() method, which is called from the move() method, now draws a line starting from the fixed support through each ball.

Run the code with different initial positions to see how the balls move under gravity and the spring forces to rearrange themselves in their equilibrium positions.

Again, don't be afraid to experiment. For example, add the following method moveSupport() and call it in move() to make the support oscillate sinusoidally, dragging the chain along with it:

```
function moveSupport(){
    support.x = 100*Math.sin(1.0*t)+0.5*canvas.width;
    center = support.pos2D;
}
```

This gives you something like what's pictured in Figure 8-10.

How about trying different masses and different spring constants? Or allowing the balls to be dragged? Or see if you can figure out how to make closed chains? We'll leave you to it.

Summary

We hope you had a lot of fun playing with the examples in this chapter. As we said at the beginning of the chapter, springs are not only fun but also extremely useful. Springs can be used creatively in many ways—for example, you could apply them to velocity, so that an object accelerates and decelerates smoothly to attain a given "equilibrium" velocity. Hopefully you'll be able to find many uses for them. Your imagination is the limit. We'll certainly bump into springs again later in this book. For now, it's time to move on to something different in the next chapter: rotational motion.

CHAPTER 9

■ ■ ■

Centripetal Forces: Rotational Motion

Circular and rotational motions are widespread both in nature and in man-made machines, from merry-go-rounds to the orbits and spins of planets. To analyze and model such types of motion, we need some special tools: the linear kinematics and dynamics presented in Chapter 5 need to be extended to rotational motion. In a nutshell, that is what the present chapter will begin to look into.

Topics covered in this chapter include the following:

- **Kinematics of uniform circular motion:** The kinematics of rotational motion can be developed in analogy with linear kinematics.

- **Centripetal acceleration and centripetal force:** An object in uniform circular motion still experiences acceleration and therefore a force directed toward the center of rotation.

- **Non-uniform circular motion:** This happens if there is a tangential component of force in addition to a centripetal component.

The material covered in this chapter will also be relevant for handling rigid body motion in Chapter 13.

Kinematics of uniform circular motion

In Chapter 4, we laid out the framework for describing motion using concepts such as displacement, velocity, and acceleration. As we said there, this framework is technically called *kinematics*. Those concepts sufficed to describe so-called linear or translational motion. But for analyzing circular or rotational motion, we need to introduce additional concepts.

In fact, the concepts of rotational kinematics can be developed in complete analogy with those of linear kinematics. For starters, we have rotational analogs of displacement, velocity, and acceleration that are called *angular displacement*, *angular velocity*, and *angular acceleration*, respectively. So let's start by looking at them.

Angular displacement

Recall that displacement was defined in Chapter 4 as distance moved in a specified direction. So what is the equivalent definition for angular displacement?

First, we need to figure out what concepts are equivalent to distance and direction in rotational motion. Take a look at Figure 9-1, which compares translational motion with rotational motion. On the left, an object moves along a distance d in a given direction. On the right, an object rotates through an angle θ about some center, in a given sense (clockwise in this case). So it's clear that in rotational kinematics, angle takes the place of distance, and rotation sense (clockwise or counterclockwise) takes the place of direction.

Figure 9-1. *Translation and rotation compared for particle motion*

Another context in which angular displacement arises is when a rigid body rotates about a fixed axis, as shown in Figure 9-2. In this case, each point on the rigid body moves through the same angle θ about the axis of rotation.

Figure 9-2. *Rotation of a rigid body about an axis*

In either case (particle rotation about a center or rigid body rotation about an axis), the idea is therefore the same. Hence, we define *angular displacement* as the angle through which an object moves about a specified center and in a specified sense.

This definition implies that the magnitude of angular displacement is an angle. The usual convention is to use radians for the angle, so we'll do that for angular displacement.

Angular velocity

In analogy with linear velocity, *angular velocity* is defined as the rate of change of angular displacement with time. The usual symbol for angular velocity is ω (the Greek letter omega), so its defining equation in calculus notation is this:

$$\omega = \frac{d\theta}{dt}$$

For a small time interval Δt and angle change $\Delta\theta$, it can be expressed in this discrete form:

$$\omega = \frac{\Delta\theta}{\Delta t}$$

The latter equation can also be written in the following form:

$$\Delta\theta = \omega\,\Delta t$$

This last form of the equation is what we'll use most frequently in code to calculate the angular displacement due to an angular velocity ω in a time interval Δt.

Angular velocity is measured in radians per second (rad/s) because we divide angle by time to calculate it.

You'll frequently deal with situations where the angular velocity is constant. For example, a particle in uniform circular motion has a constant angular velocity, although its linear velocity is not constant (because its direction of motion changes). Another example is that of an object spinning at a constant rate, such as the Earth.

Angular acceleration

Angular acceleration is the rate of change of angular velocity. It is denoted by the Greek letter α (alpha), and its defining equation is this:

$$\alpha = \frac{d\omega}{dt}$$

The definition of angular acceleration implies that it is zero if the angular velocity is constant. Therefore, an object in uniform circular motion has zero angular acceleration. That does not mean that its linear acceleration is zero. In fact, the linear acceleration cannot be zero, because the direction of motion (and therefore the linear velocity) is constantly changing. We'll come back to this point a little later in the chapter.

Period, frequency, and angular velocity

Uniform circular motion or rotation is a type of periodic motion (see "Basic Trigonometry" in Chapter 3) because the object returns to the same position at regular intervals. In fact, as discussed in Chapter 3, circular motion is related to oscillatory, sinusoidal motion. Back then, we defined the angular frequency, frequency, and period of an oscillation and showed that they were related by these equations:

$$f = \frac{1}{T}$$

$$\omega = 2\pi f = \frac{2\pi}{T}$$

The same relationships hold for circular motion, as should be evident by considering Figure 3-16, which illustrated them for both types of motion. For circular motion ω is now the angular velocity; it's the same as the angular frequency of the corresponding sinusoidal oscillation. Similarly, f is the frequency of rotation (the number of revolutions per second). Finally, T is the period of revolution (the time it takes to perform one complete revolution).

As an example, let's calculate the angular velocity of the Earth as it orbits the Sun using the formula $\omega = 2\pi/T$. We know that the period T is approximately 365 days. In seconds, it has the following value:

$$T = 365 \times 24 \times 60 \times 60 \text{ s} \approx 3.15 \times 10^7 \text{ s}$$

Therefore the angular velocity has the following value:

$$\omega = 2\pi/T = 2\pi/(3.15 \times 10^7) \approx 2.0 \times 10^{-7} \text{ rad/s}$$

This is the angle, in radians, through which the Earth moves around the Sun every second.

Let's now calculate the angular velocity of the Earth as it revolves around its axis using the same formula. In this case, the period of revolution is 24 hours, and so T has the following value:

$$T = 24 \times 60 \times 60 \text{ s} = 86400 \text{ s}$$

Therefore, the angular velocity is the following:

$$\omega = 2\pi/T = 2\pi/86400 = 7.3 \times 10^{-5} \text{ rad/s}$$

Note that this is the angular velocity of every point on the Earth, both on its surface and within it. That's because the Earth is a rigid body so that, as it revolves about its axis, every point rotates through the same angle in the same time. However, different points have different *linear velocities*. How is the angular velocity related to the linear velocity? Time to find out!

The relationship between angular velocity and linear velocity

There is a simple relationship between the linear velocity and angular velocity for an object moving in uniform circular motion. To arrive at this relationship, we first note that the displacement Δs of an object moving through an angle $\Delta\theta$ around a circle of radius r is the length of arc that subtends that angle at the center of rotation. It is therefore given by the following:

$$\Delta s = r\,\Delta\theta$$

This follows from the definition of the radian given in Chapter 3: one radian is the angle subtended at the center of a circle by an arc of length equal to the radius of the circle. So, by proportion, an arc that makes an angle of $\Delta\theta$ radians at the center must be of length $r\,\Delta\theta$ (see Figure 9-3).

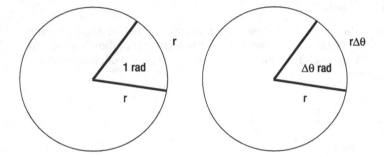

Figure 9-3. *Relationship between length of arc and angle at center*

Now we can divide this equation on both sides by the time interval Δt for the object to move through that angle:

$$\frac{\Delta s}{\Delta t} = r\,\frac{\Delta\theta}{\Delta t}$$

But $\Delta s/\Delta t = v$ and $\Delta\theta/\Delta t = \omega$, by definition. Hence, we have the following:

$$v = r\,\omega$$

This formula gives us the linear velocity of an object moving in a circle of radius r at angular velocity ω.

It also applies to a rigid body undergoing rotation about an axis. In that case, it gives the linear velocity at a distance r from the axis of rotation. For a given angular velocity ω, the formula then tells us that the velocity is proportional to the distance from the axis (the farther away you are, the faster is the linear velocity).

Let's apply this formula to the examples discussed in the previous section. First, we'll calculate the linear velocity of the Earth in its orbit around the Sun. To work this out, we need to know the radius of Earth's orbit (the distance of the Earth from the Sun): 1.5×10^{11} m. We've already worked out the angular velocity of the Earth in its orbit. It is 2.0×10^{-7} rad/s.

Therefore, the orbital velocity of the Earth is given by the following:

$$v = r\,\omega = 1.5 \times 10^{11} \times 2.0 \times 10^{-7} = 3 \times 10^{4}\,\text{m/s}$$

212

This is 30 km/s, or 100 000 km/hr. That's about 100 times the typical speed of an airplane!

As a second example, because the Earth's radius is 6.4×10^6 m, and its angular velocity about its own axis is 7.3×10^{-5} rad/s (as we worked out in the previous section) the speed of any point on the Earth's surface at the equator due to Earth's rotation has the following value:

$$v = r\,\omega = 6.4 \times 10^6 \times 7.3 \times 10^{-5} \text{ m/s} \approx 470 \text{ m/s}$$

This is about 1500 km/hr, or about one and a half times the typical speed of an airplane.

Example: A rolling wheel

We now know enough to be able to put together some simple examples. Our first example will be to create rolling wheels. Unlike most of the examples in the previous few chapters, this one will not involve any dynamics, but only kinematics. So we will not compute motion using forces, but simply tell the objects how to move by specifying the velocity directly.

To begin with, let's create a wheel. We'd like the wheel to look like that shown in Figure 9-4, with an inner and outer rim, and a number of equally spaced spokes (so that we can see it rotating).

Figure 9-4. *A rolling wheel*

Here is a Wheel object that does the job:

```
function Wheel(innerRadius,outerRadius,numSpokes){
    this.ir = innerRadius;
    this.or = outerRadius;
    this.nums = numSpokes;
    this.x = 0;
    this.y = 0;
    this.vx = 0;
    this.vy = 0;
}
Wheel.prototype = {
    get pos2D (){
        return new Vector2D(this.x,this.y);
    },
    set pos2D (pos){
        this.x = pos.x;
        this.y = pos.y;
    },
```

```
        get velo2D (){
            return new Vector2D(this.vx,this.vy);
        },
        set velo2D (velo){
            this.vx = velo.x;
            this.vy = velo.y;
        },
        draw: function (context) {
            var ir = this.ir;
            var or = this.or;
            var nums = this.nums;
            context.save();
            context.fillStyle = '#000000';
            context.beginPath();
            context.arc(this.x, this.y, or, 0, 2*Math.PI, true);
            context.closePath();
            context.fill();
            context.fillStyle = '#ffffaa';
            context.beginPath();
            context.arc(this.x, this.y, ir, 0, 2*Math.PI, true);
            context.closePath();
            context.fill();
            context.strokeStyle = '#000000';
            context.lineWidth = 4;
            context.beginPath();
            for (var n=0; n<nums; n++){
                context.moveTo(this.x,this.y);
            context.lineTo(this.x+ir*Math.cos(2*Math.PI*n/nums),this.y+ir*Math.sin(2*Math.PI*n/nums));
            }
            context.closePath();
            context.stroke();
            context.restore();
        }
    }
}
```

The constructor of Wheel takes three arguments: the inner radius, the outer radius, and the number of spokes.

Now we'll create a Wheel instance and make it roll. Take a look at the code in wheel-demo.js, from the book's downloadable files:

```
var canvas = document.getElementById('canvas');
var context = canvas.getContext('2d');
var r = 50;        // outer radius
var w = 1;         // angular velocity in radians per second
var dt = 30/1000;  // timestep = 1/FPS
var fac = 1;       // slipping/sliding factor

var wheel = new Wheel(r-10,r,12);
wheel.x = 100;
wheel.y = 200;
wheel.draw(context);
```

```
var v = fac*r*w;      // v = r w
var angle = 0;
setInterval(onTimer, 1/dt);

function onTimer(evt){
    wheel.x += v*dt;
    angle += w*dt;
    context.clearRect(0, 0, canvas.width, canvas.height);
    context.save();
    context.translate(wheel.x,wheel.y);
    context.rotate(angle);
    context.translate(-wheel.x,-wheel.y);
    wheel.draw(context);
    context.restore();
}
```

We create a Wheel instance and then set up a setInterval() loop that calls an onTimer() function, which increments the position and angular orientation of the wheel at each timestep. This is done using the linear velocity v and angular velocity w by using these formulas:

```
wheel.x += v*dt;
angle += w*dt;
```

The first formula uses the value of velocity v that is precalculated using this formula:

```
v = fac*r*w*;
```

This is basically the formula $v = r\omega$, but with an additional factor fac included to model the effect of slipping or sliding (skidding), with pure rolling if fac = 1.

The second formula comes from the definition of the angular velocity. The variable angle denotes the angle through which the wheel needs to be turned. The actual turning is handled by the rest of the code in onTimer(). The problem is that there is no way to rotate individual objects on a canvas element—you have to rotate the entire canvas! We do this using the context.rotate() method in the following line:

```
context.rotate(angle);
```

However, doing only this would rotate the canvas around the canvas origin (0,0), which is the top-left corner of the canvas element. We want to rotate the object around its center. To achieve this, we first use the context.translate() method to shift the canvas so that its origin is at the object's center before the rotation. After rotating the canvas, we then translate the canvas back to its original location before drawing the wheel:

```
context.translate(wheel.x,wheel.y);
context.rotate(angle);
context.translate(-wheel.x,-wheel.y);
wheel.draw(context);
```

Note that this whole block of code is enclosed within a pair of context.save() and context.restore() commands, in order to prevent the canvas transformations from affecting other objects that may subsequently be drawn on the same canvas.

Finally, dt is the timestep, which is given a value of 0.03. This is an estimate of the time interval between successive calls of onTimer(). We expect dt to be approximately equal to 1/FPS, where FPS is the frame rate generated by the setInterval() function, which we set at 30. We reiterate that this is just approximate (refer to the discussion of setInterval() in Chapter 2), but it is good enough for this simple demo.

Run the code with fac = 1, and you'll see the wheel move so that its translational velocity is consistent with its rotation rate. This gives the appearance of pure rolling without slipping or skidding. If you change the value of fac to less than 1, say 0.2, the wheel does not move forward fast enough in relation to its rotation; it looks like it's stuck in the mud and is slipping. If you give fac a value greater than 1, say 5, the wheel moves forward faster than it would do purely as a result of its rotation: it appears to be skidding on ice.

Example: Satellite around a rotating Earth

What we want to achieve in this example is in essence quite simple: an animation of a satellite in a circular orbit around a rotating Earth. The twist is that we want the satellite to orbit so that it is always over the same spot on Earth. This is called a *geostationary orbit*; as you might guess, it's very useful for telecommunications as well as spying.

Once again, this example will involve only kinematics and no dynamics (no forces). Later on in the chapter, we'll add in the forces.

The full code is in the file satellite-demo.js and is reproduced here:

```
var canvas = document.getElementById('canvas');
var context = canvas.getContext('2d');

var earth;
var satellite;

var r, x0, y0, omega;
var angle = 0;

window.onload = init;

function init() {
    // create a stationary earth
    earth = new Ball(70,'#0099ff',1000000,0,true,true);
    earth.pos2D = new Vector2D(400,300);
    earth.angVelo = 0.4;
    earth.draw(context);
    // create a moving satellite
    satellite = new Satellite(8,'#0000ff',1);
    satellite.pos2D = new Vector2D(600,300);
    satellite.angVelo = earth.angVelo;
    satellite.draw(context);
    // set params
    r = satellite.pos2D.subtract(earth.pos2D).length();
    omega = earth.angVelo;
    x0 = earth.x;
    y0 = earth.y;
    // make the satellite orbit the earth
    t0 = new Date().getTime();
    t = 0;
    animFrame();
};
```

```
function animFrame(){
    animId = requestAnimationFrame(animFrame,canvas);
    onTimer();
}
function onTimer(){
    var t1 = new Date().getTime();
    dt = 0.001*(t1-t0);
    t0 = t1;
    if (dt>0.2) {dt=0;};
    t += dt;
    move();
}
function move(){
    satellite.pos2D = new Vector2D(r*Math.cos(omega*t)+x0,r*Math.sin(omega*t)+y0);
    angle += omega*dt;
    context.clearRect(0, 0, canvas.width, canvas.height);
    rotateObject(earth);
    rotateObject(satellite);
}
function rotateObject(obj){
    context.save();
    context.translate(obj.x,obj.y);
    context.rotate(angle);
    context.translate(-obj.x,-obj.y);
    obj.draw(context);
    context.restore();
}
```

Most of the code is straightforward, but with some noteworthy new features. We create an Earth and a satellite object. The masses that are given to these objects are irrelevant here as there is no dynamics. You can use any value you want, and the animation will behave in exactly the same way. Note that Earth is an instance of Ball, whereas satellite is an instance of Satellite. The latter object is basically like Ball, with the addition of code that draws three lines on the satellite to give it a nice old-fashioned, Sputnik-like appearance. Both the Ball and Satellite objects have a new property called angVelo, which stores the value of the angular velocity of their instances. We have also introduced an optional Boolean parameter line in Ball that, if set to true, draws a pair of crossed lines on the Ball instance. This is so that the rotation of the ball can be observed.

We give the Earth a non-zero angular velocity. Then we assign the same angular velocity to the satellite. The distance of the satellite from the Earth is computed and stored in the variable r. This distance does not change because the orbit will be circular. Then the angular velocity and x and y position of the Earth are stored in the variables omega, x0, and y0, respectively.

The action takes place in the move() method. All we are doing here is telling the satellite where it must be at any time, using these formulas:

$$x = r\cos(\omega t) + x0$$

$$x = r\sin(\omega t) + y0$$

You might recall from Chapter 3 that using cos and sin in this way produces circular motion with angular frequency ω at a radius r. Adding x0 and y0 (the coordinates of the center of the Earth) makes the satellite orbit the Earth. The other important thing is that ω is chosen to be equal to the angular velocity of the Earth. This makes the satellite orbit the Earth at exactly the same rate as the Earth spins on its axis. Run the simulation, and you'll see that this is indeed the case.

Also, because the satellite has the same angular velocity around its axis as the Earth, its antennae always point toward the Earth (see Figure 9-5).

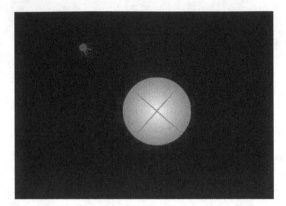

Figure 9-5. *A spy satellite orbiting the Earth*

The code that produces the rotation of the Earth and the satellite is in the `rotateObject()` method and should look familiar from the previous example. Note that here a single variable `angle` is used to compute the angle through which both objects must rotate at each time step. This is because they have the same angular velocity.

The alert reader will have noticed that we've called this example an *animation* rather than a *simulation*. That's because we basically told the satellite how to move, rather than prescribing the forces that act on it and letting them determine the motion of the satellite. Although the animation does have some physics realism, it is not completely realistic. One reason is that we have forced the satellite to orbit the Earth at the same rate (the same angular velocity) as the Earth spins around its axis. You can change the distance of the satellite from the Earth's center and it will still orbit at the same rate. In reality, satellites can only do so at a specific distance from the Earth's center; in other words, all geostationary satellites must be at the same distance from the Earth! It is not obvious why that should be so, but the next section will help clarify that and help you to build this feature into the animation.

Centripetal acceleration and centripetal force

Now that we've covered the basics, it's time to move on to some slightly more difficult concepts: centripetal acceleration and centripetal force. Actually they are not really difficult, but they are frequently misunderstood. Hence, we'll try to clear up some of the possible confusion as we go along.

Centripetal acceleration

As we pointed out in the section on angular velocity, an object moving in a circle (or in a curved path in general) has a linear velocity that is changing with time because its direction is changing all the time. Therefore, from the definition of acceleration as rate of change of velocity, that means it has a non-zero acceleration—we never said that acceleration means just a change in the magnitude of velocity (speed); it could mean a change in direction as well.

It may not be obvious at all, but for an object moving in a circle, this acceleration actually points toward the center of the circle. Therefore, it is called *centripetal acceleration* (from the Latin: *centr* = "center," and *petere* = "to seek"). One way to appreciate this is to think of the center as pulling the object, thereby changing its direction constantly (see Figure 9-6). We'll see in a moment how to calculate the centripetal acceleration.

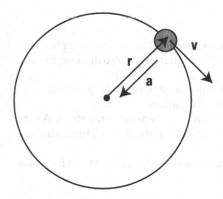

Figure 9-6. *Centripetal acceleration*

Centripetal acceleration must not be confused with angular acceleration. As explained earlier in this chapter, angular acceleration refers to the rate of change of angular velocity. In the case of uniform circular motion, the angular acceleration is zero because the angular velocity is constant (that's what "uniform" means), but the centripetal acceleration is not zero. The centripetal acceleration is a measure of the rate of change of linear velocity, when the latter is only changing in direction while its magnitude remains constant.

Centripetal acceleration, velocity, and angular velocity

How do we calculate the centripetal acceleration? Well, there is a simple formula for it. It's not easy to prove, so the best thing is just to believe us! Here is one form of the formula:

$$a = \frac{v^2}{r}$$

Referring to Figure 9-6, this formula tells us the centripetal acceleration for an object moving with velocity v in a circle or arc of radius r. From this we deduce that if the velocity is large, the acceleration is large (for the same radius); and if the radius is small, the acceleration is large (for the same velocity magnitude).

Remembering that $v = r\omega$, you can replace v in the preceding formula to come up with an alternative form for the formula in terms of r and ω:

$$a = r\,\omega^2$$

This formula now tells us that the centripetal acceleration is greater when the angular velocity is greater (for the same radius). But it also tells us that the centripetal acceleration is greater when the radius is greater, *for the same angular velocity*. This does not contradict what we said previously about the other form of the formula, but can seem confusing at first! The key point is that here the linear velocity magnitude is not assumed to be constant for different radii. In fact, if the angular velocity is constant, then the linear velocity magnitude must increase with radius because $v = r\omega$.

One consequence of the previous formula is that for a rigid body spinning about its axis, points farther away from the axis have a greater acceleration (because all points on the rigid body have the same angular velocity) as well as a greater velocity (because $v = r\omega$).

Centripetal force

We've just seen that any object in uniform circular motion must experience an acceleration toward the center of the circular trajectory. Therefore, by Newton's second law, there must be a *resultant force* on it that is also directed toward the center. This is known as the *centripetal force*.

The centripetal force is the force that is needed to keep an object in circular motion. It needs to be provided continuously by some physical agent; otherwise, the object cannot maintain circular motion.

As an example, an object whirled around by a string gets its centripetal force from the tension in the string. A car moving around a circular track gets centripetal force from friction exerted by the ground on the tires. Planets orbiting the Sun experience a centripetal force due to the Sun's gravitational attraction.

It's very easy to work out the formula for centripetal force. Because $F = ma$, you just need to multiply the formulas for centripetal acceleration by m (the mass of the moving object) to obtain this:

$$F = \frac{m v^2}{r}$$

And to get this:

$$F = m r \omega^2$$

In vector form, the first formula can be written as follows:

$$\mathbf{F} = -\frac{m v^2}{r^2} \mathbf{r}$$

Or it can be written like this, where $\mathbf{r}_u$ is a unit vector in the direction of the position vector $\mathbf{r}$ of the moving object with respect to the center:

$$\mathbf{F} = -\frac{m v^2}{r} \mathbf{r}_u$$

The minus sign arises because the force points toward the center (opposite to the vector $\mathbf{r}$). Similar vector forms also hold for the formula $F = mr\omega^2$.

Common misconceptions about centripetal force

Centripetal force is probably one of the most misunderstood concepts in physics. Let's clear up some of the confusion.

- Centripetal force is not a distinct "type" of force in the same sense that gravity and friction are types of forces. It is simply the force that must be present to make an object move in a circle. Different forces can act as centripetal forces, including gravity and friction.

- Sometimes people mistakenly talk about the need to "balance" the centripetal force. For example, a common misunderstanding is that the gravitational force on a planet in orbit around the Sun balances the centripetal force. That does not make sense for several reasons. First, the centripetal force must point toward the Sun, and so does the gravitational force, so they are both in the same direction. Second, *if* the two forces *did* balance, the resultant force on the planet would be zero; its acceleration would therefore be zero and so it would have to move in a straight line at constant velocity (by Newton's first law of motion). Third, centripetal force is not even a "type" of force. The correct thinking is that the gravitational force *provides* the centripetal force necessary for the planet to orbit the Sun.

- You may also hear about something called *centrifugal force*, which has the same magnitude as the centripetal force but acts in the opposite direction (away from the center of rotation). Centrifugal force is not a real force but a so-called pseudo force. It arises out of the attempt to analyze motion within the framework of Newton's laws but from the point of view of a rotating frame of reference. An example is the description of atmospheric motion from a reference frame on the Earth (which is, of course, rotating). Although centrifugal force certainly has its place in physics in analyzing problems like this, it can cause a lot of confusion, too. Our recommendation is therefore to avoid thinking in terms of centrifugal forces. In the section "Example: Car moving around a bend" later in the chapter we give a centripetal-force account of an example commonly thought of in terms of centrifugal force.

Example: Revisiting the satellite animation

As a first example of the application of the centripetal force concept, let's go back to the satellite animation and inject some more realism into it as promised.

Here the centripetal force is provided by the force of gravity on the satellite. Therefore we can equate the expression for centripetal force with that for the gravitational force to obtain the following equation, where m is the satellite mass, M is the Earth mass, r is the distance of the satellite from the Earth's center, and ω is the angular velocity of the satellite:

$$m\, r\, \omega^2 = \frac{G M m}{r^2}$$

It is easy to rearrange this equation to give the following:

$$r = \sqrt[3]{\frac{G M}{\omega^2}}$$

This formula tells us the radius at which the satellite must be in order to orbit at an angular velocity ω. In other words, the satellite cannot have just any angular velocity at any distance; the centripetal force dictates that it has to rotate at a fixed angular velocity for any given distance from the Earth! In particular, we can use the formula to calculate the distance at which it must be to rotate at the same angular velocity as the Earth's spin. If you substitute the values for G, M (the mass of the Earth), and ω (the Earth's angular velocity as we worked out before), you'll find that the radius of a geostationary orbit is 42,400 km, or approximately 6.6 times the radius of the Earth.

Going back to our animation, we need to make the satellite aware of the constraint between its distance from the Earth and its angular velocity around the Earth, as expressed by the previous equation. In fact, in the animation we'll specify the position of the satellite, and therefore the distance r from the Earth, and want to work out its resulting angular velocity ω instead of setting it to be equal to that of the Earth.

Therefore, we want a formula for ω in terms of r. It's easy enough to manipulate the previous equation to give the following:

$$\omega = \sqrt{\frac{G M}{r^3}}$$

That's all we need. We copied `satellite-demo.js` to create `satellite-demo2.js`. If you look at the latter file, you'll see that the main change we've made is to replace this line:

```
omega = earth.angVelo;
```

with the following line:

```
omega = Math.sqrt(G*M/(r*r*r));
```

where M is the mass of the Earth (here set at 1000000), and the value of the gravitational constant G is set to 1. We now also have separate variables omegaE and angleE to store the angular velocity and angular displacement of the Earth.

If you now run the code with the previous positions and masses of the satellite and Earth and angular velocity of the Earth, you'll see that the satellite is no longer in a geostationary orbit. In fact, by the time it completes one orbit, its antennae are already pointing the wrong way. If you use the previous formula to calculate the value of r for a geostationary orbit with the given values of $G = 1$, $M = 1000000$, and $\omega = 0.4$, you will get $r = 184.2$. This is the distance that the satellite should be from the Earth's center. Given that the Earth is located at (400,300), you just need to change the position of the satellite to a location 184.2 units away, such as (584.2,300) in satellite-demo2.js:

```
satellite.pos2D = new Vector2D(584.2,300);
```

Do this and then run the code. You'll see that the satellite does orbit at the same angular velocity as the Earth.

Example: Circular orbits with gravitational force

In this example, we go back to a full dynamic simulation. In fact, we already did that in the orbits simulation in Chapter 6, in which we simulated the motion of a planet round the Sun. The simulation already "knows" that gravity is a centripetal force, so there is nothing else to add. But if we want circular orbits, we can use the centripetal force formula to work out exactly what velocity we need to give the planet.

Again, this is simply a matter of equating the expressions for centripetal force and gravitational force. This time, we use the form $F = mv^2/r$ for the centripetal force:

$$\frac{m\,v^2}{r} = \frac{G\,M\,m}{r^2}$$

A little algebra then gives us the following, which is the velocity magnitude that the planet must have in order to have a circular orbit around the Sun at a distance r from its center:

$$v = \sqrt{\frac{G\,M}{r}}$$

Let's code this into a modified version of the orbits simulation. The new source file is called circular-orbits.js, and the code is shown in full here:

```
var canvas = document.getElementById('canvas');
var context = canvas.getContext('2d');
var canvas_bg = document.getElementById('canvas_bg');
var context_bg = canvas_bg.getContext('2d');

var planet;
var sun;
var m = 1;        // planet's mass
var M = 1000000; // sun's mass
var G = 1;
var t0,dt;
var acc, force;

window.onload = init;
```

```
function init() {
    // create a stationary sun
    sun = new Ball(70,'#ff9900',M,0,true);
    sun.pos2D = new Vector2D(400,300);
    sun.draw(context_bg);
    // create a moving planet
    planet = new Ball(10,'#0000ff',m);
    planet.pos2D = new Vector2D(400,50);
    var r = planet.pos2D.subtract(sun.pos2D).length();
    var v = Math.sqrt(G*M*m/r);
    planet.velo2D = new Vector2D(v,0);
    planet.draw(context);
    // make the planet orbit the sun
    t0 = new Date().getTime();
    animFrame();
};

function animFrame(){
    animId = requestAnimationFrame(animFrame,canvas);
    onTimer();
}
function onTimer(){
    var t1 = new Date().getTime();
    dt = 0.001*(t1-t0);
    t0 = t1;
    if (dt>0.2) {dt=0;};
    move();
}
function move(){
    moveObject(planet);
    calcForce();
    updateAccel();
    updateVelo(planet);
}
function moveObject(obj){
    obj.pos2D = obj.pos2D.addScaled(obj.velo2D,dt);
    context.clearRect(0, 0, canvas.width, canvas.height);
    obj.draw(context);
}
function calcForce(){
    force = Forces.gravity(G,M,m,planet.pos2D.subtract(sun.pos2D));
}
function updateAccel(){
    acc = force.multiply(1/m);
}
function updateVelo(obj){
    obj.velo2D = obj.velo2D.addScaled(acc,dt);
}
```

Most of the code should be very familiar. The new feature in this simulation is that we give the planet exactly the initial velocity it needs to move in a circular orbit. This is done in the two lines highlighted in bold, using the formula $v = \sqrt{(GM/r)}$ that we just derived.

223

Run the simulation with the initial values as given in the previous code listing, and you'll find that the planet indeed describes a circular orbit around the Sun. To convince yourself that this works at any distance from the Sun, change the initial position of the planet to the following:

```
planet.pos2D = new Vector2D(400,150);
```

This positions the planet closer to the Sun. If you now run the code, you'll see that the planet orbits the Sun at a faster rate, but the orbit is still circular.

Note that the velocity must be tangential with no radial component (see Figure 9-7). If there is any radial velocity component, the planet will either approach or recede from the Sun (its orbit won't be circular). For example, with the initial position of the planet at (400, 50), try the following:

```
planet.velo2D = new Vector2D(v/Math.sqrt(2), v/Math.sqrt(2));
```

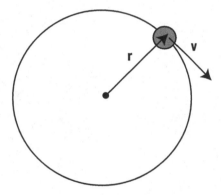

Figure 9-7. *Tangential velocity*

This gives the planet an initial velocity of the same magnitude v as before, but in a different direction, so that it has a radial component toward the Sun as well as a tangential component. You will find that the planet's orbit is now highly elliptical, with the planet getting very close to the Sun and then receding away from it.

You are encouraged to try different initial positions and velocities to see the types of orbits you get. You should find that, without using the formula $v = \sqrt{(GM/r)}$, it is rather hard to get the initial conditions just right to produce even approximately circular orbits by simple trial and error!

Example: Car moving around a bend

In the next example, we simulate the motion of a car around a circular track and use it to demonstrate skidding if the car goes too fast.

The basic physics here is that when a car moves around a curve or bend, the centripetal force it needs to do so is provided by the frictional force on the tires in contact with the road surface (see Figure 9-8).

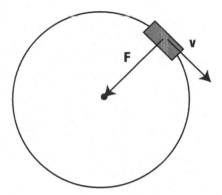

Figure 9-8. *Friction provides the centripetal force for a car to negotiate a bend*

Going back to the formula for centripetal force, the faster the car moves, the greater the centripetal force needed to keep it moving around the bend:

$$F = \frac{m\,v^2}{r}$$

Incidentally, the formula also shows that the centripetal force is greater for sharper bends, which curve with a *smaller* radius.

The frictional force is the static frictional force and, as discussed in Chapter 7, it has a maximum value given by $f = C_s N$, where N is the normal force (which here is equal to the car's weight mg), and C_s is the coefficient of static friction between the tires and the road surface. Therefore, if the centripetal force needed to negotiate a bend exceeds the maximum static friction, the car won't be able to follow the curvature of the bend—it will skid.

We now build a simulation that can handle this scenario in a natural way. The setup is shown in Figure 9-9.

Figure 9-9. *The skidding car simulation*

And here is the code that does it (in the file car-demo.js):

```
var canvas = document.getElementById('canvas');
var context = canvas.getContext('2d');
var canvas_bg = document.getElementById('canvas_bg');
var context_bg = canvas_bg.getContext('2d');
```

```
var center = new Vector2D(canvas.width/2,canvas.height/2);
var car;
var mass = 90; // car mass
var g = 10;
var Cs = 1;
var angle = 0;
var omega;
var t0,dt;
var acc, force;

window.onload = init;

function init() {
    // create a circular track, e.g. a roundabout
    context_bg.fillStyle = '#cccccc';
    context_bg.beginPath();
    context_bg.arc(canvas.width/2, canvas.height/2, 100, 0, 2*Math.PI, true);
    context_bg.closePath();
    context_bg.fill();
    context_bg.fillStyle = '#ffffff';
    context_bg.beginPath();
    context_bg.arc(canvas.width/2, canvas.height/2, 50, 0, 2*Math.PI, true);
    context_bg.closePath();
    context_bg.fill();
    // create a car
    car = new Box(10,20,'#0000ff',mass);
    car.pos2D = new Vector2D(center.x+75,center.y);
    car.velo2D = new Vector2D(0,-10);
    car.angVelo = -car.velo2D.length()/(car.pos2D.subtract(center).length());
    omega = car.angVelo;
    car.draw(context);
    // make the car move
    t0 = new Date().getTime();
    animFrame();
};

function animFrame(){
    animId = requestAnimationFrame(animFrame,canvas);
    onTimer();
}
function onTimer(){
    var t1 = new Date().getTime();
    dt = 0.001*(t1-t0);
    t0 = t1;
    if (dt>0.2) {dt=0;};
    move();
}
function move(){
    moveObject(car);
    calcForce();
    updateAccel();
    updateVelo(car);
}
```

```
function moveObject(obj){
    obj.pos2D = obj.pos2D.addScaled(obj.velo2D,dt);
    angle += omega*dt;
    context.clearRect(0, 0, canvas.width, canvas.height);
    rotateObject(obj);
}
function rotateObject(obj){
    context.save();
    context.translate(obj.x,obj.y);
    context.rotate(angle);
    context.translate(-obj.x,-obj.y);
    obj.draw(context);
    context.restore();
}
function calcForce(){
    var dist = car.pos2D.subtract(center);
    var velo = car.velo2D.length();
    var centripetalForce = dist.unit().multiply(-mass*velo*velo/dist.length());
    var radialFriction = dist.unit().multiply(-Cs*mass*g);
    if(radialFriction.length() > centripetalForce.length()) {
        force = centripetalForce;
    }
    else{
        force = radialFriction;
    }
}
function updateAccel(){
    acc = force.multiply(1/mass);
}
function updateVelo(obj){
    obj.velo2D = obj.velo2D.addScaled(acc,dt);
}
```

As shown in the figure, we begin in the init() method by drawing a circular track. The next step introduces a bit of artistic novelty. Because we are dealing with a car, a Ball instance simply won't do. Instead, our car is a Box instance. Box is a class that is essentially similar to Ball except that it draws a filled rectangle instead of a filled circle. Box takes four parameters (width, height, color, and mass), all of which have default values and are therefore optional. After creating the car as a Box instance, we position it on the track and give it an initial tangential velocity. The next line then gives the car a spin angular velocity equal to its "orbital" angular velocity by using the formula $\omega = v/r$, where v is the car's speed, and r is its distance from the center.

The rest of the code should be easy to follow. In calcForce(), we calculate the centripetal force using the formula $F = mv^2/r$ in vector form and the maximum frictional force on the car using the formula $F = C_s mg$ (see Chapter 7), where m is the mass of the car. For simplicity, we assume that static and dynamic friction are the same. Also, we assume that the resultant force on the car is friction in the radial direction. The if block checks whether the maximum friction is sufficient to provide the centripetal force. If so, the resultant force is taken to be equal to the centripetal force; if not, the resultant force is equal to the maximum friction.

If you run the simulation with an initial velocity of 10 or 20 px/s, you'll find that the car moves around the track without problem. However, if you increase the velocity beyond about 30, the car will skid!

Non-uniform circular motion

So far in this chapter we've dealt only with uniform circular motion. How do we handle rotation when the angular velocity is not constant? In this last section, we'll begin to look at this problem and illustrate it with an example. A fuller treatment of non-uniform rotation will involve delving into concepts such as angular momentum and torque. For that, you'll have to await Chapter 13.

Tangential force and acceleration

The underlying difference between uniform and non-uniform circular motion is that in the former, centripetal force is the only force; whereas in the latter there is a tangential as well as a centripetal force (see Figure 9-10). *Tangential* literally means "along a tangent" to the circle. The centripetal force in non-uniform circular motion is given by the same formulas as for the uniform case. As with centripetal force, the tangential force can be due to any number of factors such as gravity or friction.

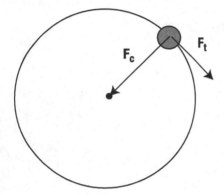

Figure 9-10. *Tangential (F_t) and centripetal (F_c) forces*

Note that centripetal force changes only the direction of motion, which is why uniform circular motion is uniform. But because tangential forces act in the direction of the velocity vector, they cause a change in the speed of the rotating object. This also means there is a non-zero angular acceleration when a tangential force is present.

The bottom line: to simulate non-uniform circular motion, we need forces that will provide both centripetal and tangential force components, as demonstrated in our next and final example.

Example: A simple pendulum

A so-called *simple pendulum* consists of a heavy bob suspended by a cord to a fixed pivot. The pendulum is set into oscillation by displacing the bob slightly and releasing it. Simulating a simple pendulum is not totally straightforward and does require a bit of thinking to get the physics right.

Figure 9-11 shows the force diagram for a simple pendulum. The cord will usually be inclined at some angle θ to the vertical. We assume that the cord has negligible mass and that there is no friction or drag. Let m denote the mass of the bob. There are then two forces acting on the bob: gravity acting vertically downward with magnitude mg; and the tension in the cord acting toward the fixed pivot with magnitude T.

Figure 9-11. *Geometrical and force diagram for a pendulum*

Obviously, the bob moves in a circular arc with the pivot as its center. But the angular velocity of the bob is non-uniform. In fact, it is zero when the bob is in its uppermost position and maximum when the bob is at its lowest point. Therefore, there is an angular acceleration because of a tangential force component. Because the tension is in the radial direction (which is perpendicular to the tangential direction), it has no tangential component. But the force of gravity in general does have a tangential component given by $mg\sin(\theta)$. This is the force that causes the angular acceleration. Note that because the angle θ changes with time, the tangential force and therefore the angular acceleration are not constant.

What is the radial force component that provides the centripetal force? From Figure 9-11, it's clear that gravity has a component $mg\cos(\theta)$ that acts away from the pivot. Hence, the net radial force component is $T - mg\cos(\theta)$, and this must be equal to the centripetal force:

$$T - m\,g\cos(\theta) = \frac{m\,v^2}{r}$$

Therefore, this implies that the magnitude of the tension T is given by the following:

$$T = m\,g\cos(\theta) + \frac{m\,v^2}{r}$$

As is clear from Figure 9-11, the direction of the tension force is opposite to the position vector **r** of the bob relative to the pivot.

Now comes the clever part. All we need to do is to specify the forces of gravity mg and tension T, as given by the last equation. Then, once we give it an initial position, the bob ought to know how to move under those two forces. Let's go ahead and code it up.

The code is in the file pendulum.js:

```
var canvas = document.getElementById('canvas');
var context = canvas.getContext('2d');

var bob;
var pivot;
var displ = new Vector2D(0,0);
var center = new Vector2D(0.5*canvas.width,50);
var mass = 1;
var g = 100;
var lengthP = 200;
var initAngle = 30;
var t0, t, dt;
var acc, force;
var animId;

window.onload = init;
```

```
function init() {
    // create a pivot
    pivot = new Ball(2,'#000000');
    pivot.pos2D = center;
    pivot.draw(context);
    // create a bob
    bob = new Ball(10,'#333333',mass);
    bob.mass = mass;
    var relativePos = new Vector2D(lengthP*Math.sin(initAngle*Math.PI/180),
lengthP*Math.cos(initAngle*Math.PI/180));
    bob.pos2D = pivot.pos2D.add(relativePos);
    bob.draw(context);
    // make the bob move
    t0 = new Date().getTime();
    t = 0;
    animFrame();
};
function animFrame(){
    animId = requestAnimationFrame(animFrame,canvas);
    onTimer();
}
function onTimer(){
    var t1 = new Date().getTime();
    dt = 0.001*(t1-t0);
    t0 = t1;
    if (dt>0.2) {dt=0;};
    t += dt;
    move();
}
function move(){
    context.clearRect(0, 0, canvas.width, canvas.height);
    drawSpring(bob);
    moveObject(bob);
    calcForce(bob);
    updateAccel();
    updateVelo(bob);
}
function drawSpring(obj){
    pivot.draw(context);
    context.save();
    context.strokeStyle = '#999999';
    context.lineWidth = 2;
    context.moveTo(center.x,center.y);
    context.lineTo(obj.x,obj.y);
    context.stroke();
    context.restore();
}
function moveObject(obj){
    obj.pos2D = obj.pos2D.addScaled(obj.velo2D,dt);
    obj.draw(context);
}
```

```
function calcForce(obj){
    displ = obj.pos2D.subtract(center);
    var gravity = Forces.constantGravity(mass,g);
    var tension;
    if (displ.length() >= lengthP) {
        tension = displ.unit().multiply(-(gravity.projection(displ)
+mass*bob.velo2D.lengthSquared()/lengthP));
    }else{
        tension = new Vector2D(0,0);
    }
    force = Forces.add([gravity, tension]);
}
function updateAccel(){
    acc = force.multiply(1/mass);
}
function updateVelo(obj){
    obj.velo2D = obj.velo2D.addScaled(acc,dt);
}
```

We begin by creating a pivot and a pendulum bob. The bob is positioned so that the cord makes an initial angle of 30 degrees with the vertical. To see this, refer to Figure 9-11, which shows that the x and y coordinates of the bob relative to the pivot are given by the following, where l is the "length" of the pendulum, defined as the distance of the center of the bob to the fixed pivot:

$$x = l\sin(\theta)$$

$$y = l\cos(\theta)$$

Physically, l is equal to the sum of the length of the cord and the radius of the bob. In the code, we denote this by the variable lengthP. This relative position vector is calculated and stored in the variable relativePos, which is then added to the pivot's pos2D property to set the position of the bob. The initial inclination angle (in degrees) is set by the parameter initAngle.

The novelty in the animation part of the code is basically what's in the calcForce() method. We calculate gravity in the usual way. The if block of code checks to see if the distance of the bob from the pivot is greater than or equal to the cord length. If so, that means the cord is taut and therefore the tension is non-zero; it is calculated using the formula $T = mg\cos(\theta) + mv^2/r$. Otherwise, the cord is not taut, so the tension is zero. In the current setup, it is not strictly necessary to check whether the cord is taut, because the simulation starts with a taut cord and it remains so all the time. But implementing this check makes the code more robust to possible future modifications. Note that the radial component of gravity $mg\cos(\theta)$ is computed using the nifty projection() method, which we introduced into the Vector2D object so that vec1.projection(vec2) gives the projection of vector vec1 in the direction of vector vec2. Here is the definition of projection():

```
function projection(vec){
    var length = this.length();
    var lengthVec = vec.length();
    var proj;
    if( (length == 0) || ( lengthVec == 0) ){
        proj = 0;
```

```
    }else {
        proj = (this.x*vec.x + this.y*vec.y)/lengthVec;
    }
    return proj;
}
```

If you run the code and play with the parameters, you'll see that the pendulum oscillates faster if the cord length is shorter and if the value of *g* is greater. This is just as it should be in reality. In fact you can test how good your simulated pendulum is by comparing the period of the oscillations with the theoretical value.

Physics theory says that for oscillations of small amplitude, the period of a simple pendulum is given approximately by the following, where *l* is the length of the pendulum:

$$T = 2\pi\sqrt{\frac{l}{g}}$$

The values we used in the simulation are $l = 200$ and $g = 100$. This gives you $T = 2\pi$, which is approximately 8.9 seconds. Check whether the simulation gives this value, by outputting the time to the console and timing to ten oscillations, for example, and then dividing the total time by ten. To make this easier, the file pendulum2.js includes some additional code to allow you to stop the simulation by clicking the mouse. You should get a value very close to 8.9 s. As you can see in Figure 9-12, it works almost like the real thing!.

Figure 9-12. *The pendulum simulation*

Summary

This chapter introduced some of the physics needed to handle circular and rotational motion, focusing on particle and simple rigid body rotation. This chapter has laid the foundations for a more detailed look at rigid body rotation, which we'll present in Chapter 13. Some of the concepts introduced here will also be applied and developed further in the next chapter, on long-range forces.

CHAPTER 10

■ ■ ■

Long-Range Forces

In this last chapter of Part II, we'll introduce yet more force laws. However, the approach and purpose here will be more playful than in previous chapters. You'll learn concepts and techniques that you may not necessarily use for making realistic simulations, but more for producing fun animations and effects.

Topics covered in this chapter include the following:

- **Particle interactions and force fields:** There are two ways of viewing forces that act at a distance: in terms of direct interactions between particles, and in terms of force fields.

- **Gravitational force:** We revisit gravity as an example of a long-range force, giving further examples and building a black hole game!

- **Electrostatic force:** This is the force between electrically charged particles at rest, which can be attractive or repulsive. Interesting effects can be produced with electric forces.

- **Electromagnetic force:** Moving charges experience a magnetic force as well as an electric force. Together, they constitute an electromagnetic force, which can be used to produce more complicated types of motion.

- **Other force laws:** There is no reason you can't invent your own force laws to produce cool effects. We'll take a look at some examples, including so-called central forces of different types.

Particle interactions and force fields

Whenever we've talked about forces so far in this book, we've thought of them as being exerted by particles on other particles. But there is another way to think of forces that are exerted at a distance—we can think of them as being due to *force fields*. This is a fairly subtle concept, so we'll take some time to explain it in the next couple of sections.

Interaction at a distance

In this chapter, we'll deal exclusively with forces that are exerted and felt at a distance; the interacting objects don't need to be in contact. Actually, at a fundamental level, all forces are like that, even contact forces. The difference is that contact forces are felt when two objects are very close together. Collisions are similar; they occur when two objects are so close together that their constituent molecules exert electric forces on each other. So the real distinction is between short-range and long-range forces. Contact forces and collisions involve short-range forces. Gravity is a long-range force. In general, both short-range and long-range forces can be attractive or repulsive.

From particle interactions to force fields

Historically, physicists were not very happy about the fact that forces like gravity appear to be exerted across empty space, with two remote objects being apparently able to influence each other instantly. This was the so-called *action-at-a-distance* problem. So they came up with the concept of a *force field* to replace the action-at-a-distance concept.

The idea of a force field, though seemingly esoteric, is actually quite simple. A *field of force* is simply a region of space where a force is felt. If you have two objects with mass, such as a star and a planet, the usual way to think of gravity is that they each exert a gravitational force on each other. In the field concept, you say that the star sets up a gravitational field that permeates the space around it. Any other object, such as a planet, then experiences a force due to the field at the point where it is located. The key idea is that the field mediates the interaction between the star and the planet. There is then no action-at-a-distance anymore; the force felt by the planet is a local one, due to the force field that exists locally. In fact, the force field exists whether or not there is a planet there to experience a force.

Note that in the previous example, the planet also sets up its own gravitational field, which then causes the star to experience a force equal and opposite to that experienced by the planet, in accordance with Newton's third law of motion.

As we know, the force felt by the planet depends on its distance from the star. In the field concept, the variation of the force with distance is encapsulated in the concept of *field strength*. In the case of gravity, the field strength decreases with distance from the source of the field (in this case, a star). In the next section we'll see the precise form of the field strength due to the star. It is also customary to refer to the field strength simply as the *field*.

Similar ideas apply to other long-range forces, such as electric forces. Particles create force fields. Other particles then experience forces in the presence of that field. The amount of force they experience depends on the field strength.

Why should you care about force fields? One important practical advantage is that force fields free us from the need to have particles just so they can exert forces. As you'll see later in the chapter, we can produce a force field without worrying about how it can be produced by particles. This gives us great flexibility in the type of forces we can subject particles to. The concepts of force field and field strength are especially useful in connection with electric and magnetic forces, but let's take a closer look at them in the context of gravity. They will then be easier to appreciate when we talk about the rather more abstract electric and magnetic fields.

Newtonian gravitation

Gravity is an archetypal example of a long-range force. The field strength in this case is defined as the force per unit mass that acts on a particle at any given point in the field. This is a sensible definition: It tells us how strong the gravity force field is by telling us the force that it exerts on an object of unit mass.

Gravitational field strength is a vector denoted by the symbol $\mathbf{g}$. The definition tells us that

$$\mathbf{g} = \frac{\mathbf{F}}{m}$$

You will recognize this as being equivalent to the familiar formula for the gravitational force on an object of mass m:

$$\mathbf{F} = m\,\mathbf{g}$$

So, the gravitational field strength is a vector with magnitude equal to the acceleration due to gravity g. In particular, that means it has the same value for all objects, regardless of their mass or other characteristics. In general, the gravitational field strength vector $\mathbf{g}$ can change with position, just like the (non-bolded) scalar g. In a uniform gravitational field, such as close to the surface of the Earth, both $\mathbf{g}$ and g are constant.

To reiterate an important point, the key thing with the definition of the gravitational field strength is that it is a property only of the field, as it exists independently of any object that may experience a force due to it. Whereas the gravitational *force on* an object will depend on its mass, the gravitational field strength $\mathbf{g}$ itself tells us the force per unit mass at any point in the field. From this, we can work out the force $\mathbf{F}$ on any mass m by multiplying by m.

Gravitational field due to a particle

The gravitational field strength due to a particle of mass M, such as a star, can be computed starting from Newton's law of gravitation:

$$\mathbf{F} = -\frac{G\,M\,m}{r^3}\,\mathbf{r}$$

Here, m is the mass of any other particle in the field generated by the mass M, and $\mathbf{r}$ is its position vector relative to the source of the field.

Because the gravitational field strength is defined by $\mathbf{g} = \mathbf{F}/m$, we just have to divide the preceding formula by m to give this:

$$\mathbf{g} = -\frac{G\,M}{r^3}\,\mathbf{r}$$

As you can see explicitly in the preceding formula, the gravitational field $\mathbf{g}$ depends only on the mass M of the particle that is producing it and the position vector from the particle, but not on any other particles that may be present. We can also deduce that the magnitude of $\mathbf{g}$ is given by $g = GM/r^2$, consistent with the variation of acceleration due to gravity derived in Chapter 6.

In general, $\mathbf{g}$ could be much more complicated than this simple formula. In a galaxy, for example, $\mathbf{g}$ is the vector sum of all the fields produced by the individual stars (all of which are, of course, moving). But simulating the motion of stars in a galaxy can be done much more efficiently using the field concept than by directly calculating all the forces between every pair of stars, as you'll see in Chapter 12. Meanwhile, it's time to start playing with some simpler examples of gravity as a long-range force.

Gravity with multiple orbiters

Our first example will involve a single gravitational attractor, which will be held fixed. We borrow the orbits simulation from Chapter 6, but we'll add more orbiting planets to make it more interesting and to illustrate the fact that each planet experiences a different gravitational field strength at any given time, and therefore moves along a different trajectory. Here is the modified code that does this in orbits.js:

```
var canvas = document.getElementById('canvas');
var context = canvas.getContext('2d');
var canvas_bg = document.getElementById('canvas_bg');
var context_bg = canvas_bg.getContext('2d');

var M = 1000000; // sun's mass
var G = 1;
var sun;

var planets;
var t;
var t0;
var dt;
var force;
var acc;
var numPlanets = 3;

window.onload = init;
```

```javascript
function init() {
    // create a stationary sun
    sun = new Ball(70,'#ff9900',M,0,true);
    sun.pos2D = new Vector2D(400,300);
    sun.draw(context_bg);
    // create planets
    planets = new Array();
    var radius = new Array(10,6,12);
    var mass = new Array(10,3,15);
    var color = new Array('#0000ff','#ff0000','#00ff00');
    var pos = new Array(new Vector2D(400,50),new Vector2D(500,300),new Vector2D(200,300));
    var velo = new Array(new Vector2D(65,0),new Vector2D(0,100),new Vector2D(0,-70));
    for (var i=0; i<numPlanets; i++){
        var planet = new Ball(radius[i],color[i],mass[i],0,true);
        planet.pos2D = pos[i];
        planet.velo2D = velo[i];
        planet.draw(context);
        planets.push(planet);
    }
    t0 = new Date().getTime();
    t = 0;
    animFrame();
}
function animFrame(){
    requestAnimationFrame(animFrame,canvas);
    onTimer();
}
function onTimer(){
    dt = 0.001*(new Date().getTime() - t0);
    t0 = new Date().getTime();
    t += dt;
    move();
}
function move(){
    context.clearRect(0, 0, canvas.width, canvas.height);
    for (var i=0; i<numPlanets; i++){
        var planet = planets[i];
        moveObject(planet);
        calcForce(planet);
        updateAccel(planet.mass);
        updateVelo(planet);
    }
}
function moveObject(obj){
    obj.pos2D = obj.pos2D.addScaled(obj.velo2D,dt);
    obj.draw(context);
}
function updateAccel(mass){
    acc = force.multiply(1/mass);
}
```

```
function updateVelo(obj){
    obj.velo2D = obj.velo2D.addScaled(acc,dt);
}
function calcForce(planet){
    force = Forces.gravity(G,M,planet.mass,planet.pos2D.subtract(sun.pos2D));
}
```

The main point here is that we are creating three planets and then initializing their positions and velocities so that they end up orbiting the sun. The planets are placed at different distances from the sun and each is then given an initial tangential velocity. The magnitudes of the velocities are chosen essentially by trial and error; or you can use the method given in Chapter 9 to choose the velocities that will give a roughly circular orbit. Note that the move() function loops over each planet, applying the functions moveObject(), calcForce(), updateAccel() and updateVelo() to each in turn.

If you run the code, you'll get a nice solar system toy simulation (see Figure 10-1). The basic physics is there. For example, the nearer a planet is to the sun, the faster it orbits. But this simulation is not completely accurate. As you saw in earlier examples, the Euler integration scheme quickly accumulates errors. If you are looking to do an accurate Solar System simulation, you'll need a better integrator. We'll do that in Chapter 16, where we'll also account for the forces between the planets as well as input accurate data on the masses, sizes, positions, and velocities of the planets.

Figure 10-1. *Multiple orbiting planets around a sun*

Gravity with multiple attractors

Let's complicate the previous simulation a little by adding another attractor. As in that example, we'll keep the attractors fixed. It's not difficult to make them move; that would produce some interesting overall motion. But we'd have to be more careful with our numerical integration scheme. We'll come back to this issue in Chapter 14.

The new code is in a file called attractors.js and differs from orbits.js essentially in the init() and calcForce() methods. Let's look at the former first:

```
var numOrbiters = 3;
var numAttractors = 2;

function init() {
    // create attractors
    attractors = new Array();
    var radiusA = new Array(20,20);
```

```
        var massA = new Array(1000000,1000000);
        var colorA = new Array('#ff9900','#ff9900');
        var posA = new Array(new Vector2D(300,300),new Vector2D(500,300));
        for (var i=0; i<numAttractors; i++){
            var attractor = new Ball(radiusA[i],colorA[i],massA[i],0,true);
            attractor.pos2D = posA[i];
            attractor.draw(context_bg);
            attractors.push(attractor);
        }
        // create orbiters
        orbiters = new Array();
        var radius = new Array(8,8,8);
        var mass = new Array(1,1,1);
        var color = new Array('#0000ff','#ff0000','#00ff00');
        var pos = new Array(new Vector2D(400,300),new Vector2D(400,400),new Vector2D(300,400));
        var velo = new Array(new Vector2D(0,60),new Vector2D(10,60),new Vector2D(90,0));
        for (var i=0; i<numOrbiters; i++){
            var orbiter = new Ball(radius[i],color[i],mass[i],0,true);
            orbiter.pos2D = pos[i];
            orbiter.velo2D = velo[i];
            orbiter.draw(context);
            orbiters.push(orbiter);
        }
        t0 = new Date().getTime();
        t = 0;
        animFrame();
}
```

The code is basically self-explanatory: We create two attractors and three orbiters, all as Ball instances. The attractors are given the same radius and mass. The initial position and velocity of the orbiters are then set. As we shall see, completely different trajectories result from those different initial conditions.

In calcForce() we calculate and then sum the forces acting on each orbiter due to all the attractors. The code can handle any number of attractors.

```
function calcForce(orbiter){
    var gravity;
    force = Forces.zeroForce();
    for (var i=0; i<numAttractors; i++){
        var attractor = attractors[i];
        gravity = Forces.gravity(G,attractor.mass,orbiter.mass,orbiter.pos2D.subtract
(attractor.pos2D));
        force = Forces.add([force, gravity]);
    }
}
```

Run the code with the initial conditions for the three orbiters as specified in attractors.js. The blue orbiter has position vector (400,300) and velocity vector (0,60). This positions the orbiter exactly in the middle of the two attractors and gives it a downward velocity of 60 px/s. You'll see that the orbiter oscillates up and down, so that it is at the same distance from each attractor.

The red orbiter has position vector (400,400) and velocity vector (10,60). You'll find that this orbiter moves in an interesting way: orbiting each attractor alternately, but doing a twist in between so that it orbits both of them in a clockwise sense. If you now keep the same initial position but change the initial velocity to (120,0), you'll see that the orbiter orbits both attractors. In general, you could have a distribution of different attractors and it would still be possible for an object to orbit the whole bunch.

The green orbiter has position vector (300,400) and velocity vector (90,0). This orbiter orbits each attractor alternately, but does so in the opposite sense by following a figure-eight trajectory.

Note that if you let the simulation run for long enough you might start seeing the orbits change due to numerical inaccuracies in the integration scheme. As discussed in the previous section, we will look at how to resolve this issue in Chapter 14.

The key lesson learned from these experiments (see Figure 10-2) is that although the gravitational field is fixed by the attractors, the actual trajectories of particles in that field will also depend on their positions and velocities.

Figure 10-2. *Orbiters moving under the gravitational influence of two attractors*

Needless to say, there are many ways you can experiment with this simulation. As an exercise, why don't you add another attractor and see what kind of motion you get?

Particle trajectories in a gravity field

In this next example, we have a number of attractors, giving rise to a complicated gravity field. The resulting trajectories of particles in such a field can be quite complex and sometimes difficult to predict. To make the example even more interesting, we assume that our attractors are black holes. We modify the attractors.js code from the previous example to implement these new features. Let us first take a look at the init() method:

```
function init() {
    // create attractors
    attractors = new Array();
    for (var i=0; i<numAttractors; i++){
        var r = 20*(Math.random()+0.5);
        var m = (0.5*c*c/G)*r;
        var attractor = new Ball(r,'#000000',m,0,false);
        attractor.pos2D = new Vector2D(Math.random()*canvas.width,Math.random()*canvas.height);
        attractor.draw(context_bg);
        attractors.push(attractor);
    }
```

```
        // create orbiters
        orbiters = new Array();
        var color = new Array('#0000ff','#ff0000','#00ff00');
        for (var i=0; i<numOrbiters; i++){
            var orbiter = new Ball(5,color[i],1,0,true);
            orbiter.pos2D = new Vector2D(Math.random()*canvas.width,Math.random()*canvas.height);
            orbiter.velo2D = new Vector2D((Math.random()-0.5)*100,(Math.random()-0.5)*100);
            orbiter.draw(context);
            orbiters.push(orbiter);
        }
        setupGraph();
        t0 = new Date().getTime();
        t = 0;
        animFrame();
}
```

In this code, we create some black holes as ball instances, place them at random positions on the canvas, and put references to them in an array named attractors. We then create three orbiters, also as ball instances (colored blue, red and green as in the previous examples), and assign them a random position and a random velocity. As you can see from the code, to set the masses of the black holes we've used the formula $M = (0.5c^2/G) R$, where M is the mass and R is the radius of the black hole (which is given a random value between 10 and 30 pixels in the code). What is c, and where does this formula come from? This is the formula for the mass of a black hole in terms of its radius. The constant c is the speed of light. Our black holes are actually hypothetical Newtonian black holes; real (Einsteinian) black holes do not obey Newton's law of gravitation, but require Einstein's General Relativity (a much more complicated theory that we have no intention of simulating in this book!). The value of c will determine the range of masses of the black holes. It's a case of playing with that value to make the black holes produce sufficient, but not too much, attraction so that the particles have a chance to do something interesting before being swallowed up by a black hole. The value we chose is 300.

The calcForce() method loops over all the attractors and sums their gravity forces as in the previous example. In addition, if the orbiter collides with any black hole it disappears and is "recycled" by calling the recycleOrbiter() method, as shown in the highlighted code within calcForce():

```
function calcForce(obj){
    var gravity;
    force = Forces.zeroForce();
    for (var i=0; i<numAttractors; i++){
        var attractor = attractors[i];
        var dist = obj.pos2D.subtract(attractor.pos2D);
        if (dist.length() > attractor.radius+obj.radius){
            gravity = Forces.gravity(G,attractor.mass,obj.mass,dist);
            force = Forces.add([force, gravity]);
        }else{
            recycleOrbiter(obj);
        }
    }
}
```

The recycleOrbiter() method simply reinitializes the position and velocity of the orbiter:

```
function recycleOrbiter(obj){
    obj.pos2D = new Vector2D(Math.random()*canvas.width,Math.random()*canvas.height);
    obj.velo2D = new Vector2D((Math.random()-0.5)*100,(Math.random()-0.5)*100);
}
```

The orbiter is also "recycled," if it goes outside of the visible stage area, by a piece of if logic in the moveObject() method:

```
function moveObject(obj){
    obj.pos2D = obj.pos2D.addScaled(obj.velo2D,dt);
    if (obj.x < 0 || obj.x > canvas.width || obj.y < 0 || obj.y > canvas.height){
        recycleOrbiter(obj);
    }
    obj.draw(context);
}
```

You'll notice that we also call a plotGraph() method in the move() method. What's this about? Well, we are not really plotting a graph, but the trajectory of the orbiter. But we can do this using a Graph instance that has the same range as the stage. This is done in the setupGraph() method, which is called within the init() method. The plotGraph() method then plots the y position of the orbiter against its *x* position. Because plotGraph() is called within move(), it executes on each timestep, so the code effectively traces out the trajectory of the orbiter:

```
function setupGraph(){
    graph = new Graph(context_bg,0,canvas.width,0,canvas.height,0,0,canvas.width,canvas.height);
}
function plotGraph(obj){
    graph.plot([obj.x], [-obj.y], obj.color, false, true);
}
```

Take a look at the file gravity-field.js if you want to see how all this code fits together. Run the code, and you'll be treated to some interesting trajectories as each orbiter moves through the complex gravity field and eventually ends up into a black hole. Each time this happens, it reappears somewhere else and traces out another trajectory that either ends into a black hole or just outside of the stage area. Figure 10-3 shows the type of result you'll be able to see. The randomness in the initial conditions of the particles has the consequence that different patterns emerge over time, so you might want to leave the simulation running for some time to see this. Moreover, each time you run the simulation you will get a different configuration of black holes that will also give different patterns of particle trajectories.

Figure 10-3. *Particle trajectories in the gravity field of black holes*

Building a simple black hole game

In this next project, we'll be a bit more adventurous and actually build a simple game by modifying the preceding simulation. Figure 10-4 shows a screenshot of what the game will look like. The objective of the game is to navigate a spaceship (the triangle) through a black hole field. The spaceship starts off near the lower end of the stage, and you win if you can pass the winning line at the top. Each time you win, a new black hole is added. The positions of the black holes are initialized randomly so that their centers all lie between the winning line and another horizontal line lower down. You lose a life each time a black hole captures the spaceship. If you go off the stage, the spaceship is repositioned at its initial location.

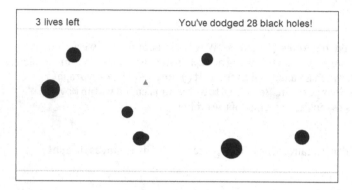

Figure 10-4. *The black hole game*

Creating the visual setup

The bits of code that create the visual setup are invoked from the init() function in the file black-holes.js:

```
function init() {
    ship = new Rocket(12,12,'#ff0000',1);
    ship.pos2D = new Vector2D(0.5*canvas.width,canvas.height-50);
    ship.draw(context);
    attractors = new Array();
    addAttractor();
    setupText();
    setupScene();
    setupEventListeners();
    t0 = new Date().getTime();
    t = 0;
    animFrame();
}
```

First we create a spaceship named ship as an instance of the Rocket object, borrowed from Chapter 6. Next we create an array called attractors, and then call a function addAttractor() that creates our first black hole and puts a reference to it in the attractors array:

```
function addAttractor(){
    var r = 20*(Math.random()+0.5);
    var m = (0.5*c*c/G)*r;
    var attractor = new Ball(r,'#000000',m,0,false);
    attractors.push(attractor);
}
```

The code that creates the black holes and assigns their properties is similar to that in the previous example. In the code in black-holes.js we reduced the speed of light to 200 px/s so that the attraction is not too strong, making it actually possible to avoid the black holes!

Next in init(), the setupText() function is called. This function sets the text properties such as font size and family.

```
function setupText(){
    context_bg.font = "18pt Arial";
    context_bg.textAlign = "left";
    context_bg.textBaseline = "top";
}
```

Then the setupScene() method is called; it displays the visual elements on canvas_bg:

```
function setupScene(){
    context_bg.clearRect(0, 0, canvas_bg.width, canvas_bg.height);
    drawLines();
    showLives();
    showScore();
    for (var i=0; i<attractors.length; i++){
        var attractor = attractors[i];
        attractor.pos2D = new Vector2D(Math.random()*canvas.width,
Math.random()*(yposEdge-yposWinning)+yposWinning);
        attractor.draw(context_bg);
    }
}
```

The setupScene() function first clears the canvas and then calls three functions, drawLines(), showLives(), and showScore(). First, the drawLines() function draws horizontal lines at the two vertical levels yposWinning and yposEdge (here set to 50 and 400, respectively). The showLives() and showScore() functions respectively display the current number of lives (initialized at 3) and the current score (which is equal to the number of black holes successfully avoided). Then setupScene() places all the black holes in random positions between the two aforementioned horizontal lines.

Back in init(), the setupEventListeners() method is called before the animation code is invoked. The corresponding event listeners are described in the next section.

Programming the game functionality

Next we look at the code sections that implement the game functionality. To start with, there are six variables that are initialized at the beginning of the code and that play a key role in the game's interactivity:

```
var applyThrust = false;
var direction = "";
var dir = new Vector2D(0,1);
var vedmdt = 10; // ve*dm/dt
var numLives = 3;
var score = 0;
```

The four variables applyThrust, direction, dir, and vedmdt work together in that they are needed to specify the thrust on the spaceship.

- The first variable, applyThrust, is a Boolean with a value of true if thrust is applied.

- The second variable, direction, is a string that tells us which direction the thrust is applied in.

- The third, dir, is a unit vector pointing downward; it will be used to work out the thrust vector.

- The fourth, vedmdt, is the value of ve*dm/dt, which gives the magnitude of the thrust on the rocket (refer to Chapter 6).

- The last two variables, numLives and score, are Number variables that store the current number of lives and the score, respectively.

The setupEventListeners() method looks as follows:

```
function setupEventListeners(){
    window.addEventListener('keydown',startThrust,false);
    window.addEventListener('keyup',stopThrust,false);
    window.addEventListener('dblclick',changeSetup,false);
}
```

The event handler startThrust() will be invoked if a key is pressed, stopThrust() is invoked if the key is released, and changeSetup() is invoked if we double-click. Here is what startThrust() and stopThrust() look like:

```
function startThrust(evt){
    applyThrust = true;
    if (evt.keyCode==38){ // up arrow
        direction = "UP";
    }
    if (evt.keyCode==40){ // down arrow
        direction = "DOWN";
    }
    if (evt.keyCode==39){ // right arrow
        direction = "RIGHT";
    }
    if (evt.keyCode==37){ // left arrow
        direction = "LEFT";
    }
}
function stopThrust(evt){
    applyThrust = false;
    direction = "";
}
```

Hence, startThrust() sets applyThrust to true and gives values of "UP", "DOWN", "RIGHT", or "LEFT" to direction based on which of the direction keys is pressed. For its part, stopThrust() resets applyThrust to false and assigns a blank string to direction.

The changeSetup() event handler, which is invoked by double-clicking anywhere on the window, looks like this:

```
function changeSetup(evt){
    setupScene();
    recycleOrbiter(ship);
}
```

We have already discussed the setupScene() method in the last section. The recycleOrbiter() method does exactly what its name suggests, re-initializing the spaceship's position and velocity to their original values:

```
function recycleOrbiter(obj){
    obj.pos2D = new Vector2D(0.5*canvas.width,canvas.height-50);
    obj.velo2D = new Vector2D(0,0);
}
```

So you can reset the positions of the black holes and the spaceship at any time by double-clicking anywhere in the browser window.

Let's now look at what calcForce() looks like:

```
function calcForce(obj){
    force = Forces.zeroForce();
    // calculate and add gravity due to all black holes
    var gravity = Forces.zeroForce();
    for (var i=0; i<attractors.length; i++){
        var attractor = attractors[i];
        var dist = obj.pos2D.subtract(attractor.pos2D);
        if (dist.length() > attractor.radius){
            gravity = Forces.gravity(G,attractor.mass,obj.mass,dist);
            force = Forces.add([force, gravity]);
        }else{
            updateLives();
            setupScene();
            recycleOrbiter(obj);
        }
    }
    // calculate and add thrust
    var thrust = Forces.zeroForce();
    if (applyThrust){
        if (direction=="UP"){
            thrust = dir.para(-vedmdt);
        }else if (direction=="DOWN"){
            thrust = dir.para(vedmdt);
        }else if (direction=="RIGHT"){
            thrust = dir.perp(vedmdt);
        }else if (direction=="LEFT"){
            thrust = dir.perp(-vedmdt);
        }else{
            thrust = new Vector2D(0,0);
        }
        force = Forces.add([force, thrust]);
    }
}
```

The force of gravity due to each black hole is calculated in a for loop and then added to the total force (here G is given the value of 1 at the beginning of the code). A collision detection test checks that the spaceship is not within the current black hole; if it is, the method updateLives() is called, and the spaceship is recycled. The thrust on the spaceship is then calculated depending on which arrow key is pressed, as determined by the string stored in the direction variable. For example, if direction=="UP", the thrust is applied opposite to the unit vector dir (which points downward) by using the para() public method of Vector2D, scaling dir by -vedmdt. If the right or left arrow key is pressed, the perp() method is used instead, to give a horizontal vector of length vedmdt. The thrust is then added to the total force.

The updateLives() method mentioned before decrements the number of lives variable numLives:

```
function updateLives(){
    numLives--;
}
```

Next we'll take a look at the moveObject() method:

```
function moveObject(obj){
    obj.pos2D = obj.pos2D.addScaled(obj.velo2D,dt);
    if (obj.x < 0 || obj.x > canvas.width || obj.y < 0 || obj.y > canvas.height){
        recycleOrbiter(obj);
    }
    if (obj.y < yposWinning){
        updateScore();
        addAttractor();
        setupScene();
        recycleOrbiter(obj);
    }
    obj.draw(context);
}
```

The new bits in here are the if blocks of code. The first if block recycles the ship if it is outside the canvas area. The second if block checks to see whether the ship has passed the winning line. If it has, it updates the score, adds a new black hole, repositions all the black holes, and recycles the orbiter. The addAttractor(), setupScene() and recycleOrbiter() methods were described previously. The updateScore() method increments the current score variable score by the current number of black holes (and so score has a value equal to the total number of black holes evaded):

```
function updateScore(){
    score += attractors.length;
}
```

For completeness we show the showLives() and showScore() methods, which are called from setupScene():

```
function showLives(){
    txtLives = numLives.toString().concat(" lives left");
    if (numLives==0){
        txtLives = "Game over";
        stop();
    }
    writeText(txtLives,50,20);
}
function showScore(){
    if (score==0){
        txtScore = "";
```

```
    }else if (score==1){
        txtScore = "You've just dodged a black hole!"
    }else{
        txtScore = "You've dodged ";
        txtScore = txtScore.concat(score.toString()," black holes!");
    }
    writeText(txtScore,400,20);
}
function writeText(txt,x,y){
    context_bg.fillText(txt,x,y);
}
```

The utility function writeText() is called from both showLives() and showScore() and simply writes text on the canvas at a specified location. The other thing to note here is that if numLives become zero, the stop() method is called in showLives() and stops the animation:

```
function stop(){
    cancelAnimationFrame(animId);
}
```

This completes the description of the game. Take a look at the source files and have fun playing around! Feel free to develop the game further. It could certainly do with enhanced graphics and perhaps some sound effects, too. In terms of functionality, see if you can improve the controls; for example, allow the user to move the spaceship diagonally by pressing an up or down key together with a left or right key.

Electrostatic force

The next long-range force we'll look at is one that exists between electrically charged particles. This is called an electric or electrostatic force. But before we get to the force law, we need to explain a few facts about electric charges.

Electric charge

Electric charge is a physical property of particles just like mass is. Elementary particles, the fundamental building blocks of matter, are frequently charged. For example, electrons are particles that orbit the nuclei of atoms, and they have negative charge. The nuclei of atoms include protons, which have positive charge, and neutrons, which have zero charge. What we call an *electric current* is actually a flow of free electrons in a metal—moving charges (whether electrons or not) constitute an electric current.

A particle with mass creates a gravitational field that exerts a force on other particles with mass. Similarly, a charged particle creates an electric field that exerts a force on other charged particles. There are two types of charges: positive and negative.

Like charges repel; unlike charges attract.

So a positive charge will attract a negative charge, and vice versa. But the positive charge will repel another positive charge; similarly, a negative charge will repel another negative charge. This is different from mass, which is always positive and always leads to an attractive gravitational force.

Coulomb's law of electrostatics

The force law for the electric force between two particles is called *Coulomb's law*. It is virtually identical in form with Newton's law of gravitation, being given by the following, where Q_1 and Q_2 are the charges on the two particles, r is the distance between them, and k is a constant analogous to G:

$$F = k \frac{Q_1 Q_2}{r^2}$$

Don't worry about the value of k; we are not going to model real electric charges, but we'll play around with the force law to see what kind of motion it produces. So we can give k any value we like.

The forces exerted on each particle by the other have the same magnitude but opposite direction, in accordance with Newton's third law. Like gravity, the force is directed along the line joining the two particles, so Coulomb's law can be written in vector form in the following two ways, where $\mathbf{r}_u$ is a unit vector in the direction of $\mathbf{r}$:

$$\mathbf{F} = k \frac{Q_1 Q_2}{r^2} \mathbf{r}_u$$

or

$$\mathbf{F} = k \frac{Q_1 Q_2}{r^3} \mathbf{r}$$

Here $\mathbf{r}$ is the position vector of the object experiencing the force relative to the object that is exerting the force, just like gravity (refer to Chapter 6).

Note the absence of a negative sign in the preceding formula (recall that the equivalent vector formula for gravity had a negative sign). That's because like charges repel, whereas masses always attract. So if Q_1 and Q_2 are both positive or both negative, their product is positive, and the force $\mathbf{F}$ is a positive number times $\mathbf{r}$. $\mathbf{F}$ then is oriented in the direction of $\mathbf{r}$ (it is repulsive). But if one of the charges is positive and the other is negative, $\mathbf{F}$ is a negative number times $\mathbf{r}$ and directed opposite to $\mathbf{r}$ (it is attractive).

Let's create an electric force function similar to the gravity function in the Forces object:

```
Forces.electric = function(k,q1,q2,r){
    return r.multiply(k*q1*q2/(r.lengthSquared()*r.length()));
}
```

This is similar in form to the gravity force function, but without the minus sign. As explained previously, the sign of the product q1*q2 determines whether we get an attractive or repulsive force. Just by allowing two different signs for charges, we get a "richer" force than gravity, although the formula is nearly identical in form.

Charged particle attraction and repulsion

To see the electric force in action, let's build a simulation similar to gravity-field.js, but with electrically charged particles instead of black holes. The new file is electric-field.js. The essential differences are as highlighted below in the init() and calcForce() methods:

```
function init() {
    // create attractors
    attractors = new Array();
    for (var i=0; i<numAttractors; i++){
        var r = 20*(Math.random()+0.5);
        var charge = (Math.random()-0.5)*1000000;
```

```
            if (charge<0){
                  color = '#ff0000';
            }else if(charge>0){
                  color = '#0000ff';
            }else{
                  color = '#000000';
            }
            var attractor = new Ball(r,color,1,charge,true);
            attractor.pos2D = new Vector2D(Math.random()*canvas.width,Math.random()*canvas.height);
            attractor.draw(context_bg);
            attractors.push(attractor);
      }
      // create orbiters
      orbiters = new Array();        for (var i=0; i<numOrbiters; i++){
            var orbiter = new Ball(5, '#0000ff',1,1,true);
            orbiter.pos2D = new Vector2D(Math.random()*canvas.width,Math.random()*canvas.height);
            orbiter.velo2D = new Vector2D((Math.random()-0.5)*100,(Math.random()-0.5)*100);
            orbiter.draw(context);
            orbiters.push(orbiter);
      }
      setupGraph();
      t0 = new Date().getTime();
      t = 0;
      animFrame();
}
```

The main difference is that we are giving the attractors random positive and negative charges, and coloring them blue if their charge is positive and red if their charge is negative (and black if they turn out to have zero charge, which would be a rare occurrence because Math.random() would have to return exactly 0.5 for that to be true). Each moving particle, still called orbiter, is given a positive charge of 1 and is colored blue. So it will be attracted by the red centers and repelled by the blue ones.

In calcForce(), we replace Forces.gravity() by Forces.electric(), and masses by charges:

```
function calcForce(obj){
      var electric;
      force = Forces.zeroForce();
      for (var i=0; i<numAttractors; i++){
            var attractor = attractors[i];
            var dist = obj.pos2D.subtract(attractor.pos2D);
            if (dist.length() > attractor.radius+obj.radius){
                  electric = Forces.electric(k,attractor.charge,obj.charge,dist);
                  force = Forces.add([force, electric]);
            }else{
                  recycleOrbiter(obj);
            }
      }
}
```

Figure 10-5 shows an example of what you should see when you run the code.

Figure 10-5. *Trajectories in the electric field of multiple charged particles*

Electric fields

As with gravity, we can invoke the concept of a force field in electrostatics. Recall that the gravitational field strength **g** was defined as the force exerted per unit mass, $\mathbf{g} = \mathbf{F}/m$. Similarly, electric field strength **E** is defined as the force exerted per unit *charge*:

$$\mathbf{E} = \mathbf{F}/q$$

Therefore, if we know the electric field strength, we can easily calculate the electric force the field exerts on a particle by multiplying by its charge:

$$\mathbf{F} = q\,\mathbf{E}$$

Compare this with the equivalent formula for gravity:

$$\mathbf{F} = m\,\mathbf{g}$$

Because we want to use the formula $\mathbf{F} = q\mathbf{E}$, why not create a force function for it? Let's call it Forces.forceField:

```
Forces.forceField = function(q,E) {
    return E.multiply(q);
}
```

Note that nothing stops us from using the same function to calculate $\mathbf{F} = m\mathbf{g}$, too, if we use m for the parameter q and **g** for **E**.

Electric field due to a charged particle

As an example, using Coulomb's law, we can calculate the electric field caused by a charged particle. Let the particle have charge Q. Then the force it exerts on a particle of charge q a distance r away is this:

$$F = \frac{kQq}{r^2}$$

Therefore, the force per unit charge is this:

$$E = \frac{kQ}{r^2}$$

In vector form, it can be written as follows:

$$\mathbf{E} = \frac{kQ}{r^3}\mathbf{r}$$

This is the formula for the electric field produced by a charged particle. But we can also play around with any form for **E** that we want, without worrying about how it is actually produced. Let's look at a couple of examples.

Time-varying electric fields

The electric field of a stationary charge is constant in time, even though it varies in space, as described in the previous section. This is similar to the gravitational field of a stationary mass. But if a charged particle moves, the electric field it sets up will vary in time. For example, an oscillating charge will produce an oscillating electric field.

A simple example is an electric field that varies in time like a sine or cosine wave. Wave concepts such as frequency and amplitude can then be applied to such a sinusoidally varying field, as discussed in Chapters 3 and 8. Moreover, because an electric field is a vector, its components can vary independently of each other. If all this sounds a bit abstract, that's because an electric field *is* an abstract concept! You can't visualize an oscillating electric field with two or more components as you can visualize an oscillating mass-spring system. Nevertheless, the same math can be applied to both.

Interesting effects can be produced with electric fields that vary in time. In the file `electric-field-examples.js`, we take a look at the types of motion that different electric fields produce:

```js
var canvas - document.getElementById('canvas');
var context = canvas.getContext('2d');
var canvas_bg = document.getElementById('canvas_bg');
var context_bg = canvas_bg.getContext('2d');

var particle;
var mass = 1;
var charge = 1;
var E;
var t0, t, dt;
var acc, force;
var graph;
var animId;
var animTime = 25;

window.onload = init;

function init() {
    particle = new Ball(5,'#ff0000',mass,charge,true);
    particle.pos2D = new Vector2D(100,300);
    particle.draw(context);
    setupGraph();
    t0 = new Date().getTime();
    t = 0;
    animFrame();
}
```

```javascript
function animFrame(){
    animId = requestAnimationFrame(animFrame,canvas);
    onTimer();
}
function onTimer(){
    dt = 0.001*(new Date().getTime() - t0);
    t0 = new Date().getTime();
    t += dt;
    if (t < animTime){
        move();
    }else{
        stop();
    }
}
function move(){
    moveObject(particle);
    calcForce();
    updateAccel();
    updateVelo(particle);
    plotGraph();
}
function moveObject(obj){
    obj.pos2D = obj.pos2D.addScaled(obj.velo2D,dt);
    context.clearRect(0, 0, canvas.width, canvas.height);
    obj.draw(context);
}
function calcForce(){
    E = new Vector2D(20*Math.sin(1*t),20*Math.cos(1*t));
    force = Forces.forceField(charge,E);
}
function updateAccel(){
    acc = force.multiply(1/mass);
}
function updateVelo(obj){
    obj.velo2D = obj.velo2D.addScaled(acc,dt);
}
function stop(){
    cancelAnimationFrame(animId);
}
function setupGraph(){
    graph = new Graph(context_bg,0,canvas.width,0,canvas.height,0,0,canvas.width,canvas.height); }
function plotGraph(){
    graph.plot([particle.x], [-particle.y], '#666666', false, true);
}
```

As the preceding code shows, we are moving a charged ball instance under the influence of an electric force specified in calcForce() and plotting its trajectory using the plotGraph() method to draw on a Graph instance previously set up in setupGraph().

Now it's play time! In the source file we included a number of different sinusoidally varying functions (as commented-out code) for E in calcForce() that you can try. Try the following function to start with:

```
E = new Vector2D(0, 50*Math.cos(1*t));
```

What we're doing is to apply an electric field with a vertical component that varies sinusoidally in time with an amplitude (maximum magnitude) of 50 and a frequency of 1 cycle per second. When you run the code, you'll see that the particle oscillates up and down in response to the applied electric field.

What happens if we change the amplitude or frequency of the oscillation? If we increase the amplitude, we'll be applying a larger force, so it's no surprise that the particle will oscillate with larger amplitude. But the effect of increasing the frequency of the applied electric field might not be so obvious. Try changing the frequency to 3, so that E becomes this:

```
E = new Vector2D(0, 50*Math.cos(3*t));
```

If you now run the code, you'll find that the particle oscillates with a much smaller amplitude. What's happening here is that the particle, because it has inertia (mass), cannot keep up with the speed of variation of the electric field.

The following function gives a more interesting pattern, by applying an electric field with a constant component of magnitude 1 in the horizontal and a sinusoidally varying vertical component with an amplitude given by 2*t:

```
E = new Vector2D(1, 2*t*Math.cos(1*t));
```

This makes the particle accelerate in the horizontal and oscillate with an increasing amplitude in the vertical (see Figure 10-6).

Figure 10-6. *Example of the effect of a time-varying electric field on a charged particle*

We'll let you play with the other example functions given in the file, as well as try your own. Of course, there is no reason to restrict yourself to sinusoidally varying functions: feel free to experiment with any function you like.

Electromagnetic force

The electric (electrostatic) force is but one aspect of charged particles. *Moving* charged particles experience and exert another force—a *magnetic force*—in addition to the electric force. Therefore, accounting for the magnetic force will change the way that charged particles move. In this section, you'll see how to compute the magnetic force and how combining it with the electric force affects the motion of charged particles.

Magnetic fields and forces

We've all experienced the fascination of magnets as kids. Part of their appeal is that you can actually feel the force acting between two magnets without them actually touching. Because of this action-at-a-distance characteristic, magnetism fits neatly into the force field concept: a magnet generates a magnetic field around it, which then exerts a force on other magnets and magnetic materials.

What is not obvious at all is that the magnetic field actually has a close connection with the electric field. Magnetic fields are generated by moving charges or by electric fields that vary in time. So, an electric current in a wire will create a magnetic field. A sinusoidally varying electric field will produce a sinusoidally varying magnetic field. The relationship between electric and magnetic fields and the precise way in which they are generated are complex; they are described mathematically by a set of vector differential equations called *Maxwell's equations*. To keep things simple, we'll simply assume given electric and magnetic fields without worrying about how they are produced or how they interact with each other, and focus on how they affect the motion of charged particles.

We already know that the force due to an electric field of strength **E** on a particle of charge q is given by $\mathbf{F} = q\mathbf{E}$. What is the equivalent force law for a magnetic field?

First we need to introduce a magnetic field strength analogous to the electric field strength. There is no need to go into the actual definition; suffice it to say that it exists and is given the symbol **B**, and that it is a vector like the electric field strength **E**.

The force on a charge q due to a magnetic field **B** is then given by the following, where **v** is the velocity vector of the charged particle and × denotes the cross (vector) product (refer to Chapter 3):

$$\mathbf{F} = q\,\mathbf{v} \times \mathbf{B}$$

As explained in Chapter 3, the cross product **v** × **B** gives a vector that is perpendicular to both **v** and **B** (it points in a direction perpendicular to the plane containing the vectors **v** and **B**). Multiplying this by q gives a vector in the same direction but with q times its magnitude. From Chapter 3, the magnetic force can also be written thus, where θ is the angle between the **v** and **B** vectors and **n** is the unit vector perpendicular to **v** and **B** vectors and oriented according to the right-hand rule (refer to Chapter 3):

$$\mathbf{F} = q\,v\,B\sin(\theta)\,\mathbf{n}$$

Note that because the magnetic force is always perpendicular to the particle velocity, it therefore acts as a centripetal force, causing rotation (refer to Chapter 9). Therefore, we can equate the magnetic force law with the centripetal force formula:

$$q\,v\,B\sin(\theta) = \frac{m\,v^2}{r}$$

Rearranging this equation gives this:

$$r = \frac{m\,v}{q\,B\sin(\theta)}$$

This gives the radius of the trajectory that the charged particle follows. The formula tells us that the radius of the circle increases if the mass or velocity increases, and it decreases if either the charge q or the magnetic field magnitude B increases.

The Lorentz force law

You can combine the electric and magnetic forces on a charged particle to give a single formula for the *electromagnetic force* on the particle:

$$F = q\left(E + v \times B\right)$$

This is called the *Lorentz force equation*.

We'll now create a static force function called `lorentz()` in the `Forces` object to implement this force law. The only problem is that the vector product is only defined in 3D, whereas our forces are currently only in 2D. But we can implement the magnetic force qv × **B** in a restricted way if we assume that the magnetic field **B** is always pointing either into or out of the screen. The magnetic force is given by qv × **B** = $qvB \sin(\theta)$ **n** (refer to the previous section), where θ is the angle between **v** and **B**, and in 2D **v** is always perpendicular to **B** if the latter is pointing into or out of the screen. Because sin (90°) = 1, this gives, in that special case, the following, where **n** is perpendicular to **v**:

$$q\, v \times B = q\, v\, B\, n$$

This means that in JavaScript the magnetic force is given by the following, where vel is the velocity vector **v** and B is the magnitude of the magnetic field:

```
vel.perp(q*B*vel.length())
```

The complete Lorentz force function is then as follows:

```
Forces.lorentz - function(q,E,B,vel) {
    return E.multiply(q).add(vel.perp(q*B*vel.length()));
}
```

Let's now play with the Lorentz force function. The file `lorentz-force.js` sets up a particle and makes it move under the Lorentz force. It is very similar to the previous code in `electric-field-examples.js`, with the significant differences being in the calcForce() method:

```
function calcForce(){
    E = new Vector2D(0,0);
    B = 0.2;
    force = Forces.lorentz(charge,E,B,particle.velo2D);
}
```

We initialized the velocity of the particle to be 40 px/s in the x direction in `init()`; different results will be obtained for different choices of initial velocity.

Let's try using different values and math functions for E and B to see what we get. To begin with, let E be a zero vector and let B = 0.2 as in the previous code snippet—in other words, we have a constant magnetic field. Run the code and you'll see that the particle traces out a circular path, as discussed in the previous section. You can verify what we said at the end of the previous section by increasing the value of B to 0.5 and noting that the radius of the circular path decreases.

You can reduce the velocity of the particle on each timestep by adding the following line in calcForce() or updateVelo():

```
particle.velo2D = particle.velo2D.multiply(0.999);
```

This will give you the spiral pattern shown in Figure 10-7.

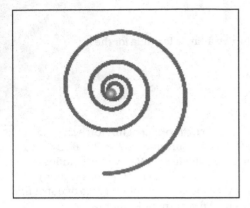

Figure 10-7. *A spiral traced by a particle with decreasing velocity in a constant magnetic field*

Now add in a non-zero electric field; for example:

```
E = new Vector2D(1,0);
B = 0.5;
```

This will produce a helical trajectory. You can also make the electric field and/or the magnetic field time-varying functions; for example:

```
E = new Vector2D(0,50*Math.cos(1*time));
B = 0.5;
```

This will produce trajectories that are not always what you might expect. Have fun experimenting!

Other force laws

So far in this chapter, we have discussed physical forces that actually exist in nature. But there is no reason why we cannot invent our own. Because our main purpose is to play around with forces and their effects, we don't have to be limited by reality. In the next few sections, we'll introduce different force laws and see what they can do. Feel free to create your own!

Central forces

A *central force* is one that satisfies the following two conditions:

- The magnitude of the force depends only on the distance from a given point.

- The direction of the force is always toward that point.

Newtonian gravity, electrostatic forces, and spring forces are all examples of central forces. Mathematically, the above two conditions can be combined to give the force vector at any point P as follows, where $\mathbf{r}_u$ is a unit vector of the point P from the force center, r is its distance from that center, and $f(r)$ is a function of r:

$$\mathbf{F} = f(r)\,\mathbf{r}_u$$

As you already know, for gravity and electrostatic forces, $f(r)$ is proportional to $1/r^2$:

$$f(r) \propto \frac{1}{r^2}$$

This is usually referred to as an *inverse square law*. Ever wondered what things would be like if gravity obeyed a different law—for example, an inverse $1/r$ or an inverse cube $1/r^3$ law? Well we can easily find out by creating a modified force function for gravity. But rather than creating special functions for these different cases, let's create a general central force function that varies according to the following, where both k and n can be positive or negative:

$$f(r) = k\,r^n$$

This gives the following vector form:

$$\mathbf{F} = k\,r^n\,\mathbf{r}_u$$

Or equivalently:

$$\mathbf{F} = k\,r^{n-1}\,\mathbf{r}$$

If k is positive, the force is repulsive (because it is in the direction of $\mathbf{r}$); if k is negative, the force is attractive (because it is in the opposite direction from $\mathbf{r}$). If n is positive, the force increases with distance; if n is negative, the force decreases with distance.

Examples include the spring force law, for which k is negative and n is 1; and gravity, for which k is negative and n is -2. The constant k is usually related to some property of the particle (for example, mass or charge).

Let's add a central force function to the `Forces` object:

```
Forces.central = function(k,n,r) {
    return r.multiply(k*Math.pow(r.length(),n-1));
}
```

The following code snippets from the file `central-forces.js` set up a particle that is subjected to a central force toward a fixed center:

```
function init() {
    center = new Ball(2,'#000000');
    center.pos2D = new Vector2D(350,250);
    center.draw(context_bg);
    particle = new Ball(5,'#ff0000',mass,0,true);
    particle.pos2D = new Vector2D(150,250);
    particle.velo2D = new Vector2D(0,-20);
    particle.draw(context);
    setupGraph();
    t0 = new Date().getTime();
    t = 0;
    animFrame();
}
function calcForce(){
    var r = particle.pos2D.subtract(center.pos2D);
    force = Forces.central(k,n,r);
}
```

The rest of the code is similar to the previous examples, and include plotting the resulting trajectory of the particle as before. You can experiment with different values for k and n, as well as different initial positions and velocities for the particle.

Can you always make a particle follow a closed orbit with an attractive central force (negative k)? We already know this is possible for an $f(r) = k/r^2$ law (for example, gravity) and an $f(r) = kr$ law (springs). But what about other force laws, such as $f(r) = k/r$ or $f(r) = r^3$? Try it out and see for yourself!

As an example, with the following initial conditions, and with $(k = -1, n = 1)$, a spring-like force, you get an elongated closed orbit:

```
center.pos2D = new Vector2D(350,250);
particle.pos2D = new Vector2D(150,250);
particle.velo2D = new Vector2D(0,-20);
```

With $(k = -100000, n = -2)$, a gravity-like law, you also get a closed elliptical orbit. But with $(k = -1000, n = -1)$, a $1/r$ law, you get a flower-like trajectory that does not close on itself (see Figure 10-8); it is a bound orbit, but not a closed one. And with a $1/r^3$ law you get trajectories that either spiral in or spiral out, but do not close: they are neither closed nor bound. Note that the magnitude of k needs to be adjusted depending on the value of n to produce displacements of the right magnitude to fit on the stage.

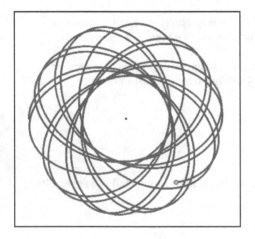

Figure 10-8. *Trajectory traced by a particle in a 1/r force field*

There is actually a mathematical theorem called *Bertrand's theorem* that says the only central force laws that give closed orbits are $f(r) = k/r^2$ and $f(r) = kr$ laws. Lucky for Earth (and us!) that gravity is a $1/r^2$ law!

In spite of the last statement, it turns out that closed circular orbits exist, as a special case, for all attractive central forces if you have just the correct tangential velocity. It's easy to work out the velocity needed for that; just equate the force law with the formula for centripetal force, where m is the mass of the particle:

$$\frac{m v^2}{r} = -k r^n$$

Solving for v gives this:

$$v = \sqrt{\frac{-k r^{n+1}}{m}}$$

You can test this formula with the simulation. It should work for any value of n, provided that k is negative.

Gravity with a spring force law?

Can you imagine what the universe would be like if gravity obeyed a different force law, for instance a spring force law? Well, let's find out!

The code is in the file spring-gravity.js, and is again adapted from previous examples in this chapter. So we'll just list it here with little explanation:

```javascript
var canvas = document.getElementById('canvas');
var context = canvas.getContext('2d');
var canvas_bg = document.getElementById('canvas_bg');
var context_bg = canvas_bg.getContext('2d');

var vmax = 100;
var m = 1; // particles' mass
var M = 1; // center's mass
var G = 1;
var k = -G*M*m;
var n = 1;
var center;
var particles;
var t;
var t0;
var dt;
var force;
var acc;
var numParticles = 50;

window.onload = init;

function init() {
    // create a stationary center
    center = new Ball(20,'#ff0000',M,0,true);
    center.pos2D = new Vector2D(400,300);
    center.draw(context_bg);
    // create particles
    particles = new Array();
    for (var i=0; i<numParticles; i++){
        var particle = new Ball(4,'#000000',m,0,false);
        particle.pos2D = new Vector2D(Math.random()*canvas.width,Math.random()*canvas.height);
        particle.velo2D = new Vector2D((Math.random()-0.5)*vmax,(Math.random()-0.5)*vmax);
        particle.draw(context);
        particles.push(particle);
    }
    t0 = new Date().getTime();
    t = 0;
    animFrame();
};

function animFrame(){
    requestAnimationFrame(animFrame,canvas);
    onTimer();
}
```

```
function onTimer(){
    dt = 0.001*(new Date().getTime() - t0);
    t0 = new Date().getTime();
    t += dt;
    move();
}
function move(){
    context.clearRect(0, 0, canvas.width, canvas.height);
    for (var i=0; i<numParticles; i++){
        var particle = particles[i];
        moveObject(particle);
        calcForce(particle);
        updateAccel(particle.mass);
        updateVelo(particle);
    }
}
function moveObject(obj){
    obj.pos2D = obj.pos2D.addScaled(obj.velo2D,dt);
    obj.draw(context);
}
function updateAccel(mass){
    acc = force.multiply(1/mass);
}
function updateVelo(obj){
    obj.velo2D = obj.velo2D.addScaled(acc,dt);
}
function calcForce(particle){
    var r = particle.pos2D.subtract(center.pos2D);
    force = Forces.central(k,n,r);
}
```

The main idea here is that we create 50 particles, give them random positions and velocities, and subject them to a central force toward a fixed center. The calcForce() method basically computes a central force, using $k = -GMm$, where the gravitational constant $G = 1$, M is the mass of the center; and m is the mass of the relevant particle (all 1 here). Now because k is negative and $n = 1$, we have a spring force. We've created spring-force gravity!

Run the code to get an interesting insight into what life might be like with gravity obeying the spring force law. You'll see that all the particles are pulled toward the center undergoing some kind of oscillation (see Figure 10-9). If you follow any individual particle you will find that it describes a closed orbit (generally elongated) around the center. If you increase the value of the velocity coefficient vmax, say to 1000, the particles will move about more, but will still be pulled into this oscillatory motion. There is just no way to escape from spring gravity!

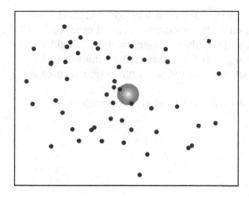

Figure 10-9. *Modeling gravity with a spring force*

Multiple attractors with different laws of gravity

In our final example, `force-fields.js`, we'll combine central forces with different values of k and n to produce a complex force field. This is a universe in which different attractors exert gravity according to different force laws.

Let us first take a look at the `init()` method:

```
function init() {
    centers = new Array();
    // k/r force
    var center1 = new Ball(20,'#ff0000',1000,-1,true);
    center1.pos2D = new Vector2D(200,500);
    center1.velo2D = new Vector2D(10,-10);
    center1.draw(context);
    centers.push(center1);
    // k/r2 force
    var center2 = new Ball(20,'#00ff00',100000,-2,true);
    center2.pos2D = new Vector2D(500,100);
    center2.draw(context_bg);
    centers.push(center2);
    // k/r3 force
    var center3 = new Ball(20,'#0000ff',10000000,-3,true);
    center3.pos2D = new Vector2D(600,300);
    center3.draw(context_bg);
    centers.push(center3);
    // create particles
    particles = new Array();
    for (var i=0; i<numParticles; i++){
        var particle = new Ball(4,'#000000',1,0,false);
        particle.pos2D = new Vector2D(Math.random()*canvas.width,Math.random()*canvas.height);
        particle.velo2D = new Vector2D((Math.random()-0.5)*vmax,(Math.random()-0.5)*vmax);
        particle.draw(context);
        particles.push(particle);
    }
    t0 = new Date().getTime();
    t = 0;
    animFrame();
}
```

261

As in `spring-gravity.js`, we set up a bunch of particles (50 in fact) and give them random positions and velocities, with the maximum velocity magnitude vmax set at 20. Then we set up three attractors, called `center1`, `center2`, and `center3`, put references to them in an array called `centers`, and give them masses of 1000, 100000, and 10000000; and charges of –1, –2, and –3, respectively. The values of the charges are used to store the values of n, the central force law index. There is no reason why we can't do that because we won't be using charge here. This means that the attractors will exert $1/r$, $1/r^2$, and $1/r^3$ force laws, respectively.

We give `center1` a non-zero velocity and make it move by including the following bolded line of code in the `move()` method:

```
function move(){
    context.clearRect(0, 0, canvas.width, canvas.height);
    moveObject(centers[0]);
    for (var i=0; i<numParticles; i++){
        var particle = particles[i];
        moveObject(particle);
        calcForce(particle);
        updateAccel(particle.mass);
        updateVelo(particle);
    }
}
```

The `calcForce()` method looks like this:

```
function calcForce(particle){
    var central;
    force = Forces.zeroForce();
    for (var i=0; i<centers.length; i++){
        var center = centers[i];
        var k = -G*center.mass*particle.mass;
        var n = center.charge;
        var r = particle.pos2D.subtract(center.pos2D);
        if (r.length() > center.radius){
            central = Forces.central(k,n,r);
        }else{
            central = Forces.zeroForce();
        }
        force = Forces.add([force, central]);
    }
}
```

This is similar to the previous example, except that we now have an array of attracting centers (see Figure 10-10), so we sum the central force that each exerts in a for loop in `calcForce()`. Note that we are setting the force to be zero if a particle happens to be within a center. This is to improve the visual effect. After all, it's a universe of our own creation, so we can do whatever we want, can't we?

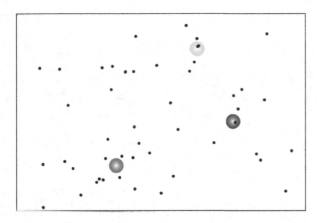

Figure 10-10. *Particles moving in a field composed of different central forces*

If you run the code, you'll see that most of the particles gravitate around the center that exerts the $1/r$ force. As it moves along, it captures more particles. The gravity of this attractor dominates because a $1/r$ force is a longer-range force than a $1/r^2$ or a $1/r^3$ force: it decays less rapidly with distance. The attractor that exerts the $1/r^3$ force holds onto very few particles: its influence decays very rapidly with distance.

There are tons of other things you could try; for example, make the attractors move in more complicated ways (for example, orbit a center or move around and bounce). You could add more attractors or include antigravity. You are limited only by your imagination.

Summary

You now have plenty of tools with a whole lot of forces for creating interesting types of motion. This concludes Part II of the book. In Part III, you will apply what you have learned in Part II to build more complex systems consisting of interacting particles or extended objects.

Multi-particle and Extended Systems

CHAPTER 11

■ ■ ■

Collisions

This chapter deals with an important subject that is bound to crop up in any animation or simulation: collisions. More precisely, it focuses primarily on *collision resolution*—how to respond to collision events—and less on *collision detection*. Both collision detection and collision resolution are vast subjects in their own right. The intricacies of collision detection for general objects are outside the scope of this book (because we focus on the physics governing motion), but the situation is much simpler for collisions between particles, which is the main subject of this chapter. Similarly, it is impossible to cover all aspects of collision resolution in a single chapter. We shall, therefore, concentrate on some of the basics that are most commonly encountered. Specifically, we shall restrict our attention to collisions of particles with fixed walls (bouncing) and with other particles.

Topics covered in this chapter include the following:

- **Collisions and their modeling:** This brief introductory section explains what collisions are and outlines the approach this chapter will take to modeling them.

- **Bouncing off horizontal or vertical walls:** By *wall*, we mean any fixed flat surface that a particle can bounce off. We start with the example of a ball bouncing off a horizontal or vertical wall. The collision resolution in this case is simple. The effects of energy loss by bouncing or wall friction can also be implemented in a straightforward way.

- **Bouncing off inclined walls:** The situation is a lot more complicated if the wall is inclined. You will see a general method to resolve collisions with walls of any inclination.

- **Collisions between particles in 1D:** When particles move along the line joining them, collisions are one-dimensional and can be resolved in a straightforward way by applying the laws of conservation of momentum and energy.

- **Collisions between particles in 2D:** The final section discusses a general method for resolving more complicated two-dimensional collisions between particles that occur at an angle to the line joining them.

Collisions and their modeling

We'll begin by defining what we mean by collisions in the context of this book. A *collision* between two objects is a brief interaction during which they come into contact and exchange forces that then modify their motion. The task of collision resolution is to determine the motion of the two colliding objects immediately after the collision has taken place.

In Part II of the book, you became accustomed to solving motion problems using forces. That is not how collisions are usually treated. It is very difficult to model the strong and brief forces that are exerted during collisions. The way collisions are normally handled is through their effect. We know from Newton's second law of motion that forces produce changes in momentum. In Chapter 5, this relationship was expressed in the following way through the concept of an impulse $\mathbf{F}\Delta t$, where $\Delta\mathbf{p}$ is the change in momentum produced by an impulse:

$$\mathbf{F}\Delta t = \Delta\mathbf{p}$$

For a particle with constant mass m:

$$\Delta\mathbf{p} = m\Delta\mathbf{v}$$

so that:

$$\mathbf{F}\Delta t = m\Delta\mathbf{v}$$

So the effect of a large and brief collision force, in other words an impulse $\mathbf{F}\Delta t$, is to produce a change of velocity given by the preceding formula.

The way to handle collisions is to directly work out that change in velocity. If you look back to Chapter 5, you will recall that this is what the principle of momentum conservation is all about. But momentum conservation on its own is not enough for collision resolution. We also have to make assumptions about what happens to the kinetic energy of the colliding objects. Hence, the physics involved in collisions consist of the two conservation principles of momentum and energy taken together. We will apply them either explicitly or tacitly in what follows.

Broadly speaking, we will simulate two types of collisions: particle-particle collisions and particle-wall collisions. A *wall* here means an immovable object, whose motion is not itself being simulated. Specifically, we'll use the word *wall* to refer to any fixed flat surface from which particles can bounce. Therefore, our walls can be horizontal or vertical or oblique; they can also be bounding barriers or barriers placed anywhere else in the simulation space.

Bouncing off horizontal or vertical walls

In the first application of collision physics, we will look at how to make a ball bounce off a straight wall that is either horizontal or vertical in a 2D simulation space such as a floor, ceiling, or room wall. For illustration, we'll use a vertical wall here, but similar principles will apply to horizontal walls as well.

We'll look at elastic and inelastic bouncing in turn (bouncing in which the kinetic energy of the ball is or is not conserved).

Elastic bouncing

If the ball bounces elastically off a wall, its kinetic energy just after bouncing must equal its kinetic energy just before bouncing. Because k.e. = ½ mv^2, this implies that its velocity magnitude is unchanged by the collision.

Consider first a special case in which the ball hits the wall perpendicularly with velocity $\mathbf{v}$ (see Figure 11-1). In that case, the ball will bounce back at a right angle as well. Therefore, because its velocity magnitude is unchanged, its velocity just after bouncing will be $-\mathbf{v}$.

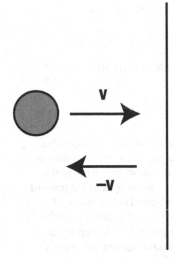

Figure 11-1. *A ball bouncing off a wall at a right angle*

This is very easy to implement in code: you just reverse the velocity direction after the collision detection. However, there is something else to consider. When collision is detected, the ball may have passed the edge of the wall, penetrating it slightly. Therefore, before you reverse the ball's velocity, you need to reposition the ball just at the edge of the wall (see Figure 11-2). This is necessary not just to avoid the visual effect of the ball penetrating into the wall but also to avoid the potential problem of the ball "getting stuck" in the wall. The latter situation might arise if the reversed velocity of the ball is not sufficient for it to get out of the wall (especially if the velocity is also reduced to account for energy loss—see the next section). In that case, the velocity of the ball would be reversed again on the next timestep, sending it back into the wall.

Figure 11-2. *Repositioning the ball after collision detection*

The following code illustrates these steps for the scenario shown in Figure 11-2, for a Ball instance named ball and a wall object named wall:

```
if (ball.x > wall.x - ball.radius){  // collision detection
    ball.x = wall.x - ball.radius;  // reposition ball at wall edge
    ball.vx *= -1; // reverse ball's velocity
}
```

These simple three lines encapsulate the whole process of handling the bouncing of a ball colliding perpendicularly with a horizontal or vertical wall:

1. Collision detection: simple in this case.

2. Reposition the particle at the point of collision: in this case, shift it horizontally or vertically so that it just touches the wall.

3. Calculate the particle's new velocity just after the collision: here, for elastic collisions normal (perpendicular) to the wall, just reverse the velocity.

Note that in steps 1 and 2 the preceding code assumes that the ball's position is taken to be that of its center. If, for instance, the ball's position is instead taken to be the upper-left corner of its bounding box, then its diameter should be subtracted in the corresponding lines of code. Also, this code covers only the situation where the ball is moving from left to right, but it is not difficult to see how you can modify it to move the ball from right to left instead.

This is all nice and simple, but what if the ball hits the wall at an oblique angle (see Figure 11-3), instead of at a right angle? In that case, in implementing step 3, we need to consider the components of velocity perpendicular and parallel to the wall separately. In the case of a vertical wall shown in Figure 11-3, the perpendicular component is ball.vx, and the parallel component is ball.vy. We need to reverse the perpendicular component as before and leave the parallel component unchanged. This is just what the previous piece of code does, so it should work well for an oblique impact as well. This technique of decomposing the velocity vector into a normal (perpendicular) and a parallel (tangential) component with respect to the wall seems entirely natural in this context. But its application is more general; you'll see in the next section that a variant of it applies to the collision between two particles.

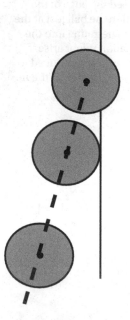

Figure 11-3. Ball bouncing off a wall at an oblique angle

If you need to be extra accurate, there is something else you need to worry about, this time in relation to step 2. Take a look again at Figure 11-3. In the previous code, we reposition the ball by moving it along the x-direction so that it just touches the wall. But when the collision is oblique, the ball's real position at the point of collision is along the line of collision. So the ball also needs to be moved a little along the y-direction. We'll devise a general method to do that in the next section. For this simple example, let's just adjust the x-position only. This should work fine and produce a smooth bouncing effect in most common situations (except perhaps if you have a slow machine, in which case you might find that the ball occasionally sticks to the wall).

The downloadable file wall-bouncing.js demonstrates this simple example. Here is the code:

```
var canvas = document.getElementById('canvas');
var context = canvas.getContext('2d');
var canvas_bg = document.getElementById('canvas_bg');
var context_bg = canvas_bg.getContext('2d');

var ball;
var wallX = 400;
var t0, dt;

window.onload = init;

function init() {
    // create a ball
    ball = new Ball(15,'#000000',1,0,false);
    ball.pos2D = new Vector2D(100,100);
    ball.velo2D = new Vector2D(200,50);
    ball.draw(context);
    // create a wall
    context_bg.strokeStyle = '#333333';
    context_bg.beginPath();
    context_bg.moveTo(wallX,50);
    context_bg.lineTo(wallX,350);
    context_bg.closePath();
    context_bg.stroke();
    // make the ball move
    t0 = new Date().getTime();
    animFrame();
};

function animFrame(){
    animId = requestAnimationFrame(animFrame,canvas);
    onTimer();
}
function onTimer(){
    var t1 = new Date().getTime();
    dt = 0.001*(t1-t0);
    t0 = t1;
    if (dt>0.2) {dt=0;};
    move();
}
function move(){
    moveObject(ball);
    checkBounce(ball);
}
function moveObject(obj){
    obj.pos2D = obj.pos2D.addScaled(obj.velo2D,dt);
    context.clearRect(0, 0, canvas.width, canvas.height);
    obj.draw(context);
}
```

```
function checkBounce(obj){
    if (obj.x > wallX - obj.radius){
        obj.x = wallX - obj.radius;
        obj.vx *= -1;
    }
}
```

As you can see, the code in `init()` simply creates a ball as a `Ball` object and draws a straight line to represent a wall. The bulk of the subsequent animation code is familiar. Here we are not imposing any forces. Therefore, the velocity of the ball is constant, except when it collides with the wall. The key functionality is provided by the `checkBounce()` method, which contains a piece of conditional code identical to the one given previously for a ball colliding perpendicularly with the wall. Note that this code would have to be modified slightly if the wall were on the left side or horizontal. And if the wall were neither horizontal nor vertical, but at some angle, you'd need a lot more code than just those three lines in the `checkBounce()` method, as you'll soon find out!

Inelastic bouncing

In the previous example, we assumed that there is no loss of kinetic energy, in other words that the collision is elastic. Doing this means the ball bounces back with the same velocity magnitude. In real-world collisions there is always some loss of kinetic energy. It is very easy to include the effect of loss of kinetic energy due to bouncing. All you have to do is multiply the velocity of the ball normal to the wall by a factor of less than 1 when reversing it.

Hence, in the previous example, the following line:

```
ball.vx *= -1;
```

would be replaced by something like this, where `vfac` is a number between 0 and 1:

```
ball.vx *= -vfac; // energy loss on bouncing
```

A value of 1 corresponds to an elastic collision, while a value of 0 corresponds to a completely inelastic collision (discussed in more detail a little later), in which the ball just sticks to the wall. You can experiment with different values of `vfac` to see what you get.

The reason for multiplying the velocity by this constant factor will become clear later, when we discuss one-dimensional collisions.

Similarly, you can model the effect of wall friction in a simple way by multiplying the tangential velocity of the ball (the velocity component parallel to the wall) by a factor between 0 and 1:

```
ball.vy *= vfac2; // wall friction
```

Note the absence of a minus sign in this case, as friction reduces but does not reverse the tangential velocity.

Bouncing off inclined walls

The situation becomes significantly more complicated if the wall on which the ball bounces is inclined at some angle to the horizontal or vertical. The same steps apply as in the case of a horizontal or vertical wall, but they are now a bit more complex to implement. Different approaches could be taken here. One common approach, described in the book *Foundation HTML5 Animation with JavaScript,* by Billy Lamberta and Keith Peters (Apress, 2011), is to perform a coordinate rotation to make the wall horizontal, do the bouncing, and then rotate the coordinate system back. This is a perfectly good way to do it, and we refer you to that book for details on the procedure. For our present purposes, because we are using vectors, we have devised an alternative method that exploits the vector formulation and avoids the two coordinate rotations. We explain the steps of the new method in detail before giving an example of how to implement it.

Collision detection with an inclined wall

Collision detection is much less straightforward when bouncing off an inclined wall because it is not simply a case of checking the *x*- or *y*-position of the ball in relation to that of the wall. But thinking in terms of vectors helps a lot. Take a look at Figure 11-4, which shows a particle approaching collision with a wall. There are basically two conditions that must be met for a collision to occur:

- The perpendicular distance of the particle from the wall must be smaller than its radius.

- The particle must be located between the end points of the wall.

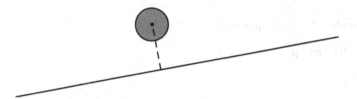

Figure 11-4. *A ball approaching a wall*

There are a number of ways to implement either condition. We describe one possible approach here. Figure 11-5 shows a diagram of the position and displacement vectors corresponding to the setup in Figure 11-4. In this diagram, **p1** and **p2** are the position vectors of the end points of the wall with respect to the origin O; **w** is a vector from the end point marked A (with position vector **p1**) to the other end point. Similarly, **p** is the position vector of the ball with respect to the origin, **b1** and **b2** are vectors from the ball to the end points of the wall, and **d** is a perpendicular vector from the ball to the wall (so that **d** is equal to the distance PQ of the ball from the wall). Note that we are taking the position of a particle to be at its center. This is true of any Ball instance created from the Ball object.

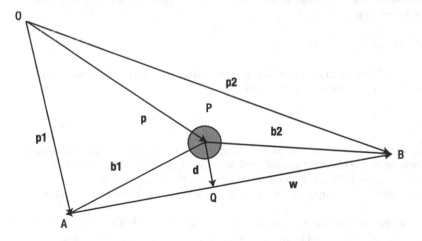

Figure 11-5. *Vector diagram for analyzing the collision of a ball with an inclined wall*

In terms of these vectors, the first condition is simply the following, where r is the radius of the ball:

$$d < r$$

The second condition can be stated in terms of the projections QA and QB of the vectors **b1** and **b2** in the direction of the wall vector **w**. If the length of both of those projections is less than the length of **w**, it means that the ball is between the end points of the wall. Otherwise, if either projection exceeds the length of **w**, the ball must be outside of that range and won't hit the wall.

It remains now to work out the length of the projections and the distance d from the known vectors **p1**, **p2**, and **p**. By using the rules of vector addition, we get the following:

$$\mathbf{w} = \mathbf{p2} - \mathbf{p1}$$

In pseudocode, this is:

```
wallVec = wall.p2.subtract(wall.p1);
```

By a similar reasoning, the vectors **b1** and **b2** are given by these equations:

$$\mathbf{b1} = \mathbf{p1} - \mathbf{p}$$

$$\mathbf{b2} = \mathbf{p2} - \mathbf{p}$$

In pseudocode, they can be written as follows:

```
ballToWall1 = wall.p1.subtract(ball.pos2D);
ballToWall2 = wall.p2.subtract(ball.pos2D);
```

Then the projection of the vectors `ballToWall1` and `ballToWall2` onto **w** is given by this:

```
proj1 = ballToWall1.projection(wallVec);
proj2 = ballToWall2.projection(wallVec);
```

The vector **d**, which we'll call `dist` in pseudocode, can then be obtained by subtracting from **b1** the projection vector of **b1** onto **w**. In pseudocode it can be written like this:

```
dist = ballToWall1.subtract(ballToWall1.project(wallVec));
```

The `project()` function will be introduced later in the chapter. You can probably express these quantities in a number of different but equivalent ways. We leave that to you as an exercise!

Repositioning the particle

The formula you saw in the previous section for repositioning the particle at collision detection is specific to a vertical wall on the right side in relation to the location of the ball. Its form will look slightly different for the walls on the left, top, or bottom. And it's no good if the wall is inclined. We need something better. That's where vectors come to the rescue again. With vector methods, it is possible to come up with a formula that works for any particle velocity and any wall orientation.

Figure 11-6 shows a ball hitting an inclined wall, and the collision being detected after the ball has gone a small distance into the wall. As the diagram indicates, the ball must be moved a distance $\Delta s = h$ back along its line of approach (opposite to its velocity vector). Here we are assuming that the direction of the velocity vector is constant during that small interval. If a force such as gravity is present, this is not strictly true, but because the time interval is so small, the velocity direction can be taken as constant to a very good approximation.

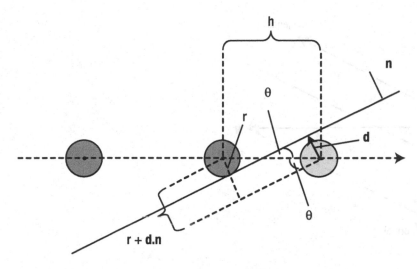

Figure 11-6. *Repositioning a particle after collision detection with an inclined wall*

Simple trigonometry then shows that the magnitude of Δs is given by the following expression, where **d** is a perpendicular vector from the particle's center at the point of collision *detection* to the wall (so that its magnitude *d* is the distance of the particle from the wall), **n** is a unit vector perpendicular to the wall and pointing into the side where the particle normally resides, and θ is the angle between the line of approach of the particle (and therefore its velocity just before collision) and the wall:

$$\Delta s = \frac{r + \mathbf{d} \bullet \mathbf{n}}{\sin(\theta)}$$

Note that if the ball's center at the point of collision detection lies in front of the wall, then **d** is opposite to **n**, and therefore $\mathbf{d} \cdot \mathbf{n} = -d$; if it lies behind the wall, then **d** points along **n**, and so $\mathbf{d} \cdot \mathbf{n} = d$. Using the dot product automatically handles both cases.

In pseudocode, the displacement vector to reposition the particle is then given by this:

```
displ = particle.velo2D.para(deltaS);
```

Therefore, the particle's position needs to be updated as follows:

```
particle.pos2D = particle.pos2D.subtract(displ);
```

This all looks nice and simple in comparison to the use of special non-vector code for each wall.

Calculating the new velocity

Just as it is with a horizontal or vertical wall, the particle's new velocity after bouncing is calculated by first decomposing the velocity before bouncing into components parallel and normal to the wall, and then reversing the normal component. But because the wall is now oblique, those components are not just the vx and vy properties of the particle. Instead, we have to specify them as Vector2D objects in their own right.

See Figure 11-7 for an illustration of how to do this. If **d** is a vector from the particle center normal to the wall at the point of collision, the normal velocity is given as a vector with magnitude equal to the projection of the particle's velocity onto **d** and in the same direction as **d**.

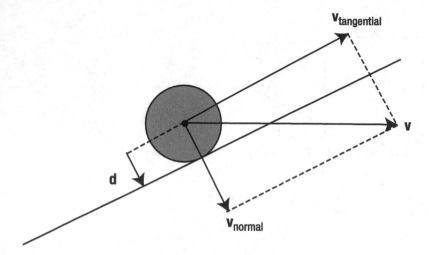

Figure 11-7. *Decomposing the velocity vector*

In pseudocode, if we calculate the perpendicular vector from the particle to the wall as dist and denote the particle as particle, the normal velocity is given by the following using the projection() and para() methods of the Vector2D object:

```
normalVelo = dist.para(particle.velo2D.projection(dist));
```

Recall that vec1.projection(vec2) gives the length of the projection of vector vec1 in the direction of vec2, and that vec.para(mag) gives a vector parallel to vector vec and of length mag.

We can make the code even simpler by creating the following project() method in the Vector2D object:

```
function project(vec) {
    return vec.para(this.projection(vec));
}
```

Thus, vec1.project(vec2) gives a vector in the direction of vector vec2 and with magnitude equal to the projection of vec1 in the direction of vec2. With this newly defined method, we can write the normal velocity simply as follows:

```
normalVelo = particle.velo2D.project(dist);
```

The tangential velocity can then be obtained simply by subtracting the normal velocity from the particle velocity (see Figure 11-7):

```
tangentVelo = particle.velo2D.subtract(normalVelo);
```

These are the precollision velocities. Assuming there is no energy loss, the collision will reverse the normal velocity while leaving the tangential velocity unchanged. Therefore, the new velocity of the particle as a result of the collision is given by this:

```
particle.velo2D = tangentVelo.addScaled(normalVelo,-1);
```

If there is energy loss due to bouncing, simply replace the –1 in the previous code by the fraction vfac discussed in the previous section.

Velocity correction just before collision

If you are creating a simulation that involves a force, such as gravity, there is something else to worry about. Whenever there is a force involved, it means that the particle is accelerating (its velocity is changing all the time). In that case, when the particle is repositioned at the edge of the wall, its velocity must also be adjusted to what it was at that point. Although this may seem like a small correction, failure to do so could in some cases result in serious loss of accuracy. This applies equally to horizontal or vertical walls if the velocity is changing with time.

Let's consider a simple example: a ball dropped from a certain height onto a horizontal floor. Suppose that collision is detected when the ball has gone slightly past the floor level. If you simply follow the procedure given so far, you would move the ball to the level of the floor and then reverse its velocity (if you assume no energy loss due to bouncing). The trouble is that because the ball is accelerating under gravity, its velocity at the point of *collision detection* is higher than it should be at the actual point of collision. By simply reversing this velocity, you are sending it off with higher kinetic energy than it's supposed to have as a result of having lost potential energy by falling from its initial height. The consequence is that the ball will end up reaching higher than the point it fell from! After a few bounces, the animation could become completely unstable. Of course, if you implement energy loss on bouncing, you may not even notice the problem—if accuracy is not important, that may be a simple trick to solve the problem. But if you want to be as accurate as possible, or if the nature of the simulation does not permit you to include energy loss, then here is the way to do it.

The aim is to compute the velocity of the particle at the point of collision given that it is accelerating. We know the velocity, acceleration, and displacement at the point of collision detection. To proceed, let's start with the calculus definition of acceleration:

$$a = \frac{dv}{dt}$$

For a reason that will become apparent shortly, we can write it as the following (you can think of the two *ds* factors as "cancelling out"):

$$a = \frac{dv}{ds}\frac{ds}{dt}$$

Now, because $v = ds/dt$, we can write it as follows:

$$a = v\frac{dv}{ds}$$

This gives us a differential equation connecting the quantities that we were just talking about. Because we are doing a discrete simulation, let's write this:

$$\frac{dv}{ds} \approx \frac{\Delta v}{\Delta s}$$

Substituting into the preceding equation gives this:

$$a \approx v\frac{\Delta v}{\Delta s}$$

And so:

$$\Delta v \approx \frac{a\,\Delta s}{v}$$

This formula gives the change in velocity Δv that results from a displacement Δs under an acceleration a. Let v be the velocity at collision detection and v' be the velocity at collision, so that:

$$\Delta v = v - v'$$

Simple algebra gives this:

$$\frac{v'}{v} \approx 1 - \frac{a\,\Delta s}{v^2}$$

This formula gives the ratio of the magnitude of the velocity at the point of collision to that at the point of collision detection in terms of the acceleration (which is constant in the case of gravity), the velocity at the point of collision detection, and the displacement of the particle from the point of collision to the position where collision is detected. The latter quantity was worked out in the section "Repositioning the particle." Therefore, the adjustment factor for the velocity can be calculated from these known quantities as given by the preceding formula. The formula was derived for a 1D case because we didn't use vectors, but it applies equally to 2D when the acceleration a and the displacement Δs are vectors that may not be in the same direction (for example, for a ball moving under gravity). In that case, we take the acceleration resolved in the direction of the displacement, so that in effect we need to replace the product $a\Delta s$ by the dot product $\mathbf{a}.\Delta\mathbf{s}$; and v is the magnitude of the velocity vector.

Let's denote the code variable corresponding to the velocity correction factor v'/v as vcor. Then, assuming that the direction of the velocity does not change much between the point of collision and the point of collision detection, we can write this in pseudocode:

```
veloAtCollision = veloAtCollisionDetection.multiply(vcor);
```

Example: a ball bouncing off an inclined wall

All that vector algebra we've been discussing is probably beginning to sound a bit heavy. So it's time to pull together all you have learned in this section to build a full example. Because we are going to do a lot of bouncing around walls, it would make sense to create a reusable Wall object. Let's do that first.

Creating a Wall object

The Wall object is a simple object that draws a line between two specified end points to represent a wall. The end points are Vector2D objects. Here is the full code of the Wall object:

```
function Wall(p1,p2){
    this.p1 = p1;
    this.p2 = p2;
    this.side = 1;
}
Wall.prototype = {
    get dir (){
        return this.p2.subtract(this.p1);
    },
    get normal (){
        return this.dir.perp(1);
    },
    draw: function (context) {
        context.save();
        context.strokeStyle = '#000000';
```

```
            context.lineWidth = 1;
            context.beginPath();
            context.moveTo(this.p1.x,this.p1.y);
            context.lineTo(this.p2.x,this.p2.y);
            context.closePath();
            context.stroke();
            context.restore();
        }
    }
```

The end points, denoted by p1 and p2, are supplied as arguments in Wall's constructor. Properties wall.dir and wall.normal are defined via getters that return the vector from p1 to p2 (the vector along the wall) and the unit vector normal to the wall, respectively. The usefulness of these properties will soon become apparent. The side property will be discussed in the section "Dealing with a potential 'tunneling' problem."

Creating a Wall instance

In the file wall-object.js, we demonstrate how to create a Wall instance that is at an oblique angle to the horizontal by the following piece of code:

```
var p1 = new Vector2D(100,200);
var p2 = new Vector2D(250,400);
var wall = new Wall(p1,p2);
wall.draw(context);
```

So the end point vectors p1 and p2 are [100, 200] and [250, 400], respectively.

Getting a ball to bounce off an inclined wall

In the bouncing-off-inclined-wall.js file we first create a ball and an inclined wall and then make the ball move under gravity onto the wall (see Figure 11-9 later in the chapter) using the usual animation code with a gravity force Forces.constantGravity in calcForce(). The move() method adds a new method, checkBounce(), which looks as follows:

```
function checkBounce(obj){
    // vector along wall
    var wdir = wall.dir;
    // vectors from ball to endpoints of wall
    var ballp1 = wall.p1.subtract(obj.pos2D);
    var ballp2 = wall.p2.subtract(obj.pos2D);
    // projection of above vectors onto wall vector
    var proj1 = ballp1.projection(wdir);
    var proj2 = ballp2.projection(wdir);
    // perpendicular distance vector from the object to the wall
    var dist = ballp1.addScaled(wdir.unit(), proj1*(-1));
    // collision detection
    var test = ((Math.abs(proj1) < wdir.length()) && (Math.abs(proj2) < wdir.length()));
    if ((dist.length() < obj.radius) &&  test){
        // angle between velocity and wall
        var angle = Vector2D.angleBetween(obj.velo2D, wdir);
```

```
                // reposition object
                var normal = wall.normal;
                if (normal.dotProduct(obj.velo2D) > 0){
                    normal.scaleBy(-1);
                }
                var deltaS = (obj.radius+dist.dotProduct(normal))/Math.sin(angle);
                var displ = obj.velo2D.para(deltaS);
                obj.pos2D = obj.pos2D.subtract(displ);
                // velocity correction factor
                var vcor = 1-acc.dotProduct(displ)/obj.velo2D.lengthSquared();
                // corrected velocity vector just before impact
                var Velo = obj.velo2D.multiply(vcor);
                // velocity vector component perpendicular to wall just before impact
                var normalVelo = dist.para(Velo.projection(dist));
                // velocity vector component parallel to wall; unchanged by impact
                var tangentVelo = Velo.subtract(normalVelo);
                // velocity vector component perpendicular to wall just after impact
                obj.velo2D = tangentVelo.addScaled(normalVelo,-vfac);
            }
        // collision at the wall boundaries
        else if (Math.abs(ballp1.length()) < obj.radius){
            bounceOffEndpoint(obj,wall.p1);
        }
        else if (Math.abs(ballp2.length()) < obj.radius){
            bounceOffEndpoint(obj,wall.p2);
        }
    }
}
```

This code closely mirrors the description given in the previous sections. Most of it should therefore be straightforward (and we've left the comments in so you can follow the logic more easily). Let's therefore focus on just a couple of features that were not covered in the preceding discussion.

First, in the code that repositions the ball after collision detection, note that we check whether the wall normal vector has a positive dot product with the ball's velocity vector; if so, we reverse the wall normal vector. To understand why this is done, refer to the section "Repositioning the particle," in which we said that the normal must point to the side where the particle resides. The latter condition is equivalent to saying that the normal vector should point so that it has a normal component in the opposite direction to the ball's velocity and so should have a negative dot product with it (see Figure 11-8). The if code enforces that condition. But why do we need to check this every timestep; can't we fix the normal once and for all? The reason is that by doing so we allow for the possibility that the ball could bounce on the bottom surface as well as on the top surface of the wall.

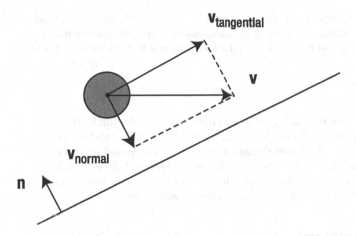

Figure 11-8. *The unit normal vector to the wall should be oriented opposite to the velocity vector*

The second thing to point out is the presence of the two `else if` blocks at the end of the `checkBounce()` function. They are there to handle the case where the ball is within a radius of either of the end points of the wall. In that case, they call a new method: `bounceOffEndpoint()`. The idea is that bouncing off the edge of the wall should give rise to a different type of motion and should therefore be handled differently. The approach we take is to handle such a collision in a similar way to that between two particles, with the additional feature that here one of the "particles," the wall end point, is fixed and has zero radius. The code within the `bounceOffEndpoint()` method probably won't make too much sense now, but it should once you've covered the material on collisions between particles later in the chapter.

To make the simulation more interactive and fun, there is also code that allows you to click and drag anywhere on the canvas to change the position and size of the ball. On releasing the mouse, the simulation resumes with the new ball.

Spend some time experimenting with the simulation. Click and drag to create balls of different sizes and see how they fall and bounce onto the inclined wall in a natural way. Avoid overlapping the ball with the wall when you are dragging as this will result in erratic behavior. Release the ball onto the end points of the wall and notice the difference in the way it bounces. Change gravity g and the energy loss factor vfac. See Figure 11-9 for a screenshot of the simulation.

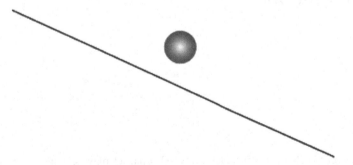

Figure 11-9. *A ball bouncing off an inclined wall*

Next release the ball just above the line, so that it starts to slide down the wall. You might find that the ball tends to get "stuck" if it just slides without bouncing. The problem is that our code handles *collision resolution* but not *contact resolution*. To fake contact resolution, you can cheat by introducing the following line in checkBounce(), just after the ball's position vector pos2D is updated:

```
obj.y -= 0.1;
```

This raises the ball very slightly (by just 0.1 px) above the wall each time it comes into contact with it. The result is that the ball then falls back onto the wall again, experiencing a series of consecutive collisions as it slides down the wall. Run the simulation again with this additional line, and see how the ball now slides down the wall, apparently smoothly. This is strongly reminiscent of the simulation of a ball sliding down an inclined plane that we did back in Chapter 7 using normal contact forces. In fact, this is a common approach to handling contact resolution: using impulses produced by "micro-collisions" rather than by explicitly including a normal contact force.

Dealing with a potential "tunneling" problem

The method of collision detection we described in the previous section and implemented in this simulation should work well under most normal circumstances. But in some cases, especially if the simulation is run on a slow machine and the ball is small and moving fast, it may be possible for the ball to cross the wall completely in a single timestep. In that case, collision detection will fail. This is known as *tunneling*. You can probably see this effect if you make the ball very small (1 px) and release it a long way above the wall so it achieves a high velocity by the time it hits the wall. The ball might then pass straight through the wall.

The collision detection algorithm outlined in the previous section fails because the first condition (that the particle is closer to the wall than its radius) is never satisfied. We need to modify the algorithm to include the new possible scenario. A simple solution is to test whether the ball's center has moved from one side of the wall to the other. If so, that means it has "tunneled," and that in itself provides the collision detection.

We have implemented this collision detection mechanism in a modified version of the simulation with source files bouncing-off-inclined-wall2.js. If you compare this modified code with the original, you will find that a key change is the inclusion of the new checkSide() and setSide() methods in the init() and onUp() methods:

```
function checkSide(){
    var wdir = wall.dir;
    var ballp1 = wall.p1.subtract(ball.pos2D);
    var proj1 = ballp1.projection(wdir);
    var dist = ballp1.addScaled(wdir.unit(), proj1*(-1));
    setSide(dist);
}
function setSide(dist){
    if (dist.dotProduct(wall.normal) > 0){
        wall.side = 1;
    }else{
        wall.side = -1;
    }
}
```

The setSide() method is also called in checkBounce(). This code provides a way to keep track of which side of each wall the ball is at any moment. To do this, it checks the sign of the dot product between the perpendicular vector dist from the particle to the wall and the wall normal vector. If the sign is negative, it sets the side property of the wall to –1; otherwise, it sets it to 1. The side property of the Wall object has been created specifically for this purpose.

Another important new piece of code in checkBounce() checks to see whether the sign of the dot product has reversed (which means the ball has tunneled); if so, it sets the testTunneling Boolean variable to true:

```
var testTunneling;
if (wall.side*dist.dotProduct(wall.normal) < 0){
    testTunneling = true;
}else{
    testTunneling = false;
}
```

The value of testTunneling is then used as part of the collision detection test:

```
if (( (dist.length() < obj.radius) || (testTunneling) ) &&  test){
    ...
}
```

This sets up the basic collision detection in the case of tunneling. The rest of the changes in the code should be easy to follow.

If you test bouncing-off-inclined-wall2.js you should find that the tunneling problem is fixed.

Example: Ball bouncing off multiple inclined walls

In bouncing-off-multiple-inclined-walls.js we generalize the preceding simulation to include several walls (see Figure 11-10). Take a look at the source files; the code extends the previous example in a straightforward way. First, you just add more walls in init() in the same way—four inclined walls, plus four bounding walls to form a box that encloses the other walls and the ball. The checkBounce() method now loops over each wall. It also includes a new hasHitAWall Boolean variable that is used to stop the looping once a collision with one of the walls is detected.

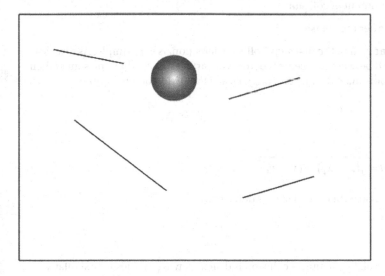

Figure 11-10. Ball bouncing off multiple walls

Experiment with the simulation, remembering that you can click and drag to reposition and resize the ball. As before, avoid positioning the ball so that it overlaps with any of the walls. Doing so will introduce an unphysical initial condition (a ball cannot physically overlap with a wall) that will cause some of the equations to give nonsensical results, resulting in erratic and unpredictable behavior.

See how the simulation handles different scenarios properly. For example, try balls of different sizes and release them at different locations: above the walls, so that they bounce off; just on the walls, so that they slide down; or just above a gap between the walls too small for them, so that they get trapped. You will see that collisions under the walls are also handled properly. Note that the four confining walls are treated in exactly the same way as the others. You can also click and drag *above* the top wall to make the ball bounce off it!

As in the previous simulation, you may encounter the tunneling problem on a slower machine. To fix this, we have modified the simulation in exactly the same way as described in the previous subsection. The modified source code is in the files `bouncing-off-multiple-inclined-walls2.js`. You might find that tunneling still sometimes happens at very high velocities (for example, try initializing the ball's velocity with a magnitude in excess of 1000 px/s). The problem there is that we are at the limit of the time resolution of the simulation, which is limited by how fast your machine can run it.

Collisions between particles in 1D

In this section, we will show you how to handle collisions between particles when the approach direction of the particles lies along the line joining them. This situation can be described as a 1D collision because the motion of the particles takes place in a straight line, both before and after the collision. In general, two particles may collide at any angle, changing their direction as they do so. Therefore, the case discussed in this section may seem like a very special case. So why study it? The reason is that the methods and formulas that hold in this special case can be readily extended to the more general case where the particles may collide at any angle. In fact, we will do that in the next section.

The steps for handling 1D particle collisions are the following (mirroring the steps for resolving the bouncing of a particle moving perpendicular to a wall):

1. Collision detection
2. Repositioning the particles at the moment of collision
3. Calculating the new velocities just after the collision

In the case of spherical particles (or circular in 2D), the first step, collision detection, is very simple. As discussed in Chapter 2, you just see whether the distance d between the centers of the two particles is less than the sum of their radii, where d is calculated from the position coordinates (x_1, y_1) and (x_2, y_2) using the Pythagorean theorem:

$$d < r_1 + r_2$$

In 2D:

$$d = \sqrt{(x_2 - x_1)^2 + (y_2 - y_1)^2}$$

Let's now look at how to reposition the particles when a collision is detected.

Repositioning the particles

Just as a particle may sink some distance into a wall by the time a collision is detected, two particles may similarly overlap. The complication in this case is that in general both particles may be moving, so both need to be moved back to their position at the actual point of contact. But how do we know how much to move each particle?

Let's begin by considering the case when the two particles are moving toward each other, as shown in Figure 11-11.

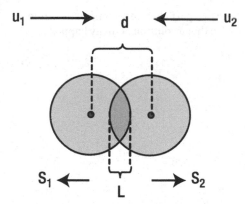

Figure 11-11. *Separating overlapping particles moving toward each other*

The amount of overlap L is given by the following, where r_1 and r_2 are the radii of the two particles, and d is the distance between their centers, as given by the Pythagorean formula discussed in the previous section:

$$L = r_1 + r_2 - d$$

Let s_1 and s_2 be the magnitudes of the displacements by which the particles must be moved, in opposite directions, so that they are just touching. These displacements must add up to give the overlap distance L:

$$s_1 + s_2 = L$$

This gives one equation relating s_1 and s_2 in terms of a known variable L. In order to be able to work out s_1 and s_2, we need a second equation connecting them. We can come up with such an equation by recalling that, in a small time interval t:

$$s_1 = u_1 t$$

and

$$s_2 = u_2 t$$

where u_1 and u_2 are the velocities of the respective particles just before the collision. That's just using the fact that displacement = velocity × time (see Chapter 4).

Dividing the first equation by the second gives this:

$$\frac{s_1}{s_2} = \frac{u_1}{u_2}$$

This is our second equation. It is now a matter of simple algebra to solve for s_1 and s_2 to give this:

$$s_1 = \frac{u_1}{u_1 + u_2} L$$

$$s_2 = \frac{u_2}{u_1 + u_2} L$$

What this result tells us is that the particles must be displaced in proportion to their velocities just before the impact.

This is great, but what if we have the other possible situation, in which the two particles are moving in the same direction (rather than toward each other) with the one behind moving faster (so that a collision actually happens), as shown in Figure 11-12.

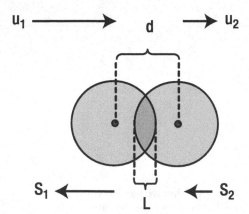

Figure 11-12. *Overlapping particles moving in the same direction*

In that case, the first equation connecting the displacement magnitudes s_1 and s_2 becomes the following, while the second equation is unchanged:

$$s_1 - s_2 = L$$

Solving them simultaneously then gives this:

$$s_1 = \frac{u_1}{u_1 - u_2} L$$

and this:

$$s_2 = \frac{u_2}{u_1 - u_2} L$$

This is a bit messy because we have different equations depending on whether the particles are moving toward each other or not. Luckily, it is possible to incorporate both cases into a single solution by thinking in terms of vector displacements. The reasoning is slightly less intuitive, but here is the final result, where the symbol $|\mathbf{v}|$ signifies the magnitude of vector $\mathbf{v}$:

$$\mathbf{s}_1 = -\frac{\mathbf{u}_1}{|\mathbf{u}_1 - \mathbf{u}_2|} L$$

$$\mathbf{s}_2 = -\frac{\mathbf{u}_2}{|\mathbf{u}_1 - \mathbf{u}_2|} L$$

Note that we always divide by the magnitude of the *relative velocity* $(\mathbf{u}_1 - \mathbf{u}_2)$. When the particles are approaching each other, this is $(u_1 + u_2)$; otherwise, it is $(u_1 - u_2)$. Hence, these equations indeed reduce to the corresponding equations for the displacement magnitudes in the two cases discussed previously. The other good thing is that here the direction of the displacements is also explicit in the formulas: the minus sign tells us that $\mathbf{s}_1$ is opposite to $\mathbf{u}_1$, and $\mathbf{s}_2$ is opposite to $\mathbf{u}_2$.

You now know how to reposition the particles once the collision is detected. The final thing to do is to calculate the new velocities of the colliding particles just after the collision. We'll do this separately for elastic and inelastic collisions.

Elastic collisions

Recall from Chapter 4 that an elastic collision is one in which kinetic energy is conserved. This means we can apply conservation of kinetic energy in addition to conservation of momentum (which is always conserved in any collision, elastic or not). For example, the collisions between billiard balls are usually modeled as elastic collisions.

Let the two colliding particles (which we can call particle1 and particle2) have masses m_1 and m_2, initial velocities u_1 and u_2, and final velocities v_1 and v_2, respectively. Note that we need only one component of velocity because the motion is 1D. Then we can write momentum conservation and energy conservation as follows:

$$m_1 v_1 + m_2 v_2 = m_1 u_1 + m_2 u_2$$

$$m_1 v_1^2 + m_2 v_2^2 = m_1 u_1^2 + m_2 u_2^2$$

Here the masses m_1 and m_2 of the particles are known, and so are the initial velocities u_1 and u_2. The aim is to calculate the final velocities v_1 and v_2 in terms of these known variables. This is a matter of solving these two equations simultaneously. The easiest method to do so involves deriving an important intermediate result involving the relative velocities of the particles before and after the collision. So let's do that now.

Relative velocity of colliding particles

The first step in deriving the relative velocity of the colliding particles is to rearrange the previous two equations by combining the terms for each particle on each side of the equation (put all the terms with a 1 subscript on one side and the terms with a 2 subscript on the other side):

$$m_1 (v_1 - u_1) = m_2 (u_2 - v_2)$$

$$m_1 (v_1^2 - u_1^2) = m_2 (u_2^2 - v_2^2)$$

Now recall the following identity from your school algebra:

$$a^2 - b^2 = (a - b)(a + b)$$

This allows you to write the second equation as follows:

$$m_1 (v_1 - u_1)(v_1 + u_1) = m_2 (u_2 - v_2)(u_2 + v_2)$$

You can now see that each side of this equation contains the corresponding side of the first equation as a factor. So you can divide this equation by the first equation to get rid of those factors, leaving us with this:

$$(v_1 + u_1) = (u_2 + v_2)$$

This can be rearranged by combining the initial velocities (the u variables) on one side and the final velocities (the v variables) on the other side of the equation to give this:

$$v_1 - v_2 = u_2 - u_1$$

Or, equivalently, this:

$$v_1 - v_2 = -(u_1 - u_2)$$

This is our result. Note that $(u_1 - u_2)$ is the initial relative velocity of particle1 from the point of view of particle2. Similarly, $(v_1 - v_2)$ is the final relative velocity of particle1 from the point of view of particle2. Therefore, the preceding result tells us that the relative velocity of separation of the two particles is the negative of their relative velocity of approach. This result does not depend on the masses of the particles, because m_1 and m_2 were cancelled out. But note that it holds only for elastic collisions. We shall see in the next section how it is modified for inelastic collisions.

As an immediate application of this result, consider the case when one of the particles, say particle2, is immovable (such as a wall). This is the same as saying that $u_2 = v_2 = 0$. Putting these values into the last equation gives us this:

$$v_1 = -u_1$$

This is elastic bouncing off an immovable object, and is the condition that we applied in the first example of a ball bouncing elastically off a wall.

Calculating velocities after an elastic collision

Using the result derived in the preceding section, it is now easy to work out the velocities of the particles after an elastic collision. The logic is that energy conservation is incorporated into the equation for relative velocities:

$$v_1 - v_2 = u_2 - u_1$$

So we need to solve this equation simultaneously with the equation expressing momentum conservation:

$$m_1 v_1 + m_2 v_2 = m_1 u_1 + m_2 u_2$$

The goal is to find the final velocities, v_1 and v_2, in terms of the other variables (the initial velocities and the masses). This can be done by eliminating either v_1 or v_2 between the two equations and then rearranging the resulting equation to find the other one. For example, we first multiply the first equation by m_2 to give this:

$$m_2 v_1 - m_2 v_2 = m_2 u_2 - m_2 u_1$$

Adding this to the second equation then gets rid of v_2, giving this:

$$(m_1 + m_2)v_1 = (m_1 - m_2)u_1 + 2m_2 u_2$$

Dividing by $(m_1 + m_2)$ then gives the final result for the velocity of particle1:

$$v_1 = \frac{(m_1 - m_2)u_1 + 2m_2 u_2}{(m_1 + m_2)}$$

You could go through a similar algebraic manipulation to calculate v_2, but there is no need to: you can just swap the 1 and 2 indices on the last equation to give this:

$$v_2 = \frac{(m_2 - m_1)u_2 + 2m_1 u_1}{(m_1 + m_2)}$$

This is the result you are after: you can now calculate the velocities of the two particles just after the impact, from the velocities just before the impact (and the masses of the particles).

Finally, note that you don't have to calculate v_2 from the second equation. Once you know v_1, you can just work out v_2 by rearranging the equation for relative velocities to give the following, which saves on CPU time:

$$v_2 = v_1 + u_1 - u_2$$

A special case: particles of equal masses

In the special case of particles that have the same mass, the formulas for their velocities after collision take a particularly simple form. To see this, simply replacing $m_1 = m_2 = m$ into the preceding equations gives this:

$$v_1 = u_2$$

and this:

$$v_2 = u_1$$

In other words, the particles simply exchange velocities after the collision! This applies regardless of the initial velocities of the particles, as long as they have the same mass and the collision is elastic. This is a very useful result. If your simulation will only ever involve elastic collisions between particles of the same mass, there is no need to code in the complicated general formula given previously, saving on valuable CPU time. You might recall that we made use of this result in the simple collision example in Chapter 5.

As a special case of this special case, if one of the particles is initially at rest ($u_2 = 0$), we get $v_1 = 0$ and $v_2 = u_1$; the other particle then stops dead in its track after the collision, while the initially stationary particle moves off at the velocity that the other one had before the collision.

Another special case: collision with a particle of much larger mass

On the other hand, if the mass of one of the particles is much larger than the other (for example, $m_2 \gg m_1$), the formulas for the final velocities reduce to this:

$$v_1 \approx -u_1 + 2u_2$$

and this:

$$v_2 = u_2 + 2\left(\frac{m_1}{m_2}\right)u_1$$

In particular, if the particle with large mass (particle2) is initially stationary, $u_2 = 0$, so

$$v_1 \approx -u_1$$

and

$$v_2 = 2\left(\frac{m_1}{m_2}\right)u_1$$

Hence, the lighter particle bounces off the heavier one, almost reversing its velocity. Noting that (m_1/m_2) is a small number much less than 1, we conclude that $v_2 \ll u_1$; hence, the heavier particle moves off at a much smaller velocity than the velocity at which the first particle hit it. This is all common sense.

Inelastic collisions

Although it is common to model collisions as elastic, most collisions in real life are rarely elastic—they usually involve a loss of kinetic energy and are therefore inelastic.

To model inelastic collisions, a useful starting point is again the relative velocity of the colliding particles—through the introduction of a concept known as the *coefficient of restitution*.

Coefficient of restitution

The coefficient of restitution (denoted by the symbol C_R) is defined as the ratio between the relative velocity after a collision and the relative velocity before the collision:.

$$C_R = \frac{v_1 - v_2}{u_2 - u_1}$$

This equation can be rewritten as follows:

$$v_1 - v_2 = C_R \left(u_2 - u_1 \right)$$

For an elastic collision, the relative velocities before and after the collision are related by the equation $v_1 - v_2 = u_2 - u_1$, so the preceding equation tells us that $C_R = 1$ for an elastic collision.

Conceptually, the coefficient of restitution is a measure of the departure from perfectly elastic collisions. Generally, the value of C_R will be less than 1. Collisions for which $C_R > 1$ are also possible; they correspond to collisions that generate explosive forces, so that the total kinetic energy of the particles after the collision is larger than their initial kinetic energy. Such collisions are called *superelastic*.

The special case when $C_R = 0$ refers to so-called *completely inelastic* collisions. In that case, the relative velocity equation reduces to this:

$$v_1 - v_2 = 0$$

So that:

$$v_1 = v_2$$

In other words, the final velocities of the particles are the same: they stick together. In a completely inelastic collision, the loss of kinetic energy is maximum, but not complete (if it were complete, the particles would just stop; this would violate momentum conservation).

As another special case, suppose that one of the particles is immovable (such as a wall). For example, if particle2 is immovable, $u_2 = v_2 = 0$, so that the relative velocity equation gives this:

$$v_1 = -C_R u_1$$

This is exactly how we modeled wall collisions involving energy loss earlier in this chapter, with C_R representing the "bounce" factor.

Calculating velocities after an inelastic collision

Starting from the relative velocity equation for inelastic collisions and using a method similar to that used to derive the corresponding elastic collision equations, it is easy to show that the final velocities due to an inelastic collision are given by this:

$$v_1 = \frac{(m_1 - C_R m_2)u_1 + (m_2 + C_R m_2)u_2}{(m_1 + m_2)}$$

and this:

$$v_2 = \frac{(m_2 - C_R m_1)u_2 + (m_1 + C_R m_1)u_1}{(m_1 + m_2)}$$

This is the most general formula for collisions, as it also includes the elastic formula as a special case (set $C_R = 1$ in the above formulas and verify that they reduce to the corresponding formulas for elastic collisions).

Completely inelastic collisions

If the collision of two particles is completely inelastic (with $C_R = 0$), the last equations reduce to this:

$$v_1 = v_2 = \frac{m_1 u_1 + m_2 u_2}{(m_1 + m_2)}$$

So the two particles stick together and move at the same velocity after the collision. Examples in which you might want to model completely inelastic collisions include hitting a character with a snowball or firing a bullet that sticks into its target.

This completes our discussion of particle collisions in 1D. You are no doubt eager to see all that math applied in a demo. You'll get to see a code example very soon, but before we do that, let's quickly discuss how this extends to 2D. Once we've covered that, we will then be able to build simulations that can handle both 1D and 2D collisions.

Collisions between particles in 2D

We are now ready to look at general 2D collisions, in which the direction of approach of the particles is not necessarily along the line joining their centers. The way to handle such collisions is to resort to a trick similar to that used for a ball colliding with a wall: at the point of collision (when the particles are just touching), resolve the velocity of each particle into a normal component along the line joining them, and a tangential component perpendicular to that line (see Figure 11-13). The revelation is that, just as in a collision with a wall, only the normal velocity components are affected by the collision; the tangential components remain the same after the collision (provided it is frictionless). What's more, the normal velocity components are changed in exactly the same way as if the collision were in 1D (as if the tangential components were zero). That's great; it means that we can treat any 2D collision as a 1D collision in terms of the normal velocity components.

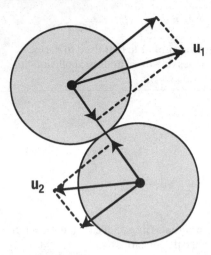

Figure 11-13. *Resolving velocity normal and parallel to line joining particles*

So the steps for handling 2D particle collisions are the following:

1. Detecting the collision

2. Decomposing the initial velocities in normal and tangential components

3. Repositioning the particles at the moment of collision

4. Calculating the new normal velocities just after the collision

5. Adding the new normal velocity components back to the tangential components

Compared with the procedure for handling 1D collisions, the extra steps are steps 2 and 5. Note also that, in step 3, the particles are repositioned using the same formula we derived for 1D collisions (see the section "Repositioning the particles"), but using the normal velocities.

As mentioned in the section "Bouncing off inclined walls," the usual method we found that people use to handle 2D collisions is to rotate the coordinate system, perform a 1D collision, and then rotate back the coordinate system. But armed with vectors, the method we suggest actually proves simpler: in place of coordinate rotations, we simply resolve vectors and later add them up again. Let's see the method in action!

Example: 2D collisions between two particles

We will create a simulation that can handle a general 2D collision between two particles. Obviously, it will also be able to handle 1D collisions simply by choosing appropriate initial positions and velocities for the particles. This example will pull together everything we have covered on collisions between particles.

Creating a two-particle collision simulator

The code for creating this two-particle collision simulator example is in the file ball-collision.js. The init() method creates the two particles as Ball instances and sets their initial sizes, masses, positions, and velocities before invoking the animation code:

```
function init() {
    // create a ball
    ball1 = new Ball(15,'#ff0000',1,0,true);
    ball1.pos2D = new Vector2D(0,200);
    ball1.velo2D = new Vector2D(250,0);
    ball1.draw(context);
    ball2 = new Ball(75,'#0000ff',125,0,true);
    ball2.pos2D = new Vector2D(300,200);
    ball2.velo2D = new Vector2D(50,0);
    ball2.draw(context);
    // make the ball move
    t0 = new Date().getTime();
    animFrame();
}
```

We are creating a small ball of radius 15 pixels and 1 mass unit and a large ball of radius 75 pixels and 125 mass units. Note that we've scaled masses on the cube of the radius, based on 3D geometry (recall that the volume of a sphere = $4\pi r^3/3$), and assuming that the two balls have the same density (recall that mass = density × volume). On this basis, because the large ball has a radius 5 times that of the smaller one, its mass should be 125 times larger.

In the animation part of the code, the move() method moves each ball in turn and then checks for collision at each timestep.

```
function move(){
    context.clearRect(0, 0, canvas.width, canvas.height);
    moveObject(ball1);
    moveObject(ball2);
    checkCollision();
}
```

The checkCollision() method looks like this:

```
function checkCollision(){
    var dist = ball1.pos2D.subtract(ball2.pos2D);
    if (dist.length() < (ball1.radius + ball2.radius) ) {
        // normal velocity vectors just before the impact
        var normalVelo1 = ball1.velo2D.project(dist);
        var normalVelo2 = ball2.velo2D.project(dist);
        // tangential velocity vectors
        var tangentVelo1 = ball1.velo2D.subtract(normalVelo1);
        var tangentVelo2 = ball2.velo2D.subtract(normalVelo2);
        // move particles so that they just touch
        var L = ball1.radius + ball2.radius-dist.length();
        var vrel = normalVelo1.subtract(normalVelo2).length();
        ball1.pos2D = ball1.pos2D.addScaled(normalVelo1,-L/vrel);
        ball2.pos2D = ball2.pos2D.addScaled(normalVelo2,-L/vrel);
```

```
        // normal velocity components after the impact
        var m1 = ball1.mass;
        var m2 = ball2.mass;
        var u1 = normalVelo1.projection(dist);
        var u2 = normalVelo2.projection(dist);
        var v1 = ((m1-m2)*u1+2*m2*u2)/(m1+m2);
        var v2 = ((m2-m1)*u2+2*m1*u1)/(m1+m2);
        // normal velocity vectors after collision
        normalVelo1 = dist.para(v1);
        normalVelo2 = dist.para(v2);
        // final velocity vectors after collision
        ball1.velo2D = normalVelo1.add(tangentVelo1);
        ball2.velo2D = normalVelo2.add(tangentVelo2);
    }
}
```

The code follows the explanations given in the previous subsections closely, and the comments in the code should make it clear what is going on at each step. In fact, this code is substantially simpler than the corresponding code for bouncing off an oblique wall. Notice also the symmetry with respect to the two balls. The simplicity and relative brevity of the code provide what we think is an attractive alternative to the usual method of rotating the coordinate system to resolve oblique collisions.

Finally, the formula for calculating the final velocities assumes elastic collisions, but it is a simple matter to replace it with the alternative (and more general) formula for inelastic collisions. We leave this as an exercise for you.

Experimenting with the particle collision simulation

If you run the particle collision simulation, you'll see the small ball in a 1D collision with the larger one (see Figure 11-14). Let's start experimenting by verifying some of the observations we made when discussing special cases in 1D elastic collisions.

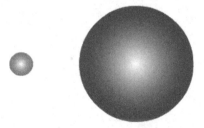

Figure 11-14. *A two-particle collision simulator*

First, set the initial velocity of the large one to zero, simply by commenting out the line that sets its velocity in `ball-collision.js`. You will see that the small ball almost reverses its velocity after the collision, while the larger one moves off with a very small velocity, just as we said before.

Next, make the second ball the same size and mass as the first by replacing the line that instantiates it with the following modified line:

```
var ball2 = new Ball(15,'#0000ff',1,0,true);
```

Keep the second ball's velocity at zero and run the code. You will see that, upon collision, the first ball stops right in its track, while the second ball moves off at the initial velocity of the first ball. Again this confirms the deductions we made previously on the basis of the governing collision equations.

This is a full 2D collision simulator, so why not get the balls to collide at an angle? For example, while keeping the masses and the sizes of the two particles the same, try the following:

```
ball1.velo2D = new Vector2D(100,-30);
ball2.velo2D = new Vector2D(-50,-30);
```

This shows that our basic 2D particle collision simulator can handle both 1D and 2D collisions properly. So let's now add a bit more complexity.

Example: multiple particle collisions

Extending the preceding simulation to handle a large number of particles is simply a matter of creating more ball instances and then checking for collisions between each pair of particles. In multiple-ball-collision.js, we create nine particles of the same size and mass, and animate each one in the move() method, which looks like this:

```
function move(){
    context.clearRect(0, 0, canvas.width, canvas.height);
    for (var i=0; i<numBalls; i++){
        var ball = balls[i];
        moveObject(ball);
    }
    checkCollision();
}
```

The checkCollision() method is very similar to the two-particle version in ball-collision.js, the main difference being a double for loop in the present version:

```
function checkCollision(){
    for (var i=0; i<balls.length; i++){
        var ball1 = balls[i];
        for(var j=i+1; j<balls.length; j++){
            var ball2 = balls[j];
                    // code in here is similar to ball-collision.js
            }
        }
}
```

The key task with the for loops is to pick all possible pairs of particles without double-counting. So the first loop iterates over all the elements of the balls array, picking the first ball, ball1, from it. The second loop then iterates over the elements of balls again to pick ball2, but this time starting from the next element from ball1. This avoids checking for collisions between ball1 and ball2, and then again between ball2 and ball1.

The nine balls are initially positioned randomly on the canvas. They are given velocities toward the center of the canvas, with a velocity magnitude proportional to their distance from the center. When you run the simulation, the balls move to the center, where they collide a number of times in quick succession, as a result of which they bounce outward. Feel free to experiment with different configurations and initial velocities.

Example: multiple particle collisions with bouncing

The previous example was interesting, but the particles only collided briefly before separating and disappearing outside the canvas area. It would be much more fun to confine them so that they collide over and over again. To do this, we need to introduce confining walls. So, let's combine everything we have learned in this chapter and build one final example involving multiple particles colliding with each other and with walls. The particles will also have different sizes and masses.

We call the new file molecules.js because the result will look like gas molecules bouncing about. Here is the init() method in molecules.js:

```
function init() {
    balls = new Array();
    for(var i = 0; i < numBalls; i++){
        var radius = Math.random()*20 + 5;
        var mass = 0.01*Math.pow(radius,3);
        var ball = new Ball(radius,'#666600',mass,0,true);
        ball.pos2D = new Vector2D(Math.random()*(canvas.width-2*radius)+radius,
Math.random()*(canvas.height-2*radius)+radius);
        ball.velo2D = new Vector2D(((Math.random()-0.5)*100),((Math.random()-0.5)*100));
        balls.push(ball);
        ball.draw(context);
    }
    walls = new Array();
    var wall1 = new Wall(new Vector2D(canvas.width,0),new Vector2D(0,0));
    wall1.draw(context_bg);
    walls.push(wall1);
    var wall2 = new Wall(new Vector2D(canvas.width,canvas.height),new Vector2D(canvas.width,0));
    wall2.draw(context_bg);
    walls.push(wall2);
    var wall3 = new Wall(new Vector2D(0,canvas.height), new Vector2D(canvas.width,canvas.height));
    wall3.draw(context_bg);
    walls.push(wall3);
    var wall4 = new Wall(new Vector2D(0,0),new Vector2D(0,canvas.height));
    wall4.draw(context_bg);
    walls.push(wall4);
    t0 = new Date().getTime();
    animFrame();
}
```

We first create a set of balls with random radius ranging from 5 px to 25 px, and with masses proportional to the cube of the radius. The balls are positioned randomly on the canvas and given random velocities with a maximum magnitude of 50 px/s. Then four walls are created at the edges of the canvas. The animation code is then called.

The rest of the code is basically a hybrid of the codes used for multiple colliding particles (the previous example) and for bouncing off multiple walls. Hence, there is nothing substantially new, except in the way they are combined. The move() method is identical to that in the previous example with multiple colliding particles.

The checkCollision() method is almost identical with that of the previous example, except for the addition of one line in the outer for loop (shown in bold in the following listing):

```
function checkCollision(){
    for (var i=0; i<balls.length; i++){
        var ball1 = balls[i];
        for(var j=i+1; j<balls.length; j++){
            var ball2 = balls[j];
            var dist = ball1.pos2D.subtract(ball2.pos2D);
            if (dist.length() < (ball1.radius + ball2.radius) ) {
                // normal velocity vectors just before the impact
                var normalVelo1 = ball1.velo2D.project(dist);
                var normalVelo2 = ball2.velo2D.project(dist);
                // tangential velocity vectors
                var tangentVelo1 = ball1.velo2D.subtract(normalVelo1);
                var tangentVelo2 = ball2.velo2D.subtract(normalVelo2);
                // move particles so that they just touch
                var L = ball1.radius + ball2.radius-dist.length();
                var vrel = normalVelo1.subtract(normalVelo2).length();
                ball1.pos2D = ball1.pos2D.addScaled(normalVelo1,-L/vrel);
                ball2.pos2D = ball2.pos2D.addScaled(normalVelo2,-L/vrel);
                // normal velocity components after the impact
                var m1 = ball1.mass;
                var m2 = ball2.mass;
                var u1 = normalVelo1.projection(dist);
                var u2 = normalVelo2.projection(dist);
                var v1 = ((m1-m2)*u1+2*m2*u2)/(m1+m2);
                var v2 = ((m2-m1)*u2+2*m1*u1)/(m1+m2);
                // normal velocity vectors after collision
                normalVelo1 = dist.para(v1);
                normalVelo2 = dist.para(v2);
                // final velocity vectors after collision
                ball1.velo2D = normalVelo1.add(tangentVelo1);
                ball2.velo2D = normalVelo2.add(tangentVelo2);
            }
        }
        checkWallBounce(ball1);
    }
}
```

The extra line tells the code to see whether ball1 is in collision with any wall. The checkWallBounce() method is given here for completeness, but it is essentially the same as in bouncing-off-multiple-inclined-walls.js, except that we got rid of the code that handled bouncing off the wall end points, because there are no free wall end points to bounce off in this example:

```
function checkWallBounce(obj){
    var hasHitAWall = false;
    for (var i=0; (i<walls.length && hasHitAWall==false); i++){
        var wall = walls[i];
        var wdir = wall.dir;
        var ballp1 = wall.p1.subtract(obj.pos2D);
```

```
        var ballp2 = wall.p2.subtract(obj.pos2D);
        var proj1 = ballp1.projection(wdir);
        var proj2 = ballp2.projection(wdir);
        var dist = ballp1.addScaled(wdir.unit(), proj1*(-1));
        var test = ((Math.abs(proj1) < wdir.length()) && (Math.abs(proj2) < wdir.length()));
        if ((dist.length() < obj.radius) &&  test){
            var angle = Vector2D.angleBetween(obj.velo2D, wdir);
            var normal = wall.normal;
            if (normal.dotProduct(obj.velo2D) > 0){
                normal.scaleBy(-1);
            }
            var deltaS = (obj.radius+dist.dotProduct(normal))/Math.sin(angle);
            var displ = obj.velo2D.para(deltaS);
            obj.pos2D = obj.pos2D.subtract(displ);
            var normalVelo = obj.velo2D.project(dist);
            var tangentVelo = obj.velo2D.subtract(normalVelo);
            obj.velo2D = tangentVelo.addScaled(normalVelo,-vfac);
            hasHitAWall = true;
        }
    }
}
```

Figure 11-15 shows a screenshot of what you will see when you run the code: gas molecules bouncing about! Notice that the little molecules generally end up moving faster than the bigger ones because they can pick up a lot of momentum when a large one collides with them. A lot of time can be wasted playing with this simulation or simply watching it! To make it even more fun, in the source code we have also included a modified version of the simulation (molecules2.js) that allows you to add your own particles by clicking and dragging. With a lot of particles, you might find that some of them, especially the smaller ones, will occasionally tunnel out of the confining walls. You can fix this by using the method described in the section "Bouncing off inclined walls."

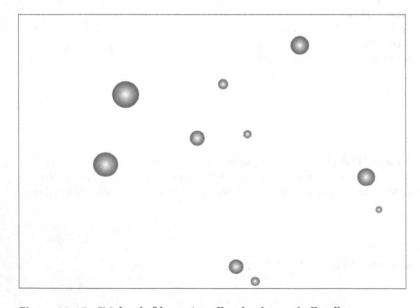

Figure 11-15. *"Molecules" bouncing off each other and off walls*

You may also find that some particles overlap when they are initially created because of the random positioning. This will result in some initial erratic behavior that should mostly sort itself out in a few timesteps. Other problems could also occur with numerous particles (apart from the obvious one of your computer not being able to cope), especially if they are crammed into a small space or if they are moving at high speed. You could, for example, have a particle colliding with two other particles in the same timestep. Or you could have a particle that is repositioned and ends up overlapping another particle close by. We could go into elaborate methods for dealing with scenarios like these, but we've already covered a lot of ground in this chapter and need to stop somewhere!

Summary

In this chapter, we have gone from a simple demonstration of a ball bouncing off a vertical wall to creating complex simulations involving particles bouncing off multiple inclined walls and particles colliding with other particles. We have covered the underlying physics in considerable detail, discussing the equations that govern different types of collisions in 1D and 2D. In implementing collision resolution, both with walls and between particles, we introduced a novel method using vector algebra that avoids the usual need for performing coordinate rotations to resolve collisions in 2D. The range of examples we looked at culminated in an interesting simulation with multiple particles colliding and behaving like the molecules of a gas. In the next chapter we continue the fun by exploring a range of visual and animated effects that can be achieved with systems involving a large number of particles.

CHAPTER 12

■ ■ ■

Particle Systems

In a nutshell, this chapter will show you how to create animated effects and simulations using systems of multiple particles. Particle systems are very popular, and a lot of creative work has been done in the animation community over the years using them. In a single chapter, we can only really scratch the surface of what is possible. Therefore, we shall content ourselves with giving you a few ideas and examples to play with and build upon.

Topics covered in this chapter include the following:

- **Introduction to particle system modeling:** This brief section will explain what we mean by a particle system and what is needed to set one up.

- **Creating animated effects using particles:** It is possible to produce some interesting animated effects such as smoke and fire using particles and some simple physics. We'll walk you through some examples in this section.

- **Particle animations with long-range forces:** Particle animations don't have to look realistic; they can be just for fun! We look at a couple of wacky examples using long-range forces such as gravity.

- **Interacting particle systems:** More complex particle systems include interactions between the particles. But this can get pretty computationally expensive with large numbers of particles. We give a couple of examples, discussing tricks to overcome this problem.

The approach in this chapter is to create animations that use some physics, but without necessarily being accurate simulations. Above all, this is a subject where experimentation and creativity pay dividends. Therefore, don't be afraid to tinker and invent, even if that means breaking a few laws of physics!

Introduction to particle system modeling

Although a precise definition of a particle system probably does not exist, an attempt to define it will help to explain what we have in mind before we do anything else. In the sense in which we use the term, a *particle system* consists of the following elements:

- A group of particles

- Rules by which they move and change

- Rules by which they interact (if any)

This definition is very general: the said "rules" could be based on physics, artificial intelligence, biology, or any such system. It won't come as a surprise that we'll limit ourselves to particles moving and interacting under physical laws (with perhaps the odd tweak here and there). Therefore, the particle systems we'll consider will animate particles according to Newton's laws of motion under the action of a subset of the forces that we discussed in Part II of the book. The different categories of interaction between the particles can include the following:

- **No mutual interaction:** In this case, the particles are unaware of each other and move independently under the action of globally prescribed forces (such as external gravity). Even though this is the simplest case, quite impressive effects can be generated using non-interacting particles. We will look at several examples in the next two sections.

- **Interaction by collision:** Here the particles do not interact except very briefly when they collide. The collisions can be resolved using the methods given in Chapter 11. In fact, the last example in Chapter 11 showed just such a system of particles interacting via collisions.

- **Short-range interactions:** In this case, the particles interact only when they are close together but not necessarily touching. They can be modeled using short-range forces of a type that exists between molecules. Using such forces it is possible to model fluid effects such as the formation and fall of a liquid drop. But these simulations require more advanced methods and will not be covered in this book.

- **Long-range interactions:** This category involves mutual interactions between the particles at any distance, such as gravitational or electric forces between the particles. Typically, every particle experiences a force due to every other particle. Clearly the number of computations that need to be performed becomes very large pretty quickly as you increase the number of particles in the system. We look at some examples in the last section of this chapter.

- **Local interactions:** These interactions are intermediate between short-range and long-range; particles within a certain local neighborhood are linked and interact. Such interactions can give rise to organized systems and connected structures. Examples include mass-spring systems, which can be used to simulate deformable bodies like ropes and clothes. These particle systems are explored in Chapter 13.

So what do we need, in terms of physics and coding, to create a particle system? The answer might surprise you: not a lot beyond what we've already covered in the previous chapters. So there won't be much theory in this chapter, but more on the application of principles that have already been discussed with a few extra tricks added in. That means you get to see code much sooner!

Creating animated effects using particles

One of the most common uses of particle systems is to create animated visual effects such as smoke and fire. In this section, we show you simple ways of producing some of these effects using physics-based animation. We start with a very simple example and then create a particle emitter that will allow us to create some more elaborate effects. The approach in this section is that we want to produce animations that *look* realistic, but that don't have to be completely accurate.

A simple example: splash effect with particles

In this example, we will drop objects in water and then create a splash effect using particles. The objects will be balls of different sizes and will be dropped one at a time from the same height. The splash will be made from a group of `Ball` objects of smaller size. Let's dive straight into the code that creates these objects. The file, downloadable from www.apress.com, is called splash.js. Here is a full listing of the code:

```
var canvas = document.getElementById('canvas');
var context = canvas.getContext('2d');
var canvas_bg = document.getElementById('canvas_bg');
var context_bg = canvas_bg.getContext('2d');
```

```
var drop;
var droplets;
var numDroplets = 20;
var m = 1;
var g = 20;
var vx = 20;
var vy = -15;
var wlevel = 510;
var fac = 1;
var t0,dt;
var acc, force;

window.onload = init;

function init() {
    makeBackground();
    makeDrop();
    makeDroplets();
    t0 = new Date().getTime();
    animFrame();
}
function makeBackground(){
    var horizon = 500;
    // the sea
    context_bg.fillStyle = '#7fffd4';
    context_bg.fillRect(0,horizon,canvas_bg.width,canvas_bg.height-horizon);
    // the sky
    gradient = context_bg.createLinearGradient(0,0,0,horizon);
    gradient.addColorStop(0,'#87ceeb');
    gradient.addColorStop(1,'#ffffff');
    context_bg.fillStyle = gradient;
    context_bg.fillRect(0,0,canvas_bg.width,horizon);
}
function makeDrop(){
    drop = new Ball(8,'#3399ff',1,0,true);
    drop.pos2D = new Vector2D(400,100);
    drop.velo2D = new Vector2D(0,100);
    drop.draw(context);
}
function makeDroplets(){
    droplets = new Array();
    for (var i=0; i<numDroplets; i++){
        var radius = Math.random()*2+1;
        var droplet = new Ball(radius,'#3399ff',m,0,true);
        droplets.push(droplet);
    }
}
function animFrame(){
    animId = requestAnimationFrame(animFrame,canvas);
    onTimer();
}
```

```
function onTimer(){
    var t1 = new Date().getTime();
    dt = 0.001*(t1-t0);
    t0 = t1;
    if (dt>0.2) {dt=0;};
    move();
}
function move(){
    context.clearRect(0, 0, canvas.width, canvas.height);
    moveObject(drop);
    checkDrop();
    for (var i=0; i<numDroplets; i++){
        var droplet = droplets[i];
        moveObject(droplet);
        calcForce(droplet);
        updateAccel();
        updateVelo(droplet);
    }
}
function moveObject(obj){
    obj.pos2D = obj.pos2D.addScaled(obj.velo2D,dt);
    if (obj.y < wlevel){// only show drops that are above water level
        obj.draw(context);
    }
}
function calcForce(obj){
    force = Forces.constantGravity(m,g);
}
function updateAccel(){
    acc = force.multiply(1/m);
}
function updateVelo(obj){
    obj.velo2D = obj.velo2D.addScaled(acc,dt);
}
function checkDrop(){
    if (drop.y > wlevel){
        for (var i=0; i<droplets.length; i++){
            var droplet = droplets[i];
            var posx = drop.x+(Math.random()-0.5)*drop.radius;
            var posy = wlevel-10+Math.random()*drop.radius;
            var velx = (Math.random()-0.5)*vx*fac;
            var vely = (Math.random()+0.5)*vy*fac;
            droplet.pos2D = new Vector2D(posx,posy);
            droplet.velo2D = new Vector2D(velx,vely);
        }
        drop.x = Math.random()*600+100;
        drop.y = 100;
        drop.radius = 4 + 8*Math.random();
        fac = Math.pow(drop.radius/8,1.5);
    }
}
```

Looking at the init() method first, we see that the initial setup code has been organized into three separate methods makeBackground(), makeDrop() and makeDroplets(), which respectively create the visual background, the Ball object to be dropped (named drop; think raindrop) and a group of 20 smaller Ball objects with random radii between 1 and 3 pixels. These will be the splash droplets, and they are not initially visible as they have not been drawn yet. They are put into an array called droplets. The drop is initially positioned above the water surface, at y = 100, and given a velocity of 100 px/s vertically downward.

The animation code is invoked by calling the animFrame() method from init() as usual. In the move() method the drop is animated first by invoking the moveObject() method passing drop as an argument. This makes it move at the constant downward velocity of 100 px/s specified earlier in the code. You may be wondering why we make the object fall at a constant velocity instead of making it accelerate under gravity. The answer is that if it is a raindrop, it would probably have reached terminal velocity anyway.

Next in move(), the checkDrop() method is called. This method checks whether the drop has fallen below the water level (set at 10 px below the top edge of the blue rectangle representing the body of water, to give a fake 3D effect). If that happens, the splash droplets are repositioned around the region of impact and given random velocities with an upward vertical component. The magnitude of the velocities depends on parameters vx and vy that are set initially in the code as well as on a factor fac, which is updated every time a splash occurs, as will be described shortly. The falling drop is repositioned at the initial height and at a new random horizontal location as soon as it hits the water level. Its radius is then changed to a random value between 4 and 12 pixels.

The velocity factor fac is updated according to the following formula, in which r_m is the mean radius of the drop (8 pixels):

$$\text{fac} = \left(\frac{r}{r_m}\right)^{3/2}$$

What is happening here? The idea is that the larger the drop is, the heavier its mass will be (its mass is proportional to its volume, or the cube of its radius, r^3). Because the drop always has the same velocity, its kinetic energy ($E_k = \frac{1}{2}mv^2$) will be proportional to its mass, and therefore to r^3. A fraction of that energy will be imparted to the splash droplets, and one can therefore expect the average kinetic energy of those droplets to be proportional to r^3. Because the masses of the droplets are constant, their kinetic energy is proportional to the square of their velocity. So we have the following:

$$E_k \propto v^2 \propto r^3$$

Therefore, we can write the following:

$$v \propto r^{3/2}$$

This shows that we expect the droplets to have a mean velocity proportional to the radius of the falling drop raised to the power of 1.5. The previous formula for fac implements this assumption, with the value of fac being set to 1 when the radius is equal to the mean radius of 8 px.

Back in the move() method, the droplets are each animated in the for loop. They are made to fall under gravity by using the Forces.constantGravity() method in calcForce(). In moveObject() there is an if condition that draws them to the canvas only if they are below the water level; otherwise, they remain invisible.

If you run the simulation, you will find that the larger the drop is, the higher the droplets will splash because of their greater initial velocities. Figure 12-1 shows a screenshot. As usual, feel free to experiment with different parameters. Of course, the visual aspects of the animation can be enhanced in many ways according to your imagination and artistic skills. We have focused on the physics and coding aspects; feel free to season the appearance to taste.

Figure 12-1. *Producing a splash!*

Creating a particle emitter

Many applications of particle systems require a continuous source of particles. This can be achieved using *particle emitters*. Creating a particle emitter is not difficult; essentially what you need is to create new particles over time. But it is also important to limit the total number of particles to avoid crashing your computer! This may mean fixing the total number of particles or recycling/removing them.

There are several approaches you could take to achieve each of these outcomes. We can only give an example here, without attempting to cover all the different approaches.

You'll find an example of our approach in the `particle-emitter.js` file, the full listing of which is given here:

```
var canvas = document.getElementById('canvas');
var context = canvas.getContext('2d');

var particles;
var maxParticles = 120;
var m = 1;
var g = 20;
var k = 0.003;
var vx = 60;
var vy = -80;
var i = 0;     // only needed for fountain effect
var fps = 30; // controls rate of creation of particles
var t0,dt;
var acc, force;
var posEmitter;

window.onload = init;

function init() {
    particles = new Array();
    posEmitter = new Vector2D(0.5*canvas.width,0.5*canvas.height);
    addEventListener('mousemove',onMouseMove,false);
    t0 = new Date().getTime();
    animFrame();
}
function onMouseMove(evt){
    posEmitter = new Vector2D(evt.clientX,evt.clientY);
}
```

```
function animFrame(){
    setTimeout(function() {
        animId = requestAnimationFrame(animFrame,canvas);
        onTimer();
    }, 1000/fps);
}
function onTimer(){
    var t1 = new Date().getTime();
    dt = 0.001*(t1-t0);
    t0 = t1;
    if (dt>0.2) {dt=0;};
    move();
}
function move(){
    context.clearRect(0, 0, canvas.width, canvas.height);
    if (particles.length < maxParticles){
        createNewParticles(posEmitter);
    }else{
        recycleParticles(posEmitter);
    }
    for (var i=0; i<particles.length; i++){
        var particle = particles[i];
        moveObject(particle);
        calcForce(particle);
        updateAccel();
        updateVelo(particle);
    }
}
function createNewParticles(ppos){
    var newParticle = new Ball(2);
    setPosVelo(newParticle,ppos);
    particles.push(newParticle);
}
function recycleParticles(ppos){
    var firstParticle = particles[0];
    firstParticle.color = '#ff0000';
    setPosVelo(firstParticle,ppos);
    particles.shift();
    particles.push(firstParticle);
}
function setPosVelo(obj,pos){
    obj.pos2D = pos;
    obj.velo2D = new Vector2D((Math.random()-0.5)*vx,(Math.random()+0.5)*vy);
}
function moveObject(obj){
    obj.pos2D = obj.pos2D.addScaled(obj.velo2D,dt);
    obj.draw(context);
}
```

```
function calcForce(obj){
     var gravity = Forces.constantGravity(m,g);
     var drag = Forces.drag(k,obj.velo2D);
     force = Forces.add([gravity, drag]);
}
function updateAccel(){
     acc = force.multiply(1/m);
}
function updateVelo(obj){
     obj.velo2D = obj.velo2D.addScaled(acc,dt);
}
```

The particles are stored in an array named particles. In this example, the calcForce() method includes gravity and drag forces. The really new features appear in the two aptly named methods createNewParticles() and recycleParticles(), either of which is called from within the move() method depending on whether the specified maximum number of particles maxParticles have already been created or not.

The createNewParticles() method creates a new particle as a Ball object and then initializes its position and velocity by calling the setPosVelo() function with the location specified as a Vector2D input parameter. The location specified is here called posEmitter, initially set in the middle of the canvas in init(), but subsequently updated to the location of the mouse cursor location through use of a mousemove event listener/handler. The particle is given a random upward initial velocity. In createNewParticles() the particles are then pushed into the particles array.

This happens once per timestep, so that a new particle is created at each timestep. Note that we have nested the requestAnimationFrame() call into a setTimeout() function in animFrame(). As discussed in Chapter 2, this allows you to control the timestep of the animation. In the example listed, the parameter fps is set at 30. This means that the animation would run at (approximately) 30 frames per second, producing one particle per frame (timestep). Hence, fps indirectly specifies the rate at which new particles are created per second, 30 in this case. You can, of course, produce more than one particle per timestep, say N. In that case, the rate at which new particles are created would be N*fps.

If the createNewParticles() method were called unconditionally at each timestep, your animation would quickly fill up with particles until your computer couldn't cope any more. Therefore, we instead call recycleParticles() if the number of particles exceeds the maximum allowed number maxParticles. In recycleParticles(), the first (and oldest) particle is identified. Its position is reset to the value of posEmitter and its velocity to a random vertical velocity as when it was created. Here we also change its color to red, but that is optional. Finally we remove the first particle's reference position in the particles array from the first to the last by successively applying the particles.shift() and particles.push() methods.

You don't want to set maxParticles too high. In the example file, a modest value of 120 is chosen. Although we have tested the animation successfully with thousands of particles, the performance on your own machine will depend of the capabilities of your hardware and browser and also on how many other processes are running on the machine.

Run the simulation and you'll have a particle emitter! Little balls are projected upward and fall back under gravity and drag, looking a bit like a spray. The position of the emitter changes with the location of the mouse cursor, so that you can move the mouse around and watch the fun.

You can produce some interesting effects by changing the parameters and initial conditions. For example, instead of giving the particles a random velocity, you can introduce the following lines of code into setPosVelo():

```
var n = i%7;
var angle = -(60+10*n)*Math.PI/180;
var mag = 100;
newBall.velo2D = Vector2D.vector2D(mag,angle);
i++;
```

Here, the variable i is initially given the value of 0. This produces a fountain-like pattern, as shown in Figure 12-2. You may need to adjust the number of particles or frame rate to reproduce the pattern shown in the screenshot.

Figure 12-2. *Creating a particle emitter*

Creating a smoke effect

Let us now use our particle emitter to create a smoke effect. This is easier than you might think; in fact, you've already done most of the work. The code in the modified file, smoke-effect.js, is essentially the same as that in particle-emitter.js, except for a few relatively small changes.

```
function Spark(radius,r,g,b,alpha,mass){
    if(typeof(radius)==='undefined') radius = 2;
    if(typeof(r)==='undefined') r = 255;
    if(typeof(g)==='undefined') g = 255;
    if(typeof(b)==='undefined') b = 255;
    if(typeof(alpha)==='undefined') alpha = 1;
    if(typeof(mass)==='undefined') mass = 1;
    this.radius = radius;
    this.r = r;
    this.g = g;
    this.b = b;
    this.alpha = alpha;
    this.mass = mass;
    this.x = 0;
    this.y = 0;
    this.vx = 0;
    this.vy = 0;
}

Spark.prototype = {
    get pos2D (){
        return new Vector2D(this.x,this.y);
    },
    set pos2D (pos){
        this.x = pos.x;
        this.y = pos.y;
    },
```

```
    get velo2D (){
        return new Vector2D(this.vx,this.vy);
    },
    set velo2D (velo){
        this.vx = velo.x;
        this.vy = velo.y;
    },
    draw: function (context) {
        context.fillStyle = "rgba("+ this.r +","+ this.g +","+ this.b +","+ this.alpha +")";
        context.beginPath();
        context.arc(this.x, this.y, this.radius, 0, 2*Math.PI, true);
        context.closePath();
        context.fill();
    }
}
```

The first modification might appear a bit weird: we are giving the gravity constant g a negative value (–5)! What's going on here? The thing is that smoke will tend to rise rather than fall because forces such as buoyancy (upthrust) will overcome the force of gravity. But instead of modeling buoyancy, it is simpler to modify gravity so that it acts upward because we are interested only in reproducing the visual effect of smoke approximately.

The second modification is that we are using a new object Spark, created especially for the next few animations. The Spark object looks similar to Ball in many respects, but it does away with extra properties like charge and gradient, which will not be needed here. More importantly, it introduces four new properties r, g, b, and alpha to replace the single property color of Ball. Spark also has a radius and a mass property.

The r, g, b, and alpha values are fed into the constructor (together with radius and mass) and have default values of 255, 255, 255 and 1 respectively. They are used in the draw() function to set the fillStyle when drawing a filled circle of the specified radius, with alpha representing transparency and r, g, b representing color in the RGB format. We specify the individual color and alpha channels separately so that we can manipulate them independently to produce visual effects (as you'll see over the next several examples).

Armed with the new object Spark, we then modify the createNewParticles() method by creating new particles as instances of Spark rather than Ball, giving them radiuses between the values of 1 and 4 pixels. Modified lines are indicated in bold in the following code snippets.

```
function createNewParticles(ppos){
    var newParticle = new Spark(1+3*Math.random(),255,255,255,1,m);
    setPosVelo(newParticle,ppos);
    particles.push(newParticle);
}
```

The next modification is to introduce a new method, modifyObject(), which is called from within the for loop in move() and is therefore executed for each particle at each timestep.

```
function move(){
    context.clearRect(0, 0, canvas.width, canvas.height);
    if (particles.length < maxParticles){
        createNewParticles(posEmitter);
    }else{
        recycleParticles(posEmitter);
    }
    for (var i=0; i<particles.length; i++){
        var particle = particles[i];
        modifyObject(particle);
        moveObject(particle);
```

```
        calcForce(particle);
        updateAccel();
        updateVelo(particle);
    }
}
```

The modifyObject() method looks like this:

```
function modifyObject(obj){
    obj.radius *= 1.01;
    obj.alpha += -0.01;
}
```

All we are doing here is increasing the size of each particle by a constant factor and reducing its transparency by a fixed amount at each timestep.

The result of the previous additions and modifications is that the particles grow and fade as they rise, before disappearing altogether and being recycled. There is one more change that must be made to ensure that the recycling works properly. Because we have been modifying the radius and transparency of the particles, we need to reset those properties to their initial values when they are recycled. This is done by introducing a new method, resetObject() into the recycleParticles() method:

```
function recycleParticles(ppos){
    var firstParticle = particles[0];
    resetObject(firstParticle);
    setPosVelo(firstParticle,ppos);
    particles.shift();
    particles.push(firstParticle);
}
 function resetObject(obj){
    obj.radius = 1+3*Math.random();
    obj.alpha = 1;
}
```

If you were to run the code as shown here, you would get an interesting effect, but you couldn't really call it smoke—see Figure 12-3.

Figure 12-3. *An interesting effect, but not quite smoke yet!*

Time to introduce filters! If you are not familiar with image filters, we encourage you to spend some time reading about them (you can find many tutorials on the Web) and playing around with them. The particular filter we want to use is the blur filter, which gives the edges of an image or HTML element a blurred appearance. There are several ways to achieve this. Since our interest here is on the physics rather than on filters *per se*, we'll make do with what is probably the simplest approach: using CSS filters. Unfortunately the specification for this technology has not yet stabilized, so browser support is rather patchy at the time of writing. The following line added to the CSS file works in Chrome (and reportedly in Safari, too):

```
-webkit-filter: blur(3px);
```

This can also be set in the JavaScript file:

```
canvas.style.webkitFilter = "blur(3px)";
```

You can obviously change the degree of blurring by changing the number of pixels in the parentheses. Feel free to experiment with different values.

If you now run the code, you will see something that looks much more like smoke, as shown on screen in Figure 12-4.

Figure 12-4. *The smoke effect at last*

This is a basic smoke effect that can be tweaked and enhanced in endless ways. Think of it as a starting point for further experimentation rather than as a final result. Moreover, there are lots of other ways to produce a smoke effect like this. The preceding method has been adapted from a tutorial in ActionScript by Seb Lee-Delisle that appeared in *Computer Arts* magazine (March 2008). It's nice because of its simplicity and the fact that it can be done with pure code alone.

Creating a fire effect

It is extremely easy to modify the smoke animation to produce something that looks like fire. The main changes are linked to the appearance of the particles; first we make them slightly bigger and orangey by modifying the first line in createNewParticles() to the following:

```
var newParticle = new Spark(3+3*Math.random(),255,100,0,1,m);
```

This makes particles with radiuses between 3 and 6 pixels. Subsequently, the particles are modified slightly differently than in the smoke simulation in `modifyObject()`:

```
function modifyObject(obj){
    obj.radius *= 1.01;
    obj.alpha += -0.04;
    obj.g = Math.floor(100+Math.random()*150);
}
```

We now change the green color channel at every timestep to range between 100 and 250. We also increase the amount by which the alpha channel is incremented. Naturally, we need to modify the `resetObject()` method to restore the initial color and radius:

```
function resetObject(obj){
    obj.radius = 3+3*Math.random();
    obj.r = 255;
    obj.g = 100;
    obj.b = 0;
    obj.alpha = 1;
}
```

We have also tweaked the values of g and k, changing them to –2 and 0.003 respectively. Feel free to experiment by changing these parameter values. You might also look at the effect of changing the frame rate—perhaps changing fps dynamically, for example randomizing it or making it respond to user events.

The final change we made is to increase the brightness by modifying the canvas style using the following line of code in line 3 of the file:

```
canvas.style.webkitFilter = "blur(3px) brightness(2)";
```

If you run the code now you'll see something like Figure 12-5. Of course, you need to see the actual animation to appreciate the effect and colors.

Figure 12-5. *Creating a fire effect*

Now that you have the basic tools at your fingertips, you can create more elaborate effects by applying the methods to different setups and by combining different techniques. For example, by attaching emitters to objects, you can create the illusion of the objects being on fire. You can also add wind, combine smoke with the fire, add sparks, and so on. Talking of sparks, let's create some now.

Creating fireworks

The end result we want to achieve in this section is an animation that looks like fireworks: a series of little explosions, each generating colorful sparks that fall under gravity with drag. In order to get there, we will first add a couple of properties to our Spark instances and then create a sparks animation before finally adding extra features to make the fireworks.

Adding lifetime and age properties to sparks

Something like a spark exists for only a certain duration, after which it will need to be removed or recycled. It makes sense therefore to introduce a couple of new properties to represent the lifetime and age of a Spark instance. We have a choice of either adding the properties to the Spark object itself or adding them to instances of Spark. We choose the latter for the next couple of examples.

As you will recall from Chapter 2, it's easy to add properties to object instances, as follows:

```
var spark = new Spark();
spark.lifetime = 10;
spark.age = 0;
```

This creates the two properties, lifetime and age, and assigns them values of 10 and 0, respectively. These represent the lifetime and age of spark in seconds. In subsequent code, you can then update its age as time progresses and to check and take the appropriate action if its age exceeds its lifetime.

Making sparks

Let us now apply the newly created lifetime and age properties to create sparks that exist for a specified duration. The code is in a file called sparks.js. We now have 200 particles and give them values of g, k, vx, and vy of 10, 0.005, 100, and –100, respectively (which you can change if you want). We have also changed the value of fps to 60 and specified a blur value of 1px and brightness factor of 2 in the corresponding CSS file. The methods that contain changes from the previous example (fire-effect.js) are reproduced here, with the modified lines highlighted in bold:

```
function move(){
    context.clearRect(0, 0, canvas.width, canvas.height);
    if (particles.length < maxParticles){
        createNewParticles(posEmitter);
    }else{
        recycleParticles(posEmitter);
    }
    for (var i=0; i<particles.length; i++){
        var particle = particles[i];
        modifyObject(particle,i);
        moveObject(particle);
        calcForce(particle);
        updateAccel();
        updateVelo(particle);
    }
}
```

```
function createNewParticles(ppos){
    var newParticle = new Spark(2,255,255,0,1,m);
    setProperties(newParticle,ppos);
    particles.push(newParticle);
}
function recycleParticles(ppos){
    var firstParticle = particles[0];
    resetObject(firstParticle);
    setProperties(firstParticle,ppos);
    particles.shift();
    particles.push(firstParticle);
}
function setProperties(obj,ppos){
    obj.pos2D = ppos;
    obj.velo2D = new Vector2D((Math.random()-0.5)*vx,(Math.random()-0.5)*vy);
    obj.lifetime = 6 + 2*Math.random();
    obj.age = 0;
}
function resetObject(obj){
    obj.alpha = 1;
}
function modifyObject(obj,i){
    obj.alpha += -0.01;
    obj.age += dt;
    if (obj.age > obj.lifetime){
        removeObject(i);
    }
}
function removeObject(num){
    particles.splice(num,1);
}
```

In createNewParticles(), each particle is given the same radius of 2 pixels and a yellowish color. The setPosVelo() method has been replaced by a setProperties() method that now does a bit more—it sets the lifetime and age of each particle in addition to its position and velocity. Because sparks can fly in any direction, each particle is given a random velocity in any direction. Then its lifetime is set to a random value between six and eight seconds. Its age is then initialized to zero.

The resetObject() method only needs to reset the transparency of each recycled particle to 1, since other properties (radius and color) are not changed during the animation.

The modifyObject() method decrements the alpha value of each spark as before, but additionally updates its age every timestep. The particle's age is then checked against its lifetime: if it exceeds the lifetime, the removeParticle() method is called, which removes the particle from the particles array.

Run the simulation and you'll see some nice sparks following the mouse (see Figure 12-6).

Figure 12-6. Making sparks

Making the fireworks animation

Now that we have sparks, we can use them to produce fireworks. Instead of producing the sparks continuously, we want to do that in a series of little explosions. We'll have an initial explosion that will create a bunch of sparks with random velocities; these sparks will then fall under gravity with drag, fading with time. When each spark reaches the end of its lifetime, it will explode, producing further sparks. Obviously, we want to stop this process at some point. The easiest way to do that is to limit the duration of the animation by imposing a global cutoff time.

Following is the source code in the file fireworks.js in full, with modified parts highlighted in bold. Note that some code has also been removed compared to the previous sparks example, including the event listener/handler code.

```
var canvas = document.getElementById('canvas');
var context = canvas.getContext('2d');

var particles;
var m = 1;
var g = 10;
var k = 0.005;
var vx = 150;
var vy = -100;
var numSparks = 10;
var minLife = 2;
var maxLife = 4;
var duration = 6;
var fps = 30;
var t0, t, dt;
var acc, force;
var posEmitter;
```

```
window.onload = init;

function init() {
    particles = new Array();
    posEmitter = new Vector2D(0.5*canvas.width,200);
    createNewParticles(posEmitter,255,255,0);
    t0 = new Date().getTime();
    t = 0;
    animFrame();
}
function animFrame(){
    setTimeout(function() {
        animId = requestAnimationFrame(animFrame,canvas);
        onTimer();
    }, 1000/fps);
}
function onTimer(){
    var t1 = new Date().getTime();
    dt = 0.001*(t1-t0);
    t0 = t1;
    if (dt>0.2) {dt=0;};
    t += dt;
    move();
}
function move(){
    context.clearRect(0, 0, canvas.width, canvas.height);
    for (var i=0; i<particles.length; i++){
        var particle = particles[i];
        modifyObject(particle,i);
        moveObject(particle);
        calcForce(particle);
        updateAccel();
        updateVelo(particle);
    }
}
function createNewParticles(ppos,r,g,b){
    for (var i=0; i<numSparks; i++){
        var newParticle = new Spark(2,r,g,b,1,m);
        setProperties(newParticle,ppos);
        particles.push(newParticle);
    }
}
function setProperties(obj,ppos){
    obj.pos2D = ppos;
    obj.velo2D = new Vector2D((Math.random()-0.5)*vx,(Math.random()-0.5)*vy);
    obj.lifetime = minLife + (maxLife-minLife)*Math.random();
    obj.age = 0;
}
```

```
function modifyObject(obj,i){
    obj.alpha += -0.01;
    obj.age += dt;
    if (obj.age > obj.lifetime){
        if (t < duration){
            explode(obj);
        }
        removeObject(i);
    }
}
function explode(obj){
    createNewParticles(obj.pos2D,0,255,0);
}
function removeObject(num){
    particles.splice(num,1);
}
function moveObject(obj){
    obj.pos2D = obj.pos2D.addScaled(obj.velo2D,dt);
    obj.draw(context);
}
function calcForce(obj){
    var gravity = Forces.constantGravity(m,g);
    var drag = Forces.drag(k,obj.velo2D);
    force = Forces.add([gravity, drag]);
}
function updateAccel(){
    acc = force.multiply(1/m);
}
function updateVelo(obj){
    obj.velo2D = obj.velo2D.addScaled(acc,dt);
}
```

First note that we've changed the value of vx from 100 to 150. This is just so that the sparks spread horizontally more than vertically. We have also added four new variables: numSparks, minLife, maxLife, and duration to store the number of sparks, their minimum and maximum lifetimes, and the duration of the animation, respectively. The next change is that the createNewParticles() method is now called from within the init() method, not from within moveObject(). This means that the particles are created initially, not at every timestep. The createNewParticles() method is modified to accept new arguments that specify the RGB color of the sparks, to create a number numSparks of particles at each timestep instead of just one, and to assign to those particles the specified RGB color. The setProperties() method called from createNewParticles() then assigns each particle a random lifetime between minLife and maxLife.

The modifyObject() method is modified so that, as long as duration has not been exceeded, any particle that exceeds its lifetime explodes before being removed. The explosion is handled by the explode() method, which simply calls the createNewParticles() method and specifies the position of the dying particle as the location for the explosion and gives a new color for the next generation of sparks.

Run the code and you will be treated to a fireworks display (see Figure 12-7). Needless to say, you can tweak the animation endlessly to improve the appearance and add further effects such as trailing sparks, smoke, and even sound effects. We've done our job of showing you how to implement the basic physics. Now go for it!

Figure 12-7. Fireworks!

In the source code, we have also included a modified version of the simulation in a file named fireworks2.js. This is an interactive version where you click and hold down the mouse anywhere on the canvas. The number of sparks numSparks will be set to equal to twice the duration in seconds for which you hold down the mouse, so the longer you press the mouse the greater the number of sparks that will be produced per explosion. When you release the mouse, the initial explosion will take place at the location of the mouse. The colors of the sparks are also randomized in this version. Try it out!

Particle animations with long-range forces

It's now time to transcend reality and start playing around with particles and physics. In this section, we'll be moving lots of particles around under the action of long-range forces to create some interesting patterns and animations.

In this section and the next, we'll generally be dealing with large numbers of particles and lots of calculations. To reduce any unnecessary overheads, we shall therefore make use of a slightly lighter version of the Ball object that we'll call Star. The Star object is similar to the Ball object, but it does not draw a gradient fill and so does away with the extra code needed to do that. It also dispenses with the charge, gradient and angVelo properties. The remaining examples in this chapter will make use of the Star object.

Particle paths in a force field

Particle trajectories are commonly used in generative art projects. We'll now set up a simple example using multiple particles that can be used as a basis for further explorations.

The idea of this animation is very simple, and it is similar in principle to the gravity field example in Chapter 10. We set up a number of stars randomly around a central attractor and give them small random velocities. The stars are subjected to a gravitational force toward the attractor and move around it, tracing trajectories.

The source file is called long-range.js and contains the following code:

```javascript
var canvas = document.getElementById('canvas');
var context = canvas.getContext('2d');
var canvas_bg = document.getElementById('canvas_bg');
var context_bg = canvas_bg.getContext('2d');

var G = 10;
var attractors;
var orbiters;
var t0;
var dt;
var force;
var acc;
var numOrbiters = 20;
var numAttractors = 5;
var graph;

window.onload = init;

function init() {
    // create attractors
    attractors = new Array();
    for (var i=0; i<numAttractors; i++){
        var attractor = new Ball(20,'#333333',10000,0,false);
        attractor.pos2D = new Vector2D(Math.random()*canvas.width,Math.random()*canvas.height);
        attractor.draw(context_bg);
        attractors.push(attractor);
    }
    // create orbiters
    orbiters = new Array();
    for (var i=0; i<numOrbiters; i++){
        var orbiter = new Star(5,'ffff00',1);
        orbiter.pos2D = new Vector2D(Math.random()*canvas.width,Math.random()*canvas.height);
        orbiter.velo2D = new Vector2D((Math.random()-0.5)*50,(Math.random()-0.5)*50);
        orbiter.draw(context);
        orbiters.push(orbiter);
    }
    setupGraph();
    t0 = new Date().getTime();
    animFrame();
}

function animFrame(){
    requestAnimationFrame(animFrame,canvas);
    onTimer();
}
function onTimer(){
    var t1 = new Date().getTime();
    dt = 0.001*(t1-t0);
```

```
            t0 = t1;
            if (dt>0.2) {dt=0;};
            move();
    }
    function move(){
            context.clearRect(0, 0, canvas.width, canvas.height);
            for (var i=0; i<numOrbiters; i++){
                var orbiter = orbiters[i];
                plotGraph(orbiter);
                moveObject(orbiter);
                calcForce(orbiter);
                updateAccel(orbiter.mass);
                updateVelo(orbiter);
            }
    }
    function moveObject(obj){
            obj.pos2D = obj.pos2D.addScaled(obj.velo2D,dt);
            if (obj.x < 0 || obj.x > canvas.width || obj.y < 0 || obj.y > canvas.height){
                recycleOrbiter(obj);
            }
            obj.draw(context);
    }
    function updateAccel(mass){
            acc = force.multiply(1/mass);
    }
    function updateVelo(obj){
            obj.velo2D = obj.velo2D.addScaled(acc,dt);
    }
    function calcForce(obj){
            var gravity;
            force = Forces.zeroForce();
            for (var i=0; i<numAttractors; i++){
                var attractor = attractors[i];
                var dist = obj.pos2D.subtract(attractor.pos2D);
                if (dist.length() > attractor.radius+obj.radius){
                    gravity = Forces.gravity(G,attractor.mass,obj.mass,dist);
                    force = Forces.add([force, gravity]);
                }
            }
    }
    function recycleOrbiter(obj){
            obj.pos2D = new Vector2D(Math.random()*canvas.width,Math.random()*canvas.height);
            obj.velo2D = new Vector2D((Math.random()-0.5)*100,(Math.random()-0.5)*100);
    }
    function setupGraph(){
            graph = new Graph(context_bg,0,canvas.width,0,canvas.height,0,0,canvas.width,canvas.height);
    }
    function plotGraph(obj){
            graph.plot([obj.x], [-obj.y], '#cccccc', false, true);
    }
```

There is little that you have not seen before in this code, and we'll focus on the few new elements. In `init()` we create multiple attractors as `Ball` instances and multiple orbiters as `Star` instances. In `calcForce()`, we are subjecting each star to the gravitational force due to the attractors using the `Forces.gravity()` function, but note that if the star happens to be within a particular attractor we do not include the force that it exerts, effectively setting that force to zero. As in the gravity field example in Chapter 10, we use a `graph` object to plot the trajectory of each orbiter.

Run the simulation and play around by changing the parameters and modifying it in any way you can think of. For example, you could add a finite particle lifetime. If you have a slow machine, you might want to reduce the number of particles. You can come up with some interesting patterns (see, for example, Figure 12-8).

Figure 12-8. *An example of particle trajectories under a central gravitational force*

Building a wormhole

In this wacky example we are going to create something that does not reflect any real physics but is nevertheless interesting to watch!

A *wormhole* is a hypothetical object in which you enter a black hole and emerge at some other location in space. In our animation, we'll have a wormhole made up of a black hole that sucks in stars and a white hole that spews them out again. To make the animation more visually interesting, the stars coming out of the black hole will be increased in size and given a randomized velocity back toward the black hole, creating a cycling system. What do you expect to happen eventually? Let's find out. First we'll show the simulation variables and parameter values and the `init()` function in the file `wormhole.js`:

```
var stars;
var numStars = 1000;
var massStar = 1;
var massAttractor = 10000;
var radiusAttractor = 20;
var posAttractor = new Vector2D(400,400);
var posEmitter = new Vector2D(400,100);
var G = 10;
```

```
var t0, dt;
var acc, force;

window.onload = init;

function init() {
    // create a stationary black hole
    var blackHole = new Star(radiusAttractor,'#222222',massAttractor);
    blackHole.pos2D = posAttractor;
    blackHole.draw(context_bg);
    // create a stationary white hole
    var whiteHole = new Star(10,'#ffffff');
    whiteHole.pos2D = posEmitter;
    whiteHole.draw(context_bg);
    // create stars
    stars = new Array();
    for (var i=0; i<numStars; i++){
        var star = new Star(2,'#ffff00',massStar);
        star.pos2D = new Vector2D(Math.random()*canvas.width,Math.random()*canvas.height);
        star.velo2D = new Vector2D((Math.random()-0.5)*50,(Math.random()-0.5)*50);
        star.draw(context);
        stars.push(star);
    }
    t0 = new Date().getTime();
    animFrame();
}
```

We create a black hole and a white hole and place them some distance from each other, at locations denoted by posAttractor and posEmitter respectively. We next create 1000 stars and place them randomly on the canvas. The stars are animated as usual by calling animFrame(). The subsequent code is standard, the only new features cropping up in the calcForce() and recycleObject() methods:

```
function calcForce(obj){
    var dist = obj.pos2D.subtract(posAttractor);
    if (dist.length() < radiusAttractor){
        recycleObject(obj);
    }else{
        var gravity;
        force = Forces.zeroForce();
        if (dist.length() > radiusAttractor+obj.radius){
            gravity = Forces.gravity(G,massAttractor,massStar,dist);
            force = Forces.add([force, gravity]);
        }
    }
}
function recycleObject(obj){
    obj.pos2D = posEmitter;
    obj.velo2D = new Vector2D((Math.random()-0.5)*50,Math.random()*10);
    obj.radius *= 1.5;
}
```

The `calcForce()` method is nearly the same as in the previous example. The novelty is that we have a new `recycleObject()` method that is called if the star enters the black hole. The `recycleObject()` method instantly moves particles that enter the black hole to the location of the white hole, gives them a random downward velocity, and increases their radius by 50 percent.

If you run the code, you'll find that the stars are sucked into the black hole, emerging larger out of the white hole. Because they are spewed around the black hole again, some of the stars are attracted back into it, while others end up in an orbit around it. Some stars might manage to escape, depending on the maximum magnitude of velocity you set. A few stars go through the wormhole a few times, growing bigger and bigger. Eventually you end up with stars of different sizes trapped in perpetual orbit around the black hole, as shown in Figure 12-9. Because those stars are in a closed orbit around the black hole and have originated from the white hole, their orbits close back on the white hole, giving the impression that the latter is also attracting them!

Figure 12-9. *Stars circulating through a wormhole!*

Interacting particle systems

So far, the particle systems we have looked at have not involved any mutual interactions between the particles. For example, you could let the particles exert a gravitational force on each other. This would create some interesting effects. The trouble is that the number of calculations then becomes very large as the number of particles is increased. For N particles, there are on the order of N^2 interactions because every particle interacts with every other particle. Even with only 100 particles, that's 10,000 extra gravity calculations per timestep! The next two examples illustrate different ways we may be able to handle this.

Multiple particles under mutual gravity

In this example, we will modify the gravity animations in the previous two examples by including mutual gravitational forces between the stars. In physics jargon, this will be a direct N-body calculation.

Again, let's start by looking at the variable declaration/initialization and init() function in the relevant file, multigravity.js:

```
var stars;
var numStars = 200;
var massStar = 100;
var vmag = 10;
var massNucleus = 1;
var radiusNucleus = 20;
var posNucleus = new Vector2D(0.5*canvas.width,0.5*canvas.height);
var G = 1;
var eps = 1;
var rmin = 100;
var t0, dt;
var acc, force;

window.onload = init;

function init() {
    // create a stationary attracting nucleus
    var nucleus = new Star(radiusNucleus,'#333333',massNucleus);
    nucleus.pos2D = posNucleus;
    nucleus.draw(context_bg);
    // create stars
    stars = new Array();
    for (var i=0; i<numStars; i++){
        var star = new Star(2,'#ffff00',massStar*(Math.random()+0.1));
        star.pos2D = new Vector2D(Math.random()*canvas.width,Math.random()*canvas.height);
        star.velo2D = new Vector2D((Math.random()-0.5)*vmag,(Math.random()-0.5)*vmag);
        star.draw(context);
        stars.push(star);
    }
    t0 = new Date().getTime();
    animFrame();
}
```

Here we are creating a central attracting nucleus as well as 200 stars that are randomly positioned around it and have small random velocities. The mass of the nucleus is made 100 times larger than that of the stars, but those are parameters that you can change to see their effect. The only substantial difference from the previous examples is in the calcForce() method:

```
function calcForce(obj,num){
    var dist = obj.pos2D.subtract(posNucleus);
    var gravityCentral;
    if (dist.length() < radiusNucleus) {
        gravityCentral = new Vector2D(0,0);
    }else{
        gravityCentral = Forces.gravity(G,massNucleus,obj.mass,dist);
    }
```

```
        var gravityMutual = new Vector2D(0,0);
        for (var i=0; i<stars.length; i++){
            if (i != num){
                var star = stars[i];
                var distP = obj.pos2D.subtract(star.pos2D);
                if (distP.length() < rmin){
                    var gravityP = Forces.gravityModified(G,star.mass,obj.mass,distP,eps);
                    gravityMutual.incrementBy(gravityP);
                }
            }
        }
        force = Forces.add([gravityCentral, gravityMutual]);
}
```

You are already familiar with the first half of the code in `calcForce()`, which computes the force `gravityCentral` on the stars due to the central nucleus. The second half of the code calculates the total force `gravityMutual` on a star due to all the other stars (excluding itself, hence the `if (i != pnum){}` condition) and adds it to the `gravityCentral` force to get the total force on each star.

There are two new features in this code, in another `if` statement nested within the first:

```
if (distP.length() < rmin){
    var gravityP = Forces.gravityModified(G,star.mass,obj.mass,distP,eps);
    gravityMutual.incrementBy(gravityP);
}
```

The first new feature is the `if` condition, which checks to see whether the distance of the current star from any other star is less than a certain minimum distance `rmin`. The gravity force due to the latter star is included only if the condition is satisfied. This is called the *local interaction approximation*. The idea is that because gravity is an inverse square law, its magnitude falls off rapidly with distance. So if the other star is very far away, including the force it exerts won't make much difference to the total force and is just a waste of resources. So you include only the influence of the nearest neighbors. In an accurate simulation, you would have to be careful to implement this approximation properly, as there are some subtleties. But because we are just playing around, so to speak, there is no need to go into those finer points. The value of `rmin` chosen in the code is 100 pixels, but you can experiment with other values. Giving `rmin` the value of 0 would effectively exclude all mutual interactions between the stars. Giving `rmin` a value larger than 800 would include interactions between all 200 stars: that's about 400,000 extra gravity calculations per timestep, and will certainly slow down your animation!

The second new feature is that we are using a modified version of the gravity function called `Forces.gravityModified()` to compute the interactions between the stars. The new function is defined as follows:

```
Forces.gravityModified = function(G,m1,m2,r,eps){
    return r.multiply(-G*m1*m2/((r.lengthSquared()+eps*eps)*r.length()));
}
```

Comparing this with the `Forces.gravity()` function, you will find that we have introduced a new parameter `eps`, whose square is added to the r^2 term in the denominator of the function. The corresponding mathematical formula is this:

$$F = G\,\frac{m_1\,m_2}{r^2 + \varepsilon^2}$$

The ε symbol (the Greek letter epsilon) stands for the eps parameter. Why do we modify the gravity function in this way? When two objects exerting gravitational forces on each other get very close, the forces become very large or even infinite (because r goes to zero, and we end up dividing by a small number or zero). This, as you will recall from Chapter 6, causes the two objects to accelerate enormously and be sent flying off in random directions. The ε factor is a common "fudge" to bring that problem under control. Because ε^2 is always positive (being the square of a real number), the denominator will never be zero. And as long as ε is small, it will not alter the force calculation much for most values of r except the very smallest. In the example, eps has a value of 1 pixel. You can also experiment with different values to see what effect it produces.

Run the simulation and experiment with different values of the parameters. For example, you can change the masses of the central nucleus and the stars to change the relative importance of the central force compared to the mutual forces between the stars. Running the code with the default values of the parameters will make the stars tend to lump together in different locations, with a few lingering around the central attractor. A screenshot is shown in Figure 12-10. Again, you may want to reduce the number of particles if the simulation runs slowly on your machine.

Figure 12-10. *Lots of stars exerting gravitational forces on one another*

A simple galaxy simulation

What would you need to do to simulate the motion of stars in a galaxy? Well, that is not a trivial job to do properly, typically requiring some serious hardware and lots of physics and code. But it is possible to cheat and come up with a very simplified approach. While the result certainly won't look like that in more sophisticated approaches, it will give you something interesting to play and experiment with further.

The most obvious problem that we hit when attempting to model a system like this is how to handle the large number of particles you'd need. We are talking at least thousands here, and possibly tens of thousands. A direct N-body calculation is impractical with such large numbers of particles, especially for an animation that's going to run in a web browser!

An alternative approach is to consider the motion of each star in the effective gravitational force field due to all the other stars taken together. This is the so-called *mean field approach*. The star system is then effectively considered as a non-interacting collisionless system with each star moving independently in that mean field. The mean field can of course evolve over time as the positions of the stars change, and this evolution needs to be incorporated in such a simulation.

There are numerical methods for calculating the mean field created by a general distribution of point masses, but they are beyond the scope of this book. However, if we make the assumption that the stars are distributed in a spherically symmetric way around the galactic center, the task becomes much simpler thanks to a neat mathematical principle. This principle says that for any spherically symmetric mass distribution, the gravitational force at any distance r from the center is the same force exerted by the total mass enclosed within a sphere of radius r, with that mass taken to be at the center. Any mass outside that radius does not have any effect. If you start a simulation with a spherically symmetric distribution of stars, it should remain spherically symmetric at all times. So you can apply this principle at each timestep.

The stars in a galaxy are not the only source of mass. Many galaxies have a central nucleus that may be a supermassive black hole. So the mass of this galactic nucleus needs to be taken into account. But that's easy; we just use the `Forces.gravity()` function with a specified mass for the nucleus.

There is also something more exotic that lurks in galaxies: dark matter. In fact, it is estimated that most of the mass in a galaxy exists in a dark matter halo around the galaxy. Again, assuming spherical symmetry, the contribution of this dark matter to the gravitational force can be calculated in the same way as that of the stars.

With these basic ingredients, let's put together a quick and dirty galaxy simulation. Much of the code in the relevant file `galaxy.js` looks similar to that in the previous examples, but we list the source code here in its full glory:

```javascript
var canvas = document.getElementById('canvas');
var context = canvas.getContext('2d');

var stars;
var numStars = 5000;
var massStar = 10;
var veloMag = 20;
var maxRadius = 300;
var nucleus;
var massNucleus = 100000;
var radiusNucleus = 20;
var posNucleus = new Vector2D(0.5*canvas.width,0.5*canvas.height);
var G = 1;
var rmax = 500;
var constDark = 1000;
var A = 1;
var alpha = 0.5;
var t0, dt;
var acc, force;
var massStars = new Array(); // total mass of stars within radius r
var massDark = new Array();  // total mass of dark matter within radius r

window.onload = init;

function init() {
    // create a stationary attracting nucleus
    nucleus = new Star(radiusNucleus,'#333333',massNucleus);
    nucleus.pos2D = posNucleus;
    nucleus.draw(context);
    // initial distribution of stars
    stars = new Array();
    for (var i=0; i<numStars; i++){
        var star = new Star(1,'#ffff00',massStar);
        var radius = radiusNucleus + (maxRadius-radiusNucleus)*Math.random();
        var angle = 2*Math.PI*Math.random();
```

```
                star.pos2D = new Vector2D(radius*Math.cos(angle),radius*Math.sin(angle)).add(posNucleus);
                var rvec = posNucleus.subtract(star.pos2D);
                star.velo2D = rvec.perp(veloMag);
                star.draw(context);
                stars.push(star);
            }
        t0 = new Date().getTime();
        animFrame();
    }

    function animFrame(){
        requestAnimationFrame(animFrame,canvas);
        onTimer();
    }
    function onTimer(){
        var t1 = new Date().getTime();
        dt = 0.001*(t1-t0);
        t0 = t1;
        if (dt>0.2) {dt=0;};
        move();
    }
    function move(){
        context.clearRect(0, 0, canvas.width, canvas.height);
        nucleus.draw(context);
        calcMass();
        for (var i=0; i<numStars; i++){
            var star = stars[i];
            moveObject(star);
            calcForce(star,i);
            updateAccel(massStar);
            updateVelo(star);
        }
    }
    function moveObject(obj){
        obj.pos2D = obj.pos2D.addScaled(obj.velo2D,dt);
        obj.draw(context);
    }
    function updateAccel(mass){
        acc = force.multiply(1/mass);
    }
    function updateVelo(obj){
        obj.velo2D = obj.velo2D.addScaled(acc,dt);
    }
    function calcForce(obj){
        var dist = obj.pos2D.subtract(posNucleus);
        if (dist.length() < radiusNucleus) {
            force = new Vector2D(0,0);
        }else{
            force = Forces.gravity(G, massNucleus + massStars[Math.ceil(dist.length())] +
massDark[Math.ceil(dist.length())], massStar, dist);
        }
    }
```

```javascript
function calcMass(){
    var distanceToCenter;
    var star;
    var massStarRing = new Array();
    var massDarkRing = new Array();
    for (var l=0; l<rmax; l++){
        massStarRing[l] = 0;
        massDarkRing[l] = constDark*l*l*Math.exp(-A*Math.pow(l,alpha));
    }
    for (var k=0; k<stars.length-1; k++){
        star = stars[k];
        distanceToCenter = star.pos2D.subtract(posNucleus).length();
        massStarRing[Math.ceil(distanceToCenter)] += star.mass;
    }
    massStars[0] = massStarRing[0];
    massDark[0] = massDarkRing[0];
    for(var j=1; j<stars.length-1; j++){
        massStars[j] = massStars[j-1] + massStarRing[j];
        massDark[j] = massDark[j-1] + massDarkRing[j];
    }
    //console.log(massNucleus,massStars[rmax-1],massDark[rmax-1]);
}
```

We first create a galactic nucleus of mass 100,000 units and radius 20 pixels and place it in the middle of the canvas. Then we create 5,000 stars (depending on your computer's speed, you might want to reduce this number), each with mass 10 units, and place them in a random circular distribution around the galactic center (that's what the lines of trigonometry code in init() achieve). Note that each "star" here really represents lots of stars; there are typically billions of stars in a galaxy, not thousands! The stars are then given an initial tangential velocity around the galactic center. The velocity magnitude for each star has the same value veloMag; that's because observed galactic rotation curves show that the velocity in a galaxy is approximately independent of the distance from the galactic center. There are already a lot of parameters to play with here, such as the mass of the galactic center, the mass of each star, the rotational velocity, and so on. You can also try out different initial positions and velocities for the stars. In the file galaxy.js there are some commented lines with different options for these initial conditions. Try them out to see how they lead to different evolutions of the galaxy.

■ **Note**   If you have a slow machine, you may need to remove the line that contains the following code: if (dt>0.2) {dt=0;}. The large number of particles in this simulation means that a large number of calculations must be performed at each timestep, which could take longer than 0.2 seconds on a slow machine. In that case no movement whatsoever would take place!

Next let's take a look at the calcForce() method. As you can see from the code, we are calculating the total gravitational force on each star at its distance from the center (dist) by using the Forces.gravity() function, with a mass that is the sum of the galactic nucleus mass and the masses of the stars and dark matter within that radius, as stored in the arrays massStars and massDark. These arrays are updated at each timestep by summing the mass at different distances from the center in the calcMass() method. A commented out line at the end of calcMass() outputs the three total masses to the console.

The mass of the stars is computed simply by locating the stars. For the dark matter, the situation is different because it is not included in the simulation as an object. Therefore, we prescribe a mass distribution based on the so-called Einasto profile, which is commonly used in computer simulations of dark matter. The mathematical form of that distribution is the following:

$$\rho(r) = \rho_0 \exp\left(-A r^\alpha\right)$$

Here ρ_0, A and α are constants that must be specified. This formula gives the mass density (mass per unit volume). To get the mass at a distance r, one must multiply this mass density by the volume of a thin spherical shell of thickness dr. This introduces an extra factor of $4\pi r^2 dr$ (surface area of sphere times the thickness of the spherical shell). This gives the formula that is coded in calcMass(). Don't worry if this dark matter material seems a bit difficult to follow. We included it because it can change the dynamics of the interacting stars in a significant way, making for a "richer" simulation. But even if you don't fully understand everything here, you can still play with the relevant parameters to explore the range of possible effects you can get with this additional physics included.

If you run the code with the default parameter values, you should find that after successive initial contractions and expansions, the star distribution settles into a quasi-steady state. Figure 12-11 shows a screenshot of what you might be able to see. One can even discern some structure in the form of rings at times, although it would take a more careful simulation to reproduce realistic physical structures properly. Again, you can change the parameters in galaxy.js, especially those of the dark matter distribution. It would be instructive to see how the simulation changes when you change the relative magnitudes of the galactic nucleus mass, the total star mass, and the total dark matter mass. Have fun!

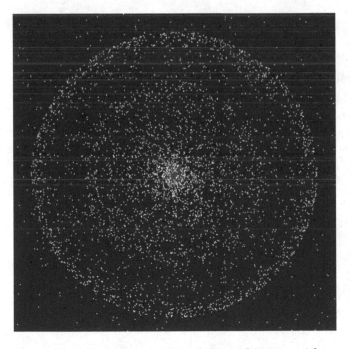

Figure 12-11. *A simple galaxy simulation with 5000 particles*

Summary

This chapter has provided a taste of what can be achieved with particles and some simple physics. In just a short chapter it is impossible to cover the subject fully. We therefore encourage you to search the Web and explore what has been achieved within the animation community and beyond. Many examples of inspiring creations by talented individuals exist, too numerous to mention here, but we've included relevant links on our web site: www.physicscodes.com.

You've had quite a lot of fun with particles in the last few chapters. In the next chapter we'll look at how to model the motion of more complex extended objects.

CHAPTER 13

■ ■ ■

Extended Objects

In much of this book, we have focused on the motion of particles. In this chapter, we will explore the physics governing the motion of extended objects. This topic is important for obvious reasons: objects in everyday life are extended in space and have all sorts of shapes, sizes and behavior. To model the motion of extended objects, we need to cover some additional physics and methods. This is a big subject that could easily have filled several chapters, or even an entire book. We have therefore been selective in our coverage, focusing on two topics that we can cover in sufficient depth to provide a good introduction, instead of giving a wider but more superficial presentation.

Topics covered in this chapter include the following:

- **Rigid bodies:** A *rigid body* is an extended object with a fixed shape and size. In addition to changing its position, such an object can also rotate to change its orientation. We will cover rigid body dynamics, rolling, and rigid body collisions, and illustrate them with a number of different examples.

- **Deformable bodies:** Objects such as ropes and clothes can change their shapes. We can model such *deformable bodies* by means of mass-spring systems, building upon the principles discussed in Chapter 8.

Most of the chapter is devoted to rigid bodies, with a much shorter discussion of deformable bodies.

Rigid bodies

A *rigid body* is defined as an object that maintains its shape and size when a force is applied to it. In other words, rigid bodies do not deform under the action of forces. The rigid body concept is an idealization because in reality, nearly all objects suffer some deformation when subjected to forces, even if it is by a minute amount. However, when modeling the motion of many objects, it is frequently possible to ignore any such deformation and still obtain good results. This is the approach we'll adopt in this section.

Basic concepts of rigid body modeling

Before we can model the motion of rigid bodies, we need to review some relevant concepts from earlier chapters and introduce some new ones. These concepts will then be brought together in the next section to formulate the laws governing rigid body rotational motion.

Rigid body motion versus particle motion

The key difference in the motion of rigid bodies compared to that of particles is that they can undergo rotation as well as translation. The translational motion of a rigid body obeys the same laws as that of particles (as described in Chapter 5). We must now discuss how the rotational motion can be analyzed.

Rotational kinematics

In Chapter 9, we looked at the kinematics of rotational motion, introducing concepts such as angular displacement θ, angular velocity ω, and angular acceleration α. As a brief recap, here are the defining equations for some of these quantities:

Angular velocity:

$$\omega = \frac{d\theta}{dt}$$

Angular acceleration:

$$\alpha = \frac{d\omega}{dt}$$

These rotational kinematics variables are related to the corresponding linear variables, for example:
Linear and angular displacements:

$$s = r\,\theta$$

Linear and angular velocities:

$$v = r\,\omega$$

Linear (tangential) and angular accelerations:

$$a = r\,\alpha$$

In the context of rigid body rotation, these formulas give the displacement, velocity, and tangential acceleration of a point on a rigid body at a distance r from the center of rotation in the absence of translational motion—or in addition to those due to translational motion.

In addition to the tangential acceleration, there is a centripetal (radial) acceleration given by this formula:

$$a = v^2/r = r\,\omega^2$$

Note that all points on a rigid body must have the same angular displacement, angular velocity, and angular acceleration, whereas the linear counterparts of these quantities depend on the distance r from the center of rotation.

We shall also use vector equivalents of the preceding quantities and formulas. For example, the angular velocity is really a vector ω with a direction perpendicular to the plane of rotation and with an orientation as shown in Figure 13-1. The angular acceleration, as the derivative of the angular velocity, is therefore also a vector α.

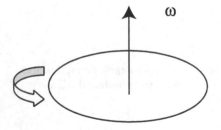

Figure 13-1. *Angular velocity as a vector*

Rotating rigid body objects on a canvas element

How do you rotate objects on a canvas element? In Chapter 9 we did it by rotating the whole canvas. Recall that we first have to shift the canvas so that its origin is at the object's center before doing the rotation. After rotating the canvas, we then translate the canvas back to its original location before drawing the object. If there are many objects being animated, this process has to be repeated for each object at each timestep. Surely there has to be a better way to do this.

Although you cannot rotate individual objects on a canvas element after they are drawn, you can control the orientation with which to draw them in the first place. In an animation, if you keep track of the orientation of the object, then you can redraw it with a slightly different orientation at each timestep.

To illustrate the application of this idea, let us dig out the `wheel-demo.js` simulation and `Wheel` object from Chapter 9 and make some small modifications to them. In `wheel.js` we add a `rotation` property in the constructor to keep track of the orientation of a wheel instance. The value of `rotation` will represent an angle in radians, with an initial value of 0:

```
this.rotation = 0;
```

Then, in the `draw()` method of `Wheel`, we modify the code that draws the spokes, as shown here in bold:

```
for (var n=0; n<nums; n++){
    context.moveTo(this.x,this.y);
    context.lineTo(this.x + ir*Math.cos(2*Math.PI*n/nums + this.rotation),
this.y + ir*Math.sin(2*Math.PI*n/nums + this.rotation));
}
```

With this modification, the `draw()` method adds the rotation of the wheel instance to the angle at which it draws each spoke.

Next we modify `wheel-demo.js` from Chapter 9, calling the new file `wheel-rotate.js`. In that file we get rid of the lines of code in `onTimer()` that perform the canvas transformations:

```
context.save();
context.translate(wheel.x,wheel.y);
context.rotate(angle);
context.translate(-wheel.x,-wheel.y);
context.restore();
```

We replace these five lines with the single line:

```
wheel.rotation = angle;
```

Run the code and you'll find it produces exactly the same animation as the one in Chapter 9. But this code is simpler, more elegant and more efficient. The performance gains may not be noticeable in this simple example, but they can be considerable if lots of rotating objects are being animated.

The Polygon object and rotating polygons

The method we used in the previous section can be adapted to rotate other types of objects besides wheels. We'll be dealing with polygons a lot in this chapter, so let's create a Polygon object and apply the method to it:

```
function Polygon(vertices,color,mass){
    if(typeof(color)==='undefined') color = '#0000ff';
    if(typeof(mass)==='undefined') mass = 1;
```

```
        this.vertices = vertices;
        this.color = color;
        this.mass = mass;
        this.x = 0;
        this.y = 0;
        this.vx = 0;
        this.vy = 0;
        this.angVelo = 0;
}

Polygon.prototype = {
    get pos2D (){
        return new Vector2D(this.x,this.y);
    },
    set pos2D (pos){
        this.x = pos.x;
        this.y = pos.y;
    },
    get velo2D (){
        return new Vector2D(this.vx,this.vy);
    },
    set velo2D (velo){
        this.vx = velo.x;
        this.vy = velo.y;
    },
    set rotation (angle){
        for (var i=0; i<this.vertices.length; i++){
            this.vertices[i] = this.vertices[i].rotate(angle);
        }
    },
    draw: function (ctx) {
        var v = new Array();
        for (var i=0; i<this.vertices.length; i++){
            v[i] = this.vertices[i].add(this.pos2D);
        }
        ctx.save();
        ctx.fillStyle = this.color;
        ctx.beginPath();
        ctx.moveTo(v[0].x,v[0].y);
        for (var i=1; i<v.length; i++){
            ctx.lineTo(v[i].x,v[i].y);
        }
        ctx.lineTo(v[0].x,v[0].y);
        ctx.closePath();
        ctx.fill();
        ctx.restore();
    }
}
```

The Polygon object takes three arguments: `vertices`, `color`, and `mass`. It is the first of those, `vertices`, that is of interest here. This is an array of `Vector2D` objects that specify the position vectors of the vertices of the polygon instance to be created. These position vectors are relative to the position of the polygon object, as specified by the x and y values. For a regular polygon, that would be at the position of its geometrical center. The `draw()` method draws a polygon by joining these vertices. The way the `rotation` property works here is different than in the `Wheel` object. Here a setter is used to rotate the vertices of the polygon by an angle assigned as the value of `rotation`. This is done using the newly created `rotate()` method of the `Vector2D` object, which rotates a vector through the angle specified as its argument (in radians). It is defined as follows:

```
function rotate(angle){
     return new Vector2D(this.x*Math.cos(angle) - this.y*Math.sin(angle),
this.x*Math.sin(angle) + this.y*Math.cos(angle));
}
```

It uses some trigonometry to do that, which you can try to figure out as an exercise.

The `polygon-rotate.js` file gives an example of how to use the `Polygon` object to create a polygon and make it rotate:

```
var canvas = document.getElementById('canvas');
var context = canvas.getContext('2d');
var v = 10;        // linear velocity in pixels per second
var w = 1;         // angular velocity in radians per second
var angDispl = 0; // initial angular displacement in radians
var dt = 30/1000; // time step in seconds = 1/FPS
// create a polygon
v1 = new Vector2D(-100,100);
v2 = new Vector2D(100,100);
v3 = new Vector2D(150,0);
v4 = new Vector2D(100,-100);
v5 = new Vector2D(-100,-100);
var vertices = new Array(v1,v2,v3,v4,v5);
var polygon = new Polygon(vertices);
polygon.x = 300;
polygon.y = 300;
polygon.draw(context);
setInterval(onTimer, 1/dt);
function onTimer(evt){
     polygon.x += v*dt;
     angDispl = w*dt;
     polygon.rotation = angDispl;
     context.clearRect(0, 0, canvas.width, canvas.height);
     polygon.draw(context);
}
```

As you can see, this code works in the same way as the modified wheel example in the previous section, simply by updating the value of the rotation property of the polygon instance inside the time loop, without needing to invoke canvas transformations.

As pointed out at the beginning of this section, you can adapt this method to deal with other types of objects. We have implemented a variation of it in the `Ball` object by defining "vertices" corresponding to the end-points of the lines drawn on a `Ball` instance when its `line` property is specified as `true`. Take a look at the modified `ball.js` file in the source code for this chapter. `Ball` instances can then be made to rotate simply by changing their `rotation` property prior to drawing them, as illustrated in the `ball-rotate.js` example file.

The turning effect of a force: torque

Suppose a rigid body is at rest and we want to translate it (give it some linear velocity). How do we do that? We need to apply a force. But what must we do if we want to rotate it about a given axis? Again we need to apply a force. But the line of action of the force must not pass through the axis. The *turning effect* of a force is known as a *moment* or *torque*, and is defined as the product of the force and the perpendicular distance of its line of action from the axis (see Figure 13-2):

$$T = F\,d = F\,r\sin(\theta)$$

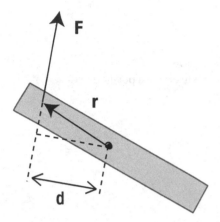

Figure 13-2. *Definition of torque due to a force*

Here, θ is the angle between the force **F** and the vector **r** from the center of rotation to the point of application of the force.

In vector form, it is the following:

$$\mathbf{T} = \mathbf{r} \times \mathbf{F}$$

Note that the vector product is not commutative, so the order in which the product is performed matters. Because the vector product of two vectors gives a vector that is perpendicular to both, if **r** and **F** are in the plane of the paper, the torque will point either into or out of the paper (see the section "Multiplying vectors: Vector or cross product" in Chapter 3 for how to work out the direction of the resulting vector).

From this definition, it is clear that the torque is zero if the line of action of the force passes through the axis. In general, a force will produce both a linear acceleration and a turning effect.

Center of mass

From what we have said in the previous section, you can see that if an object is free to move (without any constraints) and you apply a force on it, it will undergo both a translation and a rotation. An exception arises if the line of action of the force passes through a special point known as the *center of mass* of the object. In that case, the applied force produces only translation, but no rotation.

Center of mass is a general concept that applies to collections of point particles as well as to extended objects. In both cases, it represents the location at which the overall mass of the system appears to act. For a collection of point particles of mass m_1, m_2, ... located at positions $\mathbf{r}_1$, $\mathbf{r}_2$, ..., the position vector of the center of mass is given by the following formula:

$$\mathbf{r} = \frac{m_1\,\mathbf{r}_1 + m_2\,\mathbf{r}_2 + \ldots}{m_1 + m_2 + \ldots}$$

So we add the products $m\mathbf{r}$ of the particles vectorally and divide the sum by their total mass. Using the symbol Σ, which stands for sum, we can write this formula in the following shorthand form:

$$\mathbf{r} = \frac{\sum m_i\,\mathbf{r}_i}{\sum m_i}$$

For a rigid body, a generalization of this formula is used by considering the body as being composed of a continuous distribution of particles. The center of mass of a rigid body can then be computed using the calculus formula:

$$\mathbf{r} = \frac{\int \mathbf{r}\,dm}{\int dm}$$

The denominator of this formula is simply equal to the total mass of the rigid body. The location of the center of mass will depend on the shape of the body as well as on how its mass is distributed. For objects that are symmetrical and with a uniform mass distribution, the center of mass is located at their geometrical center. For example, the center of mass of a sphere is located at its center. It is similar for other objects such as cuboids, discs, and rectangles.

The center of mass is important for two reasons. First, it provides a connection between particle dynamics and rigid body dynamics: in terms of its translational motion, a rigid body can be thought of as a particle located at its center of mass. Second, the analysis of rigid body motion is much simpler if expressed in terms of a coordinate system with the center of mass as the origin.

Moment of inertia

We said that torque is the analog of force for rotational motion: torque is the cause of angular acceleration. What is the rotational analog of mass (inertia)? This may not be obvious, but, as will be demonstrated in the next section, it is a quantity known as the *moment of inertia*. The moment of inertia is defined as the sum of mr^2 for all the particles comprising the particle system or rigid body, where m is the mass of the particle and r is its distance from the axis of rotation. For a discrete system of particles, the definition of the moment of inertia (denoted by the symbol I) is therefore the following:

$$I = \sum m_i\,r_i^2$$

This formula tells us that the larger the mass of the particles or the greater their distance from the axis, the larger the moment of inertia.

For a continuous distribution of mass such as a rigid body, the corresponding calculus definition is the following:

$$I = \int r^2\,dm$$

Both of these formulas tell us that the moment of inertia is a property that quantifies the mass distribution in a rigid body. Using the calculus formula, one can work out the moment of inertia of a variety of regular rigid bodies in both 2D and 3D. The result is a formula in terms of the total mass and some linear dimensions of the rigid body.

For example, the moment of inertia of a hollow sphere of mass m and radius r about an axis through its center is given by the following formula:

$$I = \frac{2}{3} m r^2$$

Because the moment of inertia depends on the mass distribution, a solid sphere of the same mass m and radius r has a different moment of inertia, being given by this formula:

$$I = \frac{2}{5} m r^2$$

So a hollow sphere has a larger moment of inertia (and is therefore harder to rotate) than a solid sphere of the same mass and radius.

The moment of inertia also depends on the axis around which the rotation takes place. For example, the solid cylinder shown in Figure 13-3 has a moment of inertia around the x-axis and y-axis given by the following formula (where m is its mass, r is the radius of its circular cross-section and h is its height):

$$I = \frac{1}{12} m \left(3 r^2 + 4 h^2 \right)$$

Figure 13-3. *Rotation of a solid cylinder about different axes*

The corresponding moment of inertia of the same cylinder around the z-axis is given by a different formula:

$$I = \frac{1}{2} m r^2$$

You can find the moments of inertia of a wide variety of 2D and 3D objects in physics or engineering textbooks and web sites.

Angular momentum

Another important concept is that of *angular momentum*, which is the rotational analog of linear momentum. For a particle rotating about a center at a distance r from it, the angular momentum (denoted by the symbol L) is defined as the product of its linear momentum and the distance r:

$$L = pr = mvr$$

In vector form, the angular momentum vector is the vector product of the position and momentum vectors:

$$\mathbf{L} = \mathbf{r} \times \mathbf{p}$$

Using the relationship between linear and angular velocity $v = r\omega$, gives this:

$$L = mr^2 \omega$$

Therefore, for a collection of particles all rotating with the same angular velocity ω, the total angular momentum is given by the following:

$$L = \sum m_i r_i^2 \omega$$

Using the definition of moment of inertia, this gives the following result:

$$L = I\omega$$

In vector form, it is this:

$$\mathbf{L} = I\omega$$

This result also applies to rigid bodies, with the appropriate calculus definition of moment of inertia.

Modeling rigid bodies

Armed with our knowledge of rigid body concepts, we can now build some basic JavaScript objects that will help us create rigid bodies.

Creating a RigidBody object

The first object we'll create is the RigidBody object. Because a rigid body has all the properties of a particle plus more, it might make sense to "extend" the Particle object using the method emulating classical inheritance described in Chapter 4. This would be the recommended approach if you were to develop a large library with numerous objects inheriting properties from other objects. But in the interest of clarity we'll just modify the code for the Particle object in particle.js and save it as rigidbody.js.

In fact, our RigidBody object will just replace the charge property of the Particle object by the im property, which represents moment of inertia (with a default value of 1). So here is the RigidBody object code:

```
function RigidBody(mass,momentOfInertia){
    if(typeof(mass)==='undefined') mass = 1;
    if(typeof(momentOfInertia)==='undefined') momentOfInertia = 1;
    this.mass = mass;
    this.im = momentOfInertia;
    this.x = 0;
```

```
        this.y = 0;
        this.vx = 0;
        this.vy = 0;
}

RigidBody.prototype = {
    get pos2D (){
        return new Vector2D(this.x,this.y);
    },
    set pos2D (pos){
        this.x = pos.x;
        this.y = pos.y;
    },
    get velo2D (){
        return new Vector2D(this.vx,this.vy);
    },
    set velo2D (velo){
        this.vx = velo.x;
        this.vy = velo.y;
    }
}
```

The position of a rigid body instance will always be taken to be that of its center of mass, and is specified by the x and y properties or equivalently by the pos2D property.

Extending the RigidBody object

Like Particle, the RigidBody object has no graphics. To do anything with it in practice, you need to "extend" it and include some graphics. Let's create a couple of examples that we will use later in this chapter.

The BallRB object

Just as RigidBody replaced the charge property in Particle by the im (moment of inertia) property, we do the same with the Ball object and call the new object BallRB. So the constructor of BallRB looks like this:

```
function BallRB(radius,color,mass,momentOfInertia,gradient,line){}
```

All the parameters are optional, with default values of 20, '#0000ff', 1, 1, false, and false respectively.

The PolygonRB object

Next we create a PolygonRB object in a similar way to the BallRB class, essentially by just adding a moment of inertia property to Polygon. The parameters in the constructor of this object are therefore as follows:

```
function PolygonRB(vertices,color,mass,momentOfInertia){}
```

As with the Polygon object, vertices is an array of Vector2D values that corresponds to the locations of the vertices relative to the position of the PolygonRB instance, hence *relative to the center of mass* of the polygon.

Like Polygon, the PolygonRB object draws a polygon with a fill of the specified color. The order in which the vertices are specified is important. The code draws the polygon by joining the vertices in the specified order, so that different shapes result from different orderings of the vertices.

Using the rigid body objects

The file `rigid-body-test.js` contains code that demonstrates the use of these rigid body classes. This code produces a BallRB object rotated by 45° and a square PolygonRB object and makes them rotate at different rates and in opposite senses. The square is also made to move slowly to the right as it rotates. Comparing this example with the earlier rotating polygon in `polygon-rotate.js` shows that we haven't done anything substantially new yet— we haven't made use of the moment of inertia property of either BallRB or PolygonRB. To do this we need to implement rotational dynamics into our simulations. But before we can do that we need a bit more theory.

Rotational dynamics of rigid bodies

Having developed relevant rotational motion concepts in analogy with their linear counterparts, we are now in a position to formulate the laws of rotational dynamics. Let's start with the most important one: the rotational equivalent of Newton's second law of motion.

Newton's second law for rotational motion

Consider a rigid body that is rotating about an axis under the action of a force F (which produces a torque T), as shown in Figure 13-4.

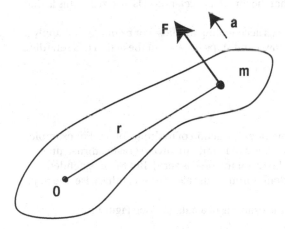

Figure 13-4. *A rotating rigid body*

Let's think of the rigid body as being composed of little particles, each of mass m, each undergoing a tangential acceleration a (ignore any radial acceleration, which does not contribute to rotation). Then, applying Newton's second law to such a particle gives the following:

$$F = m a$$

Recalling the formula relating the tangential acceleration to the angular acceleration, a = $r\alpha$, we can write the previous formula as follows:

$$F = mr\alpha$$

Therefore, the torque $T = Fr$ on the particle is obtained by multiplying the previous formula by r to give this:

$$T = mr^2\alpha$$

To get the total torque on the rigid body, we sum the torques on each particle to give the following formula:

$$T = \sum mr^2\alpha$$

Strictly speaking, we should use an integral rather than a discrete sum for a rigid body, but the reasoning and final answer are the same because an integral is nothing but a continuous sum. So we'll use the simpler discrete summation notation here.

Because all points on a rigid body have the same angular acceleration, α is a constant, and we can take it out of the sum. Recognizing $\sum mr^2$ as the moment of inertia I, we then obtain the following final result:

$$T = I\alpha$$

In vector form, it is this:

$$\mathbf{T} = I\boldsymbol{\alpha}$$

This formula is the equivalent of Newton's second law $\mathbf{F} = m\mathbf{a}$ for rotational motion, with torque, moment of inertia, and angular acceleration replacing force, mass, and linear acceleration, respectively. The formula enables us to calculate the angular acceleration of a rigid body from the torque exerted on it.

As a special case, if the torque T is zero, the formula implies that the angular acceleration is also zero. This is the analog of Newton's first law of motion.

Just as in linear motion, you can have retarding torques as well as accelerating torques. For example, you apply an accelerating torque to make a merry-go-round spin. It then slows down and stops because of the action of a retarding torque applied by friction.

Rigid bodies in equilibrium

In Chapter 4, we discussed the situation of an object in equilibrium under the action of multiple forces. For example, an airplane moving at constant velocity is in equilibrium under the action of four main forces (gravity, thrust, drag, and lift). The condition for equilibrium is that the forces balance (the resultant force is zero). But for an extended object, such as a rigid body, this condition is not enough. The resultant torque must also be zero; otherwise, the object will undergo rotational acceleration.

This concept of rotational equilibrium is well illustrated with the example of a balance (see Figure 13-5).

Figure 13-5. *Rotational equilibrium illustrated by a balance*

Assuming that the balance is in equilibrium, the downward force exerted by the combined weights on either side of the pivot is balanced by the upward contact force exerted by the pivot. Also, the clockwise torque or moment generated by one weight is balanced by the counterclockwise torque generated by the other weight: this is known as the *principle of moments*. In vector terms, one of the torques points out of the paper and the other points into the paper.

An example of a situation in which the resultant force may be zero and the resultant torque is not is when you turn a knob (see Figure 13-6). In that case, there are two opposite forces applied to either side of the knob. If their magnitudes are equal, they will give a zero resultant force. However, their torques will be in the same direction (into the paper) because they both generate clockwise rotations. This is an example of a *couple*: a pair of equal and opposite forces that have parallel non-coincident lines of action that therefore generate a resultant torque.

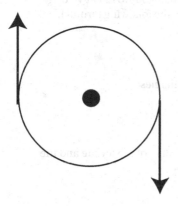

Figure 13-6. *A couple*

Conservation of angular momentum

Just as there is a rotational analog of Newton's second law, rotational analogs of other laws exist, too. We shall now state these laws without proof, starting with the principle of conservation of angular momentum.

This principle states that the angular momentum of a rigid body or a system of particles is conserved if no external torque acts on it. For example, if an object is spinning at constant angular velocity, it will continue to do so unless an external torque is applied to it. That's the reason the Earth continues to spin on its axis. On the other hand, a spinning top soon stops spinning because of opposing frictional torque.

Angular impulse-momentum theorem

The conservation of angular momentum is a special case of the angular impulse-momentum theorem. Recall the linear impulse-momentum theorem from Chapter 5. The formula expressing that theorem looks like this:

$$\mathbf{F}\,\Delta t = \Delta \mathbf{p}$$

This formula tells us that the impulse applied to an object is equal to the change in momentum produced.

The rotational analog of the previous equation is obtained by taking the vector product of $\mathbf{r}$ with each side of the equation to give the following (because $\mathbf{T} = \mathbf{r} \times \mathbf{F}$ and $\mathbf{L} = \mathbf{r} \times \mathbf{p}$):

$$\mathbf{T}\,\Delta t = \Delta \mathbf{L}$$

In other words, the angular impulse applied to an object is equal to the change in angular momentum it produces. Recall that, for a rigid body, angular momentum $\mathbf{L} = I\omega$. This result will be useful when we consider collisions between rigid bodies.

If the torque $\mathbf{T} = 0$, the theorem gives $\Delta \mathbf{L} = 0$, angular momentum conservation. Therefore, the principle of angular momentum conservation is a special case of the angular impulse-momentum theorem as stated earlier.

Rotational kinetic energy

Because a rigid body can rotate as well as translate, there is kinetic energy associated with rotational motion in addition to the kinetic energy associated with linear motion. Recall that the linear kinetic energy is given by the following formula:

$$E_k = \frac{1}{2}mv^2$$

We said that the moment of inertia is analogous to mass, and angular velocity is analogous to linear velocity. Therefore, you might not be surprised to learn that rotational kinetic energy is given by the following formula:

$$E_k = \frac{1}{2}I\omega^2$$

Therefore, the total kinetic energy of a rigid body is the sum of these two kinetic energies.

Work-energy theorem for rotational motion

In an analogy of the work done by a force, the work done by a torque is equal to the product of the torque and the angular displacement it produces:

$$W = T\theta$$

We can then apply the work-energy theorem (see Chapter 4) to the case of rotational motion, concluding that the work done by a torque is equal to the change in rotational kinetic energy that it produces:

$$\Delta W = \Delta E_k$$

In that case, the kinetic energy is given by $E_k = \frac{1}{2} I\omega^2$.

Simulating rigid body dynamics

We are now ready to implement rigid body dynamics in code. To do this, we will need to modify relevant bits of the animation loop code that we have so far been using in this book.

Modifying the animation loop to include rotational dynamics

The animation code needs to be modified in a straightforward way to include torque and angular acceleration, in exact analogy to force and linear acceleration. The following listing shows typical code to achieve this, with the added bits highlighted in bold:

```
function moveObject(obj){
    obj.pos2D = obj.pos2D.addScaled(obj.velo2D,dt);
    obj.rotation = obj.angVelo*dt;
    context.clearRect(0, 0, canvas.width, canvas.height);
    obj.draw(context);
}
```

```
function calcForce(obj){
    force = Forces.zeroForce();
    torque = 0;
}
function updateAccel(obj){
    acc = force.multiply(1/obj.mass);
    alp = torque/obj.im;
}
function updateVelo(obj){
    obj.velo2D = obj.velo2D.addScaled(acc,dt);
    obj.angVelo += alp*dt;
}
```

In this code, torque represents the *magnitude* of the torque and alp represents the *magnitude* of the angular acceleration. Hence, they are both numbers rather than Vector2D objects like the corresponding force and acc variables. The reason we only represent the magnitudes of the torque and angular acceleration is that in the 2D examples that we'll consider, the rotation can only take place in the *x–y* plane (there *is* only one plane), so the direction of any associated angular velocity, angular acceleration, and torque will always be in a hypothetical third dimension that sticks either into or out of that plane. The sign of the relevant quantity will determine which way it points.

A simple test

Let's test the new rotational dynamics code with a simple example. In rigid-body-dynamics.js, we create a square rigid body using the PolygonRB object and then subject it to an imposed torque. The setup code in the init() method looks like this:

```
function init() {
    var v1 = new Vector2D(-100,100);
    var v2 = new Vector2D(100,100);
    var v3 = new Vector2D(100,-100);
    var v4 = new Vector2D(-100,-100);
    var vertices = new Array(v1,v2,v3,v4);
    rigidBody = new PolygonRB(vertices);
    rigidBody.mass = 1;
    rigidBody.im = 5;
    rigidBody.pos2D = new Vector2D(200,200);
    rigidBody.velo2D = new Vector2D(10,0);
    rigidBody.angVelo = 0;
    rigidBody.draw(context);
    t0 = new Date().getTime();
    animFrame();
}
```

The body's mass and moment of inertia are set and its velocity and angular velocity are initialized. The subsequent animation code looks like this:

```
function animFrame(){
    animId = requestAnimationFrame(animFrame,canvas);
    onTimer();
}
```

```
function onTimer(){
    var t1 = new Date().getTime();
    dt = 0.001*(t1-t0);
    t0 = t1;
    if (dt>0.2) {dt=0;};
    move();
}
function move(){
    moveObject(rigidBody);
    calcForce(rigidBody);
    updateAccel(rigidBody);
    updateVelo(rigidBody);
}
function moveObject(obj){
    obj.pos2D = obj.pos2D.addScaled(obj.velo2D,dt);
    obj.rotation = obj.angVelo*dt;
    context.clearRect(0, 0, canvas.width, canvas.height);
    obj.draw(context);
}
function calcForce(obj){
    force = Forces.zeroForce();
    force = force.addScaled(obj.velo2D,-kLin); // linear damping
    torque = 1;
    torque += -kAng*obj.angVelo; // angular damping
}
function updateAccel(obj){
    acc = force.multiply(1/obj.mass);
    alp = torque/obj.im;
}
function updateVelo(obj){
    obj.velo2D = obj.velo2D.addScaled(acc,dt);
    obj.angVelo += alp*dt;
}
```

As you can see in the calcForce() method, a torque of magnitude 1 unit is applied at each timestep. If that was all that was done, the square would undergo continuous angular acceleration, rotating faster and faster. Therefore, an angular damping term proportional to the angular velocity is also applied to limit its angular velocity. A linear damping term is also added to the force. The values of the corresponding damping factors kLin and kAng are set to 0.05 and 0.5 respectively.

If you run the simulation, you will find that the square translates to the right while rotating in a clockwise sense. As time progresses, its linear velocity decreases until it stops (because there is no driving force but a retarding force proportional to its velocity), whereas its angular velocity increases to a constant value (you can check this by tracing the angular velocity at each timestep). The latter happens because the applied torque of 1 unit tends to increase the angular velocity whereas the angular damping term grows as the angular velocity increases. Therefore, at some point the damping term balances the applied torque and rotational equilibrium is achieved (as well as linear equilibrium). It's the equivalent of terminal velocity for rotational motion. You can calculate the "terminal angular velocity" in the following way.

Start with the equation of angular motion relating torque and angular acceleration:

$$T = I\alpha$$

In the present simulation, because there is a driving torque of 1 unit and a retarding torque proportional to the angular velocity, the resultant torque T is given by this:

$$T = 1 - k\omega$$

Using the previous equation of motion then gives the following:

$$I\alpha = 1 - k\omega$$

At equilibrium, the angular acceleration α is zero. Therefore, the left side of this equation is zero. Rearranging gives the following result:

$$\omega = 1/k$$

This is the "terminal" angular velocity. Using the value of $k = 0.5$ in the code gives a value of 2 for this angular velocity. If you trace the body's angular velocity at each timestep in the simulation you will find that it indeed converges to this value.

Experiment by changing the mass and moment of inertia of the body. You will find that they affect the time it takes to achieve linear and rotational equilibrium respectively, but do not affect the final linear velocity (0) or final angular velocity (2).

We can now simulate rotational dynamics! Let's build some more interesting examples.

Example: a simple wind turbine simulation

In this example we'll simulate the motion of more than one rigid body. The objects we'll simulate are wind turbines. So we start by creating a turbine function that makes use of PolygonRB to draw a filled polygon consisting of six vertices. Three of the vertices lie equidistant along the circumference of an inner circle, and the other three lie on an outer circle. The vertices on the inner and outer circle alternate so that the resulting Polygon looks like a wind turbine. The turbine function takes five parameters corresponding to the radius of the inner and outer circles (ri and ro), the turbine color (col), its mass (m) and moment of inertia (im), and it looks like this:

```
function turbine(ri,ro,col,m,im){
    var vertices = new Array();
    for (var i=0; i<3; i++){
        var vertex = getVertex(ro,i*120);
        vertices.push(vertex);
        vertex = getVertex(ri,i*120+60);
        vertices.push(vertex);
    }
    return new PolygonRB(vertices,col,m,im);
}
```

The function getVertex() returns the vertex position as a Vector2D object given its distance from the turbine center and its angle from the horizontal:

```
function getVertex(r,a){
    a *= Math.PI/180;
    return new Vector2D(r*Math.cos(a),r*Math.sin(a));
}
```

In the file wind-turbines.js we use the turbine function to create three turbines of different sizes, as shown in Figure 13-7.

Figure 13-7. *Creating wind turbines!*

This is done in the init() method of wind-turbines.js:

```
function init() {
    turbines = new Array();
    var turbine1 = turbine(4,50,'#000000',1,1);
    turbine1.pos2D = new Vector2D(200,150);
    turbines.push(turbine1);
    var turbine2 = turbine(6,75,'#000000',2.25,5);
    turbine2.pos2D = new Vector2D(150,400);
    turbines.push(turbine2);
    var turbine3 = turbine(12,150,'#000000',9,81);
    turbine3.pos2D = new Vector2D(500,300);
    turbines.push(turbine3);
    addEventListener('mousedown',onDown,false);
    t0 = new Date().getTime();
    animFrame();
}
```

The code assigns different masses and moments of inertia to the turbines. The masses are assigned in proportion to the square of the outer radius of the turbines (treating them as two-dimensional), while the moments of inertia are in proportion to the fourth power of the outer radius (because I is proportional to mr^2, and m is proportional to r^2). The masses are really irrelevant because the turbines will only rotate. Changing their values to anything else won't make any difference to the rotation. But we set appropriate values for physical consistency.

Part of the animation code is shown here:

```
function move(){
    context.clearRect(0, 0, canvas.width, canvas.height);
    for (var i=0; i<turbines.length; i++){
        var windTurbine = turbines[i];
        moveObject(windTurbine);
        calcForce(windTurbine);
        updateAccel(windTurbine);
        updateVelo(windTurbine);
    }
}
```

```
function moveObject(obj){
    obj.pos2D = obj.pos2D.addScaled(obj.velo2D,dt);
    obj.rotation = obj.angVelo*dt;
    obj.draw(context);
}
function calcForce(obj){
    force = Forces.zeroForce();
    torque = tq;
    torque += -k*obj.angVelo; // angular damping
}
function updateAccel(obj){
    acc = force.multiply(1/obj.mass);
    alp = torque/obj.im;
}
function updateVelo(obj){
    obj.velo2D = obj.velo2D.addScaled(acc,dt);
    obj.angVelo += alp*dt;
}
```

This code should look familiar from the previous example. In the calcForce() method, we specify a zero resultant force and a driving torque of magnitude tq as well as an angular damping term proportional to the angular velocity. The value of the torque magnitude tq is controlled by mouse-click event handlers: if the mouse is pressed, tq is given a value tqMax (which is 2 by default); if not, it has a value of 0. This means any time the mouse is clicked, a constant driving torque is applied to each turbine; otherwise, the driving torque is zero.

```
function onDown(evt){
    tq = tqMax;
    addEventListener('mouseup',onUp,false);
}
function onUp(evt){
    tq = 0;
    removeEventListener('mouseup',onUp,false);
}
```

Run the simulation and click anywhere on the canvas. What do you see? The smallest turbine starts turning almost immediately while the largest one only starts turning slowly. This illustrates the concept of rotational inertia: a rigid body with a larger moment of inertia will accelerate less than one with a smaller moment of inertia for the same torque. This is, of course, nothing but the consequence of $T = I\alpha$. Similarly, if you stop pressing the mouse, the smallest turbine will stop quickly; the largest one will stop only after a long time.

While this simulation captures the basic dynamics of a rotating turbine, more work is needed to make a more realistic simulation of how it operates in practice with wind forcing. For example, the torque and damping coefficient for each turbine will depend on characteristics such as its surface area. Wind modeling is another subject in its own right. We won't dwell on these complicating factors; instead we'll move to another example!

Example: Rolling down an inclined plane

Rolling involves an interesting and particularly instructive application of rotational dynamics, but it can be fairly complex to understand. Therefore we'll approach the subject through a specific example.

In Chapter 7, we simulated the motion of a ball sliding down an inclined plane. It was noted there that the ball would slide only if the incline were steeper than a certain critical angle that depends on the coefficient of static friction. The simulation worked well, but there was a major defect: the ball would not move if the angle was not high enough. This is hardly realistic; in reality balls *roll* down inclined planes whatever their angle of inclination!

From a particle to a rigid body simulation

We are now in a position to incorporate rolling into the ball sliding down an inclined plane simulation. But first we need to treat the ball as a rigid body instead of a particle. So let's dig out that old code, sliding.js, and modify it to make use of our new rigid body object BallRB. The setup part of the file, rolling.js, initially looks like this:

```
var ball;
var r = 20; // radius of ball
var m = 1;  // mass of ball
var g = 10; // acceleration due to gravity
var ck = 0.2;  // coeff of kinetic friction
var cs = 0.25; // coeff of static friction
var vtol = 0.000001 // tolerance
// coordinates of end-points of inclined plane
var xtop = 50; var ytop = 150;
var xbot = 450; var ybot = 250;
var angle = Math.atan2(ybot-ytop,xbot-xtop); // angle of inclined plane
var acc, force;
var alp, torque;
var t0, dt;
var animId;

window.onload = init;

function init() {
    // create a ball
    ball = new BallRB(r,'#0000ff',m,0,true,true);
    ball.im = 0.4*m*r*r; // for solid sphere
    ball.pos2D = new Vector2D(50,130);
    ball.velo2D = new Vector2D(0,0);
    ball.draw(context);
    // create an inclined plane
    context_bg.strokeStyle = '#333333';
    context_bg.beginPath();
    context_bg.moveTo(xtop,ytop);
    context_bg.lineTo(xbot,ybot);
    context_bg.closePath();
    context_bg.stroke();
    // make the ball move
    t0 = new Date().getTime();
    t = 0;
    animFrame();
}
```

This is similar to the code in Chapter 7, and it produces the setup shown in Figure 13-8. In addition, we have specified the mass and moment of inertia of the ball. For the latter, we are using the formula for the moment of inertia of a solid sphere ($I = 2mr^2/5$), assuming we are simulating a solid spherical ball.

Figure 13-8. *A ball rolling down an inclined plane*

The animation part of the code is standard, except for the calcForce() method, which initially looks like this (we will soon modify it):

```
function calcForce(){
    var gravity = Forces.constantGravity(m,g);
    var normal = Vector2D.vector2D(m*g*Math.cos(angle),0.5*Math.PI-angle,false);
    var coeff;
    if (ball.velo2D.length() < vtol){  // static friction
        coeff = Math.min(cs*normal.length(),m*g*Math.sin(angle));
    }else{  // kinetic friction
        coeff = ck*normal.length();
    }
    var friction = normal.perp(coeff);
    force = Forces.add([gravity, normal, friction]);
}
```

If you compare this code with the corresponding calcForce() method for the sliding.js example from Chapter 7, you'll find that it does the same thing, with identical forces and parameter values. All that we've done so far is to replace Ball with BallRB so that we can introduce rigid body dynamics. If you were to run the code in its current form, the ball would not move, just as in Chapter 7, unless you made the incline steeper (for example, by changing the value of ybot in the setup file to 260 or more). We know that in real life the ball would roll down the slope even if it can't slide. So what's missing?

Simulating rolling without slipping

You might be tempted to just add a torque to calcForce() and see whether that makes the ball roll. As you can see from the last line of code, there are three forces included in the simulation: gravity, the normal force, and friction (see the force diagram in Figure 13-9). Because both gravity and the normal force act through the center of mass, they do not have any associated torque about the center of mass. Only the frictional force has a torque about the center of mass of the ball, and the magnitude of that torque is fr, where f is the magnitude of the friction force, and r is the radius of the ball.

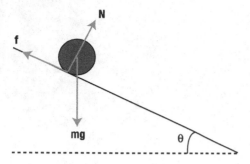

Figure 13-9. *Force diagram for a ball rolling down an inclined plane*

Add the following line of code after the last line in `calcForce()`:

```
torque = r*friction.length();
```

Now run the code. What do you find? Sure the ball rotates faster and faster under the action of the torque generated by the frictional force, but it does not go anywhere! We are still missing something. Leave the torque code because it is correct. But we need to do a bit more thinking.

Let's take another look at Figure 13-9. What else needs to change apart from accounting for the torque due to friction? The only other thing is whether the three forces are still the same with rolling. Now gravity is a fixed force that depends only on the mass of the object, so it will remain exactly the same, with magnitude *mg* and acting vertically downward; so will the normal force because it must still be equal and opposite to the component of gravity normal to the plane (there is no motion in that direction). Therefore, the normal force still has magnitude $mg \cos(\theta)$ and acts normal to the plane, as implemented in the code.

The frictional force needs to change. Rolling friction is generally smaller than static or kinetic friction (that's what makes the wheel such a useful invention!). At the moment, the frictional force is generally too large. So the problem really boils down to specifying the correct frictional force that will produce rolling without slipping.

The point is that the condition for rolling without slipping constrains the linear and rotational motion to "work together," and this in turn constrains the magnitude of the frictional force. By formulating the constraint from first principles (that is, starting from basic physics laws) and working out its implications using the equations of linear and rotational motion, it is possible to deduce what the frictional force must be. Let's do that now.

To make it easier to visualize (but without loss of generality) think of a ball or wheel of radius *r* that is rolling on flat ground with an angular velocity ω, as shown in Figure 13-10.

Figure 13-10. *A ball or wheel rolling without slipping*

If the ball or wheel rolls without slipping (let's call this *pure rolling*), when it completes one revolution it has moved forward a distance equal to $2\pi r$. It does that in a time equal to its period T, which is equal to $2\pi/\omega$ (see Chapter 9). The velocity of its center of mass is given by the ratio of the distance moved to the time taken, which is therefore given by the following:

$$v = r\omega$$

Recall that this is just the formula for the linear velocity of any point on the circumference of a circle; in pure rolling it also gives the velocity with which the whole object moves forward. This formula holds at any time, even if the angular velocity (and therefore the linear center of mass velocity) is changing. Differentiating with respect to time then gives the equivalent formula relating the linear center of mass acceleration to the angular acceleration:

$$a = r\alpha$$

This is the crucial constraint that will help us calculate the pure rolling frictional force (denoted by **f**). The way that force comes into play is of course through the equations of motion. Applying the linear equation of motion $\mathbf{F} = m\mathbf{a}$ along the slope gives (see Figure 13-9):

$$mg\sin(\theta) - f = ma$$

Applying the angular equation of motion $T = I\alpha$ gives the following:

$$fr = I\alpha$$

We need to solve for the frictional force f, but we don't know the acceleration a or the angular acceleration α. But we do have the constraint $a = r\alpha$ that relates them, so we can use that together with the previous equation to eliminate α and obtain the following relationship between the acceleration a and the frictional force f:

$$a = fr^2/I$$

We can now substitute this into the previous equation that arose from the linear equation of motion and, after rearranging, obtain the following final result:

$$f = \frac{mg\sin(\theta)}{1 + mr^2/I}$$

We can also then use the previous equation connecting a and f to deduce the following formula for the acceleration of the rolling object:

$$a = \frac{g\sin(\theta)}{1 + I/(mr^2)}$$

Comparing this with the acceleration of a freely falling object, g, we find that the acceleration of a rolling object is reduced by a factor that depends on the ratio I/mr^2 for the body, as well as on the angle of inclination of the plane (the latter is just because we are looking at the acceleration component down the slope, rather than vertically downward).

Now that we have the formula for the frictional force for pure rolling, it's a simple matter to include it in the code. Remove the `if` block of code that computes the magnitude of the friction `coeff` in `calcForce()` and replace it by the following line, which is exactly the formula for f:

```
coeff = m*g*Math.sin(angle)/(1+m*r*r/ball.im);
```

Now run the code, and you'll have the ball rolling down the slope without slipping!

Allowing both slipping and rolling

Now increase the slope by changing the value of ybot to 850 and rerun the simulation. The slope is now very steep, but the ball will still roll down without slipping. Now we have the opposite problem: the ball does not know how to slip!

To make the simulation more realistic, we need to implement the possibility of both rolling and slipping in a simple way just by adding the following if block just after the line that computes coeff:

```
if (coeff > cs*normal.length()){
    coeff = ck*normal.length();
}
```

This imposes a limit on the maximum magnitude that the rolling friction can have; it resets the magnitude of the computed friction to the kinetic friction if it exceeds the static friction. Run the code and you'll see that the ball now slips as it rolls down. If you change ybot back to 250 you will find that the ball undergoes pure rolling as before. In fact, you can add a console.log("slipping") line inside the if block and run the code for different values of ybot. This will tell you unequivocally when the ball is slipping. With the given parameter values, you should find that pure rolling occurs up to the value of ybot = 500, corresponding to a slope angle of approximately 41.2°.

More experiments with the simulation

A classic college physics problem is the following: suppose you release two solid cylinders, a light one and a heavy one, at the same height on a slope. Assuming that they both roll down the slope without slipping, which one will reach the bottom first? Well, you can use your simulation to find out!

First, change the value of ybot in rolling.js back to 250, so that you have pure rolling. Then change the moment of inertia formula to the following:

```
ball.im = 0.5*m*r*r;
```

This differs from the previous formula for a sphere only in the factor of 0.5; the moment of inertia of a cylinder is $I = mr^2/2$.

Experiment with the simulation using different values for the mass and the radius of the cylinder and make a note of the time it takes for it to reach the bottom. What do you notice?

Well, counterintuitive as it may seem, you should find that the cylinder always takes the same time to reach the bottom of the slope, regardless of its mass or its radius. To see why that is so, refer to the formula for the acceleration derived in the previous subsection. Because the moment of inertia of a cylinder is given by $I = mr^2/2$, the ratio I/mr^2 that appears in that formula has the value of 0.5, giving the acceleration of a solid cylinder down the slope as

$$a = \frac{2}{3}g\sin(\theta)$$

This interesting result tells us that the acceleration is completely independent of the properties of the cylinder such as mass and radius or moment of inertia: they've all cancelled out! So, as long as two cylinders are both solid, they should always roll down a slope at the same rate!

However, a hollow cylindrical tube has a moment of inertia given by approximately $I = mr^2$. Going through the same calculation then gives the following acceleration:

$$a = \frac{1}{2}g\sin(\theta)$$

So a hollow cylindrical tube would accelerate more slowly and therefore take longer to reach the bottom of the slope.

Rigid body collisions and bouncing

In Chapter 11, we spent a considerable amount of time discussing particle collisions and bouncing. You might perhaps have felt that the math got a bit complicated then. Well, with rigid bodies, the math gets even more complicated! With rigid bodies you have to take into account both the linear motion and the rotation of the objects involved in the collision. Particles, spheres, and circular objects don't rotate as a result of collisions (at least if we assume the collisions are frictionless). That's because for such objects the line of collision is always through their center of mass (see Figure 13-11), so the impulsive force due to collision does not generate torque.

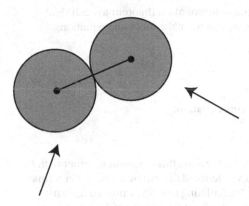

Figure 13-11. *Colliding spheres*

For an object with a more complicated shape, this won't be true in general. As with a sphere, the line of collision is normal to the surface of an object, but it may not pass through the center of mass of the object (see Figure 13-12). Hence, a torque about the center of each of the colliding objects is generated in this case, causing them to rotate.

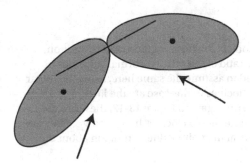

Figure 13-12. *Collision between two rigid bodies of arbitrary shape*

The task of collision resolution in this more general case is therefore to calculate the final linear velocities v_1^f and v_2^f *and* angular velocities ω_1^f and ω_2^f of the two objects, given their initial linear velocities v_1^i and v_2^i and angular velocities ω_1^i and ω_2^i (the objects could already be rotating before the collision) just before the impact. That is what we shall do in this section.

Linear impulse due to collision

The linear velocities $\mathbf{v}_1^i$, $\mathbf{v}_2^i$, $\mathbf{v}_1^f$, and $\mathbf{v}_2^f$ are the initial and final linear velocities of the center of mass of the two colliding rigid bodies (denoted by the subscript 1 and 2, respectively). The angular velocities ω_1^i, ω_2^i, ω_1^f, and ω_2^f are the corresponding angular velocities about the respective center of mass of each rigid body.

The starting point is to apply the impulse-momentum theorem:

$$\mathbf{F}\,\Delta t = \Delta \mathbf{p} = m\,\Delta \mathbf{v}$$

Let's denote the impulse $\mathbf{F}\Delta t$ by the symbol $\mathbf{J}$. Then, applying the impulse-momentum theorem to each rigid body and remembering that they experience equal and opposite impulse, we can write the following equations:

$$\mathbf{J} = m_1\left(\mathbf{v}_1^f - \mathbf{v}_1^i\right)$$

$$-\mathbf{J} = m_2\left(\mathbf{v}_2^f - \mathbf{v}_2^i\right)$$

We note in passing that together these two equations imply the following equation:

$$m_1\mathbf{v}_1^i + m_2\mathbf{v}_2^i = m_1\mathbf{v}_1^f + m_2\mathbf{v}_2^f$$

This is nothing but conservation of momentum, as we saw in Chapter 11. We used this equation together with the one for the coefficient of restitution C_R to obtain the final velocities $\mathbf{v}_1^f$ and $\mathbf{v}_2^f$ (denoted therein by $\mathbf{v}_1$ and $\mathbf{v}_2$) in terms of the initial velocities (denoted therein by $\mathbf{u}_1$ and $\mathbf{u}_2$). Refer to the section "Calculating velocities after an inelastic collision" in Chapter 11. Here the situation is more complicated because we also have the angular velocities to worry about, and we need to proceed via a slightly different route.

The approach we'll adopt is to express the final velocities in terms of the impulse $\mathbf{J}$ and then to work out what $\mathbf{J}$ is. For the linear velocities, this is simply a matter of rearranging the previous equations involving $\mathbf{J}$ to obtain the following:

$$\mathbf{v}_1^f = \mathbf{v}_1^i + \mathbf{J}/m_1$$

$$\mathbf{v}_2^f = \mathbf{v}_2^i - \mathbf{J}/m_2$$

As with particle collisions, we can supplement these equations with one involving a coefficient of restitution. In the particle case, the coefficient of restitution was equal to the negative ratio of the relative normal velocities of the colliding particles before and after the collision. One might be tempted to assume the same here, using the linear velocities of the center of mass of each particle. But, in fact, the relevant velocities in this case are the linear velocities of the points of contact on each body normal to the contact surfaces. Referring again to Figure 13-12, these are the velocities at the point P where the two rigid bodies make contact. Let's denote these velocities by $\mathbf{v}_{p1}$ and $\mathbf{v}_{p2}$. They are each given by the vector sum of the center of mass velocity and the velocity at the point P due to rotation about the center of mass.

So we have the following equations:

$$\mathbf{v}_{p1} = \mathbf{v}_1 + \omega_1 \times \mathbf{r}_{p1}$$

$$\mathbf{v}_{p2} = \mathbf{v}_2 + \omega_2 \times \mathbf{r}_{p2}$$

These equations are valid at any time and, in particular, just before and just after the collision. Hence, they can be written with the "i" and "f" superscripts we have used before. The vectors $\mathbf{r}_{p1}$ and $\mathbf{r}_{p2}$, which are the position vectors of the point P relative to the center of mass of each body, are the same during that brief interval, so they do not require these superscripts.

The relative velocities before and after the collision are given by the following:

$$\mathbf{v}_r^i = \mathbf{v}_{p1}^i - \mathbf{v}_{p2}^i$$

$$\mathbf{v}_r^f = \mathbf{v}_{p1}^f - \mathbf{v}_{p2}^f$$

The coefficient of restitution is then given by the negative ratio of the normal components of these relative velocities (where **n** is the unit normal vector):

$$C_R = -\frac{\mathbf{v}_r^f \bullet \mathbf{n}}{\mathbf{v}_r^i \bullet \mathbf{n}}$$

The problem is that this involves the final angular velocities as well, which we don't know. So we need to solve for the angular velocities simultaneously. That means we need more equations. The extra equations come from applying the angular impulse-momentum theorem.

Angular impulse due to collision

Let's now apply the angular impulse-momentum theorem:

$$\mathbf{T}\,\Delta t = \Delta \mathbf{L}$$

Because $\mathbf{T} = \mathbf{r} \times \mathbf{F}$ and $\mathbf{L} = I\omega$, this is equivalent to the following:

$$\mathbf{r} \times \mathbf{J} = I\,\Delta\omega$$

Applying this to each body and again remembering that they experience equal and opposite impulses gives us the following equations:

$$\mathbf{r}_{p1} \times \mathbf{J} = I_1\left(\omega_1^f - \omega_1^i\right)$$

$$-\mathbf{r}_{p1} \times \mathbf{J} = I_2\left(\omega_2^f - \omega_2^i\right)$$

These equations can be rearranged to give the final angular velocities in terms of the initial angular velocities and the impulse:

$$\omega_1^f = \omega_1^i + \mathbf{r}_{p1} \times \mathbf{J}/I_1$$

$$\omega_2^f = \omega_2^i - \mathbf{r}_{p2} \times \mathbf{J}/I_2$$

The only thing we need now is the impulse **J**, and we can then obtain both the linear and angular velocities.

The final result

It is possible to solve all of the preceding equations together to obtain an expression for the impulse **J**. We'll spare you the detailed algebra and just provide the final answer. Writing $\mathbf{J} = J\mathbf{n}$, where J is the magnitude of the impulse, and **n** is the unit normal vector as before (because the impulse is along the direction of the normal), we obtain the following expression for the magnitude of the impulse:

$$J = -\frac{\left(1 + C_R\right)\mathbf{v}_r^i \bullet \mathbf{n}}{1/m_1 + 1/m_2 + \left(\mathbf{r}_{p1} \times \mathbf{n}\right)^2/I_1 + \left(\mathbf{r}_{p2} \times \mathbf{n}\right)^2/I_2}$$

In the preceding equation, the square of each of the cross product terms (which are vector quantities) refers to taking the dot product with itself.

In the case in which the second rigid body is an immovable object, such as a wall, we can make m_2 and I_2 infinite in the previous equation (which eliminates the terms involving them). Note that the relative velocity $\mathbf{v}_r^i$ in that case is just the velocity $\mathbf{v}_{p1}^i$ of point P on body 1. We then end up with the following:

$$J = -\frac{(1+C_R)\mathbf{v}_{p1}^i \bullet \mathbf{n}}{1/m_1 + (\mathbf{r}_{p1} \times \mathbf{n})^2 / I_1}$$

For easy reference, let's repeat the equations that allow you to then calculate the final linear and angular velocities:

$$\mathbf{v}_1^f = \mathbf{v}_1^i + J/m_1$$

$$\mathbf{v}_2^f = \mathbf{v}_2^i - J/m_2$$

$$\omega_1^f = \omega_1^i + \mathbf{r}_{p1} \times J/I_1$$

$$\omega_2^f = \omega_2^i - \mathbf{r}_{p2} \times J/I_2$$

In the case of the second object being an immovable wall, $\mathbf{v}_2^f$ and ω_2^f are zero.

Having been through that complex-looking math, you'll be glad to know that the previous formulas are not actually very hard to code. In coding terms, the trickier aspects of simulating rigid body collisions are probably those of collision detection and repositioning, which are equally important and require careful consideration when creating realistic simulations.

Note that these equations are valid for collisions between rigid bodies of any shape. In the examples we will put together shortly, we are going to consider polygons. In that case, the most common collision event is the collision of a vertex of one polygon with an edge of another. The line of collision is then the normal to the relevant edge. But collisions between the vertices of two polygons are also quite common, and it is important to have a method to handle them. Other less-common collision scenarios include two vertices of an object hitting two different objects at the same time.

To avoid complications associated with these different collision scenarios and the collision detection and handling methods needed to deal with them, we will start with a simple example of a single polygon bouncing off a floor. This will allow us to focus on implementing the collision resolution method that was developed in the preceding sections. Afterward we will build a more complex simulation involving multiple colliding and bouncing objects, which will require us to confront some of the trickier issues mentioned here.

Example: Simulating a single bouncing block

We will now build a simple simulation of a rectangular block bouncing off a floor, so that we have a single movable object. The setup code for this simulation, rigid-body-bouncing.js, looks like this:

```
var block;
var wall;
var m = 1;
var im = 5000;
var g = 20;
var cr = 0.4;
var k = 1;
```

```
var acc, force;
var alp, torque;
var t0, dt;
var animId;

window.onload = init;

function init() {
    // create a block
    block = makeBlock(100,50,'#0000ff',m,im);
    block.rotation = Math.PI/4;
    block.pos2D = new Vector2D(400,50);
    block.draw(context);
    // create a wall
    wall = new Wall(new Vector2D(100,400),new Vector2D(700,400));
    wall.draw(context_bg);
    // make the block move
    t0 = new Date().getTime();
    animFrame();
}
function makeBlock(w,h,col,m,im){
    var vertices = new Array();
    var vertex = new Vector2D(-w/2,-h/2);
    vertices.push(vertex);
    vertex = new Vector2D(w/2,-h/2);
    vertices.push(vertex);
    vertex = new Vector2D(w/2,h/2);
    vertices.push(vertex);
    vertex = new Vector2D(-w/2,h/2);
    vertices.push(vertex);
    return new PolygonRB(vertices,col,m,im);
}
```

We create a rectangular block as a PolygonRB instance and a floor object using the Wall class in Chapter 11. The block is given a moment of inertia of 5000 and an initial orientation of π/4 radians (45°).

The animation part of the code is fairly standard, with an unremarkable looking calcForce() method:

```
function calcForce(obj){
    force = Forces.constantGravity(m,g);
    torque = 0; // no external torque since gravity is the only force
    torque += -k*obj.angVelo; // damping
}
```

The calcForce() method prescribes gravity as the only force on the block and specifies a zero external torque because gravity does not generate torque about its center of mass. We do include a damping torque, though, the magnitude of which is controlled by the damping parameter k (which you can set to zero if you wish).

The really new physics in the code is contained in the checkBounce() method, which is called from the move() method at each timestep, and looks like this:

```
function checkBounce(obj){
    // collision detection
    var testCollision = false;
    var j;
    for (var i=0; i<obj.vertices.length;i++){
        if (obj.pos2D.add(obj.vertices[i].rotate(obj.rotation)).y >= wall.p1.y){
            if (testCollision==false){
                testCollision = true;
                j = i;
            }else{ // that means one vertex is already touching
                stop(); // block is lying flat on floor, so stop simulation
            }
        }
    }
    // collision resolution
    if (testCollision == true){
        obj.y += obj.pos2D.add(obj.vertices[j].rotate(obj.rotation)).y*(-1) + wall.p1.y;
        var normal = wall.normal;
        var rp1 = obj.vertices[j].rotate(obj.rotation);
        var vp1 = obj.velo2D.add(rp1.perp(-obj.angVelo*rp1.length()));
        var rp1Xnormal = rp1.crossProduct(normal);
        var impulse = -(1+cr)*vp1.dotProduct(normal)/(1/obj.mass + rp1Xnormal*rp1Xnormal/obj.im);
        obj.velo2D = obj.velo2D.add(normal.multiply(impulse/obj.mass));
        obj.angVelo += rp1.crossProduct(normal)*impulse/obj.im;
        testCollision = false;
    }
}
```

As you can see, the code looks surprisingly short given the apparent complexity of the preceding discussion of the theory. The code is split into two parts, one specifying the collision detection and the other the collision resolution. The collision detection code loops over the vertices of the block and tests to see whether any of them is lower than the floor using the following condition:

```
if (obj.pos2D.add(obj.vertices[i].rotate(obj.rotation)).y >= wall.p1.y){}
```

This line might look a bit complicated, so let's break it down. First the easy bit: wall.p1.y just gives the y position of the wall. Next, obj.vertices[i] is the position vector of the vertex currently being tested relative to the center of mass of the block. You have already encountered the rotate() method of the Vector2D object earlier in this chapter.

We are therefore rotating the position vector of the current vertex through an angle equal to the angular displacement obj.rotation of the block to account for the block's orientation. Then we add this to the block's (center of mass) position. We do this because we need the position vector of the vertex in the canvas coordinate system, not in the center of mass coordinate system. Finally, we test whether the y component of this vector is greater than the y location of the wall. If it is, a collision is detected, and the Boolean parameter testCollision is set to true and the index of the vertex is stored in the variable j. But this is only done provided testCollision is currently false (another collision has not already been detected in the same timestep). If testCollision was already true, that means another vertex is already in collision with the floor. Physically, it means that the block is now lying flat on the floor.

The reasonable thing to do then is to stop the simulation. We do this using the stop() method, which stops the animation loop:

```
function stop(){
    cancelAnimationFrame(animId);
}
```

The collision resolution code executes if a collision is detected (if testCollision is true). The first line repositions the block by simply moving it up by the amount that it fell below the wall. The next few lines of code simply implement the equations given at the end of the last section and should be straightforward to follow. The only subtlety is the use of the crossProduct() method, which is another newly created method of the Vector2D class defined as follows:

```
function crossProduct(vec) {
    return this.x*vec.y - this.y*vec.x;
}
```

This might confuse you if you recall that the cross product of two vectors is only supposed to exist in 3D and to be itself a vector. Because our simulation is in 2D, we've defined the analog of the cross product, but can only give its magnitude because the cross product of two vectors should be perpendicular to both and should therefore need a third dimension to exist. The bottom line is that this trick enables us to use the formulas involving vector products in the last section pretty much as they are, as long as we keep in mind that it will only give us the magnitude of the cross product (which, in fact, is all that we need in those formulas).

There is not much more to say about this simulation. Run it and enjoy! See Figure 13-13 for a screenshot. As usual, try out the effects of changing the parameters like the moment of inertia, the coefficient of restitution, and the angular damping factor. As an additional exercise, try replacing the rectangle with another polygon, such as a triangle or a pentagon.

Figure 13-13. *A falling block bouncing off a floor*

Example: Colliding blocks

As discussed earlier, with multiple blocks colliding together, care is needed to detect collisions between the objects and then keep them apart. So let's spend some time discussing how they are applied in a specific example—a group of polygons with different sizes and orientations dropped from a height so that they fall onto and bounce off a floor, colliding with one another as they do so.

Figure 13-14 illustrates the most common scenario when a vertex *P* of one block (object 1) collides with an edge of another (object 2). At the moment of collision detection, *P* is inside the second polygon. If you consider the position vectors of the vertices of the second polygon relative to *P*, they should all have positive dot products with the normal from *P* to the side adjacent to them (by convention, we'll consider the side that is in a counterclockwise direction from the relevant vertex). So if you test all these dot products and any one of them is negative, you know that no collision has taken place. You could also do a weaker test first by seeing whether the distance between the centers of mass of the two objects is larger than the distance to their farthest vertices. If so, you don't have to bother doing the more detailed collision detection test.

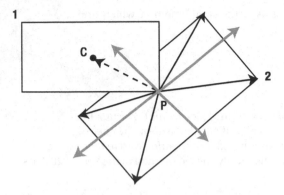

Figure 13-14. *Vertex-edge collision between two polygons*

To reposition an object after a vertex-edge collision, you simply move it back along the normal to the edge where the collision took place by an amount equal to the perpendicular distance from the point P to the relevant edge. The correct normal is determined by checking which one has the minimum angle with the position vector of P relative to the center of mass of object 1 (refer to Figure 13-14).

Another scenario is when a vertex of one object collides with a vertex of another. You might think that would be a rare event, but it tends to happen more often than you'd think. For example, a vertex of one polygon can slide along an edge of another until it hits the vertex at the end. In the case of vertex-vertex collisions, a simple collision detection method is to check for the distance between two vertices; if it's smaller than a certain amount (let's say 1 pixel), that's counted as a collision.

We apply these methods in our example simulation. The code for the simulation is in the file `rigid-body-collisions.js`. This code produces a number of polygons of different sizes and orientations and assigns them masses proportional to their areas and moments of inertia based on their masses and dimensions. A `Wall` object is also produced to represent the floor. We won't list all the code here, but only show the amended `move()` method so you get an idea of the main logic:

```
function move(){
    context.clearRect(0, 0, canvas.width, canvas.height);
    for (var i=0; i<blocks.length; i++){
        var block = blocks[i];
        checkWallBounce(block);
        for(var j=0;j<blocks.length;j++){
            if(j!==i){
                checkObjectCollision(block,blocks[j]);
            }
        }
        moveObject(block);
        checkWallBounce(block);
        calcForce(block);
        updateAccel(block);
        updateVelo(block);
    }
}
```

As in the previous simulation, there is only gravity as an external force on each object and no external torque, so that `calcForce()` is the same as before. At each timestep, the `checkWallBounce()` method checks whether the current object is colliding with a wall and handles the collision if necessary. This method is in essence very similar to the code we saw in the previous example for detecting and resolving wall collisions. Then the `checkObjectCollision()` method sees whether the current object is colliding with any other object and resolves the collision if it takes place. The collision resolution code is along the same lines as that of the wall collision, but of course using the corresponding formulas for two-body collisions. The rest of the code in `checkObjectCollision()` detects any vertex-side or vertex-vertex collisions between two objects and repositions them according to the methods described previously. See the source code in the file `rigid-body-collisions.js` for the detailed implementation.

If you run the code you will find that the simulation generally works well, correctly handling the collision scenarios it is designed to detect. But because we kept the simulation simple, you may notice some problems every now and then, especially when objects get crowded and multiple collisions are involved. The problems can get worse if higher velocities are involved; for example, if g is increased. You could improve the simulation by devising methods to handle more of these possible collision scenarios. You could also introduce friction to make it look more realistic at the moment the blocks slide along the floor once they have settled due to the lack of friction. Figure 13-15 shows a screenshot of the simulation.

Figure 13-15. *The multiple colliding blocks simulation*

Deformable bodies

You now know how to simulate rigid body motion, but how do you simulate the motion of deformable bodies such as ropes and clothes, whose shapes can change? There are various ways to do that, but we'll introduce one particular approach based on the spring physics that we covered in Chapter 8. Let's begin with a brief recap of the main principles and formulas of spring physics and a discussion of how those principles can be applied to model deformable bodies.

Mass-spring systems

The basic modeling approach is to represent a deformable extended object as a series of particles with mass joined together by virtual springs. Hence we generally refer to such models as mass-spring systems. As an illustration of the method, consider the simple one-dimensional chain of particles and springs shown in Figure 13-16.

Figure 13-16. *A 1D chain of particles connected by springs*

Each particle experiences a spring force that depends on its distance from the adjacent particles. We can impose a certain equilibrium distance L between the particles. If two particles are closer together than the distance L, they repel; if they are farther apart than L, they attract. The length can be thought of as the natural unstretched length of the virtual spring connecting the two particles.

As described in Chapter 8, the spring force between any two particles is given by the following equation, in which k is the spring constant and $\mathbf{x}$ is the extension:

$$\mathbf{F} = -k\,\mathbf{x}$$

The magnitude of the extension $\mathbf{x}$ is the amount by which the spring is stretched beyond its unstretched length L. In the case of two adjacent particles connected by a spring, it is therefore equal to the distance d between the particles minus L:

$$x = d - L$$

In vector form, it is this:

$$\mathbf{x} = (d - L)\frac{\mathbf{d}}{d}$$

Here $\mathbf{d}$ is the distance vector between the two particles. For example, the ith particle in the preceding 1D chain experiences a force due to the $(i+1)^{\text{th}}$ particle given by the following equation, where $\mathbf{r}$ is the position vector of the respective particle:

$$\mathbf{F} = -k\left(\left|\mathbf{r}_i - \mathbf{r}_{i+1}\right| - L\right)\frac{\mathbf{r}_i - \mathbf{r}_{i+1}}{\left|\mathbf{r}_i - \mathbf{r}_{i+1}\right|}$$

Similarly, the ith particle experiences a force due to the $(i-1)^{\text{th}}$ particle given by the following:

$$\mathbf{F} = -k\left(\left|\mathbf{r}_i - \mathbf{r}_{i-1}\right| - L\right)\frac{\mathbf{r}_i - \mathbf{r}_{i-1}}{\left|\mathbf{r}_i - \mathbf{r}_{i-1}\right|}$$

This 1D model can be extended to 2D or 3D, and each particle can then be subjected to a spring force due to more neighbors according to the previous formulas.

You also want to have damping in your mass-spring system; otherwise, the particles would just oscillate forever. The damping term is usually linear in the relative velocity with a constant coefficient c (which can be chosen to minimize the time it takes to reach equilibrium), as we discussed in Chapter 8:

$$\mathbf{F} = -c\,\mathbf{v}_\mathbf{r}$$

In the specific context of our connected mass-spring system, the velocity $\mathbf{v}_r$ is the velocity of the relevant particle relative to the particle exerting the force on it. Therefore, the damping force on the ith particle relative to the $(i+1)^{\text{th}}$ particle is given by this:

$$\mathbf{F} = -c\left(\mathbf{v}_i - \mathbf{v}_{i+1}\right)$$

Similarly, the damping force on the ith particle relative to the $(i+1)^{\text{th}}$ particle is given by the following:

$$\mathbf{F} = -c\left(\mathbf{v}_i - \mathbf{v}_{i-1}\right)$$

To get a mass-spring system to work properly, it is frequently necessary to adjust the mass, stiffness, and damping coefficient. Generally you'll want the stiffness k to be high to reduce the stretchiness of your object. The problem is that the resulting spring system becomes more unstable, and it is not unusual to see a simulation explode before your very eyes! Let's put together an example, and you'll soon get to see what we mean!

Rope simulation

This example builds upon the last example in Chapter 8, where we simulated a chain of particles connected together by springs (see the "Coupled Oscillations" code). We will now make some small but significant changes to that simulation to make it behave more like a rope. The modified code is in the file rope.js and is reproduced here in full, with the most significant changes highlighted in bold:

```javascript
var canvas = document.getElementById('canvas');
var context = canvas.getContext('2d');

var balls;
var support;
var center = new Vector2D(100,100);
var g = 10;
var kDamping = 20;
var kSpring = 500;
var springLength = 20;
var spacing = 20;
var numBalls = 15;
var drop = false;
var t0, dt;
var acc, force;
var animId;

window.onload = init;

function init() {
    // create a support
    support = new Ball(2,'#000000');
    support.pos2D = center;
    support.draw(context);
    // create a bunch of balls
    balls = new Array();
    for (var i=0; i<numBalls; i++){
        var ball = new Ball(2,'#000000',10,0,true);
        ball.pos2D = new Vector2D(support.x+spacing*(i+1),support.y);
        ball.draw(context);
        balls.push(ball);
    }
    addEventListener('mousedown',onDown,false);
    t0 = new Date().getTime();
    animFrame();
}
function onDown(evt){
    drop = true;
    addEventListener('mouseup',onUp,false);
}
function onUp(evt){
    drop = false;
    removeEventListener('mouseup',onUp,false);
}
```

367

```javascript
function animFrame(){
    animId = requestAnimationFrame(animFrame,canvas);
    onTimer();
}
function onTimer(){
    var t1 = new Date().getTime();
    dt = 0.001*(t1-t0);
    t0 = t1;
    if (dt>0.2) {dt=0;};
    move();
}
function move(){
    context.clearRect(0, 0, canvas.width, canvas.height);
    drawSpring();
    for (var i=0; i<numBalls; i++){
        var ball = balls[i];
        moveObject(ball);
        calcForce(ball,i);
        updateAccel(ball.mass);
        updateVelo(ball);
    }
}
function drawSpring(){
    support.draw(context);
    context.save();
    context.lineStyle = '#009999';
    context.lineWidth = 2;
    context.moveTo(center.x,center.y);
    for (var i=0; i<numBalls; i++){
        var X = balls[i].x;
        var Y = balls[i].y;
        context.lineTo(X,Y);
    }
    context.stroke();
    context.restore();
}
function moveObject(obj){
    obj.pos2D = obj.pos2D.addScaled(obj.velo2D,dt);
    obj.draw(context);
}
function calcForce(obj,num){
    var centerPrev;
    var centerNext;
    var veloPrev;
    var veloNext;
    if (num > 0){
        centerPrev = balls[num-1].pos2D;
        veloPrev = balls[num-1].velo2D;
    }else{
        centerPrev = center;
        veloPrev = new Vector2D(0,0);
    }
```

```
        if (num < balls.length-1){
            centerNext = balls[num+1].pos2D;
            veloNext = balls[num+1].velo2D;
        }else{
            centerNext = obj.pos2D;
            veloNext = obj.velo2D;
        }
        var gravity = Forces.constantGravity(obj.mass,g);
        var velo = obj.velo2D.multiply(2).subtract(veloPrev).subtract(veloNext);
        var damping = Forces.damping(kDamping,velo);
        var displPrev = obj.pos2D.subtract(centerPrev);
        var displNext = obj.pos2D.subtract(centerNext);
        var extensionPrev = displPrev.subtract(displPrev.unit().multiply(springLength));
        var extensionNext = displNext.subtract(displNext.unit().multiply(springLength));
        var restoringPrev = Forces.spring(kSpring,extensionPrev);
        var restoringNext = Forces.spring(kSpring,extensionNext);
        force = Forces.add([gravity, damping, restoringPrev, restoringNext]);
        if (num==balls.length-1 && drop==false){
            force = new Vector2D(0,0);
            obj.velo2D = new Vector2D(0,0);
        }
    }
}
function updateAccel(mass){
    acc = force.multiply(1/mass);
}
function updateVelo(obj){
    obj.velo2D = obj.velo2D.addScaled(acc,dt);
}
```

Most of the code is unchanged from that in coupled-oscillations.js, and we therefore refer you to the relevant discussion in Chapter 8 if it is not completely obvious and you need a refresher of how it works. We'll instead focus on the key changes.

First, notice that we are storing the velocities of the particles before and after the current one in the variables veloPrev and veloNext. They are then combined with the velocity of the current particle to give the parameter velo, which is used to compute the damping force using the Forces.damping() function. You might be wondering why we are combining the velocities in that way. Referring to the formulas for the damping force given in the previous subsection, we are adding up the damping force on the current particle relative to the two neighboring particles to give this:

$$\mathbf{F}=-c(\mathbf{v}_i-\mathbf{v}_{i+1})+-c(\mathbf{v}_i-\mathbf{v}_{i-1})=-c(2\mathbf{v}_i-\mathbf{v}_{i+1}-\mathbf{v}_{i-1})$$

The variable velo is just the combined effective velocity that results from that sum. Note that in coupled-oscillations.js we used the absolute velocity of the current particle (not the velocities relative to its neighbors) to compute the damping force on it. You might want to experiment by comparing the behavior of the simulation if you do the same here.

Another change is that we are fixing the last particle in the chain by setting the force on it and its velocity to zero, unless the Boolean parameter drop is true:

```
if (num==balls.length-1 && drop==false){
    force = new Vector2D(0,0);
    obj.velo2D = new Vector2D(0,0);
}
```

The parameter drop, initially set to false, is controlled by user interaction through the event handlers onDown() and onUp() that respond to a mousedown and mouseup event, respectively. As long as the user holds the mouse down, drop is true, and the last particle can move under the action of forces like the rest of the particles (except the first). If the mouse is released, the last particle stops wherever it is. There is a slightly modified version of the simulation in the source file rope2.js that responds in a different way to mouse clicks: when the mouse is held down, a force is applied toward the mouse with a magnitude proportional to the distance from the mouse to the last particle; the force is removed when the mouse is released. Although we refer to the first version of the simulation in the following discussion, much of it applies equally well to the modified version.

Note the values of the parameters that we specify in rope.js: gravity is 10 units, spring length is 20 pixels, and the mass of the particles is 10 units. Most importantly, note the high values used for the spring damping coefficient (20) and the spring constant (500) compared to what they were in the coupled oscillations simulation in Chapter 8, where these parameters had values of 0.5 and 10, respectively. As you experiment with this simulation, do try different values for these parameters to see how they change its behavior.

Run the simulation with the default values of these parameters. Notice how the particles fall from their initial positions under the effect of gravity, but are held together by the spring force. After some brief oscillations and slight stretching, they settle down into a curved shape that hangs down like a rope (see Figure 13-17). This is a characteristic mathematical curve known as a *catenary*: it's the shape that a chain fixed at both ends naturally takes under the effect of its own weight. After it has settled down, click and hold down the mouse so that the end of the string falls down: see how the "rope" can readjust itself. Now release the mouse and notice that the rope again settles into a characteristic curve: this is a different section of the catenary.

Figure 13-17. *A rope simulation*

Experiment by changing the values of the parameters. First, increase the value of the spring constant kSpring to 1000. See how the rope now stretches less. You might be tempted to try a much larger value to see whether you can get an even tighter rope. Go ahead and increase kSpring to 10000 (just don't say we didn't warn you) and rerun the simulation. Whoops! Your rope just blew up! Welcome to numerical instability. Unfortunately, this is a common problem with mass-spring systems: they are prone to blow up, especially for high values of the spring constant. This arises because of an underlying issue with integration schemes known as numerical instability, which we'll discuss in more detail in the next chapter.

You can similarly play with the damping coefficient kDamping and note that its value affects how quickly the oscillations stop. Problems can get nasty here, too. For example, keep kSpring at its initial value of 500 and decrease the value of kDamping to 1. The simulation seems to be well-behaved initially, apparently settling down as before. But wait a little longer and you soon start seeing little fluctuations growing and distorting the rope into something that you can't call a rope any more.

To conclude: mass-spring systems are easy to create and fun to watch, but they can prove highly unstable in certain parameter regimes. Some steps can be taken to improve their stability, for example by using an improved integration scheme (see the next chapter), but they should be used with care.

Cloth simulation

It is fairly straightforward to extend our rope simulation to 2D to create a simple cloth simulation. Of course, to create a realistic simulation of a cloth that can bend we really need a 3D simulation, even if the cloth is 2D, to allow for movement and bending of the cloth in the third dimension. But we can quickly make a 2D version that will reproduce at least some elements of the behavior of a moving cloth. So let's make some quick modifications to the rope simulation and create a 2D version of it. The new file is called cloth.js, the setup part of which is reproduced here:

```
var balls;
var rows = 10;
var cols = 15;
var refPoint = new Vector2D(120,50);
var fixedPoints = new Array(0,70,140);
var g = 10;
var kDamping = 10;
var kSpring = 100;
var kWind = 10;
var windMag = 10;
var springLength = 20;
var spacing = 20;
var w = 0;
var t0, dt;
var acc, force;
var animId;

window.onload = init;

function init() {
    // create the masses
    balls = new Array();
    for (var i=0; i<cols*rows; i++){
        var ball = new Ball(2,'#000000',10,0,true);
        var ncol = Math.floor(i/rows);
        ball.pos2D = new Vector2D(refPoint.x+ncol*spacing,refPoint.y+(i-ncol*rows-1)*spacing);
        ball.draw(context);
        balls.push(ball);
    }
    addEventListener('mousedown',onDown,false);
    t0 = new Date().getTime();
    animFrame();
}
function onDown(evt){
    w = windMag;
    addEventListener('mouseup',onUp,false);
}
function onUp(evt){
    w = 0;
    removeEventListener('mouseup',onUp,false);
}
```

Apart from the obvious generalization of the setup to 2D, note that we have also specified an array of points on the cloth that we want to remain fixed. In the listing, we are holding the cloth fixed at three points, giving the appearance of a piece of cloth that is hung on a line.

The calcForce() method that drives the simulation is fairly long, but it is an obvious generalization of that in the rope.js code and so we won't list it here. Take a look at the code in the source file, though. Arguably some of the coding in that file could be done more concisely and elegantly by using arrays instead of different variables (such as extensionUp, extensionDown, and so on) that do the same thing in different directions. But the code is probably easier to understand in the current inelegant form, and the comments should also help. The main idea is that now each particle is experiencing a force due its four nearest neighbors to the left, right, up, and down, respectively. If a particle is on the edge of the cloth, it obviously does not have one or more of these forces. All the particles are subject to gravity. The other change is in terms of user interaction; clicking and holding down the mouse now applies a steady wind blowing to the right.

Run the simulation and you'll have a hanging piece of cloth that you can blow the wind over by clicking the mouse (see Figure 13-18). Experiment with the parameters of the simulation to see what they do. For example, you can try and increase the number of particles, reduce their spacing, and so on. You might also want to increase the spring constant and see how far you can go before you tear the cloth to pieces!

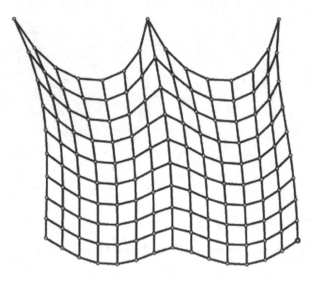

Figure 13-18. *A simple cloth simulation*

Needless to say, this is a very basic cloth simulation that can be enhanced in endless ways. Functionally, the most important improvement is probably to make the cloth move in 3D, but we haven't talked about how to simulate physics in 3D yet. You could also connect each particle to more neighbors; for example, the four nearest diagonal neighbors and the next nearest neighbors up, down, left, and right. That would improve the way the cloth behaves. Visually, you could fill up the areas between the particles, as well as add texture, lighting, and so on. Over to you!

Summary

This chapter introduced rigid body dynamics and collisions, and showed you how to model deformable bodies using mass-spring systems. Needless to say, what we have covered in this chapter is only the tip of the iceberg. There are many more topics on the general subject of extended systems that we can only briefly mention here: constrained systems, forward and inverse kinematics, and Verlet systems. Some of them can provide alternative approaches to simulating both rigid bodies and deformable bodies, but we do not have the space to include a discussion of them in this book.

This chapter completes Part III. In the first chapter of Part IV, we will look at advanced numerical schemes and considerations of stability and accuracy involved in creating complex simulations.

PART IV

Building More Complex Simulations

CHAPTER 14

■ ■ ■

Numerical Integration Schemes, Accuracy, and Scaling

In the previous two parts of this book we have covered a lot of physics. In the process we have largely managed to avoid getting into complex numerical issues. In this chapter we will focus on the important subject of *numerical integration schemes* and considerations of numerical stability and accuracy. Because no new physics will be presented, there won't be any new simulations in this chapter, but just some simple code examples to test the different schemes. At the end of the chapter we also include a short section on building scale models.

Numerical integration is a branch of numerical analysis that deals with the solution of differential equations. An *integration scheme* is a particular method for doing numerical integration in a form that you can readily write into code. We need an integration scheme to simulate motion because it involves solving Newton's second law of motion (which is a differential equation; see Chapter 5).

Topics covered in this chapter include the following:

- **General principles:** We begin by stating the general problem to be solved and explain the different types of integration schemes available and their characteristics.

- **Euler integration:** This is the simplest integration method and is the one we have been using throughout the book so far. It is fast and very easy to code, but it is inaccurate and can be unstable, which can lead to problems with some types of simulations.

- **Runge-Kutta integration:** This method is much more accurate than the Euler scheme, but it involves a lot of calculations and can therefore slow down your simulation. It is particularly suited to highly accurate simulations.

- **Verlet integration:** This method is not as accurate as Runge-Kutta, but is generally better than the Euler scheme. It is well suited to a number of game programming and animation applications.

- **Tips for achieving accuracy:** This section reviews some of the factors you need to take into account if you want to create a simulation that needs to be highly accurate.

- **Building scale models:** Numerical accuracy is not the only consideration when you are building realistic simulations. This section discusses how to choose units and parameter values to create a scale model of the system you are trying to simulate.

General principles

Before we look at specific integration schemes, it is useful to start by posing the problem of numerical simulation in a general way and then looking at how numerical integration approaches its solution. We then discuss the general characteristics of integration schemes and review some terminology associated with different types of schemes.

Statement of the problem

Numerical integration is a method to solve a problem. So what is the problem we are trying to solve?

Motion of a particle as an initial-value problem

To simplify the discussion, consider the problem of simulating the motion of a single particle under the action of forces. Suppose the particle starts out at a location given by its initial position vector $\mathbf{x}(0)$ with respect to an origin O and with an initial velocity $\mathbf{v}(0)$ (see Figure 14-1). The problem is then to determine the trajectory as a function of time. Mathematically, this is equivalent to determining the position and velocity vectors $\mathbf{x}(t)$ and $\mathbf{v}(t)$ as a function of time. This is called an *initial-value problem.*

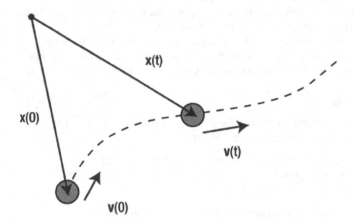

Figure 14-1. The initial-value problem for particle motion simulation

In this problem, the velocity of the particle $\mathbf{v}$ could itself be changing in time (in other words, the particle could be accelerating). That is why we need Newton's second law:

$$\mathbf{a} = \frac{\mathbf{F}}{m}$$

Knowing the acceleration at any time then allows us to calculate the velocity $\mathbf{v}$ by integrating the equation that defines acceleration:

$$\frac{d\mathbf{v}}{dt} = \mathbf{a}$$

Similarly, applying the definition of velocity, we can obtain the position by integrating the velocity in time:

$$\frac{d\mathbf{x}}{dt} = \mathbf{v}$$

As discussed in Chapter 5, these differential equations can sometimes be solved analytically to give closed-form expressions for $\mathbf{x}(t)$ and $\mathbf{v}(t)$ as functions of time. In computer simulation, the integration needs to be done numerically.

Numerical integration means that the position and velocity of the particle, which change continuously, can be calculated and updated only in small discrete steps. To do this, we must first *discretize* the equations of motion just shown.

Numerical discretization and difference schemes

You saw an example of the discretization procedure back in Chapter 3 when we discussed the numerical calculation of gradient functions in general mathematical terms. You may want to refer to the section "Simple calculus ideas" there for a refresher.

In the current context, you can apply numerical discretization to the previous two equations to convert them into a form that can be put into code and solved on a computer.

This is done by approximating the derivatives in those equations by algebraic fractions. For example, we can approximate the acceleration $d\mathbf{v}/dt$ using small changes $\Delta\mathbf{v}$ and Δt in $\mathbf{v}$ and t like this:

$$\mathbf{a} = \frac{d\mathbf{v}}{dt} \approx \frac{\Delta\mathbf{v}}{\Delta t}$$

The next step is to represent the discrete step changes $\Delta\mathbf{v}$ and Δt in terms of values at definite times because that is what you know (or rather what your computer knows). This can be done in different ways, known as *difference schemes*.

As an example, you can take Δt to be the time at the next timestep minus the current time, and similarly for the velocity interval $\Delta\mathbf{v}$. This gives a forward difference scheme, as discussed in Chapter 3 (note that n here denotes the timestep number):

$$\mathbf{a}(n) = \frac{\mathbf{v}(n+1) - \mathbf{v}(n)}{t(n+1) - t(n)}$$

Similarly, the velocity can be approximated by a forward difference scheme in the following way:

$$\mathbf{v}(n) = \frac{\mathbf{x}(n+1) - \mathbf{x}(n)}{t(n+1) - t(n)}$$

Now you've converted the differential equations into algebraic equations that you can understand and manipulate easily. More importantly, it's in a form that a computer can calculate. This is the role of discretization.

But before you can put anything into code, there is one more step: you need to convert the preceding difference scheme to an integration scheme.

Numerical integration and integration schemes

Numerical integration was also introduced in general terms in Chapter 3. The key idea is that we need to find the velocity and position at the new time in terms of those values at the old time. So, just as we did in Chapter 3, we manipulate the previous equations to give the following expressions for $\mathbf{v}(n+1)$ and $\mathbf{x}(n+1)$, in which we have written the time difference $t(n+1) - t(n)$ as Δt (the timestep):

$$\mathbf{v}(n+1) = \mathbf{v}(n) + \mathbf{a}(n) \cdot \Delta t$$

$$\mathbf{x}(n+1) = \mathbf{x}(n) + \mathbf{v}(n) \cdot \Delta t$$

This gives a forward integration scheme known as the Euler scheme, as you know. With these equations, you can obtain the new velocity and position of your particle in terms of its velocity and position at the previous timestep. You can now put these equations directly into code and simulate the motion of the particle by repeating that calculation at each timestep. This will give you a discrete approximation of the true trajectory of the particle, as shown schematically in Figure 14-2. A good simulation means that this approximated trajectory is as close to the real one as needed for your particular purpose. How good the approximation turns out to be will depend on a number of factors, including the following:

- **Physics of the problem:** Effectively, this is captured by how the acceleration **a** varies with time. Some physical problems are easier to simulate accurately than others, especially if the acceleration does not vary much with time.

- **Simulation timestep:** Generally, the smaller the timestep the better the approximation will be. But reducing the timestep comes at a cost because your simulation may run more slowly. Referring to Figure 14-2, smaller timesteps mean that the distance between the dots is reduced and that the approximated curve is closer to the true one.

- **Integration scheme:** The choice of integration scheme generally has a significant effect on the accuracy, stability, and speed of execution of your simulation. But there is often a trade-off between these desirable characteristics.

Figure 14-2. *Numerical integration gives an approximation of the true trajectory*

Characteristics of numerical schemes

When you are deciding which integration scheme to use, there is a set of characteristics that you need to bear in mind, as they determine how "good" that scheme is and how well suited it is to the application you have in mind. We'll briefly discuss some of these characteristics separately, but remember that they are connected.

Consistency

Consistency of a numerical scheme is the property that the numerical scheme is consistent with the original differential equation in the sense that it approximates the differential equation. Formally, in the limit of indefinitely small timesteps, the numerical solution should be identical to the true solution of the differential equation. This can be viewed as a necessary condition for any numerical scheme. If it's not true, the scheme will give the wrong physics and be essentially useless.

Stability

In the previous chapter you saw a spectacular example of numerical instability as the rope simulation "blew up" when the spring stiffness was too high. Formally, the *stability* of a numerical scheme is its capability to reduce errors (or "perturbations," as they are usually called) over time. A scheme is stable if an error or perturbation at any time decays with time; it is unstable if the error grows with time. A scheme can be conditionally stable (meaning that it is stable under certain conditions) or unconditionally stable (always stable, regardless of the conditions).

Convergence

Convergence is the requirement that as we reduce the timestep, the resulting numerical solution should approach the true solution. Consistency is a necessary condition for convergence, but not a sufficient condition. Again, clearly a numerical scheme is of no use if it is not convergent. For convergence, a scheme must also be stable.

Accuracy

Replacing a differential equation by finite differences inevitably introduces errors (known as *discretization errors*). Needless to say, it is desirable to keep these errors as small as possible. The *accuracy* of a numerical scheme determines how small or large these errors will be. The timestep also has an important effect on the numerical errors; errors are generally smaller the smaller the timestep (if the scheme is convergent). The *order* of a numerical scheme determines how quickly the errors diminish as you reduce the timestep. A *first-order* scheme has an error that is proportional to the timestep Δt, a second-order scheme has an error proportional to $(\Delta t)^2$, and so on. Therefore, as the timestep Δt is reduced, a second-order scheme will converge faster to the real solution, making it more accurate.

Efficiency

The *efficiency* of a numerical scheme quantifies how quickly (in wall clock time) it can compute a solution per unit simulation time. For the same timestep, the more complex a numerical scheme is, the lower is its efficiency because it has to perform a greater number of calculations and associated operations to produce a given solution per timestep. More accurate schemes are usually more complex and therefore less efficient. There is, therefore, usually a trade-off to achieve between accuracy and efficiency. However, in an actual implementation, the overall efficiency of a numerical method depends on the size of timestep that it can allow while preserving stability and accuracy. It could turn out that a simple scheme requires a much larger timestep to remain stable than a more complicated one, making it effectively less efficient in terms of overall computing time per simulation time.

Types of integration schemes

The terminology of numerical analysis can sound confusing because of the plethora of schemes, their associated names, and the different ways to classify them. Following are very brief descriptions of some of the terminology associated with the classification of integration schemes. Note that the categories mentioned here are not mutually exclusive; they overlap.

- **Forward/backward schemes:** You may come across scheme names such as *forward Euler* and *backward Euler*. These names show that the scheme is derived from a corresponding forward or backward difference scheme.

- **Implicit/explicit schemes:** An *explicit scheme* is one in which the values of the state variables at the new timestep are computed in terms of only the variables at the previous timestep; this makes an explicit scheme straightforward to apply. In an *implicit scheme*, an equation involving variables at both the old and the new timestep must be solved to calculate the variables at the new timestep; this makes such schemes less efficient.

- **Single-step/multistep methods:** A *single-step method* uses information from a single previous timestep to calculate variables at the new timestep. A *multistep method* uses information from more than one previous timestep.

- **Predictor-corrector methods:** As its name suggests, a predictor-corrector method involves two stages: a step that predicts a value at the new timestep, followed by another step that applies a correction to the estimated value.

- **Runge-Kutta methods:** This refers to a class of higher-order methods that proceed by employing intermediate stages and can be explicit as well as implicit. We will consider two examples of such methods, including the fourth-order Runge-Kutta (RK4) method, which is often referred to simply as *the* Runge-Kutta method.

A simple example to demonstrate different integration schemes

In the next sections we discuss a number of different schemes and then write code that will implement them. It would be helpful to be able to switch between different schemes easily, which would be convenient for comparing different schemes and for choosing an appropriate scheme for each problem.

Enabling that switching is best demonstrated in a simple example that modifies the structure of the animation code we have been using in most of the examples in this book so far. Specifically, we will modify the basic forces-test.js example from way back in Chapter 5, which demonstrated the motion of a ball under the forces of gravity and drag, to handle switching. We call the modified file schemes-test.js. The beginning of the code looks like this:

```
var canvas = document.getElementById('canvas');
var context = canvas.getContext('2d');

var ball;
var m = 1;
var g = 10;
var k = 0.1;
var t, t0, dt;
var force, acc;
var animId;
var animTime = 10;

window.onload = init;

function init() {
    ball = new Ball(15,'#0000ff',m,0,true);
    ball.pos2D = new Vector2D(50,400);
    ball.velo2D = new Vector2D(60,-60);
    ball.draw(context);
    t0 = new Date().getTime();
    t = 0;
    animFrame();
};

function animFrame(){
    animId = requestAnimationFrame(animFrame,canvas);
    onTimer();
}
function onTimer(){
    var t1 = new Date().getTime();
    dt = 0.001*(t1-t0);
    t0 = t1;
```

```
        if (dt>0.2) {dt=0;};
        t += dt;
        if (t < animTime){
            move();
        }else{
            stop();
        }
    }
    function stop(){
        cancelAnimationFrame(animId);
    }
    function move(){
        myFavoriteScheme(ball);
        context.clearRect(0, 0, canvas.width, canvas.height);
        ball.draw(context);
    }
    function calcForce(pos,vel){
        var gravity = Forces.constantGravity(m,g);
        var drag = Forces.linearDrag(k,vel);
        force = Forces.add([gravity, drag]);
    }
    function getAcc(pos,vel){
        calcForce(pos,vel);
        return force.multiply(1/m);
    }
    function myFavoriteScheme(obj){
        // scheme-specific code goes in here
    }
```

The key structural changes to the code are indicated with boldface type. The calcForce() method now takes two arguments, pos and vel, which reference position and velocity vectors. This will be needed because some schemes require the evaluation of the acceleration (and hence the force) at different times. In the listed example the pos parameter is not used, but it may be needed in future examples and so is included for generality. Those schemes will do that evaluation by calling the private getAcc() method, which calculates the acceleration, also with position and velocity vectors as arguments. The move() method will call the method that implements the integration scheme. All the scheme-specific code will be in its own method, here named generically as myFavoriteScheme(). In this way it will be easy to implement new schemes and to switch between schemes. Note that we are only applying the changes to the linear motion because we will only use the new integration schemes for particle motion; as a further exercise you could also implement them on the rotational motion along the same lines.

Euler integration

We have talked about and used the Euler integration scheme a lot in this book, so you are very familiar with it by now. But what you might not know is that there are several different versions of the Euler scheme. Let's take a look at some of them and their properties.

Explicit Euler

The Euler integration scheme that we derived earlier in this section from the forward difference scheme is called (appropriately enough) the *forward Euler scheme*. And because it is an explicit scheme, it is also known as the *explicit Euler scheme*. Here are the equations again:

$$\mathbf{v}(n+1) = \mathbf{v}(n) + \mathbf{a}(n) \cdot \Delta t$$

$$\mathbf{x}(n+1) = \mathbf{x}(n) + \mathbf{v}(n) \cdot \Delta t$$

Because it is simple, the explicit Euler scheme is fast, but it has only first-order accuracy and is often unstable.

Note that when implementing this scheme in code, we update the position based on the current velocity before updating the velocity based on the current acceleration, to be consistent with the previous equations.

The relevant code in the file `schemes-test.js` is in the `EulerExplicit()` method, which looks like this:

```
function EulerExplicit(obj){
    acc = getAcc(obj.pos2D,obj.velo2D);
    obj.pos2D = obj.pos2D.addScaled(obj.velo2D,dt);
    obj.velo2D = obj.velo2D.addScaled(acc,dt);
}
```

Implicit Euler

The explicit Euler scheme was obtained by starting from a forward difference approximation to the derivative. You can instead start from a backward difference scheme:

$$\mathbf{a}(n+1) = \frac{\mathbf{v}(n+1) - \mathbf{v}(n)}{t(n+1) - t(n)}$$

$$\mathbf{v}(n+1) = \frac{\mathbf{x}(n+1) - \mathbf{x}(n)}{t(n+1) - t(n)}$$

Rearranging these difference equations then gives the following:

$$\mathbf{v}(n+1) = \mathbf{v}(n) + \mathbf{a}(n+1) \cdot \Delta t$$

$$\mathbf{x}(n+1) = \mathbf{x}(n) + \mathbf{v}(n+1) \cdot \Delta t$$

This looks similar to the corresponding equation for the explicit Euler scheme, except for one crucial difference: the right sides of those equations contain the acceleration as well as the velocity at the new timestep. We therefore have an implicit equation that needs to be solved first before we can obtain the velocity at the new timestep. This involves further calculations, which make implicit schemes less efficient (as well as a pain to code up!). A major advantage of the implicit scheme is that it is unconditionally stable. If you want to make sure that your simulation will never blow up, it's worth considering using an implicit scheme. But because we don't use the implicit Euler scheme in this book, we won't bother coding it up.

Semi-implicit Euler

The *semi-implicit Euler scheme*, as its name suggests, is somewhere between the explicit and implicit Euler schemes. In one common variant, the velocity is advanced based on the acceleration at the previous timestep, as in the explicit scheme, but the position is advanced based on the updated velocity at the new timestep, as in the implicit scheme:

$$\mathbf{v}(n+1) = \mathbf{v}(n) + \mathbf{a}(n) \cdot \Delta t$$

$$\mathbf{x}(n+1) = \mathbf{x}(n) + \mathbf{v}(n+1) \cdot \Delta t$$

The advantage of the semi-implicit scheme is that it is more stable than the explicit scheme and also conserves energy. This energy-conserving property makes it more accurate than the explicit scheme, although it is still first-order.

Compared with the implementation of the explicit scheme, the semi-implicit scheme is simple to implement. You just reverse the order in which you update the position and velocity. Here is the corresponding function EulerSemiImplicit():

```
function EulerSemiImplicit(obj){
    acc = getAcc(obj.pos2D,obj.velo2D);
    obj.velo2D = obj.velo2D.addScaled(acc,dt);
    obj.pos2D = obj.pos2D.addScaled(obj.velo2D,dt);
}
```

There is another variant of the semi-implicit Euler scheme (with properties similar to the first version), in which the position is advanced based on the current velocity instead of the updated velocity, and the velocity is advanced based on the updated acceleration (and therefore at the updated position):

$$\mathbf{x}(n+1) = \mathbf{x}(n) + \mathbf{v}(n) \cdot \Delta t$$

$$\mathbf{v}(n+1) = \mathbf{v}(n) + \mathbf{a}(n+1) \cdot \Delta t$$

Note that because the acceleration potentially depends on the position and must be evaluated at the new time, the position must be updated first in code. This version of the semi-implicit Euler scheme is the one that we have been using throughout most of the book, and it has mostly worked quite well, at least for the purpose of creating simple demos of various types of physics effects.

We've coded this in the function EulerSemiImplicit2():

```
function EulerSemiImplicit2(obj){
    obj.pos2D = obj.pos2D.addScaled(obj.velo2D,dt);
    acc = getAcc(obj.pos2D,obj.velo2D);
    obj.velo2D = obj.velo2D.addScaled(acc,dt);
}
```

Comparing the explicit and semi-implicit Euler schemes

To compare the explicit and semi-implicit Euler schemes, let's put together a very simple simulation of a particle oscillating under the effect of a spring force. The file spring.js sets up a particle and a center toward which a spring force acts, and it creates two other particles at the points where its trajectory should theoretically end. The calcForce() method then applies the spring force and simulates the motion of the moving particle, tracing out its trajectory. There is nothing new in terms of physics or coding in those files, so we won't list any code here. But the key point is that you can change the integration scheme in the move() method.

Run the simulation in turn with the EulerExplicit(), EulerSemiImplicit(), and EulerSemiImplicit2() methods. You can choose an integration scheme by uncommenting the relevant line in the moveObject() method in springs.js and commenting out the other lines (as an alternative, you may want to modify the code to run multiple schemes at the same time). You will find that the particle oscillates as expected and remains nicely within the bounds of the endpoints with either of the two semi-implicit schemes. The semi-implicit Euler method nearly conserves energy; it's a so-called *symplectic method*. However, the explicit Euler scheme behaves very badly: the oscillations grow larger and larger (see Figure 14-3). The simulation blows up: explicit Euler creates energy! The stability is improved if you introduce some physics that can remove energy, such as drag or friction. However, the scheme can't simulate pure periodic oscillatory motion.

Figure 14-3. *The explicit Euler scheme is too unstable to simulate spring motion properly*

As another test of the stability of these schemes, try running the rope simulation from the previous chapter with the explicit Euler scheme by changing the order of the position and velocity updates in the move() method. This is done in the file rope-explicit-euler.js: it's not a pretty sight! The explicit Euler scheme can't simulate the rope even at a much lower stiffness. Interestingly, even the first version of the semi-implicit scheme does not do as well as the second version; it becomes unstable for much smaller values of the stiffness. By comparison, the second version of the semi-implicit scheme is quite robust, although it also eventually fails, as you saw in Chapter 13.

Why use Euler and why not?

Many programmers use nothing but Euler integration, whereas others keep as far away from Euler as they can. So should you use Euler or not?

To answer this question wisely, it is important to distinguish between the different versions of the Euler method. People often talk of the Euler scheme as if there were only one. But we've just seen that different versions of Euler have very different properties, which can lead to vastly different performance depending on the nature of your simulation. There is bad Euler and there is better Euler. You should definitely avoid the bad, explicit Euler. Semi-implicit Euler is actually not that bad (after all, we've survived for most of the book with it!). It is as easy to code as the explicit Euler scheme, but has much nicer properties. In code, the difference between the explicit and semi-implicit Euler schemes simply amounts to swapping the order in which you compute variables (so be careful!). So there really is no reason to use the explicit Euler scheme. The semi-implicit Euler scheme is widely used in rigid-body physics engines.

If you need absolute stability, the fully implicit Euler scheme is worth considering, although we haven't really shown you how to solve an implicit equation. But now that you have a better insight into numerical schemes, it shouldn't be hard to figure it out from books or online sources. The extra computational cost involved in solving the resulting implicit equation makes the implicit Euler scheme seem less attractive in terms of efficiency. But you can use large timesteps without worrying about numerical instability, which would improve the efficiency. However, large timesteps would then result in poor accuracy, especially given that Euler is only first-order. That's probably fine if accuracy is not important compared to stability (for example, if you just want your simulation not to blow up, without worrying about its accuracy).

However, if you really need accuracy, the first-order Euler schemes we have discussed won't serve you well. What you probably need then is something like a Runge-Kutta scheme.

Runge-Kutta integration

Runge-Kutta schemes are more complex than the Euler scheme, but they pay off in terms of considerably greater accuracy. If accuracy is critical for your simulation, you should seriously consider Runge-Kutta. This accuracy does come at a performance price, though, especially if you opt for the higher-order schemes. We'll describe two of the most popular Runge-Kutta schemes.

Second-order Runge-Kutta scheme (RK2)

The second-order Runge-Kutta method (RK2) is also known as Heun's method or the improved Euler method. It is a two-stage predictor-corrector method that uses the explicit Euler's method as predictor and a so-called trapezoidal method as corrector. Here are the equations defining the method:

$$\mathbf{p}_1 = \mathbf{x}(n)$$

$$\mathbf{v}_1 = \mathbf{v}(n)$$

$$\mathbf{a}_1 = \mathbf{a}(\mathbf{p}_1, \mathbf{v}_1)$$

$$\mathbf{p}_2 = \mathbf{p}_1 + \mathbf{v}_1 \cdot \Delta t$$

$$\mathbf{v}_2 = \mathbf{v}_1 + \mathbf{a}_1 \cdot \Delta t$$

$$\mathbf{a}_2 = \mathbf{a}(\mathbf{p}_2, \mathbf{v}_2)$$

$$\mathbf{x}(n+1) = \mathbf{x}(n) + \frac{(\mathbf{v}_1 + \mathbf{v}_2)}{2} \cdot \Delta t$$

$$\mathbf{v}(n+1) = \mathbf{v}(n) + \frac{(\mathbf{a}_1 + \mathbf{a}_2)}{2} \cdot \Delta t$$

The temporary variables $\mathbf{p}_1$, $\mathbf{v}_1$, and $\mathbf{a}_1$ are the initial position, velocity, and acceleration vectors; similarly, $\mathbf{p}_2$, $\mathbf{v}_2$, and $\mathbf{a}_2$ are the corresponding variables at the end of the timestep as computed by the forward Euler scheme. That's the predictor part. The last two equations apply the corrector by updating the position and velocity using (respectively) the average velocity and average acceleration over the timestep interval.

RK2 is more accurate than Euler because the Euler scheme uses only the velocity and acceleration at the old timestep to work out the new velocity and position of the particle. That would be fine if there were no acceleration, so that the velocity remained constant during a timestep, but both the velocity and the acceleration could be changing. For example, for a projectile the velocity changes both in magnitude and in direction. The Euler scheme takes into account the velocity only at the beginning of a timestep, but the RK2 scheme takes the average of the velocities at the beginning and the end of the timestep. So the position at the end of the timestep as predicted by RK2 ends up being closer to the real position.

The accuracy of this method is second order, so it is significantly more accurate than the Euler method. Here is the relevant RK2() function:

```
function RK2(obj){
    var pos1 = obj.pos2D;
    var vel1 = obj.velo2D;
    var acc1 = getAcc(pos1,vel1);
    var pos2 = pos1.addScaled(vel1,dt);
    var vel2 = vel1.addScaled(acc1,dt);
    var acc2 = getAcc(pos2,vel2);
    obj.pos2D = pos1.addScaled(vel1.add(vel2),dt/2);
    obj.velo2D = vel1.addScaled(acc1.add(acc2),dt/2);
}
```

The RK2() function involves a few more lines of code than the semi-implicit Euler schemes. For the same timestep an increase in accuracy is therefore achieved at the expense of reduced speed.

Fourth-order Runge-Kutta scheme (RK4)

The fourth-order Runge-Kutta scheme (RK4) is the best-known Runge-Kutta scheme, and is often called *the* Runge-Kutta scheme. As its name suggests, it is fourth-order accurate. So if you halve the timestep, the error should be reduced by a factor of one-sixteenth! The idea is similar to that of RK2, but there are more intermediate steps, and the intermediate variables and their averages are computed differently. Here is the full set of equations:

$$\mathbf{p}_1 = \mathbf{x}(n)$$

$$\mathbf{v}_1 = \mathbf{v}(n)$$

$$\mathbf{a}_1 = \mathbf{a}(\mathbf{p}_1, \mathbf{v}_1)$$

$$\mathbf{p}_2 = \mathbf{p}_1 + \mathbf{v}_1 \cdot \Delta t / 2$$

$$\mathbf{v}_2 = \mathbf{v}_1 + \mathbf{a}_1 \cdot \Delta t / 2$$

$$\mathbf{a}_2 = \mathbf{a}(\mathbf{p}_2, \mathbf{v}_2)$$

$$\mathbf{p}_3 = \mathbf{p}_1 + \mathbf{v}_2 \cdot \Delta t / 2$$

$$\mathbf{v}_3 = \mathbf{v}_1 + \mathbf{a}_2 \cdot \Delta t / 2$$

$$\mathbf{a}_3 = \mathbf{a}(\mathbf{p}_3, \mathbf{v}_3)$$

$$\mathbf{p}_4 = \mathbf{p}_1 + \mathbf{v}_3 \cdot \Delta t$$

$$\mathbf{v}_4 = \mathbf{v}_1 + \mathbf{a}_3 \cdot \Delta t$$

$$\mathbf{a}_4 = \mathbf{a}(\mathbf{p}_4, \mathbf{v}_4)$$

$$\mathbf{x}(n+1) = \mathbf{x}(n) + \frac{(\mathbf{v}_1 + 2\mathbf{v}_2 + 2\mathbf{v}_3 + \mathbf{v}_4)}{6} \cdot \Delta t$$

$$\mathbf{v}(n+1) = \mathbf{v}(n) + \frac{(\mathbf{a}_1 + 2\mathbf{a}_2 + 2\mathbf{a}_3 + \mathbf{a}_4)}{6} \cdot \Delta t$$

Following is the corresponding RK4() method:

```
function RK4(obj){
    var pos1 = obj.pos2D;
    var vel1 = obj.velo2D;
    var acc1 = getAcc(pos1,vel1);
    var pos2 = pos1.addScaled(vel1,dt/2);
    var vel2 = vel1.addScaled(acc1,dt/2);
    var acc2 = getAcc(pos2,vel2);
    var pos3 = pos1.addScaled(vel2,dt/2);
    var vel3 = vel1.addScaled(acc2,dt/2);
    var acc3 = getAcc(pos3,vel3);
    var pos4 = pos1.addScaled(vel3,dt);
    var vel4 = vel1.addScaled(acc3,dt);
    var acc4 = getAcc(pos4,vel4);
    var velsum = vel1.addScaled(vel2,2).addScaled(vel3,2).add(vel4);
    var accsum = acc1.addScaled(acc2,2).addScaled(acc3,2).add(acc4);
    obj.pos2D = pos1.addScaled(velsum,dt/6);
    obj.velo2D = vel1.addScaled(accsum,dt/6);
}
```

That's a lot of calculations to do in a single timestep! So let's see what RK4 can do for us. We'll compare the Euler, RK2, and RK4 methods for three different problems.

Stability and accuracy of RK2 and RK4 compared with Euler

To check the stability of RK2 and RK4, you can repeat the springs test, using the RK2() and RK4() methods. You'll find that the oscillatory motion is perfectly simulated by both: there isn't even a slight decrease or increase in the amplitude of oscillation (and therefore of energy) as far as the eye can tell (if you want, you can perform more quantitative tests by plotting a graph).

To test the accuracy of the schemes and compare it with that of the previous schemes in a simple way, let's put together a simple orbit simulation. The file is called orbits.js. Again there is nothing that you haven't seen in earlier files, and we won't list any code from it here. The test is that the orbits should close on themselves; if they don't, the scheme is introducing significant errors.

Run the code with different integration schemes as before. With the explicit Euler integrator, the orbit will end up all over the place: it never closes on itself (see Figure 14-4). That should be enough to convince you never to use the explicit Euler scheme!

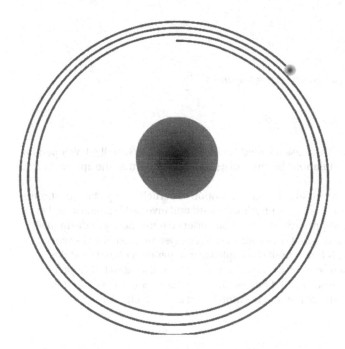

Figure 14-4. *The explicit Euler scheme is too inaccurate to produce a closed orbit*

All the other schemes do a pretty decent job. But if you were to run the simulation for a long time, you would find that even the semi-implicit Euler schemes start losing accuracy and tracing slightly non-overlapping circles because they are only first-order accurate (see Figure 14-5). By comparison, we ran the RK4 scheme for a much longer duration, but could not notice any loss of accuracy. The RK2 scheme is intermediate in accuracy between the semi-implicit Euler scheme and the RK4 scheme. For this simple example you will hardly notice any difference between RK2 and RK4.

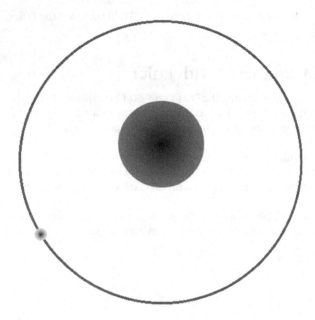

Figure 14-5. *The semi-implicit Euler scheme accumulates errors after a few orbits*

Verlet integration

The third and final class of integration schemes that we'll discuss is called *Verlet integration*. Originally developed for handling complex and variable molecular dynamics simulations because of its stability properties, the approach is now widely used in game programming and animation.

Verlet integration is employed in so-called *Verlet systems* to simulate the motion of particles subject to constraints. This technique can be applied to connected structures as in ragdoll physics, forward and inverse kinematics, and even rigid body systems. We do not have space to explore this approach. We mention Verlet systems merely to distinguish them from the Verlet integration scheme because they are sometimes confused: Verlet systems are named as such because they use the Verlet integration scheme. But the scheme itself is completely independent of that modeling approach; in fact, it can be used with any other approach, such as the rigid body dynamics discussed in Chapter 13.

Verlet integration schemes are generally not as accurate as RK4 but, on the other hand, are very efficient in comparison. Let's take a look at two common variants of the method: Position Verlet and Velocity Verlet.

The Position Verlet Method

In the *Position Verlet method*, also known as the *Standard Verlet method*, the velocity of a particle is not stored. Instead, the last position of the particle is stored, and its velocity can then be computed as needed by subtracting the last position from the current position and dividing by the timestep.

Just as the explicit Euler scheme can be derived starting from the forward difference approximation of the first derivative, the standard Verlet scheme can be derived from the central difference approximation to the second derivative (see Chapter 3). We won't show the derivation here but only quote the final result:

$$\mathbf{x}(n+1) = 2\mathbf{x}(n) - \mathbf{x}(n-1) + \mathbf{a}(n) \cdot (\Delta t)^2$$

This equation gives the position at the new timestep in terms of the positions at the previous two timesteps without using the velocity.

If desired, the velocity can be computed from the positions—for example, using backward differencing:

$$\mathbf{v}(n+1) = \frac{\mathbf{x}(n+1) - \mathbf{x}(n)}{\Delta t}$$

Alternatively you can use the central differencing scheme, because the previous position is also known, to give a more accurate estimate of the velocity:

$$\mathbf{v}(n+1) = \frac{\mathbf{x}(n+1) - \mathbf{x}(n-1)}{2\Delta t}$$

One problem with the Position Verlet equation as given previously is that it assumes that the timestep is constant. But in general the timesteps in your simulation could be variable. In fact, the timesteps will usually vary slightly in your JavaScript simulations. To allow for variable timesteps, a modified version of the equation is used:

$$\mathbf{x}(n+1) = 2\mathbf{x}(n) - \mathbf{x}(n-1)\Delta t(n)/\Delta t(n-1) + \mathbf{a}(n) \cdot \left(\Delta t(n)\right)^2$$

In this equation, $\Delta t(n)$ denotes the current timestep, and $\Delta t(n-1)$ denotes the previous timestep. This form can be called the time-corrected or time-adjusted Position Verlet scheme.

Another potential problem that arises in the implementation of the Position Verlet scheme is the specification of the initial conditions. Because the scheme does not use velocity but the position at the previous timestep, you cannot directly specify the initial velocity together with the initial position as you would normally do. Instead, you need to specify the initial position $\mathbf{x}(0)$ as well as the previous position $\mathbf{x}(-1)$ *before* the initial position! That might sound like nonsense, but you can actually infer the value of that hypothetical position from the initial velocity by applying the backward difference formula for the velocity given previously. Setting $n = -1$ in that formula gives the following:

$$\mathbf{v}(0) = \frac{\mathbf{x}(0) - \mathbf{x}(-1)}{\Delta t}$$

Solving this equation for $\mathbf{x}(-1)$ then gives this:

$$\mathbf{x}(-1) = \mathbf{x}(0) - \mathbf{v}(0)\Delta t$$

We can now write a `PositionVerlet()` function as follows:

```
function PositionVerlet(obj){
    var temp = obj.pos2D;
    if (n==0){
        acc = getAcc(obj.pos2D,obj.velo2D);
        oldpos = obj.pos2D.addScaled(obj.velo2D,-dt).addScaled(acc,dt*dt/2);
        olddt = dt;
    }
    acc = getAcc(obj.pos2D,obj.velo2D);
    obj.pos2D = obj.pos2D.addScaled(obj.pos2D.subtract(oldpos),dt/olddt).addScaled(acc,dt*dt);
    obj.velo2D = (obj.pos2D.subtract(oldpos)).multiply(0.5/dt);
    oldpos = temp;
    olddt = dt;
    n++;
}
```

Note that we have new variables `oldpos` and `olddt` for storing the previous position and the previous timestep. There is also a variable n that represents the number of timesteps that have elapsed since the last call to that function. As you can see from the code, the first time the function is called, the position $\mathbf{x}(-1)$ is set.

The Velocity Verlet Method

One of the problems with the Position Verlet method is that the velocity estimation is not very accurate. The *Velocity Verlet method* fixes this, albeit at some cost in efficiency. The Velocity Verlet is the more commonly used version of the two. The scheme equations are these:

$$\mathbf{x}(n+1)=\mathbf{x}(n)+\mathbf{v}(n)\cdot\Delta t+\frac{1}{2}\mathbf{a}(n)\cdot(\Delta t)^2$$

$$\mathbf{v}(n+1)=\mathbf{v}(n)+\frac{1}{2}\Big[\mathbf{a}(n)+\mathbf{a}(n+1)\Big]\Delta t$$

Comparing the first equation with the corresponding equation in the Euler scheme shows that we now have an additional term that includes the acceleration. The Euler scheme therefore assumes that the acceleration is zero in the interval of one timestep, whereas the Velocity Verlet method takes into account the acceleration but assumes it is constant during that interval. Perhaps you recall the equation $s = ut + \frac{1}{2} at^2$ from Chapter 4. The equation for the position update in the Velocity Verlet is exactly of that form (the displacement is $s = \mathbf{x}(n+1) - \mathbf{x}(n)$).

Also note that the velocity update equation uses the average of the acceleration at the old and the new timestep rather than the acceleration just at the old timestep. Hence, it is a better approximation of the velocity. For these reasons the Velocity Verlet scheme is more accurate than the Euler scheme, as well as having other nice properties such as greater stability and conservation of energy.

Here is the VelocityVerlet() method:

```
function VelocityVerlet(obj){
    acc = getAcc(obj.pos2D,obj.velo2D);
    var accPrev = acc;
    obj.pos2D = obj.pos2D.addScaled(obj.velo2D,dt).addScaled(acc,dt*dt/2);
    acc = getAcc(obj.pos2D,obj.velo2D);
    obj.velo2D = obj.velo2D.addScaled(acc.add(accPrev),dt/2);
}
```

Testing the stability and accuracy of the Verlet schemes

You can now run the spring and orbit simulations using the Verlet schemes. You should find that they do quite a good job in both cases. Verlet schemes are stable, but they are less accurate than RK4.

A simple test to illustrate the differences in the accuracy of all the different schemes can be done by performing a simulation for a problem with a known analytical solution, against which the numerical solutions can then be compared. You might recall that we did such a test for the Euler scheme for a projectile simulation back in Chapter 4. Let's do something similar now for all the different schemes.

The file projectile.js contains the code. Once again we won't show any code listings because you've seen similar code tons of times by now. The main point is that it creates a ball and initializes its position and velocity such that the ball is thrown upward at an angle, and then subjects the ball to gravity.

Run the simulation with different integrators. The code plots the analytical trajectory as well as the numerically computed trajectory (which, of course, the ball follows). You will find that the time-corrected Position Verlet and all the Euler integrators give a trajectory that deviates slightly from the analytical trajectory (see Figure 14-6). On the other hand, the trajectories predicted using the Velocity Verlet, RK2, and RK4 schemes are so close to the analytical trajectory that they cannot be distinguished. Like RK2, the Velocity Verlet scheme is a second-order scheme. Note that these comparisons are for a specific problem, involving constant acceleration. Different schemes might be more or less accurate with different problems.

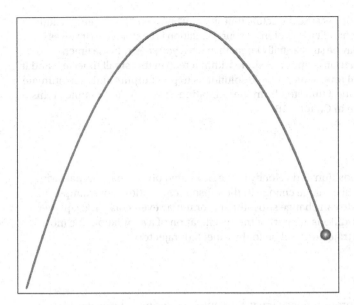

Figure 14-6. *Projectile trajectory simulated with Position Verlet scheme (slightly lower curve)*

Finally, you might want to check how well the standard Position Verlet scheme does without the time correction. To do this, replace the line of code that updates the position in `PositionVerlet()` with the following one:

```
obj.pos2D = obj.pos2D.add(obj.pos2D).subtract(oldpos).addScaled(acc,dt*dt);
```

If you then run the code you will find that the simulation gets it completely wrong! The message is that time correction is essential if you have variable timesteps in your simulation.

Tips for achieving accuracy

If you want to build very accurate simulations, you need to consider several aspects carefully. We briefly review here what you have learned about the subject in this chapter as well as in previous chapters.

Choosing an appropriate integration scheme

We have spent a lot of time in this chapter discussing numerical integration schemes and their characteristics such as accuracy and stability. Therefore, there is not much more to be said here. Just to reiterate briefly, the usual Euler scheme is not very accurate, being only a first-order scheme; the fourth-order Runge-Kutta scheme, RK4, is generally a good choice for simulations where accuracy is important, although this comes at the price of reduced efficiency. The RK2 and Velocity Verlet schemes offer a good compromise between accuracy and speed, being second-order (and therefore more accurate than the Euler scheme) and at the same time being substantially simpler than RK4.

Using an appropriate timestep

Together with the integration scheme, you need to choose an appropriate timestep for your simulation. Numerical schemes are more accurate with smaller timesteps. Higher-order schemes such as RK4 converge faster than lower-order schemes such as Euler. This implies that RK4 is more accurate for a given timestep. You can control the timestep to some extent.

393

However, there is a limit to how small the timestep can be because the actual time interval between `timer` events includes the time it takes to execute all the code within the event handler. Therefore, if your simulation is complex and involves lots of calculations or animation, the actual timestep may be substantially larger than what you specify in the timer.

Some simulations are so complex that the calculations cannot be done within a reasonably small timestep, and it may not therefore be possible to perform them in real time. One possible solution is to precompute and then animate afterward. In this way, you can "decouple" the simulation timestep from the animation timestep. An example of this method will be applied in the solar system simulation in Chapter 16.

Using accurate initial conditions

Some simulations are sensitive to the values for the position and velocity of the simulated object that you start with. A small change in these initial conditions could produce a large change in the subsequent motion. For example, in simulations involving orbits, the trajectory of a satellite can change substantially, or it may even crash into a planet with the wrong choice of initial conditions. Initial conditions are part of the specification of a simulation: the more accurately they are specified, the closer the resulting trajectory will be to the expected trajectory.

Dealing with boundaries carefully

Simulations that involve boundaries are particularly prone to inaccuracy. Such interactions must be dealt with using special methods to detect and handle collisions at specific instants, and they introduce additional sources of error that can become even more important over time than those associated with numerical integration. In Chapter 11, we described how to deal with some of those problems in special cases, including repositioning and velocity correction at a boundary. Another source of inaccuracy arises from uncertainties about the time of collision. In the next section you will see an example where a ball is detected and stopped after it has gone "through" the ground. The time for it to fall to the ground is therefore slightly over-estimated. This error can get larger at higher velocities. For extra accuracy, these errors need to be accounted for and corrected.

Building scale models

Let's begin this section by clarifying the meaning of the title. By *scale model* we do not mean a physical scale model like that of an airplane. We mean a computer model in which all the relevant physical parameters are in appropriate proportion relative to the real system it is meant to simulate. In this sense, a scale model may include representing physical objects to scale, but it goes well beyond that simple visual aspect; it must also, in some sense that we'll make more precise soon, scale the physics correctly.

Scaling for realism

Why is scale modeling important? Correct scale modeling is necessary for a simulation to replicate realistically the behavior of a system that is being modeled. Having the correct physics equations and appropriate visual representations as well as added effects like 3D are obviously important for realism in your games and simulations. Perhaps less obvious is the need to choose appropriate parameter values consistently so that all the aspects of your simulation work together with the right length and time scales to produce a realistic model of the real world.

How do we do this? First, we'll illustrate the process of scale modeling with a very simple example; then at the end of this section we'll give you a general formal method for dealing with more complex simulations.

A simple example

Suppose you want to create a 2D game of volleyball: characters will be tossing the ball around and for much of the time it will therefore be moving under gravity, like a projectile. There will be scenery and buildings around, and you want your game to be a scale model visually and functionally. To proceed, let's consider a simple hypothetical scene where the ball is at the height of a building and is falling down under gravity. You want the ball to fall down at a rate that is consistent with the length scales in the surrounding scenery; in this case, the building height. Assuming that the only force is pure gravity without drag or friction or wind effects, and considering only the vertical motion for simplicity (but without loss of generality), the underlying physics can be described by a single equation. Applying Newton's second law, $F = ma$, with the force F given by mg, we arrive at this equation:

$$a = g$$

This equation, of course, merely expresses the fact that all objects fall with the same vertical acceleration of g, regardless of their mass or other characteristics. As you know, your simulation will integrate this equation twice: the first time to obtain the velocity of the ball and the second time to obtain its displacement. The whole problem is controlled by a single parameter: the acceleration due to gravity g. The question therefore boils down to this: what value of g must you use in your simulation so that the ball falls at a realistic rate, consistent with the sizes and distances in the game? The actual value of g is 9.8 m/s², or approximately 10 m/s². But this is not the value you can use in your simulation, because you are not using the same units in your simulation. See Figure 14-7.

Figure 14-7. *Simulating a falling ball to scale*

Choosing units

First you need to choose the units for relevant physical quantities in your simulation. The most important units you need are those for time, length, and mass. They are called *base quantities* in physics. Other quantities, such as velocity and acceleration, depend on these base quantities, and their units can be derived from those of the base quantities by using their defining equations; they are therefore called *derived quantities*.

In this case, because mass drops out of the equations, it's completely irrelevant what unit or indeed what value you use for the mass of the ball. So that leaves two base quantities we need to worry about: time and length (or distance).

Let's assume that you want *real-time simulation*: in other words, the simulation should proceed at the same rate as real "wall-clock" time. (Sometimes you might not want this: for example, if you are simulating the solar system, you may not want to wait a year for the Earth to go around the Sun once!) In Figure 14-7, the ball in your simulation would then take exactly the same time to fall as it would if falling from the height of a real building. Therefore, you choose to measure time in seconds, as in real life. Not only that, but you want 1 second of simulation time to be equal to 1 second of real time: your scaling factor for time is 1.

The natural unit of distance to use for a screen-based visual simulation is the pixel (px). You also need to decide on an appropriate scaling factor to convert actual distances to pixels.

Scaling factors and parameter values

Suppose that the building in your scene would be 5 m tall in real life, and that you represent it by a rectangle of height 200 px. That means your scaling factor is 0.025 m/px; each pixel represents 0.025 m or 2.5 cm. You can use this length scale factor to scale other objects accordingly. So if your ball is a volleyball of radius 10 cm, its radius in the simulation would be 4 pixels.

Going back to our original question: what value should you give to g? The way you figure this out is as follows. Being an acceleration, g is measured in m/s^2. Now, each second is an actual second in the simulation, but each meter is 40 px in the simulation. Therefore, scaling the approximate value of $g = 10$ m/s^2 would give $g = 400$ in the simulation!

The file `scale-model.js` implements these values in this simple simulation. In the code, the ball is made to stop when it falls the 200 px (equivalent to 5 m in reality) to the ground. The time since the beginning of the simulation is then traced. Run the simulation and you'll find that the ball takes approximately 1 second to fall to the ground. Is this realistic? It's easy to find out using the old formula you met in Chapter 4:

$$s = u\,t + \frac{1}{2}a\,t^2$$

Here the displacement s is the height fallen (5 m), u is the initial velocity magnitude (zero), and a is the acceleration due to gravity g (10 m/s^2). Substituting these values indeed gives $t = 1$ s. We have a real-time scale model! The value traced in the simulation is not exactly 1, but it is close enough. One of the reasons it's not exactly 1 is that the ball is detected to be past the ground level slightly later because it's moving so fast. When you run the simulation, you'll see that it stops slightly below the "ground."

Suppose you naively gave g the value of 10 in the simulation. What would be the consequence? Do this now, and you should find that the ball takes more than 6 seconds to reach the ground—hardly realistic!

Of course, you may not always need to be as careful as this in fixing the parameters of your simulation. You may not care about having a scale model at all; perhaps you are just interested in creating an animation that looks roughly right. But it's useful to know how to do this when realism is really important. In more complex simulations it helps to have a systematic method to work out the values of your parameters.

Rescaling equations

The method of *rescaling* an equation is a formal procedure that can help to work out appropriate values for the parameters in your simulation. It is especially useful when you have more than one parameter whose value you need to work out or if there are multiple scale factors, but we'll demonstrate the method for the simple example we've just looked at.

Rescaling involves scaling the variables in a system, re-expressing the equations in terms of the new scaled variables, and then comparing the scaled equation with the original one. The procedure is as follows.

First, write down the governing equation or equations (algebraic or differential), identifying all the variables. In our example, the equation is $a = g$, but this is really the following differential equation:

$$\frac{d^2s}{dt^2} = g$$

Next, define scaling factors for each of the variables as follows:

$$s = \lambda\,\hat{s} \qquad t = \tau\,\hat{t}$$

Here, the variables with hats are the new scaled variables, and the Greek letters are the corresponding scaling factors.

Then substitute the old variables into the original equation. In the preceding differential equation, note that the second derivative means that we are dividing a displacement increment by a time increment twice. Making the substitution, we therefore arrive at this:

$$\frac{\lambda}{\tau^2}\frac{d^2\hat{s}}{d\hat{t}^2} = g$$

We can rewrite this transformed equation as the following:

$$\frac{d^2\hat{s}}{d\hat{t}^2} = \frac{\tau^2 g}{\lambda}$$

Comparing this with the original equation, we deduce that the equation in terms of the scaled variables will be exactly the same form as the original equation, provided that the right side is equal to the rescaled value of g:

$$\hat{g} = \frac{\tau^2 g}{\lambda}$$

This equation gives a constraint between the scaling factors and the rescaled value of the parameter g. So if we choose two of them, we can obtain the third. In this example, we chose the scaling factors for distance and time. So we can get the rescaled value of g by substituting the values of the scaling factors τ and λ. The scaling factor τ for time t is 1, as discussed previously, while the scaling factor λ for distance s is 5/200 or 0.025 m/px, as shown in the previous subsection. Therefore, the scaled value of g that we need for the simulation is given by the following:

$$\hat{g} = \tau^2 g/\lambda = 10/0.025 = 400$$

This is just as we reasoned earlier.

Note that we could alternatively fix the rescaled value of g together with the scaling factor of one of the variables (either time or length). The previous constraint would then give us the scaling factor for the remaining variable.

For this simple example, the formal procedure just outlined is certainly overkill, but add in more variables and a more complex system of equations, and it will come in handy indeed.

Summary

If you plan to get into physics simulation seriously, sooner or later you need to worry about the accuracy and stability of your integration scheme. This chapter has presented some of the most common options at your disposal. The choice of a particular scheme depends on the problem as well as on other practical factors. In the previous chapters of the book we used the Euler scheme exclusively. In Chapter 16 you'll see an example in which you need a more accurate integration scheme.

■ ■ ■

Doing Physics in 3D

So far in this book you have built simulations in two dimensions. But in the real world there are three dimensions: what does it take to extend the hard work you've already done into the 3D realm? In this penultimate chapter we introduce you to the exciting world of 3D physics-based animation.

Topics covered in this chapter include the following:

- **3D physics and math**: This section discusses how to extend our existing code framework to create 3D simulations. In the process we'll explore some additional math concepts that will help to handle both translational and rotational motion in 3D, which will be used in the examples later in the chapter.

- **3D rendering: Introducing WebGL and three.js**: This section discusses 3D rendering and the WebGL API, and it introduces the three.js JavaScript library, which simplifies the process of creating 3D simulations with WebGL.

- **Simulating particle motion in 3D**: This section gives examples of using the three.js library to create physics simulations of particle motion in 3D. The methods used here will then be applied in developing an accurate solar system simulation in Chapter 16.

- **Simulating rigid body motion in 3D**: Taking a rotating cube as an example, this section shows how to simulate rigid body motion in 3D. In Chapter 16 we will build upon this example to create a flight simulator.

Please note that the focus in this chapter will be very much on *doing physics in 3D*, rather than on 3D programming in general. Thus, although we'll inevitably have to discuss some aspects of 3D coding using JavaScript libraries, this chapter is *not* about the latest cutting-edge 3D technology.

3D physics and math

Before we can create simulations in 3D, we need to generalize some of the math and physics concepts we have been using so far, and introduce new ones along the way.

3D versus 2D physics

Most of the physics we've discussed so far in this book is essentially unchanged in going from 2D to 3D. The fundamental laws of motion for linear and rotational motion remain the same when expressed in their vector forms. Particle motion is treated in a similar way, with the difference that in 3D particles can move in an extra dimension (that's obvious, isn't it?). Hence, the math and code have to be generalized to include the extra space dimension. So we'll look at vectors and vector algebra in 3D, and construct a Vector3D JavaScript object. We'll also create a Forces3D object that, together with the Vector3D object, will enable us to write code to handle the motion of particles under a variety of forces in 3D space.

Rigid body dynamics is more complicated because rotation in 3D is complex and requires some more advanced math. So we shall also present the math background needed to handle 3D rotations, introducing new math concepts like matrices and quaternions.

Vectors in 3D

We have used vectors extensively in this book. Just as a reminder of their usefulness, vectors enable the equations that represent physical laws to be written in an economical way. Code written in terms of vector objects is also more concise, more intuitive, and less error-prone. The good news is that vectors in 3D are not very different from their 2D counterparts.

Vector algebra in 3D

Vectors in 3D are straightforward extensions of their 2D counterparts. In Chapter 3, we reviewed vector algebra in 2D and in 3D side by side. You may wish to read that section again if you need a refresher. The most important difference between vector algebra in 2D and 3D, apart from the obvious fact that there are three components instead of two, is that you can do cross products in 3D.

The Vector3D object

Back in Chapter 3, we built a Vector2D object that we have steadily been enhancing with new methods. It is straightforward to modify it to create a Vector3D object. The code is in the file vector3D.js downloadable from www.apress.com, and we list it here in full:

```
function Vector3D(x,y,z) {
    this.x = x;
    this.y = y;
    this.z = z;
}

// PUBLIC METHODS
Vector3D.prototype = {
    lengthSquared: function(){
        return this.x*this.x + this.y*this.y + this.z*this.z;
    },
    length: function(){
        return Math.sqrt(this.lengthSquared());
    },
    clone: function() {
        return new Vector3D(this.x,this.y,this.z);
    },
    negate: function() {
        this.x = - this.x;
        this.y = - this.y;
        this.z = - this.z;
    },
```

```
    unit: function() {
        var length = this.length();
        if (length > 0) {
            return new Vector3D(this.x/length,this.y/length,this.z/length);
        }else{
            return new Vector3D(0,0,0);
        }
    },
    normalize: function() {
        var length = this.length();
        if (length > 0) {
            this.x /=length;
            this.y /=length;
            this.z /=length;
        }
        return this.length();
    },
    add: function(vec) {
        return new Vector3D(this.x + vec.x,this.y + vec.y,this.z + vec.z);
    },
    incrementBy: function(vec) {
        this.x += vec.x;
        this.y += vec.y;
        this.z += vec.z;
    },
    subtract: function(vec) {
        return new Vector3D(this.x - vec.x,this.y - vec.y,this.z - vec.z);
    },
    decrementBy: function(vec) {
        this.x -= vec.x;
        this.y -= vec.y;
        this.z -= vec.z;
    },
    multiply: function(k) {
        return new Vector3D(k*this.x,k*this.y,k*this.z);
    },
    addScaled: function(vec,k) {
        return new Vector3D(this.x + k*vec.x, this.y + k*vec.y, this.z + k*vec.z);
    },
    scaleBy: function(k) {
        this.x *= k;
        this.y *= k;
        this.z *= k;
    },
    dotProduct: function(vec) {
        return this.x*vec.x + this.y*vec.y + this.z*vec.z;
    },
    crossProduct: function(vec) {
        return new Vector3D(this.y*vec.z-this.z*vec.y,this.z*vec.x-this.x*vec.z,this.x*vec.y-
        this.y*vec.x);
    }
};
```

```
// STATIC METHODS
Vector3D.distance =  function(vec1,vec2){
    return (vec1.subtract(vec2)).length();
}
Vector3D.angleBetween = function(vec1,vec2){
    return Math.acos(vec1.dotProduct(vec2)/(vec1.length()*vec2.length()));
}
Vector3D.scale = function(vec,sca){
    vec.x *= sca;
    vec.y *= sca;
    vec.z *= sca;
}
```

The Vector3D methods are straightforward generalizations of their Vector2D counterparts. Note that the crossProduct() method returns a Vector3D object, as it should.

Forces in 3D

Because forces are vector quantities, it won't surprise you to learn that the newly created Vector3D object makes it a straightforward matter to include forces in 3D simulations.

Newton's laws of motion in 3D

In Chapter 5, we introduced the laws governing motion, including Newton's laws of motion. To recap, these laws allow us to compute the motion of objects under the action of forces. If you take a look back at Chapter 5, you will find that these laws were expressed in vector form. Crucially, we did not specify whether we were talking about vectors in 2D or in 3D: the laws are the same. The same is true of the motion concepts we introduced in Chapter 4, such as velocity and acceleration. Therefore, all we have to do when writing 3D code is to define these physical quantities as Vector3D objects instead of Vector2D objects. The laws that we must apply remain the same, and therefore the resulting physics code is virtually identical to its 2D counterpart!

The Forces3D object

Before we can write analogous code for 3D particle motion, we need to update one more key piece of code: the Forces object. Again, this is mostly quite straightforward. We call the new object Forces3D, and list here the code in the corresponding file forces3D.js:

```
function Forces3D(){
}

// STATIC METHODS
Forces3D.zeroForce = function() {
    return (new Vector3D(0,0,0));
}
Forces3D.constantGravity = function(m,g){
    return new Vector3D(0,m*g,0);
}
Forces3D.gravity = function(G,m1,m2,r){
    return r.multiply(-G*m1*m2/(r.lengthSquared()*r.length()));
}
```

```
Forces3D.gravityModified = function(G,m1,m2,r,eps){
    return r.multiply(-G*m1*m2/((r.lengthSquared()+eps*eps)*r.length()));
}
Forces3D.electric = function(k,q1,q2,r){
    return r.multiply(k*q1*q2/(r.lengthSquared()*r.length()));
}
Forces3D.forceField = function(q,E) {
    return E.multiply(q);
}
Forces3D.lorentz = function(q,E,B,vel) {
    return E.multiply(q).add(vel.perp(q*B*vel.length()));
}
Forces3D.central = function(k,n,r) {
    return r.multiply(k*Math.pow(r.length(),n-1));
}
Forces3D.linearDrag = function(k,vel){
    var force;
    var velMag = vel.length();
    if (velMag > 0) {
        force = vel.multiply(-k);
    }else {
        force = new Vector3D(0,0,0);
    }
    return force;
}
Forces3D.drag = function(k,vel) {
    var force;
    var velMag = vel.length();
    if (velMag > 0) {
        force = vel.multiply(-k*velMag);
    } else {
        force = new Vector3D(0,0,0);
    }
    return force;
}
Forces3D.upthrust = function(rho,V,g) {
    return new Vector3D(0,-rho*V*g,0);
}
Forces3D.spring = function(k,r){
    return r.multiply(-k);
}
Forces3D.damping = function(c,vel){
    var force;
    var velMag = vel.length();
    if (velMag>0) {
        force = vel.multiply(-c);
    }
    else {
        force = new Vector3D(0,0,0);
    }
    return force;
}
```

```
Forces3D.add = function(arr){
    var forceSum = new Vector3D(0,0,0);
    for (var i=0; i<arr.length; i++){
        var force = arr[i];
        forceSum.incrementBy(force);
        }
    return forceSum;
}
```

Matrices and rotation

Vectors help us to handle translational motion, whereby an object changes its position in space. You need a more complicated mathematical entity to handle rotations, whereby an extended object changes its orientation in space—you need a matrix.

Introducing matrices

We've done a good job of avoiding matrices so far, even when discussing rigid body rotation in Chapter 13. While it was fine to do so in 2D, it is more difficult to ignore matrices in 3D. But before we discuss matrix algebra and rotations in 3D, it would help a lot to do so first in the simpler 2D context.

A matrix is essentially an array of numbers, pretty much like a vector. But although a vector is a one-dimensional array, you can have higher-dimensional matrices. We'll only ever need to worry about two-dimensional matrices, which look something like this:

$$\begin{pmatrix} 1 & 3 & 4 & 5 \\ 3 & 2 & 5 & 2 \\ 0 & -2 & 7 & 2 \end{pmatrix}$$

This matrix has 3 rows and 4 columns; it's a 3 × 4 matrix. Let's call it **A**. Then we can identify particular matrix elements by the row and column number. For example, $A(3,2) = -2$.

Just like arrays, matrices are useful when you have to deal with a group of similar quantities and you have to perform the same operations on them. They provide a compact way to perform calculations; for example, when you have to do rotations and other transformations. But just as a math vector is more than an array in the sense that it has definite rules for vector algebra (such as vector addition or multiplication), so is a matrix. Let's take a look at the rules of matrix algebra.

Matrix algebra

You can add and subtract matrices by adding and subtracting the corresponding elements. This means that you can only add or subtract matrices with the same size, for example for 2 × 2 matrices:

$$\begin{pmatrix} a_1 & b_1 \\ c_1 & d_1 \end{pmatrix} + \begin{pmatrix} a_2 & b_2 \\ c_2 & d_2 \end{pmatrix} = \begin{pmatrix} a_1 + a_2 & b_1 + b_2 \\ c_1 + c_2 & d_1 + d_2 \end{pmatrix}$$

Matrix addition can be applied to represent translations, or displacements, where the position of an object is shifted in space; for example, the following shifts the position of a point by an amount dx and dy along the x and y directions, respectively. This can be represented using 2 × 1 matrices as follows:

$$\begin{pmatrix} x \\ y \end{pmatrix} + \begin{pmatrix} dx \\ dy \end{pmatrix} = \begin{pmatrix} x + dx \\ y + dy \end{pmatrix}$$

Matrix multiplication is a bit more complicated. When you multiply two matrices **A** and **B**, you multiply each row of **A** by each column of **B**, element by element, and add the results. Here's an example for 2 × 2 matrices:

$$\begin{pmatrix} a_1 & b_1 \\ c_1 & d_1 \end{pmatrix}\begin{pmatrix} a_2 & b_2 \\ c_2 & d_2 \end{pmatrix} = \begin{pmatrix} a_1\,a_2 + b_1\,c_2 & a_1\,b_2 + b_1\,d_2 \\ c_1\,a_2 + d_1\,c_2 & c_1\,b_2 + d_1\,d_2 \end{pmatrix}$$

This means that you can only multiply matrix **A** by matrix **B** if **A** has the same number of columns as **B** has rows. In other words, you can multiply an $M \times N$ matrix only by an $N \times P$ matrix.

Note that multiplying the mth row by the nth column gives you the (m,n) matrix element in the product. Also, the result of multiplying an $M \times N$ matrix by an $N \times P$ matrix is an $M \times P$ matrix.

Matrix multiplication can transform objects in all sorts of ways, depending on the form of the matrix we're multiplying with. We're especially interested in rotation matrices.

Rotation matrices in 2D

Matrices are especially useful for doing rotations. To see this, let's say you have an object that you want to rotate through an angle θ about an axis perpendicular to the xy plane through the origin (see Figure 15-1). Let's use the math coordinate system so that the y-axis points upward and angles are measured in a counterclockwise sense.

Figure 15-1. *Rotating an object in 2D*

Using trigonometry, you can show that each point on the object with coordinates (x, y) will be moved to a new position with coordinates (x', y') given by the following equations:

$$x' = x\cos(\theta) - y\sin(\theta)$$
$$y' = x\sin(\theta) + y\cos(\theta)$$

By the way, this is the math behind the `rotate()` method of the `Vector2D` object that we introduced in Chapter 13. You can represent this relationship between the new and old coordinates as a single matrix equation:

$$\begin{pmatrix} x' \\ y' \end{pmatrix} = \begin{pmatrix} \cos(\theta) & -\sin(\theta) \\ \sin(\theta) & \cos(\theta) \end{pmatrix}\begin{pmatrix} x \\ y \end{pmatrix}$$

What we have done here is to represent each of the position vectors **r** and **r'** of points (x, y) and (x', y') as a matrix with a single column (called a *column matrix* or *column vector*). If you multiply out the matrices on the right side and equate the elements of the resulting column vector with those on the left side of the equation, you will recover the previous two equations.

We can write this matrix equation in a convenient shorthand form as follows:

$$\mathbf{r}' = \mathbf{R}\,\mathbf{r}$$

The matrix **R** is called the *rotation matrix* and is given by the following:

$$\mathbf{R} = \begin{pmatrix} \cos(\theta) & -\sin(\theta) \\ \sin(\theta) & \cos(\theta) \end{pmatrix}$$

Instead of rotating the object, you could also rotate the coordinate system (axes):

$$\mathbf{R} = \begin{pmatrix} \cos(\theta) & \sin(\theta) \\ -\sin(\theta) & \cos(\theta) \end{pmatrix}$$

What's happening here is that rotating the coordinate axes by angle θ is the same as rotating the object by angle –θ. So, if you replace θ by –θ in the original matrix and use the fact that sin (–θ) = –sin (θ), and cos (–θ) = cos (θ), you end up with the second matrix. So, the rule for swapping between object and coordinate system rotations is to "reverse the signs of the sines."

Rotation matrices in 3D

In 3D, the situation is complicated by the fact that you have three components and also three independent directions about which you can perform rotations. The rotation matrix is a 3 × 3 matrix, and for rotation about the *z*-axis it is given by this:

$$\begin{pmatrix} \cos(\theta) & -\sin(\theta) & 0 \\ \sin(\theta) & \cos(\theta) & 0 \\ 0 & 0 & 1 \end{pmatrix}$$

The rotation matrix about the *x*-axis is given by this:

$$\begin{pmatrix} 1 & 0 & 0 \\ 0 & \cos(\theta) & -\sin(\theta) \\ 0 & \sin(\theta) & \cos(\theta) \end{pmatrix}$$

A rotation about the *y*-axis is given by this matrix:

$$\begin{pmatrix} \cos(\theta) & 0 & \sin(\theta) \\ 0 & 1 & 0 \\ -\sin(\theta) & 0 & \cos(\theta) \end{pmatrix}$$

As in the 2D case, the signs of the sines are reversed if the coordinate axes are rotated instead.

Rotation matrices can be combined by multiplying them together. So a rotation with matrix $\mathbf{R}_1$ followed by a rotation with matrix $\mathbf{R}_2$ is equivalent to a rotation with matrix $\mathbf{R}_2\,\mathbf{R}_1$. Note that the order of the rotation matters in 3D. For example, rotating a cuboid by 90° clockwise about the *x*-axis and then 90° clockwise about the *z*-axis will have the cuboid end up in a different orientation than a corresponding rotation about the *z*-axis followed by a rotation about the *x*-axis. Try it with a book! Mathematically, this corresponds to the fact that matrix multiplication is not commutative. In other words:

$$\mathbf{R}_1\,\mathbf{R}_2 \neq \mathbf{R}_2\,\mathbf{R}_1$$

On the other hand, very small incremental (infinitesimal) rotations *are* commutative, so it does not matter in what order infinitesimal rotations about different axes are performed. This has important implications for how we can represent angular orientation and angular velocity in 3D. The noncommutativity of rotations about the *x*-, *y*-, and *z*-axes means that there is no unambiguous meaning to angular orientation as a vector with three components. So you cannot form a true vector from angular rotation θ in 3D. However, you *can* form a vector for small angular increments Δθ and therefore for angular velocity ω = dθ/dt.

As the preceding discussion has shown, rotation matrices are very useful mathematical objects that can be implemented in code to allow objects to be rotated in 3D. However, in practice dealing with matrix operations is generally not very efficient from a computational point of view. Without going into details, suffice it to say that a 3 × 3 matrix has nine components, and matrix operations such as multiplication involve a lot of calculations, some of which are redundant. Fortunately, there is a more efficient method to perform rotations in 3D—using even more exotic math objects known as *quaternions*.

Quaternions

The most convenient way to handle rotations in 3D involves the use of quaternions, which belong to an abstract number system. These rather mysterious mathematical entities are not frequently covered in college or university math courses—so chances are you may not have come across them before. Let's therefore spend a little time on an informal introduction to quaternions.

Introducing quaternions

Quaternions were invented by an Irish mathematician named William Hamilton in the nineteenth century as an extension of the so-called complex (or imaginary) numbers. As you might imagine, this makes them rather abstract constructs. For our purposes, it is more useful to think of a quaternion as a combination of a scalar and a vector (see Chapter 3 for a refresher on scalars and vectors). We can write a quaternion symbolically as

$$q = (s, \boldsymbol{v})$$

Where s is the scalar part and $\boldsymbol{v}$ is the vector part. We can also write the vector components explicitly, like this:

$$q = (s, v_1, v_2, v_3)$$

There are alternative notations, but this is probably the simplest. In this notation, it is tempting to think of a quaternion as a vector with four components. For many purposes this is quite helpful, as long as you keep in mind that the rules for manipulating and combining quaternions (that is, quaternion algebra) are somewhat different from those of vectors. Let's take a look at quaternion algebra now.

Quaternion algebra

The operations that you will need to know for handling 3D rotations are addition of two quaternions, multiplication of a quaternion by a scalar, and multiplication of two quaternions. Additionally, you will need to know about the magnitude of a quaternion, the conjugate and inverse of a quaternion, and the identity quaternion.

To add or subtract two quaternions, you simply add or subtract their respective components:

$$(r, u_1, u_2, u_3) + (s, v_1, v_2, v_3) = (r + s, u_1 + v_1, u_2 + v_2, u_3 + v_3)$$

To multiply or divide a quaternion by a scalar, you multiply or divide each of the components of the quaternion by the scalar:

$$\lambda(s, v_1, v_2, v_3) = (\lambda s, \lambda v_1, \lambda v_2, \lambda v_3)$$

The previous rules are similar to those for combining vectors. To multiply a quaternion by another quaternion is more complicated and is done using a combination of the dot and cross products. It is most conveniently written in terms of the following notation:

$$(r,\mathbf{u})(s,\mathbf{v})=(rs-\mathbf{u}\cdot\mathbf{v},r\mathbf{v}+s\mathbf{u}+\mathbf{u}\times\mathbf{v})$$

Note that quaternion multiplication is not commutative—the order of multiplication matters.

The *identity quaternion* is a special quaternion with a scalar part equal to unity and a vector part equal to zero: $1 = (1,0,0,0)$. It is so called because multiplying any quaternion by the identity quaternion leaves it unchanged (we leave the proof as an exercise!).

The *magnitude* or *norm* of a quaternion $q = (s,v_1,v_2,v_3)$ is defined in a similar way to that of a vector:

$$|q|=\sqrt{s^2+v_1^2+v_2^2+v_3^2}$$

Dividing a quaternion by its magnitude gives a quaternion of unit magnitude, also called a *unit quaternion*. This process is called normalization.

For any quaternion $q = (s,v_1,v_2,v_3)$ there is a *conjugate quaternion* defined by $q^* = (s,-v_1,-v_2,-v_3)$. It is easy to show that the product of a quaternion and its conjugate gives a quaternion with a zero vector part and with a scalar part equal to the norm squared of the quaternion (again, we leave this as an exercise):

$$qq^*=\left(|q|^2,0,0,0\right)$$

The *inverse* q^{-1} of a quaternion q is equal to its conjugate divided by the square of its norm:

$$q^{-1}=\frac{q^*}{|q|^2}$$

Multiplying a quaternion with its inverse gives the identity quaternion:

$$qq^{-1}=1$$

Quaternions and rotation

Like matrices, quaternions can be used for rotating vectors. In the previous section we saw that a rotation matrix $\mathbf{R}$ transforms a vector $\mathbf{r}$ to a vector $\mathbf{r'}$ according to the formula $\mathbf{r'} = \mathbf{R}\,\mathbf{r}$. That is, we simply premultiply the vector by the rotation matrix to get the rotated vector. The equivalent formula for rotating a vector $\mathbf{r}$ with a quaternion q is a little more complicated:

$$r'=qrq^{-1}$$

Here r is a quaternion with a scalar part of zero and with the vector part equal to $\mathbf{r}$: $r = (0,\mathbf{r})$.

If q is a unit quaternion, then that is the same as the following equation:

$$r'=qrq^*$$

In this case, the rotation quaternion can always be written in the following form, to represent a rotation through an angle θ around an axis represented by the unit vector $\mathbf{u}$:

$$q=(\cos(\theta/2),\sin(\theta/2)\mathbf{u})$$

Like rotation matrices, two rotation quaternions q_1 and q_2 can be combined by multiplying (or *composing*) them together to give a quaternion q' representing the combined rotation:

$$q' = q_2 q_1$$

This represents a rotation represented by q_1 followed by one represented by q_2. Recall that quaternion multiplication is not commutative, so the order of the product will give different rotations in 3D space.

Rotational dynamics in 3D

The final piece of background theory you need is about how to implement rigid body dynamics in 3D. To do this, we first need to establish how key concepts such as angular orientation, angular velocity, torque, and so on generalize to 3D.

Orientation in 3D

In 2D the orientation of an object can be straightforwardly described by an angle in the x-y plane, which can be interpreted as a rotation about a virtual z-axis perpendicular to that plane. It is tempting to generalize this method to 3D by specifying orientation as a combination of rotations through angles about the x, y, and z axes. These angles are known as *Euler angles*. Unfortunately there are serious problems with this approach. First, as discussed in the section "Rotation matrices in 3D", the orientation of an object as defined in this way would depend on the order of the rotations about the three axes. This is hardly satisfactory. Second, certain configurations can result in the dreaded "gimbal lock" problem, whereby no rotation is possible about one of the axes (search for "gimbal lock" on the Web for more details); this proved to be an issue during the Apollo 11 mission.

A better solution is to use a rotation matrix to characterize orientation—because a rotation matrix tells us how to rotate an object with respect to a fixed set of axes, it can also be thought of as holding information on the orientation of the rotated object. The problem then becomes one of computing the evolution in time of the rotation matrix. This is certainly doable and is a very common method of animating rotations. But it suffers from the slight disadvantage that one has to deal with matrix algebra, which is not generally computationally efficient.

Our preferred method is to use a unit quaternion to represent orientation. This is possible for the same reason that a rotation matrix can be used to represent orientation. To illustrate how that might work, suppose the initial orientation of a rigid body is described by a unit quaternion q. We then subject the rigid body to a rotation described by a unit quaternion p. The new orientation q' of the rigid body is then obtained simply by multiplying q by p:

$$q' = qp$$

The question we face in a physics animation is: how do we find the quaternion p that we need to multiply q with at each timestep? In discrete form, we are looking for p such that:

$$q(n+1) = q(n)p(n)$$

Time to go back to angular velocity.

Angular velocity and orientation

In the section "Rotation matrices in 3D" we made the point that an infinitesimal angular displacement is a vector, and hence so is the angular velocity $\omega = d\theta/dt$. It turns out that there is a particularly simple evolution equation relating the orientation quaternion with the angular velocity. In a coordinate frame attached to a rotating object (the so-called body frame), it can be written as:

$$\frac{dq}{dt} = \frac{1}{2}q\omega$$

Here ω is the angular velocity quaternion, constructed by setting the vector part of the quaternion equal to the angular velocity vector and the scalar part to zero. This equation tells us how the orientation quaternion q of an object changes in time: its rate of change is equal to half the product of q and the angular velocity ω.

To apply this equation in code, we first have to discretize it. Using the Euler method we can write:

$$q(n+1) - q(n) = \frac{1}{2}\Delta t\, q(n)\omega(n)$$

Rearranging, we can write this equation as:

$$q(n+1) = q(n)\left[1 + \frac{1}{2}\Delta t\, \omega(n)\right]$$

This equation relates the orientation quaternion at the new timestep $q(n+1)$ to that at the old timestep $q(n)$. The quantity in the square brackets is the expression for $p(n)$ that we were looking for. This is the rotation quaternion by which we need to multiply q at each timestep to update the orientation. Note that the first 1 in the square brackets denotes the identity quaternion.

A key requirement is that q must be a unit quaternion at all times; otherwise, the object will be scaled or distorted as the animation progresses. Because there will inevitably be numerical errors that will accumulate over time and cause the norm of q to deviate from unity, it is wise to normalize q frequently, possibly at every timestep.

Torque, angular acceleration, and the moment of inertia matrix

Just like angular velocity, angular acceleration, $\alpha = d\omega/dt$, is also a vector in 3D. A rigid body will experience an angular acceleration if there is a resultant torque $\mathbf{T}$ acting on it. In 3D the angular equation of motion can be written in the body frame as the following matrix equation:

$$\mathbf{T} = \mathbf{I}\alpha + \omega \times (\mathbf{I}\omega)$$

Recall that torque is given by the cross product of the position vector of the point of application of a force from the center of rotation and the force vector: $\mathbf{T} = \mathbf{r} \times \mathbf{F}$. This equation can be solved numerically to give the angular velocity at each timestep. The additional complication is that in 3D the moment of inertia $\mathbf{I}$ is a 3×3 matrix. In the special case where $\mathbf{I}$ is diagonal and the diagonal elements are all equal, $I_{xx} = I_{yy} = I_{zz} = I$, the previous equation simplifies to $\mathbf{T} = I\alpha$, similar to the 2D case in Chapter 13.

3D rendering: Introducing WebGL and three.js

After this fairly lengthy introduction to 3D math and physics, you are no doubt impatient to see it all in action. But how do you produce 3D graphics and animation in the browser? It's time to introduce WebGL and `three.js`.

Canvas, WebGL, and WebGL frameworks

The HTML5 canvas element is an inherently 2D environment. So how can we extend its capabilities to render 3D? It is possible to simulate 3D on a 2D canvas by applying perspective distortion—this is sometimes known as 2.5D. This is the approach taken in the book *Foundation HTML5 Animation with JavaScript* by Billy Lamberta and Keith Peters. However, it is a rather laborious process, and there are issues with performance. Fortunately, there is now an easier and more powerful alternative—WebGL.

WebGL: extending canvas to 3D

WebGL originated from attempts at Mozilla to add 3D capabilities to the canvas element. It is essentially a JavaScript API for rendering both 2D and 3D graphics within the web browser. WebGL is based on OpenGL ES 2.0 and allows GPU (Graphics Processing Unit) acceleration in compatible browsers. At the time of this writing, WebGL is now supported by most of the major web browsers. To check if your browser or device supports WebGL, you can visit one of the following web sites:

```
http://webglreport.com/
http://get.webgl.org/
```

A WebGL program consists of JavaScript control code and shader code executed on a computer's GPU (a shader is a program that performs shading of 3D models for depth perception and visual effects). Coding in pure WebGL can be a rather laborious process and is outside the scope of this book. Instead, we shall make use of a framework that will avoid the need to write raw shader code altogether.

WebGL frameworks

So far we've done very well without needing to use external libraries or frameworks. But we'll make an exception for 3D, as we're not particularly keen on spending hours with low-level WebGL commands! There are a number of JavaScript frameworks and libraries that build on top of WebGL to simplify the process of coding in 3D. Three.js and babylon.js are just two among the more popular ones. In this book we will use the three.js library.

A quick three.js primer

The purpose of this section is to present the absolute minimum you need to know to get up and running with three.js. There are many books and online sources on three.js that we encourage you to consult if you want to get a more in-depth knowledge. The first place to head to is, of course, the official project web page at http://three.org, where you will find documentation and examples, and will be able to download the latest version of the library. For convenience we have included a copy of the three.min.js file, which contains the full library, in the downloadable source code for this chapter. Needless to say, you will have to include this file in a <script> tag in your HTML files in all the examples in this chapter.

The renderer

First you need to choose a renderer. You have a choice of renderers, including a CanvasRenderer and the much better-performing WebGLRenderer, which uses the GPU. You can create a WebGLRenderer and add it to the DOM with the following lines of code:

```
var renderer = new THREE.WebGLRenderer();
renderer.setSize(window.innerWidth, window.innerHeight);
document.body.appendChild(renderer.domElement);
```

The last line creates a canvas element that will display the scene.

The scene

A scene sets an area where visual elements, cameras, lights, and so on can be placed. Creating a scene couldn't be simpler:

```
var scene = new THREE.Scene();
```

The camera

Next you need a camera. There are different choices of camera available, and we refer you to the documentation for details. Here we just pick a PerspectiveCamera, set its position, and add it to the scene thus:

```
var camera = new THREE.PerspectiveCamera(45, window.innerWidth/window.innerHeight, 0.1, 10000);
camera.position.set(100,0,400);
scene.add(camera);
```

You need to specify four arguments in PerspectiveCamera: fov (field of view), aspect, near, and far. The field of view is here set at 45 degrees, and the aspect ratio as the ratio between the browser window's width and height. The near and far parameters are respectively the closest and farthest distance at which the camera will render objects (here set at 0.1 and 10000).

The second line of code in the previous listing sets the position of the camera using (x,y,z) coordinates. The last line adds the camera to the scene.

Lighting

You need a light to see the objects on the scene. Several different choices are possible (see the documentation), and you can use more than one light. Let's pick a DirectionalLight:

```
var light = new THREE.DirectionalLight();
light.position.set(-10,0,20);
scene.add(light);
```

Objects: mesh, geometry, and material

Next you need to populate the scene with one or more objects. In three.js, you create an object with a Mesh, which takes two arguments, Geometry and Material. Again, there are many choices of Geometry and Material depending on the shape and appearance of the objects you want to create. Let's create a sphere and give it a MeshLambertMaterial with a red color:

```
var sphereGeometry = new THREE.SphereGeometry(50,20,20);
var sphereMaterial = new THREE.MeshLambertMaterial({color: 0xff0000});
var ball = new THREE.Mesh(sphereGeometry,sphereMaterial);
ball.position.set(100,0,0);
scene.add(ball);
```

The SphereGeometry takes three arguments: radius, number of horizontal segments (similar to latitude lines), and number of vertical segments (similar to longitude lines).

The 3D coordinate system

In WebGL and `three.js` the coordinate system is as shown in Figure 15-2. The *x*-axis points from left to right, the *y*-axis from bottom to top, and the *z*-axis points out of the screen. The origin is at the center of the display area. The location of the origin and the direction of the *y*-axis are different than in the 2D canvas coordinate system. These differences must be taken into consideration in your code.

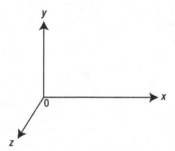

Figure 15-2. *The 3D coordinate system*

Animation with three.js

To animate objects in 3D using `three.js` is essentially the same as in 2D. You first create an animation loop using any of the methods described in Chapter 2 and used throughout the book. Within the animation loop you then update the position and/or orientation of objects at each timestep.

You have already seen how the position of an object (obj say) can be set using the `obj.position.set()` method. You can also set or update individual coordinates separately, as in this example:

```
obj.position.x = 100;
```

In `three.js`, an object's orientation can be specified by a `rotation` property, which is an Euler angle representation with three components *x*, *y*, and *z*. For example:

```
obj.rotation.y = Math.PI/2;
```

It is also possible to specify an object's orientation using its quaternion property. You will see an example in the section "Simulating rigid body motion in 3D."

Simulating particle motion in 3D

Okay, after all this background material, it's finally time for some code examples. Let's start with our "hello world" physics simulation—a bouncing ball!

A bouncing ball simulation in 3D

Because this is our first 3D example, it is useful to see the code in full. The code is in bouncing-ball.js and is listed here:

```
var width = window.innerWidth, height = window.innerHeight;
var scene, camera, renderer;
var ball;
var t0, dt;
var g = -20;
var fac = 0.9;
var radius = 20;
var x0 = -100, y0 = -100, z0 = -100;

window.onload = init;

function init() {
    renderer = new THREE.WebGLRenderer();
    renderer.setSize(width, height);
    document.body.appendChild(renderer.domElement);

    scene = new THREE.Scene();

    var angle = 45, aspect = width/height, near = 0.1, far = 10000;
    camera = new THREE.PerspectiveCamera(angle, aspect, near, far);
    camera.position.set(100,0,400);
    scene.add(camera);

    var light = new THREE.DirectionalLight();
    light.position.set(-10,0,20);
    scene.add(light);

    var sphereGeometry = new THREE.SphereGeometry(radius,20,20);
    var sphereMaterial = new THREE.MeshLambertMaterial({color: 0x006666});
    ball = new THREE.Mesh(sphereGeometry,sphereMaterial);
    scene.add(ball);
    ball.pos = new Vector3D(100,0,0);
    ball.velo = new Vector3D(-20,0,-20);
    positionObject(ball);

    var plane1 = new THREE.Mesh(new THREE.PlaneGeometry(400, 400), new THREE.MeshNormalMaterial());
    plane1.rotation.x = -Math.PI/2;
    plane1.position.set(0,y0,0);
    scene.add(plane1);

    var plane2 = new THREE.Mesh(new THREE.PlaneGeometry(400, 400), new THREE.MeshNormalMaterial());
    plane2.position.set(0,0,z0);
    scene.add(plane2);

    var plane3 = new THREE.Mesh(new THREE.PlaneGeometry(400, 400), new THREE.MeshNormalMaterial());
    plane3.rotation.y = Math.PI/2;
    plane3.position.set(x0,0,0);
    scene.add(plane3);
```

```
        t0 = new Date().getTime();
        animFrame();
}

function animFrame(){
        requestAnimationFrame(animFrame);
        onTimer();
}
function onTimer(){
        var t1 = new Date().getTime();
        dt = 0.001*(t1-t0);
        t0 = t1;
        if (dt>0.2) {dt=0;};
        move();
}
function move(){
        moveObject(ball);
}
function positionObject(obj){
        obj.position.set(obj.pos.x,obj.pos.y,obj.pos.z);
}
function moveObject(obj){
        obj.velo.y += g*dt;
        obj.pos = obj.pos.addScaled(obj.velo,dt);
        if (obj.pos.x < x0 + radius){
                obj.pos.x = x0 + radius;
                obj.velo.x *= -fac;
        }
        if (obj.pos.y < y0 + radius){
                obj.pos.y = y0 + radius;
                obj.velo.y *= -fac;
        }
        if (obj.pos.z < z0 + radius){
                obj.pos.z = z0 + radius;
                obj.velo.z *= -fac;
        }
        positionObject(obj);
        renderer.render(scene, camera);
}
```

We begin by storing the width and height of the browser window in the variables width and height, which we'll use in a couple of places. Then we create variables for the scene, camera, and renderer, and a ball object. The radius of the ball is stored in the variable radius, which we'll use in a number of places. Note that the variable g, which represents acceleration due to gravity, is given a negative value. The reason is that WebGL's vertical (y) axis points upward rather than downward.

In the init() method we set up the renderer, scene, camera, and light as discussed in the previous section. We then create a ball using SphereGeometry. Next we create new properties pos and velo for the ball object and assign them Vector3D values to hold its initial position and velocity. Note that you must include the vector3D.js file in your HTML file. The ball.pos and ball.velo variables will be used for performing the physics calculations. But we also need to tell WebGL to set the ball's position on the canvas each time these variables are updated. This is done by calling the positionObject() method, which updates the position property of the ball using the pos values:

```
function positionObject(obj){
    obj.position.set(obj.pos.x,obj.pos.y,obj.pos.z);
}
```

Next in init(), we create three walls using the PlaneGeometry object, and orient and position them suitably using the rotation and position properties of the instances.

The animation code looks very similar to what you are already used to for creating 2D canvas simulations. The new pieces of code are in the moveObject() method. In the first two lines we update the vertical velocity and the position vector of the ball. Then we check for collisions with each of the three walls in a similar way to what we did in the very first example in Chapter 1. We then call positionObject() to update the position property of the ball before rendering the scene.

Run the code and you should see something similar to the screenshot in Figure 15-3. As ever, feel free to experiment by changing the parameters and visual elements.

Figure 15-3. *Bouncing ball in 3D*

A rotating Earth animation

Creating rotating animations is easily achieved with three.js. To illustrate how to do it, let's make a rotating Earth animation. The code for this example is actually simpler than the previous example, and you'll find it in the file earth. js. Here is the full listing:

```
var width = window.innerWidth, height = window.innerHeight;
var renderer = new THREE.WebGLRenderer();
renderer.setSize(width, height);
document.body.appendChild(renderer.domElement);

var scene = new THREE.Scene();
```

```
var angle = 45, aspect = width/height, near = 0.1, far = 10000;
var camera = new THREE.PerspectiveCamera(angle, aspect, near, far);
camera.position.set(100,0,500);
scene.add(camera);

var light = new THREE.DirectionalLight();
light.position.set(-10,0,20);
scene.add(light);

var radius = 100, segments = 20, rings = 20;
var sphereGeometry = new THREE.SphereGeometry(radius,segments,rings);
var sphereMaterial = new THREE.MeshLambertMaterial();
sphereMaterial.map = THREE.ImageUtils.loadTexture('images/earth.jpg');
var sphere = new THREE.Mesh(sphereGeometry,sphereMaterial);
scene.add(sphere);

function animFrame(){
    requestAnimationFrame(animFrame);
    onEachStep();
}
function onEachStep() {
    sphere.rotation.y += 0.01;
    camera.position.z -= 0.1;
    renderer.render(scene, camera);
}
animFrame();
```

As you can see, we have simplified the animation code considerably. Aside from this, the novelty lies in just three lines of code, which appear in boldface type. The first line loads an image that it uses as a texture map for the SphereGeometry object created, giving the appearance of a 3D Earth that you can see in Figure 15-4. Note that your code may not work properly if you simply open the HTML file in a web browser, because of a security feature in JavaScript that stops externally hosted files from loading. If that happens, a helpful three.js page at https://github.com/mrdoob/three.js/wiki/How-to-run-things-locally explains how to circumvent the problem.

Figure 15-4. *Rotating Earth in 3D*

In the function onEachStep( ), the first two lines increment the *y* component of the rotation property of the Earth and decrement the *z* component of the camera's position. Run the code to see the resulting effect.

Forces: gravity and orbits in 3D

Next, we'll add a Moon and some gravity physics to make it orbit the Earth! We will need accurate time-keeping, so will restore the full animation loop that we've used for most of the examples in the book. You will also need to add the forces3D.js file in your HTML file.

The resulting code is in earth-moon.js and is reproduced here:

```
var width = window.innerWidth, height = window.innerHeight;
var acc, force;
var t0, dt;
var animId;
var G = 1;
var M = 50000;
var m = 1;
var scene, camera, renderer;
var earth, moon;

window.onload = init;

function init() {
    renderer = new THREE.WebGLRenderer();
    renderer.setSize(width, height);
    document.body.appendChild(renderer.domElement);

    scene = new THREE.Scene();

    var angle = 45, aspect = width/height, near = 0.1, far = 10000;
    camera = new THREE.PerspectiveCamera(angle, aspect, near, far);
```

```
    camera.position.set(0,100,1000);
    scene.add(camera);

    var light = new THREE.DirectionalLight();
    light.position.set(-10,0,20);
    scene.add(light);

    var radius = 100, segments = 20, rings = 20;
    var sphereGeometry = new THREE.SphereGeometry(radius,segments,rings);
    var sphereMaterial = new THREE.MeshLambertMaterial({color: 0x0099ff});
    sphereMaterial.map = THREE.ImageUtils.loadTexture('images/Earth.jpg');
    earth = new THREE.Mesh(sphereGeometry,sphereMaterial);
    scene.add(earth);
    earth.mass = M;
    earth.pos = new Vector3D(0,0,0);
    earth.velo = new Vector3D(0,0,0);
    positionObject(earth);

    moon = new THREE.Mesh(new THREE.SphereGeometry(radius/4,segments,rings),
    new THREE.MeshLambertMaterial());
    scene.add(moon);
    moon.mass = m;
    moon.pos = new Vector3D(300,0,0);
    moon.velo = new Vector3D(0,0,-12);
    positionObject(moon);

    t0 = new Date().getTime();
    animFrame();
}

function animFrame(){
    requestAnimationFrame(animFrame);
    onTimer();
}
function onTimer(){
    var t1 = new Date().getTime();
    dt = 0.001*(t1-t0);
    t0 = t1;
    if (dt>0.2) {dt=0;};
    move();
}
function move(){
    positionObject(moon);
    moveObject(moon);
    calcForce(moon);
    updateAccel(moon);
    updateVelo(moon);
}
function positionObject(obj){
    obj.position.set(obj.pos.x,obj.pos.y,obj.pos.z);
}
```

419

```
function moveObject(obj){
    obj.pos = obj.pos.addScaled(obj.velo,dt);
    positionObject(obj);
    earth.rotation.y += 0.001;
    renderer.render(scene, camera);
}
function calcForce(obj){
    var r = obj.pos.subtract(earth.pos);
    force = Forces3D.gravity(G,M,m,r);
}
function updateAccel(obj){
    acc = force.multiply(1/obj.mass);
}
function updateVelo(obj){
    obj.velo = obj.velo.addScaled(acc,dt);
}
```

You should be able to follow this code without any difficulty. The init() method sets up the scene and 3D objects, and the animation code works as in the 2D examples, substituting Vector3D variables for Vector2D ones as needed.

Run the code and you will be treated to a visually appealing 3D simulation of the Moon orbiting the Earth, as shown in Figure 15-5. You can change the position of the camera to view the system from different points of view. For example, add the following line in init() to view the Moon from the Earth's position:

```
camera.position = earth.position;
```

Figure 15-5. *Earth-Moon simulation*

Or add the following line in moveObject() to view the Earth from the Moon:

```
camera.position = moon.position;
```

We leave you to develop the code further and add interactivity, for example to change the camera location or add zooming effects and so on.

Needless to say, the simulation is not to scale, but it does contain the essential physics. In Chapter 16, you will build an accurate and much more realistic simulation of the solar system.

Simulating rigid body motion in 3D

We are now ready to simulate rigid body motion in 3D. Let us choose a simple object–a rotating cube–for which the moment of inertia matrix has equal diagonal elements and the nondiagonal elements equal to zero. As we saw in the section "Rotational dynamics in 3D," the relationship between torque and angular acceleration then simplifies to $\mathbf{T} = I\,\alpha$, where I is the value of each diagonal element of the moment of inertia matrix.

A rotating cube animation

As a starting point, let us go back to the `rigid-body-dynamics.js` simulation of Chapter 13 and make a few modifications to replace the rotating square we had there with a rotating cube. The modified code is in `cube-rotation.js` and is reproduced here in full:

```
var width = window.innerWidth, height = window.innerHeight;
var t0, dt;
var cube;
var scene, camera, renderer;
var alp, torque;
var t0, dt;
var animId;
var k = 0.5; // angular damping factor
var tqMax = 2;
var tq = 0;

window.onload = init;

function init() {
    renderer = new THREE.WebGLRenderer();
    renderer.setSize(width, height);
    document.body.appendChild(renderer.domElement);

    scene = new THREE.Scene();

    var angle = 45, aspect = width/height, near = 0.1, far = 10000;
    camera = new THREE.PerspectiveCamera(angle, aspect, near, far);
    camera.position.set(100,0,500);
    scene.add(camera);

    var light = new THREE.DirectionalLight();
    light.position.set(30,0,30);
    scene.add(light);

    cube = new THREE.Mesh(new THREE.CubeGeometry(100, 100, 100), new THREE.MeshNormalMaterial());
    cube.overdraw = true;
    scene.add(cube);
    cube.im = 1;
    cube.angVelo = 0;

    addEventListener('mousedown',onDown,false);
    t0 = new Date().getTime();
    animFrame();
}
```

```
function onDown(evt){
    tq = tqMax;
    addEventListener('mouseup',onUp,false);
}
function onUp(evt){
    tq = 0;
    removeEventListener('mouseup',onUp,false);
}
function animFrame(){
    animId = requestAnimationFrame(animFrame);
    onTimer();
}
function onTimer(){
    var t1 = new Date().getTime();
    dt = 0.001*(t1-t0);
    t0 = t1;
    if (dt>0.2) {dt=0;};
    move();
}
function move(){
    moveObject(cube);
    calcForce(cube);
    updateAccel(cube);
    updateVelo(cube);
}
function moveObject(obj){
    obj.rotation.x += obj.angVelo*dt;
    renderer.render(scene, camera);
}
function calcForce(obj){
    torque = tq;
    torque += -k*obj.angVelo; // angular damping
}
function updateAccel(obj){
    alp = torque/obj.im;
}
function updateVelo(obj){
    obj.angVelo += alp*dt;
}
```

In the init() method, we have added new code to set up the scene and related objects with the help of three.js commands. We then create a cube with CubeGeometry and give it new properties of im (moment of inertia) and angVelo (angular velocity), with values set to 1 and 0 respectively. The animation part of the code closely follows that in the rigid-body-dynamics.js code of Chapter 13. Here we have removed bits of code relating to forces, as we are only applying a torque and no force. For simplicity, both the torque and the angular acceleration are treated as scalars, exactly as they are in the 2D case. This is fine for now, as we shall rotate the cube about either the x-, y-, or z-axis. In the code listing we have the following line, which makes the cube rotate around the x-axis:

```
obj.rotation.x += obj.angVelo*dt;
```

You can change this line to rotate about one of the other two axes instead. There are event listeners and handlers that apply a constant torque that makes the cube rotate when you click the mouse, and set the torque to zero otherwise. An angular damping term has been included as in the 2D example. Run the code and click the mouse to experiment with the simulation. A screenshot is shown in Figure 15-6.

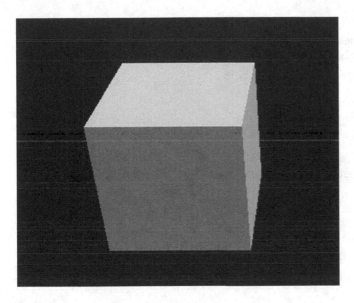

Figure 15-6. *A rotating cube in 3D*

Applying a force to the rotating cube

Let us now develop the rotating cube simulation further by treating the torque and the angular acceleration as vectors instead of scalars. In this example we'll handle the rotation using Euler angles. We'll also include code to deal with forces. To compensate for the increased length of the code, we remove the event handlers and listeners, thus losing interactivity. The new code (cube-euler-angles.js) now looks like this:

```
var width = window.innerWidth, height = window.innerHeight;
var t0, dt;
var cube;
var scene, camera, renderer;
var acc, force;
var alp, torque;
var t0, dt;
var animId;
var k = 0.5;
var kSpring = 0.2;
var tq = new Vector3D(1,0,0);
var center = new Vector3D(0,0,-500);

window.onload = init;
```

```
function init() {
    renderer = new THREE.WebGLRenderer();
    renderer.setSize(width, height);
    document.body.appendChild(renderer.domElement);

    scene = new THREE.Scene();

    var angle = 45, aspect = width/height, near = 0.1, far = 10000;
    camera = new THREE.PerspectiveCamera(angle, aspect, near, far);
    camera.position.set(100,0,500);
    scene.add(camera);

    var light = new THREE.DirectionalLight();
    light.position.set(30,0,30);
    scene.add(light);

    cube = new THREE.Mesh(new THREE.CubeGeometry(100, 100, 100), new THREE.MeshNormalMaterial());
    cube.overdraw = true;
    scene.add(cube);
    cube.mass = 1;
    cube.im = new Vector3D(1,1,1);
    cube.pos = new Vector3D(0,0,0);
    cube.velo = new Vector3D(0,0,0);
    cube.eulerAngles = new Vector3D(0,0,0);
    cube.angVelo = new Vector3D(0,0,0);

    t0 = new Date().getTime();
    animFrame();
}
function animFrame(){
    animId = requestAnimationFrame(animFrame);
    onTimer();
}
function onTimer(){
    var t1 = new Date().getTime();
    dt = 0.001*(t1-t0);
    t0 = t1;
    if (dt>0.2) {dt=0;};
    move();
}
function move(){
    positionObject(cube);
    moveObject(cube);
    calcForce(cube);
    updateAccel(cube);
    updateVelo(cube);
}
function positionObject(obj){
    obj.position.set(obj.pos.x,obj.pos.y,obj.pos.z);
    obj.rotation.set(obj.eulerAngles.x,obj.eulerAngles.y,obj.eulerAngles.z);
}
```

```
function moveObject(obj){
    obj.pos = obj.pos.addScaled(obj.velo,dt);
    obj.eulerAngles = obj.eulerAngles.addScaled(obj.angVelo,dt);
    positionObject(obj);
    renderer.render(scene, camera);
}
function calcForce(obj){
    var r = obj.pos.subtract(center);
    force = Forces3D.spring(kSpring,r);
    torque = tq;
    torque = torque.addScaled(obj.angVelo,-k);
}
function updateAccel(obj){
    acc = force.multiply(1/obj.mass);
    alp = torque.div(obj.im);
}
function updateVelo(obj){
    obj.velo = obj.velo.addScaled(acc,dt);
    obj.angVelo = obj.angVelo.addScaled(alp,dt);
}
```

There are a number of new features in this code. First, we include a spring force in calcForce(), using the Forces3D.spring() method. Torque is now a vector and is assigned a constant Vector3D value throughout the simulation, which is set in the variable tq. In init() we create and initialize various physical properties for the cube: a mass property, a moment of inertia vector (instead of a matrix, assuming the matrix is diagonal), position and velocity vectors, an angular velocity vector, and a vector storing the Euler angles describing the cube's orientation.

In updateAccel() we compute the angular acceleration by dividing each component of the torque by the corresponding moment of inertia component; this is a simplification of the math that is only possible when the moment of inertia matrix is diagonal, as it is in this case. We perform this division using a newly created div() method of Vector3D. The div() method allows you to divide a vector by another vector by dividing their respective components (not a standard mathematical operation!):

```
div: function(vec) {
    return new Vector3D(this.x/vec.x,this.y/vec.y,this.z/vec.z);
}
```

Finally, we treat the eulerAngles variable just like the position variable pos in moveObject() and positionObject(). This is fine for rotation about the x-, y-, or z-axis, but not about an arbitrary oblique axis, as you are about to see.

If you run the code as it is, you will see a cube rotating about its x-axis while oscillating along the z-axis. You can change the axis of rotation and center of oscillation simply by changing the values of the Vector3D variables tq and center. First change the value of tq to Vector3D(0,1,0) and then to Vector3D(0,0,1); this applies a torque in the y and z directions respectively, and makes the cube rotate about the respective axes. Now try making the cube rotate about an oblique axis by changing the value of tq to Vector3D(1,1,1). This applies a torque along a diagonal axis and, physically, ought to make the cube rotate around that axis. But if you run the code you will find that the cube behaves rather differently. Our simple attempt with Euler angles has trouble handling rotations about oblique axes. Let's see how we can deal with this using quaternions.

Rotating the cube about an arbitrary axis

Our focus here is on how to handle rotations about an arbitrary axis. So let us strip the previous code of the parts that deal with forces so we can focus on the parts that deal with the rotation. Also, instead of working with the eulerAngles property that we created, we instead work with the quaternion property, which is a built-in three.js property that stores an object's orientation as a quaternion. The new code is called cube-rotation-quaternion.js, and is listed here:

```
var width = window.innerWidth, height = window.innerHeight;
var t0, dt;
var cube;
var scene, camera, renderer;
var alp, torque;
var t0, dt;
var animId;
var k = 0.5;
var tqMax = new Vector3D(1,1,1);
var tq = new Vector3D(0,0,0);

window.onload = init;

function init() {
    renderer = new THREE.WebGLRenderer();
    renderer.setSize(width, height);
    document.body.appendChild(renderer.domElement);

    scene = new THREE.Scene();

    var angle = 45, aspect = width/height, near = 0.1, far = 10000;
    camera = new THREE.PerspectiveCamera(angle, aspect, near, far);
    camera.position.set(100,0,500);
    scene.add(camera);

    var light = new THREE.DirectionalLight();
    light.position.set(30,0,30);
    scene.add(light);

    cube = new THREE.Mesh(new THREE.CubeGeometry(100, 100, 100), new THREE.MeshNormalMaterial());
    cube.overdraw = true;
    scene.add(cube);
    cube.im = new Vector3D(1,1,1);
    cube.angVelo = new Vector3D(0,0,0);

    addEventListener('mousedown',onDown,false);
    t0 = new Date().getTime();
    animFrame();
}
function onDown(evt){
    tq = tqMax;
    addEventListener('mouseup',onUp,false);
}
```

```
function onUp(evt){
    tq = new Vector3D(0,0,0);
    removeEventListener('mouseup',onUp,false);
}
function animFrame(){
    animId = requestAnimationFrame(animFrame);
    onTimer();
}
function onTimer(){
    var t1 = new Date().getTime();
    dt = 0.001*(t1-t0);
    t0 = t1;
    if (dt>0.2) {dt=0;};
    move();
}
function move(){
    moveObject(cube);
    calcForce(cube);
    updateAccel(cube);
    updateVelo(cube);
}
function moveObject(obj){
    var p = new THREE.Quaternion;
    p.set(obj.angVelo.x*dt/2,obj.angVelo.y*dt/2,obj.angVelo.z*dt/2,1);
    obj.quaternion.multiply(p);
    obj.quaternion.normalize();
    renderer.render(scene,camera);
}
function calcForce(obj){
    torque = tq;
    torque = torque.addScaled(obj.angVelo,-k);
}
function updateAccel(obj){
    alp = torque.div(obj.im);
}
function updateVelo(obj){
    obj.angVelo = obj.angVelo.addScaled(alp,dt);
}
```

Note that we have reintroduced event listeners and handlers so that a torque is applied only when the mouse is clicked. By default the torque applied has the value Vector3D(1,1,1); so it is applied along a diagonal axis. The key new bits of code are the first four lines in moveObject(); this is all that is required to implement the quaternion rotation technology we discussed in the section "Rotational dynamics in 3D." The first line simply creates a new quaternion p by instantiating the THREE.Quaternion object. The next line uses the set() method of Quaternion to give p a value equal to the quaternion quantity that appears in the square bracket of the following equation:

$$q(n+1) = q(n)\left[1 + \frac{1}{2}\Delta t\ \omega(n)\right]$$

427

Recall that, in this equation, 1 represents the identity quaternion with a scalar component of 1 and vector components of 0; similarly, ω is the quaternion form of the angular velocity, with a scalar component equal to 0 and a vector component equal to the angular velocity vector. The third line of code in moveObject() employs the multiply() method of Quaternion to multiply and update the object's orientation quaternion (obj.quaternion, q in the previous equation) by p. The last line normalizes the object's orientation quaternion to avoid distortions due to numerical rounding errors.

Run the code and you'll find that the cube behaves perfectly, rotating about the diagonal axis. Experiment by changing the value of the applied torque tqMax to make it rotate about any arbitrary axis.

Summary

Well done for making it this far into the book! You now know how to create physics simulations in 3D—in principle there is nothing stopping you from converting any of the 2D examples in the book to 3D. In the final chapter you will apply what you have learned here to create two 3D simulations—a flight simulator and a solar system simulation.

■ ■ ■

CHAPTER 16

Simulation Projects

This final chapter consists of three simulation projects that will illustrate how the physics and methods you've learned in this book can be used for different types of applications. The examples are quite different from one another, reflecting differences not only in the underlying physics but also in the purposes for which they are built.

The three examples include the following:

- **Building a submarine**: The aim here is to show how easily you can modify some of the existing code you've already come across to create a submarine that you could incorporate in a 2D game.

- **Building a flight simulator**: In this example we'll create a 3D flight simulator that could be further developed in many interesting ways just for pure fun!

- **Creating an accurate solar system model**: This project is to create an accurate 3D model of the solar system that could be used as an e-learning tool. We will then compare the simulation with data generated from a simulation by NASA.

The idea is that these are *your* projects, so we will describe the relevant physics and help you build a basic version, but then leave it to you to develop and enhance them in any ways you might want. Have fun!

Building a submarine

In Chapter 7 we had a simple but interesting example of a ball floating in water. It is actually quite easy to modify that example and turn it into an interactive submarine of a type that can be used in simple 2D games. Let's first quickly review the main physics involved.

Brief review of the physics

In the floating-ball example, we identified three main forces that acted on the ball: gravity, upthrust, and drag, which are given respectively by the following formulas:

$$\mathbf{W} = m\mathbf{g}$$

$$\mathbf{U} = -\rho V \mathbf{g}$$

$$\mathbf{F} = -k v \mathbf{v}$$

Note that we have written the upthrust formula in vector form: the minus sign is needed because upthrust acts upward, opposing the gravity vector $\mathbf{g}$. Just as a reminder, in that formula ρ is the density of water and V is the volume of water displaced by the object.

With a submarine you have a fourth force: the thrust **T** that pushes the sub, allowing it to move horizontally through the water. This will be modeled as a horizontal force of constant magnitude when power is applied.

Another relevant piece of physics (as discussed in Chapter 7), is that an object will float if its density (mass per unit volume) is less than or equal to that of water, and it will sink otherwise. A submarine functions on the principle that its effective density can be varied by filling ballast tanks with sea water or pressurized air: its density (mass/volume ratio) varies because its mass thus changes while its volume remains the same.

The visual setup

The visual background is quite simple, consisting of a rectangle with a gradient fill to represent the sky and another one to represent the sea—both are created using the drawing API. A screenshot of the simulation is shown in Figure 16-1. There is also some text on the screen that displays the ratio of the density of the submarine to that of the water.

Figure 16-1. Screenshot of the submarine simulation

The submarine is created, using the drawing API, as a JavaScript object Sub—the code is in the file sub.js, available along with all of the source code and related files at www.apress.com. Figure 16-2 takes a closer look at it. The blue rectangle within the sub represents water in the ballast tanks. By controlling its height, we create the illusion of changing the water level, with the mass of the submarine being adjusted accordingly.

Figure 16-2. A closer look at the submarine

The setup code

The setup code is in the init() method of the simulation's file submarine.js. The code in init() is listed here:

```
function init() {
    // create the sky
    gradient = context_bg.createLinearGradient(0,0,0,yLevel);
    gradient.addColorStop(0,'#0066ff');
    gradient.addColorStop(1,'#ffffff');
    context_bg.fillStyle = gradient;
    context_bg.fillRect(0,0,canvas_bg.width,yLevel);
    // create the sea
    context_fg.fillStyle = "rgba(0,255,255,0.5)";
    context_fg.fillRect(0,yLevel,canvas.width,canvas.height);
    // create a sub
    sub = new Sub(160,60,'#0000ff',emptySubMass);
    sub.pos2D = new Vector2D(250,300);
    sub.velo2D = new Vector2D(40,-20);
    sub.draw(context);
    // set water height in sub
    setWaterHeight();
    // set up text formatting
    setupText();
    // set up event listener
    window.addEventListener('keydown',keydownListener,false);
    // initialise time and animate
    initAnim();
}
```

Note that we are using three canvas instances (see the markup in the associated HTML file, submarine.html). The sky is drawn on a background canvas, and the sea is drawn on a foreground canvas. The sub is placed on a canvas instance in the middle. Naturally, the last two canvas elements are made transparent (see the associated style file, style7.css). The water level in the sub is set in the setWaterHeight() method, and the text formatting is set up in the setupText() method. A keydown event listener is then set up, and finally the initAnim() method, which initiates the animation code, is called.

The Sub object is created with four arguments, specifying its width, height, color, and mass, respectively. In addition to these properties it has a tankWidth and a tankHeight property, which are by default set to half of its width and height, respectively. It also has a waterHeight property, with a default value of 0. It has position (x and y) and velocity (vx and vy) properties, and associated pos2D and velo2D getters and setters. Finally, it has a draw() method, which draws the sub's body, the tank, and the water level. See the code in sub.js.

The basic motion code

The rest of the code is a modification of the floating simulation floating-ball.js that we created back in Chapter 7. The main changes have to do with the visual effects and controls (they are described in the next section). The basic motion code, as implemented in the calcForce() method, is not actually very different from that in floating-ball.js. Here is the calcForce() method:

```
function calcForce(){
    var rheight = 0.5*sub.height;
    var ysub = sub.y + rheight;
    var dr = (ysub-yLevel)/rheight;
    var ratio; // volume fraction of object that is submerged
    if (dr <= -1){ // object completely out of water
        ratio = 0;
    }else if (dr < 1){ // object partially in water
        ratio = 0.5+0.5*dr; // for cuboid
    }else{ // object completely in water
        ratio = 1;
    }
    var gravity = Forces.constantGravity(sub.mass,g);
    var upthrust = Forces.upthrust(rho,V*ratio,g);
    var drag = Forces.drag(k*ratio,sub.velo2D);
    force = Forces.add([gravity, upthrust, drag, thrust]);
}
```

The variable dr is the fraction of the height of the sub that is submerged under the water level. The variable ratio is the volume fraction that is submerged (which determines the upthrust and drag on the sub) and depends on the shape of the sub in a complex way. Because this simulation is meant for a simple game, it makes sense to deal with it in an approximate way. So we simply treat the sub like a cuboid, in which case the volume ratio is equal to 0.5 + 0.5*dr as long as the value of dr is between 0 and 1. If dr is negative (in which case the sub is completely outside the water), ratio is set to zero. If dr is greater than 1 (in which case the sub is fully immersed), ratio is set to 1.

The variable ratio is used to adjust the upthrust and drag, and they are then added to the weight of the sub. There is a fourth force, thrust, that is added and that obviously did not appear in the floating-ball example of Chapter 7. This is a Vector2D variable whose value is set according to user interaction. So let's take a look at how the user controls the simulation.

Adding controls and visual effects

The aim is to control the submarine by means of the arrow keys on the keyboard. The right arrow will apply a forward thrust; the left arrow will apply a backward thrust; the down arrow will introduce water in the ballast tanks; and the up arrow will remove water from the ballast tanks and fill them with air. This is done via the following two event handlers, which respond to the keydown and keyup keyboard events, respectively:

```
function keydownListener(evt){
    if (evt.keyCode == 39) { // right arrow
        thrust = new Vector2D(thrustMag,0);
    } else if (evt.keyCode == 37) { // left arrow
        thrust = new Vector2D(-thrustMag,0);
    }
```

```
        if (evt.keyCode == 40) { // down arrow
            ballastInc = incMag;
        } else if (evt.keyCode == 38) { // up arrow
            ballastInc = -incMag;
        }
        window.addEventListener('keyup',keyupListener,false);
}
function keyupListener(evt){
        thrust = new Vector2D(0,0);
        ballastInc = 0;
        window.removeEventListener('keyup',keyupListener,false);
}
```

The variables thrustMag and incMag control the amount of thrust and the amount by which the water level is to be increased or decreased per timestep. The default values in the code are 20 and 0.01, respectively. The current values of thrust and water level increment are stored in the variables thrust and ballastInc, respectively. The thrust and water level increment are both reset to zero when the keys are up again.

The necessary visual changes are controlled by individual methods that are called at each timestep from the updateSub() method in the move() method:

```
function updateSub(){
        adjustBallast();
        updateInfo();
}
```

The adjustBallast() method increments the waterFraction variable, which keeps track of the amount of water in the ballast tank as a fraction of the amount when it is full. Obviously, that fraction cannot be made less than 0 or more than 1; hence the code also makes sure that never happens:

```
function adjustBallast(){
        if (ballastInc != 0){
            waterFraction += ballastInc;
            if (waterFraction < 0){
                waterFraction = 0;
            }
            if (waterFraction > 1){
                waterFraction = 1;
            }
            setWaterHeight();
        }
}
```

The final line of code in adjustBallast() calls a setWater() method, whose task it is to adjust the height of the water level and the mass of the sub as a result of the change in the mass of the water in the tank:

```
function setWaterHeight(){
        sub.waterHeight = sub.tankHeight*waterFraction;
        sub.mass = emptySubMass + waterMass*waterFraction;
}
```

The final method called from updateSub() is the updateInfo() method, which computes and displays the updated ratio of the density of the submarine to that of water:

```
function updateInfo(){
    var ratio = sub.mass/V/rho; // ratio of submarine density to water density
    ratio = Math.round(ratio*100)/100; // round to 2 d.p.
    var txt = "[sub density] / [water density] = ";
    txt = txt.concat(ratio.toString());
    context_fg.clearRect(0,0,700,100);
    context_fg.fillText(txt,20,20);
}
```

The full code

To show how everything fits together, we list here the full code of submarine.js:

```
var canvas = document.getElementById('canvas');
var context = canvas.getContext('2d');
var canvas_bg = document.getElementById('canvas_bg');
var context_bg = canvas_bg.getContext('2d');
var canvas_fg = document.getElementById('canvas_fg');
var context_fg = canvas_fg.getContext('2d');

var sub;
var g = 10;
var rho = 1;
var V = 1;
var k = 0.05;
var yLevel = 200;
var thrustMag = 20;
var thrust = new Vector2D(0,0);
var waterMass = 1;
var emptySubMass = 0.5;
var waterFraction = 0.4; // must be between 0 and 1
var ballastInc = 0; // ballast increment
var incMag = 0.01; // magnitude of the ballast increment
var t0, dt
var force, acc;
var animId;

window.onload = init;

function init() {
    // create the sky
    gradient = context_bg.createLinearGradient(0,0,0,yLevel);
    gradient.addColorStop(0,'#0066ff');
    gradient.addColorStop(1,'#ffffff');
    context_bg.fillStyle = gradient;
    context_bg.fillRect(0,0,canvas_bg.width,yLevel);
```

```
        // create the sea
        context_fg.fillStyle = "rgba(0,255,255,0.5)";
        context_fg.fillRect(0,yLevel,canvas.width,canvas.height);
        // create a sub
        sub = new Sub(160,60,'#0000ff',emptySubMass);
        sub.pos2D = new Vector2D(250,300);
        sub.velo2D = new Vector2D(40,-20);
        sub.draw(context);
        // set water height in sub
        setWaterHeight();
        // set up text formatting
        setupText();
        // set up event listener
        window.addEventListener('keydown',keydownListener,false);
        // initialize time and animate
        initAnim();
};
function setupText(){
        context_fg.font = "12pt Arial";
        context_fg.textAlign = "left";
        context_fg.textBaseline = "top";
}
function keydownListener(evt){
        if (evt.keyCode == 39) { // right arrow
            thrust = new Vector2D(thrustMag,0);
        } else if (evt.keyCode == 37) { // left arrow
            thrust = new Vector2D(-thrustMag,0);
        }
        if (evt.keyCode == 40) { // down arrow
            ballastInc = incMag;
        } else if (evt.keyCode == 38) { // up arrow
            ballastInc = -incMag;
        }
        window.addEventListener('keyup',keyupListener,false);
}
function keyupListener(evt){
        thrust = new Vector2D(0,0);
        ballastInc = 0;
        window.removeEventListener('keyup',keyupListener,false);
}

function initAnim(){
        t0 = new Date().getTime();
        animFrame();
}

function animFrame(){
        animId = requestAnimationFrame(animFrame,canvas);
        onTimer();
}
```

```
function onTimer(){
    var t1 = new Date().getTime();
    dt = 0.001*(t1-t0);
    t0 = t1;
    if (dt>0.2) {dt=0;};
    move();
}
function move(){
    updateSub();
    moveObject();
    calcForce();
    updateAccel();
    updateVelo();
}
function stop(){
    cancelAnimationFrame(animId);
}
function updateSub(){
    adjustBallast();
    updateInfo();
}
function adjustBallast(){
    if (ballastInc != 0){
        waterFraction += ballastInc;
        if (waterFraction < 0){
            waterFraction = 0;
        }
        if (waterFraction > 1){
            waterFraction = 1;
        }
        setWaterHeight();
    }
}
function setWaterHeight(){
    sub.waterHeight = sub.tankHeight*waterFraction;
    sub.mass = emptySubMass + waterMass*waterFraction;
}
function updateInfo(){
    var ratio = sub.mass/V/rho; // ratio of submarine density to water density
    ratio = Math.round(ratio*100)/100; // round to 2 d.p.
    var txt = "[sub density] / [water density] = ";
    txt = txt.concat(ratio.toString());
    context_fg.clearRect(0,0,700,100);
    context_fg.fillText(txt,20,20);
}
function moveObject(){
    sub.pos2D = sub.pos2D.addScaled(sub.velo2D,dt);
    context.clearRect(0, 0, canvas.width, canvas.height);
    sub.draw(context);
}
```

```
function calcForce(){
    var rheight = 0.5*sub.height;
    var ysub = sub.y + rheight;
    var dr = (ysub-yLevel)/rheight;
    var ratio; // volume fraction of object that is submerged
    if (dr <= -1){ // object completely out of water
        ratio = 0;
    }else if (dr < 1){ // object partially in water
        ratio = 0.5+0.5*dr; // for cuboid
    }else{ // object completely in water
        ratio = 1;
    }
    var gravity = Forces.constantGravity(sub.mass,g);
    var upthrust = Forces.upthrust(rho,V*ratio,g);
    var drag = Forces.drag(k*ratio,sub.velo2D);
    force = Forces.add([gravity, upthrust, drag, thrust]);
}
function updateAccel(){
    acc = force.multiply(1/sub.mass);
}
function updateVelo(){
    sub.velo2D = sub.velo2D.addScaled(acc,dt);
}
```

The submarine is now ready for a test drive! Have fun playing around and experimenting with the parameter values as you've done with examples throughout the book.

It's your turn

That wasn't too bad, was it? You now have a basic but functional submarine that you can add in a game. Now that it's in your hands, you can further develop it as you see fit. You can enhance the visual appearance of the sub, add scenery such as a nice background with aquatic creatures and plants, add bubbles, and so on. You could add a sea floor and handle contact with it using a normal force. It should also not be very difficult to convert this simulation to 3D. If you do that, you would, of course, also need to include code to handle rotation.

Building a flight simulator

This project is quite a bit more complicated than the preceding example because we'll be working in 3D, and also because the physics and operation of aircraft are fairly complex. Therefore, we'll need to spend a bit more time on theory before we can get to the coding.

Physics and control mechanisms of aircraft

There are two aspects of theory to understand in order to simulate aircraft flight. The first is the underlying physics, which includes an understanding of the forces and torques acting on the aircraft and how they affect the aircraft's motion. The second aspect is the mechanism by which aircraft control these forces and torques; this requires an understanding of the relevant parts of the aircraft and their associated maneuvers.

Forces on an aircraft

We discussed the forces that act on an airplane in Chapter 7: gravity, thrust, drag, and lift. Figure 16-3 shows a force diagram for a plane at an angle to the horizontal. This is a generalization of the force diagram shown in Figure 7-15, which was for the special case of an airplane in horizontal flight. Therefore, the directions of the thrust and drag are not necessarily horizontal, and the lift is not necessarily vertical. As a result, the force balance is a little more complex in this case. It is clearly important to get the magnitudes as well as the directions of these different forces right at all times (during ascent and descent, not just during horizontal flight), so we need robust equations for computing them in general.

Figure 16-3. *The four forces acting on an airplane during flight*

The force of gravity $\mathbf{W} = m\mathbf{g}$ still acts downward and is constant, of course; so that one is easy. The thrust $\mathbf{T}$, whether generated by a propeller or by a jet engine, will usually act along the axis of the plane in the forward direction (unless you are considering an aircraft model such as the Harrier, in which the direction of the thrust can be varied). The magnitude of the thrust depends on many factors such as engine type, engine efficiency, and altitude effects. In our simulation, we'll disregard all these effects, simply prescribing a value that can be changed by the user.

The drag and lift forces are more subtle. Strictly speaking, they are defined relative to the direction of the airflow over the relevant aircraft part such as the wing. Assuming there is no wind, we can approximate this as the direction of the aircraft's velocity. The drag force can then be defined as the component of the aerodynamic force (force exerted as a result of the airflow) that acts opposite to the aircraft's velocity. The lift force is the component perpendicular to the aircraft's velocity.

The drag formula is the same as that given in Chapter 7, in which $\mathbf{v}$ is now interpreted as the velocity of the aircraft:

$$\mathbf{F} = -\frac{1}{2}\rho\, A\, C_d\, v\, \mathbf{v}$$

The lift formula that we gave in Chapter 7 is generalized to the following formula, in which $\mathbf{k}$ is a unit vector perpendicular to the plane's velocity and oriented to point upward from the plane's wings:

$$\mathbf{F} = \frac{1}{2}\rho\, A\, C_L\, v^2\, \mathbf{k}$$

These are general formulas that need to be adapted once we look at the aircraft parts in more detail. In particular, the relevant areas for use in those equations should be defined. We also need to specify the drag and lift coefficients, which can vary depending on several factors.

Torques on an aircraft: rotation

The forces on an aircraft are not sufficient to compute its motion. As you know, the resultant force determines the translational motion, but these forces can also exert torques if their lines of action do not pass through the center of mass. The weight of an object acts through a point known as its *center of gravity*. In uniform gravitational fields such as near the surface of the Earth (and an airplane is near enough the Earth's surface for that purpose), the center of gravity coincides with the center of mass. Therefore, the weight of an airplane never generates a torque. However, the drag and lift forces act through a point known as the *center of pressure*. This is a similar concept to that of center of gravity, but it depends on the shape and inclination of the airplane, and does not in general coincide with its center of mass. So it can produce a torque that can send the aircraft spinning if unbalanced. An aircraft therefore needs to have stability mechanisms in place to balance this torque.

Of course, you do sometimes want an airplane to rotate. Figure 16-4 shows three ways in which an airplane can rotate about its center of mass and the axes about which it does so. It can *pitch* by moving its nose and tail up and down; it can *roll* by moving its wing tips up and down; and it can *yaw* by moving its nose and tail sideways. The axes are defined relative to the shape of the aircraft, and they all pass through its center of gravity. The *pitch axis* is oriented in a direction parallel to the wingspan, the *roll axis* is along the length of the aircraft, and the *yaw axis* is perpendicular to the other two axes. An aircraft is designed so that it has special parts that can produce these types of motion by controlling the lift and drag forces. Let's look at those now.

Figure 16-4. *Pitch, roll, and yaw*

Aircraft parts and controls

Aircraft can control their motion by modifying the thrust, drag, and lift forces acting on them. This section briefly describes the parts of an aircraft that do this and how they do it. The thrust is controlled by the engine (which can be of different types, such as propeller or jet) and will propel the plane forward. Figure 16-5 shows a schematic of an airplane emphasizing those parts that are relevant to drag and lift and their control.

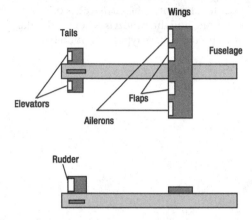

Figure 16-5. *Aircraft parts*

Fixed "main" parts include these:

- **Fuselage**: This is the main body of the aircraft. It is responsible for much of the drag. It also creates lift and pitching torque, but only for large angles of inclination, and they can usually be neglected. It can also create yawing torque for large lateral inclination; again this can usually be neglected.

- **Wings**: The two wings of an aircraft contribute most of the lift and drag forces on it. Without wings, an airplane just wouldn't fly. The center of pressure of the lift and drag forces on the main wings is close to the center of mass, so one can assume that they contribute no torque, just like the fuselage. However, they have movable parts called flaps and ailerons that can be maneuvered to modify the lift and drag force and generate rolling torque.

- **Tails**: The tails consist of two parts: a horizontal and a vertical tail, which help in maintaining horizontal and vertical stability of the airplane. They also have movable parts called elevators and rudders that generate pitching and yawing torques.

Movable "control" parts include the following:

- **Flaps**: Flaps are attached to the rear of the wings and are rotated downward during takeoff and landing to increase the lift force (and also the drag force during landing to slow down the fast-moving aircraft).

- **Ailerons**: Ailerons are also attached to the rear of the wing, but farther along toward the wing tips. Rotating an aileron downward increases the lift, and rotating it upward decreases the lift. The two ailerons are rotated in opposite directions to produce a rolling torque (couple). Because the ailerons are far from the center of mass, large torques can be produced by relatively small changes in lift on either side of the wings (recall that moment = force × distance). Ailerons are usually controlled by a control stick; moving the stick to the right or left causes the aircraft to roll to the right or left.

- **Elevators**: Elevators are hinged to the rear side of the horizontal tail. Unlike ailerons, the elevators move together (both upward or both downward), thereby generating a pitching torque. Elevators are controlled by moving a stick forward to raise the nose of the aircraft and moving the stick backward to cause the aircraft nose to dip.

- **Rudder**: The rudder is attached to the rear of the vertical tail fin. It can rotate to either side, causing a yawing torque. The rudder is controlled by two foot pedals so that depressing the left or right pedal moves the aircraft's nose to the left or right, respectively.

Airfoil geometry and angle of attack

The shape and inclination of aircraft wings are important factors that determine the magnitude of lift. Figure 16-6 shows the shape of a cross-section of a wing, called an *airfoil*. The shape of an airfoil is usually rounded at the front and sharp at the rear. The line joining the centers of curvature of the front and rear edges is called the *chord line*.

Figure 16-6. *Flow over an aircraft wing (airfoil)*

The angle between the chord line and the incident air flow (which is generally along the velocity of the plane) is called the *angle of attack*, usually denoted by the Greek letter α. The drag and lift coefficients of an airfoil depend on the angle of attack, and flight models generally use experimental data or a simple function to evaluate those coefficients as a function of angle of attack.

Takeoff and landing

An airplane can take off only if its velocity exceeds a certain threshold. That threshold value corresponds to the point at which the lift force balances the weight of the plane. In that case, you can equate the expressions for the lift force and the weight:

$$\frac{1}{2} \rho A C_L v^2 = mg$$

You can then rearrange this formula to give a formula for the velocity, which is the threshold velocity for takeoff:

$$v = \sqrt{\frac{2mg}{\rho A C_L}}$$

During landing you have the opposite problem. You don't want the velocity with which the plane touches the ground to be too high; otherwise, the plane will crash. You can set a reasonable threshold velocity in your game or simulation. Another consideration during landing is that the pitch angle must be zero or slightly positive; otherwise, the nose of the plane will hit the ground.

Turning

Turning is achieved by banking to give a horizontal *unbalanced* component of the lift force that, because it is always perpendicular to the velocity, generates a centripetal force that makes the plane move in a circle (see Figure 16-7). Banking is achieved by rolling the plane using the ailerons. The yawing motion produced by a rudder is not used for turning, but for aligning the plane in the direction of the velocity.

Figure 16-7. *Force diagram for a banked plane*

What we will create

The simulation we will create will include the essential physics needed to make an airplane fly, with the ability to undergo the different types of motion (straight flight, pitch, roll, and yaw) and maneuvers (takeoff, landing, and turning) discussed. The user will be able to control a very simple airplane model using the keyboard, in a similar way to a pilot controlling an airplane. The operation of the elevators, ailerons, and rudder in creating pitching, rolling, and yawing torque will be simulated. The user can also adjust the amount of thrust. For simplicity we won't include flaps—however, they can easily be added.

Creating the visual setup

The visual setup is minimalist, consisting of just the ground and a very simple airplane model represented with a cuboid. The code is in the file airplane.js and the init() method looks like this:

```
function init() {
    setupObjects();
    setupOrientation();
    setupText();
    renderer.render(scene,camera);
    window.addEventListener('keydown',startControl,false);
    t0 = new Date().getTime();
    animFrame();
}
```

The first two methods setupObjects() and setupOrientation() are responsible for creating the display objects and initializing the airplane's orientation respectively. Let's look at setupObjects() first:

```
function setupObjects(){
    renderer = new THREE.WebGLRenderer({clearColor: 0xff0000, clearAlpha: 1});
    renderer.setClearColor( 0x82caff, 1);
    renderer.setSize(width, height);
    document.body.appendChild(renderer.domElement);

    scene = new THREE.Scene();

    var angle = 45, aspect = width/height, near = 0.1, far = 10000;
    camera = new THREE.PerspectiveCamera(angle, aspect, near, far);
    camera.position.set(100,0,1000);
    scene.add(camera);

    var light = new THREE.DirectionalLight();
    light.position.set(30,0,30);
    scene.add(light);

    var geom = new THREE.PlaneGeometry(5000, 100000, 50, 500);
    var wireframeMat = new THREE.MeshBasicMaterial();
    wireframeMat.wireframe = true;
    var ground = new THREE.Mesh(geom, wireframeMat);
    ground.rotation.x = -Math.PT/2;
    ground.position.set(0,groundLevel,0);
    scene.add(ground);

    airplane = new THREE.Mesh(new THREE.CubeGeometry(400, 100, 100), new
THREE.MeshNormalMaterial());
    airplane.overdraw = true;
    scene.add(airplane);
    airplane.mass = massAirplane;
    airplane.pos = new Vector3D(0,200,0);
    airplane.velo = new Vector3D(0,0,0);
    airplane.angVelo = new Vector3D(0,0,0);
}
```

The "ground" is created using PlaneGeometry with MeshBasicMaterial and a wireframe option, and is rotated around the x-axis by 90 degrees. The airplane is created using CubeGeometry and is given a mass, a position vector, a velocity vector, and an angular velocity. The moment of inertia of the airplane is specified in the variable I, which is initialized in the list of variables at the beginning of the code. As discussed in the previous chapter, the moment of inertia is a 3 × 3 matrix in 3D. Here we consider the inertia matrix to consist of only three diagonal components: Ixx, Iyy, and Izz, the other components of the matrix being taken to be zero. In order to implement the required matrix algebra (see the following section on "Coding up the physics") we have coded a very simple Matrix3D object that creates a 3 × 3 matrix by considering each row of the matrix as a Vector3D object. Matrix3D therefore takes three Vector3D arguments in its constructor. We have endowed Matrix3D with two methods, multiply() and scaleBy(), which multiply it with a Vector3D object and a scalar, respectively. See the code in the file matrix3D.js for the detailed implementation.

Note that the airplane is created such that it is initially oriented with its length along the *x*-axis. In the simulation, we'll want it to point along the –*z*-axis so that it flies into the screen. To achieve this, the setupOrientation() method rotates the plane by 90 degrees about the *y*-axis:

```
function setupOrientation(){
    // initialize airplane orientation
    var qRotate = new THREE.Quaternion();
    qRotate.setFromAxisAngle(new THREE.Vector3( 0, 1, 0 ), Math.PI/2);
    airplane.quaternion.multiply(qRotate);

    // airplane local axes
    ix = new Vector3D(1,0,0);
    iy = new Vector3D(0,1,0);
    iz = new Vector3D(0,0,1);
}
```

We also define three vectors ix, iy, and iz to represent the airplane's three axes in its own frame of reference. These will be needed for calculating the lift forces and torques on the airplane in calcForce(). Referring to Figure 16-4, these axes correspond to the roll, yaw and pitch axes respectively. They are defined relative to the airplane, and will therefore change relative to the ground, in so-called "world frame."

Coding up the physics

The animation loop is set up by a call to the animFrame() method in init(). This produces calls to familiar methods such as moveObject(), calcForce(), updateAccel(), and updateVelo(), which handle the updating of both the translational and rotational motion of the airplane as in previous examples. In addition there is a controlRotation() method that applies a bit of a hack to impose stability on the airplane's rotational motion, preventing it from spinning out of control. In reality, the stability mechanism is quite complex, and would be rather difficult to implement properly. So we cheat a little in controlRotation(), simply applying a damping factor to the plane's angular velocity.

The guts of the code consist of the calculation of the forces and torques on the airplane, which is done in the calcForce() method. This looks quite complicated at first sight, but it will make sense when you go through it step by step. We have also included plenty of comments in the downloadable source file; some of them are included in the following listings. Let us list the whole of calcForce() before discussing it:

```
function calcForce(obj){
    // *** rotate airplane velocity vector to airplane's frame ***
    var q = new THREE.Quaternion;
    q.copy(airplane.quaternion);
    var rvelo = rotateVector(obj.velo,q);

    // *** forces on whole plane ***
    force = new Vector3D(0,0,0);
    var drag = Forces3D.drag(kDrag,rvelo);
    force = force.add(drag);
    var thrust = new Vector3D(-thrustMag,0,0); // thrust is assumed along roll axis
    force = force.add(thrust);

    // *** torques on whole plane ***
    torque = new Vector3D(0,0,0); // gravity, drag and thrust don't have torques
```

```
    // *** lift forces and torques on wings and control surfaces ***
    if (rvelo.length() > 0){ // no lift if velocity is zero
        var viXY = new Vector3D(rvelo.x,rvelo.y,0); // velocity in the airplane xy plane
        var viZX = new Vector3D(rvelo.x,0,rvelo.z); // velocity in the airplane xz plane

        // *** calculate angle of attack and lateral angle ***
        calcAlphaBeta(rvelo);

        // *** Wing ***
        // force: lift on the Wing; no overall torque
        var liftW = liftforce(viXY,iz,areaWing,clift(alphaWing+alpha));
        force = force.add(liftW);

        // *** Ailerons ***
        // force: ailerons; form a couple, so no net force
        var liftAl = liftforce(viXY,iz,areaAileron,clift(alphaAl));
        var torqueAl = (iz.multiply(distAlToCM*2)).crossProduct(liftAl); // T = r x F
        torque = torque.add(torqueAl);

        // *** Elevators ***
        // force: horizontal tail (elevators)
        var liftEl = liftforce(viXY,iz,areaElevator,clift(alphaEl));
        torqueEl = (ix.multiply(-distTlToCM)).crossProduct(liftEl);  // T = r x liftHt;
        force = force.add(liftEl);
        torque = torque.add(torqueEl);

        // *** Rudder ***
        // force: vertical tail (rudder)
        var liftRd = liftforce(viZX,iy.multiply(-1),areaRudder,clift(alphaRd+beta));
        torqueRd = (ix.multiply(-distTlToCM)).crossProduct(liftRd); // T = r x liftVt
        force = force.add(liftRd);
        torque = torque.add(torqueRd);
    }

    // *** rotate force back to world frame ***
    force = rotateVector(force,q.conjugate());

    // *** add gravity ***
    var gravity = Forces3D.constantGravity(massAirplane,g);
    force = force.add(gravity);
}
```

A key feature of this simulation is that most of the force and moment calculations are performed in the airplane's frame of reference. So we begin by rotating the airplane's velocity vector into the airplane's frame by applying the rotateVector() method, which makes use of the applyQuaternion() method in three.js. The drag force is then computed as opposite to this rotated velocity vector. The drag force is computed assuming a constant drag coefficient. This is a simplification; generally, the drag coefficient will depend on the angle of attack, but this dependence is not modeled here for simplicity. The thrust is applied in the direction of the plane's ix (roll) axis, and its magnitude is controlled by the user by updating the thrustMag variable (as will be described later). The net torque due to these forces is assumed to be zero so that the plane maintains rotational equilibrium.

The next section of code computes the lift forces on the various surfaces of the airplane (wings, ailerons, elevators and rudder) and the moments produced by these forces. Because the lift force is zero if the plane is not moving, the whole calculation is only done if the plane's velocity is non-zero. The lift forces consist of vertical lift on the wings, elevators, and ailerons and of horizontal lift on the rudder. They depend on the velocities in the xy and xz planes relative to the airplane. These velocities are therefore calculated first. Then they are used to compute the angle of attack α and lateral angle β (the angle between the x and z components of the plane's velocity) in the calcAlphaBeta() function. Note that we are here assuming that there is no wind. It would be straightforward to add in the effect of the wind, but that would only complicate the code further.

Next, the lift force on the wings is calculated. The cross product is used because the lift force on the wings is perpendicular to the velocity in the xy plane and the wing axis (the pitch axis). The lift coefficient is calculated assuming a linear dependence on the angle of attack, with a constant gradient $dC_L/d\alpha$:

$$C_L = \left(\frac{dC_L}{d\alpha}\right)\alpha$$

Note that we add the inclination of the wing relative to the plane's roll axis (alphWing) to the value of α calculated previously to obtain the actual angle of attack. We also impose a limiting value on the lift force because in reality the lift force does not increase indefinitely with the angle of attack, but reaches a maximum value. The lift coefficient is calculated in the clift() function and the lift force in liftforce().

The lift force on the main wings is assumed to generate no torque when the plane is in equilibrium, just like drag and thrust (or, more accurately, the combined torques of these forces are made to cancel out in practice).

The next blocks of code compute the lift forces on the movable control surfaces (elevators, ailerons, and rudder) and the torques they generate. The lift calculation is done in the same way as for the main wings. The torques are calculated as usual by taking the cross product of the distance vector of the lift force from the center of mass and the lift force:

$$\mathbf{T} = \mathbf{r} \times \mathbf{F}$$

The appropriate distance vector needs to be specified for each control surface.

After all the lift forces are added to the force vector, the latter is then rotated back to the world frame and the gravity is added as a constant downward force. The subsequent calculation of the acceleration and velocity updates are then performed in the world frame as usual.

Note that the angular motion calculation is done in the airplane's frame throughout the code. Here we have to be a little careful in how we apply the angular equation of motion (that is, the relationship between torque and angular acceleration). Because the airplane is in a rotating frame of reference, the latter has an additional term, and looks like this (see the section "Torque, angular acceleration, and the moment of inertia matrix" in Chapter 15):

$$\mathbf{T} = \mathbf{I}\alpha + \omega \times (\mathbf{I}\omega)$$

Recall that this is a matrix equation, with the moment of inertia $\mathbf{I}$ being a 3×3 matrix and the torque $\mathbf{T}$, angular velocity ω, and angular acceleration $\alpha = d\omega/dt$ being vectors. This equation can be easily manipulated to give a matrix equation for the angular acceleration:

$$\alpha = \mathbf{I}^{-1}\left[\mathbf{T} - \omega \times (\mathbf{I}\omega)\right]$$

Here $\mathbf{I}^{-1}$ is the inverse of the moment of inertia matrix. This equation can be discretized using a forward scheme and implemented in code as shown in the bold lines in the following listing of the updateAccel() method:

```
function updateAccel(obj){
    acc = force.multiply(1/obj.mass);
    var omega = obj.angVelo;
    alp = Iinv.multiply(torque.subtract(omega.crossProduct(I.multiply(omega))));
}
```

The inverse moment of inertia matrix Iinv is precomputed in the code from the specified components of the moment of inertia matrix I.

Finally, the airplane's orientation and position are updated in moveObject():

```
function moveObject(obj){
    var p = new THREE.Quaternion;
    p.set(obj.angVelo.x*dt/2,obj.angVelo.y*dt/2,obj.angVelo.z*dt/2,1);
    obj.quaternion.multiply(p);
    obj.quaternion.normalize();
    obj.pos = obj.pos.addScaled(obj.velo,dt);
    positionObject(obj);
    positionCamera(obj);
    renderer.render(scene,camera);
}
```

Note also the addition of the new positionCamera() method in moveObject(), which controls the camera position and movement, and which you are welcome to customize.

Implementing the controls

In the init() method an event listener is set up for keydown events. The airplane is controlled by using the arrow, X, and Z keys to control the elevators, ailerons, and rudder; and the spacebar and Enter key to control the thrust. This is done in the startControl() event listener. (We won't list the code here because it's quite straightforward.) The down-arrow key increases the pitch, raising the airplane's nose upward, and the up key lowers it. The left- and right-arrow keys make the plane roll to the left and right, respectively. These movements are similar to the way the control stick is used by a pilot to control the elevators and ailerons. The rudder is controlled using the X and Z keys. The maximum angles and increments for these movable parts are set at the beginning of the program. The thrust magnitude is increased and decreased by pressing the spacebar and Enter keys, respectively. Again, the maximum magnitude of the thrust and its increment are set at the beginning of the code.

The camera position is controlled by pressing the A key to follow the airplane or the W key to remain at a fixed point in the world frame. Finally, pressing the Esc key stops the simulation.

Displaying flight information

The updateInfo() method, called at each timestep from the onTimer() method, contains code to write text on a separate canvas element as the simulation progresses. Information is displayed about the airplane's altitude, vertical velocity, and horizontal velocity as well as the aileron, elevator, and rudder angles. The first two pieces of information are important to bear in mind when you are trying to keep the plane in flight without crashing it. A positive vertical velocity means that the plane is rising; if the vertical velocity is negative, it is losing altitude, so you better watch out.

You can easily add additional information such as the current position of the airplane (useful if you want to go somewhere).

Test flying the simulator

The airplane is now ready to fly! Run it with the default parameter values. When the simulation starts, the plane will have an initial velocity of zero, but there is an applied thrust. If you don't do anything, the airplane will initially fall under gravity, and then start rising as the applied thrust increases its horizontal velocity and hence provides lift. Increase the thrust by pressing and holding down the spacebar. Then increase the elevators' angle by pressing the down-arrow key. You will see the plane gradually rising as it moves forward. Then decrease the pitch angle by pressing the up-arrow key, which will reduce the lift and decrease the ascent of the plane, or even make it descend. See if you can make the airplane rise up to a given altitude and remain there. To do that you need to play with the thrust and/or the pitch angle, and you need to make the vertical velocity reach close to zero at your desired altitude. Once you've achieved that, you can sit back and relax; the plane will take care of itself.

Restart the simulation and try out the aileron and rudder controls. Note that the plane turns when the plane rolls, just as described in the "Turning" section. Too much rolling or yawing might make the airplane behave somewhat unpredictably, though. See also the detailed comments included in the source code. Figure 16-8 shows a screenshot of the simulation with the plane in flight.

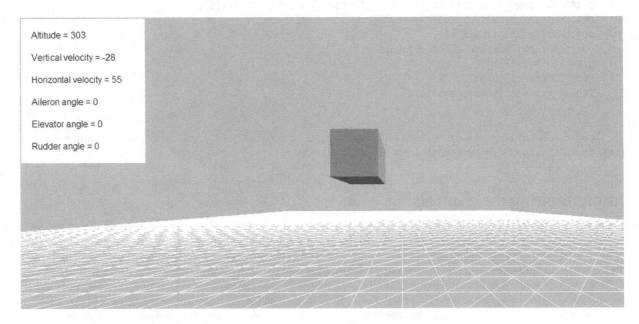

Figure 16-8. *The airplane in flight*

It's your turn

You probably already have several ideas about how to improve this simulator. Creating a much more impressive 3D model airplane is probably one of them, and possibly more visually appealing scenery, too. You could go much further with the 3D effects, and also incorporate a more extensive terrain, which could be either generated or based on real aerial information. You could also improve the control of the airplane by adding flaps, include visual elements in the model to represent the control surfaces, add crash scenarios, and so on. You probably have even better ideas of your own!

Creating an accurate solar system model

This project will be somewhat different from most of the examples in the book. The aim here is to create an accurate computer model of the solar system that could be used as an e-learning tool for students. The key word here is *accurate*: the visual and animation effects are less important than the correctness of the physics and the accuracy of the simulation. Consequently, we will depart from our usual animation framework and adopt a somewhat different coding approach from the outset that will reflect the simulation rather than the animation aspect of the project.

What we will create

Our aim is to create a scale model of the solar system that includes the Sun and the planets. In the supplied source code we include the innermost four planets (Mercury, Venus, Earth, and Mars)—the so-called *terrestrial planets*. We leave it as an exercise for you to add the other four (Jupiter, Saturn, Uranus and Neptune)—the so-called *gas giants*. This should be easy to do, and will give you valuable hands-on experience with the code.

Note that Pluto is no longer classified as a planet. In the simulation we'll pretend that smaller celestial bodies like these do not exist, including asteroids and moons. We can omit them because their effects on the motion of the planets are pretty negligible.

The project will proceed in different stages:

- **Step 1**: First, we'll set up a simulation loop using the fourth-order Runge-Kutta scheme (RK4, introduced in Chapter 14) in 3D, which we'll test with a simple example. The source code for this is in the file rk4test3d.js.

- **Step 2**: Second, we'll use that simulation loop to model the motion of a single planet in a simple idealized way. The source code for that step is in the file single-planet.js.

- **Step 3**: Third, we will include the four inner planets and set their properties and initial conditions based on mean astronomical data, so that we'll end up with a reasonably realistic solar system model (or rather half of it). We'll also need to set up appropriate scales carefully. The corresponding file is named solar-system-basic.js.

- **Step 4**: Fourth, in the file solar-system.js, we will include accurate initial conditions and run the simulation for a year.

- **Step 5**: Fifth, in solar-system-nasa.js we'll compare the results with corresponding simulation data from NASA to see how good our simulation is.

- **Step 6**: Finally, in solar-system-animated.js, we'll introduce some basic animation to make the simulation more visually appealing.

The physics

The simulation will involve modeling the motion of each planet under the action of the combined gravitational force exerted on it by the Sun and the other planets. The effect of the Sun will, of course, be much larger because of its very large mass compared with those of any of the planets. We'll adopt a coordinate system in which the Sun is fixed, so that we don't have to model the motion of the Sun itself. The planets will be able to move in 3D space under the action of those forces.

Let m be the mass of a planet, $\mathbf{r}_i$ its position vector relative to each of the other planets and the Sun (with $\mathbf{r}_i^u$ being the corresponding unit vector), and m_i the mass of each of the other planets and the Sun. Then the total force on each planet is given by the following formula:

$$\mathbf{F} = \sum_i -G \frac{m_i\, m}{r_i^2}\, \mathbf{r}_i^u$$

Dividing by the mass, we obtain the acceleration of each planet:

$$\mathbf{a} = \sum_i -G \frac{m_i}{r_i^2} \mathbf{r}_i^{\,u}$$

This is the equation that the numerical integration code will solve. That's it. The physics of this problem is pretty simple! But there are other issues that make the simulation nontrivial: implementing an accurate numerical integration scheme, scaling the model properly, and incorporating accurate initial conditions. We'll handle each of these requirements one step at a time.

Coding up an appropriate integration scheme

Because accuracy is our prime concern, it makes complete sense to use the RK4 integration method. To implement RK4, we'll first create a simple "simulation loop" that will do the timestepping, but we'll do that independently of the "animation loop" that we've been using so far. It's easier to do this than to explain it, so let's just do it and we'll explain afterward.

We borrow the RK4 code from the examples in Chapter 14 and modify it to come up with the following code, which is in the file rk4test3d.js:

```
var dt = 0.05;
var numSteps = 20;
var t = 0;
var g = 10;
var v = new Vector3D(0,0,0);
var s = new Vector3D(0,0,0);

window.onload = init;

function init(){
    simulate();
}
function simulate(){
    console.log(t,s.y);
    for (var i=0; i<numSteps; i++){
        t += dt;
        RK4();
        console.log(t,s.y);
    }
}
function RK4(){
    // step 1
    var pos1 = s;
    var vel1 = v;
    var acc1 = getAcc(pos1,vel1);
    // step 2
    var pos2 = pos1.addScaled(vel1,dt/2);
    var vel2 = vel1.addScaled(acc1,dt/2);
    var acc2 = getAcc(pos2,vel2);
    // step 3
```

```
        var pos3 = pos1.addScaled(vel2,dt/2);
        var vel3 = vel1.addScaled(acc2,dt/2);
        var acc3 = getAcc(pos3,vel3);
        // step 4
        var pos4 = pos1.addScaled(vel3,dt);
        var vel4 = vel1.addScaled(acc3,dt);
        var acc4 = getAcc(pos4,vel4);
        // sum vel and acc
        var velsum = vel1.addScaled(vel2,2).addScaled(vel3,2).addScaled(vel4,1);
        var accsum = acc1.addScaled(acc2,2).addScaled(acc3,2).addScaled(acc4,1);
        // update pos and velo
        s = pos1.addScaled(velsum,dt/6);
        v = vel1.addScaled(accsum,dt/6);
        //acc = accsum.multiply(1/6);
}
function getAcc(ppos,pvel){
        return new Vector3D(0,g,0);
}
```

Okay, let's start with the familiar. As stated earlier, the RK4() method is a modification of the RK4() method that we first saw in Chapter 14. If you compare the two versions, you will notice one crucial difference: this code deals with the current position and velocity through abstract variables s and v, instead of actual particle position and velocity properties as before. This is the first sign of the separation of the animation aspect from the simulation.

The getAcc() method that previously invoked calcForce() has been simplified here to simply return a constant acceleration vector pointing downward in the y direction. That means here we are specializing the code to a simple gravity problem. The other remaining piece of code is the simulate() method, which is called once upon initialization. The core of the code is incredibly simple. It is the following for loop that does all the timestepping, incrementing the current time and calling the RK4() method, which updates the position and velocity vectors s and v at each timestep:

```
for (var i=0; i<numSteps; i++){
    t += dt;
    RK4();
}
```

From an animation perspective, this code and the associated timestepping will execute all in one go: effectively we'll be precomputing the motion before doing any animation of existing display objects. There isn't even a display object in this code. The advantage of doing this is that it "decouples" the simulation loop from the animation loop (if there's going to be one), so that either can do its job unhindered by any time delays introduced by the other. However, this approach doesn't work if your simulation needs to be interactive.

Looking at how the variables are initialized, we can see that we are simulating the fall of an object from rest (v is initially zero) under gravity for one time unit (because dt * numSteps = 0.05 × 20 = 1). For example, choosing units of seconds for dt and m/s² for g, this corresponds to letting an object fall from rest for 1 second under gravity with g equal to 10 m/s². Using the formula $s = ut + \frac{1}{2}at^2$ then tells us that the object falls a distance of 5 m in that time. In the code, we output to the console the pair of values t and s.y at each timestep, which tells us how far the object has fallen at each time. Run the code and you'll find that the final distance is indeed 5. You can try different timesteps (adjusting the number of steps accordingly) and you'll find that RK4 is doing a pretty good job, pretty much whatever the timestep. For example, even with a timestep of 0.5 and with 2 steps (so that the duration is still 1 time unit), it still gives exactly 5!

Now that we've got a good integrator and a basic simulation loop set up, we're ready to move on and create something closer to a planetary system.

Building an idealized single-planet simulation

It is straightforward to modify the basic RK4 simulator we just created to simulate a planetary orbit: you essentially have to modify the getAcc() method according to Newton's $1/r^2$ formula for gravitational force and choose appropriate initial conditions for s and v. But we also want to see something on the canvas! So, with a little help from three.js, we also add a sun and a planet using sphereGeometry, and include some code that will show us how their positions change with time. The result is the following code, saved as single-planet.js:

```
var width = window.innerWidth, height = window.innerHeight;
var dt = 0.05;
var numSteps = 2500;
var animFreq = 40;
var t = 0;
var v = new Vector3D(5,0,14);
var s = new Vector3D(0,250,0);
var center = new Vector3D(0,0,0);
var G = 10;
var massSun = 5000;
var scene, camera, renderer;
var sun, planet;

window.onload = init;

function init(){
    setupObjects();
    simulate();
    renderer.render(scene, camera);
}
function setupObjects(){
    renderer = new THREE.WebGLRenderer();
    renderer.setSize(width, height);
    document.body.appendChild(renderer.domElement);

    scene = new THREE.Scene();

    var angle = 45, aspect = width/height, near = 0.1, far = 10000;
    camera = new THREE.PerspectiveCamera(angle, aspect, near, far);
    camera.position.set(0,0,1000);
    scene.add(camera);

    var light = new THREE.DirectionalLight();
    light.position.set(-10,0,20);
    scene.add(light);

    var radius = 80, segments = 20, rings = 20;
    var sphereGeometry = new THREE.SphereGeometry(radius,segments,rings);
    var sphereMaterial = new THREE.MeshLambertMaterial({color: 0xffff00});
    sun = new THREE.Mesh(sphereGeometry,sphereMaterial);
    scene.add(sun);
```

```
        sun.mass = massSun;
        sun.pos = center;
        positionObject(sun);

        var sphereGeometry = new THREE.SphereGeometry(radius/10,segments,rings);
        var sphereMaterial = new THREE.MeshLambertMaterial({color: 0x0099ff});
        planet = new THREE.Mesh(sphereGeometry,sphereMaterial);
        scene.add(planet);
        planet.mass = 1;
        planet.pos = s;
        positionObject(planet);
}
function positionObject(obj){
        obj.position.set(obj.pos.x,obj.pos.y,obj.pos.z);
}
function simulate(){
        for (var i=0; i<numSteps; i++){
                t += dt;
                RK4();
                if (i%animFreq==0){
                        clonePlanet(planet);
                }
        }
}
function clonePlanet(){
        var p = planet.clone();
        scene.add(p);
        p.pos = s;
        positionObject(p);
}
function getAcc(ppos,pvel){
        var r = ppos.subtract(center);
        return r.multiply(-G*massSun/(r.lengthSquared()*r.length()));
}
function RK4(){
        // code as in previous example
}
```

The first novel piece of code is in the setupObjects() method, which implements the three.js functionality and creates the sun and planets. Note that the rendering is done just once, at the end in the init() method, after setupObjects() and simulate() have executed. We have added an if block of code in the simulate() function that calls a clonePlanet() method at intervals of animFreq. The clonePlanet() method creates a copy of the planet and places it at the new position. The net result is a series of cloned planets at locations where the planet has been after equal amounts of time (see Figure 16-9). Not quite "animation," because if you run the code you will see everything displayed at once, but it does convey some sense of stepping through time. This is a planetary trajectory in 3D; you can see the perspective effect causing the planet to appear smaller when its z-coordinate is greater. In terms of the physics, the most significant modification is that the getAcc() method now applies an acceleration due to the sun's attraction on the planet. This produces the orbit that we see in Figure 16-9.

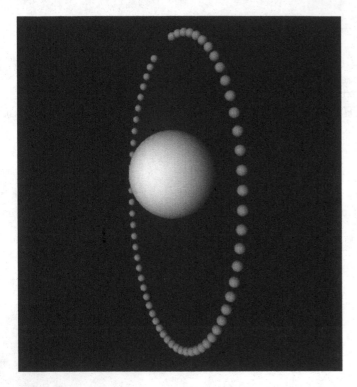

Figure 16-9. *A planetary trajectory in 3D*

Choosing appropriate scaling factors

Now that we have an accurate orbit simulator, it's time to represent the real solar system to scale as the next step toward a realistic simulation. To do this, we need to go back to the governing equation. For the purpose of choosing appropriate scaling factors, it is the form of the equation that matters instead of the details of the various terms. So it will be fine to consider only the portion of the equation reflecting the effect of the sun. Also, it's the magnitude of the relevant quantities that matters, not their direction. The last equation therefore leads to the following approximate equation for the acceleration of each planet, in which M_s is the mass of the Sun and r is the distance of the planet from it:

$$\frac{d^2s}{dt^2} = G\frac{M_s}{r^2}$$

We now define scaling factors for time, distance, and mass in a similar way to the example in the previous chapter:

$$s = \lambda\,\hat{s} \qquad t = \tau\,\hat{t} \qquad m = \mu\,\hat{m}$$

Substituting these factors into the previous equation and rearranging gives the following corresponding equation in terms of the rescaled variables:

$$\frac{d^2\hat{s}}{d\hat{t}^2} = \left(\frac{G\mu\tau^2}{\lambda^3}\right)\frac{\hat{M}_s}{\hat{r}^2}$$

Comparing the two equations then tells us that the value of the gravitational constant G in the rescaled system is given by this:

$$\hat{G} = \frac{G\mu\tau^2}{\lambda^3}$$

We now need to choose appropriate scaling factors μ, τ, and λ for the base units for converting quantities from the usual SI units to corresponding simulation units. In any given problem a sensible choice for the scaling factors should reflect scales relevant to the physics. In this case, for example, it makes no sense to think of mass values in terms of kg but instead in terms of the mass of the Sun or the mass of the Earth. Let's choose the latter. Similarly, it makes little sense to stick with the second as a unit of time, because we will be interested in seeing the planets complete at least one revolution around the Sun (the duration of the simulation will be on the order of years). Therefore, we'll choose 1 day as the unit of time. Finally, we could choose the mean distance of the Earth from the Sun (known as an *astronomical unit* or *au*) as the distance unit. That's about 150 million km, or 150×10^9 m. This would make the distance between the Earth and the Sun 1 unit in the simulation by definition. However, because we are building a visual simulation, we'll be thinking of distance in terms of pixels and want to see the Earth a decent number of pixels away from the Sun. A more suitable choice of scaling factor in that case is 1 million km (10^9 m) per pixel, which would make the Earth-Sun distance around 150 pixels. Table 16-1 summarizes these choices of scaling factors.

Table 16-1. *Scaling Factors for Base Units*

Scaling factor	Value
μ (mass)	Earth mass = 5.9736×10^{24} kg
τ (time)	Earth day = 86400 s
λ (length)	1 million km = 10^9 m

Scaling factors for derived quantities such as velocity can be worked out from those of the base quantities. For example, the scale factor for velocity is given by λ/τ.

Obtaining planetary data and initial conditions

Next we need to obtain some planetary data such as the masses of the planets and some suitable values for the initial conditions (planets' positions and velocities). This web page from NASA's web site has all the required information: http://nssdc.gsfc.nasa.gov/planetary/planetfact.html.

For easy access, we have saved some of the data that we'll be using as static constants in the Astro object. This includes, for example, the constants EARTH_MASS, EARTH_RADIUS, EARTH_ORBITAL_RADIUS, and EARTH_ORBITAL_VELOCITY and similar constants for other planets. Take a look at the file astro.js. There is a related class called Phys, in the file phys.js, which contains values of a few physical constants such as the gravitational constant G (GRAVITATIONAL_CONSTANT) and the standard value of the acceleration due to gravity on Earth (STANDARD_GRAVITY). These values were obtained from the following web page on the NIST web site: http://physics.nist.gov/cuu/Constants/.

The values of the mean orbital radius and the orbital velocity of the planets in the Astro object will be used as approximate initial conditions in the basic version of the solar system model that we will construct next.

Creating a basic solar system model

We are now ready to put together a basic solar system model that will include all the essential aspects of the simulation. The relevant file, `solar-system-basic.js`, contains a fair amount of code. So we'll break it down a bit. Let's begin by listing the variables and the `init()` method:

```
// rendering
var width = window.innerWidth, height = window.innerHeight;
var scene, camera, renderer;

// time-keeping variables
var dt = 1/24; // simulation time unit is 1 day; time-step is 1 hr
var numSteps = 8760; // 1 year; 365*24
var animFreq = 168; // once per week; 24*7
var t = 0;

// gravitational constant
var G;

// sun variables
var center;
var massSun;
var radiusSun = 30;

// arrays to hold velocity and position vectors for all planets
var v;
var s;

// visual objects
var sun;
var planets;
var numPlanets = 4;

// planets' properties
var colors;
var radiuses;
var masses;
var distances;
var velos;

// scaling factors
var scaleTime;
var scaleDist;
var scaleMass;
var scaleVelo;

window.onload = init;

function init(){
    setupScaling();
    setupPlanetData();
    setInitialConditions();
```

```
        setupObjects();
        simulate();
        renderer.render(scene, camera);
}
```

First, take a look at the variable definitions. Note in particular that s and v are now arrays that will hold the Vector3D positions and velocities of the planets. Note also the arrays colors, radiuses, and so on that will hold the properties of the planets. Next take a look at the init() function. The following methods are called in succession before the final rendering: setupScaling(), setupPlanetData(), setInitialConditions(), setupObjects(), and simulate(). Let's briefly discuss each one in turn.

The setupScaling() method does exactly what its name suggests: it defines the scale factors and then uses them to rescale the mass of the sun and the gravitational constant to their simulation values:

```
function setupScaling(){
        scaleMass = Astro.EARTH_MASS;
        scaleTime = Astro.EARTH_DAY;
        scaleDist = 1e9; // 1 million km or 1 billion meters
        scaleVelo = scaleDist/scaleTime; // million km per day

        massSun = Astro.SUN_MASS/scaleMass;

        G = Phys.GRAVITATIONAL_CONSTANT;
        G *= scaleMass*scaleTime*scaleTime/(scaleDist*scaleDist*scaleDist);
}
```

The setupPlanetData() method puts the appropriate values for the planets' properties in the five arrays radiuses, colors, masses, distances, and velos. The values we chose for radiuses are in proportion to the four planets' real radii. But please note that they are not in proportion to the radius of the Sun (which in reality would be much larger compared with those of the planets). Moreover, neither the radii of the planets nor the radius of the Sun are in proportion to the distances between them. If we did that, the planets would all be tiny dots in the space available in the browser window. The masses, distances, and velocities are scaled values of those read in from the Astro object for each planet.

```
function setupPlanetData(){
        radiuses = [1.9, 4.7, 5, 2.7];
        colors = [0xffffcc, 0xffcc00, 0x0099ff, 0xff6600];

        masses = new Array();
        distances = new Array();
        velos = new Array();

        masses[0] = Astro.MERCURY_MASS/scaleMass;
        masses[1] = Astro.VENUS_MASS/scaleMass;
        masses[2] = Astro.EARTH_MASS/scaleMass;
        masses[3] = Astro.MARS_MASS/scaleMass;

        distances[0] = Astro.MERCURY_ORBITAL_RADIUS/scaleDist;
        distances[1] = Astro.VENUS_ORBITAL_RADIUS/scaleDist;
        distances[2] = Astro.EARTH_ORBITAL_RADIUS/scaleDist;
        distances[3] = Astro.MARS_ORBITAL_RADIUS/scaleDist;
```

```
      velos[0] = Astro.MERCURY_ORBITAL_VELOCITY/scaleVelo;
      velos[1] = Astro.VENUS_ORBITAL_VELOCITY/scaleVelo;
      velos[2] = Astro.EARTH_ORBITAL_VELOCITY/scaleVelo;
      velos[3] = Astro.MARS_ORBITAL_VELOCITY/scaleVelo;
}
```

The setInitialConditions() method uses the distances and velocities set up in setupPlanetData() to set the initial values of the position and velocity vectors in s and v for each planet relative to the Sun.

```
function setInitialConditions(){
      center = new Vector3D(0,0,0);

      s = new Array();
      s[0] = new Vector3D(distances[0],0,0);
      s[1] = new Vector3D(distances[1],0,0);
      s[2] = new Vector3D(distances[2],0,0);
      s[3] = new Vector3D(distances[3],0,0);

      v = new Array();
      v[0] = new Vector3D(0,velos[0],0);
      v[1] = new Vector3D(0,velos[1],0);
      v[2] = new Vector3D(0,velos[2],0);
      v[3] = new Vector3D(0,velos[3],0);
}
```

As in the single-planet example, the setupObjects() method then makes use of three.js to create the Sun and planets, giving each one the appropriate radius, color, and mass and setting the initial positions and velocities with the aid of the positionObject() method.

```
function setupObjects(){
      renderer = new THREE.WebGLRenderer();
      renderer.setSize(width, height);
      document.body.appendChild(renderer.domElement);

      scene = new THREE.Scene();

      var angle = 45, aspect = width/height, near = 0.1, far = 10000;
      camera = new THREE.PerspectiveCamera(angle, aspect, near, far);
      camera.position.set(0,0,1000);
      scene.add(camera);

      var light = new THREE.DirectionalLight();
      light.position.set(-10,0,20);
      scene.add(light);

      var sphereGeometry = new THREE.SphereGeometry(radiusSun,10,10);
      var sphereMaterial = new THREE.MeshLambertMaterial({color: 0xffff00});
      sun = new THREE.Mesh(sphereGeometry,sphereMaterial);
      scene.add(sun);
      sun.mass = massSun;
      sun.pos = center;
      positionObject(sun);
```

```
        planets = new Array();

        for (var n=0; n<numPlanets; n++){
            sphereGeometry = new THREE.SphereGeometry(radiuses[n],10,10);
            sphereMaterial = new THREE.MeshLambertMaterial({color: colors[n]});
            var planet = new THREE.Mesh(sphereGeometry,sphereMaterial);
            planets.push(planet);
            scene.add(planet);
            planet.mass = masses[n];
            planet.pos = s[n];
            planet.velo = v[n];
            positionObject(planet);
        }
    }
}
function positionObject(obj){
    obj.position.set(obj.pos.x,obj.pos.y,obj.pos.z);
}
```

Finally we have the simulate() method, together with the associated clonePlanet() method that we had in the previous version of the code. These are all natural generalizations of their previous counterparts to multiple planets, effected with the addition of a parameter n that represents the array index of the relevant planet. The RK4() and getAcc() methods are also updated to include this planet index parameter n, so that they know which planet they are calculating for. Note that getAcc() now includes the gravitational force exerted by each of the other planets in addition to that exerted by the Sun in calculating the resultant force and acceleration of each planet.

```
function simulate(){
    for (var i=0; i<numSteps; i++){
        t += dt;
        for (var n=0; n<numPlanets; n++){
            RK4(n);
            if (i%animFreq==0){
                clonePlanet(n);
            }
        }
    }
}
function clonePlanet(n){
    var planet = planets[n];
    var p = planet.clone();
    scene.add(p);
    p.pos = s[n];
    positionObject(p);
}
function getAcc(ppos,pvel,pn){
    var massPlanet = planets[pn].mass;
    var r = ppos.subtract(center);
    // force exerted by sun
    var force = Forces3D.gravity(G,massSun,massPlanet,r);
    // forces exerted by other planets
    for (var n=0; n<numPlanets; n++){
        if (n!=pn){ // exclude the current planet itself!
```

```
            r = ppos.subtract(s[n]);
            var gravity = Forces3D.gravity(G,masses[n],massPlanet,r);;
            force = Forces3D.add([force, gravity]);
        }
    }
    // acceleration
    return force.multiply(1/massPlanet);
}

function RK4(n){
    // step 1
    var pos1 = s[n];
    var vel1 = v[n];
    var acc1 = getAcc(pos1,vel1,n);
    // step 2
    var pos2 = pos1.addScaled(vel1,dt/2);
    var vel2 = vel1.addScaled(acc1,dt/2);
    var acc2 = getAcc(pos2,vel2,n);
    // step 3
    var pos3 = pos1.addScaled(vel2,dt/2);
    var vel3 = vel1.addScaled(acc2,dt/2);
    var acc3 = getAcc(pos3,vel3,n);
    // step 4
    var pos4 = pos1.addScaled(vel3,dt);
    var vel4 = vel1.addScaled(acc3,dt);
    var acc4 = getAcc(pos4,vel4,n);
    // sum vel and acc
    var velsum = vel1.addScaled(vel2,2).addScaled(vel3,2).addScaled(vel4,1);
    var accsum = acc1.addScaled(acc2,2).addScaled(acc3,2).addScaled(acc4,1);
    // update pos and velo
    s[n] = pos1.addScaled(velsum,dt/6);
    v[n] = vel1.addScaled(accsum,dt/6);
}
```

Run the simulation. Note that it might take a few seconds to run, depending on the speed of your computer and what other processes are currently running; nothing will seem to happen while it's calculating. That's because it goes through the whole timestepping loop before doing any rendering. The default values in the code for the timekeeping variables are dt = 1/24, numSteps = 8760, and animFreq = 168. Recalling that in the simulation the unit of time is 1 day, dt = 1/24 corresponds to a timestep of 1 hr. Doubling it will mean that the simulation can run for twice as long in the same wall clock time or can run for the same simulated time in half the wall clock time.

You can experiment with the timestep to see how large you can make it without losing accuracy significantly. The value of 8760 for numSteps equals 365 × 24; so we are doing an Earth year's worth of simulation. The animFreq value of 168 is equal to 7 × 24, and so the planets' positions are visually updated once per week. Running the simulation with the default values will produce the trajectories shown in Figure 16-10. Earth is, of course, the third planet from the Sun, and it completes a full orbit in the 1 year of simulation time, which is reassuring! Venus and Mercury complete more than one orbit, and as a result you can see some overlap between the clones. On the other hand, Mars completes only slightly more than half an orbit. If you reduce the simulation time to 8500 timesteps (about 354 days), you will find that Earth just fails to complete one orbit, as expected. This is a good indication that we got the simulation at least approximately right.

Figure 16-10. *A basic solar system model that looks a bit artificial*

This is a fully functional and physically quite realistic scale model of the solar system. Apart from the minor fact that the sizes of the planets and Sun are not visually represented in proportion to the distances between them, the real limitation of the model is that the initial conditions chosen for the planets are not actual instantaneous values; they are based on mean values of their distances from the Sun and their mean orbital velocities. Also, the planets are all aligned in a straight line to start with, which is a bit artificial. Let's fix these limitations now.

Incorporating accurate initial conditions

We're almost there, but to create a truly realistic solar system simulation you need to use accurate data as initial conditions. The only code that needs to change is really the setInitialConditions() method. You need to put some real data in there; you can get that data from NASA's HORIZONS system here: http://ssd.jpl.nasa.gov/horizons.cgi.

This system generates highly accurate trajectory data (known as *ephemerides*) for a large number of objects in the solar system. The data is generated by NASA's own simulation to extremely high accuracy (typically 16 significant figures!). You can choose the data type, coordinate origin, time span, and other settings. The file initial_conditions.txt, included with this example's source code, contains some data that we downloaded for the positions and velocities of the eight planets at the time of 00:00 on 1 January 2012. Next to the name of each planet there are six fields that contain values of x, y, z, vx, vy, and vz, respectively. The positions are in km and the velocities in km/s, both relative to the Sun. We have used this data as initial conditions for the four planets we are simulating in the version of the code with the filename solar-system.js. Note that the setupPlanetData() method has also been simplified by removing the distances and velos arrays, which are no longer needed.

If you run the simulation you will find that the simulated trajectories now look more realistic with proper initial conditions (see Figure 16-11). Note in particular the characteristic eccentricity of Mercury's orbit. Because we have access to NASA's simulation data, why not compare our simulation with theirs?

Figure 16-11. *Planets' trajectories in a 1-year simulation with our code*

Comparing the model results with NASA data

We have also downloaded and saved position data from the HORIZONS web site for a whole year's worth of simulation, from 1 Jan 2012 to 1 Jan 2013. The data is saved in CSV format in a separate file for each planet and is located in a subdirectory in the source code folder for this simulation. Note that the HORIZONS system is frequently updated as new measurement data is incorporated. The implication is that if you download data at a different time you may not obtain exactly the same figures to 16-digit accuracy. For most purposes, you wouldn't even notice the difference, though!

To enable us to compare our simulation results with NASA's data, we make a few small modifications to the previous code in solar-system.js. The new code is the file solar-system-nasa.js. The first change is to run the simulation for 366 days, by changing the value of numSteps to 8784. Next we change the value of animFreq to numSteps, so that the new planets' positions are displayed only at the end of the 366 days. In the init() method just before rendering, we introduce a call to a new method, compareNASA(), which creates clones of the planets and places them at locations given by the NASA data on day 366. The remaining changes are in the simulate() method (see the bold lines in the following listing), with the replacement of the clonePlanet() method by a movePlanet() method, which moves the original planets to the new position instead of cloning them. Note also that the index i is replaced by i+1 in the if statement—this ensures that movePlanet() is not called initially (when i = 0) but on the last timestep.

```
function simulate(){
    for (var i=0; i<numSteps; i++){
        t += dt;
        for (var n=0; n<numPlanets; n++){
            RK4(n);
            if ((i+1)%animFreq==0){
                movePlanet(n);
            }
        }
    }
}
```

```
function movePlanet(n){
    var planet = planets[n];
    planet.pos = s[n];
    positionObject(planet);
}
```

The result of these changes is that two copies of each planet are placed on the canvas on day 366 of the simulation. One set of planets is located based on the calculations of our simulation and the other set is located at the positions read from NASA's data, each after exactly one year from the initial conditions. So how do they compare?

Run the simulation and you'll see the planets in the locations shown in the screenshot in Figure 16-12. But why is there only one set of planets? The answer is that there are actually two sets—they are on top of each other! To convince yourself, add the following line of code just before the last line in the compareNASA() method:

```
p.pos = sN[i].multiply(2);
```

Figure 16-12. *Planet positions after one year of simulated time compared with NASA data*

What this does is to double the distance of each planet from the Sun for the cloned set of planets corresponding to the NASA data. Re-run the code and you will now find that there are indeed two sets of planets, one at double the distance from the Sun. So this shows that the NASA clones were on top of the original planets in the first run, and you just couldn't distinguish between the two sets of planets at this resolution. Not bad, eh?

Although we have neglected a whole host of effects, such as the gas giants (especially Jupiter, the largest planet and the closest to the four terrestrial planets), asteroids, and relativistic effects, the results look pretty good. Of course, NASA's simulation has all these and a lot more, together with much more advanced numerical methods, which make it much more accurate. It would be interesting to run the simulation longer or reduce the timestep to see at what point it starts to show visible differences compared with the NASA data. There are, of course, small differences, and bearing in mind that 1 px on the screen is a million km in reality, they may be significant in absolute terms. Nevertheless, while you may not necessarily be able to use this simulation to send your homemade space probe to Mars, you can most certainly use it to teach school kids or college students about how the solar system works.

Animating the solar system simulation

It is not difficult to modify the solar-system.js simulation to introduce some basic animation. This is done in the modified file solar-system-animated.js. First we replace the call to the simulate() method in init() by a call to the animFrame() method. We then introduce the following modified code, much of which should look very familiar:

```
function animFrame(){
    animId = requestAnimationFrame(animFrame);
    onTimer();
}
function onTimer(){
    if (nSteps < numSteps){
        simulate();
        moveCamera();
        renderer.render(scene, camera);
    }else{
        stop();
    }
    nSteps++;
}
function simulate(){
    t += dt;
    for (var n=0; n<numPlanets; n++){
        RK4(n);
        movePlanet(n);
    }
}
function movePlanet(n){
    var planet = planets[n];
    planet.pos = s[n];
    positionObject(planet);
}
function moveCamera(){
    camera.position.x += -0.1;
    camera.position.z += -0.5;
}
function stop(){
    cancelAnimationFrame(animId);
}
```

Note that the line that calls the renderer is now included in the time loop in onTimer(), so that the planets are re-rendered at their new location each timestep, producing the animation. We have also introduced a new moveCamera() method, which moves the camera as the animation progresses. Run the simulation to see the interesting visual effect this produces. You can experiment by making the camera move in different ways. For example, you can view the simulation from the perspective of a fixed Earth by replacing the two lines in moveCamera() with the following line:

```
camera.position.set(planets[2].position.x,planets[2].position.y,planets[2].position.z+200);
```

Figure 16-13 shows a screenshot of the resulting animation with this modification.

Figure 16-13. *Animated version of the solar system simulation*

It's your turn

There are many ways in which you could develop or extend this simulation. The most obvious (and most straightforward) improvement would be to add in the four outer planets. You could also add in interactivity, dynamic scaling, enhanced animation effects, and so on.

There is also a whole host of 3D features waiting to be exploited here. Perhaps you can use actual image maps of the planets wrapped on them. Then you could add functionality to rotate and scale the view. Perhaps you could even show the planets spinning when they are close up. We'll leave you to it.

Summary

With the completion of this book you now have a powerful set of tools at your disposal that will help you build more realistic and engaging games and animations as well as some pretty powerful simulations. From the simple bouncing ball simulation in Chapter 1, you've come a long way, indeed!

Let's have a quick recap of all the ground covered in this book. In Part I, you went through a good deal of background material in JavaScript, math, and physics to establish the key concepts and techniques relating to physics-based motion and simulation.

Part II covered the basic laws of motion, and you encountered a wide variety of forces, building lots of examples that showed the interesting types of motion those forces produce.

In Part III, you simulated systems consisting of multiple particles or extended objects, including particle collisions, rigid bodies, and deformable bodies.

Finally, in Part IV you looked into how to create more complex simulations that require greater attention to numerical accuracy or that involve 3D or scale modeling.

That's a lot of material.

This final chapter provided just a tiny glimpse of the possibilities that lie ahead for bringing all that physics together and putting it to use. We hope you will continue to have some serious fun with these projects as well as many others that you'll build from scratch. We invite you to share your creations on the book's website at www.physicscodes.com!

Index

Get the eBook for only $10!

Now you can take the weightless companion with you anywhere, anytime. Your purchase of this book entitles you to 3 electronic versions for only $10.

This Apress title will prove so indispensible that you'll want to carry it with you everywhere, which is why we are offering the eBook in 3 formats for only $10 if you have already purchased the print book.

Convenient and fully searchable, the PDF version enables you to easily find and copy code—or perform examples by quickly toggling between instructions and applications. The MOBI format is ideal for your Kindle, while the ePUB can be utilized on a variety of mobile devices.

Go to www.apress.com/promo/tendollars to purchase your companion eBook.

Apress®
THE EXPERT'S VOICE™